Vietnam

a travel survival kit

D0368243

Robert Storey

Vietnam – a travel survival kit

2nd edition

Published by .
   Lonely Planet Publications
   Head Office: PO Box 617, Hawthorn, Vic 3122, Australia
   Branches: PO Box 2001A, Berkeley, CA 94702, USA
                  12 Barley Mow Passage, Chiswick, London W4 4PH, UK

Printed by
   Singapore National Printers Ltd, Singapore

Photographs by
   Richard I' Anson (RI), Glenn Beanland (GB), Mason Florence (MF), Robert Storey (RS)
   Front cover: Montagnard girl with baskets (Guido Alberto Rossi), The Image Bank
   Back cover: Man with bike, Quan Cong Temple, Hoi An (MF)

First Published
   February 1991

This Edition
   September 1993

**Although the authors and publisher have tried to make the information as
accurate as possible, they accept no responsibility for any loss, injury or
inconvenience sustained by any person using this book.**

National Library of Australia Cataloguing in Publication Data

   Robinson, Daniel
   Vietnam : a travel survival kit.

   Includes index.
   ISBN 0 86442 197 4.

   1. Vietnam – Guidebooks. I. Storey, Robert. I. Title.
   (Series : Lonely Planet travel survival kit).

915.970444

text & maps © Lonely Planet 1993
photos © photographers as indicated 1993
climate charts compiled from information supplied by Patrick J Tyson © Patrick J Tyson, 1993

Robert Storey

Robert has pursued a number of distinguished careers, including monkeykeeper at a zoo, Texas urban cowboy and slot machine repairman in a Las Vegas casino. After graduating from the University of Nevada in Las Vegas, Robert went to Taiwan, learned to speak Chinese, finally found a decent job and has become a respectable citizen and a pillar of the community. His hobbies include mountaineering, bungee jumping and computer hacking.

Daniel Robinson

Daniel, researcher and writer of the first edition's Vietnam and Cambodia sections, grew up in the USA (the San Francisco Bay Area and Glen Ellyn, Illinois) and Israel. He has travelled extensively in the Middle East and South, South-East and East Asia. Daniel holds a BA in Near Eastern Studies from Princeton University. He has contributed to Lonely Planet's shoestring series and is also co-author of our guide to France. Daniel lives in Tel Aviv.

From the Authors

The first edition of this book was entitled *Vietnam, Laos & Cambodia – a travel survival kit.* Daniel Robinson did the Vietnam and Cambodia sections and Joe Cummings researched and wrote the Laos section. Laos and Cambodia have now been spun off to their own books, and this new update by Robert Storey deals exclusively with Vietnam.

For this edition, special thanks to Rocky Dang and Billy Chan of Hong Kong. There are a number of Vietnamese people who served as guides, translators and travelling companions whom we'd love to thank. But sadly we feel it is more prudent to leave their names out of this book. However, we are especially grateful to them.

Daniel would like to add that he has lost touch with Mr Hung and Mr Long, who were of much assistance in producing the last edition, and would very much appreciate information on how to contact them.

From the Publisher

This book was edited by Diana Saad. Proofing and editorial layout were done by Greg Alford. Mapping, design, illustrating and layout was by Louise Keppie. Additional illustrations by Kathy Yates. Thanks also to Valerie Tellini and Chris Lee Ack for artistic assistance. Indexing was by Sharon Wertheim. Vietnamese script was provided by Nguyen Xuan Thu, and keyed and bromided by Diana Saad and Louise Keppie.

Thanks to all the travellers who wrote in with advice, tips and travellers' tales:

Denise & Zeke (Aus), MM Adams (HK), Maria Almerda (UK), Gunter Annaert (B), Mayor Victor Ashe (USA), Ian Baird (T), David Begg (NZ), Barry Behrstock (USA), Amir Bem (T), Paul Bishop (Aus), Johan Borchert (NL), C Botschuijver (NL), Martin Bottenberg (NL), Mrs Gayle Bowman (Aus), David Boyall (Aus), Andy Brown (UK), Odile Buclez (F), C Noel Bunting (UK), Thorsten Burmeister (HK), Charlotte Calhoun (USA), Lene Callesen (DK), Dona Chamblin (USA), David Chandler, Peter Clarke (UK), Augusta Cobbold (HK), F Gale Connor (USA), Earl Cooper, Lawrence Cox (UK), AM Crawford, Nguyen Huy Cuong (V)

Des Davis (Aus), Gijs de Graaff (NL), F de Vooys (NL), Douglas Dean (Aus), Maxine Degraaf (Aus), Alice T Diamond (USA), Andrew Dinwoodie (UK), Thang N Do (USA), Shirley Dockerill, Brian Duffy (UK), David Elfick (Aus), Mark Elliott, Jim Ellis, Frank Engelen (NL), Jeff Essen (NL), Caroline & Martin Evans (UK), Clare & John Evenson (Aus), Tim Farnsworth (UK), David Fitzstevens (USA), Jules Flach (CH), Tatyana Flade (D), Mary Flaharty, David W Fleming (NZ), Marie Flynn (Aus), Marianne Foley (NL), Kim Furqueron (USA), John Jansen van Galen (NL), Nan Gallagher (Aus), Xavier Galland (F), Jonathan Gat (Isr), Naomi Geer, Greg Giannis (Aus), Eddie Gilbert (UK), Thomas Grenne (DK), Mauro Grusovin (I), Marc Grutering (B), Miss

Hang (V), Kerry Hart (Aus), Richard Henderson (UK), Jenny Herbert (UK), Maria Herceg (Aus), Andreas Hessberger (D), Ha Minh Hien (V), Steve Hodgkiss (NL), Rob Hofman (NL), Lies Pott Hofstede (NL), Kristin Holbrook (USA), John Holland (Aus), Alan Mark Holt (UK), Harry Hunter (USA), Iain Hutchison (UK)

Marie-Line J-Lestang (F), Eline Jagtenberg (NL), Teixeira Jean (F), Hilary Jeffcote (Aus), Chiara Jibhas, Jorgen Johanson (N), Howard Jones (UK), Paul Jungnitsch (C), Ivan Kasimoff (USA), Keiko Katohira (J), Kryss Katsiavrades (UK), Geoffrey Kelsall (UK), Karim Khalil (Lao), Bill Kimball (USA), Rick Koken (NL), Kiros Kokkas (G), Charlie Krey (F), Sarah Kydel (M), Andrew Lamb (T), Jan Lambert (USA), Lan (UK), Dave Landis (HK), Jean Lebel (C), Jo Lerner (B), Damien Leruste (F), Nguyen Lieu (V), Howard Limbest (UK), Dieter Lohr (D), Marilyn Long (Aus), Julie Luckman (UK), Larry Lustig (USA)

James MacGregor (USA), Michael Mackey (UK), George Maeda (Aus), Tom Malia, Luu Minh Man (V), Alain Maniciati (CH), Janet Martin (Aus), J Mason Florence, Anita Mathur (UK), William McCloskey (USA), David McGrath (USA), Frank Meire (B), Mike Merritt (UK), John & Ann Michener (USA), Gergely Miklos (H), D Milsom (UK), Deio Miners (UK), Nick Morgan (UK), Don Morrisey (Aus), Adrian Moyes (UK), Ingrid Muan (USA), Nicole Nathan (T), Francois Navarro (F), Charles Neary (USA), Peter Nestmann (D), R H Newton (Aus), Paul Nicholls (UK), Andrea O'Brien (Aus), Tom O'Neill (USA), Ken Opprann (N), DM Parkin (UK), Bryna Parkin, Tania Paul (Aus), Harry M Pearson (USA), Edward Peters (UK), Ed & Philippa Peters, P Petitgas (V), Mark Pettit (Aus), Peter Pfingst, Steve Pottinger (UK), Reggie Pugh (UK)

Tong Manh Quan, Richard Quayle (UK), Tran Quoc Cong (V), CP Raine (UK), Clifford C Raisbeck MD (USA), Nis Ranken (UK), Yves Rault (F), AM Reynalds (HK), Keith Richmond, Kim Le Riding (V), Jason Roberts (USA), Christopher Roberts, Amit Rochvarger (Isr), Bo Rosen (S), Ingrid Rosenberg (S), Andy Rother, Jeff Rothman (USA), Tom Rowan (Aus), Dorothy Ruef (USA), Mark Russell (Aus), Terri Ruyter (USA), Catherine Ryan (Aus), Florence Samson (F), Anton Segal, Luc Selleslagh (B), Owen Shaffer (USA), Val Shingleton (Aus), Le Van Sinh (V), Johan Sjoberg (S), David Sloper (Aus), Humphrey Smith (UK), Dierdre Smith (Aus), Peter Smolanko (Aus), Susanne Stoger (A), Julia Stone (Aus), Edmund Tan (S), Judith Teichman (USA), Eric Telfer (USA), Lim Sin Thai (Sin), Zip Tone (V), Quoc Cong Tran (V), Pham Thi Tuyet, AD Urquart (UK), Jacqueline van Campen (C), Twan van de Kerkhof (NL), Frans Vellema (NL), Andrew Warmington (UK), M Wells (UK), Lisa Wilkes (UK), Robert Wilkinson (USA), Stephen Williams, Leonard Wolfe (USA), Will Young, Robert Zwerner (USA)

Aus – Australia, B – Belgium, C – Canada, CH – Switzerland, D – Germany, DK – Denmark, F – France, G – Greece, H – Hungary, HK – Hong Kong, I – Italy, Lao – Laos, N – Norway, NL – Netherlands, NZ – New Zealand, Sin – Singapore, T – Thailand, UK – United Kingdom, USA – United States of America, V – Vietnam

Warning & Request

A travel writer's job is never done. Before the ink is dry on a new book, things change, and few places change more quickly than Vietnam. At Lonely Planet we get a steady stream of mail from travellers and it all helps – whether it's a few lines scribbled on the back of a used paper plate or a stack of neat word processed pages spewing forth from our fax machine. Prices go up, new hotels open, old ones degenerate, some burn down, others get renovated and renamed, bus routes change, bridges collapse and recommended travel agents get indicted for fraud.

Remember, this book is meant to be a guide, not a gospel – since things go on changing we can't tell you exactly what to expect all the time. Hopefully this book will point you in a few of the right directions and save you some time and money whilst you're at it! So if you find things aren't like they're described herein, don't get upset – get out your pen and write to Lonely Planet. Your input will help make the next edition better. As usual, the writers of useful letters will score a free copy of the next edition, or another Lonely Planet guide if you prefer. We give away lots of books, but unfortunately not every letter/postcard receives one.

Contents

Map Legend

BOUNDARIES

—·—·—·—	International Boundary
—·—·—·—	Internal Boundary
+++++++	National Park or Reserve
— — — —	The Equator
············	The Tropics

SYMBOLS

◉ NATIONAL	National Capital
● PROVINCIAL	Provincial or State Capital
● Major	Major Town
● Minor	Minor Town
■	Places to Stay
▼	Places to Eat
✉	Post Office
✈	Airport
i	Tourist Information
⊖	Bus Station or Terminal
66	Highway Route Number
⚱✝⛪⛩	Mosque, Church, Cathedral
∴	Tomb
✚	Hospital
✳	Lookout
Δ	Camping Area
⊼	Picnic Area
⌂	Hut or Chalet
▲	Mountain or Hill
⊢■⊣	Railway Station
≡	Road Bridge
++++++	Railway Bridge
⇒ ⇐	Road Tunnel
⇥ ⇤	Railway Tunnel
⁀⁀⁀	Escarpment or Cliff
‿	Pass
⊓⊓⊓	Ancient or Historic Wall

ROUTES

————	Major Road or Highway
— — — —	Unsealed Major Road
————	Sealed Road
– – – –	Unsealed Road or Track
≡≡≡≡	City Street
+++++++	Railway
●————	Subway
············	Walking Track
·· ·· ··	Ferry Route
++++++++++	Cable Car or Chair Lift

HYDROGRAPHIC FEATURES

	River or Creek
	Intermittent Stream
	Lake, Intermittent Lake
	Coast Line
	Spring
	Waterfall
	Swamp
	Salt Lake or Reef
	Glacier

OTHER FEATURES

	Park, Garden or National Park
	Built Up Area
	Market or Pedestrian Mall
	Plaza or Town Square
	Cemetery

Note: not all symbols displayed above appear in this book

Introduction

In the decades following WW II the name 'Vietnam' came to signify to many Westerners either a brutal jungle war or a spectacular failure of American power – or both. Bumper stickers in the USA demanded that there be 'No more Vietnams in Central America'. Half-a-dozen major motion pictures, several TV drama series, countless university courses and hundreds of books about Vietnam captivated audiences around the globe, but virtually all were about the American war in Indochina, not Vietnam the country. The real Vietnam, with its unique and rich civilisation, spectacular scenery and highly cultured and friendly people was almost entirely ignored.

After the fall of South Vietnam to Communist North Vietnamese forces in 1975, xenophobia on the part of the leadership in Hanoi and a US-led campaign to isolate Vietnam internationally resulted in a sharp reduction in the quality and quantity of information available in Vietnam, especially that which transcended the narrowly political. But towards the end of the 1980s, the Cold War thawed and the Hanoi government began trying to reduce Vietnam's international isolation, in part by opening the country's doors to foreign visitors. Not long thereafter, the dramatic collapse of the Eastern Bloc and the ending of the Cambodian civil war greatly reduced tensions in Indochina.

At the same time, a change of presidential administration in the USA has resulted in a perceptible shift in US policy towards Vietnam in 1993. The reasons for this are for the most part political and economic, but the results have given travellers the first opportunity in over a generation to visit a Vietnam at peace with itself and its neighbours.

Most visitors to Vietnam are overwhelmed by the sublime beauty of the country's natural setting. The Red River Delta in the north, the Mekong Delta in the south and almost the entire coastal strip are a patchwork of brilliant green rice paddies tended by peasant women in conical hats. Vietnam's 3260 km of coastline – considerably longer than the West Coast of the USA – include countless km of unspoiled beaches and a number of stunning lagoons; some sections are shaded by coconut palms and casuarinas, others bounded by seemingly endless expanses of sand dunes or rugged spurs of the Truong Son Mountains.

Between the two deltas, the coastal paddies lining the South China Sea give way to soaring mountains, some of whose slopes are cloaked with the richest of rainforests. A bit further from the littoral are the refreshingly cool plateaus of the Central Highlands, which are dotted with waterfalls. The area is home to dozens of distinct ethno-linguistic

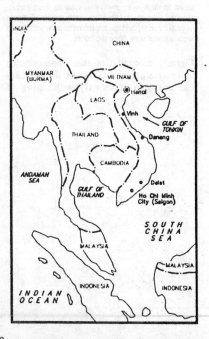

9

groups (hill tribes), more than almost any other country in Asia.

Visitors to Vietnam have their senses thrilled by all the sights, sounds, tastes and smells of a society born of over a century of contact between an ancient civilisation and the ways of the West. There's nothing quite like grabbing a delicious lunch of local delicacies at a food stall deep inside a marketplace, surrounded by tropical fruit vendors and legions of curious youngsters. Or sitting by a waterfall in the Central Highlands, sipping soda water with lemon juice and watching newly wed couples on their honeymoon tiptoe up to the streambank in their 'Sunday finest'. Or being invited by a Buddhist monk to attend prayers at his pagoda conducted, according to ancient Mahayana rites, with chanting, drums and gongs.

Of the 30 or so countries I have been to, Vietnam is easily the most beautiful. I saw more shades of green then I knew existed. Rice fields manually tended from dawn to dusk were always in view as were forest-covered mountains. I also frequently caught glimpses of pristine deserted beaches from the train window as we made our way along the coast...

Fiercely protective of their independence and sovereignty for 2000 years, the Vietnamese are also graciously welcoming of foreigners who come as their guests rather than as conquerors. No matter what side they or their parents were on during the war, the Vietnamese are, almost without exception, extremely friendly to Western visitors (including Americans) and supportive of more contact with the outside world. People who visit Vietnam during the first years of the country's renewed interaction within the West will play an important role in conveying to the Vietnamese the potentialities of such contact. And now that 'capitalism' is no longer a four-letter word, private Vietnamese businesses have mushroomed, adding an atmosphere of hustle and bustle to Ho Chi Minh City and other cities whose resurgent dynamism is reviving the moribund Vietnamese economy.

Visiting Vietnam involves a bit more red tape than is usual when travelling abroad, but this country is changing at the speed of light – what was strictly prohibited yesterday has now become mundane. If present liberalising trends continue, travel should keep getting easier. In any case, Vietnam is rapidly becoming a popular travel destination – the number of foreign tourists seems to double every year. However, many remote parts of the country have hardly been explored by travellers – if you hurry, you can still be amongst the pioneers.

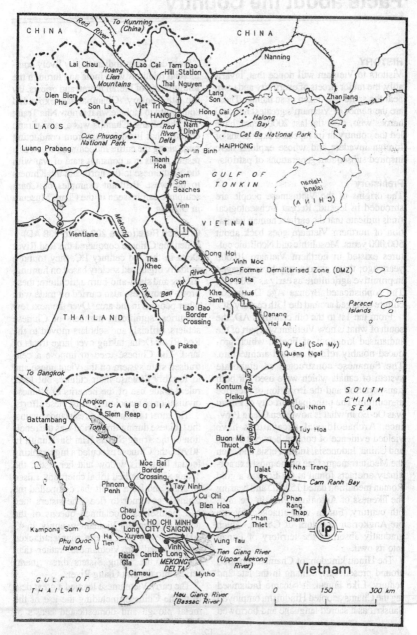

Vietnam

CHINA

Red River
To Kunming
(China)

CHINA

Nanning

Lai Chau
Hoang Lien Mountains
Lao Cai
Tam Dao Hill Station
Thai Nguyen

Dien Bien Phu
Son La
Viet Tri
Lang Son
Hong Gai
Zhanjiang

LAOS
HANOI
Red River Delta
Nam Dinh
Halong Bay
Cat Ba National Park

Cuc Phuong National Park

Luang Prabang
Ninh Binh
HAIPHONG

Thanh Hoa

Sam Son Beaches

Hainan Island
(CHINA)

GULF OF TONKIN

Vinh

Vientiane

Mekong River

VIETNAM

Tha Khec

Dong Hoi
Vinh Moc
Former Demilitarised Zone (DMZ)
Dong Ha
Khe Sanh
Hué

Ben River

Lao Bao Border Crossing

Paracel Islands

Danang
Hoi An

THAILAND

Pakse

My Lai (Son My)
Quang Ngai

To Bangkok

Kontum
Pleiku

SOUTH CHINA SEA

Angkor
Siem Reap

CAMBODIA

Battambang

Tonle Sap

Qui Nhon

Tuy Hoa

Buon Ma Thuot

Central Highlands

Moc Bai Border Crossing

Nha Trang
Cam Ranh Bay

Phnom Penh

Tay Ninh

Cu Chi
Bien Hoa

Dalat

Chau Doc

Long Xuyen

HO CHI MINH CITY (SAIGON)

Phan Rang - Thap Cham

Phan Thiet

Kampong Som

Ha Tien

Vung Tau

Phu Quoc Island

Rach Gia
Cantho
Vinh Long
MEKONG DELTA

Tien Giang River (Upper Mekong River)

Camau
Mytho

Hau Giang River (Bassac River)

GULF OF THAILAND

0   150   300 km

Facts about the Country

HISTORY

Visitors to Vietnam will notice that, invariably, the major streets of every city and town bear the same two dozen or so names. These are the names of Vietnam's greatest national heroes who, over the last 2000 years, have led the country in its repeated expulsions of foreign invaders and whose exploits have inspired subsequent generations of patriots.

Prehistory

The origins of the Vietnamese people are shrouded in legend. Recent archaeological finds indicate that the earliest human habitation of northern Vietnam goes back about 500,000 years. Mesolithic and Neolithic cultures existed in northern Vietnam 10,000 years ago; these groups may have engaged in primitive agriculture as early as 7000 BC. The sophisticated Bronze Age Dong Son culture emerged around the 13th century BC.

From the 1st to the 6th centuries AD, the south of what is now Vietnam was part of the Indianised kingdom of Funan, which produced notably refined art and architecture. The Funanese constructed an elaborate system of canals which were used for both transportation and the irrigation of wet rice agriculture. The principal port city of Funan was Oc-Eo in what is now Kien Giang Province. Archaeological excavations have yielded evidence of contact between Funan and China, Indonesia, India, Persia and even the Mediterranean. One of the most extraordinary artefacts found at Oc-Eo was a gold Roman medallion dated 152 AD and bearing the likeness of Antoninus Pius. In the mid-6th century, Funan was attacked by the pre-Angkorian kingdom of Chenla, which gradually absorbed the territory of Funan into its own.

The Hindu kingdom of Champa appeared around present-day Danang in the late 2nd century. Like Funan, it became Indianised (eg the Chams adopted Hinduism, employed Sanskrit as a sacred language and borrowed a great deal from Indian art) by lively commercial relations with India and through the immigration of Indian literati and priests. By the 8th century, Champa had expanded southward to include what is now Nha Trang and Phan Rang. Champa was a semi-piratic country that lived in part from conducting raids along the entire Indochinese coast; as a result, it was in a constant state of war with the Vietnamese to the north and the Khmers to the west. Brilliant examples of Cham sculpture can be seen in the Cham Museum in Danang.

Chinese Rule (circa 200 BC to 938 AD)

When the Chinese conquered the Red River Delta in the 2nd century BC, they found a feudally organised society based on hunting, fishing and slash-and-burn agriculture; these proto-Vietnamese also carried on trade with other peoples in the area. Over the next few centuries, significant numbers of Chinese settlers, officials and scholars moved to the Red River Delta, taking over large tracts of land. The Chinese tried to impose a centralised state system on the Vietnamese and to forcibly Sinicise their culture, but local rulers made use of the benefits of Chinese civilisation to tenaciously resist these efforts.

The most famous act of resistance against the Chinese during this period was the rebellion of the Trung Sisters (Hai Ba Trung). In 40 AD, the Chinese executed a high-ranking feudal lord. His widow and her sister, the Trung Sisters, rallied tribal chieftains, raised an army and led a revolt that compelled the Chinese governor to flee. The sisters then had themselves proclaimed queens of the newly independent Vietnamese entity. In 43 AD, however, the Chinese counterattacked and defeated the Vietnamese; rather than surrender, the Trung Sisters threw themselves into the Hat Giang River.

The early Vietnamese learned a great deal from the Chinese, including the use of the metal plough and domesticated beasts of burden and the construction of dikes and irrigation works. These innovations made possible the establishment of a culture based on rice growing, which remains the basis of the Vietnamese way of life to this day. As food became more plentiful, the population grew, forcing the Vietnamese to seek new lands on which to grow rice.

During this era, Vietnam was a key port of call on the sea route between China and India. The Vietnamese were introduced to Confucianism and Taoism by Chinese scholars who came to Vietnam as administrators and refugees. Indians sailing eastward brought Theravada (Hinayana) Buddhism to the Red River Delta while, simultaneously, Chinese travellers introduced Mahayana Buddhism. Buddhist monks carried with them the scientific and medical knowledge of the civilisations of India and China; as a result, Vietnamese Buddhists soon counted among their own great doctors, botanists and scholars.

There were major rebellions against Chinese rule – which was characterised by tyranny, forced labour and insatiable demands for tribute – in the 3rd and 6th centuries, but all (along with numerous minor revolts) were crushed. In 679, the Chinese named the country Annam, which means the Pacified South. But ever since this era, the collective memory of those early attempts to throw off the Chinese yoke has played an important role in shaping Vietnamese identity.

Independence from China (10th Century)

In the aftermath of the collapse of the Tang Dynasty in China in the early 10th century, the Vietnamese revolted against Chinese rule. In 938 AD, Ngo Quyen vanquished the Chinese armies at a battle on the Bach Dang River, ending 1000 years of Chinese rule. Ngo Quyen established an independent Vietnamese state, but it was not until 968 that Dinh Bo Linh ended the anarchy that followed Ngo Quyen's death and, following the custom of the times, reached an agreement with China: in return for recognition of their de facto independence, the Vietnamese accepted Chinese sovereignty and agreed to pay triennial tribute.

The dynasty founded by Dinh Bo Linh survived only until 980, when Le Dai Hanh overthrew it, beginning what is known as the Early Le Dynasty (980-1009).

The dynasties of independent Vietnam were:

Ngo Dynasty	939-65
Dinh Dynasty	968-80
Early Le Dynasty	980-1009
Ly Dynasty	1010-1225
Tran Dynasty	1225-1400
Ho Dynasty	1400-07
Post-Tran Dynasty	1407-13
Chinese Rule	1414-27
Later Le Dynasty (nominally until 1788)	1428-1524
Mac Dynasty	1527-92
Trinh Lords of the North	1539-1787
Nguyen Lords of the South	1558-1778
Tay Son Dynasty	1788-1802
Nguyen Dynasty	1802-1945

Ly Dynasty (1010-1225)

From the 11th to the 13th centuries, the independence of the Vietnamese Kingdom (Dai Viet) was consolidated under the emperors of the Ly Dynasty, founded by Ly Thai To. They reorganised the administrative system, founded the nation's first university (the Temple of Literature in Hanoi), promoted agriculture and built the first embankments for flood control along the Red River. Confucian scholars fell out of official favour because of their close cultural links to China; at the same time the early Ly monarchs, whose dynasty had come to power with Buddhist support, promoted Buddhism.

The Confucian philosophy of government and society, emphasising educational attainment, ritual performance and government authority, reasserted itself with the graduation of the first class from the Temple of Literature in 1075. Following years of study which emphasised classical education, these scholars went into government service, becoming what the West came to call mandarins. The outlines of the Vietnamese mandarinal system of government – according to which the state was run by a scholar class recruited in civil service examinations – date from this era.

During the Ly Dynasty, the Chinese, Khmers and Chams repeatedly attacked Vietnam but were repelled, most notably under the renowned strategist and tactician Ly Thuong Kiet (1030-1105), a military mandarin of royal blood who is still revered as a national hero.

Vietnamese conquests of Cham territory, which greatly increased the acreage under rice cultivation, were accompanied by an aggressive policy of colonisation that reproduced social structures dominant in the north in the newly settled territories. This process did not make allowances for the potential technological and cultural contributions of the Chams (and indeed destroyed Cham civilisation), but it did result in a chain of homogeneous villages that eventually stretched from the Chinese border to the Gulf of Thailand.

Tran Dynasty (1225-1400)

After years of civil strife, the Tran Dynasty overthrew the Ly Dynasty. The Tran increased the land under cultivation to feed the growing population and improved the dikes on the Red River.

After the dreaded Mongol warrior Kublai Khan completed his conquest of China in the mid-13th century, he demanded the right to cross Vietnamese territory on his way to attack Champa. The Vietnamese refused this demand but the Mongols – 500,000 of them – came anyway. The outnumbered Vietnamese under Tran Hung Dao attacked the invaders and forced them back to China, but the Mongols returned, this time with 300,000 men. Tran Hung Dao then lured them deep into Vietnamese territory; at high tide he attacked the Mongol fleet as it sailed on the Bach Dang River, ordering a tactical retreat of his forces to lure the Mongols into staying and fighting. The battle continued for many hours until low tide when a sudden Vietnam-

ese counteroffensive forced the Mongol boats back, impaling them on steel-tipped bamboo stakes set in the river bed the night before. The entire fleet was captured or sunk.

When the Tran Dynasty was overthrown in 1400 by Ho Qui Ly, both the Tran loyalists and the Chams (who had sacked Hanoi in 1371) encouraged Chinese intervention. The Chinese readily complied with the request and took control of Vietnam in 1407, imposing a regime characterised by heavy taxation and slave labour; Chinese culture and ways of doing things were forced on the population. The Chinese also took the national archives – and some of the country's intellectuals as well – to China, an irreparable loss to Vietnamese civilisation. Of this period, the great poet Nguyen Trai (1380-1442) would write:

Were the water of the Eastern Sea to be exhausted, the stain of their ignominy could not be washed away; all the bamboo of the Southern Mountains would not suffice to provide the paper for recording all their crimes.

Later Le Dynasty (1428-1524)

Le Loi was born into a large and prosperous family in the village of Lam Son in Thanh Hoa Province and earned a reputation for using his wealth to aid the poor. The ruling Chinese invited him to join the mandarinate but he refused. In 1418, Le Loi began to organise what came to be known as the Lam Son Uprising, travelling around the countryside to rally the people against the Chinese. Despite several defeats, he persisted in his efforts, earning the respect of the peasantry by ensuring that even when facing starvation his guerrilla troops did not pillage the land. After his victory in 1428, Le Loi declared himself Emperor Ly Thai To, thus beginning the Later Le Dynasty. To this day, Le Loi is revered as one of Vietnam's greatest national heroes.

After Le Loi's victory over the Chinese, Nguyen Trai, a scholar and Le Loi's companion in arms, wrote his famous *Great Proclamation (Binh Ngo Dai Cao)*, extra-

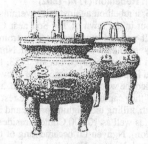

Dynastic Urns

ordinary for the compelling voice it gave to Vietnam's fierce spirit of independence:

Our people long ago established Vietnam as an independent nation with its own civilisation. We have our own mountains and our own rivers, our own customs and traditions, and these are different from those of the foreign country to the north...We have sometimes been weak and sometime powerful, but at no time have we suffered from a lack of heroes.

The Later Le Dynasty ruled until 1524 and, nominally, up to 1788. Le Loi and his successors instituted a vast programme of agrarian reform and land redistribution. They also launched a campaign to take over Cham lands to the south. In the 15th century Laos was forced to recognise Vietnamese suzerainty.

Under the Le Dynasty, an attempt was made to break free of the cultural and intellectual domination of Chinese civilisation. In the realms of law, religion and literature, indigenous traditions were brought to the fore. The Vietnamese language gained favour among scholars – who had previously disdained it, preferring Chinese – and a number of outstanding works of literature were produced. Legal reforms gave women almost-equal rights in the domestic sphere, but two groups were excluded from full civil rights: slaves (many of them prisoners of war) and, oddly, actors. In the culture of the elite, however, Chinese language and traditions continued to hold sway, and

neo-Confucianism remained dominant in the areas of social and political morality.

Trinh & Nguyen Lords

Throughout the 17th and 18th centuries, Vietnam was divided between the Trinh Lords, who ruled in the north under the titular kingship of the Later Le monarchs, and the Nguyen Lords, who controlled the south and also nominally recognised the Later Le Dynasty. The Trinh Lords repeatedly failed in attempts to take over areas under Nguyen control, in part because the Portuguese weaponry used by the Nguyen was far superior to the Dutch armaments supplied to the Trinh. During this period the Nguyen extended Vietnamese control into the Khmer territories of the Mekong Delta, populating the area with Vietnamese settlers. Cambodia was forced to accept Vietnamese suzerainty in the mid-17th century.

Buddhism enjoyed the patronage and support of both the Trinh and the Nguyen, and pagodas were built all over the country. But by this time Vietnamese Buddhism was no longer doctrinally pure, having become intermingled with animism, ancestor-worship and popularised Taoism.

Early Contact with the West

According to Chinese records, the first Vietnamese contact with Europeans took place in 166 AD when travellers from the Rome of Marcus Aurelius arrived in the Red River Delta.

The first Portuguese sailors landed in Danang in 1516; they were followed by Dominican missionaries 11 years later. During the next few decades the Portuguese began to trade with Vietnam, setting up a commercial colony alongside those of the Japanese and Chinese at Faifo (present-day Hoi An near Danang).

Franciscan missionaries from the Philippines settled in central Vietnam in 1580, followed in 1615 by the Jesuits who had just been expelled from Japan. In 1637, the Dutch were authorised to set up trading posts in the north, and one of the Le kings even took a Dutch woman as one of his six wives. The first English attempt to break into the Vietnamese market ended with the murder of an agent of the East India Company in Hanoi in 1613.

One of the most illustrious of the early missionaries was the brilliant French Jesuit Alexandre de Rhodes (1591-1660). He is most recognised for his work in devising *quoc ngu*, the Latin-based phonetic alphabet in which Vietnamese is written to this day. Over the course of his long career, de Rhodes flitted back and forth between Hanoi, Macau, Rome and Paris, seeking support and funding for his missionary activities and battling both Portuguese colonial opposition and the intractable Vatican bureaucracy. In 1645, he was sentenced to death for illegally entering Vietnam to proselytise but was expelled instead; two of the priests with him were beheaded.

By the late 17th century most of the European merchants were gone; trade with Vietnam had not proved particularly profitable. But the missionaries remained, and the Catholic Church eventually had a greater impact on Vietnam than on any country in Asia except the Philippines, which was ruled by the Spanish for 400 years. The Vietnamese – especially in the north – proved highly receptive to Catholicism, but mass conversions were hindered by the Catholic stand against polygamy and by the opposition of the Vatican to ancestor-worship. The Catholic emphasis on individual salvation undermined the established Confucian order, and wary officials of the mandarinate often restricted the activities of missionaries and persecuted their followers. But despite this friction, the imperial court retained a contingent of Jesuit scholars, astronomers, mathematicians and physicians.

The European missionaries did not hesitate to use secular means to help them achieve their goal – the conversion to Catholicism of all of Asia. Towards this end, French missionaries, who had supplanted the Portuguese by the 18th century, actively campaigned for a greater French political and military role in Vietnam.

Tay Son Rebellion (1771-1802)

In 1765, a rebellion against misgovernment broke out in the town of Tay Son near Qui Nhon. It was led by three brothers from a wealthy merchant family: Nguyen Nhac, Nguyen Hue and Nguyen Lu. By 1773, the Tay Son Rebels (as they came to be known) controlled the whole of central Vietnam, and in 1783 they captured Saigon and the rest of the south, killing the reigning prince and his family (as well as 10,000 Chinese residents of Cholon). Nguyen Lu became king of the south, and Nguyen Nhac became king of central Vietnam.

Prince Nguyen Anh, the only survivor of the defeated Nguyen clan, fled to Thailand and requested military assistance from the Thais. He also met the French Jesuit missionary Pigneau de Behaine (the Bishop of Adran), whom he eventually authorised to act as his intermediary in seeking assistance from the French. As a sign of good faith, Nguyen Anh sent his four-year-old son Canh with Pigneau de Behaine to France. The exotic entourage created quite a sensation when it arrived at Versailles in 1787, and Louis XVI authorised a military expedition. Louis XVI later changed his mind, but the bishop managed to convince French merchants in India to buy him two ships, weapons and supplies. With a force of 400 French deserters he had recruited, de Behaine set sail from Pondicherry, India, in June 1789.

Meanwhile, the Tay Son overthrew the Trinh Lords in the north and proclaimed allegiance to the Later Le Dynasty. The weak Le emperor, however, proved unable to retain his control of the country, but rather than calling on the Tay Son, he asked the Chinese for help. Taking advantage of the unstable situation, the Chinese sent 200,000 troops to Vietnam under the pretext of helping the emperor. In 1788, with popular sentiment on his side, one of the Tay Son brothers, Nguyen Hue, proclaimed himself Emperor Quang Trung and set out with his army to expel the Chinese. In 1789, Nguyen Hue's forces overwhelmingly defeated the Chinese army at Dong Da (near Hanoi) in one of the most celebrated military achievements in Vietnamese history.

In the south, Nguyen Anh, whose forces were trained by Pigneau de Behaine's young French adventurers, gradually pushed back the Tay Son. In 1802, Nguyen Anh proclaimed himself Emperor Gia Long, thus beginning the Nguyen Dynasty. When he captured Hanoi, his victory was complete, and for the first time in two centuries, Vietnam was united. Hué became the new national capital.

Nguyen Dynasty (1802-1945)

Emperors of the Nguyen Dynasty:

Gia Long	1802-1819
Minh Mang	1820-1840
Thieu Tri	1841-1847
Tu Duc	1848-1883
Duc Duc	1883
Hiep Hoa	1883
Kien Phuc	1883-1884
Ham Nghi	1884-1885
Dong Khanh	1885-1889
Thanh Thai	1889-1907
Duy Tan	1907-1916
Khai Dinh	1916-1925
Bao Dai	1925-1945

Emperor Gia Long (reigned 1802-19) initiated what historian David Marr has called 'a policy of massive reassertion of Confucian values and institutions' in order to consolidate the dynasty's shaky position by appealing to the conservative tendencies of the elite, who had felt threatened by the atmosphere of reform stirred up by the Tay Son Rebels.

Gia Long also began a large-scale programme of public works (dikes, canals, roads, ports, bridges, land reclamation) to rehabilitate the country, which had been devastated by almost three decades of warfare. The Mandarin Road linking the national capital, Hué, to both Hanoi and Saigon was constructed during this period, as was a string of star-shaped citadels – built according to the principles of the French military architect Vauban – in provincial capitals. All

these projects imposed a heavy burden on the population in the forms of taxation, military conscription and *corvée* (forced labour).

Gia Long's son, Emperor Minh Mang (reigned 1820-40), worked to consolidate the state and establish a strong central government. Because of his background as a Confucian scholar, he emphasised the importance of traditional Confucian education which consisted of the memorisation and orthodox interpretation of the Confucian classics and texts of ancient Chinese history. As a result, education and spheres of activity dependent on it stagnated.

Minh Mang was profoundly hostile to Catholicism, which he saw as a threat to the Confucian state, and he extended this antipathy to all Western influences. Seven missionaries and an unknown number of Vietnamese Catholics were executed in the 1830s, inflaming passions among French Catholics who demanded that their government intervene in Vietnam.

Serious uprisings broke out in both the north and the south during this period, growing progressively more serious in the 1840s and 1850s. To make matters worse, the civil unrest in the deltas was accompanied by smallpox epidemics, tribal uprisings, drought, locusts and – most serious of all – repeated breaches in the Red River dikes, the result of government neglect.

The early Nguyen emperors continued the expansionist policies followed by preceding dynasties, pushing into Cambodia and westward into the mountains along a wide front. They seized huge areas of Lao territory and clashed with Thailand over control of the lands of the weak Khmer Empire.

The first half of the 19th century was marked by a great deal of literary activity. It was during this period that Nguyen Du (1765-1820), a poet, scholar, mandarin and diplomat, wrote one of Vietnam's literary masterpieces, *The Tale of Kieu (Kim Van Kieu)*.

Minh Mang was succeeded by Emperor Thieu Tri (reigned 1841-47), who expelled most of the foreign missionaries. He was followed by Emperor Tu Duc (reigned 1848-

83), who continued to rule according to conservative Confucian precepts and in imitation of Qing practices in China. Both responded to rural unrest with repression.

French Rule (1859-1954)

Ever since Pigneau de Behaine's patronage of Nguyen Anh in the late 18th century and his son Canh's appearance at Versailles in 1787, certain segments of French society had retained an active interest in Indochina. But it was not until the Revolution of 1848 and the advent of the Second Empire that there arose a coalition of interests – Catholic, commercial, patriotic, strategic and idealistic (fans of the *mission civilisatrice*) – with sufficient influence to initiate large-scale, long-term colonial efforts. However, for the next four decades, the French colonial venture in Indochina was carried out haphazardly and without any preconceived plan. In fact, it was repeatedly on the verge of being discontinued altogether, and at times only the insubordinate and reckless actions of a few adventurers kept it going.

France's military activity in Vietnam began in 1847, when the French Navy attacked Danang harbour in response to Thieu Tri's actions against Catholic missionaries. In 1858, a joint military force of 14 ships from France and the Spanish colony of the Philippines stormed Danang after the killing of several missionaries. As disease began to take a heavy toll and the expected support from Catholic Vietnamese failed to materialise, the force left a small garrison in Danang and followed the monsoon winds southward, seizing Saigon in early 1859. Huge quantities of Vietnamese cannon, firearms, swords, saltpetre, sulphur, shot and copper coins were seized; a fire set in rice storage granaries is said to have smouldered for three years.

The French victory in the 1861 Battle of Ky Hoa (Chi Hoa) marked the beginning of the end of formal, organised Vietnamese military action against the French in the south and the rise of popular guerrilla resistance led by the local scholar-gentry, who had refused en masse to collaborate with the French administration. This resistance took the form of ambushing French rivercraft, denying food supplies to French bases and assassinating collaborators.

In 1862, Tu Duc signed a treaty that gave the French the three eastern provinces of Cochinchina. In addition, missionaries were promised the freedom to proselytise everywhere in the country, several ports were opened to French and Spanish commerce, and Tu Duc undertook to pay a large indemnity. To raise the necessary cash he authorised the sale of opium in the north and sold the monopoly to the Chinese. Additionally, he debased the meritocratic mandarinate by putting low-ranking mandarinal posts up for sale.

The French offensive of 1867 broke the morale of the resistance, causing the scholar-gentry who had not been killed to flee the delta. Cochinchina became a French colony, and the peasantry assumed a position of nonviolent resignation. At the same time, voices among the more educated classes of Vietnamese began to advocate cooperation with and subordination to the French in the interest of technical and economic development.

During this era, the Vietnamese might have been able to reduce the impact of the arrival of the European maritime powers and to retain their independence, but this would have required a degree of imagination and dynamism lacking in Hué. Indeed, until the mid-19th century, the imperial court at Hué, which was dominated by extreme Confucian conservatism, behaved almost as if Europe did not exist, though events such as the Opium War of 1839 in China should have served as a warning. In addition, resistance to colonialism was severely handicapped by an almost total lack of political and economic intelligence about France and the French.

The next major French action came in the years 1872 to 1874, when Jean Dupuis, a merchant seeking to supply salt and weapons to a Yunnanese general by sailing up the Red River, seized the Hanoi Citadel. Captain Francis Garnier, ostensibly dispatched to reign in Dupuis, instead took over where Dupuis left off. After capturing Hanoi, Garnier's gunboats proceeded to sail around the Red River Delta demanding tribute from provincial fortresses, an activity that ended only when Garnier was killed by the Black Flags (Co Den), a semi-autonomous army of Chinese, Vietnamese and hill-tribes troops who fought mostly for booty but resisted the French in part because of a strong antipathy toward Westerners.

These events threw the north into chaos: the Black Flags continued their piratic activities; local bands were organised to take vengeance on the Vietnamese – especially Catholics – who had helped the French; Chinese militias in the pay of both the French and the Nguyen emperors sprung up; Le Dynasty pretenders began asserting their claims; and the hill tribes revolted. As central government authority collapsed and all established order broke down, Tu Duc went so far as to petition for help from the Chinese and to ask for support from the British and even the Americans.

In 1882, a French force under Captain Henri Rivière seized Hanoi, but further conquests were stubbornly resisted by both Chinese regulars and the Black Flags, especially the latter. The following year, Black Flags units ambushed Rivière at Cau Giay, killing him and 32 other Frenchmen, and triumphally paraded his severed head from hamlet to hamlet.

Meanwhile, only a few weeks after the death of Tu Duc in 1883, the French attacked Hué and imposed a Treaty of Protectorate on the imperial court. There then began a tragicomic struggle for royal succession notable for its palace coups, mysteriously dead emperors and heavy-handed French diplomacy. Emperors Duc Duc and Hiep Hoà were succeeded by Kien Phuc (reigned 1883-84), who was followed by 14-year-old Emperor Ham Nghi (reigned 1884-85). By the time Ham Nghi and his advisors decided to relocate the court to the mountains and to lead resistance activities from there, the French had rounded up enough mandarin collaborators to give his French-picked successor, Emperor Dong Khanh (reigned 1885-89), sufficient legitimacy to survive.

Ham Nghi held out against the French until 1888 when he was betrayed, captured by the French and exiled to Algeria. Although the Indochinese Union (consisting of Cochinchina, Annam, Tonkin, Cambodia, Laos and the port of Qinzhouwan in China), proclaimed by the French in 1887, effectively ended the existence of an independent Vietnamese state, active resistance to colonialism continued in various parts of the country for the duration of French rule. The establishment of the Indochinese Union ended Vietnamese expansionism, and the Vietnamese were forced to give back lands taken from Cambodia and Laos.

Continuing in the tradition of centuries of Vietnamese dynasties, the French colonial authorities carried out ambitious public works, constructing the Saigon-Hanoi railway as well as ports, extensive irrigation and drainage systems, improved dikes, various public services and research institutes. To fund these activities, the government heavily taxed the peasants, devastating the traditional rural economy. The colonial administration also ran alcohol, salt and opium monopolies for the purpose of raising revenues. In Saigon, they produced a quick-burning type of opium which helped increase addiction and thus revenues.

And since colonialism was supposed to be a profitable proposition, French capital was invested for quick returns in anthracite coal, tin, tungsten and zinc mines and in tea, coffee and rubber plantations, all of which became notorious for the abysmal wages they paid and the subhuman treatment to which their Vietnamese workers were subjected. Out of the 45,000 indentured workers at one Michelin rubber plantation, 12,000 died of disease and malnutrition between 1917 and 1944.

As land, like capital, became concentrated in the hands of a tiny percentage of the population (in Cochinchina, 2.5% of the population came to own 45% of the land), a subproletariat of landless and uprooted peasants was formed. In the countryside these people were reduced to sharecropping, paying up to 60% of their crop in rents. Whereas the majority of Vietnamese peasants had owned their land before the arrival of the French, by the 1930s about 70% of them were landless. Because French policies impoverished the people of Indochina, the area never became an important market for French industry.

Vietnamese Anti-Colonialism

Throughout the colonial period, the vast majority of Vietnamese retained a strong desire to have their national independence restored. Seething nationalist aspirations often broke out into open defiance of the French, which took forms ranging from the publishing of patriotic periodicals and books to an attempt to poison the French garrison in Hanoi.

The imperial court in Hué, though corrupt, was a centre of nationalist feeling, a fact most evident in the game of musical thrones orchestrated by the French. Upon his death the subservient Dong Khanh was replaced by 10-year-old Emperor Thanh Thai (reigned 1889-1907), whose rule the French ended when he was discovered to have been plotting against them. He was deported to the Indian Ocean island of Réunion, where he remained until 1947.

His son and successor, Emperor Duy Tan (reigned 1907-16), was only in his teens in 1916 when he and the poet Tran Cao Van planned a general uprising in Hué that was discovered the day before it was scheduled to begin; Tran Cao Van was beheaded and Duy Tan was exiled to Réunion. Duy Tan was succeeded by the docile Emperor Khai Dinh (reigned 1916-25). On his death he was followed by his son, Emperor Bao Dai (reigned 1926-45), who at the time of his accession was 12 years old and in school in France.

Some Vietnamese nationalists (such as the scholar and patriot Phan Boi Chau who rejected French rule but not Western ideas and technology) looked to Japan and China for support and political inspiration, especially after Japan's victory in the Russo-Japanese war of 1905 showed all of Asia that Western powers could be defeated. Sun Yatsen's 1911 revolution in China was also closely followed in Vietnamese nationalist circles.

The Viet Nam Quoc Dan Dang (VNQDD), a largely middle-class nationalist party modelled after the Chinese Kuomintang, was founded in 1927 by nationalist leaders including Nguyen Thai Hoc, who was guillotined along with 12 comrades in the savage French retribution for the abortive 1930 Yen Bai uprising.

Another source of nationalist agitation was among those Vietnamese who had spent time in France where they were not hampered by the restrictions on political activity in force in the colonies. In addition, over 100,000 Vietnamese were sent to Europe as soldiers during WW I.

Ultimately, the most successful anti-colonialists proved to be the Communists, who were uniquely able to relate to the frustrations and aspirations of the population – especially the peasants – and to effectively channel and organise their demands for more equitable land distribution.

The institutional history of Vietnamese Communism – which in many ways is the political biography of Ho Chi Minh – is rather complicated. In brief, the first Marxist grouping in Indochina was the Vietnam Revolutionary Youth League (Viet Nam Cach Menh Thanh Nien Dong Chi Hoi), founded by Ho Chi Minh in Canton, China, in 1925. The Revolutionary Youth League was succeeded in February 1930 by the Vietnamese Communist Party (Dang Cong San Viet Nam), a union of three groups effected by Ho which was renamed the Indochinese Communist Party (Dang Cong San Dong Duong) in October 1930. In 1941, Ho Chi Minh formed the League for the Independence of Vietnam (Viet Nam Doc Lap Dong Minh Hoi), better known as the Viet Minh, which resisted the Japanese occupation (and thus received Chinese and American aid) and carried out extensive political organising during WW II. Despite its broad nationalist programme and claims to the contrary, the

Viet Minh was, from its inception, dominated by Ho's Communists.

Communist successes in the late 1920s included major strikes by urban workers. During the Nghe Tinh Uprising (1930-31), revolutionary committees (or soviets) took control of parts of Nghe An and Ha Tinh provinces (thus all the streets named 'Xo Viet Nghe Tinh'), but after an unprecedented wave of terror, the French managed to re-establish control. A 1940 uprising in the south was also brutally suppressed, seriously damaging the Party's infrastructure. French prisons, filled with arrested cadres, were turned by the captives into revolutionary 'universities' in which Marxist-Leninist theory was taught.

WW II

When France fell to Nazi Germany in 1940, the Indochinese government of Vichy-appointed Admiral Jean Decoux concluded an agreement to accept the presence of Japanese troops in Vietnam. For their own convenience the Japanese, who sought to exploit the area's strategic location and its natural resources, left the French administration in charge of the day-to-day running of the country. The only group that did anything significant to resist the Japanese occupation was the Communist-dominated Viet Minh, which from 1944 received funding and arms from the US Office of Strategic Services (OSS), predecessor of the CIA. This affiliation offered the Viet Minh the hope of eventual US recognition of their demands for independence; it also proved useful to Ho in that it implied that he had the support of the Americans.

In March 1945, as a Viet Minh offensive was getting under way and Decoux's government was plotting to resist the Japanese – something they hadn't tried in the preceding 4½ years – the Japanese overthrew Decoux, imprisoning both his troops and his administrators. Decoux's administration was replaced with a puppet regime – nominally independent within Japan's Greater East-Asian Co-Prosperity Sphere – led by Emperor Bao Dai, who abrogated the 1883 treaty that made Annam and Tonkin French protectorates. During the same period, Japanese rice requisitions and the Japanese policy of forcing farmers to plant industrial crops – combined with floods and breaches in the dikes – caused a horrific famine in which two million of northern Vietnam's 10 million people starved to death.

By the spring of 1945 the Viet Minh controlled large parts of the country, especially in the north. In mid-August – after the atomic bombing of Japan – Ho Chi Minh formed the National Liberation Committee and called for a general uprising, later known as the August Revolution (Cach Mang Thang Tam), to take advantage of the power vacuum. Almost immediately, the Viet Minh assumed complete control of the north. In central Vietnam, Emperor Bao Dai abdicated in favour of the new government (which later appointed him as its 'Supreme Advisor', whatever that means). In the south, the Viet Minh soon held power in a shaky coalition with non-Communist groups. On 2 September 1945, Ho Chi Minh – with American OSS agents at his side and borrowing liberally from the stirring prose of the American Declaration of Independence – declared the Democratic Republic of Vietnam independent at a rally in Hanoi's Ba Dinh Square. During this period, Ho wrote no fewer than eight letters to US President Truman and the State Department asking for US aid but did not receive replies.

A minor item on the agenda of the Potsdam Conference of 1945 was the procedure for disarming the Japanese occupation forces in Vietnam. It was decided that the Chinese Kuomintang (Nationalist Party) would accept the Japanese surrender north of the 16th parallel and the British would do the same south of that line.

When the British arrived in Saigon chaos reigned, with enraged French settlers beginning to take matters into their own hands and competing Vietnamese groups on the verge of civil war. With only 1800 British, Indian and Ghurka troops at his disposal, British General Gracey ordered the defeated Japanese troops (!) to help him restore order. He also released and armed 1400 imprisoned French paratroopers who immediately went on a rampage around the city, overthrowing the Committee of the South government, breaking into Vietnamese homes and shops and indiscriminately clubbing men, women and children. The Viet Minh and allied groups responded by calling a general strike and by beginning a guerrilla campaign against the French. On 24 September, French General Jacques Philippe Leclerc arrived in Saigon, declaring, 'We have come to reclaim our inheritance'.

Meanwhile, in Hué, the imperial library was demolished (priceless documents were being used in the marketplace to wrap fish), and in the north 180,000 Chinese Kuomintang troops were fleeing the Chinese Communists, pillaging their way southward towards Hanoi. Ho tried to placate them, but as the months of Chinese occupation dragged on, he decided to accept a temporary return of the French in order to get rid of the anti-Communist Kuomintang, who, in addition to everything else, were supporting the Viet Minh's nationalist rivals. Most of the Kuomintang soldiers were packed off to Taiwan. The French were to stay for five years in return for recognising Vietnam as a free state within the French Union. As Ho put it at the time:

The last time the Chinese came, they stayed a thousand years. The French are foreigners. They are weak. Colonialism is dying. The white man is finished in Asia. As for me, I prefer to sniff French shit for five years than eat Chinese shit for the rest of my life.

The British wanted out, the French wanted in, Ho Chi Minh wanted the Chinese to go and the Americans under President Truman were not as actively opposed to colonialism as they had been under President Roosevelt. So the French, employing their usual duplicitous methods (such as ignoring the provisions of solemnly signed agreements), managed to regain control of Vietnam, at least in name. But when the French shelled Haiphong in November 1946 after an obscure customs dispute, killing hundreds of civilians, the patience of the Vietnamese people ended. A few weeks later fighting broke out in Hanoi, marking the start of the Franco-Viet Minh War. Ho and his forces fled to the mountains where they would remain for eight years.

Franco-Viet Minh War (1946-54)

In the face of Vietnamese determination that their country regain its independence, the French proved unable to reassert their control. Despite massive American aid and the existence of significant indigenous anti-Communist elements – who in 1949 rallied to support Bao Dai's 'Associated State' within the French Union – it was an unwinnable war. As Ho said to the French at the time: 'You can kill 10 of my men for every one I kill of yours, but even at those odds, you will lose and I will win'.

After eight years of fighting, the Viet Minh controlled much of Vietnam and neighbouring Laos. On 7 May 1954, after a 57-day siege, over 10,000 starving French troops surrendered to the Viet Minh at Dien Bien Phu – a catastrophic defeat that shattered the remaining public support for the war in France. The next day, the Geneva Conference opened to negotiate an end to the conflict; 2½ months later, the Geneva Accords were signed. The Geneva Accords provided for an exchange of prisoners, the temporary division of Vietnam into two zones at the Ben Hai River (near the 17th parallel), the free passage of people across the 17th parallel for a period of 300 days, and the holding of nationwide elections on 20 July 1956. In the course of the Franco-Viet Minh War, more than 35,000 men were killed and 48,000 wounded on the French side, but Vietnamese casualties were much greater.

South Vietnam

After the signing of the Geneva Accords, the South was ruled by a government led by Ngo Dinh Diem (pronounced 'zee-EM'), a fiercely anti-Communist Catholic whose brother had been killed by the Viet Minh in 1945. His power base was significantly strengthened by some 900,000 refugees –

many of them Catholics – who fled the Communist North during the 300-day free-passage period.

In 1955 Diem, convinced that if elections were held Ho Chi Minh would win, refused – with US encouragement – to implement the Geneva Accords; instead, he held a referendum on his continued rule. Diem claimed to have won 98.2% of the vote in an election that was by all accounts rigged (in Saigon, he received a third more votes that there were registered voters!). After Diem declared himself president of the Republic of Vietnam, the new regime was recognised by France, the USA, Great Britain, Australia, New Zealand, Italy, Japan, Thailand and South Korea.

During the first few years of his rule, Diem consolidated power fairly effectively, defeating the Binh Xuyen crime syndicate and the private armies of the Hoa Hao and Cao Dai religious sects. During a 1957 official visit to the USA President Eisenhower called Diem the 'miracle man' of Asia. But as time went on he became increasingly tyrannical in dealing with dissent. Running the government became a family affair (Diem's much-hated sister-in-law became Vietnam's powerful 'first lady' while his father-in-law was appointed US ambassador).

Such blatant nepotism was offensive enough, but worse still, Diem's land-reform programme ended up reversing land redistribution effected by the Viet Minh in the '40s. The favouritism he showed to Catholics alienated many Buddhists. In the early 1960s, the South was rocked by anti-Diem unrest led by university students and Buddhist clergy, including several self-immolations by monks that shocked the world. When Diem used French contacts to explore negotiations with Hanoi, the USA threw its support behind a military coup; in November 1963, he was overthrown and killed. Diem was succeeded by a succession of military rulers who continued his repressive policies.

North Vietnam

The Geneva Accords allowed the leadership of the Democratic Republic of Vietnam to return to Hanoi and to assert control of all territory north of the 17th parallel. The new government immediately set out to eliminate elements of the population that threatened its power. A radical land-reform programme was implemented, providing about half a hectare of land to some 1.5 million peasants. Tens of thousands of 'landlords', some with only tiny holdings – and many of whom had been denounced to 'security committees' by envious neighbours – were arrested; hasty 'trials' resulted in 10,000 to 15,000 executions and the imprisonment of 50,000 to 100,000 people. In 1956, the Party, faced with serious rural unrest caused by the programme, recognised that the People's Agricultural Reform Tribunals had gotten out of hand and began a 'Campaign for the Rectification of Errors'.

On 12 December 1955 – shortly after Diem had declared the South a republic – the USA closed its consulate in Hanoi. Since then there has been no American diplomatic representation in the North.

The Vietnam War

Though there were Communist-led guerrilla attacks on Diem's government during the mid-1950s, the real campaign to 'liberate' the South began in 1959 when Hanoi, responding to the demands of Southern cadres that they be allowed to resist the Diem regime, changed from a strategy of 'political struggle' to one of 'armed struggle'. Shortly thereafter, the Ho Chi Minh Trail, which had been in existence for several years, was expanded. In April 1960, universal military conscription was implemented in the North. Eight months later, Hanoi announced the formation of the National Liberation Front (NLF), whose platform called for a neutralisation of Vietnam, the withdrawal of all foreign troops and gradual reunification. In the South, the NLF came to be known derogatorily as the 'Viet Cong' or just the 'VC'; both are abbreviations for Viet Nam Cong San, which means 'Vietnamese Communist' (today, the words 'Viet Cong' and 'VC' are no longer considered pejoratives). American soldiers nicknamed the Viet Cong 'Charlie'.

When the NLF campaign got under way, the military situation of the Diem government rapidly deteriorated. To turn things around, the Strategic Hamlet Programme (Ap Chien Luoc) was begun in 1962. Following tactics employed successfully by the British in Malaya during the '50s, peasants were forcibly moved into fortified 'strategic hamlets' in order to deny the Viet Cong bases of support. The incompetence and brutality with which the programme was carried out created new enemies for the Saigon government, and many of the strategic hamlets were infiltrated by the VC and fell under their control. The Strategic Hamlets Programme was widely criticised in the West and finally abandoned by the South Vietnamese government, but after the war ended the VC admitted that the programme had caused them very serious concern and that they had expended a major effort sabotaging it.

And it was no longer just a battle with the VC. In 1964, Hanoi began infiltrating regular North Vietnamese Army (NVA) units into the South. By early 1965, the Saigon government was in desperate straits; desertions from the ARVN (Army of the Republic of Vietnam), whose command was notorious for corruption and incompetence, had reached 2000 per month. It was losing 500 men and a district capital each week, yet since 1954, only one senior South Vietnamese Army officer had been wounded. The army was getting ready to evacuate Hué and Danang, and the Central Highlands seemed about to fall. The South Vietnamese general staff even prepared a plan to move its headquarters from Saigon to the Vung Tau peninsula, which was easy to defend and was only minutes from ships that could spirit them out of the country. It was at this point that the USA committed its first combat troops.

Enter the Americans

The first Americans to set foot in Vietnam were the crew of the clipper ship *Franklin* under the command of Captain John White

of Salem, Massachusetts, which docked at Saigon in 1820. Edmund Roberts, a New Englander selected by President Andrew Jackson, led the first official American mission to Vietnam in 1832. In 1845, the USS *Constitution* under Captain 'Mad Jack' Percival sent an armed party ashore at Hué to rescue a French bishop who was under sentence of death, taking several Vietnamese officials hostage. When this failed to convince Emperor Thieu Tri to free the bishop, Percival's men opened fire on a crowd of civilians. In the 1870s, Emperor Tu Duc sent a respected scholar, Bui Vien, to Washington in an attempt to garner international support to counter the French. Bui Vien met President Ulysses S Grant but, lacking the proper documents of accreditation, was sent back to Vietnam empty-handed.

The theory was rapidly gaining acceptance in the West that there was a worldwide Communist movement intent on overthrowing one government after another by waging various 'wars of liberation' (the 'Domino Theory' as it came to be known). The Domino Theory gained considerable support after the start of the Korean War in 1950, and the Americans saw France's colonial war in Indochina as an important part of the worldwide struggle to stop Communist expansion. By 1954, US military aid to the French war effort topped two billion dollars (and that's 1950s dollars). In 1950, 35 US soldiers arrived in Vietnam as part of the US Military Assistance Advisory Group (MAAG), ostensibly to instruct troops receiving US weapons how to use them; there would be American soldiers on Vietnamese soil for the next 25 years.

The People's Republic of China established diplomatic relations with the Democratic Republic of Vietnam in 1950; shortly thereafter, the Soviet Union did the same. Only then did Washington recognise Bao Dai's French-backed government. The circumstances of this event are instructive: though Ho's government had been around since 1945, the USSR didn't get around to recognising it until the Communist Chinese did so, and the US State Department – which at the time was reverberating with recriminations over who was to blame for 'losing China' to Communism – recognised Bao Dai's government as a reaction to these events. From that point on, US policy in Indochina has usually been a kneejerk reaction against whatever the Communists do.

When the last French troops left Vietnam in April 1956, the MAAG, now numbering several hundred men, assumed responsibility for training the South Vietnamese military; the transition couldn't have been neater. The first American troops to die in the Vietnam War were killed at Bien Hoa in 1959 at a time when about 700 US military personnel were in Vietnam.

As the military position of the South Vietnamese government continued to deteriorate, the Kennedy administration (1961-63) sent more and more military advisors to Vietnam. By the end of 1963, there were 16,300 US military personnel in the country.

The Vietnam War became a central issue in the USA's 1964 presidential election. The candidate for the Republican Party, Senator Barry Goldwater of Arizona, took the more aggressive stance – he warned that if elected he would tell Ho Chi Minh to stop the war 'or there won't be enough left of North Vietnam to grow rice on it'. Many Americans, with bitter memories of how Chinese troops came to the aid of North Korea during the Korean War, feared the same would happen again. The thought of a possible nuclear confrontation with Russia could not be ruled out, either. With such horrors in mind, voters overwhelming supported Lyndon Baines Johnson.

Ironically, it was 'peace candidate' Johnson who rapidly escalated the USA's involvement in the war. A major turning-point in American strategy was precipitated by the August 1964 Tonkin Gulf Incidents in which two American destroyers, the *Maddox* and the *Turner Joy*, claimed to have come under 'unprovoked' attack while sailing off the North Vietnamese coast. Subsequent research indicates that the first attack took place while the *Maddox* was in North Vietnamese territorial waters assisting a secret South Vietnamese commando raid and that the second attack simply never took place.

But on President Johnson's orders, carrier-based jets flew 64 sorties against the North, the first of thousands of such missions that would hit every single road and rail bridge in the country as well as 4000 of North Vietnam's 5788 villages. Two American aircraft were lost, and the pilot of one, Lieutenant Everett Alvarez, became the first American prisoner of war (POW) of the conflict; he would remain in captivity for eight years.

A few days later, an indignant (and misled) Congress almost unanimously (two Senators dissented) passed the Tonkin Gulf Resolution, which gave the President the power to 'take all necessary measures' to 'repel any armed attack against the forces of the United States and to prevent further aggression'. Only later was it established that the Johnson administration had in fact drafted the resolution before the 'attacks' had actually taken place. Until its repeal in 1970, the resolution was treated by US presidents as a blank cheque to do whatever they chose in Vietnam without congressional oversight.

As the military situation of the Saigon government reached a new nadir, the first US combat troops splashed ashore at Danang in March 1965, ostensibly to defend Danang air base. But once you had 'American boys' fighting and dying, you had to do everything necessary to protect and support them, including sending over more American boys. By December 1965, 184,300 American military personnel were in Vietnam, and American dead numbered 636. Twelve months later, the totals were 385,300 US troops in Vietnam and 6644 dead. By December 1967, 485,600 US soldiers were in-country and 16,021 had died. In 1967, with South Vietnamese and 'Free World Forces' counted in, there were 1.3 million men – one for every 15 people in South Vietnam – under arms for the Saigon government.

By 1966, the failed Strategic Hamlets Programme of earlier years was replaced with a policy of 'pacification', 'search and destroy' and 'free-fire zones'. Pacification meant building a pro-government civilian infrastructure of teachers, health-care workers and officials in each village, as well as soldiers to guard them and keep the VC away from the villagers. To protect the villages from VC raids, mobile 'search and destroy' units of soldiers moved around the country (often by helicopter) to hunt bands of VC guerrillas. In some cases, villagers were evacuated so the Americans could use heavy weapons like bombs, napalm, artillery and tanks in areas that were declared 'free-fire zones'. A relatively little-publicised strategy was dubbed 'Operation Phoenix', a controversial programme run by the CIA aimed at eliminating VC cadres by assassination, capture or defection.

These strategies were only partially successful – US forces could control the countryside by day while the VC usually controlled it by night. The VC proved adept at infiltrating 'pacified' villages. Although lacking heavy weapons like tanks and aircraft, VC guerrillas still continued to inflict heavy casualties on US and ARVN troops in ambushes and by using mines and booby traps. Although free-fire zones were supposed to prevent civilian casualties, plenty of villagers were nevertheless bombed, strafed and napalmed to death – their surviving relatives often joined the Viet Cong.

The Turning Point

In January 1968, North Vietnamese troops launched a major attack at Khe Sanh (see the DMZ & Vicinity chapter for details). This battle, the single largest of the war, turned out to be a massive diversion for what was to come only a week later: the Tet Offensive.

The Tet Offensive of early 1968 marked a crucial turning point in the war. On the evening of 31 January, as the country celebrated the New Year, the Viet Cong launched a stunning offensive in over 100 cities and towns, including Saigon. As the TV cameras rolled, a VC commando team took over the courtyard of the downtown-Saigon US Embassy building.

The American forces had long been wanting to engage the VC in an open battle rather than a guerrilla war where the enemy couldn't be seen. The Tet Offensive provided the opportunity. Though taken by complete surprise (a major failure of US military intelligence), the South Vietnamese and Americans quickly counterattacked with massive firepower, bombing and shelling heavily populated cities as they had the open jungle. The effect was devastating on the VC but also on the civilian population. In Ben Tre, an American officer bitterly explained that 'we had to destroy the town in order to save it'.

The Tet Offensive killed about 1000 American soldiers and 2000 ARVN troops, but Viet Cong losses were more than 10 times higher at approximately 32,000 deaths. In addition, some 500 Americans and 10,000 North Vietnamese troops died at the battle of Khe Sanh a week before the Tet Offensive began. According to American estimates, 165,000 civilians also died in the three weeks following the start of the Tet Offensive; two million more became refugees.

The VC only held the cities for three or four days (with the exception of Hué which they held for 25 days). The surviving VC then retreated to the jungles. General Westmoreland, commander of US forces in Vietnam, insisted that the uprising had been a decisive military blow to the Communists (and he was right – by their own admission, the VC never recovered from their high casualties). Westmoreland then asked for an additional 206,000 troops – he didn't get them and was replaced in July by General Creighton W Abrams.

Perhaps the VC lost the battle, but they were far from losing the war. After years of hearing that they were winning, many Americans – having watched the killing and chaos in Saigon on their nightly TV newscasts – stopped believing what they were being told by their government. While US generals were proclaiming a great victory, public tolerance of the war and its casualties reached the breaking point. For the VC, the Tet Offensive proved to be a big success after all – it made the cost of fighting the war (both in dollars and in lives) unbearable for the Americans.

Antiwar demonstrations rocked US campuses and spilled out into the streets. Seeing his political popularity plummet in the polls, President Lyndon Johnson decided not to stand for re-election.

Richard Nixon was elected president of the USA, in part because of a promise that he had a 'secret plan' to end the war. The plan, later to be labelled the 'Nixon Doctrine', was unveiled in July 1969 and called on Asian nations to be more 'self-reliant' in defence matters and not expect the USA to become embroiled in future civil wars. Nixon's strategy called for 'Vietnamisation' – making the South Vietnamese military fight the war without American troops.

Nixon Doctrine or not, the first half of 1969 saw still greater escalation. In April, the number of US soldiers in Vietnam reached an all-time high of 543,400. By the end of 1969, US troop levels were down to 475,200; 40,024 Americans had been killed in action as had 110,176 ARVN troops. While the fighting raged, Nixon's chief negotiator, Henry Kissinger, pursued talks in Paris with his North Vietnamese counterpart Le Duc Tho.

In 1969, the USA began secretly bombing Cambodia. The following year, American ground forces were sent into Cambodia to extricate ARVN units whose fighting ability was still unable to match the enemy's. This new escalation infuriated previously quiescent elements of the American public, leading to bitter antiwar protests. The TV screens of America were almost daily filled with scenes of demonstrations, student strikes and even deadly acts of self-immolation. A peace demonstration at Kent State University in Ohio resulted in four protesters being shot dead by National Guard troops.

The rise of organisations like 'Vietnam Veterans Against the War' demonstrated that it wasn't just 'cowardly students fearing military conscription' who wanted the USA out of Vietnam. It was clear that the war was ripping the USA apart. Nor were the protests just confined to the USA – huge anti-American demonstrations in Western Europe were shaking the NATO alliance. There was even a Vietnamese peace movement – at great risk to themselves, idealistic young students in Saigon protested against the US presence in their country.

In 1971, excerpts from a scandalous top secret study of US involvement in Indochina were published in the New York Times after a legal battle which went to the US Supreme Court. The study, known as the 'Pentagon Papers', was commissioned by the US Defense Department and detailed how the military and former presidents had systematically lied to Congress and the American public. The Pentagon Papers infuriated the US public and caused antiwar sentiment to reach new heights. The New York Times obtained the study from one of its authors, Dr Daniel Ellsberg, who had turned against the war. Ellsberg was subsequently prosecuted for espionage, theft and conspiracy. A judge dismissed the charges after Nixon's notorious 'White House Plumbers' (so called because they were supposed to stop 'leaks') burglarised the office of Ellsberg's psychiatrist to obtain evidence.

In the spring of 1972, the North Vietnamese launched an offensive across the 17th parallel; the USA responded with increased bombing of the North and mined seven North Vietnamese harbours. The 'Christmas Bombing' of Hanoi and Haiphong at the end of 1972 was meant to wrest concessions from North Vietnam at the negotiating table. Finally, Henry Kissinger and Le Duc Tho reached agreement. The Paris Agreements, signed by the USA, North Vietnam, South Vietnam and the Viet Cong on 27 January 1973, provided for a cease-fire, the establishment of a National Council of Reconciliation and Concord, the total withdrawal of US combat forces and the release of 590 American POWs. The agreement made no mention of approximately 200,000 North Vietnamese troops then in South Vietnam.

Richard Nixon was re-elected president in November 1972, shortly before the Paris peace agreements were signed. By 1973, he became hopelessly mired in the 'Watergate Scandal' resulting from illegal activities regarding his re-election campaign. The Pentagon Papers and Watergate contributed to such a high level of public distrust of the military and presidents that the US Congress passed a resolution prohibiting any further US military involvement in Indochina after 15 August 1973. Nixon resigned in disgrace in 1974.

In total, 3.14 million Americans (including 7200 women) served in the US armed forces in Vietnam during the war. Officially, 58,183 Americans (including eight women) were killed in action or are listed as missing-in-action. The US losses were nearly double that of the Korean War. Pentagon figures indicate that by 1972, 3689 fixed-wing aircraft and 4857 helicopters had been lost and 15 million tonnes of ammunition had been expended. The direct cost of the war was officially put at US$165 billion though its true cost to the economy was at least twice that. By comparison, the Korean War had cost America US$18 billion.

By the end of 1973, 223,748 South Vietnamese soldiers had been killed in action; North Vietnamese and Viet Cong fatalities have been estimated at 440,000 with about twice that many wounded. Approximately four million civilians – 10% of the population of Vietnam – were killed or injured during the war, many in the North due to the American bombing. Over 2200 Americans and 300,000 Vietnamese are still listed as missing-in-action.

As far as anyone knows, the Soviet Union and China – who supplied all the weapons to North Vietnam and the Viet Cong – did not suffer a single casualty.

Other Foreign Involvement

Australia, New Zealand, South Korea, Thailand and the Philippines sent military personnel to South Vietnam as part of what the Americans called the 'Free World Military Forces', whose purpose was to internationalise the American war effort and thus confer upon it legitimacy. The Koreans (who numbered nearly 50,000), Thais and Filipino forces were heavily subsidised by the Americans.

Australia's participation in the Vietnam War constituted the most significant commitment of Australian military forces overseas since the 1940s. At its peak strength, the Australian forces in Vietnam – which included army, navy and air force units – numbered 8300, two-thirds larger than the size of the Australian contingent in the Korean War. Overall, 46,852 Australian military personnel served in Vietnam, including 17,424 draftees; Australian casualties totalled 496 killed and 2398 wounded.

Most of New Zealand's contingent, which numbered 548 at its high point in 1968, operated as an integral part of the Australian Task Force which was stationed near Baria (just north of Vung Tau).

The Australian foreign affairs establishment decided to commit Australian troops to the Vietnam War in order to encourage US military involvement in South-East Asia, thus, they argued, furthering Australia's defence interests by having the Americans play an active role in an area of great importance to Australia's long-term security. The first Australian troops in Vietnam were 30 guerrilla warfare specialists with experience in Malaya and Borneo sent to Vietnam in May 1962. Australia announced the commitment of combat units in April 1965, only a few weeks after the first American combat troops arrived in Danang. The last Australian combat troops withdrew in December 1971; the last advisors returned home a year later. The Australian and New Zealand forces preferred to operate independently of US units, in part because they felt that the Americans took unnecessary risks and were willing to sustain unacceptably high numbers of casualties.

Royal Thai army troops were stationed in Vietnam from 1967 to 1973; Thailand also allowed the US Air Force to base B-52s and fighter aircraft on its territory. The Philippines sent units for non-combat 'civic action' work. South Korea's soldiers, who operated in the South between 1965 and 1971, were noted for both their exceptional fighting ability and extreme brutality.

Taiwan's brief role was one of the most under-reported facts of the war because it was such an embarassment. At that time, the USA still recognised Taiwan's ruling Kuomintang as the legitimate government of all China. Ever since 1949, when the Kuomintang troops were defeated by the Communists, Taiwan's President Chiang Kai-shek had been promising to 'retake the mainland'. When US President Johnson asked Taiwan to supply around 20,000 troops, Chiang was happy to comply, and some troops were immediately dispatched to Saigon. Chiang then rapidly tried to increase the number to 200,000! It soon became apparent that Chiang was planning to use Vietnam as a stepping stone to invade mainland China and draw the USA into his personal war against the Chinese Communists. The USA wanted no part of this and asked Chiang to withdraw his troops from South Vietnam – it was promptly done and the whole incident was hushed up.

Fall of the South (1975)

For a while, things were looking up for the South. The pacification programme was having some success. Although there were sporadic clashes, the Viet Cong seemed to be losing their grip, at least around major population centres. American and South Vietnamese leaders were being cautiously optimistic. They couldn't have been more wrong.

The guerrilla war was over. In January 1975, the North Vietnamese army launched a massive conventional ground attack across the 17th parallel, using tanks and heavy artillery. The NVA quickly occupied a large section of the Central Highlands. The invasion – a blatant violation of the Paris Agreements – panicked the South Vietnamese army and government, which in the past had always depended on the Americans. In the absence of US military support or advice, President Nguyen Van Thieu personally decided on a strategy of tactical withdrawal to more defensible positions. This proved to

be a spectacular military blunder. South Vietnamese troops interpreted the order to retreat as a decisive military defeat – the 'tactical withdrawal' turned into a chaotic rout as soldiers deserted en masse in order to try to save their families.

Whole brigades disintegrated and fled southward, joining the hundreds of thousands of civilians clogging National Highway 1. City after city – Buon Ma Thuot, Quang Tri, Hué, Danang, Qui Nhon, Tuy Hoa, Nha Trang – were simply abandoned by the defenders with hardly a shot fired. So quickly did the ARVN troops flee that the North Vietnamese army could barely keep up with them. The US Congress, fed up with the war and its drain on the treasury, refused to send emergency aid that President Nixon (who had resigned the previous year because of Watergate) had promised would be forthcoming in the event of such an invasion.

President Nguyen Van Thieu, in power since 1967, resigned on 21 April 1975 and fled the country, allegedly taking with him millions of dollars in ill-gotten wealth. He moved to Britain rather than the USA because he felt 'abandoned' by the Americans. For a while he lived in a stately London mansion called 'the White House', but later he sold it and has been keeping a very low profile. He is said to fear assassination and lives as a recluse.

Thieu's main political rival and former vice president, Nguyen Cao Ky, also fled Vietnam and has since been living in California. Unlike Thieu, he is outspoken and very willing to talk to reporters. He denies reports that he stole millions from Vietnam, and in 1984 he filed for bankruptcy in a US court.

President Thieu was replaced by Vice President Tran Van Huong, who quit a week later, turning the presidency over to General Duong Van Minh, who surrendered on the morning of 30 April 1975 in Saigon's Independence Hall (now Reunification Hall) after only 43 hours in office.

The last Americans were evacuated to US ships stationed offshore, transported by helicopter from the US Embassy roof just a few hours before South Vietnam surrendered. Thus came to an end more than a decade of US military involvement. Throughout the entire episode, the USA had never declared war on North Vietnam.

The Americans weren't the only ones who left. As the South collapsed, 135,000 Vietnamese also fled the country; in the next five years, at least 545,000 of their compatriots would do the same. Those who left by sea would become known to the world as 'boat people'.

It's a much less publicised fact that there were a number of 'reverse refugees'. Some South Vietnamese students in the USA who were closet socialists rushed back home at the news of their country's liberation by the North – only to be persecuted upon returning because of their tainted association with America.

Since Reunification

The sudden success of the 1975 North Vietnamese offensive surprised the North almost as much as it did the South. As a result, Hanoi had not prepared specific plans to deal with integrating the two parts of the country whose social and economic systems could hardly have been more different. Until the formal reunification of Vietnam in July 1976, the South was nominally ruled by a Provisional Revolutionary Government.

Because the Communist Party did not really trust the Southern urban intelligentsia – even those of its members who had supported the Viet Cong – large numbers of Northern cadres were sent southward to manage the transition. This created enormous resentment among Southerners who had worked against the Thieu government and then, after its overthrow, found themselves frozen out of positions of responsibility (even today, most of the officials and police in Saigon are from the North).

After months of debates, those in Hanoi who wanted to implement a rapid transition to socialism (including the collectivisation of agriculture) in the South gained the upper hand. Great efforts were made to deal with the South's social problems: millions of illiterates and unemployed, several hundred thousand prostitutes and drug addicts, and tens of thousands of people who made their living by criminal activities. Many of these people were encouraged to move to the newly collectivised farms in the countryside. This may have had some beneficial effects, but the results of the transition to socialism were mostly disastrous to the South's economy.

Reunification was accompanied by large-scale political repression which destroyed whatever trust and goodwill the Southerners might have felt towards the North. Despite repeated promises to the contrary, hundreds of thousands of people who had ties to the previous regime had their property and homes confiscated, and were subsequently rounded up and imprisoned without trial in forced-labour camps euphemistically known as 're-education camps'. Tens of thousands of intellectuals, artists, journalists, writers and trade-union leaders – many of whom had opposed both Thieu and the war – as well as Buddhist monks, Catholic priests and Protestant clergy were also detained; many were tortured. While the majority of the detainees were released within a few years, some (declared to be 'obstinate and counter- revolutionary elements') were to spend the next decade or more in what has been called the 'Vietnamese gulag'. The purge prompted hundreds of thousands of Southerners to flee their homeland by sea and overland through Cambodia.

The purge affected not only former opponents of the Communists, but also their families. Even today, the children of former 'counter-revolutionaries' are treated as if they have some hereditary disease and thus are kept at arm's length from society. One common way to do this is to deny a *ho khao*, a sort of residence permit needed for attending school, seeking employment, owning farmland, a home or a business and so on. Many people you see in Ho Chi Minh City living on the margin of Vietnamese society – not attending school, sleeping in the street, begging, peddling cigarettes and lottery tickets and driving cyclos to survive – do not have a residence permit to live in the city and their presence is technically illegal. Should they dare to start a business, they could easily have it taken away from them. Despite the fact that the war ended nearly two decades ago, these policies have not changed – now the grandchildren of older former ARVN soldiers are starting be be affected.

An anti-capitalist campaign was launched in March 1978, during which private property and businesses were seized. Most of the victims were ethnic-Chinese – hundreds of thousands soon became refugees, and relations with China soured. Meanwhile, repeated attacks on Vietnamese border villages by Khmer Rouge forces caused Vietnam to invade Cambodia at the end of 1978. The Vietnamese drove the murderous Khmer Rouge from power in early 1979 and set up a pro-Hanoi regime in Phnom Penh.

China – already angered by Vietnam's ill treatment of ethnic-Chinese – viewed the attack on the Khmer Rouge (China's allies) as the final insult. In February 1979, Chinese

forces invaded Vietnam and fought a brief 17-day war before withdrawing (for details, see The North chapter).

Khmer Rouge forces, with support from China and Thailand, continued a costly guerrilla war against the Vietnamese on Cambodian soil for the next decade. Vietnam pulled its forces out of Cambodia in September 1989. The Cambodian civil war was officially settled in 1992 and United Nations peace-keeping forces were called in to monitor the peace agreement. Although Khmer Rouge units continue to violate the terms of the peace plan, Vietnam is no longer involved in the conflict. For the first time since WW II began, Vietnam is finally at peace.

Opening the Door

The recent liberalisation of foreign investment laws and the relaxation of visa regulations for tourists seem to be part of a general Vietnamese opening-up to the world.

After becoming almost totally isolated from Western nations, Vietnam's Foreign

Ministry launched a concerted campaign to improve the country's international standing. Sweden, the first Western country to establish diplomatic relations with Hanoi, did so in 1969; since that time, most Western nations have followed suit. The major holdout is the USA, though this is expected to change shortly.

The Soviet Union began its first cautious opening to the West in 1984 with the appointment of Mikhail Gorbachev as Secretary General of the Communist Party. Vietnam followed suit in 1986 by chosing reform-minded Nguyen Van Linh as General Secretary of the Vietnamese Communist Party. However, the dramatic changes in Eastern Europe and the USSR have not been viewed with favour in Hanoi. The Vietnamese Communist Party has denounced the participation of non-Communists in Eastern Bloc governments as 'bourgeois liberalisation', calling the democratic revolutions 'a counterattack from imperialist circles' against socialism.

General Secretary Linh declared at the end of 1989 that 'we resolutely reject pluralism, a multiparty system and opposition parties'. But in February 1990, the government called for more openness and criticism. The response came swiftly, with an outpouring of news articles, editorials and letters from the public condemning corruption, inept leadership and the high living standards of senior officials while most people lived in extreme poverty. Taken aback by the harsh criticism, official control over literature, the arts and the media were tightened once again in a campaign against 'deviant ideological viewpoints'. Xenophobia reasserted itself and an effort was made to blame public dissatisfaction on foreign imperialists. Interior Minister Mai Chi Tho wrote in the army's newspaper:

Through modern communications means and news-papers, letters and video tapes brought to Vietnam, they have conducted virulent attacks against Marxism-Leninism and the Party's leadership, blaming all socio-economic difficulties on the Communist Party in order to demand political pluralism, a multiparty system and bourgeois-type democracy.

The Party was also concerned that the Vietnamese students and workers in the USSR and East European countries (estimated to number somewhere between 60,000 and several hundred thousand) would return home with politically unacceptable ideas. As it has turned out, most of these Vietnamese workers have been unwilling to return home, with many fleeing to Western Europe to seek political asylum.

At age 75, ailing Party Secretary General Nguyen Van Linh was replaced in June 1991 by Prime Minister Do Muoi (age 74). Regarded as a conservative, Muoi nevertheless vowed to continue the economic reforms started by Linh. At the same time, a major shake-up of the ruling Politburo and Central Committee of the Communist Party saw many members forcibly retired and replaced by younger, more liberal-minded leaders. The sudden collapse of the USSR just two months later caused the government to reiterate its stand that political pluralism would not be tolerated, but at the same time economic reforms were speeded up.

Secretary General Do Muoi and Prime Minister Vo Van Kiet visited Beijing in November 1991 to heal Vietnam's 12-year rift with China. The visit was reciprocated in December 1992 when Chinese Prime Minister Li Peng visited Hanoi. Although it was all toothy-smiles and warm handshakes in front of the cameras, relations between Vietnam and China still remain tense. On the other hand, trade across the China-Vietnam border (both legal and otherwise) is booming.

Foreign business involvement with Vietnam is increasing rapidly; however, the USA still has trade restrictions in place and so is missing out on opportunities. See the Economy section later in this chapter for more details.

GEOGRAPHY

Vietnam stretches over 1600 km along the eastern coast of the Indochinese Peninsula (from 8°34' N to 23°22' N). The country's land area is 329,566 sq km, making it slightly larger than Italy and a bit smaller than Japan. Vietnam has 3260 km of coastline; and land borders of 1650 km with Laos, 1150 km with China and 950 km with Cambodia.

Vietnamese often describe their country as resembling a bamboo pole supporting a basket of rice on each end. The country is S-shaped, broad in the north and south and very narrow in the centre, where at one point it is only 50 km wide.

The country's two main cultivated areas are the Red River Delta (15,000 sq km) in the north and the Mekong Delta (60,000 sq km) in the south. Silt carried by the Red River and its tributaries, which are confined to their paths by 3000 km of dikes, has raised the level of the river beds above that of the surrounding plains. Breaches in the levees result in disastrous flooding. The Mekong Delta is very fertile where drainage is adequate. It was created by silt deposited by the Mekong River.

Three-quarters of the country consists of mountains and hills, the highest of which is 3143-metre-high Fansipan (also spelled Phan Si Pan) in the Hoang Lien Mountains in the far north-west of northern Vietnam. The Truong Son Mountains (Annamite Cordillera), which form the Central Highlands, run almost the full length of the country, along Vietnam's borders with Laos and Cambodia. Spurs of the Truong Son Mountains stretch eastward to the South China Sea, segmenting the fertile coastal plain.

The Vietnamese speak of their country as having three distinct geographical areas: Bac Bo (the north), Trung Bo (the central region) and Nam Bo (the south), which correspond to the French administrative divisions of Tonkin (Nam Ky), Annam (Trung Ky) and Cochinchina (Bac Ky). Between 1954 and 1975, the country was divided at the Ben Hai River (the 17th parallel) into the Republic of Vietnam, with its capital at Saigon, and the Democratic Republic of Vietnam, which was governed from Hanoi.

Offshore Islands

Vietnam claims assorted offshore islands in the Gulf of Thailand and the South China Sea, including Phu Quoc Island off the Cambodian coast, the Tho Chu Islands

south-west of Phu Quoc, the Con Dao Islands south-east of the Mekong Delta, the Paracel Islands (Quan Dao Hoang Xa) 300 km east of Danang and the Spratly Islands (Quan Dao Thruong Xa) 475 km south-east of Nha Trang.

Several of the Paracel Islands, which historically have been occupied only sporadically, were seized by the People's Republic of China in 1951. In the 1960s a few of the islands were occupied by the South Vietnamese, who were driven out by Chinese forces in 1964, an action protested by both the Saigon and Hanoi governments.

The Spratlys, which consist of hundreds of tiny islets, are closer to Borneo than to Vietnam. They are claimed by virtually every country in the vicinity, including the Philippines, Malaysia, Indonesia, China, Taiwan and Vietnam. In 1988, Vietnam lost two ships and 70 sailors in a clash with China over the Spratlys. In mid-1992, Chinese military patrol boats reportedly opened fire on several occasions on Vietnamese cargo vessels leaving Hong Kong, bringing trade between Vietnam and Hong Kong to a near halt. The weak explanation was that China was trying to prevent smuggling.

Both archipelagos have little intrinsic value but the country that has sovereignty over them can claim huge areas of the South China Sea – reported to hold vast oil reserves – as its territorial waters. China pushed tensions to a new high in 1992 by signing contracts with a US company (Crestone Corporation) to explore for oil in the disputed areas. In June 1992, Chinese forces occupied one of the islets claimed by Vietnam.

CLIMATE

There are no good or bad seasons for visiting Vietnam. When one region is wet or cold or steamy hot, there is always somewhere else that is sunny and pleasantly warm.

Vietnam has a remarkably diverse climate because of its wide range of latitudes and altitudes. Although the entire country lies in the intertropical zone, local conditions vary from frosty winters in the far northern hills

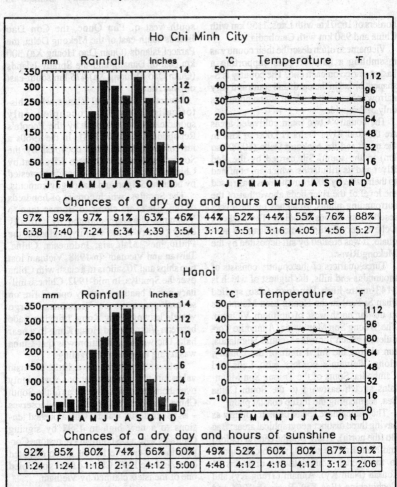

Ho Chi Minh City

Rainfall

J	F	M	A	M	J	J	A	S	O	N	D

Temperature

Chances of a dry day and hours of sunshine

97%	99%	97%	91%	63%	46%	44%	52%	44%	55%	76%	88%
6:38	7:40	7:24	6:34	4:39	3:54	3:12	3:51	3:16	4:05	4:56	5:27

Hanoi

Rainfall

Temperature

Chances of a dry day and hours of sunshine

92%	85%	80%	74%	66%	60%	49%	52%	60%	80%	87%	91%
1:24	1:24	1:18	2:12	4:12	5:00	4:48	4:12	4:18	4:12	3:12	2:06

to the year-round subequatorial warmth of the Mekong Delta. At sea level, the mean annual temperature is about 27°C in the south, falling to about 21°C in the extreme north. There is a drop in mean annual temperature of about half a degree for each increase of 100 metres in elevation. Because about one-third of Vietnam is more than 500 metres above sea level, much of the country

enjoys a subtropical or – above 2000 metres – even a temperate climate.

Vietnam lies in the South-East Asian intertropical monsoon zone. Its weather is determined by two monsoons, which set the rhythm of rural life. The relatively dry winter monsoon, which mainly affects the part of Vietnam north of Danang, comes from the north-east between October or November and March. From April or May to October, the south-western monsoon blows, its winds laden with moisture picked up while crossing the Indian Ocean and the Gulf of Thailand. The south-western monsoon brings warm, damp weather to the whole country except those areas sheltered by mountains (such as the central coastal lowlands and the Red River Delta).

Between July and November, violent and unpredictable typhoons often develop over the ocean east of Vietnam, hitting central and northern Vietnam with devastating results. The frequency of such storms has increased in recent years, possibly because of changes in local climatic conditions resulting from the massive deforestation of Vietnam during the last three decades.

Most of Vietnam receives about 2000 mm of rain annually, though parts of the Central Highlands get approximately 3300 mm of precipitation per annum.

The South

The south, whose climate is subequatorial, has two main seasons: the wet and the dry. The wet season, brought by the south-west monsoon, lasts from May to November. During this period, there are heavy but short-lived downpours almost daily, usually in the afternoon. The dry season runs from December to April. February, March and April are hot and very humid.

In Ho Chi Minh City, the average annual temperature is 27°C. In April, daily highs are usually in the low 30s. In January, the daily lows average 21°C. Average humidity is 80% and annual rainfall averages 1979 mm. The coldest temperature ever recorded in Ho Chi Minh City is 14°C.

Central Vietnam

The coastal lowlands are denied significant rainfall from the south-west monsoon (April or May to October) by the Truong Son Mountains, which are very wet during this period. Much of the coastal strip's precipitation is brought between December and February by the north-east monsoon, the southern part of which picks up moisture over the South China Sea. Thus, Nha Trang's dry season lasts from June to October while Dalat's dry season goes from December to March.

Dalat, like the rest of the Central Highlands, is much cooler than the Mekong Delta and the coastal strip. From November to March, Dalat's daily highs are usually in the low to mid-20s.

The cold and dry winter weather of the north-central coastal lowlands is accompanied by fog and fine drizzle *(crachin)*. Because typhoons account for a significant part of the area's precipitation, annual rainfall totals are erratic (at Hué they average 2890 mm).

The North

Areas north of the 18th parallel (Ha Tinh Province) have two seasons: winter and

Temperature Chart											
Ho Chi Minh City											
Month	Jan	Feb	Mar	Apr	May	Jun	Jul	Aug	Sep	Oct	Nov	Dec
°C	25	26	27	28	28	27	26	27	26	26	26	26
Rain mm	16	3	13	42	220	331	314	269	336	269	115	56
Hanoi											
Month	Jan	Feb	Mar	Apr	May	Jun	Jul	Aug	Sep	Oct	Nov	Dec
°C	15	17	19	23	27	29	28	28	27	24	21	18
Rain mm	22	36	45	89	216	254	335	339	276	115	48	27

summer. Winter, which is quite cool (and even cold), is brought by the irregular north-eastern monsoon and usually lasts from about November to April. During January (the coldest month of the year), the mean temperature in Hanoi is 17°C. February and March are marked by a persistent drizzling rain the Vietnamese call 'rain dust'. The hot summers run from May to October. Precipitation, which falls erratically, averages 1678 mm per year in Hanoi. The north is subject to occasional devastating typhoons during the summer months.

FLORA & FAUNA
Flora
Originally, almost the whole of Vietnam was covered with dense forests. Since the arrival of the first human beings many millennia ago, Vietnam has been progressively denuded of forest cover. The first to lose their trees were coastal and low-lying areas, which were ideal for rice growing. Over the centuries, human exploitation has spread higher and higher into the hills and mountains, a process accelerated by the wars and population growth. While 44% of the original forest cover was extant in 1943, by 1976 only 29% remained and by 1983 only 24% was left.

The forests of Vietnam are estimated to contain 12,000 plant species, only 7000 of which have been identified and 2300 of which are known to be useful to humans for food, medicines, animal fodder, wood products and other purposes.

Currently, an estimated 2000 sq km are deforested every year because of slash-and-burn agriculture by Montagnards, forest fires (made all the fiercer by the dead wood of trees killed by the herbicide Agent Orange), relentless firewood collection, the processing of trees into charcoal and the massive harvesting of exportable hardwood (the country's third largest hard currency earner after rice and crude oil). Along the forest periphery, firewood gathering greatly exceeds regeneration capacity, causing the forest edge to recede. Environmentalists warn that unless these patterns of use are changed, Vietnam's forests will almost completely disappear by the year 2000. At present only 21% of the country is forested and just 8 to 9% of Vietnam's land area retains its primary forest cover.

Each hectare of land denuded of vegetation contributes to the flooding of areas downstream from water catchment areas, irreversible soil erosion (upland soils are especially fragile), the silting up of rivers, streams, lakes and reservoirs, and unpredictable climatic changes.

For many years, Vietnam has had an active reafforestation programme in which Ho Chi Minh himself is said to have taken a keen interest. However, only 36% of the 8720 sq km of trees planted between 1955 and 1979 were still forested at the end of the period. Currently, about 1600 sq km are planted with some 500 million trees each year. The Ministry of Education has made the planting and taking care of trees by pupils part of the curriculum. However, even at this rate, reafforestation is not keeping up with forest losses. There are plans to try to reafforest the bald midland hills, which have little or no agricultural value.

In 1992, Vietnam announced the banning of unprocessed timber exports. The Vietnamese press touted this as an attempt to prevent deforestation, but cynical foreign observers were less sure. The real reason, according to these sources, was so Vietnam could gain foreign investment to develop its own wood processing industry – 'value-added' wood exports are still allowed if the timber is first processed into paper, furniture, etc.

Some have found it suspicious that Australian aid in the field of forestry has been accompanied by the sudden appearance of large tracts of young eucalyptus trees in the Vietnamese countryside. Are we witnessing a form of ecological imperialism?

Fauna
Because Vietnam includes a wide range of habitats – ranging from equatorial lowlands to high, temperate plateaus and even alpine peaks – the country's wild fauna is enor-

mously diverse. Vietnam is home to 273 species of mammals, 773 species of birds, 180 species of reptiles, 80 species of amphibians, hundreds of species of fish and thousands of kinds of invertebrates. Larger animals of special importance in conservation efforts include the elephant, rhinoceros, tiger, leopard, black bear, honey bear, snub-nosed monkey, douc langur (remarkable for its variegated colours), concolour gibbon, macaque, rhesus monkey, serow (a kind of mountain goat), flying squirrel, kouprey (a blackish-brown forest ox), banteng (a kind of wild ox), deer, peacock, pheasant, crocodile, python, cobra and turtle.

Tragically, Vietnam's wildlife is in a precipitous decline as forest habitats are destroyed and waterways become polluted. In addition, uncontrolled illegal hunting – many people in remote areas have access to weapons left over from the war – has exterminated the local populations of various animals, in some cases eliminating entire species from the country. Officially, the government has recognised 54 species of mammals and 60 species of birds as endangered. The tapir (a large perissodactyl ungulate) and Sumatran rhinoceros are already extinct in Vietnam, and there are thought to be less than 20 koupreys and 20 to 30 Javan rhinoceros left in the country.

It is encouraging that some wildlife seems to be returning to reafforested areas. For example, birds, fish and crustaceans have reappeared in replanted mangrove swamps. But unless the government takes immediate remedial measures – including banning the sale and export of tiger skins and ivory – hundreds of species of mammals, birds and plants will become extinct within the next decade.

Ecological Impact of the War
During the Vietnam War, the USA employed deliberate destruction of the environment (ecocide) as a military tactic on a scale unprecedented in the history of warfare. In an effort to deny bases of operation to the VC, 72 million litres of the herbicides known as Agent Orange, Agent White and Agent Blue were sprayed on 16% of South Vietnam's land area (including 10% of the inland forests and 36% of the mangrove forests). It is said that the deforestation caused by spraying these chemicals would have been enough to supply Vietnam's timber harvesters for 30 years. The most seriously affected regions were the provinces of Dong Nai, Song Be and Tay Ninh. Another environmentally disastrous method of defoliation employed by the military involved the use of enormous bulldozers called 'Rome plows' to rip up the jungle floor.

The 40 million litres of Agent Orange used contained 170 kg of dioxin (2,3,7,8-TCDD). Dioxin is the most toxic chemical known, highly carcinogenic and mutagenic. Today, almost 20 years after the spraying, dioxin is still present in the food chain. Researchers report elevated levels of dioxin in samples of human breast milk collected in affected areas, where about 7.5% of the population of the south now lives. Vietnamese refugees living in the USA who were exposed to Agent Orange have been showing unusually high rates of cancer. Ditto for American soldiers, who have filed a class action lawsuit against the US government to seek compensation.

In addition to the spraying, large tracts of forests, agricultural land, villages and even cemeteries were bulldozed, removing both the vegetation and topsoil. Flammable melaleuka forests were ignited with napalm. In mountain areas, landslides were deliberately created by bombing and by spraying acid on limestone hillsides. Elephants, useful for transport, were attacked from the air with bombs and napalm. By war's end, extensive areas had been taken over by tough weeds (known locally as 'American grass') that prevent young trees from receiving enough light to survive. The government estimates that 20,000 sq km of forest and farmland were lost as a direct result of the American war effort.

Overall, some 13 million tonnes of bombs – equivalent to 450 times the energy of the atomic bomb used on Hiroshima – were dropped on the region. This comes to 265 kg for every man, woman and child in Indochina. If the Americans had showered the people of Indochina with the money all those bombs cost (the war cost US$2000 per resident of Indochina), they might have won.

The long-term results of this onslaught have been devastating. The lush tropical forests have not grown back, fisheries (even those in coastal waters) remain depleted in both variety and productivity, wildlife populations have not recovered, cropland productivity is still below its prewar levels, and among the human population the incidence of various cancers and toxin-related diseases has greatly increased. The land is scarred by 25 million bomb craters up to 30 metres in diameter, many of which have filled up with water and become breeding grounds for malarial mosquitoes (though some of the craters are said to have been converted into ponds for raising fish). In any case, the deep craters – from which tonnes of earth were blown – make significant parts of many rice paddies unplantable.

National Parks

At the present time, Vietnam has only two national parks, Cuc Phuong and Cat Ba, which are both in the north. Cat Ba is an island and considered Vietnam's most beautiful national park and, increasingly, a favourite with foreign travellers. Cuc

Phuong is less visited and has suffered more ecological damage from logging and burning.

In an attempt to prevent an ecological and hydrological catastrophe, the government has plans to set aside tens of thousands of sq km of forest land and to create 87 national parks and nature reserves. Fourteen reserves (including Cuc Phuong and Cat Ba national parks) totalling 1600 sq km have already received government approval. Ecologists hope that because tropical ecosystems have a high species diversity but low densities of individual species, reserve areas will be large enough to contain viable populations of each species. However, there are development interests which are not amenable to increasing the size of Vietnam's national parks and forest reserves – it is possible the whole plan will come to naught.

GOVERNMENT

The Socialist Republic of Vietnam (SRV; Cong Hoa Xa Hoi Chu Nghia Viet Nam) came into existence in July 1976 as a unitary state comprising the Democratic Republic of Vietnam (DRV; North Vietnam) and the defeated Republic of Vietnam (RVN; South Vietnam). From April 1975 until the declaration of the SRV, the South had been ruled – at least in name – by a Provisional Revolutionary Government.

The SRV espouses a Marxist-Leninist political philosophy. Its political institutions have borrowed a great deal from the Soviet and Chinese models, but in many respects have developed to meet Vietnam's particular circumstances.

Flag & National Anthem

The flag of the Socialist Republic of Vietnam consists of a yellow star in the middle of a red field. Until 1976 this was the flag of the Hanoi-based Democratic Republic of Vietnam. The significance of the yellow star and red field are explained in the national anthem, *Marching to the Front (Tien Quan Ca)*, which reflects the martial history and outlook of the present government. The words are as follows:

Soldiers of Vietnam, we go forward
With the one will to save our Fatherland.
Our hurried steps are sounding on the long and
arduous road.
Our flag, red with the blood of victory, bears the spirit
of our country.
The distant rumbling of the guns mingles with our
marching song.
The path to glory passes over the bodies of our foes.
Overcoming all hardships, together we build our
resistance bases.
Ceaselessly for the people's cause we struggle,
Hastening to the battlefield!
Forward! All together advancing!
Our Vietnam is strong eternal.

Soldiers of Vietnam, we go forward,
The gold star of our flag in the wind
Leading our people, our native land, out of misery and
suffering.
Let us join our efforts in the fight for the building of
a new life.
Let us stand up and break our chains.
For too long we have swallowed our hatred.
Let us keep ready for all sacrifices and our life will be
radiant.
Ceaselessly for the people's cause we struggle,
Hastening to the battlefield!
Forward! All together advancing!
Our Vietnam is strong eternal.

From 1973 to 1975, virtually every house in
the South had either a South Vietnamese flag
(three horizontal red stripes on a yellow
field) or a National Liberation Front flag (a
yellow star in the centre of a red and blue
field split horizontally) painted near the door.
The Paris Agreements of 1973 gave equal
status in the South to the South Vietnamese
government and the Provisional Revolutionary Government (a group set up in 1969 by
the Viet Cong). Because the areas under the
control of each were noncontiguous and had
no clear boundaries between them, the
control of each village and neighbourhood
was indicated by flags painted on roofs and
near the doorways of every building. When
the international observer force investigated
alleged cease-fire violations the flags provided instant publicly acknowledged
information on who was supposed to control
the area.

When the Communists took over the
South they painted over the old flags with

flags of their own – first that of the National
Liberation Front and then the SRV flag. Over
the years, the flags of the SRV faded away or
chipped off, revealing the NLF flags (which
remind southerners of their forcible incorpo-
ration into a unitary state) and, underneath,
the flags of the old Saigon regime. To this
day, if you look carefully, you will see South
Vietnamese flags painted on many buildings,
bridges and other structures in south and
central Vietnam. Is the government too poor
to afford a new coat of paint, or is it that no
one really cares about the old flags any
more?

The Orwellian national slogan, which
appears at the top of every official document,
is *Doc Lap, Tu Do, Hanh Phuc*, which means
'Independence, Freedom, Happiness'. It is
based on one of Ho Chi Minh's sayings.

The Communist Party

Vietnam's political system is dominated by
the 1.8 million-member Communist Party
(Dang Cong San Viet Nam), whose influence
is felt at every level of the country's social
and political life. The leadership of the Party
has been collective in style and structure ever
since its founding by Ho Chi Minh in 1930.
The Party's decentralised structure, though
originally necessitated by the difficulty of
communications between Party headquarters and its branches, has allowed local
leaders considerable leeway for initiative. It
has also encouraged local cesspools of corruption, notable examples being the Vung
Tau-Con Dao Special Economic Zone (now
abolished) and Thanh Hoa Province (where
local Party Chief Ha Trong Hoa set up his
own Mafia-style fiefdom and ruled for four
years before finally being ousted by Hanoi).

Relatively speaking, the policies of the
Vietnamese Communist Party have been
characterised by a flexible and non-doctri-
naire approach. For the most part, the Party
has tried to take into account prevailing
material and political limitations when carrying out its revolutionary programmes.

The most powerful institution in the Party
is the Political Bureau (Politburo), which has
about a dozen members. It oversees the

Party's day-to-day functioning and has the power to issue directives to the government. The Politburo is formally elected by the Central Committee, whose 125 or so full members and about 50 alternate members meet only once or twice a year.

Party Congresses, at which major policy changes are ratified after a long process of behind-the-scenes discussions and consultations, were held in 1935, 1951, 1960, 1976, 1982, 1986 and 1991. The last few Party Congresses have reflected intense intra-Party disagreements over the path Vietnamese Communism should take, with changing coalitions of conservatives and dogmatists squaring off against more pragmatic elements. The position of Party Chairman has been left vacant since Ho Chi Minh's death.

During the 1980s and early 1990s thousands of Party members were expelled, in part to reduce corruption (seen by a fed-up public as endemic) and in part to make room for more young people and workers. As in China, Vietnam has been ruled by a gerontocracy. At the time of this writing, the average age of Politburo members is 64 years, down from 71 in 1990.

Despite official rhetoric about the equality of women, females are under-represented in the Party, especially at the highest levels (there have been no female members of the Politburo since 1945).

Constitutions

The Socialist Republic of Vietnam and its Hanoi-based predecessor have had three constitutions. The 1946 Constitution, drafted by a committee headed by Ho Chi Minh, was designed to appeal to a broad spectrum of Vietnamese society while at the same time pre-empting criticism from abroad, especially from France and the USA (with this goal in mind, it contained material taken from the American Declaration of Independence).

The 1959 Constitution was drawn up after it became clear that the 1956 national elections, called for in the Geneva Agreement of 1954, were not going to take place as sched-

uled. Three years of intense debate over the question of armed struggle in the South produced the 1959 Constitution, which made the goal of creating a Communist society, characterised by central planning and collective property ownership, explicit. Following the Chinese example on ethnic minorities policy, two 'autonomous regions', complete with their own zonal assemblies, administrations and militia forces, were created in northern and north-western North Vietnam.

After reunification in 1975, it was decided that the country again needed a new Constitution. The 1980 Constitution was the result of four years of debate on how the south, with its radically different social and economic structure, should be absorbed. It reflects the victory of those who favoured rapid collectivisation. The 1980 Constitution, which borrows heavily from the 1977 Soviet Constitution, declared the Party to be 'the only force leading the State and society, and the main factor in determining all successes of the Vietnamese revolution'. Fearing the implications of creating a third minority autonomous region in the Central Highlands (where the government feared unrest by Montagnard insurgents backed, over the years, by France, the USA, China and Thailand), the two autonomous regions in the north were abolished.

Administration

The Vietnamese governmental structure administers the country but the main decision-making bodies are those of the Party, especially the Politburo, which can, independently of the government, issue decrees with the force of law. Party cadres dominate the higher echelons of government, and at all levels, promotion in the bureaucracy often depends more on party affiliation than on strict criteria of competence.

The unicameral National Assembly (Quoc Hoi) is Vietnam's highest legislative authority. Its 500 or so deputies, whose terms last five years, each represent 100,000 voters. The National Assembly's role is to rubber-stamp – usually unanimously – Politburo decisions and party-initiated legislation during its biannual sessions, which last about a week. During elections, the number of National Assembly candidates (all Party-approved) running in a given constituency usually exceeds the number of contested seats by 20 to 30%. Relative to the population, white-collar workers are over-represented in the National Assembly while peasants and women are greatly under-represented.

The Council of State functions as the country's collective presidency. Its members, who currently number 15, are elected by the National Assembly. The Council of State carries out the duties of the National Assembly when the latter is not in session. The Council of Ministers is also elected by the National Assembly. It functions as does a Western-style cabinet. Among its current members are the Prime Minister, nine deputy premiers, a secretary-general, 22 ministers with portfolio (Construction, Culture, Education, Finance, Information, Justice, Supply, Transport, etc), the heads of seven State Commissions (Planning, External Economic Relations, etc) and the directors of the State Bank and the Government Inspectorate. During the economic crises and reforms that began in 1975, cabinet shuffles have been frequent.

Though Hanoi has been promoting the idea that local governments play a greater role in planning, most such administrative units have been unable to come up with the requisite funds to make this possible. Indeed, even agricultural cooperatives, the regime's ideological backbone, have been unable to make ends meet without resorting to corruption and the black market. In the early 1980s, the provinces were allowed to establish their own import-export concerns, but when provisional governments showed a propensity to hoard foreign currency in order to buy goods from abroad, regulations allowing them to keep only part of their hard currency were implemented.

The Law
The French gave the Vietnamese the Napoleonic Code, much of which has not been repealed though these laws may conflict with later statutes. From about 1960 to 1975, South Vietnam modified much of its commercial code to resemble that of the USA. Since reunification, Soviet-style laws have been applied to the whole country, with devastating consequences for private property owners. The recent economic reforms have seen a flood of new property legislation, much of it the result of advice from the United Nations (UN), International Monetary Fund (IMF) and other international organisations. The rapid speed at which legislation is being enacted is a challenge for those who must interpret and enforce the law, especially when there are recalcitrant bureaucrats who prefer to make their own law.

Political Divisions
Vietnam is divided into 50 provinces (tinh) which have a significant degree of autonomy. Thus, provinces vary widely in their approach to foreign investment, economic development, economic liberalisation, political reform, tourism, etc. Listed from north to south, Vietnam's provinces are:

Far North: Ha Giang, Tuyen Quang, Cao Bang, Lao Cai, Yen Bai, Lai Chau, Lang Son, Bac Thai, Son La, Vinh Phu, Ha Bac, Hoa Binh and Quang Ninh.

Red River Delta Area: Ha Tay, Hai Hung, Thai Binh, Nam Ha and Ninh Binh.

North-Central Vietnam: Thanh Hoa, Nghe An, Ha Tinh, Quang Binh, Quang Tri and Thua Thien-Hue.

South-Central Coast: Quang Nam-Danang, Quang Ngai, Binh Dinh, Phu Yen, Khanh Hoa, Ninh Thuan and Binh Thuan.

Central Highlands: Kontum, Gia Lai, Dac Lac (Dak Lak) and Lam Dong.

South: Song Be, Tay Ninh, Dong Nai, Ba Ria-Vung Tau, Long An, Dong Thap, An Giang, Tien Giang, Ben Tre, Vinh Long, Tra

Vinh, Kien Giang, Cantho, Soc Trang and Minh Hai.

In addition, there are three independent municipalities: Greater Hanoi, Greater Ho Chi Minh City (which includes Saigon) and Greater Haiphong.

The provinces and municipalities are divided into rural and urban districts. Rural districts are subdivided into village-level communes made up of hamlets while urban districts are divided into wards.

The government seems to have a hard time deciding how to carve the turkey. After reunification, the provincial structure of the south was completely reorganised. Then on 1 July 1989, several provinces that were joined after 1975 were split apart. Since then there have been even more splits. Don't be surprised if what you find on the ground differs from what your map says – even the Vietnamese have difficulty keeping up with the redrawing of political boundaries.

ECONOMY

Vietnam is one of the poorest countries in the world, with an estimated per capita income of US$200 per year and US$1.4 billion in hard currency debts (owed mainly to the IMF and Japan) it is unable to repay. To put it in a word, the country is broke. About the only good news in the foreign debt situation is that much is owed to the former Soviet Union – this is denominated in roubles which are losing value even faster than the Vietnamese dong.

Despite its hard-working, educated workforce, the country's economy is beset by weak exports, a lack of raw materials for industry, chronic shortages of spare parts, a limited supply of consumer goods, unemployment (estimated at 40%) under-employment and, until recently, erratic runaway inflation (700% in 1986, 30% in 1989 and 50% in 1991). The people are so poor that it is said that many able-bodied men and women have become weak and lost the desire to work solely as a result of long-term malnutrition. The economy was hurt by wartime infrastructure damage (not a single bridge in the North survived American

air-raids, while in the South many bridges were blown up by the VC), but by the government's own admission the present economic fiasco is the result of ideologically driven policies followed after reunification and the fact that half the government's budget goes to the military.

Just how the average Vietnamese manages to survive economically is a mystery. Salaries in Ho Chi Minh City are in the neighbourhood of US$30 per month, but elsewhere they're about half that. Salaries in the north are generally lower than in the south. You simply can't survive on such wages unless you can grow your own food and build your own house (possible in the countryside but not in Ho Chi Minh City or Hanoi). So people scrounge on the side, finding some odd job they can do. In the case of women, many are forced to resort to part-time prostitution, while government officials and police often turn to corruption.

Until very recently, one of Vietnam's most valuable exports has been its people. Desperate for foreign currency, Vietnamese were given jobs that not even Russians would take – in Siberia, for instance. USSR-bound flights used to leave Hanoi full of excited young people, many of them young women, off to places like Novosibirsk where they earned US$500 per month, US$400 of which was paid to the Vietnamese government. Despite the harsh working conditions and low pay, competition for these dismal jobs was keen – one had to be of the right class background or have political connections. Many Vietnamese workers also went to the former East Germany, and when the Berlin Wall fell most of them fled to the West where they continue to live and work, often illegally. Recently, many have become targets of abuse by Germany's notorious 'skinhead' gangs. Now that the Russian economy is in possibly worse condition than Vietnam's, interest in Siberian employment has fallen to zero.

Although Vietnam and Russia are still officially as close as lips and teeth, Vietnamese from all parts of the country seem to harbour an unreserved hostility towards the few remaining Russian experts in their country. This bitterness is an outgrowth of the popular feeling that Soviet economic policies are to blame for Vietnam's economy going straight down the toilet after reunification. The once ubiquitous posters of those two White guys, Marx and Lenin, served to underline the foreign origin of much of the

The Economic Embargo

Vietnam's economic problems have no doubt been worsened by an economic embargo imposed by the USA, Western countries, ASEAN (Association of South-East Asian Nations) and China. Except for China's participation, the embargo probably had little effect on Vietnam's economy in the decade following reunification, largely because Vietnam deliberately conducted all its foreign trade with the Eastern Bloc to avoid dependency on capitalist countries. However, since capitalist-style economic reforms began in 1987, the embargo has effectively blocked loans from the IMF, trade and investment with the West and the importation of high-tech goods.

The embargo had its roots in the Vietnam War. Of course, the USA was not going to trade with its North Vietnamese enemy. But why the embargo has continued for two decades after US troops left Vietnam – and has involved so many other countries besides Vietnam and the USA – is a twisted story of political manoeuvres in the world power game.

In May 1977, the USA (under the newly elected Carter administration) opened negotiations in Paris to normalise relations with Vietnam. US opposition to Vietnamese membership in the United Nations was dropped, and Vietnam became the UN's 149th member-state. However, the discussions failed to solve other outstanding difference between the two countries. Political pressure applied by groups in the USA demanding Vietnamese cooperation in the search for 2265 Americans listed as 'missing in action' in Indochina upset the negotiations. Vietnam's demand for billions of dollars in war reparations finally shattered the talks.

Vietnam's mistreatment of ethnic Chinese and the invasion of Cambodia at the end of 1978 triggered a war with China. For the next decade, China severed all economic relations with Vietnam. The Cambodian adventure renewed fears that Vietnam would carry its war into decidedly pro-Western Thailand. With this in mind, Thailand called on its allies in ASEAN to support an embargo against Vietnam. The USA fully supported the embargo and assumed the leadership role, applying pressure to America's Western allies to isolate Vietnam economically.

The Soviet invasion of Afghanistan and the election of fervently anti-communist Ronald Reagan to the US presidency in 1980 guaranteed that there would be no East-West cooperation on economic issues. Under the Reagan administration, the US Treasury Department started vigorously enforcing the Trading with the Enemy Act, effectively prohibiting American companies from doing any business at all with Vietnam.

Vietnam's withdrawal from Cambodia in 1989 and the collapse of the USSR in 1991 should have heralded a new era of cooperation between Vietnam and the USA. However, then-President George Bush was already locked in a life-or-death struggle for re-election (which he lost) and apparently he didn't want to be seen as being 'soft on communism'. So the 'no compromise' stance continued.

Meanwhile, America's allies have – one by one – quietly been re-establishing diplomatic and economic relations with Vietnam. China normalised cross-border trade in 1990 and ASEAN countries have become major investors in Vietnam. In 1992 Japan dropped its support for the embargo, the last major American ally to do so. A number of Western nations have begun minor aid programmes to Vietnam. President Mitterand of France visited Vietnam in 1992, the first Western leader to do so since the war. At the time of this writing, the only country still trying to economically isolate Vietnam is the USA.

American business people have been strongly urging the US government to end the embargo quickly – if not, all those lucrative business contracts that the Vietnamese are ready to sign will go to the Japanese, Taiwanese, French and other non-American entrepreneurs. 'Lift the Embargo' T-shirts have become a popular item in Ho Chi Minh City with everyone from cyclo drivers to foreign business travellers. Even many staunchly anti-communist Vietnamese refugees in the USA now say the embargo has outlived its purpose, and at this point is counter-productive and vindictive. US President Clinton is expected to take a different approach to Vietnam, and it is entirely possible that by the time you read this, the embargo will be history. ∎

Party's unpopular ideology, including collectivisation and centralised planning. Perhaps not surprisingly, the posters disappeared almost overnight when the Soviet Union also disappeared in 1991.

In addition, the Vietnamese know that much of Vietnam's best products are sold or bartered to Russia just to pay off the huge national debt. Furthermore, attempts by the government to solve the debt problem with the printing press has led to devastating inflation.

Economic Reforms

The Vietnamese are keenly aware that while their centrally planned economy has been stagnating (despite billions of roubles in Soviet aid), the free market economies of their capitalist neighbours (Thailand, Malaysia, Singapore, Hong Kong and Taiwan) have been flourishing. And whereas 25 years ago Bangkok and Saigon were economically comparable, today the former is one of Asia's boom towns while the latter has hardly changed except that it has become run-down. The Vietnamese also realise that the South-East Asian technological revolution is passing them by.

Vietnam's efforts to restructure the economy really got under way with the Sixth Party Congress held in December 1986. At that time, Nguyen Van Linh (a proponent of reform) was appointed General Secretary of the Communist Party. Recent reforms have cut state subsidies, allowed limited private enterprise, reduced centralised planning, rationalised exchange rates and liberalised foreign investment.

Immediately upon the legalisation of limited private enterprise, family businesses began popping up all over the country. But it is in the south, with its experience with capitalism, where the entrepreneurial skills and managerial dynamism needed to effect the reforms are to be found. With 'new thinking' in Hanoi now remaking the economic life of the whole country in the mould of the pre-reunification south, people have been remarking that, in the end, the South won the war.

The overall five-year economic growth rate for 1987-92 was estimated at around 5.2%, exactly half of neighbouring Thailand's 10.4%, but a welcome relief after more than a decade of negative growth. But these figures don't tell the whole story; there is a growing 'black economy' not recorded in official statistics. Indeed, the amount of smuggling going on across the Cambodian-Vietnamese border (much of it done by the army and police) easily exceeds official trade between those two countries. Another fact the government doesn't like to admit is that the southern economy is improving much faster than that of the north, widening the already-significant gap in standards of living.

Business people in Vietnam – especially in Ho Chi Minh City – are generally optimistic. Ho Chi Minh City at least seems to be booming; every major hotel in Saigon and Cholon is filled with enthusiastic importers, investors, international lawyers and specialists of all stripes. Business people in the north – who have had to face titanic bureaucratic impediments – are somewhat gloomier. However, it is fair to say that there have been recent significant improvements in the north too; success tends to be contagious.

Before 1991, Vietnam's major trading partners were the USSR and other members of COMECON (Council for Mutual Economic Assistance – the East Bloc's equivalent to the European Community). Most of the trade with COMECON was on a barter basis; Vietnam traded its crude oil, wood and sugar cane for refined oil, machinery and weapons. Because the value of Vietnam's agricultural products was not nearly enough to pay for expensive value-added goods, the USSR had to subsidise the Vietnamese economy, leaving Vietnam with an enormous rouble-denominated debt.

The disintegration of COMECON and the USSR in 1991 could have brought complete economic collapse to Vietnam. Almost miraculously, this was avoided because Vietnam moved quickly to establish hard currency trade relations with China, Hong

Kong, Japan, Singapore, South Korea, Taiwan, Thailand and Western nations. This explains why Vietnamese officials have suddenly become so anxious to do business with the West. Many other former Eastern Bloc countries have not fared as well as Vietnam – their economies collapsed along with the USSR.

The transition from an isolated socialist barter economy to a free market, hard currency trading economy is not complete and has not been easy. Many of Vietnam's manufactured goods (bicycles, shoes, even laundry detergent) are of such poor quality that they are practically unsaleable, especially in the face of competition from foreign goods. One of the first effects of free (or free-ish) trade with capitalist countries was to wipe out many state-run enterprises, leading to job lay-offs and increased unemployment. Even Vietnam's sugar-cane growers have been hurt – shoddy equipment at state-run sugar refineries produces such a low-quality product that imported refined sugar is taking over Vietnam's domestic market.

The Vietnamese government has responded with a number of 'temporary import bans' (protectionism). Such bans theoretically give a boost to struggling domestic industries but also lead to increased smuggling. But, slowly, the country is regaining its ability to compete in foreign markets; low wages and the strong Vietnamese work ethic (when given incentives) bodes well for Vietnam's export industries.

The more liberal rules have had a dramatic effect on foreign joint-venture operations – foreign investors have been tripping over themselves to get into the country. Foreign-owned trading companies have been proliferating like locusts. Some of the most successful joint ventures to date have involved hotels, though some of these 'investments' are clear cases of real-estate speculation (foreigners cannot buy land directly but businesses can with a Vietnamese partner). The leading foreign investor is Taiwan, followed by Hong Kong and Australia – the French are also very active. Now that foreign business people are taking an interest in Vietnam, prospects for developing highly competitive industries look certain if the reforms aren't derailed by politics.

Unfortunately, political meddling hasn't stopped completely. The bureaucracy is plagued by middle-level functionaries whose jobs are essentially worthless (or counterproductive) and should be eliminated. Such bureaucrats view the reforms as a serious threat and would like to see them fail, though on the other hand they are not averse to accepting bribes in exchange for the rubber stamps and permits which businesses need to operate. Recalcitrant bureaucrats or not, the reforms have already gained enough momentum that it's hard to imagine reversing them – putting the toothpaste back in the tube might well be impossible.

Foreign investors say that their biggest obstacles include the formidable Vietnamese bureaucracy, official incompetence, corruption and the ever-changing rules and regulations. On paper, intellectual property rights are protected, but enforcement is lax – patents, copyrights and trademarks are openly pirated. Tax rates and government fees are frequently revised. Some municipalities have forced foreign companies to hire employees from state employment agencies, with the only employees available being the 'spoiled brats' of cadres. Not surprisingly, such problems are worse in the north.

Privatisation of large state industries has not yet begun but is being considered. Likely candidates would be Vietnam Airlines, the banking industry, telecommunications, etc. Whether or not the generation of socialist leaders can bring themselves to put the state's prime assets on the auction block remains to be seen. At the present time, Vietnam has no stock market – establishing one would be a prerequisite to any privatisation moves. In 1992, government officials held discussions with foreign experts to gain advice on establishing a capital market in Vietnam.

Vietnam's ageing revolutionary leaders generally have a good record in eschewing luxurious living, but economic liberalisation has led to an increase in corruption and access to previously unobtainable luxuries. Ironically, it is the children of the high-ranking cadres whom you see – dressed in jeans and miniskirts – enjoying the discos and karaokes that have sprung up in the last few years.

In 1992, Vietnam took the first steps towards joining ASEAN. Observers are nearly unaminous that the connection with ASEAN will greatly benefit Vietnam's economy.

Hanoi is intent on limiting Vietnam's restructuring (doi moi) to the economic sphere, keeping ideas such as pluralism and democracy from undermining the present power structure. Whether it is possible to have economic liberalisation without a concurrent liberalisation in the political sphere remains to be seen. Vietnam's role model at the moment is China, where economic liberalisation coupled with harsh political controls seems to be at least partially successful in reviving the economy. The role model of the former Soviet Union -- where political liberalisation preceded economic restructuring – is pointed to as an example of the wrong way to reform.

Agriculture & Forestry

About 70% of Vietnam's people earn their living from agriculture. Vietnam's most important crop is rice, which is cultivated using both irrigated paddy and dry field culture on 75% of cropped land. Other important food crops include sugar cane, maize, manioc, potatoes and sweet potatoes. Among Vietnam's cash crops are peanuts, soy beans, pepper, tobacco, coffee, tea, rubber, coconuts and mulberry leaves (to feed silkworms). About 21% of Vietnam's land area is used for agriculture.

Very little agricultural machinery (such as tractors) is in use. Because threshing equipment is in short supply, you often see piles

of rice stalks placed in the middle of the highway. As passing vehicles drive over them, the rice is separated from the stalks. Rice and other crops are often dried in the sun at the side of the road.

In 1978, collectivisation and natural disasters reduced food production to a low of 12.9 million tonnes, necessitating a cut in the food ration from 18 to 13 kg per person per month, a level two kg below the minimum subsistence level set by the UN. Urban residents had to stand in long lines to get their meagre ration of rice, a scene not uncommon in the USSR from which Vietnam borrowed many economic ideas. The massive 1979 exodus of boat people from Vietnam was inspired in part by a simple lack of food.

Agricultural policies have reversed course. Reforms allowing peasants to acquire small land holdings and more market-oriented policies have increased food production dramatically. The government has instructed officials to return land which was arbitrarily confiscated from peasants in southern Vietnam between 1978 and 1983. The new agricultural policies also emphasise family farming over state-run collectives.

Directly as a result of the reforms, Vietnam moved from being a rice importer in the mid-1980s to become the world's third-largest rice exporter in 1991 (after Thailand and the USA).

Because Vietnam's population is growing at the rapid rate of 2.3% per year, the land available for agricultural use per capita continues to fall.

The main source of energy in Vietnam is wood harvested from the country's shrinking natural forests. In the recent past, Vietnam earned needed foreign currency by exporting rare hardwoods. Officially, this is now prohibited but smuggling continues.

Minerals

Vietnam has an unusually wide range of mostly untapped mineral resources, but an unexpected source of mineral wealth has been created by the war. Vietnam is now the world's largest supplier of scrap metal, much of which is sold to Japan and returned to Vietnam in the form of Honda motorcycles. Local industries use some of the aluminium, brass and steel as well. The aluminium in that spoon you ate lunch with was almost certainly once part of an American aircraft, and the bronze from which newly cast Buddhas are fashioned most likely came to Vietnam in the form of American artillery shell casings.

Fishing

Fish, which constitutes the main source of protein in the diets of many Vietnamese, is the most important staple food after rice. Fishing employs 550,000 people.

Manufacturing

Following the traditions of their Soviet mentors, the Vietnamese placed great emphasis on heavy industry in the five-year plans of 1976-80 and 1981-85 – while sacrificing the production of quality consumer products. While cooking the books produced some impressive statistics on paper, many shoddy products failed to find a market. Shortages of fuel and capital, under-utilisation of industrial capacity, insufficient maintenance and inadequate standards all created production bottlenecks and led to shortages of essential items which no amount of creative accounting could hide.

Since the war, a metal-casting industry based on melting down old war materiel has developed (who says war isn't profitable?). Fireworks are produced using the gunpowder from left-over American munitions.

POPULATION

In 1992, Vietnam's population reached 70.8 million, making it the 12th most populous country in the world. Eighty-four percent of the population is ethnic-Vietnamese, 2% ethnic-Chinese and the rest Khmers, Chams and members of some 60 ethno-linguistic groups.

Vietnam has an overall population density of 200 persons per sq km, one of the world's highest for an agricultural country. Much of the Red River Delta has a population density of 1000 people per sq km or more. The current rate of population growth is 2.3% per year. Overall life expectancy is 66 years and infant mortality is 46 per 1000.

There is no government-sponsored family planning programme and most couples rely on condoms or abortion to limit family size. Abortions can be performed at government hospitals, but the complex bureaucratic procedures and waiting lists cause many women to seek private 'back alley' abortions.

PEOPLE
Ethnic-Vietnamese

The Vietnamese people (called 'Annamites' by the French) developed as a distinct ethnic group between 200 BC and 200 AD through the fusion of a people of Indonesian stock with Viet and Tai immigrants from the north and Chinese who arrived, along with Chinese rule, as of the 2nd century AD. Vietnamese civilisation was profoundly influenced by China and, via Champa and the Khmers, India, but the fact that the Vietnamese were never absorbed by China indicates that a strong local culture existed prior to the 1000 years of Chinese rule, which ended in 938 AD.

The Vietnamese have lived for thousands of years by growing rice and, as a result, have historically preferred to live in lowland areas suitable for rice growing. Over the past two millennia, they have slowly pushed southward along the narrow coastal strip, defeating the Chams in the 15th century and taking over the Mekong Delta from the Khmers in the 18th century. The Vietnamese have tended to view highland areas (and their inhabitants) with suspicion.

Vietnamese who have emigrated abroad are known as Overseas Vietnamese (Viet Kieu). They are intensely disliked by the locals, who accuse them of being cowards, arrogant, pampered, privileged and so on. These negative judgements are likely coloured by jealousy.

Ethnic-Chinese

The ethnic-Chinese (Hoa) constitute the largest single minority group in Vietnam. Today, most of them live in the south, especially in and around Saigon's sister-city Cholon. Though the families of most of Vietnam's ethnic-Chinese have lived in Vietnam for generations, they have historically tried to maintain their separate Chinese identities, languages, school systems and even citizenships. The Chinese have organised themselves into communities, known as 'congregations' *(bang)*, according to their ancestors' province of origin and dialect. Important congregations include Fujian (Phuoc Kien in Vietnamese), Cantonese (Quang Dong in Vietnamese or Guangdong in Chinese), Hainan (Hai Nam), Chaozhou (Tieu Chau) and Hakka (Nuoc Hue in Vietnamese or Kejia in Mandarin Chinese).

During the 1950s, President Diem tried without much success to forcibly assimilate South Vietnam's ethnic-Chinese population. In the North, too, the ethnic-Chinese have resisted Vietnamisation.

The Chinese are well known for their entrepreneurial abilities – before the fall of South Vietnam in 1975, ethnic-Chinese controlled nearly half of the country's economic activity. Historical antipathies between China and Vietnam and the prominence of ethnic-Chinese in commerce have generated a great deal of animosity towards them. In March 1978, the Vietnamese communists launched a campaign against 'bourgeois elements' (considered a euphemism for the ethnic-Chinese) which turned into open racial persecution. The campaign influenced China's decision to attack Vietnam in 1979 and caused about one-third of Vietnam's ethnic-Chinese to flee to China and the West. Vietnamese officials now admit that the anti-Chinese and anti-capitalist campaign was a tragic mistake which cost the country heavily.

Other Minorities

Vietnam has one of the most complex ethno-linguistic mixes in all of Asia. The country's 60 minority groups, many of whom are related to Thailand's hill tribes, live mostly in the Central Highlands and the mountainous regions of the north. The French called them *montagnards* (which means 'highlanders'), a term they themselves still use when speaking English or French. The Vietnamese often refer to the hill-tribe people as *Moi*, a derogatory word meaning 'savages' that unfortunately reflects all-too-common popular attitudes. The present government, which prefers the term 'national minorities', is trying to 'integrate' the Montagnards, which means that it is attempting to Vietnamise them culturally, linguistically, socially and ideologically.

Linguistically, the Montagnards can be divided into three main groups: those whose languages are of the Austro-Asian family (the Bru, Pacoh, Katu, Cua, Hre, Rengao, Sedang, Bahnar, M'nong, Maa and Stieng who speak Mon-Khmer languages, and the Tai (Thai or Thay) groups); the Malayo-Polynesian family (the Jarai, Hroi, Raday, Raglai, Chru, Chams); and the Sino-Tibetan family (the Hmong and Mien). Religiously, the minority groups are very diverse, practising ancestor-worship, animism and – as a result of proselytising in recent decades – Protestantism and Catholicism.

Some of the national minorities have lived in Vietnam for thousands of years while others have migrated into the region in the last few centuries. The areas inhabited by each group are often delimited by altitude, with later arrivals settling at higher elevations. Many of the groups have little in common with each other except a history of intertribal warfare.

Historically, the highland areas were allowed to remain virtually independent as long as their leaders recognised Vietnamese sovereignty and paid tribute and taxes. The 1980 Constitution abolished two vast autonomous regions established for the ethnic minorities in the northern mountains in 1959. During the Vietnam War, both the Communists and the USA actively recruited fighters among the Montagnards of the Central Highlands.

Many of the hill tribes are semi-nomadic, living by slash-and-burn agriculture. Because such practices destroy the ever-dwindling forests, the government is trying to turn them to settled agriculture.

Chams Vietnam's 60,000 Chams are the remnant of the once-vigorous Indianised kingdom of Champa which flourished from the 2nd to the 15th centuries and was destroyed as the Vietnamese expanded southward. Most of them live along the coast between Nha Trang and Phan Thiet and in the Mekong Delta province of An Giang.

Today, the Chams are best known for the many brick sanctuaries (known as 'Cham towers') they constructed all over the southern half of the country. The Cham language is of the Malayo-Polynesian (Austronesian) group. It can be written either in a traditional script of Indian origin or in a Latin-based script created by the French. Most of the Chams, who were profoundly influenced by both Hinduism and Buddhism, are now Muslims. There is a superb collection of Cham statues at the Cham Museum in Danang.

Khmers The Khmers (ethnic-Cambodians) numbers are estimated at about 700,000 and are concentrated in the south-western Mekong Delta. They practise Hinayana (Theravada) Buddhism.

Indians Almost all of South Vietnam's population of Indians, most of whose roots were in southern India, left in 1975. The remaining community in Saigon worship at the Mariamman Hindu temple and the Central Mosque.

Amerasians One of the most tragic legacies of the Vietnam War is the plight of thousands of Amerasians, most of whom are now around age 20. Marriages and other less formal unions between American soldiers and Vietnamese women – as well as prostitution – were common during the war. But when the Americans were rotated home, all

Orderly Departure Programme

The Orderly Departure Programme (ODP), which is carried out under the auspices of the United Nations High Commission for Refugees (UNHCR), was designed to allow orderly resettlement in the West (mostly in the USA) of Vietnamese political refugees who otherwise might have tried to flee the country by land or sea. After years of stalling by Hanoi, the programme finally began functioning properly at the end of the 1980s, and thousands of Amerasians and their families were flown via Bangkok to the Philippines where they underwent six months of English instruction before proceeding to the USA.

The ODP failed to stem the flow of refugees from the north. After the Vietnam-China border opened in 1990, many refugees simply took the train to China from where they only had to take a short boat ride across the Pearl River to Hong Kong to be declared 'boat people'. As the refugee camps in Hong Kong swelled to the bursting point, the public's patience ran out. Most of Hong Kong's population have relatives in the Chinese mainland who would like to come to Hong Kong but are quickly deported if they manage to sneak in. Meanwhile, Vietnamese arriving literally by the boatload were being permitted to stay.

Since all but a handful of the arrivals were declared to be economic migrants rather than political refugees, the Hong Kong government experimented with forcible repatriations in 1990. This prompted a vehement protest from the USA and the UNHCR. The Hong Kong government backed off temporarily, but held negotiations with Vietnam and reached an agreement in October 1991 on a programme of combined voluntary and forced repatriation. Under the agreement, those willing to return would not be penalised by Vietnam and would receive a resettlement allowance of US$30 per month for several months to be paid by the UNHCR. Vietnam also had to agree to give refugees back their citizenship (the previous policy was to strip all refugees of their citizenship, thus rendering them stateless).

The voluntary repatriations didn't go quite as planned, some of the volunteers were back in Hong Kong a few months later seeking another resettlement allowance. In such cases, forcible repatriation swiftly followed. The programme seems to be working – by the end of 1992 practically no Vietnamese refugees were arriving in Hong Kong. However, human rights activists continue to oppose the plan. ■

too often they abandoned their 'wives' and mistresses, leaving them to raise children who were half-White or half-Black in a society not particularly tolerant of such racial mixing.

After 1975, the Amerasians – living reminders of the American presence – were often mistreated by Vietnamese society and even abandoned by their mothers and other relatives. Many were forced to live on the street. When, in the early 1980s, it became known that the US government would resettle the Amerasians in the USA, Amerasian children were adopted by people eager to emigrate. After the adopted family arrived in America, many of these Amerasian children were subsequently dumped again and left to fend for themselves, creating a new social problem for the USA. At the end of the 1980s, the Orderly Departure Programme finally began to function as planned and the crowds of Amerasian street kids began to disappear from downtown Saigon.

Europeans Vietnam has a handful of ethnic-European citizens, most of whom are in fact racially mixed French-Vietnamese or French-Chinese.

Until about 1990, the only Caucasians most younger Vietnamese had ever seen were Russians. Unfortunately, the Russians have earned a reputation for being unfriendly and cheap. Should you be mistaken for a Russian, you may be snubbed.

EDUCATION

Compared to other desperately poor countries, Vietnam's population is very well educated. Vietnam's literacy rate is estimated at 82%, though official figures put it even higher (95%). Before the colonial period, the majority of the population possessed some degree of literacy, but by 1939 only 15% of school-age children were receiving any kind of instruction and 80% of the population was illiterate.

Today, almost all children receive primary education and 30 to 40% go on to secondary school, though a significant number of children are barred from enrolling in school because of their parents' political background. The country's 94 universities, technical colleges and other institutes enrol 30,000 students each year. Until recently, approximately 500 students per year went abroad for advanced training, mostly to the now defunct USSR and East Germany.

During the late 19th century, one of the few things that French colonial officials and Vietnamese nationalists agreed on was that the traditional Confucian educational system, on which the mandarinal civil service was based, was in desperate need of reform. Mandarinal examinations were held in Tonkin until WW I and in Annam until the war's end.

Many of Indochina's independence leaders were educated in elite French-language secondary schools such as the Lycée Albert Sarraut in Hanoi and the Lycée Chasseloup Laubat in Saigon.

ARTS
Film
One of Vietnam's first cinematographic efforts was a newsreel of Ho Chi Minh's 1945 proclamation of independence. After Dien Bien Phu, parts of the battle were restaged for the benefit of movie cameras.

Prior to reunification the South Vietnamese movie industry concentrated on producing sensational, low-budget flicks. Until recently, most North Vietnamese filmmaking efforts have been dedicated to 'the mobilisation of the masses for economic reconstruction, the building of socialism and the struggle for national reunification'. Predictable themes include 'workers devoted to socialist industrialisation', 'old mothers who continuously risk their lives to help the people's army' and 'children who are ready to face any danger'.

The relaxation of ideological censorship of the arts has proceeded in fits and starts, but in the last few years, the gradual increase in artistic freedoms has affected film-making as well as other genres. But paranoia about the changes sweeping Eastern Europe has caused a return to greater government control of the arts.

Music & Dancing
Though heavily influenced by the Chinese and, in the south, the Indianised Cham and Khmer musical traditions, Vietnamese music has a high degree of originality in style and instrumentation. The traditional system of writing down music and the five note (pentatonic) scale are of Chinese origin. Vietnamese choral music is unique in that the melody must correspond to the tones; it cannot be rising during a word that has a falling tone.

There are three broad categories of Vietnamese music:

- Folk, which includes children's songs, love songs, work songs, festival songs, lullabies, lamentations and funeral songs. It is usually sung without instrumental accompaniment.
- Classical (or 'learned music'), which is rather rigid and formal. It was performed at the imperial court and for the entertainment of the mandarin elite. A traditional orchestra consists of 40 musicians. There are two main types of classical chamber music: Hat A Dao (from the north) and Ca Hue (from central Vietnam).
- Theatre, which includes singing, dancing and instrumentation (see the Theatre subsection for more information).

Each of Vietnam's ethno-linguistic minorities has its own musical and dance traditions which often include colourful costumes and instruments such as reed flutes, lithophones (similar to xylophones), bamboo whistles, gongs and stringed instruments made from gourds. While in most hill tribes the majority of the dancers are women, a few Montagnard groups allow only the men to dance. A great deal of anthropological research has been carried out in recent years in order to preserve and revive minority traditions. At present, there are music conservatories teaching both traditional Vietnamese and Western classical musics in Hanoi, Hué and Ho Chi Minh City.

Theatre & Puppetry

Vietnamese theatre integrates music, singing, recitation, declamation, dance and mime into a single artistic whole. There are five basic forms:

- Classical theatre is known as *Hat Tuong* in the north and *Hat Boi* ('songs with show dress') in the south. It is based on Chinese opera and was probably brought to Vietnam by the 13th century Mongol invaders chased out by Tran Hung Dao. Hat Tuong is very formalistic, employing gestures and scenery similar to Chinese theatre. The accompanying orchestra, which is dominated by the drum, usually has six musicians. Often, the audience also has a drum so it too can comment on the on-stage action.

  Hat Tuong has a limited cast of typical characters who establish their identities using combinations of make-up and dress that the audience can readily recognise. For instance, red face-paint represents courage, loyalty and faithfulness. Traitors and cruel people have white faces. Lowlanders are given green faces; highlanders have black ones. Horizontal eyebrows represent honesty, erect eyebrows symbolise cruelty and lowered eyebrows belong to characters with a cowardly nature. A male character can express emotions (pensiveness, worry, anger, etc) by fingering his beard in various ways.

  Popular theatre *(Hat Cheo)* often engages in social protest through the medium of satire. The singing and declamation are in everyday language and include many proverbs and sayings. Many of the melodies are of peasant origin.

- Modern theatre *(Cai Luong)* originated in the south in the early 20th century and shows strong Western influences.
- Spoken drama *(Kich Noi* or *Kich)*, whose roots are Western, appeared in the 1920s. It's popular among students and intellectuals.
- Conventional puppetry *(Roi Can)* and that uniquely Vietnamese art form, water puppetry *(Roi Nuoc)*, draw their plots from the same legendary and historical sources as other forms of traditional theatre. It is thought that water puppetry developed when determined puppeteers in the Red River Delta managed to carry on with the show despite flooding.

Water Puppet

These days, the various forms of Vietnamese theatre are performed by dozens of state-funded troupes and companies around the country. Water puppetry can be seen at the Saigon Zoo, in Hanoi and at Thay Pagoda (near Hanoi).

Literature

Vietnamese literature can be divided into three types:

- Traditional oral literature *(Truyen Khau)* which was begun long before recorded history and includes legends, folk songs and proverbs.

Sino-Vietnamese literature *(Han Viet)*, which was written in Chinese characters *(chu nho)*. It dates from 939 AD, when the first independent Vietnamese kingdom was established. Sino-Vietnamese literature was dominated by Confucian and Buddhist texts and was governed by strict rules of metre and verse.

Modern Vietnamese literature *(Quoc Am)* includes anything recorded in *nom* characters or the Romanised quoc ngu script. The earliest extant text written in nom is the late 13th century *Van Te Ca Sau (Ode to an Alligator)*. Literature written in quoc ngu has played an important role in Vietnamese nationalism.

Architecture

The Vietnamese have not been great builders like their neighbours the Khmers, who erected the monuments of Angkor in Cambodia, and the Cham, whose graceful brick towers, constructed using sophisticated masonry technology, grace many parts of the southern half of the country. For more information on Cham architecture, see Po Klong Garai under Phan Rang/Thap Cham in the South-Central Coast chapter, Po Nagar in the section on Nha Trang (in the same chapter) and My Son in the Danang chapter.

Most of what the Vietnamese have built has been made of wood and other materials that proved highly vulnerable in the tropical climate. Because almost all of the stone structures erected by the Vietnamese have been destroyed in countless feudal wars and invasions, very little pre-modern Vietnamese architecture is extant.

Plenty of pagodas and temples founded hundreds of years ago are still functioning but their physical plan has usually been rebuilt many times with little concern for making the upgraded structure an exact copy of the original. As a result, modern elements have been casually introduced into pagoda architecture, with neon haloes for statues of the Buddha only the most glaring example of this.

Because of the Vietnamese custom of ancestor-worship – and despite the massive dislocations of populations during the Vietnam War – many graves from previous centuries are still extant. These include temples erected in memory of high-ranking mandarins, members of the royal family and emperors.

Memorials for Vietnamese who died in the wars against the French, Americans and Chinese are usually marked by cement obelisks inscribed with the words *To Quoc Ghi Cong* (The country will remember their exploits). Many of the tombstones were erected over empty graves; most Viet Minh and Viet Cong dead were buried where they fell.

Sculpture

Vietnamese sculpture has traditionally centred on religious themes and functioned as an adjunct to architecture, especially that of pagodas, temples and tombs. Many inscribed stelae, erected hundreds of years ago to commemorate the founding of a pagoda or important national events, can still be seen (eg at Thien Mu Pagoda in Hué and the Temple of Literature in Hanoi).

The Cham civilisation produced spectacular carved sandstone figures for its Hindu and Buddhist sanctuaries. Cham sculpture was profoundly influenced by Indian art but, over the centuries, also incorporated Indonesian and Vietnamese elements. The largest single collection of Cham sculpture in the world is at the Cham Museum in Danang. For more information on Cham sculpture, see the Cham Museum section in the Danang chapter.

Lacquerware

The art of making lacquerware was brought to Vietnam from China in the mid-15th century. Before that time, the Vietnamese used lacquer solely for practical purposes (such as making things watertight). During the 1930s, the Fine Arts School in Hanoi employed several Japanese teachers who introduced new styles and production methods. Their influence can still be seen in the noticeably Japanese elements in some Vietnamese lacquerware, especially that made in the north. Although a 1985 government publication declares that 'at present, lacquer painting deals boldly with realistic and revolutionary themes and forges unceasingly ahead', most of the lacquerware for sale is inlaid with mother-of-pearl and seems of traditional design.

Lacquer is a resin extracted from the *son* tree *(cay son)*. It is creamy white in raw form but is made black *(son then)* or brown *(canh dan,* 'cockroach wing') by mixing it with resin in an iron container for 40 hours. After the object to be lacquered (traditionally made of teak) has been treated with a fixative, 10 coats of lacquer are applied. Each coat must be dried for a week and then thoroughly sanded with pumice and cuttle-bone before the next layer can be applied. A specially refined lacquer is used for the 11th and final coat, which is sanded with a fine coal powder and lime wash before the object is decorated. Designs may be added by engraving in low relief, by painting, or by inlaying mother-of-pearl, egg shell, silver or even gold.

Ceramics

The production of ceramics *(gom)* has a long history in Vietnam. In ancient times, ceramic objects were made by coating a wicker mould with clay and baking it. Later, ceramics production became very refined, and each dynastic period is known for its particular techniques and motifs.

For more information on Vietnamese folk art, see *Handicrafts* (published by Xunhasaba, Hanoi), number 62 in the English and French-language *Vietnamese Studies* series.

Painting

Traditional Painting done on frame-mounted silk dates from the 13th century. Silk-painting was at one time the preserve of scholar-calligraphers, who also painted scenes from nature. Before the advent of photography, realistic portraits for use in ancestor-worship were produced. Some of

these – usually of former head monks – can still be seen in Buddhist pagodas.

Modern During this century, Vietnamese painting has been influenced by Western trends. Much of the recent work done in Vietnam has had political rather than aesthetic or artistic motives. According to an official account, the fighting of the Vietnam War provided painters with 'rich human material: People's Army combatants facing the jets, peasant and factory women in the militia who handled guns as well as they did their production work, young volunteers who repaired roads in record time...old mothers offering tea to anti-aircraft gunners...' There's lots of this stuff at the Fine Arts Museum in Hanoi.

The recent economic liberalisation has convinced many young artists to abandon the revolutionary themes and concentrate on producing commercially saleable paintings. Some have gone back to the traditional silk paintings, while others are experimenting with new subjects. There is a noticeable tendency now to produce nude paintings, which might indicate either an attempt to appeal to Western tastes or an expression of long-suppressed kinky desires.

The cheaper stuff (US$10 to US$50) gets spun off to hotel gift shops and street markets. Supposedly, the higher standard works are put on display in one of two government-run art galleries: the Vietnamese Art Association, 511 Tran Hung Dao, Hanoi; and the Ho Chi Minh City Association of Fine Arts (☎ 230025), 218 Nguyen Thi Minh Khai, District 1. Typical prices are in the US$30 to US$50 range, though the artists may ask 10 times that. It's important to know that there are quite a few forgeries around – just because you spot a painting by a 'famous Vietnamese artist' does not mean that it's an original, though it may still be an attractive work of art.

CULTURE
Traditions & Customs

Dress The graceful national dress of Vietnamese women is known as the *ao dai* (pronounced 'ow-zai' in the north and 'ow-yai' in the south). It consists of a close-fitting blouse with long panels in the front and back that is worn over loose black or white trousers. One sees fewer and fewer women wearing ao dais these days, though they are still popular for formal occasions.

Traditionally, men have also worn ao dais. The male version is shorter and looser fitting. Before the end of dynastic rule, the colours of the brocade and embroidery indicated the rank of the wearer. Gold brocade accompanied by embroidered dragons was reserved for the emperor. High-ranking mandarins wore purple while lower ranking mandarins had to settle for blue.

Mourners usually wear either white or black ao dais (white is the traditional colour of mourning).

The famous 'black pajamas' of the VC, immortalised in numerous Hollywood movies, are really just a common form of rural dress. You will see plenty of people in the countryside wearing them.

Face Having 'big face' is synonymous with prestige, and prestige is important in the Orient. All families, even poor ones, are expected to have big wedding parties and throw around money like water, in order to gain face. This is often ruinously expensive, but the fact that the wedding results in bankruptcy for the young couple is far less important than losing face.

Beauty Concepts The Vietnamese consider pale skin to be beautiful. On sunny days trendy Vietnamese women can often be seen strolling under the shade of an umbrella in order to keep from tanning. As in 19th century Europe, peasants get tanned and those who can afford it do not. Women who work in the fields will go to great lengths to preserve their pale skin by wearing long-sleeved shirts, gloves, a conical hat and wrapping their face in a towel.

Greetings The traditional Vietnamese form of greeting is to press your hands together in front of your body and to bow slightly. These days, the Western custom of shaking hands has taken over, but the traditional greeting is still sometimes used by Buddhist monks and nuns, to whom it is proper to respond in kind.

Name Cards Name cards are very popular in Vietnam, and like elsewhere in eastern Asia, exchanging business cards is an important part of even the smallest transaction or business contact. Get some printed before you arrive in Vietnam and hand them out like confetti. In Bangkok, shops using the latest laser-printing technology can make inexpensive (US$12 for 200) custom-designed business cards in 20 minutes. They can be found in Sogo Department Store in Amarin Plaza and in the Central Department Store, both of which are on Ploenchit Rd. You need to put your occupation on your name card; if you don't have one, try 'backpacker'.

Geomancy Geomancy is the art (or science if you prefer) of manipulating or judging the environment. If you want to build a house or find a suitable site for a grave then you call in a geomancer. The orientation of houses, communal meeting halls *(dinh)*, tombs and pagodas is determined by geomancers, which is why cemeteries have tombstones turned every which way. The location of an ancestor's grave is an especially serious matter – if the grave is in the wrong spot or facing the wrong way, then there is no telling what trouble the spirits might cause.

Businesses that are failing may call in a geomancer. Sometimes the solution is to move the door or a window. If this doesn't do the trick, it might be necessary to move an ancestor's grave. Distraught spirits may have to be placated with payments of cash (donated to a temple), especially if one wishes to erect a building or other structure which blocks the spirits' view.

The concept of geomancy is believed to have originated with the Chinese. Although the communists (both Chinese and Vietnamese) have disparaged geomancy as superstition, it still has influence on people's behaviour.

Staring Squads If you are doing something interesting (such as just standing there), many curious people – especially children – may gather round you to watch. When you get fed up with being the perennial centre of attention, hotel restaurants are a good place of refuge.

If you keep a diary or take notes, just about everyone will stick their nose into your notebook. Some people might even lift it out of your hands just to get a better look. On the other hand, other people get very paranoid if you take notes, especially if you're writing down what they're saying. This can be a problem if you want to take notes at a museum – you might have to assuage the museum guides with a tip.

Lien Xo! The main reason children shout *Lien Xo!* (literally 'Soviet Union') at Caucasians – all of whom are assumed to be Soviets – has something to do with people's motivations for tapping on aquarium fish tanks and catching the attention of primates at the zoo: they want to be recognised by an exotic being and to provoke some kind of reaction. The intent is also to annoy the Russians residing in Vietnam, whose unpopularity is legendary.

Russian tourists and technical advisors are far less common now than they used to be – few of them can afford a holiday in Vietnam anymore and their technical skills are considered inferior to those available from the West. But the expression *Lien Xo* is still used and seems to mean something like 'Hey, look, a white person!' and is intended to alert other curious youngsters that a strange-looking human is in the vicinity. Often, children will unabashedly come up to you and pull the hair on your arms or legs (they want to test if it's real) or dare each other to touch your skin. Some travellers have been pinched or kicked without provocation.

Taboos
Police Paranoia When dealing with local people, it is important to be extremely sensitive to indications that they are concerned that contact with you is likely to get them into trouble with the police. Vietnamese are much less afraid of being seen with Westerners than they were a few years ago, but there are still reports – especially in the north – of conversations with Westerners resulting in questioning and harassment by the police.

Sweet Beggars A good way to anger adult Vietnamese is to offer sweets to a group of shy children you come across. You may have to practically force them to take it, but children know a good thing when they see it, and soon they may be tagging along behind tourists demanding gifts. US soldiers used to do this during the war, creating gangs of six-year-old beggars and causing a great deal of resentment.

Mean Feet Like the Chinese and Japanese, Vietnamese are obsessed with clean floors and it's usual to remove shoes when entering somebody's home. If you are entering a 'shoes off' home, your host will provide a pair of slippers.

Shoes must be removed inside most Buddhist temples, but this is not universal so watch what others do. Be sure not to let the bottoms of your feet point towards other people or anything sacred, especially figures of Buddhas.

Short Shorts Short pants are generally worn only by small children and extremely casually dressed men labouring in the tropical heat (like ditch-diggers and farm workers). Vietnamese women never wear shorts, even when labouring in the rice paddies under the sweltering sun. For them to wear shorts would be considered indecent, though ironically many wear see-through trousers.

The Vietnamese are starting to get used to foreigners wearing shorts, but they consider it as appropriate as wearing a swim suit to a funeral. If you wear particularly skimpy shorts, that is especially offensive.

On the other hand, Vietnamese are less formal in dress than in many neighbouring countries (they can't afford the tailored suits and dresses yet). If you see someone walking around wearing a tie, he's more likely to be a Chinese businessman than a local.

Deadly Chopsticks Leaving a pair of chopsticks sticking vertically in a rice bowl looks very similar to the incense sticks which are burned for the dead. This is a powerful death sign and is not appreciated anywhere in the Orient.

Avoiding Offence

Vernon Weitzel of the Australian National University sends these 10 tips for successfully dealing with Vietnamese officials, business people, etc:

- Always smile and be pleasant.
- Don't run around complaining about everything.
- If you want to criticise someone, do it in a joking manner to avoid confrontation.
- Expect delays – build them into your schedule.
- Never show anger – ever! Getting visibly upset is not only rude – it will cause you to lose face.
- Don't be competitive. Treating your interaction as a cooperative enterprise works much better.
- Don't act as though you deserve service from anyone. If you do, it's likely that you will be delayed.
- Don't be too inquisitive about personal matters.
- Sitting and sipping tea and the exchange of gifts (sharing cigarettes, for instance) are an important prelude to any business interaction.
- The mentality of officialdom is very Confucian, especially in the north. Expect astounding amounts of red tape.

Sport

The Vietnamese government emphasises gymnastics which is a mandatory subject at all schools from the elementary level through university. Given the tropical climate and abundant water resources, swimming is popular. Other sports include tennis, badminton, table tennis and handball.

RELIGION

Four great philosophies and religions have shaped the spiritual life of the Vietnamese people: Confucianism, Taoism, Buddhism and Christianity. Over the centuries, Confucianism, Taoism and Buddhism have fused with popular Chinese beliefs and ancient Vietnamese animism to form what is known

collectively as the 'Triple Religion', or *Tam Giao*. Confucianism, more a system of social and political morality than a religion, took on many religious aspects. Taoism, which began as an esoteric philosophy for scholars, mixed with Buddhism among the peasants, and many Taoist elements became an intrinsic part of popular religion. If asked their religion the Vietnamese are likely to say that they are Buddhist, but when it comes to family or civic duties they are likely to follow Confucianism while turning to Taoist conceptions in understanding the nature of the cosmos.

Mahayana Buddhism

Mahayana Buddhism (Dai Thua or Bac Tong, which means From the North, ie China; also known as the Greater Wheel school, Greater Vehicle school and Northern Buddhism) is the predominant religion in Vietnam. The largest Mahayana sect in the country is Zen (Dhyana; in Vietnamese, Thien), also known as the school of meditation. Dao Trang (the Pure Land school), the second-largest Mahayana sect in Vietnam, is practised mainly in the south.

Mahayana Buddhism differs from Theravada Buddhism in several important ways. Whereas the Theravadin strives to become a perfected saint (Arhat) ready for Nirvana, the Mahayanist ideal is that of the Bodhisattva, one who strives to perfect himself or herself in the necessary virtues (generosity, morality, patience, vigour, concentration and wisdom) but even after attaining perfection chooses to remain in the world in order to save others.

Mahayanists consider Gautama Buddha to be only one of the innumerable manifestations of the one ultimate Buddha. These countless Buddhas and Bodhisattvas, who are as numberless as the universes to which they minister, gave rise in popular Vietnamese religion – with its innumerable Taoist divinities and spirits – to a pantheon of deities and helpers whose aid can be sought through invocations and offerings.

Mahayana Buddhist pagodas in Vietnam usually include a number of elements. In front of the pagoda is a white statue of a standing Quan The Am Bo Tat (Avalokiteçvara Bodhisattva in Hindi, Guanyin in Chinese, Goddess of Mercy in English). A variation of the Goddess of Mercy shows her with multiple arms and sometimes multiple eyes and ears, permitting her to touch, see and hear all. This version of the Goddess of Mercy is called Chuan De (Qianshou Guanyin in Chinese).

Inside the main sanctuary are representations of the three Buddhas: A Di Da (pronounced 'AH-zee-dah'; Amitabha), the Buddha of the Past; Thich Ca Mau Ni (Sakyamuni, or Siddhartha Gautama), the Historical Buddha; and Di Lac (pronounced 'zee-lock'; Maitreya), the Buddha of the Future. Nearby are often statues of the eight Kim Cang (Genies of the Cardinal Directions), the La Han (Arhats) and various Bo Tat (bodhisattvas) such as Van Thu (Manjusri), Quan The Am Bo Tat (Avaloketeçvara) and Dia Tang (Ksitigartha). Sometimes, an altar is set aside for Taoist divinities such as Ngoc Hoang (the Emperor of Jade) and Thien Hau Thanh Mau (the Queen of Heaven), who is also known as Tuc Goi La Ba (the Goddess of the Sea and Protector of Fishermen & Sailors). Thien Hau is known as Tin Hau in Hong Kong and Matsu in Taiwan. Every pagoda has an altar for funerary tablets memorialising deceased Buddhist monks (who are often buried in stupas near the pagoda) and lay people.

The function of the Vietnamese Buddhist monk *(bonze)* is to minister to the spiritual and superstitious needs of the peasantry, but it is largely up to him whether he invokes the lore of Taoism or the philosophy of Buddhism. A monk may live reclusively on a remote hilltop or he may manage a pagoda on a busy city street. And he may choose to fulfil any number of functions: telling fortunes, making and selling talismans *(fu)*, advising where a house should be constructed, reciting incantations at funerals or even performing acupuncture.

History Theravada Buddhism was brought to Vietnam from India by pilgrims at the end of the 2nd century AD. Simultaneously, Chinese monks introduced Mahayana Buddhism. Buddhism did not become popular with the masses until many centuries later.

Buddhism received royal patronage during the 10th to 13th centuries. This backing included recognition of the Buddhist hierarchy, financial support for the construction of pagodas and other projects, and the active participation of the clergy in ruling the country. By the 11th century, Buddhism had filtered down to the villages. Buddhism was proclaimed the official state religion in the mid-12th century.

During the 13th and 14th centuries, Confucian scholars gradually replaced Vietnamese monks as advisors to the Tran Dynasty. The Confucians accused the Buddhists of shirking their responsibilities to family and country because of the Buddhist doctrine of withdrawal from worldly matters. The Chinese invasion of 1414 reinvigorated Confucianism while at the same time resulting in the destruction of many Buddhist pagodas and manuscripts. The Nguyen Lords (1558-1778), who ruled the southern part of the country. reversed this trend.

A revival of Vietnamese Buddhism began throughout the country in the 1920s, and Buddhist organisations were begun in various parts of the country. In the 1950s and '60s, attempts were made to unite the various streams of Buddhism in Vietnam. During the early 1960s, South Vietnamese Buddhist monks and lay people played an active role in opposing the regime of Ngo Dinh Diem.

Over the centuries, the Buddhist ideals and beliefs held by the educated elite touched only superficially the rural masses (90% of the population), whose traditions were transmitted orally and put to the test by daily observance. The common people were far less concerned with the philosophy of good government than they were with seeking aid from supernatural beings for problems of the here and now.

Gradually, the various Mahayana Buddhas and Bodhisattvas became mixed up with mysticism, animism, polytheism and

Buddha statue

Hindu tantrism as well as the multiple divinities and ranks of deities of the Taoist pantheon. The Triple Religion flourished despite clerical attempts to maintain some semblance of Buddhist orthodoxy and doctrinal purity. Although most of the population has only a vague notion of Buddhist doctrines they invite monks to participate in such life-cycle ceremonies as funerals. And Buddhist pagodas have come to be seen by many Vietnamese as a physical and spiritual refuge from an uncertain world.

After 1975, many monks, including some who actively opposed the South Vietnamese government and the war, were rounded up and sent to re-education camps. Temples were closed and the training of young monks was prohibited. In the last few years, most of these restrictions have been lifted and a religious revival of sorts is taking place.

Theravada Buddhism

Theravada Buddhism (Tieu Thua or Nam Tong, which means From the South); also known as Hinayana, the Lesser Wheel school, the Lesser Vehicle school and Southern Buddhism) came to Vietnam directly from India. It is practised mainly in the Mekong Delta region, mostly by ethnic-

Khmers. The most important Theravada sect in Vietnam is the disciplinary school, Luat Tong.

Basically, the Theravada school of Buddhism is an earlier and, according to its followers, less corrupted form of Buddhism than the Mahayana schools found in most of East Asia and the Himalayan region. The Theravada school is called the 'Southern School' because it took the southern route from India, its place of origin, through South-East Asia (it came directly from India to Vietnam), while the 'Northern School' proceeded north into Nepal, Tibet, China, Korea, Mongolia, Vietnam and Japan. Because the southern school tried to preserve or limit the Buddhist doctrines to only those canons codified in the early Buddhist era, the northern school gave Theravada Buddhism the name Hinayana, or Lesser Vehicle. They considered themselves Great Vehicle because they built upon the earlier teachings, 'expanding' the doctrine in such a way so as to respond more ot the needs of lay people.

Confucianism

While it is more a religious philosophy than an organised religion, Confucianism (Nho Giao or Khong Giao) has been an important force in shaping Vietnam's social system and the everyday lives and beliefs of its people.

Confucius (in Vietnamese: Khong Tu) was born in China around 550 BC. He saw people as social beings formed by society yet capable of shaping their society. He believed that the individual exists in and for society and drew up a code of ethics to guide the individual in social interaction. This code laid down a person's specific obligations to family, society and the state. Central to Confucianism are an emphasis on duty and hierarchy.

According to Confucian philosophy, which was brought to Vietnam by the Chinese during their 1000-year rule (111 BC to 938 AD), the emperor alone, governing under the mandate of heaven, can intercede on behalf of the nation with the powers of heaven and earth. Only virtue, as acquired through education, gave one the right (the mandate of heaven) to wield political power. From this it followed that an absence of virtue would result in the withdrawal of this mandate, sanctioning rebellion against an unjust ruler. Natural disasters or defeat on the battlefield were often interpreted as a sign that the mandate of heaven had been withdrawn.

Confucian philosophy was in some senses democratic: because virtue could be acquired only through learning, education rather than birth made a person virtuous. Therefore, education had to be widespread. Until the beginning of this century, Confucian philosophy and texts formed the basis of Vietnam's educational system. Generation after generation of young people – in the villages as well as the cities – were taught their duties to family (including ancestor-worship) and community and that each person had to know their place in the social hierarchy and behave accordingly.

A system of government-run civil service examinations selected from among the country's best students those who would join the non-hereditary ruling class, the mandarins. As a result, education was prized not only as the path to virtue but as a means to social and political advancement. This system helped create the respect for intellectual and literary accomplishment for which the Vietnamese are famous to this day.

The political institutions based on Confucianism finally degenerated and became discredited, as they did elsewhere in the Chinese-influenced world. Over the centuries, the philosophy became conservative and backward-looking. This reactionary trend became dominant in Vietnam in the 15th century, suiting despotic rulers who emphasised the divine right of kings rather than their responsibilities under the doctrine of the mandate of heaven.

Taoism

Taoism (Lao Giao or Dao Giao) originated in China and is based on the philosophy of Laotse (Thai Thuong Lao Quan). Laotse (literally The Old One) lived in the 6th century BC. Little is known about Laotse, and some question whether or not he really existed. He is believed to have been the custodian of the imperial archives for the Chinese government and Confucius is supposed to have consulted him.

It is doubtful that Laotse ever intended his philosophy to become a religion. Chang Ling has been credited with formally establishing the religion in 143 BC. Taoism later split into two divisions, the Cult of the Immortals and The Way of the Heavenly Teacher.

Understanding Taoism is not easy. The philosophy emphasises contemplation and simplicity of life. Its ideal is returning to the Tao (the Way – the essence of which all things are made). Only a small elite in China and Vietnam has ever been able to grasp Taoist philosophy, which is based on various correspondences (eg the human body, the microcosmic replica of the macrocosm) and complimentary contradictions (am and duong, the Vietnamese equivalents of Yin and Yang). As a result, there are very few pure Taoist pagodas in Vietnam, yet much of Taoist ritualism has been absorbed into Chinese and Vietnamese Buddhism. You are most likely to notice the Taoist influence on temples in the form of dragons and demons which decorate the temple rooftops.

According to the Taoist cosmology, Ngoc Hoang, the Emperor of Jade (in Chinese: Yu Huang), whose abode is in heaven, rules over a world of divinities, genies, spirits and demons in which the forces of nature are incarnated as supernatural beings and great historical personages have become gods. It is this aspect of Taoism that has become assimilated into the daily lives of most Vietnamese as a collection of superstitions and mystical and animistic beliefs. Much of the sorcery and magic that are now part of popular Vietnamese religion have their origins in Taoism.

Ancestor-Worship

Vietnamese ancestor-worship, which is the ritual expression of filial piety (hieu), dates from long before the arrival of Confucianism or Buddhism. Some people consider it to be a religion unto itself.

The cult of the ancestors is based on the belief that the soul lives on after death and becomes the protector of its descendants. Because of the influence the spirits of one's ancestors exert on the living, it is considered not only shameful for them to be upset or restless but downright dangerous. A soul with no descendants is doomed to eternal wandering because it will not receive homage.

Traditionally, the Vietnamese venerate and honour the spirits of their ancestors regularly, especially on the anniversary of the ancestor's death when sacrifices are offered to both the god of the household and the spirit of the ancestors. To request intercession for success in business or on behalf of a sick child, sacrifices and prayers are offered to the ancestral spirits. The ancestors are informed on occasions of family joy or sorrow, such as weddings, success in an examination, or death. Important elements in the cult of the ancestor are the family altar, a plot of land whose income is set aside for the support of the ancestors, and the designation of a direct male descendent of the deceased to assume the obligation to carry on the cult.

Many pagodas have altars on which memorial tablets and photographs of the deceased are displayed. One may look at the young faces in the photographs and ponder the tragedy of so many people having had their lives cut short. Some visitors wonder if they died as a result of the wars. The real explanation is less tragic: most of the dead had passed on decades after the photos were taken, but rather than use a picture of an aged, infirm parent, survivors chose a more flattering (though slightly outdated) picture of the deceased in their prime.

Caodaism

Caodaism is an indigenous Vietnamese sect that seeks to create the ideal religion by fusing the secular and religious philosophies of both East and West. It was founded in the early 1920s based on messages revealed in seances to Ngo Minh Chieu, the group's founder. The sect's colourful headquarters is in Tay Ninh, 96 km north-west of Ho Chi Minh City. There are currently about two million followers of Caodaism in Vietnam. For more information about Caodaism, see Tay Ninh in the Around Ho Chi Minh City chapter.

Hoa Hao Buddhist Sect

The Hoa Hao Buddhist sect (Phat Giao Hoa Hao) was founded in the Mekong Delta in 1939 by Huynh Phu So, a young man who had studied with the most famous of the region's occultists. After he was miraculously cured of sickliness, So began preaching a reformed Buddhism based on the common people and embodied in personal faith rather than elaborate rituals. His philosophy emphasised simplicity in worship and denied the necessity for intermediaries between human beings and the Supreme Being.

In 1940 the French, who called Huynh Phu So the 'mad monk', tried to silence him. When arresting him failed, they committed him to an insane asylum where he soon converted the Vietnamese psychiatrist assigned to his case. During WW II, the Hoa Hao Sect continued to grow and to build up a militia with weapons supplied by the Japanese. In 1947, after clashes between Hoa Hao forces and the Viet Minh, Huynh Phu So was assassinated by the Viet Minh, who thereby earned the animosity of what had by then become a powerful political and military force in the Mekong Delta, especially around Chau Doc. The military power of the Hoa Hao was broken in 1956 when one of its guerrilla commanders was captured by the Diem government and publicly guillotined. Subsequently, elements of the Hoa Hao army joined the Viet Cong.

There presently are thought to be about 1½ million followers of the Hoa Hao sect.

Catholicism

Catholicism was introduced into Vietnam in the 16th century by missionaries from Portugal, Spain and France. Particularly active during the 16th and 17th centuries were the

French Jesuits and Portuguese Dominicans. Pope Alexander VII assigned the first bishops to Vietnam in 1659, and the first Vietnamese priests were ordained nine years later. According to some estimates, there were 800,000 Catholics in Vietnam by 1685. Over the next three centuries, Catholicism was discouraged and at times outlawed. The first known edict forbidding missionary activity was promulgated in 1533. Foreign missionaries and their followers were severely persecuted during the 17th and 18th centuries.

When the French began their efforts to turn Vietnam into a part of their empire, the treatment of Catholics was one of their most important pretexts for intervention. Under French rule the Catholic church was given preferential status and Catholicism flourished. Though it incorporated certain limited aspects of Vietnamese culture, Catholicism (unlike Buddhism, for instance) succeeded in retaining its doctrinal purity.

Today, Vietnam has the highest percentage of Catholics (8 to 10% of the population) in Asia outside the Philippines. Many of the 900,000 refugees who fled North Vietnam to the South in 1954 were Catholics, as was the then South Vietnamese President Ngo Dinh Diem. Since 1954 in the North and 1975 in the South, Catholics have faced restrictions on their religious activities, including strict limits on the ordination of priests and religious education. Most churches you see in Vietnam are closed and dilapidated, though some effort is now being made to reopen them. Lack of funds for restoration is part of the problem, but local officials (most of whom come from the north) are also generally uncooperative, viewing the Catholic church as both a form of Western cultural pollution and a possible instrument of subversion.

Protestantism

Protestantism was introduced to Vietnam in 1911. The majority of Vietnam's Protestants, who number about 200,000, are Montagnards living in the Central Highlands. Until 1975, the most active Protestant group in South Vietnam was the Christian & Missionary Alliance. After reunification, many Protestant clergymen – especially those trained by American missionaries – were imprisoned. The religious activities of Protestant churches are still restricted by the government.

Islam

Muslims – mostly ethnic-Khmers and Chams – constitute about 0.5% of Vietnam's population. There were small communities of Malaysian, Indonesian and south Indian Muslims in Saigon until 1975, when almost all of them fled. Today, Saigon's 5000 Muslims (including a handful of south Indians) congregate in about a dozen mosques, including the large Central Mosque in the city centre.

Arab traders reached China in the 7th century and may have stopped in Vietnam on the way, but the earliest evidence of an Islamic presence in Vietnam is a 10th century pillar inscribed in Arabic which was found near the coastal town of Phan Rang. It appears that Islam spread among Cham refugees who fled to Cambodia after the destruction of their kingdom in 1471 but that these converts had little success in propagating Islam among their fellow Chams still in Vietnam.

The Vietnamese Chams consider themselves Muslims despite the fact that they have only a vague notion of Islamic theology and laws. Their communities have very few copies of the Koran and even their religious dignitaries can hardly read Arabic. Though Muslims the world over pray five times a day, the Chams pray only on Fridays and celebrate Ramadan (a month of dawn to dusk fasting) for only three days. Their worship services consist of the recitation of a few Arabic verses from the Koran in a corrupted form. Instead of performing ritual ablutions, they make motions as if they were drawing water from a well. Circumcision is symbolically performed on boys at age 15; the ceremony consists of a religious leader making the gestures of circumcision with a wooden knife. The Chams of Vietnam do not make the pilgrimage to Mecca and though they do not eat pork, they do drink alcohol. In addition, their Islam-based religious rituals exist side-by-side with animism and the worship of Hindu deities. The Chams have even taken the Arabic words of common Koranic expressions and made them into the names of deities.

Cham religious leaders wear a white robe and an elaborate turban with gold, red or brown tassels. Their ranks are indicated by the length of the tassels.

Hinduism

Champa was profoundly influenced by Hinduism and many of the Cham towers, built as Hindu sanctuaries, contain lingams (phallic symbols of Shiva) that are still worshipped by ethnic-Vietnamese and ethnic-Chinese alike. After the fall of Champa in the 15th century, most Chams who remained in Vietnam became Muslims but continued to practise various Brahmanic (high-cast Hindu) rituals and customs.

LANGUAGE

The Vietnamese language *(kinh)* is a fusion of Mon-Khmer, Tai and Chinese elements. From the monotonic Mon-Khmer languages, Vietnamese derived a significant percentage of its basic words. From the Tai languages, it adopted certain grammatical elements and tonality. Chinese gave Vietnamese most of its philosophical, literary, technical and governmental vocabulary as well as its traditional writing system.

From around 1980 to about 1987, anyone caught studying English was liable to get be arrested. This was part of a general crackdown against people wanting to flee to the West. That attitude has changed and today the study of English is being pursued with a passion. The most widely spoken foreign languages in Vietnam are Chinese (Cantonese and Mandarin), English, French and Russian, more or less in that order. To a large extent, the divisions between who speaks each is generational. People in their 50s and older (who grew up during the colonial period) are much more likely to understand

some French than southerners of the following generation, for whom English was indispensable for professional and commercial contacts with the Americans. Some southern Vietnamese men – former combat interpreters – speak a quaint form of English peppered with all sorts of charming southern-American expressions like 'ya'll come back' and 'it ain't worth didley-squat' and pronounced with a perceptible drawl. Apparently, they worked with Americans from the deep south, carefully studied their pronunciation and diligently learned every nuance.

Many of the Vietnamese who speak English – especially former South Vietnamese soldiers and officials – learned it while working with the Americans during the Vietnam War. After reunification, almost all of them spent periods of time ranging from a few months to 14 years in 're-education camps'. Many such former South Vietnamese soldiers and officials will be delighted to renew contact with Americans, with whose compatriots they spent so much time, often in very difficult circumstances, half-a-lifetime ago. Former long-term prisoners often have friends and acquaintances all over the country (you meet an awful lot of people in 10 or more years), constituting an 'old-boys' network' of sorts.

Spoken Chinese (both Cantonese and Mandarin dialects) is making a definite comeback after years of being repressed. The large number of free-spending tourists and investors from Taiwan and Hong Kong provides the chief motivation for studying Chinese. In addition, cross-border trade with mainland China has been increasing rapidly and those who can speak Chinese are well positioned to profit from it.

After reunification, the teaching of Russian was stressed all over the country. With the collapse of the USSR in 1991, all interest in studying Russian has ground to a screeching halt.

Writing

For centuries, the Vietnamese language was written in standard Chinese characters *(chu nho)*. Around the 13th century, the Vietnamese devised their own system of writing (*chu nom* or just *nom*), which was derived by combining Chinese characters or using them for their phonetic significance only. Both writing systems were used simultaneously until the 20th century: official business and scholarship was conducted in chu nho while chu nom was used for popular literature.

The Latin-based quoc ngu script, in wide use since WW I, was developed in the 17th century by Alexandre de Rhodes, a brilliant French Jesuit scholar who first preached in Vietnamese only six months after arriving in the country in 1627. By replacing nom characters with quoc ngu, Rhodes facilitated the propagation of the gospel to a wide audience. The use of quoc ngu served to undermine the position of mandarin officials, whose power was based on traditional scholarship written in chu nho and chu nom and largely inaccessible to the masses.

Pronunciation & Tones

Most of the names of the letters of the quoc ngu alphabet are pronounced as are the letters of the French alphabet. Dictionaries are alphabetised as in English except that each vowel/tone combination is treated as a different letter. The consonants of the Romanised Vietnamese alphabet are pronounced more or less as they are in English with a few exceptions.

c	Like a 'K' but with no aspiration.
d	With a crossbar; like a hard 'D'.
d	Without a crossbar; like a 'Z' in the north and a 'Y' in the south.
gi-	Like a 'Z' in the north and a 'Y' in the south.
kh-	Like '-ch' in the German *buch*.
ng-	Like the '-nga-' in 'long ago'.
nh-	Like the Spanish 'Ñ' (as in *mañana)*
ph-	Like an 'F'.
r	Like 'Z' in the north and 'R' in the south.
s	Like an 'S' in the north and 'Sh' in the south.
tr-	Like 'Ch-' in the north and 'Tr-' in the south.
th-	Like a strongly aspirated 'T'.
x	Like an 'S'.
-ch	Like a 'K'.
-ng	Like '-ng' in 'long' but with the lips closed.
-nh	Like '-ng' in 'sing'.

The hardest part of studying Vietnamese for Westerners is learning to differentiate between the tones. Each of the six tones in Vietnamese is represented by a different diacritical mark. Thus, every syllable in Vietnamese can be pronounced six different ways. Depending on the tones, the word *ma* can be read to mean phantom, but, mother, rice seedling, tomb or horse. *Ga* can mean railroad station and chicken as well several other things.

Grammar

Vietnamese grammar is fairly straightforward, with a wide variety of sentence structures possible. The numbers and genders of nouns are generally not explicit nor are the tenses and moods of verbs. Instead, tool words (such as *cua*, which means 'belong to') and classifiers are used to show a word's relationship to its neighbours. Verbs are turned into nouns by adding *su*.

Questions are asked in the negative, as with *n'est-ce pas?* in French. When the Vietnamese ask 'Is it OK?' they say 'It is OK, is it not?' The answer 'no' means 'Not OK it is not,' which is the double-negative form of 'Yes, it is OK'. The answer 'yes', on the other hand, means 'Yes, it is not OK' or as we would say in English 'No, it is not OK'. The result is that when negative questions ('It's not OK, is it?') are posed to Vietnamese great confusion often results.

Proper Names

Most Vietnamese names consist of a family name, a middle name and a given name, in that order. Thus, if Henry David Thoreau had been Vietnamese, he would have been named Thoreau David Henry. He would have been addressed as Mr Henry – people are called by their given name but to do so without the title Mr, Mrs or Miss is consid ered as expressing either great intimacy or arrogance of the sort a superior would use with his or her inferior.

In Vietnamese, Mr is *Ong* if the man is of your grandparents' generation, *Bac* if he is of your parents' age, *Chu* if he is younger than your parents and *Anh* if he is in his teens or early 20s. Mrs is *Ba* if the woman is of your grandparents' age and *Bac* if she is of your parents' generation or younger. Miss is *Co* unless the woman is very young, in which case *Chi* might be more appropriate. Other titles of respect are Buddhist monk *(thay)*, Buddhist nun *(ba)*, Catholic priest *(cha)* and Catholic nun *(co)*.

There are 300 or so family names in use in Vietnam, the most common of which is Nguyen (pronounced something like 'nwyen'). About half of all Vietnamese have the surname Nguyen! When women marry, they usually (but not always) take their husband's family name. The middle name may be purely ornamental, may indicate the sex of its bearer or may be used by all the male members of a given family. A person's given name is carefully chosen so that it forms a harmonious and meaningful ensemble with his or her family and middle names and with the names of other family members.

Pronouns

I
   tôi
you (to an older man/men)
   (các) ông
you (to an older woman/women)
   (các) bà
you (to a man/men) of your own age
   (các) anh
you (to a woman or women of your own age)
   (các) cô
he
   cậu ấy, anh ấy
she
   cô ấy
we
   chúng tôi
they
   họ

Useful Words & Phrases

come
   tới
give
   cho
fast
   nhanh (in north)
   mau (in south)
slow
   chậm
man
   nam
woman
   nữ
understand
   hiểu
I don't understand.
   Tôi không hiểu
I need...
   Tôi cần...
change money
   đổi tiền

Greetings & Civilities

Hello.
   Chào.
How are you?
   (appropriate 'you') *Có khỏe không?*
Fine, thank you.
   Khỏe, cám ơn.
Good night.
   Chúc ngủ ngon.
Excuse me. (often used before questions)
   Xin lỗi.
Thank you.
   Cám ơn.
Thank you very much.
   Cám ơn rất nhiều.
Yes.
   Vâng. (north)
   Có, Phải. (south)
No.
   Không.

Small Talk

What is your name?
   Tên (appropriate 'you') *là gì?*
My name is...
   Tên tôi là...

I like...
   Tôi thích...
I don't like...
   Tôi không thích...
I want...
   Tôi muốn...
I don't want...
   Tôi không muốn...

Getting Around

What time does the first bus depart?
   Chuyến xe buýt sớm nhất sẽ chạy lúc mấy giờ?
What time does the last bus depart?
   Chuyến xe buýt cuối cùng sẽ chạy lúc mấy giờ?
How many km is it to...
   ...cách xa đây bao nhiêu kilomet
How many hours does the journey take?
   Chuyến đi sẽ mất bao lâu?
Go.
   Đi.
I want to go to...
   Tôi muốn đi...
What time does it arrive?
   Xe sẽ đến lúc mấy giờ?
What time does it depart?
   Xe sẽ chạy lúc mấy giờ?
hire an automobile
   mướn xe hơi (south)
   thuê xe hơi (north)
bus
   xe buýt
bus station
   bến xe
cyclo (pedicab)
   xe xích-lô
map
   bản đồ
railway station
   ga xe lửa
receipt
   biên lai
sleeping berth
   giường ngủ
timetable
   thời biểu
train
   xe lửa

Around Town

office
   văn phòng
post office
   bưu điện
restaurant
   nhà hàng
telephone
   điện thoại
tourism
   du lịch

Accommodation

hotel
   khách sạn (Chinese construct)
hotel
   nhà khách (Vietnamese construct)
Where is there a (cheap) hotel?
   Ở đâu có khách sạn (rẻ tiền)?
How much does a room cost?
   Giá một phòng bao nhiêu?
I would like a cheap room.
   Tôi thích một phòng loại rẻ.
I need to leave at (5) o'clock tomorrow morning.
   Tôi phải đi lúc (năm) giờ sáng mai.
air-conditioning
   máy lạnh
bathroom
   phòng tắm
blanket
   chăn (north)
   mền (south)
fan
   quạt
hot water
   nước nóng
laundry
   tiệm giặt quần áo
mosquito net
   màn (north)
   mùng (south)
reception
   tiếp tân
room
   phòng
room key
   chìa khóa phòng
1st-class room
   phòng loại nhất

2nd-class room
  phòng loại nhì
sheet
  ra trải giường
toilet
  nhà vệ sinh
toilet paper
  giấy vệ sinh
towel
  khăn tấm

Geographical Terms & Directions

street
  đường, phố
boulevard
  đại lộ
bridge
  cầu
highway
  xa lộ
island
  đảo
mountain
  núi
National Highway 1
  Quốc Lộ 1
river
  sông
square (in a city)
  công trường
east
  đông
north
  bắc
south
  nam
west
  tây

Shopping

For words useful for buying food and drinks, see those sections in the Facts for the Visitor chapter.

Don't have...
  Không có...
How much is this?
  Cái này giá bao nhiêu?
I want to pay in dong.
  Tôi muốn trả bằng tiền Việt Nam.

buy
  mua
sell
  bán
cheap
  rẻ tiền
expensive
  đắt tiền
really expensive
  rất đắt
market
  chợ
mosquito incense coils
  hương đốt chống muỗi
sanitary pads
  băng vệ sinh

Times & Dates

evening
  chiều
now
  bây giờ
today
  hôm nay
tomorrow
  ngày mai
Monday
  thứ hai
Tuesday
  thứ ba
Wednesday
  thứ tư
Thursday
  thứ năm
Friday
  thứ sáu
Saturday
  thứ bảy
Sunday
  chủ nhật

Numbers

1
  một
2
  hai
3
  ba
4
  bốn

5
năm
6
sáu
7
bảy
8
tám
9
chín
10
mười
11
mười một
19
mười chín
20
hai mươi
21
hai mươi mốt
30
ba mươi
90
* *chín mươi*
100
một trăm
200
hai trăm
900
chín trăm
1000
một nghìn
10,000
mười nghìn
100,000
một trăm nghìn
1 million
một triệu
first
thứ nhất
second
thứ nhì

From three upwards, the cardinal and ordinal numbers are the same.

Health
I'm sick.
Tôi bị bệnh. (south)
Tôi bị ốm. (north)

Please take me to the hospital.
Làm ơn đưa tôi đến bệnh viện.
Please call a doctor.
Làm ơn gọi bác sĩ.
dentist
nha sĩ
doctor
bác sĩ
hospital
bệnh viện
pharmacy
nhà thuốc tây
backache
đau lưng
diarrhoea
ia chảy
dizziness
chóng mặt
fever
cảm, cúm
headache
nhức đầu
malaria
sốt rét
stomachache
đau bụng
toothache
nhức răng
vomiting
ói, mửa

Emergencies
Help!
Cứu tôi với!
Thief!
Cướp, Cắp!
Pickpocket!
Móc túi!
Police.
Công an.
Immigration police station.
Phòng quản lý người nước ngoài.

Books for Language Study
A number of pocket English-Vietnamese (*Anh-Việt*) and Vietnamese-English (*Việt-Anh*) dictionaries (*tu dien*) have been published in Vietnam over the years. Used

copies may be available in the bookshops listed in the text.

Among the best scholarly dictionaries are the 992-page *Tu Dien Viet-Anh (Vietnamese-English Dictionary)* (Hanoi University Press (Truong Dai Hoc Tong Hop Ha Noi Xuat Ban), Hanoi, 1986); and the massive 1960-page English-Vietnamese *Tu Dien Anh-Viet (Nha Xuat Ban Khoa Hoc Xa Hoi*, Hanoi, 1975). It is worth taking a look at Nguyen Dinh Hoa's *Essential English-Vietnamese Dictionary* (Charles E Tuttle Co, Rutland, Vermont, and Tokyo, Japan, 1983) and *Essential Vietnamese-English Dictionary* (Charles E Tuttle Co, Rutland, Vermont, and Tokyo, Japan, 1966) before you go.

There are several fairly useful phrasebooks around, many of which you may be able to pick up at Asia Books in Bangkok or in Vietnam. Lonely Planet's *Vietnamese Phrasebook* (1993) has useful cultural tips and words and phrases for any travel situation, as well as a guide to pronunciation and grammar. *Speak Vietnamese (Hay Noi Tieng Viet*; Foreign Languages Publishing House, Hanoi, 1982) gives phrases in Vietnamese, English, French and Russian and might prove useful in dealing with Soviets and French people as well as the locals.

Say it in Vietnamese (Charles E Tuttle Co, Rutland, Vermont, and Tokyo, Japan, 1966) by Nguyen Dinh Hoa includes such phrases – sure to generate goodwill – as 'Raise your hands!' and 'Obey or I'll fire!' But aside from such signs of the times during which it was published, it has solid information on pronunciation as well as useful word lists. A larger, updated version is *Hoa's Vietnamese Phrase Book* by Nguyen Dinh Hoa (Charles E Tuttle Co, Rutland, Vermont, and Tokyo, Japan).

A two-volume set for serious students of Vietnamese, there's *Introductory Vietnamese* and *An Intermediate Vietnamese Reader* (South-East Asia Program, Cornell University, Ithaca, New York, 1972) by Robert M Quinn. Two other works still available are *Speak Vietnamese* and *Read Vietnamese* by Nguyen Dinh Hoa (Charles E Tuttle Co, Rutland, Vermont, and Tokyo, Japan, 1966). All four books are available in the USA through Schoenhof's Foreign Books (☎ (617) 547-8855), 76A Mount Auburn St, Cambridge, Massachusetts 02138.

Facts for the Visitor

VISAS & EMBASSIES

While more creativity and perseverance are necessary to travel to Vietnam than to non-socialist countries in the region, arranging the necessary paperwork is not all that daunting. And as Vietnamese officialdom gets more used to 'capitalist tourists' exploring the country on their own – and leaving behind their hard currency – getting into Vietnam will probably become easier.

Visas are normally issued on a separate piece of paper so you don't even need to leave your passport with the travel agent or embassy while your application is being processed. Apparently you can request that your tourist visa be stamped right in your passport, but this is *not* a good idea. The reason is because within Vietnam itself you will often be required to leave your visa with the hotel reception desk (they need to register your presence with the police), or with a travel agency (to get a local travel permit), or with bureaucratic ministries of every sort. With so many hands shuttling your visa from one place to another, this valuable piece of paper could get lost. Replacing a lost visa will be a hassle but still *much* easier than replacing your entire passport.

These days, the most convenient place to get Vietnamese visas is Bangkok. Even travel agents in Hong Kong send the paperwork to Bangkok for processing (in part because the Hong Kong visa office is so corrupt). Several types of visas are available: tourist, business, long-term multiple-entry business, journalist, official and family-visit. In Bangkok, single-entry tourist visas cost US$60 at most travel agencies. An 'express visa' takes half the time and is arranged by fax to Hanoi – the drawback is a greater chance of things going awry (paperwork not done properly on the Vietnamese end and the visa being declared 'invalid' on arrival). Many travel agencies offer package deals costing US$365 to US$400 for both visa and round-trip air ticket (Bangkok-Ho Chi Minh City, returning Hanoi-Bangkok). The place to look for competitive prices is Khao San Rd in Bangkok.

In Thailand at least, you *must* go to a travel agency rather than to the Vietnamese Embassy in order to secure a visa. Just why the Vietnamese Embassy in Bangkok doesn't issue the visas directly is a mystery.

In other countries which have Vietnamese embassies (there aren't many), you can get a Vietnamese visa more cheaply. In Mongolia, for example, it only costs US$15, and in this case you get it directly from the embassy. In Bangkok, two passport-style photos are required (either B&W or colour are acceptable); in Taiwan, for some strange reason six photos are needed.

Tourist Visas

Processing a visa application takes four working days in Bangkok (two days for an express visa), five days in Malaysia, six days in Mongolia and 10 to 14 days in Hong Kong or Taiwan.

Visas are normally valid for 30 days from the date you specify, so you must let your travel agent know just when you plan to enter Vietnam. You must also decide on your port of entry (Ho Chi Minh City or Hanoi) because this will be written on the visa and cannot be changed later. Vietnamese visas also specify where you must exit the country, though this can be changed within Vietnam at the Foreign Ministry Office.

Formerly, you could enter Vietnam with an official sponsor's letter and then pick up your visa on arrival. This process is no longer available; if you enter without a visa you'll be put on the next plane out, at your own expense.

If planning on seeing Vietnam after Cambodia, make sure you get your visa before you leave Bangkok, where you'll pay about $40. Leave it until Phnom Penh and the Vietnamese Consulate will demand US$60 and take a week to process the application;

$80, if you want it in three or four days. Under no circumstances should you trust a Phnom Penh travel agency to procure your visa for you. I found this out the hard way when I paid $80 to the Vietnamese Consulate for the quickie visa, only to return at the appointed hour to find that there were 'communication problems' with their office in Saigon and that they couldn't promise me a visa until the end of the next week. On the consulate's advice, I sought out a travel agent near the Monophnom Hotel, off Achar Mean Rd, who could possibly process a faster visa for me. Well, they did, giving me a three-day transit visa for Vietnam and assuring me that it was no problem to extend the visa once I got to their sister office in Saigon.

You can guess the rest. The manager of the sister office shook her head sadly and told me that their Phnom Penh office is staffed by bar girls who should know better than to tell customers that transit visas for Vietnam can be extended; you always have to leave the country to get them renewed. But if I wanted to pay US$100, she had a friend in the government who could 'do something' for me. I declined and went to the immigration police to plead my story, confident that he wouldn't be able to turn away a tearful young woman. He had no problem, I soon found out. The officer looked at me stonily and waved me away to book my plane ticket back to Bangkok, warning me that if I stayed even a day longer, I would be arrested for overstaying my three-day visa. Sigh. The lesson of the story? Make sure your paperwork's spot-on before going to Vietnam. At this time, there's no way around it if you have problems, unless you have the cash to buy your way out.

Lori McDougall

Business Visas

Business visas are a bit more complicated. But there are several advantages in having a business visa: such visas are usually valid for longer periods; can be issued for multiple-entry journeys for a three to six month period; and, finally, it's easier to arrange travel permits within Vietnam if you have a business visa. Once all the necessary documents are in order, actually stamping the visa in your passport is faster than for a tourist visa – you bring it to the embassy in Bangkok in the morning and get it back at about 3 pm.

Before issuing a business visa, the embassy must have a letter, fax, telex or telegram of invitation from some official body in Vietnam which is sponsoring you. Getting this sort of letter is more difficult than the sponsor's letter needed for a quickie tourist visa. To get a sponsor's letter for a business visa, you need the right contacts in Vietnam, and then you can expect a waiting period for the invitation to arrive in Bangkok. Sometimes, official invitations from Vietnamese companies or ministries telexed to the Bangkok Embassy are mislaid. Many busy business people end up spending frustrating days or even weeks stranded in Thailand because of foul-ups with their documents. Complaining to consular officials is of limited efficacy because they see their role as issuing visas, not helping you procure official invitations.

If you need to get in touch with your contacts in Vietnam quickly, it is possible to telephone or fax Vietnam from Bangkok for US$7.80 per three minutes. Sending a telex costs US$2.60 per minute. It is not possible to place person-to-person calls to Vietnam, but phone calls from abroad are treated with sufficient seriousness that chances are messages will be passed on – just make sure they know where you're calling from. In any case, after a few calls you should be able to track down your contact, and nothing beats actually talking to someone to get the ball rolling. Mail service between Thailand and Vietnam is slow and unreliable.

If you can't seem to confirm that things are moving on your visa, it might be worthwhile to consider going in on a tourist visa and working things out from Ho Chi Minh City or Hanoi. However, there may later be a problem changing your visa status without leaving the country and re-entering.

Other Visas

The procedure for getting journalist, official and family-visit visas is similar to that for business visas except that the embassy may also need ministerial authorisation from Hanoi. Journalists are often hosted by either the Ministry of Information or the Foreign Ministry. To a certain degree, these ministries compete with each other for guests because of the tidy profit – in US dollars, of course – they make from charging you for a car, driver, guide, etc.

Family-visit visas take about twice as long to process as tourist visas.

Visas to Laos

Hanoi is a great place to pick up a five-day Lao transit visa. The Laotian Embassy is theoretically open Monday to Friday from 8 to 11 am and from 2 to 4.30 pm. There is also a Laotian Consulate in Ho Chi Minh City. Three photos and plane tickets are required for a five-day transit visa which costs US$10.

It takes at least 24 hours to issue a visa at the embassy but some travellers have obtained the visa in just a few hours through travel agents in Ho Chi Minh City. If you're heading to Thailand after Laos, get your Thai visa in advance because the Thai Embassy in Vientiane makes you wait three days.

Visas to Cambodia

Vietnam has become the transport and paperwork gateway to Cambodia, mostly because the Phnom Penh government, originally set up by the Vietnamese, has legations in less than a dozen countries, almost all of them in Eastern Europe.

The Cambodian Embassy in Hanoi is open from 8 to 11 am and 2 to 4.30 pm daily except Sunday. Visas take seven working days to issue. You will need to supply a photocopy of your passport and four passport-style photos. Many travellers have successfully applied for visas in Hanoi and picked them up at the Cambodian Consulate in Ho Chi Minh City but don't count 100% on this (communication between the two offices can go awry).

The Cambodian Consulate in Ho Chi Minh City is open Monday to Saturday from 8 to 11 am and 2 to 5 pm. The visa costs US$20 and is normally valid for 10 days (be sure to specify on the application when you wish to enter and leave). If you are planning to return to Vietnam, you will need a re-entry visa (US$10).

Vietnamese Embassies

Afghanistan
    Number 27 Peace St, Shar-i-Nua, Kabul (☎ (93) 23671)
Albania
    Rruga Lek Dukagjini, Tirana (☎ 2556)
Algeria
    30 Rue de Chenoua, Hydva, Algiers (☎ 600752)
Australia
    6 Timbarra Crescent, O'Malley, Canberra, ACT 2603 (☎ (062) 866509; telex 62756)
Bulgaria
    Ilia Petrov St 1, Sofia (☎ 639043, 658486)
Cambodia
    Son Ngoc Minh area (opposite 749 Achar Mean Blvd), Phnom Penh (☎ 25481)
China
    32 Guangua Lu, Jianguomen Wai, Beijing (☎ 5321125)
Congo
    BP 988, Brazzaville (☎ 81-2621)
Cuba
    Avenida 5a, Numero 1802, Miramar, Havana (☎ 296262)
Czech
    Holeçkova 6, Prague 5 (☎ (2) 546498, 531723)
Egypt
    47 Noned Heshmet St, Zamalek, Cairo (☎ (02) 3402401)
Ethiopia
    Kebele No 12, House No 161-123, Addis Ababa (☎ 201147)
France
    62 Rue de Boileau, 750,16 Paris (☎ 75016)
Germany
    Konstantinstrasse 37, 5200 Bonn (☎ (0228) 3570201; telex 8861122)
Guinea
    BP 551, Conakry
Hungary
    Benczúr U 18, Budapest VI (☎ 429943)
India
    42F South Extension, New Delhi 110011 (☎ (11) 624586, 623823)
Indonesia
    Jalan Teuku Umar 25, Jakarta (☎ (021) 325347)
Iraq
    Dawoodi Al-Mansour No 71/7/17, Baghdad (☎ 5511388)
Italy
    Piazza Barberini 12, 00187 Rome (☎ (06) 4754098, 4755286; telex 610121)
Japan
    50-11 Moto Yoyogi-Cho, Shibuya-ku, Tokyo 151 (☎ 34663311)
Laos
    1 Thap Luang Rd, Vientiane (☎ 2707, 5578)

A (LG)
B (OT)
C (RM)
D (DR)
E (PS)
F (PS)

A	B
C	D
E	F

A (DR)
B (LG)
C (DR)
D (LG)
E (LG)
F (LG)

Libya
    Sharia Addhu 1/Bon-Ashun (PO Box 587),
    Tripoli (☎ 45753)
Madagascar
    2 Rue Vy Zatindravolo, Antananarivo (☎ 27651)
Malaysia
    4 Pesiaran Stonor, Kuala Lumpur (☎ (03)
    2484036; fax 2483270)
Mexico
    Calle Sierra Ventana 255, 11000 Mexico, DF
    (☎ 5401612, 5401632)
Mongolia
    Enkhe-Taivan Oudomjni 47, Ulaan Baatar
    (☎ 50465, 50547)
Mozambique
    Avenida Julius Nyerere 1555, CP 1150, Maputo
    (☎ 741948)
Myanmar (Burma)
    40 Komin Kochin Rd, Yangon (☎ (01) 50631)
Nicaragua
    Zona Residencial la Planetarium, Calle Saturno
    40, Managua, (☎ 52168)
Pakistan
    60 Embassy Rd, Ramna 6/3, Islamabad
Philippines
    54 Victor Cruz, Malate, Metro Manila (☎ (02)
    500364, 508101)
Poland
    Kawalerii 5, 00-468 Warsaw (☎ 413369,
    415867)
Romania
    Str Gr Alexandrescu 86, Bucharest (☎ 116120,
    113170)
Russia
    Bolshaya Pirogovskaya ul 13, Moscow (☎ (095)
    2450925)
Yugoslavia (Serbia)
    6 Lackoviceva St, 11000, Belgrade (☎ 663527)
Sweden
    Örby Slottsväg 26, 125 36 Älvsjö, Stockholm
    (☎ (8) 861214; telex 10332)
Syria
    Mezzeh Villas West, El Aksan Ben Saifi St,
    Damascus (☎ 667026)
Tanzania
    9 Ocean Rd, PO Box 2194, Dar-es-Salaam
Thailand
    83/1 Wireless Rd, Bangkok (☎ (02) 2517201,
    2515836)
UK
    12-14 Victoria Rd, London W8 5RD (☎ 071-
    9371912; telex 887361; fax 071-9376108)
USA
    Vietnamese Mission to the United Nations, 20
    Waterside Plaza (lobby), New York, NY 10010
    (☎ (212) 6858001, 67 3779) (no visas issued)
Yemen
    Maala Box 5186, Aden

Visa Extensions

If you've got the dollars, they've got the rubber stamp. Visa extensions are granted for 15 days at a time, and you can get extensions up to a maximum stay of three months. The cost is US$20 or US$30, depending on whether the relevant officials in charge of such matters need a new colour TV or a new refrigerator. Either way, visa extensions are not something you can handle directly. Rather, a Vietnamese travel agent or your hotel can make the arrangements. Many hotels have a sign on the front desk indicating that they have a visa extension service. The procedure takes one or two days and one photo is needed. You can apply for your extension even several weeks before it's necessary.

Although you can try, don't count on being able to extend your visa anywhere other than in Ho Chi Minh City and Hanoi. While officials in the provinces would also like to make money selling visa extensions, it is not clear that they have the power to do so – you could wind up buying a rubber stamp which will not be recognised by the immigration authorities when you try to depart the country.

Re-Entry Visas

If you wish to visit Cambodia, Laos or any other country, it is possible to do this and then re-enter Vietnam using your original single-entry Vietnamese visa. However, you must apply for a re-entry visa before departing Vietnam. If you do not have a re-entry visa, then you will have to go through the whole expensive and time-consuming procedure of applying for a new Vietnamese visa. Re-entry visas are easy enough to arrange in Hanoi or Ho Chi Minh City, but you will almost certainly have to ask a travel agent to do the paperwork for you. Travel agents charge about US$10 to US$20 for this service and can complete the procedure in one or two days. Although travellers can theoretically secure the re-entry visa without going through a travel agent, Vietnamese bureaucrats usually thwart such individual efforts.

Foreign Embassies in Vietnam

With the exception of visas for Laos and Cambodia, Hanoi's 37 embassies and Ho Chi Minh City's 13 consulates do very little visa business. For their addresses, see the Hanoi and Ho Chi Minh City chapters.

DOCUMENTS

For people on organised tours, the paperwork is all taken care of. That's part of what they pay for. But foreigners travelling independently must take care of local travel permits themselves. These permits are a nuisance and no one is likely to explain what needs to be done or how to go about it (see below for more details).

Hotels are required to register their guests – foreign and domestic – with the police, which is why they collect tourists' visas and locals' identity papers. Travellers not staying at a hotel might consider registering themselves, especially since it is unlikely that they have escaped police notice.

Formerly, foreigners had to have internal travel permits (giay phep di lai) to go anywhere outside the city in which they arrived. From 1975 to 1988, even citizens of Vietnam needed these permits to travel around their own country (to prevent them from fleeing). Recently, the central government changed the rules, so you no longer need an internal travel permit. (There are still some con artists around, however, who will insist you still need one and will happily sell you a fake 'internal travel permit'.)

Travel Permits

Although internal travel permits have been abolished, uncertainty still prevails in small towns and villages. Unfortunately, the police in many places seem to make up their own rules as they go along, no matter what the Interior Ministry in Hanoi says. In addition, more and more municipalities are chasing foreign dollars by charging for local travel permits. The bottom line is that you may have to enquire locally to see if a permit is needed.

In general, logic rarely prevails – greed does. Many local provincial and city governments are demanding that you secure a permit on arrival to visit the surrounding area, pay an additional fee for this permit, and rent another car from the local government even if you've already arrived in an official government rental car! For example, if you visit Dalat in the Central Highlands, no permit is necessary. However, to visit the nearby Lat Village (12 km away), you need to get a permit from the Dalat police (US$10), but this won't be issued unless you also rent a car from the municipal government (US$15).

Besides the Lat Village, some other places currently requiring permits include the Cham Towers at My Son (near Danang), villages around the DMZ, My Lai (Son My subdistrict near Quang Ngai), Chau Doc (in the Mekong Delta) and Ha Tien (also in the Mekong Delta). Additional information about obtaining these permits is provided in the relevant chapters.

However, don't be absolutely sure that the information in this book is correct because the policies change frequently. This tendency to require extra permits seems to be escalating as more and more local governments decide to get on the 'bilk the foreigners' bandwagon. However, all this is driving away tourists and hurting Vietnam's image, and there is the possibility that the Interior Ministry in Hanoi will eventually get fed up and try to put a stop to all this nonsense. No telling just when/if that might happen, though.

In the meantime, keep your ear to the ground to learn the latest erratic rules and regulations. Remember that being caught in an area without the necessary paperwork means a 'fine'.

Passport

A passport is essential, and if yours is within a few months of expiry, get a new one now – many countries will not issue a visa if your passport has less than six months of validity remaining. Although Vietnam doesn't stamp your passport, other countries do, so be sure it has at least a few blank pages for visas and entry and exit stamps. It could be embarassing to run out of blank pages when you are too far away from an embassy to get a new passport issued or extra pages added.

Losing your passport is very bad news indeed. Getting a new one takes time and money. However, if you will be staying in Vietnam or any foreign country for a long period of time, it helps tremendously to register your passport with your embassy. This will eliminate the need to send telexes back to your home country to confirm that you really exist. It's wise to have a driver's licence, student card, ID card or some such thing with your photo on it – some embassies want this picture ID before issuing a replacement passport even if you've registered. Having an old expired passport is also very useful – as a backup ID and to give to hotels who demand your documents as 'security', or to corrupt police who are trying to shake you down.

If you're not able to register your passport, it certainly helps to at least have a separate record of your passport number, issue date and photocopy of the passport or birth certificate. While your compiling that info, add the serial number of your travellers' cheques, details of health insurance and US$100 or so as emergency cash, and keep all that material separate from your passport and money (better hotels have a safe for valuables – that might be a good place to keep this stuff).

If you are a national of a country without diplomatic relations with Vietnam and lose your passport while in the country the situation is not good but still not hopeless. If the Immigration Police are unable to locate the passport, you will be issued documents allowing you to leave the country. You may be allowed to stay in Vietnam until your visa (the validity of which is on record with the police) expires.

Miscellaneous

If you're actually thinking about working in Vietnam (possible but highly unlikely) or anywhere else along the way, photocopies of university diplomas, transcripts and letters of recommendation could prove helpful. If you're travelling with your spouse, a photo-

copy of your marriage licence might just come in handy should you become involved with the law, hospitals or other bureaucratic authorities. Useful, though not essential, is an International Health Certificate to record your vaccinations.

The International Student Identity Card (ISIC) can get you a 15% discount for services bought through Vietnam Tourism, and you can sometimes use it to obtain cheap air fares in other parts of Asia. However, it helps to back up the ISIC with a regular student card and an official-looking letter from your school's registrar. The extra back-up documents are necessary because there's quite a worldwide trade in fake ISIC cards. Additionally, there are now maximum age limits (usually 26) for some concessions, and the fake-card dealers have been clamped down on. Nevertheless, fake cards are widely available and usable, but some are of quite poor quality.

CUSTOMS

Until very recently, the Vietnamese customs service was run by mid-level bureaucrats who had received their managerial training in China. Their bureaucratic spirit lives on in the form of unpredictable hassles.

You are permitted to bring in duty-free 200 cigarettes, 50 cigars or 250 grams of tobacco; one litre of liquor; and a reasonable quantity of luggage and personal effects. Items which you cannot bring in include opium (competes with local suppliers?), weapons, explosives and 'cultural materials unsuitable to Vietnamese society'. That last category seems to include pornographic videos and the movie *Rambo*, both of which are hot items on the thriving black market.

Tourists can bring an unlimited amount of foreign currency into Vietnam but they are required to declare it on their customs form upon arrival. Theoretically, when you leave the country you should have exchange receipts for all the foreign currency you have spent if you spent more than US$300. In practice, though, the authorities rarely check.

When entering Vietnam, visitors must also

declare all precious metals (especially gold), jewellery, cameras and electronic devices in their possession. Declaring means that when you leave, you will have no hassles taking these items out with you. It also means that you may be asked to show these items so that customs officials know you didn't sell them on the black market.

The import and export of dong and live animals is forbidden. When exiting the country, the one hassle many travellers have is with antiques (or something which looks antique), especially if they don't have a receipt:

Luggage is being x-rayed going into and out of the country. On leaving the country my sister and I declared to customs several pieces of china and ornaments which we had purchased from the tourist/antique shops along Dong Khoi St. They were all modest purchases bought for their souvenir value not collectors' items. Rice bowls had cracks and other pieces showed signs of wear. With the excepton of three items they were all confiscated and it was implied they were 'national treasures'. We asked for an expert to confirm their lowly status but this was not available. Just what they do with these 'national treasures' after confiscating them is an intriguing question – similar items could be bought in any of the forty or so similar shops that we saw including the airport's duty-free shop.

Val Shingleton

If your luggage weighs less than 25 kg, you can go through the 'express' customs lane.

MONEY
Currency

The currency of Vietnam is the dong (abbreviated by a 'd' following the amount), which is sometimes still called the piastre by old-timers. Banknotes in denominations of 200d, 500d, 1000d, 2000d, 5000d and 10,000d are presently in circulation. The red-coloured 10,000d notes are new and still very rare, but should eventually become more common. Now that Ho Chi Minh has been canonised, his picture appears on every banknote. There are no coins currently in use in Vietnam, though the dong used to be subdivided into 10 hao and 100 xu. All

dong-denominated prices in this book are from a time when US$1 was worth 10,850d.

It may seem ironic, but after having fought a bitter war with the Americans, the currency of choice in Vietnam is the US dollar. Gold is also used extensively, especially for major transactions such as the sale of homes or cars. During the Vietnam War, the Americans introduced Western banking practices – personal cheques were commonly used for large purchases, at least in Saigon. When the north took over, cheques and credit cards became instantly worthless. As the Vietnamese dismantled the banking system, telegraphic transfers into Vietnam became practically impossible, though later a company called Cosevina was set up to allow Overseas Vietnamese to send money to their relatives.

That was then and this is now. The necessity to attract tourist dollars has made the government think again about how to run the banking system. Capitalist-style monetary instruments like travellers' cheques, credit cards, telegraphic transfers and even letters of credit are all experiencing a revival. Domestic personal cheques have still not been re-introduced yet, but that should be coming soon.

For travellers, US dollars cash and travellers' cheques are still the best things to have. The black market is interested only in US dollars. Up-market hotels also require payment in US dollars, and ditto for the railway booking offices. But for everywhere else, you can pay in Vietnamese dong.

Large-denomination bills (US$100) are preferred on the black market, but a small supply (say US$20 worth) of ones and fives will prove useful during the chaos of arrival, especially when you need to hire a taxi into the city. US dollars are in such wide circulation now that many hotels and restaurants can accept a US$20 bill (or even US$100) and give you change in dollars. It's best to keep a reasonable supply of US$20 bills. It's also a good idea to check that the dollars you bring to Vietnam do not have anything scribbled on them or look too tattered, lest they be summarily rejected by uptight clerks.

Be sure to bring enough US dollars cash

for your whole visit and to keep it safe, preferably in a money belt. Try not to keep the whole lot in one place (if the money belt goes then everything goes with it). Unless you borrow from a Westerner or get someone to wire money to you (which is only possible in Ho Chi Minh City and Hanoi); losing your cash could put you in a really bad situation. Of course, you could always try begging your embassy for help (if your country has one in Vietnam), but our experience has been that most embassy staff have little sympathy and will leave you twisting in the wind.

Exchange Rates

The dong has certainly experienced its ups and downs. In 1991, it lost close to half its value. In 1992, the dong gained 35% against the US dollar, making it one of the best currency investments of the year. The surge in the dong's value was due to the turnaround in Vietnam's chronic trade deficit – in 1992, the country experienced what is believed to be its first trade surplus since reunification.

Country	Unit		Dong
Australia	A$1	=	7550d
Canada	C$1	=	8770d
China	Y1	=	1960d
France	FFr1	=	2080d
Germany	DM1	=	7060d
Hong Kong	HK$1	=	1400d
Indonesia	1 Rp	=	5d
Japan	Y1	=	88d
Malaysia	M$1	=	4330d
New Zealand	NZ$1	=	5710d
Singapore	S$1	=	6690d
Switzerland	SFr1	=	7910d
Taiwan	NT$1	=	428d
Thailand	B1	=	428d
UK	£1	=	16,930d
USA	US$1	=	10,850d

Changing Money

Although changing money is feasible in some backwaters, you'll find it considerably easier in major population centres like Hanoi, Ho Chi Minh City or Danang. Well-touristed places like Nha Trang and Hué also have functioning foreign exchange banks, but the situation is decidedly less clear in secluded hamlets like Kontum and Dien Bien Phu.

Vietcombank is another name for the state-owned Bank for Foreign Trade of Vietnam (Ngan Hang Ngoai Thuong Viet Nam). Some other banks can change foreign currency (cash only), but Vietcombank is by far the best organised for this activity. Banking hours are normally from 8 am to 3 pm on weekdays, 8 am to noon on Saturdays and closed on Sundays and holidays. Many banks also close for 1½ hours during lunch.

Foreign currency can be exchanged for dong in one of four ways: at the bank, through authorised exchange bureaus, at hotel reception desks and on the black market.

The best legal rate is offered by banks, many of which accept US dollars as well as other hard major currencies and dollar-denominated travellers' cheques. The catch is that the number of banks which can change money are few and far between. Hotel reception counters are convenient; some will charge you a 1% commission but some will actually give you a better rate than the bank (in this latter case, this means you've found the black market).

It is always best to get a receipt for exchange transactions – this can be useful to satisfy any customs officials when you depart the country. At present, you *cannot* reconvert dong back to dollars on departure even with an official receipt and you cannot legally take the dong out with you. So if you have excessive Vietnamese money left over, you'll either have to spend it, give it away or use it for toilet paper. Alternatively, you can try to change it on the black market or sell it to another traveller who will be spending additional time in Vietnam.

For details on exchange options around the country, look under the Information sections in each chapter.

The relatively low values of Vietnamese banknotes mean that almost any currency exchange will leave you with hundreds of banknotes to count. Notes are usually presented in brick-sized piles bound with rubber bands, but even so, counting them is a slow but necessary process. Changing US$100 will net you over one million dong – a large brick of 5000d notes which will not fit in a money belt. You'll have to give some thought about just where you are going to keep these bricks as you cart them around the country.

Black Market There is a thriving black market in Vietnam for gold and US dollars cash. Large notes (US$50 and US$100) are preferred and get a slightly higher rate. Much of the black market is to be found in jewellery shops, which also exchange gold for cash, but other shops sometimes engage in this business. The black market rate is only about 3% better than the official legal rate.

If you choose to squeeze that last few percent out of your dollars, be aware that black market transactions are illegal (though conducted very openly). The manifold ripoff techniques (bait-and-switch, etc) perfected years ago to separate American soldiers from their pay are still being used, especially in Ho Chi Minh City. Many travellers who have changed money on the street (rather than in a shop) have fared poorly. Offers that are way out of line with the going rate are a sure sign of trouble.

Travellers' Cheques Travellers' cheques denominated in US dollars can only be exchanged in major cities which have a branch of Vietcombank. There is a 1½ to 2% commission for exchange transactions involving travellers' cheques. The commission does not depend on the number of cheques, so Vietnam is a good place to get rid of low-denomination travellers' cheques. When you cash the cheque you can be paid in either US dollars, Vietnamese dong, or both.

At present, travellers' cheques are not very practical in Vietnam. If they get lost or stolen, you won't be able to have them replaced until you leave the country. Travellers' cheques are not yet accepted by hotels and restaurants. Vietnam Airlines has started accepting travellers' cheques for buying air tickets, but only after charging a 5% commission. Furthermore, it is not necessarily true that every branch office of Vietnam Airlines will do so.

Among the travellers' cheques acceptable at Vietcombank are those issued by American Express, Bank of America, Citicorp, First National City Bank, Thomas Cook and Visa. Don't even think of bringing travellers' cheques denominated in anything other than US dollars.

Credit Cards Until recently, credit cards were useless in Vietnam; upon arriving in the country, they reverted back to their natural state of being mere pieces of worthless plastic. This is changing: Visa, MasterCard and JCB cards are now acceptable in Ho Chi Minh City and Hanoi, but nowhere else.

The US Treasury Department forbids individuals under its jurisdiction to use credit cards in Vietnam. What this means is that if your credit card is issued by a US bank, it cannot be used in Vietnam, even if you are not a US citizen. And if you are a US citizen but have a credit card issued on a non-American bank, you are also not supposed to use it though it's hard to see how the US government would catch you in that case. The Vietnamese know the rules and will read the fine print on the credit card carefully – if it's American-issued, the card will not be accepted.

Getting a cash advance from Visa, MasterCard and JCB is possible at Vietcombank in Ho Chi Minh City and Hanoi. At no other place (yet) in Vietnam can this magic be performed.

Telegraphic Transfers

It took the Vietnamese government a long time to realise that all those Vietnamese refugees living in the West are a potential gold mine because they like to send money home to their relatives still in Vietnam. Even once the government recognised the potential, before 1990 sending money to Vietnam from abroad was a painful process that took three weeks or longer and involved massive amounts of red tape. When the money finally arrived, the recipient was only allowed to receive dong which quickly lost its value due to the 700% or so annual inflation rate. This has all changed.

Money can be cabled into Vietnam quickly and cheaply and the recipient can be paid in US dollars. However, sending money by wire is fast only if the overseas office is a 'correspondent bank' with Vietcombank. The list of correspondent banks is not extensive, but is growing. Right now, only the branches of Vietcombank in Ho Chi Minh City and Hanoi are equipped to handle wire transfers.

Correspondent banks which can cable money directly to Vietcombank are as follows:

Australia
   Commonwealth Trading Bank of Australia, GPO Box 2719, Martin Place & Pitt St, Sydney 2001, NSW
   ANZ Bank, 55 Collins St, Melbourne, 3000, Victoria (In February 1993, the ANZ became the first foreign bank to open a full office in Hanoi, on the west side of Hoan Kiem Lake, near the intersection of Hang Trong and Le Thai To Sts.)
Belgium
   Banque Bruxelles Lambert SA, 24 Avenue Marnix, B-1050, Brussels
Canada
   Royal Bank of Canada, PO Box 6001, Montreal, Quebec H3C3A9
   Bank of Montreal, PO Box 6002, Montreal, Quebec H3C3B1
France
   Crédit Lyonnais SA, 19 Blvd des Italiens, 75002, Paris
   Banque Nationale de Paris, 16 Blvd des Italiens, 75009, Paris
   Banque Commerciale pour l'Europe du Nord (Eurobank), 79-81 Blvd Haussmann 75382, Paris
   Banque Française du Commerce Extérieur, 21 Blvd Haussmann 75009, Paris
   Banque Worms SA, 45 Blvd Haussman 75427, Paris
Germany
   Deutsche Bank AG, Junghofstrasse 5-11, 6000, Frankfurt
Hong Kong
   Hong Kong & Shanghai Banking Corporation, 1 Queen's Rd, Central

   NMB Postbank Groep NV Hong Kong, 25th floor, Connaught Centre
Japan
   Mitsuitaiyokobe Bank, 3-1 Kudan Minami 1-chome Chiyoda-ku, Tokyo
   Mitsubishi Bank, 7-3 Marunouchi 2-chome Chiyoda-ku, Tokyo 100
   Sanwa Bank, 10 Fushimimachi, 4-chome Higashiku, Osaka 541
   Sanwa Bank, 1-1 Otemachi 1-chome Chiyoda-ku, Tokyo 100
   Sanwa Bank, 2-chome, Nishiki, Naka-ku, Nagoya 460
Singapore
   Dresdener Bank AG, 20 Collyer Quay, 22-00 Tung Centre
   Standard Chartered Bank, 6 Battery Rd
   Barclays Bank, PO Box 887, Maxwell Rd
   Banque Nationale de Paris, 01-01 Tung Centre, 20 Collyer Quay
   Banque Française du Commerce Extérieur, 50 Raffles Place, 35-01 Shell Tower
   Banque Indosuez, Shenton House 3, Shenton Way
Switzerland
   Swiss Bank Corporation, 8022 Zurich Paradeplatz
Thailand
   The Thai Military Bank Ltd, 34 Phayathai Rd, Bangkok 10400
UK
   Standard Chartered Bank (International Division), 38 Bisho Pogate, London EC2N 40E/22
   Standard Chartered Bank, Billiter St, London EC3A 2BE
   Barclays Bank, 54 Lombard St, London
   Midland Bank, London
USA
   contact Bankers Trust Company, New York, for special instructions

Bank Accounts

Foreigners who spend much time in Vietnam working, doing business or just hanging around, can open bank accounts at Vietcombank. The accounts can be denominated in Vietnamese dong or US dollars. Both demand-deposit and time-deposit accounts are available and interest is paid.

Vietcombank can arrange letters of credit for those doing import and export business in Vietnam. It is even possible to borrow money from Vietcombank.

Costs

A survey taken in the early 1970s found that

Ho Chi Minh City was the most expensive city in the world for travellers. Back then, it cost 63% more to visit Ho Chi Minh City than it did New York! This reflects the fact that 'capitalist tourists' were simply being ripped off by the Vietnamese government.

Things have changed. The government has finally figured out that outrageous prices means no tourist business at all. Today, Vietnam is one of the best travel bargains in the world, with decent hotels, excellent food and serviceable transport all available at very reasonable rates.

Vietnam has experienced astronomical levels of inflation in recent years, with equally severe devaluation of the dong (the old 20d notes are literally not worth the paper they are printed on). However, prices in US dollars have not appreciated greatly, and in many cases have even decreased because the government's monopoly has been eroded by new competition from the budding private sector. For this reason, we quote prices in this book in US dollars. We would rather quote prices in dong, but if we did that you might have to multiply prices by three or four times!

Your best bet is to pay for things in dong whenever possible. Dollar-denominated tariffs (such as at tourist-class hotels) are set for wealthy foreigners (and if you can afford to come to Vietnam, you are rich by Vietnamese standards). But you can pay for most things in dong, even hotels. Only at the most expensive hotels are US dollars demanded.

The cost of travelling in Vietnam depends on your tastes and susceptibility to luxuries. Ascetics can get by on US$7 a day, and for US$10 to US$15 a backpacker can live fairly well. Transport is likely to be the biggest expense if you rent a car, which many travellers wind up doing. If you choose to travel by bus or train, you can save a considerable sum but will also suffer some discomfort and lengthy delays – Vietnam's public transport is in very flimsy condition.

Foreigners are sometimes overcharged in restaurants – especially when unaccompanied by a Vietnamese – on the assumption that they cannot read either the menu or the bill. Such incidents are especially frequent in heavily touristed areas, such as downtown Saigon.

Tipping

Tipping according to a percentage of the bill is not expected in Vietnam but it is enormously appreciated. For someone making US$30 per month, 10% of the cost of your meal can equal half a day's wages. Government-run hotels and restaurants that specifically cater to tourists usually have an automatic 10% service charge. It's also not a bad idea to tip the chambermaids who clean your room if you stay a couple of days in the same hotel – US$0.50 to US$1 should be enough.

If you spend any length of time in Vietnam, someone will almost certainly ask you for a tip. It might be the security guard at your hotel, a museum guide or a car park attendant. Some foreigners get all upset at such requests, thinking that these people get a salary anyway and 'what right do they have to demand a tip'? But then ask yourself what you would do if you earned US$1 per day in a country where a soft drink costs US$0.25.

Men you deal with will also greatly appreciate small gifts such as a pack of cigarettes (women almost never smoke), but make sure it's a foreign brand of cigarettes. People will be insulted if you give Vietnamese cigarettes. The 555 brand (said to be Ho Chi Minh's favourite) is popular, as are most US brands (especially in the south). If you run out in Vietnam, don't worry – every street corner seems to have a little stand selling foreign cigarettes, sometimes for less than you paid duty-free!

It is considered proper to make a small donation at the end of a visit to a pagoda, especially if the monk has shown you around; most pagodas have contribution boxes for this purpose.

Bargaining

Always bargain in dong – then it is clear to everyone involved in the transaction what you are paying relative to what everything else in the country costs.

Remember, in the Orient, 'face' is important. Bargaining should be good-natured – smile, don't scream and argue. Many Westerners seem to take bargaining too seriously, and get all offended if they don't get the goods for less than half the original asking price. In some cases you will be able to get a 50% discount, at other times only 10%, but by no means should you get angry during the bargaining process. And once the money is accepted, the deal is done – if you harbour hard feelings because you later find out that someone else got it cheaper, the only one you are hurting is yourself.

Consumer Taxes
On all goods you pay, the marked or stated price includes any relevant taxes. Only in some hotels and restaurants is there an additional 10% tax or service charge, and this should be made clear to you from the beginning (ask if not sure).

The police love to fine foreigners for every minor real or imagined offence – this might be thought of as a tax of sorts.

WHEN TO GO
There are no especially good or bad seasons for visiting Vietnam. When one region is wet, cold or steaming hot, there is always somewhere else that is sunny and pleasantly warm.

Visitors should take into account that around Tet, the colourful Vietnamese New Year celebration which falls in late January or early February, flights into, out of and around the country are likely to be booked solid, and accommodation can be almost impossible to find. The New Year festival is more than just a one-day event – it goes on for at least a week. For at least a week before and two weeks after Tet you are likely to encounter some difficulties in booking hotels and flights; this applies also to the whole of eastern Asia.

WHAT TO BRING
'Junk' is the stuff you throw away. 'Stuff' is the junk you keep.

Bring as little as possible. Many travellers try to bring everything and the kitchen sink. Keep in mind that you can and will buy things in Vietnam, so don't burden yourself with a lot of unnecessary junk.

Nevertheless, there are things you will want to bring from home. But the first thing to consider is what kind of bag you will use to carry all your goods.

Backpacks are the easiest type of bag to carry and a frameless or internal-frame pack is the easiest to manage on buses and trains. Packs that close with a zipper can usually be secured with a padlock. Of course, any pack can be slit open with a razor blade, but a padlock will usually prevent pilfering by hotel staff and baggage handlers at airports.

A daypack can be handy. Leave your main luggage at the hotel or left-luggage room in the train stations. A beltpack is OK for maps, extra film and other miscellanea, but don't use it for valuables such as your travellers' cheques and passport, as it's an easy target for pickpockets.

If you don't want to use a backpack, a shoulder bag is much easier to carry than a suitcase. Some cleverly designed shoulder bags can also double as backpacks by rearranging a few straps. Forget suitcases.

Inside? Lightweight and compact are two words that should be etched in your mind when you're deciding what to bring. Saw the handle off your toothbrush if you have to – anything to keep the weight down! You only need two sets of clothes – one to wear and one to wash. Dark coloured clothing is preferred because it doesn't show the dirt – white clothes will force you to do laundry daily. You will, no doubt, be buying clothes along the way – you can find some real bargains in Vietnam and neighbouring countries. However, don't believe sizes – 'large' in Asia is often equivalent to 'medium' in the West. Asian clothing manufacturers would be wise to visit a Western tourist hotel to see what 'large' really means.

Nylon running or sports shoes are best – comfortable, washable and lightweight. Sandals are appropriate footwear in the tropical heat – even Ho Chi Minh wore them during his public appearances. Rubber thongs are somewhat less appropriate for formal occasions, but are nevertheless commonly worn in the south. In the north, many people will laugh at foreigners wearing rubber thongs (even if the laughers are wearing thongs themselves).

A Swiss army knife (even if not made in Switzerland) comes in handy, but you don't need one with 27 separate functions. Basically, you need one small sharp blade, a can opener and bottle opener – a built-in magnifying glass or backscratcher isn't necessary.

You can easily buy toilet paper in Vietnam, but the local product feels like sandpaper and disintegrates when wet.

The secret of successful packing is plastic bags or nylon 'stuff bags' – they keep things not only separate and clean but also dry.

The following is a checklist of things you might consider packing. You can delete whatever you like from this list (though unlike on a computer, there will be no warning like 'Are you sure?'). If you do forget to bring some 'essential' item, most likely it can be bought in Vietnam, at least in Ho Chi Minh City.

Passport, visa, documents (vaccination certificate, diplomas, marriage licence photocopy, student ID card), money, money belt, air ticket, address book, name cards, visa photos (about 20), Swiss army knife, camera & accessories, extra camera battery, colour slide film, video camera & blank tapes, radio, Walkman & rechargeable batteries, battery recharger (220 volt), reading material, padlock, cable lock (to secure luggage on trains), sunglasses, contact lens solution, alarm clock, leakproof water bottle, torch (flashlight) with batteries & bulbs, comb, compass, daypack, long pants, short pants, long shirt, T-shirt, nylon jacket, sweater (only in winter), raincover for backpack, umbrella or rain poncho, razor, razor blades, shaving cream, sewing kit, spoon, sunhat, sunscreen (UV lotion), toilet paper, tampons, toothbrush, toothpaste, dental floss, deodorant, shampoo, laundry detergent, underwear, socks, thongs, nail clipper, tweezers, mosquito repellent, moist towellets, vitamins, laxative, Lomotil, condoms, contraceptives, special medications you use and medical kit (see the Health section).

If you'll be doing any cycling, bring all necessary safety equipment (helmet, reflectors, mirrors, etc) as well as an inner tube repair kit.

A final thought: airlines do lose bags from time to time – you've got much better chance of it not being yours if it is tagged with your name and address *inside* the bag as well as outside. Other tags can always fall off or be removed.

TOURIST OFFICES
Local Tourist Offices
Vietnam's tourist offices are not like those found in capitalist countries. If you were to visit a government-run tourist office in Australia, Western Europe, Japan or decidedly free-market Hong Kong, you'd get lots of free, colourful, glossy brochures, maps and helpful advice on transport, places to stay, where to book tours and so on. Such tourist offices make no profit – indeed, they are big money losers, though they may be supported by a tax on travel agencies or hotels which benefit from the tourist office's services.

Vietnam's tourist offices operate on a different philosophy. They are government-owned enterprises whose primary interest is earning a profit. In fact, they are amongst the most profitable hard-currency cash cows the Vietnamese government has. Don't come here looking for freebies; even the colourful brochures and maps – when they have them – are for sale.

Vietnam Tourism (Tong Cong Ty Du Lich Viet Nam) and Ho Chi Minh City's Saigon Tourist (Cong Ty Du Lich Thanh Pho Ho Chi Minh) are the best examples of this genre. These large, state-run organisations are responsible for all aspects of a tourist's stay in Vietnam – arranging everything from visa extensions, accommodation, transport, guides and various kinds of tours, including to Cambodia.

Vietnam Tourism and Saigon Tourist can handle many of the bureaucratic headaches that come with travel in Vietnam, but they have neither the inclination nor indeed the staff to keep tabs on you (though the police often seem to have both). The local low-down on both bodies and their functioning is listed in the Ho Chi Minh City and Hanoi chapters.

Every province has some sort of provincial tourism authority with which Vietnam Tourism coordinates its activities. As a result, if you book a tour to Danang with Vietnam Tourism, you'll have a Vietnam Tourism guide as well as a Quang Nam-Danang Province Tourism guide (in addition to a driver) – quite an entourage! Because every organisation in Vietnam – from the Foreign Ministry on down to the local taxi drivers – desperately wants US dollars, it is entirely possible to bypass Vietnam Tourism by working either directly with provincial tourism authorities or the budding free market travel agencies. Addresses of these organisations are listed under Information in the capital city of each province.

Foreign Representatives

There are precious few foreign representatives for Vietnam's government-run tourist organisations.

Saigon Tourist has the following two representatives abroad:

Germany
    Fremdenverkehrsamt Der Sr Vietnam, Hamburger Strasse 132, 200 Hamburg 76 (Postfach 761163; ☎ (040) 295345; telex 213968 HT-D; fax (49-40) 296705)
Japan
    7th floor, Crystal Building 1-2, Kanda Awajicho, Chiyoda-ku, Tokyo 101 (☎ (03) 32589363; telex 2222611 IDITYOJ; fax (81-3) 32535757)

Vietnam Tourism also has two overseas representatives:

France
    Vietnamese Tourism-France, 54 rue Sainte Anne/4 rue Cherubini 75002, Paris (☎ (01) 42868637; telex DULIVNT 213 173 VNTF; fax (33-1) 42604332)
Thailand
    Air People Tour & Travel Co, 2nd floor, Regent House Building, 183 Rajdamri Rd, Bangkok

10500 (☎ 2543921; telex 82419 APT TH; fax (66-2) 2553750)

USEFUL ORGANISATIONS
Chamber of Commerce

Vietcochamber, the Chamber of Commerce & Industry, is supposed to initiate and facilitate contacts between foreign business people and Vietnamese companies. They may also be able to help with receiving and extending business visas. Vietcochamber publishes *Vietnam Foreign Trade* magazine and the *Trade Directory*, a listing of government companies and how to contact them.

They have offices in Ho Chi Minh City, Hanoi and Danang (for addresses see the respective chapters).

Nongovernmental Organisations

Among the nongovernmental humanitarian aid organisations working in Vietnam are: American Friends Service Committee, Catholic Charities, Committee Twee (Netherlands), Church World Services, Enfance Espoir, the International Mission of Hope (Denver, USA), Kinderhilf EV (West Germany), the Mennonites, Need International, Terre des Hommes, World Rehabilitation Fund and World Vision. Other foreign organisations active in Vietnam include the US-Indochina Reconciliation Project, based in Philadelphia, and the Veterans' Vietnam Restoration Project of Garberville, California.

Orderly Departure Programme

The Ho Chi Minh City offices of the Orderly Departure Programme (ODP) are at 184 BIS Nguyen Thi Minh Khai St (Pasteur St), across Le Duan Blvd from Notre Dame Cathedral. This is a UN programme through which Vietnamese seeking to emigrate can do so without floating around the South China Sea in small boats.

Processing of emigration requests made via the ODP is a two-stage process. First, prospective emigrants submit request papers to the Vietnamese government. Periodically, the Vietnamese government turns over lists of people whose applications have been approved to the ODP office in Bangkok. ODP then reviews the files and invites the prospective departees to interviews that are held in Vietnam.

Tourists are often asked to help expedite the processing of ODP cases, many of which have been pending since the early 1980s. Vietnamese law prohibits tourists from taking ODP documents out of the country. Overseas Vietnamese are sometimes thoroughly searched as they leave the country to make sure that they are not carrying such documents.

BUSINESS HOURS & HOLIDAYS

Vietnamese rise early (and consider sleeping in to be a sure indication of illness), in part because Vietnam's location within its time zone causes the sun to rise early and set early Offices, museums and many shops open between 7 and 8 am (depending on the season – things open a bit earlier in the summer) and close between 4 and 5 pm. They shut down for a one or two-hour lunch break sometime between 11 or 11.30 am and 1 or 2 pm. Most government offices are open on Saturday until noon. Sunday is a holiday. Most museums are closed on Mondays. Temples are usually open all day every day,

but it is considered rude to show up at mealtimes. Many small privately owned shops, restaurants and street stalls stay open seven days a week, often until late at night – they need the money.

Lunar Calendar

The Vietnamese lunar calendar closely resembles the Chinese one. Year 1 of the Vietnamese lunar calendar corresponds to 2637 BC, and each lunar month has 29 or 30 days, resulting in years with 355 days. Approximately every third year is a leap year; an extra month is added between the third and fourth months to keep the lunar year in sync with the solar year. If this weren't done, you'd end up having the seasons gradually rotate around the lunar year, playing havoc with all elements of life linked to the agricultural seasons. To find out the Gregorian (solar) date corresponding to a lunar date, check any Vietnamese or Chinese calendar.

Instead of dividing time into centuries, the Vietnamese calendar uses units of 60 years called *hoi*. Each hoi consists of six 10-year cycles *(can)* and five 12-year cycles *(ky)*. The name of each year in the cycle consists of the *can* name followed by the *ky* name, a

---

Vietnamese Zodiac

If you want to know your sign in the Vietnamese zodiac, look up your year of birth in the following chart (future years included so you can know what's coming). However, it's a little more complicated than this because Vietnamese astrology goes by the lunar calendar. The Vietnamese Lunar New Year usually falls in late January or early February, so the first month will be included in the year before.

Rat	1924	1936	1948	1960	1972	1984	1996
Ox/Cow	1925	1937	1949	1961	1973	1985	1997
Tiger	1926	1938	1950	1962	1974	1986	1998
Rabbit	1927	1939	1951	1963	1975	1987	1999
Dragon	1928	1940	1952	1964	1976	1988	2000
Snake	1929	1941	1953	1965	1977	1989	2001
Horse	1930	1942	1954	1966	1978	1990	2002
Goat	1931	1943	1955	1967	1979	1991	2003
Monkey	1932	1944	1956	1968	1980	1992	2004
Rooster	1933	1945	1957	1969	1981	1993	2005
Dog	1934	1946	1958	1970	1982	1994	2006
Pig	1935	1947	1959	1971	1983	1995	2007

system which never produces the same combination twice.

The 10 heavenly stems of the *can* cycle are as follows:

Giap	water in nature
At	water in the home
Binh	lighted fire
Dinh	latent fire
Mau	wood
Ky	wood prepared to burn
Canh	metal
Tan	wrought metal
Nham	virgin land
Quy	cultivated land

The 12 zodiacal stems of the *ky* are as follows:

Ty	rat
Suu	cow
Dan	tiger
Mau	rabbit
Thin	dragon
Ty	snake
Ngo	horse
Mui	goat
Than	monkey
Dau	rooster
Tuat	dog
Hoi	pig

Public Holidays

Politics affects everything, including public holidays. As an indication of Vietnam's new openness, Christmas, New Year, Tet (the lunar new year) and Buddha's birthday have been added as holidays after a 15-year lapse. The following are Vietnam's public holidays:

1 January
New Year's Day (Tet Duong Lich)
1st to 7th days of the 1st moon (late January to mid-February)
Tet (Tet Nguyen Dan), the Vietnamese lunar new year
3 February
Anniversary of the Founding of the Vietnamese Communist Party (Thanh Lap Dang CSVN) The Vietnamese Communist Party was founded on this date in 1930.

30 April
Liberation Day (Saigon Giai Phong) The date on which Saigon surrendered is commemorated nationwide as Liberation Day. Many cities and provinces also commemorate the anniversary of the date in March or April of 1975 on which they were 'liberated' by the North Vietnamese Army.
1 May
International Workers' Day (Quoc Te Lao Dong) Also known as *May Day*, this falls back to back with Liberation Day giving everyone a two-day holiday.
19 May
Ho Chi Minh's Birthday (Sinh Nhat Bac Ho) Ho Chi Minh is said to have been born on this date in 1890 near Vinh, Nghe An Province.
8th day of the 4th moon (usually June)
Buddha's Birthday (Dan Sinh)
2 September
National Day (Quoc Khanh) This commemorates the proclamation in Hanoi of the Declaration of Independence of the Democratic Republic of Vietnam by Ho Chi Minh on 2 September 1945.
25 December
Christmas (Giang Sinh)

Until 1990, 3 September (the anniversary of Ho Chi Minh's death) was a public holiday. The holiday was eliminated when officials admitted that Ho actually died on 2 September 1969. The reason for reporting the date of his death as 3 September was so that it wouldn't coincide with National Day.

CULTURAL EVENTS

Special prayers are held at Vietnamese and Chinese pagodas on days when the moon is either full or just the thinnest sliver. Many Buddhists eat only vegetarian food on these days which, according to the Chinese lunar calendar, fall on the 14th and 15th days of the month and on the last (29th or 30th) day of the month just ending and the 1st day of the new month.

The following major religious festivals are listed by lunar date:

1st to 7th days of the 1st moon
Tet (Tet Nguyen Dan), the Vietnamese New Year, is the most important festival of the year. Marking the new lunar year as well as the advent of spring, the public holiday is officially three days, but many people take off an entire week.

This holiday usually falls in late January or early February.

Tet is a time for family reunions, the payment of debts, the avoidance of arguments, special foods, new clothes, flowers and new beginnings. Great importance is attached to starting the year properly because it is believed that the first day and first week of the new year will determine one's fortunes for the rest of the year. Homes are decorated with sprigs of plum tree blossoms (cay mai).

The first pre-Tet ceremony, Le Tao Quan, is designed to send the Spirit of the Hearth (Tao Quan) off to report to the Emperor of Jade (Ngoc Hoang) in a positive frame of mind. A New Year's Tree (Cay Neu) is constructed to ward off evil spirits. Later, a sacrifice (Tat Nien) is offered to deceased family members. Finally, at midnight, the old year is ushered out and the new welcomed in with the ritual of Giao Thua, which is celebrated both in homes and in pagodas. Firecrackers, gongs and drums commemorate the new year and welcome back the Spirit of the Hearth. The first visitor of New Year's Day is considered very important and great care is taken to ensure that they be happy, wealthy and of high status.

The Tet celebration continues for seven days, with special events and commemorations for each day. A seasonal favourite is banh chung, which is sticky rice, yellow beans, pig fat and spices wrapped in leaves and boiled for half a day.

Visitors to Vietnam around Tet should take into account that flights into, out of and around the country are likely to be booked solid and accommodation impossible to find. Ditto for all of north-east Asia (China, Hong Kong, Macau, Taiwan, Korea and Japan).

5th day of the 3rd moon
  Holiday of the Dead (Thanh Minh) People pay solemn visits to graves of deceased relatives – specially tidied up a few days before – and make offerings of food, flowers, joss sticks and votive papers.

8th day of the 4th moon
  Buddha's Birth, Enlightenment & Death This day is celebrated at pagodas and temples which, like many private homes, are festooned with lanterns. Processions are held in the evening. This has recently be redesignated as a public holiday.

5th day of the 5th moon
  Summer Solstice Day (Doan Ngu) Offerings are made to spirits, ghosts and the God of Death to ward off epidemics. Human effigies are burned to satisfy the requirements of the God of Death for souls to staff his army.

15th day of the 7th moon
  Wandering Souls Day (Trung Nguyen) This is the second-largest festival of the year. Offerings of food and gifts are made in homes and pagodas for the wandering souls of the forgotten dead.

15th day of the 8th moon
  Mid-Autumn Festival (Trung Thu) This festival is celebrated with moon cakes of sticky rice filled with such things as lotus seeds, watermelon seeds, peanuts, the yolks of duck eggs, raisins and sugar. Colourful lanterns in the form of boats, unicorns, dragons, lobsters, carp, hares, toads, etc are carried by children in an evening procession accompanied by drums and cymbals.

28th day of the 9th moon
  Confucius' Birthday

POST & TELECOMMUNICATIONS

International postal service from Vietnam is not unreasonably priced when compared to most countries. However, international telecommunications charges are amongst the highest in the world – unless you have some matter of earthshaking importance, it's better to wait until you reach Hong Kong, Bangkok or Singapore to call the loved ones at home.

Postal Rates

To send a postcard to the USA costs US$0.50; to Australia, it's US$0.40; to east Asia (Hong Kong, Taiwan, etc), the rate is US$0.40.

Stamp values have had a difficult time keeping pace with inflation: until a few years ago, 50d stamps were the highest denomination available. Since there is no space on a 10-gram letter for many dozens of stamps (and all those stamps might weigh several tens of grams, necessitating additional postage, which would make the letter yet heavier, requiring more stamps, and so on), the post office began using postal meters which were issued only to major post offices. Fortunately, inflation is slowing down and larger denomination stamps now make it possible to send postcards and letters with real stamps rather than a metered number.

If international postal rates in Vietnam seem expensive to you, just think about how the Vietnamese feel. The tariffs are so out of line with most salaries that locals *literally* cannot afford to send letters to their friends and relatives abroad. If you would like to correspond with Vietnamese whom you meet during your visit, try leaving them enough stamps to cover postage for several letters, explaining that the stamps were extras you didn't use and would be of no value to you at home.

Sending Mail

Items mailed from anywhere other than large towns and cities are likely to take over a month to arrive at their destinations. In addition, postal authorities in the provinces may enforce censorship rules more strictly. The fastest way to get correspondence to friends outside the country is to ask another foreigner to mail it for you in Bangkok. The second-fastest way is to use the Saigon GPO, which takes about two weeks to most Western countries. The 'express' service available in Ho Chi Minh City is quicker.

Vietnamese stamps do not have gum on them; use the paste provided in little pots at post offices. And make sure that the clerk cancels them *while you watch* so that someone for whom the stamps are worth a day's salary does not soak them off and throw your letters away.

Foreigners sending parcels out of Vietnam have reported having to deal with time-consuming inspections of the contents.

Express Mail Service (EMS) is available to most developed countries and a few less developed ones like Mozambique and Ethiopia. It's perhaps 30% faster to use EMS than

to use regular airmail, but the big advantage is that the letter or small parcel will be registered. There is also domestic EMS between Ho Chi Minh City and Hanoi promising next-day delivery. The domestic EMS rates are very reasonable: US$0.35 for a letter weighing under 20 grams.

Private Carriers DHL Worldwide Express offers express document delivery from the Saigon GPO (☎ 96203, 90446; telex 8270 or 8271) and the Hanoi GPO (☎ 57124; telex 4324 HN).

TNT has also entered the Vietnamese market under the name 'TNT Vietrans', offering both domestic and international service. The telephone numbers for collection are: Hanoi (☎ 257615, 265750); Ho Chi Minh City (☎ 225520); Haiphong (☎ 47180, 47165); Danang (☎ 21685, 22582); Qui Nhon (☎ 2193, 2600); and Nha Trang (☎ 21043).

The rates charged by these private carriers for document and parcel delivery are listed below (prices in US dollars).

Receiving Mail

Every city, town, village and rural subdistrict in Vietnam has some sort of post office, but international mail is accepted only at the larger urban post offices and at some tourist

Document Service (International)					
Zone 1	Zone 2	Zone 3	Zone 4	Zone 5	Zone 6
Thailand	Hong Kong	Australia	UK	USA	Africa

	Zone 1	Zone 2	Zone 3	Zone 4	Zone 5	Zone 6
1st 500 g	30	40	45	50	55	60
Add 500 g	5	5	10	15	15	15

Small Parcel Service (International)						
1st 500 g	40	50	55	60	65	70
Add 500 g	5	5	10	15	15	15

Domestic Service		
	Major Cities	Other Cities
1st 500 g	20	30
Add 500 g	5	5

hotels. All post offices are marked with the words 'Buu Dien'.

Mailing anything larger than an envelope into Vietnam is a dicey proposition, especially if the destination is outside either Ho Chi Minh City or Hanoi.

Telephone

International and domestic long-distance calls can be booked at many hotels, but this is expensive.

It's somewhat less expensive to book long-distance phone calls from the post office. For operator-assisted calls, you will be charged for three minutes even if you only talk for one minute, plus the rate per minute will be higher. As in most countries, the cheapest way to make a long-distance call is to dial direct.

International Calls International telephone service from Vietnam is extremely expensive and, outside of Ho Chi Minh City, Danang and Hanoi, unreliable. However, service is slowly improving now that Vietnam has installed four new earth stations which link the country to the International Telecommunications Satellite Organization (INTELSAT) system.

The cheapest and simplest way by far to make an international direct-dial (IDD) call is to buy a telephone card, known in Vietnam as a 'UniphoneKad'. They are on sale at the telephone company. UniphoneKads can only be used in special telephones which are mainly found in Ho Chi Minh City, usually in the lobbies of major hotels. The cards are issued in two denominations; 30,000d (US$2.76) and 300,000d (US$27.64). The 300,000d card can be used to make both domestic and international calls, while the 30,000d card will only work for domestic calls.

To make an IDD call, you must first dial the international prefix (00) followed by the country code, area code (if any) and the local number. Note that in many countries (Australia, for example), area codes start with a zero, but this zero must not be dialled when

calling internationally. So to call Melbourne (area code 03) in Australia (country code 61) from Vietnam, you would dial 00-61-3-1234567. Some useful country codes include:

Australia-61, New Zealand-64, Belgium-32, Norway-47, Canada-1, Singapore-65, Denmark-45 Sweden-46, France-33, Switzerland-41, Germany-49, Taiwan-886, Hong Kong-852, Thailand-66, Japan-81 UK-44, Korea (South)-82, USA-1, Netherlands-31, Vietnam-84

Calls are charged by one-minute increments; any fraction of a minute is charged as a full minute. The cost for making IDD calls is as follows (prices in US dollars):

Country	1st min	each additional
Africa	5.97	4.96
Australia	4.00	3.30
Cambodia & Laos	3.20	2.70
Canada	5.46	4.55
China	4.00	3.30
Eastern Europe	4.00	3.30
Hong Kong	3.80	3.10
India	4.60	3.82
Indonesia	4.60	3.82
Japan	4.60	3.82
Korea	4.00	3.30
Malaysia	3.80	3.10
New Zealand	4.60	3.82
Philippines	4.60	3.82
Russia & Cuba	4.00	3.30
Singapore	4.00	3.30
South America	5.97	4.96
Taiwan	4.00	3.30
Thailand	3.80	3.10
UK	5.46	4.55
USA	5.97	4.96

Domestic Calls Local calls can usually be made from any hotel or restaurant phone and are usually free.

Domestic direct-dialling is known as 'subscriber trunk dialling' (STD). To place an STD call, you must first dial the national trunk prefix (01) followed by the area code and local number. For example, to call Hanoi (area code 4), you would dial 01-4-123456. Some notable area codes in Vietnam include the following:

City	Area Code
Bai Chay	33
Buon Ma Thuot	50
Camau	78
Cantho	71
Chau Doc	76
Dalat	63
Danang	51
Dien Bien Phu	23
Dong Ha	53
Dong Hoi	52
Ha Tien	77
Haiphong	31
Hanoi	4
Ho Chi Minh City	8
Hoi An	51
Hué	54
Kontum	59
Long Xuyen	76
Mytho	73
Nha Trang	58
Phan Rang	62
Phan Thiet	62
Pleiku	59
Quang Ngai	55
Qui Nhon	56
Rach Gia	77
Tay Ninh	66
Vinh	38
Vinh Long	74
Vung Tau	6

Local telephone books, available at most hotel reception desks, are listed by subject (like the yellow pages). For example, to find the phone numbers of hotels look under *khach san*.

Domestic long-distance calls are reasonably priced, but will be cheapest if you dial direct. You can save up to 20% by calling at night (10 pm to 5 am).

An STD call between Hanoi and Ho Chi Minh City at the full daytime rate will cost 5000d (US$0.46) per minute. An operator-assisted call would cost 9000d (US$0.83) per minute but there is a three-minute minimum.

Paging Service Paging networks are now available in Ho Chi Minh City and this service is expected to catch on quickly. Business travellers who have an account with PhoneLink in Bangkok might be interested to know that someone in Bangkok can page you in Ho Chi Minh City.

Fax, Telex & Telegraph

Most GPOs and many tourist hotels in Vietnam offer domestic and international fax, telegraph and telex services. Hotels are likely to charge more than the post office.

Telex is old technology and fading into disuse in the West, so unless the person you need to reach has access to a telex number, it won't be much use. Telexes are charged by the minute with a one-minute minimum. Considering the slow transmission speed of telex (about 50 words per minute) you'd best keep the message short. The cost for telex transmission is as follows (prices in US dollars):

Country	1 min	2 min	3 min	each extra
Africa	5.34	9.67	14.00	4.33
Australia	4.34	7.66	11.00	3.32
Cambodia & Laos	3.73	6.45	9.17	2.71
Canada	5.34	9.67	14.00	4.33
China	4.34	7.66	11.00	3.32
Eastern Europe	4.34	7.66	11.00	3.32
Hong Kong	4.13	7.26	10.38	3.12
India	4.70	8.47	12.20	3.73
Indonesia	4.70	8.47	12.20	3.73
Japan	4.70	8.47	12.20	3.73
Korea	4.34	7.66	11.00	3.32
Malaysia	4.13	7.26	10.38	3.12
New Zealand	4.70	8.47	12.20	3.73
Philippines	4.70	8.47	12.20	3.73
Russia & Cuba	4.34	7.66	11.00	3.32
Singapore	4.34	7.66	11.00	3.32
South America	5.34	9.67	14.00	4.33
Taiwan	4.34	7.66	11.00	3.32
Thailand	4.13	7.26	10.38	3.12
UK	5.34	9.67	14.00	4.33
USA	5.34	9.67	14.00	4.33
Western Europe	5.34	9.67	14.00	4.33

The telegraph windows of major GPOs are open 24 hours a day seven days a week. Telegrams are charged for each word (including each word of the address) and there is a seven-word minimum charge. The cost per word is as follows (prices in US dollars):

Country	Cost Per Word
Africa	0.67
Australia	0.59
Cambodia & Laos	0.23
Canada	0.65
China	0.34

Hong Kong	0.59
Japan	0.59
Korea	0.59
New Zealand	0.59
Russia	0.34
Singapore	0.59
South America	0.67
Taiwan	0.59
Thailand	0.59
UK	0.65
USA	0.67
Western Europe	0.65

Fax machines are rapidly proliferating in Vietnam. Major hotels and many companies doing international business already have them. The main post offices in Ho Chi Minh City, Danang and Hanoi offer fax services too. Currently, the rates at the GPO for international fax transmission is as follows (prices in US dollars):

Country	1st Page	Each Extra Page
Australia	8.00	6.60
Cambodia & Laos	6.40	5.40
Canada	10.92	9.10
Eastern Europe	8.00	6.60
Hong Kong	7.60	6.20
Indonesia	9.20	7.64
Japan	9.20	7.64
Malaysia	7.60	6.20
Middle East	10.00	8.30
New Zealand	9.20	7.64
Philippines	9.20	7.64
Singapore	8.00	6.60
South America	11.94	9.92
Taiwan	8.00	6.60
Thailand	7.60	6.20
UK	10.92	9.10
USA	11.94	9.92
Western Europe	10.92	9.10

TIME

Vietnam, like Thailand, is seven hours ahead of Greenwich Mean Time (Coordinated Universal Time). Because it is so close to the equator, Vietnam does not have daylight saving time (summer time). Thus, when it's 12 noon in Hanoi or Ho Chi Minh City it is 10 pm the previous day in San Francisco, 1 am in New York, 5 am in London, 1 pm in Perth and 3 pm in Sydney. When the above-listed cities are on daylight saving time, these times are one hour off.

ELECTRICITY

Electric current in Vietnam is mostly 220 volts at 50 Hertz (cycles), but often you'll still find 110 volts (also at 50 Hertz). Unfortunately, looking at the shape of the outlet on the wall gives no clue as to what voltage is flowing through the wires. In the south, most outlets are US-style flat pins. Despite the American-inspired design, the voltage is still likely to be 220 volts. In the north, most outlets are the Russian-inspired round pins and also *usually* carrying 220 volts. If the voltage is not marked on the socket try finding a lightbulb or appliance with the voltage written on it. All sockets are two-prong only – in no case will you find a third wire for ground (earth).

Much of the electrical wiring in Vietnam is improvised. It is not uncommon to find, in place of a wall switch, two exposed wires you are supposed to connect together when you want the fan to work. If you get up in the middle of the night to go to the bathroom and accidentally touch the bare ends of the wires you could easily electrocute yourself.

In Ho Chi Minh City during the dry season (January to May) when reservoirs are low, there are frequent electricity outages because hydroelectric power is used, and the situation is getting worse due to the increase in air-conditioners and power-hungry factories. By contrast, Hanoi has considerable excess hydroelectric capacity and no problem with power outages. In rural areas, power is usually supplied by diesel generators which frequently are shut down and restarted. This means you should keep your torch (flashlight) handy. More seriously, it also means that there are probably frequent surges in the current. Sensitive electronic equipment should be shielded with a surge suppressor, or better yet, run on rechargeable batteries.

LAUNDRY

It is usually easy to find a hotel attendant who will get your laundry spotlessly clean (and perceptibly thinner) for the equivalent of a US dollar or two. Be sure that they have laundry detergent – in some of the poorer backwaters, people occasionally use friction alone to separate the dirt from the cloth (and often part of the cloth from the rest of the cloth). Allow at least a day and a half for washing and drying, especially in the wet season.

WEIGHTS & MEASURES

Vietnam uses the international metric system. For a metric conversion table, see the back of the book. In addition, there are two measurements for weight borrowed from the Chinese, the tael and the catty. A catty is 0.6 kg (1.32 pounds). There are 16 taels to the catty, so one tael is 37.5 grams (1.32 ounces). Gold is always sold by the tael.

Some Vietnamese words for measurements are:

gram	(same as English)
hectare	hec-ta
kg	(same as English)
km	cay so
litre	(same as English)
metre	met
metric tonne	ton
square metre	met vuong
tael	luong
catty	can

BOOKS & MAPS

A large number of English-language books about Vietnam have been published in the last three decades. They range from popular paperbacks to outstanding works of scholarship. Most focus on American involvement in Indochina (rather than on Vietnam itself) but quite a few also cover various aspects of Vietnamese culture, history, political development, etc. A sampling of the best are listed here.

People & Society

During the colonial period, French researchers wrote quite a number of works on Vietnam's cultural history and archaeology that remain unsurpassed. Several good ones on the Chams are *Les États Hinduisés d'Indochine et d'Indonésie* by Georges Coedes (Paris, 1928), *L'Art du Champa et Son Evolution* by Philippe Stern (Toulouse, 1942), and *Le Royaume du Champa* by Georges Maspero (Paris & Brussels, 1928).

Les Arts du Champa: Architecture et Sculpture by Tran Ky Phuong, curator of the Cham Museum in Danang and Vietnam's foremost scholar of the Chams, was to be published in Paris in the early 1990s.

Two collections of Vietnamese legends are *Land of Seagull & Fox* by Ruth Q Sun (Charles E Tuttle, Rutland, VT & Tokyo, 1967) and *Vietnamese Legends* by George F Schultz (Charles E Tuttle, Rutland, Vermont & Tokyo, 1965).

One of the most scholarly works on Caodaism is *Caodai Spiritism: A Study of Religion in Vietnamese Society* by Victor L Oliver (E J Brill, Leiden, 1976).

Vietnamese Studies is a series of books published quarterly in both English and French by Xunhasaba (Hanoi). Each issue has a number of in-depth articles dealing with a particular subject, ranging from recent history to archaeology and ethnography. Histories and essays on political topics tend to be polemical.

Graham Greene's 1954 novel *The Quiet American*, which is set during the last days of French rule, is probably the most famous Western work of fiction on Vietnam. Much of the action takes place at Saigon's Continental Hotel and at the Caodai complex in Tay Ninh.

The Lover by Marguerite Duras is a fic-

tional love story set in Saigon during the 1930s. The book has been made into a major motion picture.

Vietnam: Politics, Economics and Society by Melanie Beresford (Pinter Publishers, London & New York, 1988) gives a good overview of the aspects of post-reunification Vietnam mentioned in its title. You'll find out more than you ever wanted about life in the Red River Delta in *Hai Van: Life in a Vietnamese Commune* by François Houtard & Geneviève Lamercinier (Zed Books, London, 1984).

For business types, there's *Foreign Investment & Trade Law in Vietnam* by Laurence J Brahm (Asia 2000), a relatively recent work (1992) with a self-explanatory title.

History

The Birth of Vietnam by Keith Weller Taylor (University of California Press, Berkeley, 1983) covers the country's early history.

The Vietnamese Gulag by Doan Van Toai (Simon & Schuster, New York, 1986) tells of one man's experiences in the post-reunification 're-education camps'.

An excellent little book by Ellen Hammer, *Vietnam: Yesterday & Today* (Holt, Rinehart & Winston, New York, 1966) is one of the few American works on Vietnam from the mid-60s to have retained its usefulness. For a very readable account of Vietnamese history from prehistoric times until the fall of Saigon (with a focus on the American war) try Stanley Karnow's *Vietnam: A History* (Viking Press, New York, 1983), which was published as a companion volume to the American Public Broadcasting System series 'Vietnam: A Television History'. *The Socialist Republic of Vietnam* (Foreign Languages Publishing House, Hanoi, 1980) gives the pre-perestroika Hanoi line on Vietnam's history, economy, etc.

If you're having trouble keeping your dynasties, emperors and revolutionary patriots straight, Danny J Whitfield's solid *Historical & Cultural Dictionary of Vietnam* (Scarecrow Press, Metuchen, NJ, 1976) and William J Duiker's *Historical Dictionary of Vietnam* (Scarecrow Press, Metuchen, NJ &

London, 1989) will be of great help. Duiker's book has a comprehensive bibliography in the back.

Vietnamese Nationalism *Vietnamese Anticolonialism 1885-1925* by David G Marr (University of California, Berkeley, Los Angeles & London, 1971) has become a classic in its field. *Tradition on Trial 1920-1945* (University of California Press, Berkeley, 1981) is another work by Marr, who is one of the most outstanding Western scholars of Vietnam (he is now at the Australian National University).

William J Duiker's *The Communist Road to Power in Vietnam* (Westview Press, Boulder, Colorado, 1981) and *The Rise of Nationalism in Vietnam 1900-1941* (Cornell University Press, Ithaca, New York & London, 1976) trace the development of Vietnam's 20th century anti-colonialist and nationalist movements.

A number of biographies of Ho Chi Minh have been written, including *Ho Chi Minh: A Political Biography* by Jean Lacouture (Random House, New York, 1968) and *Ho* by David Halberstam (Random House, New York, 1971).

Franco-Viet Minh War On this topic it's worth taking a look at Peter M Dunn's *The First Vietnam War* (C Hurst & Company, London, 1985); or two works by Bernard B Fall: *Street Without Joy: Indochina at War 1946-54* (Stackpole Company, Harrisburg, Pennsylvania, 1961) and *Hell in a Very Small Place: The Siege of Dien Bien Phu* (Lippincott, Philadelphia, 1967).

American War The earliest days of US involvement in Indochina – when the OSS, predecessor of the CIA, was providing funding and weapons to Ho Chi Minh at the end of WW II – are recounted in *Why Vietnam?*, a riveting work by Archimedes L Patti (University of California Press, Berkeley, Los Angeles & London, 1980). Patti was the head of the OSS team in Vietnam and was at Ho Chi Minh's side when he declared Vietnam independent in 1945.

Three of the finest essays on the Vietnam War are collected in *The Real War* by Jonathan Schell (Pantheon Books, New York, 1987). An overview of the conflict is provided by George C Herring's *America's Longest War*, 2nd edition (Alfred A Knopf, New York, 1979 & 1986). *Fire in the Lake* by Francis Fitzgerald (Vintage Books, New York, 1972) is a superb history of American involvement in Vietnam; it received the Pulitzer Prize, the National Book Award and the Bancroft Prize for History.

A highly acclaimed biographical account of the US war effort is *A Bright Shining Lie: John Paul Vann & America in Vietnam* by Neil Sheehan (Random House, New York, 1988); it won both the Pulitzer Prize and the National Book Award. Another fine biography is Tim Bowden's *One Crowded Hour* (Angus & Robertson, 1988), which is the life of Australian film journalist Neil Davis. He shot some of the most famous footage of the war, including that of the North Vietnamese tank crashing through the gate of the presidential palace in Saigon in 1975.

Ellen J Hammer's *A Death in November* (E P Dutton, New York, 1987) tells of the US role in Diem's overthrow in 1963.

The Making of a Quagmire by David Halberstam (Ballantine Books, New York) is one of the best accounts of America's effort in the war during the early 1960s.

Two accounts of the fall of South Vietnam are *The Fall of Saigon* by David Butler (Simon & Schuster, New York, 1985) and *55 Days: The Fall of South Vietnam* by Alan Dawson (Prentice Hall, Englewood Cliffs, New Jersey, 1977).

An oft-cited analysis of where US military strategy in Vietnam went wrong is *On Strategy* by Colonel Harry G Summers Jr (Presidio Press, Novato, California, 1982 & Dell Publishing, New York, 1984). *The Pentagon Papers* (paperback version by Bantam Books, Toronto, New York & London, 1971), a massive, top-secret history of the US role in Indochina, were commissioned by Defence Secretary Robert McNamara in

1967 and published amidst a great furore by the *New York Times* in 1971.

Australia Australia's involvement in the Vietnam War is covered in *Australia's Vietnam* (Allen & Unwin, Sydney, London & Boston, 1983), a collection of essays edited by Peter King; *Australia's War in Vietnam* by Frank Frost (Allen & Unwin, Sydney, London & Boston, 1987); Gregory Pemberton's *All the Way: Australia's Road to Vietnam* (Allen & Unwin, Sydney & Boston, 1987); *Desperate Praise: The Australians in Vietnam* by John J Coe (Artlook Books, Perth, 1982); and *Vietnam: The Australian Experience* (Time-Life Books of Australia, Sydney, 1987).

Soldiers' Experiences Some of the better books about what it was like to be an American soldier in Vietnam include: *Born on the Fourth of July* by Ron Kovic (Pocket Books, New York, 1976), which has recently been made into a powerful movie; the journalist Michael Herr's superb *Dispatches* (Avon Books, New York, 1978); *Chickenhawk* by Robert Mason (Viking Press, New York, 1983 & Penguin Books, Middlesex, UK, 1984), a stunning autobiographical account of the helicopter war; *A Rumor of War* by Philip Caputo (Ballantine Books, New York, 1977); and *Nam* by Mark Baker (Berkley Books, New York, 1981). *A Piece of My Heart* by Keith Walker (Ballantine Books, New York, 1985) tells the stories of American women who served in Vietnam.

Two oral histories are: *Everything We Had*, by Al Santoli (Ballantine Books, New York, 1981) and *Bloods: An Oral History of the Vietnam War by Black Veterans* by Wallace Terry (Ballantine Books, New York, 1984).

Some of the horror of the My Lai massacre of 1968 comes through in Lieutenant General W R Peers' *My Lai Inquiry* (W W Norton & Company, New York & London, 1979).

Some of the horror of what American POWs endured comes through in *Chained Eagle* by Everett Alvarez, Jr (Dell, 1989).

Alvarez was a US pilot who spent 8½ years as a prisoner in North Vietnam.

Brothers in Arms by William Broyles Jr (Avon Books, New York, 1986) is the story of the 1984 visit to Vietnam by an American journalist who served as an infantry lieutenant during the war.

Viet Cong Memoir by Truong Nhu Tang (Harcourt Brace Jovanovich, San Diego, 1985) is the autobiography of a VC cadre who later became disenchanted with post-1975 Vietnam. *Portrait of a Vietnamese Soldier* (Red River Press, Hanoi) was written from the perspective of the North Vietnamese who fought against the Americans.

National Geographic Since its first article on Indochina in 1912, *National Geographic* has kept up a lively interest in the region. Listed chronologically, articles on Vietnam include:

The French Period: 'Glimpses of Asia' (May 1921, pp 553-68); 'Along the Old Mandarin Road of Old Indochina' (Aug 1931, pp 157-99); 'Under the French Tricolor in Indochina' (Aug 1931, pp 166-99); 'By Motor Trail Across French Indochina' (Oct 1935, pp 487-534); 'Tricolor Rules the Rainbow in French Indochina' (Oct 1935, pp 495-518); 'Portrait of Indochina' (April 1951) and 'Indochina Faces the Dragon' (Sept 1952, pp 287-328).

During the Vietnam War: 'South Vietnam Fights the Red Tide' (Oct 1961, pp 445-89); 'Helicopter War in South Vietnam' (Nov 1962, pp 723-54); 'Slow Train Through Vietnam's War' (Sept 1964, pp 412-44), 'American Special Forces in Action' (January 1965, pp 38-65); 'Saigon, Eye of the Storm' (June 1965, pp 834-72); 'Of Planes & Men' (Sept 1965, pp 298-349); 'Water War in Vietnam' (Feb 1966, pp 272-96); 'Behind the Headlines in Vietnam' (Feb 1967, pp 149-89); 'Vietnam's Montagnards' (April 1968, pp 443-87) and 'The Mekong River of Terror & Hope' (Dec 1968, pp 737-87).

Since reunification: 'Hong Kong's Refugee Dilemma' (Nov 1979, pp 709-32); 'Thailand: Refuge From Terror' (May 1980, pp 633-42); 'Troubled Odyssey of Vietnamese Fishermen' (Sept 1981, pp 378-95); and 'Vietnam: Hard Road to Peace' (Nov 1989, pp 561- 621).

Travel Guides

We don't mean to toot our own horn, but you hold in your hands what is by far the most comprehensive travel guidebook to Vietnam on the market today. However, there are other books which can give you a different perspective.

Vietnam: Opening Doors to the World by Rick Graetz (Graetz Publications, 1989) is a full-colour coffee table book on Vietnam and its people today.

Another effort in this direction is *Ten Years After* by Tim Page. This impressive book boasts '12 months worth of photos taken 10 years after the war'.

The *Vietnam Insight Guide* by Apa Publications of Singapore is a more portable coffee table book with much information about Vietnamese culture.

This is Vietnam is a business travellers' guide with only scant information on sightseeing places. This book is published twice annually so it should be reasonably up to date on the frequent changes in Vietnam's many business rules and regulations. The guide is available from Beca Investments (☎ 5231658, 8122614), Room 3201, Bank of America Building, Harcourt Rd, Central, Hong Kong.

Guide to Vietnam by John R Jones (Bradt Publications, UK, 1989 & Hunter Publishing, Edison, New Jersey, 1989) does a better job conveying how things used to be than giving hands-on, how-to-travel information.

A Dragon Apparent is – despite the name – not about China, but about author Norman Lewis's journeys through Vietnam, Laos and Cambodia in 1982.

In 1974, Jeanne M Sales of the American Women's Association of Saigon wrote *Guide to Vietnam* without once mentioning the war! *Customs & Culture of Vietnam* by Ann Caddell Crawford (Charles E Tuttle, Rutland, Vermont & Tokyo, 1966) is a bit dated.

The classic guidebooks to Indochina were published by Claudius Madrolle before WW II. The English edition, *Indochina* (Société d'Éditions Géographiques, Maritimes et Coloniales, Paris, 1939) is a much condensed version of the outstanding two-volume set in French, *Indochine du Sud* and *Indochine du Nord*. The 2nd augmented edition of *Indochine du Sud* and the 3rd augmented edition of *Indochine du Nord* were published in 1939 by the Société d'Éditions Géographiques, Maritimes et Coloniales in Paris. Earlier editions of both books were published by Librairie Hachette, Paris, in the 1920s. The only place to find the Madrolle guides these days is in major university libraries and antiquarian bookshops.

Bookshops

Within Vietnam In major cities, bookshops have a decent selection of maps but most of the books are in Vietnamese. In Ho Chi Minh City and Hanoi, you can find some books in English about the Vietnamese economy, but the information is scant and often out of date. About the only English-language books you can be sure of finding in Vietnamese bookshops are dictionaries.

Abroad Ironically, the best selection of books dealing with Vietnam are to be found outside the country. You should certainly have a look at the bookshops in your own country before leaving home, but Bangkok and Hong Kong bookstores are also worth exploring.

Asia Books has three locations in Bangkok: 221 Sukhumvit Rd, between Soi 15 and Soi 17 (☎ 252-7277, 250-1822, 252-4373, 251-6042); 2nd Floor, Peninsula Plaza, Rajdamri Rd between the Erawan and Regent hotels (☎ 253-9786/7/8); and 3rd Floor, Landmark Plaza, Sukhumvit Rd between Soi 4 and Soi 6, open 10 am to 8 pm (☎ 252-5654/5).

In Hong Kong, check out Wanderlust Books (☎ 5232042), 30 Hollywood Rd, Central, Hong Kong Island. The store is on the corner of Hollywood Rd and Shelley St.

Maps

Urban orienteering is very easy in Vietnam. Like Indonesian, Vietnamese is written with a Latin-based alphabet. You can read the street signs and maps! In addition, finding out where you are is easy: street signs are plentiful, and almost every shop and restaurant has the street name and number right on its sign. Street names are sometimes abbreviated on street signs with just the initials ('DBP' for 'Diên Bien Phu St,' etc). Most street numbering is sequential with odd and even numbers on opposite sides of the street (although there are important exceptions in Ho Chi Minh City and Danang – see Orientation in those sections for details), but unfortunately, number 75 is often three blocks down the street from number 76.

A few tips: many restaurants are named after their street addresses. For instance, 'Nha Hang 51 Nguyen Hue' (*nha hang* means restaurant) is at number 51 Nguyen Hue St. If you are travelling by bus or car, a good way to find out where you are is to look for the post office – the words following Buu Dien (post office) on the sign are the name of the district, town or village you're in.

Excellent maps of Ho Chi Minh City, Hanoi, Danang, Hué and a few other places are issued in slightly different forms every few years. If you will be travelling by road outside of the main cities and towns, it is worthwhile purchasing a map of the whole country in booklet form entitled *Tap Ban Do Viet Nam Hanh Chinh Va Hinh The* (Cuc Do Dac Va Ban Do Nha Nuoc, Hanoi, 1986). It is not easy to find this atlas, but look around and you might get lucky.

The best place in the country to get all the maps you'll need during your stay is Ho Chi Minh City. First try the bookshops (where prices are lowest), then explore the street markets where entrepreneurs selling virtually every map in existence can be found behind little stands on the sidewalks along Nguyen Hue Blvd and on Le Loi Blvd between the Municipal Theatre and the Rex Hotel. In the finest capitalist tradition these map-mongers offer their wares at vastly inflated prices, but for the tourist the cost – especially after a bit of bargaining – is still reasonable. Other places to look for maps include central post offices (often at the street stalls just outside) and hotel gift shops.

War of the Names

One of the primary battlegrounds for the hearts and minds of the Vietnamese people during the last four decades has been the naming of Vietnam's provinces, districts, cities, towns, streets and institutions. Some places have been known by three or more names since WW II, and in many cases more than one name is still used.

Urban locations have borne: 1) French names (often of the generals, administrators and martyrs who made French colonialism possible); 2) names commemorating the historical personages chosen for veneration by the South Vietnamese government; and 3) the alternative set of heroes selected by the Hanoi government. Buddhist pagodas have formal names as well as one or more popular monikers. Chinese pagodas bear various Chinese appellations – most of which also have Vietnamese equivalents – based on the titles and celestial ranks of those to whom they are consecrated. In the highlands, both Montagnard and Vietnamese names for mountains, villages, etc are in use. The slight differences in vocabulary and pronunciation between the north, centre and south sometimes result in the use of different words and spellings (such as 'Pleiku' and 'Playcu').

When French control of Vietnam ended in 1954, almost all French names were replaced in both the North and the South. For example, Cap St Jacques became Vung Tau, Tourane was rechristened Danang and Rue Catinat in Saigon was renamed Tu Do (Freedom) St (since reunification it has been known as Dong Khoi (Uprising) St). In 1956, the names of some of the provinces and towns in the South were changed as part of an effort to erase from popular memory the Viet Minh's anti-French exploits, which were often known by the places where they took place. The village-based southern communists, who by this time had gone underground, continued to use the old designations and boundaries in running their regional, district and village organisations. The peasants quickly adapted to this situation, using one set of names for where they lived when dealing with the communists and a different set of names when talking to representatives of the South Vietnamese government.

Later, the US soldiers in Vietnam gave nicknames (such as China Beach near Danang) to places whose Vietnamese names they found inconvenient or difficult to remember or pronounce. This helped to make a very foreign land seem to them a bit more familiar.

After reunification, the first order of Saigon's provisional municipal Military Management Committee changed the name of the city to 'Ho Chi Minh City', a decision confirmed in Hanoi a year later. The new government immediately began changing street names considered inappropriate – a process which is still continuing – and renamed almost all the city's hotels, dropping English and French names in favour of Vietnamese ones. The only French names still in use are those of Albert Calmette (1893-1934; developer of a tuberculosis vaccine), Marie Curie (1867-1934; she won the Nobel Prize for her research into radioactivity), Louis Pasteur (1822-95; chemist and bacteriologist) and Alexandre Yersin (1863-1943; discoverer of the plague bacillus).

All this renaming has had mixed results. Streets, districts and provinces are usually known by their new names. But most residents of Ho Chi Minh City still prefer to call the place Saigon, especially since Ho Chi Minh City is in fact a huge area that stretches from near Cambodia all the way to the South China Sea. And visitors will find that the old names of the city's hotels are making a comeback.

All this makes using anything but the latest street maps a risky proposition, though fortunately most of the important street-name changes were made before any of the maps currently on sale were published. ∎

MEDIA

Newspapers & Magazines

English Language Most of Vietnam's English language press is geared towards attracting the foreign investor and business traveller rather than peddling the news. While you may not be interested in knowing how many tons of bricks or fertiliser were produced last month, these publications can give you some idea of what's happening in Vietnam.

The English-language *Vietnam Weekly* is published in Hanoi. Other English periodicals include the *Vietnam Economic News*, *Saigon Times*, *Vietnam Business* and *Vietnam Foreign Trade*.

A limited selection of imported newspapers and magazines is available in Ho Chi

Minh City. (much less so in Hanoi). The *Bangkok Post* and *New Nation* are available later the same day for US$1. The *International Herald Tribune* is also available but costs more. *Newsweek* and *Time* can be found at numerous locations in Ho Chi Minh City.

Business News Indochina is an outstanding English-language periodical published every two weeks. It is available both inside and outside Vietnam. If you are genuinely interested in Vietnam's economy, this is *the* publication to read. It's most readily available by subscription: contact Business News Indochina (☎ 8800307, fax (852) 8561184) GPO Box 9794, Hong Kong. At over US$10 per copy, it's not cheap but the price may fall as circulation increases.

Vietnamese-Language There are now about 135 periodicals published in Vietnam, all but 35 of them in Hanoi. Daily newspaper circulation is eight per 1000 people. *Nhan Dan* (The People), published in Hanoi, is the daily newspaper of the Communist Party of Vietnam. *Quan Doi Nhan Dan* (The People's Army), also published in Hanoi, is the daily paper of the army. *Saigon Giai Phong* (Liberated Saigon) is the daily of the Ho Chi Minh City section of the Vietnamese Communist Party and is published in both Vietnamese and Chinese. *Giai Phong Nhat Bao (Jiefang Ribao* in Chinese) is published daily in Chinese by the Fatherland Front. The recent liberalisation has yet to significantly reduce party and government control of the press.

Radio & TV
The Voice of Vietnam broadcasts in 11 foreign langu es: Cantonese, English, French, Indonesian, Japanese, Khmer, Lao, Mandarin, Russian, Spanish and Thai. In Hanoi, the daily English broadcast can be picked up from 6 to 6.30 pm on 1010 kHz in the medium-wave (AM) band. Elsewhere in the country, only short-wave reception of foreign-language broadcasts may be available. The Voice of Vietnam can be picked up

around the world when short-wave propagation is good.

The first broadcast of the Voice of Vietnam took place in 1945. During the Vietnam War, the Voice of Vietnam broadcast a great deal of propaganda programming to the South, including special English programmes for American GIs. From 1968 to 1976, the Voice of Vietnam used the transmitters of Radio Havana-Cuba to deliver its message direct to the American people. In 1984, there were six million radio sets in Vietnam.

Vietnamese domestic national radio broadcasts news and music programmes from 7 am until 11 pm. In Ho Chi Minh City, frequencies to try include 610 kHz and 820 kHz in the AM band and 78.5 MHz, 99.9 MHz and 103.3 MHz in the FM band. Amongst Vietnamese, radio is popular with older people, but the younger generation is mostly interested in TV and video tapes.

Because up-to-date Western magazines and newspapers are virtually unavailable in Vietnam except from other travellers or embassies, visitors interested in keeping up on events in the rest of the world – and in Vietnam itself – may want to bring along a small short-wave receiver. News, music and features programmes in a multitude of languages can easily be picked up, especially at night. Reception of any given broadcast depends on a variety of variable factors, including ionospheric conditions and sunspot activity. Frequencies you might try for English-language broadcasts include:

Radio Australia
17,750 kHz, 15,415 kHz, 15,395 kHz, 15,240 kHz, 15,140 kHz, 11,705 kHz, 9770 kHz 9645 kHz and 7205 kHz
BBC World Service
15,360 kHz (in the early morning); 15,280 kHz (during the day); and 15,310 kHz, 11,750 kHz, 9740 kHz and 6195 kHz (at night). Other frequencies to try include 11,955 kHz, 7145 kHz, 5975 kHz and 3915 kHz.
Voice of America
17,730 kHz and 15,215 kHz (in the morning); 11,755 kHz (in the evening); 6110 kHz, 9760 kHz and 15,760 kHz (at night)

Christian Science Monitor Radio
      17,780 kHz (around noon)

Vietnamese TV, which began broadcasting in 1970, consists of news and propaganda programming as well as sports and music. There are currently only two channels in Ho Chi Minh City and broadcast hours are very short. News and weather is broadcast from 7 to 8.30 pm. From 8.30 to 10.30 pm there is usually a movie (sometimes a foreign movie). On Sunday there is an extra broadcast from 3 to 4 pm. Vietnamese TV was blessedly free of commercial advertising until recently, but that too has arrived with the new economic reforms.

FILM & PHOTOGRAPHY
Airport X-Ray Machines
Some of Vietnam's airports are still equipped with the latest 1950s x-ray machines that will severely damage or destroy *any* film, whether it is exposed or unexposed and no matter how low the ASA or Din rating is. Prints made from irradiated negatives will come out all reddish (makes for colourful sunsets though) while slides get washed out.

Efforts are being made to upgrade airport facilities, however, and Noi Bai Airport, Hanoi, has recently had new x-ray machines installed (they're the same brand as those used at Bangkok airport, so they should be safe enough). At other airports, though, if you're not sure, no matter what the customs people tell you, do *not* let them x-ray your film as you leave the country.

And remember that baggage is x-rayed when it *arrives* in Vietnam (to check for 'contraband' that the customs agents would like to take home, especially electronic equipment). Do not put your film in your checked luggage! Your best bet, even on domestic flights, is to keep all film on your person.

Film & Developing
Fresh Kodacolor print film, imported in bulk, is widely available, as are 35-mm colour print films made by Konica, Fuji and Agfa. A 36-exposure 100 ASA roll of Kodacolor costs US$3.40; Konica costs US$2.60. Western-made slide films, which cannot be developed in Vietnam, are hard to find but some hotel gift shops stock them.

Impoverished photographers may want to experiment with inexpensive Russian products, sold under the 'Foto' label. Sometimes you can find 'ORWO' print and slide films from the old East Germany, or 'Lucky' from China. But note that few such films are 'DX' compatible – that is, they will not work in automatic cameras which need to sense the ASA (Din) rating of film being used. Check the box for the letters 'DX' if you aren't sure. Cameras which allow you to manually set the ASA rating do not require DX film.

If you buy film in Vietnam, be sure to check the expiry date. This is especially important if the film has been stored in a warm environment, which is very likely. A tattered and scuffed film box is a sign that the product was resold by a tourist who may have inadvertantly allowed it to be exposed to airport x-rays.

Photoprocessing shops have become ubiquitous in Ho Chi Minh City and other places where tourists congregate. Most of these places are equipped with the latest Japanese one-hour colour-printing equipment. Cost for developing is about US$0.50 per roll plus US$0.12 per 9x13 cm (3½x5 inch) print.

Photography Restrictions & Etiquette
The Vietnamese police can be troublesome about what you photograph. Obviously, don't photograph something that is militarily sensitive (airports, seaports, military bases, border checkpoints, soldiers and police accepting bribes, etc). The cops in Mytho (Mekong Delta region) must think there are spies everywhere – it seems that half the buildings have a sign (in Vietnamese) saying that photography and video recording is prohibited. Photography from aircraft is also prohibited – if you're going to try it, do it on a foreign carrier during your flight out of the country. Don't even think of trying to get a snapshot of Ho Chi Minh in his glass sar-

cophagus! Taking pictures inside pagodas and temples is usually all right, but as always it is better to ask permission from the monks.

Perhaps it would be wise for you to memorise the following message which appears on signs in various places: 'Cam Chup Hinh Va Quay Video', which means 'No Photography or Video Taping'.

Many of the touristy sites now charge a 'camera fee' of at least US$0.50, or a 'video fee' of US$2. If the staff refuses to issue a receipt for the camera fee, then you should refuse to pay – the 'fee' in that case is likely to go into their pocket.

If your camera uses a lithium battery (most do these days) it's wise to bring an extra as they can be hard to come by in Vietnam.

Like their Japanese and Chinese counterparts, Vietnamese people have a near obsession with collecting hundreds (or thousands) of photos of themselves posing in front of something. The pose is always the same; a stiff, frontal shot, hands at the sides, etc. The result is that all of their photos look nearly identical. The purpose of the photos seems to be to prove that they've been to a particular place. Since many Vietnamese cannot afford their own camera, virtually every site of tourist potential has a legion of photographers always ready to snap a few pictures. Some photographers will get the film processed and mail it to their customers, while others will shoot a roll and hand it over unprocessed. Most Vietnamese cannot understand why Westerners shoot dozens of rolls of film without posing themselves in each and every frame. Furthermore, when Westerners show off their best photographs, Vietnamese look at them and say the photos are 'boring'.

Vietnamese aren't much different from Westerners when it comes to have their photos taken by strangers. In general they won't care, though a few might get upset. People will sometimes pose for you if you give a tip or buy something from them (like the old women selling bananas by the streetside, for example). For a small tip, we've even had soldiers pose for us in full battle dress, but be discreet when handing money to someone in uniform (they are not supposed to look like they are accepting bribes).

One of the best things you can do for Vietnamese friends who don't own a camera is to take pictures of them or their families and send the photos to them after processing (or give them the roll of film and let them process it).

HEALTH

If you've heard of it, chances are someone in Vietnam's got it. Common diseases, victims of which you'll find in virtually every provincial hospital, include diarrhoeal diseases, pneumonia, malaria, measles, diphtheria, hepatitis, tetanus, plague, tuberculosis, rabies, polio and leprosy. It is important to note, however, that the local population's susceptibility to most of these diseases is the result of endemic deficiencies in immunisation, nutrition, sanitation and medical treatment – factors that are unlikely to affect travellers if they are careful.

Even the most basic nutritional supplements, antibiotics and other medicines, antitoxins, vaccines and medical equipment (everything from scalpels to diagnostic gadgets) are either in chronic short supply or totally lacking. Many of the medicines that are available in pharmacies were sent by Overseas Vietnamese to their relatives for resale – check expiry dates. Though foreigners with hard currency will receive the best treatment available, even US dollars will not make what doesn't exist magically appear. If you become seriously ill while in Vietnam, get to Bangkok, Hong Kong or some other reasonably developed country as soon as possible.

Vietnam's children are the most seriously affected by this situation and routinely die from eminently curable infectious diseases. It is estimated that 50% are malnourished. Protein and vitamin deficiencies often cause blindness, dermatitis, rickets and slowed physical and mental development. When contracted by children under four, malaria is either fatal or stunts physical and intellectual development.

For information on helping Vietnam's

hospitals and orphanages, contact the International Mission of Hope at PO Box 38909, Denver, CO 80238, USA (☎ (303) 466-2448 or care of FCVN, 1818 Gaylord St, Denver, CO 80218, USA (☎ (303) 321-4224).

The Traveller's Health Guide by Dr Anthony C Turner (Roger Lascelles, London) or *Staying Healthy in Asia, Africa & Latin America* (Moon Publications) are guides to staying healthy while travelling, or what to do if you fall ill. For the technically oriented, the classical medical reference is the *Merck Manual*, a weighty volume which covers virtually every illness known to humanity.

Children, particularly babies and unborn children, present their own peculiar problems when travelling. Lonely Planet's *Travel with Children* by Maureen Wheeler gives a rundown on health precautions to be taken with kids and advice on travel during pregnancy.

You can buy plenty of dangerous drugs across the counter in Vietnam without a prescription, but if you need some special medication then take it with you. On any medicines you buy, take a look at expiration dates – drugs may not be of the same strength as in other countries or may have deteriorated due to age or poor storage conditions. Chinese shops often sell Chinese herbal medicines.

In Ho Chi Minh City, most expatriates use Cho Ray Hospital (Benh Vien Cho Ray) at 201B Nguyen Chi Thanh Blvd, District 5 (Cholon). In Hanoi, the place to go is the International Hospital (Benh Vien Quoc Te) on the western side of Giai Phong St. In Hanoi, you could also try waking up the staff at your embassy or consulate – they just might be able to refer you to some competent medical facility. Another possibility for referral are the staff at some of the better-appointed hotels. There's a good chance that they'll all tell you to head for Bangkok.

Pre-Departure Preparations
Vaccinations Very few people will be required to have vaccinations but there are several vaccinations that are certainly recommended. If you're arriving within six days after leaving or transiting a yellow fever infected area then a vaccination is required.

Vaccinations which have been recommended by various health authorities include: meningitis, rabies, hepatitis A, hepatitis B, BCG (tuberculosis), polio, and TABT (protects against typhoid, paratyphoid A and B, and tetanus) and diphtheria.

Plan ahead for getting your vaccinations: some of them require an initial shot followed by a booster, while some vaccinations should not be given together. Most travellers from Western countries will have been immunised against various diseases during childhood but your doctor may still recommend booster shots against measles or polio, diseases still prevalent in many developing countries. The period of protection offered by vaccinations differs widely and some are contraindicated if you are pregnant.

In some countries immunisations are available from airport or government health centres.

You should have your vaccinations recorded in an International Health Certificate. If you are travelling with children, it's especially important to be sure that they've had all necessary vaccinations.

Get your teeth checked and any necessary dental work done before you leave home. Always carry a spare pair of glasses or your prescription in case of loss or breakage.

Health Insurance Although you may have medical insurance in your own country, it is probably not valid in Vietnam. A travel insurance policy is a very good idea – to protect you against cancellation penalties on advance purchase flights, against medical costs through illness or injury, against theft or loss of possessions, and against the cost of additional air tickets if you get really sick and have to fly home. Read the small print carefully since it's easy to be caught out by exclusions.

If you undergo medical treatment, be sure to collect all receipts and copies of your medical report, in English if possible, for your insurance company.

If you purchase an International Student Identity Card (ISIC) or Teacher Card (ISTC), you may be automatically covered depending on which country you purchased the card in. Check with the student travel office to be sure. If you're neither a student or a teacher, but you're between the ages of 15 and 25, you can purchase an International Youth Identity Card (YIEE) which entitles you to the same benefits. Some student travel offices also sell insurance to people who don't hold these cards.

Medical Kit You should assemble some sort of basic first-aid kit. You won't want it to be too large and cumbersome for travelling, but some items which could be included are:

Anti-malarial tablets; Band-Aids or gauze bandage with plaster (adhesive tape); a thermometer; tweezers; scissors; suncreen; insect repellent; multi-vitamins; water sterilisation tablets; chapstick; antibiotic ointment; an antiseptic agent (Dettol or Betadine); Caladryl (for sunburn and itchy bites); any medication you're already taking; diarrhoea medication (Lomotil or Imodium); rehydration mixture for treatment of severe diarrhoea; paracetemol (Panadol), ibuprofen or aspirin for pain and fever; antihistamine (such as Benadryl), useful as a decongestant for colds and allergies and to ease the itch from insect bites or stings; a course of antibiotics (probably 30 tablets of 250 mg tetracycline, but check with your doctor); and contraceptives (including condoms), if necessary. Most of these medications are available in Vietnam at low cost, but it's still not a bad idea to come prepared.

Ideally antibiotics should be administered only under medical supervision and should never be taken indiscriminately. Overuse of antibiotics can weaken your body's ability to deal with infections naturally and can reduce the drug's efficacy on a future occasion. Take only the recommended dose as prescribed. It's important that once you start a course of antibiotics, you finish it even if the illness seems to be cured earlier. If you stop taking the antibiotics after one or two days, a complete relapse is more than likely. If you think you are experiencing a reaction to any antibiotic, stop taking it immediately and consult a doctor.

Basic Rules

Food & Water In Ho Chi Minh City and Hanoi, tap water is not too bad (it's chlorinated) but it's still recommended that you boil it before drinking. In other parts of Vietnam, the water varies from pretty safe to downright dangerous. Especially after a typhoon and the subsequent flooding, there is a problem with sewers overflowing into reservoirs, thus contaminating the tap water used for drinking and bathing. Outbreaks of cholera and typhoid occur most often after floods so you must be particularly careful at such times – do not even brush your teeth with unboiled water after flooding.

Reputable brands of bottled water (both imported and domestic) or soft drinks are generally fine, although in some places bottles refilled with tap water are not unknown. Take care with fruit juice, particularly if water may have been added. Milk should be treated with suspicion, as it is often unpasteurised. Boiled milk is fine if it is kept hygienically and yoghurt is always good.

Tea and coffee should both be OK since the water should have been boiled. You can also boil your own water if you carry an electric immersion coil and a large metal cup (plastic will melt). You can safely plug a 220 volt immersion coil into a 110 volt socket (not vice versa!), but the boiling time will be much longer. For emergency use, water purification tablets will help. Water is more effectively sterilised by iodine than by chlorine tablets, because iodine kills amoebic cysts. However, iodine is not safe for prolonged use, and also tastes horrible. Bringing water to a boil is sufficient to kill most bacteria, but 20 minutes of boiling is required to kill amoebic cysts. Fortunately, amoebic cysts are relatively rare and you should not be overly concerned about these. If you have nothing to boil or purify your water, you have to consider the risks of drinking possibly contaminated water against the risks of dehydrating – the first is possible, the second is definite.

It's a good idea to carry a water bottle with you. You are dehydrating if you find you are urinating infrequently or if your urine turns a deep yellow or orange; you may also find yourself getting headaches. Dehydration is a real problem if you go hiking in Vietnam – if you can't find water along the way or can't carry enough with you, then you will soon learn just how hot this place really is!

While boiling will kill nasty microbes, freezing will not. Since most small eateries in Vietnam lack refrigeration equipment, factory-frozen ice is delivered daily. In Ho Chi Minh City and Hanoi, the ice comes from a factory which has to meet certain standards of hygiene (the water is at least chlorinated), while in rural areas the ice could be made from river (sewer?) water. Another problem is that even clean ice often makes its way to its destination in a filthy sack carried on the bare backs of delivery men. The filthy outer layer may melt off, but then again it may not, though any thoughtful restaurant will at least wash the ice before cracking it into pieces. If you do not want to risk a possibly serious gut infection, avoid ice in rural backwaters – admittedly easier said than done in a hot tropical country.

When it comes to food, use your best judgement. To be absolutely safe, everything should be throughly cooked – you can get dysentery from salads and unpeeled fruit. Ice cream is usually OK if it is a reputable brand name, but beware of ice cream that has melted and been refrozen. Thoroughly cooked food is safest but not if it has been left to cool or if it has been reheated. Take great care with shellfish or fish and avoid undercooked meat.

Other Precautions Sunglasses not only give you that fashionable 'Hollywood look' but will protect your eyes from the scorching Vietnamese sun. Amber and grey are said to be the two most effective colours for filtering out harmful ultraviolet rays.

Sunburn can be more than just uncomfortable. Among the undesirable effects of frying your hide are premature skin ageing and possible skin cancer in later years. Bring sunscreen (UV) lotion and wear something to cover your head.

If you're sweating profusely, you're going to lose a lot of salt and that can lead to fatigue and muscle cramps for some people. If necessary you can make it up by putting extra salt in your food (a teaspoon a day is plenty), but don't increase your salt intake unless you also increase your water intake.

Take good care of all cuts and scratches. In this climate they take longer to heal and can easily get infected. Treat any cut with care; wash it out with sterilised water, preferably with an antiseptic (Betadine), keep it dry and keep an eye on it – they really can turn into tropical ulcers! It would be worth bringing an antibiotic cream with you. Cuts on your feet and ankles are particularly troublesome – a new pair of sandals can quickly give you a nasty abrasion which can be difficult to heal. Try not to scratch mosquito bites for the same reason.

The climate may be tropical, but you *can* catch a cold in Vietnam. One of the easiest ways is leaving a fan on at night when you go to sleep, and air-conditioners are even worse. You can also freeze by going up to mountainous areas without warm clothes. Antihistamines can give symptomatic relief, but the way to cure a cold is to rest, drink lots of liquids, keep warm (easy to do in Vietnam!) and wait it out.

Medical Problems & Treatment

Diarrhoea Diarrhoea is often due simply to a change of diet. A lot depends on what you're used to eating and whether or not you've got an iron gut. If you do get diarrhoea, the first thing to do is wait – it rarely lasts more than a few days.

Diarrhoea will cause you to dehydrate, which will make you feel much worse. The solution is not simply to drink water, since it will run right through you. You'll get much better results by mixing your water with oral rehydration salt, a combination of salts (both NaCl and KCl) and glucose. Dissolve the powder in *cool* water (never hot!) and drink, but don't use it if the powder is wet. The quantity of water is specified on the packet. Oralit is also useful for treating heat exhaustion caused by excessive sweating.

If the diarrhoea persists then the usual

treatment is Lomotil or Imodium tablets. The maximum dose for Lomotil is two tablets three times a day. Both Lomotil and Imodium are prescription drugs in the West but are available over the counter in most Asian countries. Anti-diarrhoeal drugs don't cure anything, but they slow down the digestive system so that the cramps go away and you don't have to go to the toilet all the time. Excessive use of these drugs is not advised, as they can cause dependency and other side effects. Furthermore, the diarrhoea serves one useful purpose – it helps the body expel unwanted bacteria.

Activated charcoal – while not actually considered a drug – can provide much relief from diarrhoea and is a time-honoured treatment.

Fruit juice, tea and coffee can aggravate diarrhoea – again, water with oral rehydration salts is the best drink. It will help tremendously if you eat a light, fiber-free diet. Yoghurt or boiled eggs with salt are basic staples for diarrhoea patients. Later you may be able to tolerate rice porridge or plain white rice. Keep away from vegetables, fruits and greasy foods for awhile. If you suddenly decide to pig out on a pepperoni pizza with hot sauce, you'll be back to square one. If the diarrhoea persists for a week or more, it's probably not simple travellers' diarrhoea – it could be dysentery and it might be wise to see a doctor.

Dysentery Dysentery is considerably more serious than the usual garden-variety diarrhoea. Dysentery causes diarrhoea, often accompanied by fever, blood and pus in the stool. The victim usually feels faint, totally lacking in energy, can barely eat and can hardly get out of bed. It's a real drag! Dysentery comes in two varieties, amoebic and bacillary.

Diarrhoea with blood or pus and fever is usually bacillary dysentery. It's quite common in Vietnam and many travellers fall prey to it. Since it's caused by bacteria infecting the gut, it can be treated with antibiotics like tetracycline, or a sulfa drug. The usual dose is 250 mg tablets, taken four times daily

for about a week. In most cases, bacillary dysentery will eventually clear up without treatment, but in some cases it's actually fatal, especially in children. Be sure to use water and Oralit (see previous section on Diarrhoea) to prevent dehydration.

Antibiotics are heavy artillery, so don't start swallowing tetracycline at the first sign of diarrhoea. The main problem is that antibiotics upset the balance of intestinal flora. The problem is more serious for women since this can lead to yeast infections, and tetracycline is also contraindicated in women who are pregnant or breastfeeding.

Diarrhoea with blood or pus but without fever is usually amoebic dysentery. This is a disease you should not neglect because it will not go away by itself. In addition, if you don't wipe out the amoeba while they are still in your intestine, they will eventually migrate to the liver and other organs, causing abscesses which could require surgery.

There are several ways to cure this disease. If you treat it promptly, the amoeba will still be restricted only to the intestine. In this case, tetracycline is effective. The dosage is 250 mg, four times daily for a *minimum* of 10 days.

The most sure-fire cure for amoebic dysentery is metronidazole (Flagyl), an anti-amoebic drug. It will wipe out amoeba no matter where they reside in the body, even in the liver and other organs. The dosage is three 250 mg tablets (750 mg) three times daily for seven to 10 days. Flagyl is also available in 500 mg tablets, so in that case you take 1½ tablets per dose. If you take Flagyl, do not under any circumstances consume alcohol at the same time, not a drop! Flagyl and alcohol together can cause a severe reaction.

Herbal medicine fanatics will be pleased to know that dried papaya seeds can actually cure amoebic dysentery, but only if it hasn't gone beyond the intestine. The dosage is one heaping tablespoon daily for eight days. If you're really worried about catching amoebic dysentery, papaya seeds can be used as a preventive measure – one heaping tablespoon weekly is usually effective.

Remember that the seeds must be thoroughly dried and that they taste awful. Just because something is 'natural' doesn't mean it's harmless – papaya seeds can cause miscarriage in pregnant women and they may have other unknown side effects. Treat papaya seeds as you would any other medicine – with caution.

Giardia This is another type of amoeba which causes severe diarrhoea, nausea and weakness, but doesn't produce blood in the stool or cause fever. Giardia is very common throughout the world.

Although the symptoms are similar to amoebic dysentery, there are some important differences. On the positive side, giardia will not migrate to the liver and other organs – it stays in the intestine and therefore is much less likely to cause long-term health problems.

The bad news is that tetracycline and papaya seeds are no help whatsoever. It can only be cured with an anti-amoebic drug like metronidazole (Flagyl) – again, never drink alcohol while taking Flagyl. Without treatment, the symptoms may subside and you might feel fine for awhile, but the illness will return again and again, making your life miserable.

To treat giardia, the proper dosage of Flagyl is different than for amoebic dysentery. Take one 250 mg tablet three times daily for 10 days. It can sometimes be difficult to rid yourself of giardia, so you might need laboratory tests to be certain you're cured.

Cholera Cholera tends to travel in epidemics (usually after floods) and outbreaks are generally widely reported, so you can often avoid such problem areas. This is a disease of insanitation, so if you've heard reports of cholera be especially careful about what you eat, drink and brush your teeth with.

Symptoms include a sudden onset of acute diarrhoea with 'rice water' stools, vomiting, muscular cramps, and extreme weakness. You need medical help – but treat for dehydration, which can be extreme, and if there is an appreciable delay in getting to hospital then begin taking tetracycline. See the Dysentery section for dosages and warnings.

Cholera vaccination is not very effective and is no longer recommended by the World Health Organisation (WHO). If you get cholera, it's probably best to get on a plane to Bangkok – fast.

Typhoid Typhoid fever is another gut infection that travels the fecal-oral route – ie, contaminated water and food are responsible. Like cholera, epidemics can occur after floods because of sewage backing up into drinking water supplies.

Vaccination against typhoid is not totally effective and it is one of the most dangerous infections, so medical help must be sought.

In its early stages typhoid resembles many other illnesses: sufferers may feel like they have a bad cold or flu on the way, as early symptoms are a headache, a sore throat, and a fever which rises a little each day until it is around 40°C or more. The victim's pulse is often slow relative to the degree of fever present and gets slower as the fever rises – unlike a normal fever where the pulse increases. There may also be vomiting, diarrhoea or constipation.

In the second week the high fever and slow pulse continue and a few pink spots may appear on the body; trembling, delirium, weakness, weight loss and dehydration are other symptoms. If there are no further complications, the fever and other symptoms will slowly go during the third week. However you must get medical help before this because pneumonia (acute lung infection) or peritonitis (from burst appendix) are common complications, and because typhoid is very infectious.

The fever should be treated by keeping the victim cool and dehydration should also be watched for. Chloramphenicol is the recommended antibiotic but there are fewer side affects with ampicillin. The adult dosage is two 250 mg capsules, four times a day. Children aged between eight and 12 years should have half the adult dose; younger children should have ⅓ the adult dose.

Patients who are allergic to penicillin should not be given ampicillin.

Polio Polio is also a disease spread by insanitation and is found more frequently in hot climates. The effects on children can be especially devastating – they can be crippled for life. Fortunately, an excellent vaccination is available, but a booster every five years is recommended by many doctors.

Tetanus Tetanus is due to a bacillus which usually enters the blood system through a cut, or as the result of a skin puncture by a rusty nail, wire, etc. It is worth being vaccinated against tetanus since there is more risk of contracting the disease in warm climates where cuts take longer to heal. A tetanus booster shot should be given every five years.

Malaria The parasite that causes this disease is spread by the bite of the *Anopheles* mosquito, though it can *rarely* get passed by blood transfusion. Malaria has a nasty habit of recurring in later years, even if you're cured at the time, and it can kill you.

In the 1950s, the World Health Organisation launched a two-prong attack against malaria, spraying with the pesticide DDT and treating victims with the drug chloroquine. Health authorities confidently predicted that by the year 2000, the malaria parasite would be extinct.

It hasn't worked out that way. The mosquitos developed resistance against DDT and the malaria parasite developed resistance to chloroquine. Aside from breeding super mosquitos, DDT has also proven harmful to the environment and human health. For awhile it seemed that the war against malaria was being won; now it is obvious that malaria is staging a comeback throughout the tropics.

There are four different types of malaria, but 95% of all cases are one of two varieties. The most serious of these two types is *P falciparum* malaria, which is widespread in the southern part of Vietnam.

The illness develops 10 to 14 days after being bitten by the mosquito and symptoms consist of high fever with alternate shivering and sweating, intense headaches, and usually nausea or vomiting. Without treatment the condition is fatal within two weeks in up to 25% of cases. It is this variety of malaria which is now showing widespread resistance to the most common anti-malarial drug, chloroquine. The problem is especially serious in the Mekong River delta.

P vivax malaria is the other main type and the two rarer types are similar to *vivax*. *P vivax* malaria may be severe, but is not dangerous to life. However, if not adequately treated, the illness will continue to recur, causing chronic ill-health.

Malaria is a risk year-round in most parts of Vietnam below 1200 metres. The locals have some natural immunity to malaria resulting from generations of exposure; foreigners from nontropical countries have no such resistance. While it is not yet possible to be inoculated against malaria, limited protection is simple: either a daily or weekly tablet (the latter is more common). The tablets kill the parasites in your bloodstream before they have a chance to multiply and cause illness.

If you're travelling with children or if you're pregnant then the story with anti-malarial tablets is more complex (see Lonely Planet's *Travel with Children* for more details). Basically, the problem is that some anti-malarials may stay in your system for up to a year after the last dose is taken and may cause birth defects. So if you get pregnant or are planning to get pregnant within 12 months of taking anti-malarials your unborn child could be endangered. With newer drugs there's not much information around on the effects of long-term use. It should be noted that malaria *can* be passed from mother to child at birth.

A sensible precaution is to avoid being bitten in the first place. Most Vietnamese hotels are equipped with mosquito nets and you'd be wise to use them. In the evenings when mosquitoes are most active, cover bare skin, particularly the ankles. Use an insect repellent – any brand that contains the magic ingredient diethyl-toluamide ('deet') should work well. Autan and Off! are two such popular brands widely available in Asia. The liquid form of this stuff often comes in a leaky bottle, making for a rather messy backpack – you can avoid this hassle if you buy it in stick form. Mosquito coils work well, though the smoke thus produced irritates the lungs and eyes. Having an electric fan blowing on you while you sleep is very effective at keeping the mossies away, but you might wind up with a cold instead. Finally, it's been found that large doses of vitamin B complex are excreted through the skin and seem to act as a mild mosquito repellent, but don't count on this alone.

Treating malaria is complicated and something you should not undertake yourself except in an emergency. Blood tests are needed to determine if you in fact have malaria rather than dengue fever (see next section), and the choice of drugs depends on how well you react to them (some people are allergic to quinine, for example). However, if you are far from hospitals and doctors, you may have no other choice than self-treatment, except to die. The most common drugs for treatment are fansidar and quinine (often taken in combination), but note that these drugs are not candy – allergic reactions can occur and are sometimes fatal. And even if you think you've cured yourself, you still need to get to a hospital and have blood tests – otherwise there is the strong possibility of relapse.

For prevention, the most common antimalarial drugs are chloroquine, maloprim and doxycycline (the latter for very short-term use only), but new drugs are constantly under development. Chloroquine and maloprim are often prescribed by doctors to be taken in combination in order to guard against resistance to either one, but in the long term this is not a good practice. A lot of travellers are confused about what they should and should not be taking for malaria prevention – you should definitely consult a doctor before taking anything.

A brief rundown on common anti-malarial drugs follows (note that all dosages are for adults):

Chloroquine The most commonly prescribed drug for malaria prevention, it is extremely effective against *P vivax* malaria but only about 60% effective against *P falciparum*. Chloroquine is safe in pregnancy. Long-term use (over five years) of chloroquine has caused permanent retinal damage to the eyes in some people. Other side effects which have been reported include nausea, dizziness, headache, blurred vision, confusion, and itching, but such problems are rare.

Chloroquine tablets are available in at least two sizes, small (250 mg) or large (500 mg). Make sure you know which you have. The preventative dose is 500 mg weekly (either two small tablets or one large). You have to start taking the tablets two weeks before entering the malarial zone and continue taking them for about four to six weeks after you've left it.

Chloroquine can be used as a treatment for *P vivax*. Treatment dose is 1000 mg initially, then 500 mg at six, 24 and 48 hours.

Maloprim This is an effective malarial preventative especially if combined with chloroquine. This drug can cause severe (even life-threatening) allergic reactions in sensitive people. Because of the danger of such side effects, maloprim should be taken only once a week even though higher dosages would be more effective. It is not recommended during pregnancy. Long-term use (over three months) can reduce the white blood cell count in some people. This drug is fairly expensive.

Doxycycline This is a good preventative for the short-term (under one month) traveller. It's definitely not recommended for long-term use.

Doxycycline is a long-acting tetracycline (antibiotic). It is not recommended during pregnancy, breastfeeding or for children under age 10. Side effects include nausea, photosensitivity (severe sunburn) and vaginal yeast infections in women. It should not be taken with milk products.

The preventative dose is 100 mg (one pill) daily. Treatment dose (with quinine) is 100 mg two times daily for seven days. You should start taking doxycycline the day you enter the malarial area, and stop taking it the day you leave. Doxycycline is often taken in combination with chloroquine.

Fansidar This is an effective treatment against *P falciparum* malaria but fansidar is a poor drug against *P vivax*. It is only used as a treatment (*not* a preventative) because of the risk of severe allergic reactions. Also it is not recommended during pregnancy, especially the last trimester. It should not be taken at all if there is a history of sulfa allergy.

For treatment, three tablets are taken in a single

dose. Fansidar is usually taken in combination with quinine.

Quinine This is the drug of choice for treating severe and resistant *P falciparum* malaria and cerebral malaria. It should *only* be used as a treatment, not as preventative.

Quinine is taken for at least five days with tetracycline, doxycycline or fansidar. The dose is 600 mg every eight hours. If given alone, it should be continued for at least eight days (until blood slide is clear) or for 14 days if no blood test is available. It is safe in pregnancy, but should be used sparingly. Side effects include ringing in the ears, headache, nausea, decreased hearing, tremor, and allergic reactions (sometimes severe).

There is some resistance to quinine and it is a bit less effective against *P vivax* than chloroquine.

Qing Haosu (Artemesinine) This herbal medicine from China has generated much interest in medical circles recently. Qing haosu has been known since at least the 4th century when it was used to treat fevers, but only recently has its anti-malarial properties been established. It's important to note that just because this is an 'herbal medicine' it does not mean that it's harmless. Quinine – made from the bark of the cinchona tree – is also an herbal medicine but it is certainly not harmless. At the time of this writing, qing haosu was only available in China because studies have not yet been completed to determine the proper dosage and possible side effects. Preliminary testing in animals suggest it is toxic to the fetus and therefore not recommended in pregnancy.

Dengue Fever This is a mosquito-borne disease which resembles malaria, but is not fatal and doesn't recur once the illness has passed.

A high fever, severe headache and pains in the joints are the usual symptoms – the aches are so bad that the disease is also called breakbone fever. The fever usually lasts two to three days, then subsides, then comes back again and takes several weeks to pass. People who have had this disease say it feels like imminent death.

Despite the malaria-like symptoms, antimalarial drugs have no effect whatsoever on dengue fever. Only the symptoms can be treated, usually with complete bed rest, aspirin, codeine and an intravenous drip. There is no means of prevention other than to avoid getting bitten by mosquitos, but once you've had dengue fever, you're

immune for about a year. The patient should be kept under a mosquito net until after the fever passes – otherwise there is the risk of infecting others.

Eye Infections Trachoma is a common eye infection which is easily spread by contaminated towels which are handed out by restaurants and even airlines. The best advice about wiping your face is to use disposable tissue paper or moist towelettes ('Wet Ones' or similar brands). If you think you have trachoma, you need to see a doctor – the disease can damage your vision if untreated. Trachoma is normally treated with antibiotic eye ointments for about four to six weeks. Be careful about diagnosing yourself – simple allergies can produce symptoms similar to eye infections, and in this case antibiotics can do more harm than good.

Sexually Transmitted Diseases Vietnam, once famous for its legions of wartime prostitutes, will once again be famous for prostitution if present trends continue. Despite repeated declarations by the government that communism has eliminated such vices, prostitution is flourishing in Vietnam. The largest hotels in Ho Chi Minh City have massage services that can provide more than just relief from aching muscles. Some cheaper hotels have turned into veritable brothels and don't even offer a good night's sleep. The policies of ever-greedy local governments have allowed and even encouraged the proliferation of 'massage parlours' so that some towns are beginning to resemble the seedy sections of Thailand's provincial capitals. Beach resorts like Vung Tau and Nha Trang are starting to become famous for 'sex tours'. These cater mostly to the Japanese market but all with cash are welcome.

During the war, prostitutes often tried to cure themselves of sexually transmitted diseases (STDs), but by under-medicating themselves with antibiotics, penicillin-resistant strains of gonorrhoea and syphilis were created. During the Vietnam War, American soldiers referred to these diseases as 'Vietnam Rose'.

Sexual contact with an infected sexual partner spreads these diseases. While abstinence is the only 100% preventative, using condoms is also effective. Gonorrhoea and syphilis are the most common of these diseases; sores, blisters or rashes around the genitals, discharges or pain when urinating are common symptoms. Symptoms may be less marked or not observed at all in women. Syphilis symptoms eventually disappear completely but the disease continues and can cause severe problems in later years, and if untreated can be fatal. The treatment of gonorrhoea and syphilis is by antibiotics.

There are numerous other sexually transmitted diseases, for most of which effective treatment is available. However, there is neither a cure nor a vaccine for herpes and AIDS. Using condoms is the most effective preventative.

Given Vietnam's reputation for prostitution, AIDS (SIDA in Vietnamese) should be a major source of concern. In fact, almost no attention has been paid to AIDS until very recently. The first case of HIV infection (the virus which causes AIDS) detected in Vietnam was found in a 14-year-old girl when she applied for the Orderly Departure Program in 1990 (her application was rejected). Very little AIDS testing is going on because Vietnam has no money for it and no one wants to scare off the tourists.

AIDS can also be spread through infected blood transfusions; most developing countries cannot afford to screen blood for transfusions. It can also be spread by dirty needles – vaccinations, acupuncture, ear piercing and tattooing can potentially be as dangerous as intravenous drug use if the equipment is not clean. If you do need an injection it may be a good idea to provide the doctor with a new needle and syringe.

Hepatitis A Hepatitis is a disease which affects the liver. There are several varieties, the most common being hepatitis A and B, but there is another strain called non-A non-B. Hepatitis A occurs in countries with poor sanitation, of which Vietnam is definitely one. It's spread from person to person via infected food or water, or contaminated cooking and eating utensils. Salads which have been washed in infected water, or fruit which has been handled by an infected person, might carry the disease.

Symptoms appear 15 to 50 days after infection (generally around 25 days) and consist of fever, loss of appetite, nausea, depression, complete lack of energy, and pains around the bottom of your rib cage (the location of the liver). Your skin turns progressively yellow and the whites of your eyes change from white to yellow to orange.

The best way to detect hepatitis is to watch the colour of your urine, which will turn a deep orange no matter how much liquid you drink. If you haven't drunk much liquid and/or you're sweating a lot, don't jump to conclusions since you may just be dehydrated.

The severity of hepatitis A varies; it may last less than two weeks and give you only a few bad days, or it may last for several months and give you a few bad weeks. You could feel depleted of energy for several months afterwards. If you get hepatitis, rest and good food is the only cure; don't use alcohol or tobacco since that only gives your liver more work to do. It's important to keep up your food intake to assist recovery.

A vaccine for hepatitis A came on the market in 1992. It's not widely available yet, but it should be possible to get it. Check with your doctor.

Hepatitis B Hepatitis B is transmitted the same three ways the AIDS virus spreads: by sexual intercourse, contaminated needles, or genetically by an infant from an infected mother. Vietnamese 'health clinics' often reuse needles without proper sterilisation – no one knows how many people have been infected this way. Innocent use of needles – ear piercing, tattooing and acupuncture – can also spread the disease.

There is a vaccine for hepatitis B, but it must be given before you've been exposed. Once you've got the virus, you're a carrier for life and the vaccine is useless. Therefore, you need a blood test before the vaccine is

Top: Cholon Market, Cholon (RI)
Left: Notre Dame Cathedral, Saigon (DR)
Right: Museum, Saigon (OT)

Top: Reunification Hall, Saigon (RS)
Left: Nghia An Hoi Quan Pagoda, Cholon (TW)
Right: Cholon Market, Cholon (RI)

administered to determine if you're a carrier. The vaccine requires three injections, each given a month apart. Unfortunately, the vaccine is expensive.

As for those 'health clinics', it might be wise to buy your own needle and syringe if you need injections or must have blood samples taken while in Vietnam.

Hepatitis Non-A Non-B This is a blanket term formerly used for several different strains of hepatitis which have now been separately identified. Hepatitis C is similar to B but is less common. Hepatitis D (the 'delta particle') is also similar to B and always occurs in concert with it; it's occurrence is currently confined to IV drug users. Hepatitis E, however, is similar to A and is spread in the same manner, by water or food contamination.

Tests are available for these strands (except Hepatitis E) but are very expensive. Travellers shouldn't be too paranoid about this apparent proliferation of hepatitis strains; they are fairly rare (so far) and following the same precautions as for A and B should be all that's necessary to avoid them.

Rabies Even if you're a devout dog lover, you aren't likely to go around petting the stray dogs you encounter in Vietam. Third world dogs are not like the cute little fluffy creatures that play with children in the backyards of Western suburbia – they are often half-starved, badly mistreated and have been known to take a bite out of tourism.

Fido is likely to be even less friendly if infected with rabies. Although your chances of getting it is small, rabies is a disease worth guarding against. A vaccine is available but few people bother to get it. The vaccination requires three injections – once a week for three weeks – and is good for about two years. However, if you're bitten, the vaccine by itself is *not* sufficient to prevent rabies; it will only increase the time you have to get treatment, and you will require fewer injections if you've been vaccinated.

The rabies virus infects the saliva of the animal and is usually transferred when the rabid animal bites you and the virus passes through the wound into your body. It's important to realise that not only dogs carry rabies – any mammal which bites (like a rat) can transmit the virus. Also, if you have a scratch, cut or other break in the skin you could catch rabies if an infected animal licked that break in the skin. If you are bitten or licked by a possibly rabid animal you should wash the wound thoroughly (but without scrubbing since this may push the infected saliva deeper into the your body) and then start on a series of injections which will prevent the disease from developing. Once it reaches the brain, rabies has a 100% fatality rate. New rabies vaccines have been developed which have fewer side effects than the older animal-derived serums and vaccines.

The incubation period for rabies depends on where you're bitten. If on the head, face or neck then it's as little as 10 days, on the arms 40 days and on the legs 60 days. This allows plenty of time to be given the vaccine and for it to have a beneficial effect. With proper treatment administered quickly after being bitten, rabies will not develop.

Bilharzia Bilharzia (schistosomiasis) is not very common in Vietnam but occasional cases have been reported. Bilharzia is carried in water by minute worms. The larvae infect certain varieties of freshwater snails, found in rivers, streams, lakes and particularly behind dams or in irrigation ditches. The worms multiply and are eventually discharged into the water surrounding the snails.

They attach themselves to your intestines or bladder, where they produce large numbers of eggs. The worm enters through the skin, and the first symptom may be a tingling and sometimes a light rash around the area where it entered. Weeks later, when the worm is busy producing eggs, a high fever may develop. A general feeling of being unwell may be the first symptom; once the disease is established abdominal pain and blood in the urine are other signs.

Avoiding swimming or bathing in freshwater where bilharzia is present is the main method of preventing the disease. Even deep water can be infected. If you do get wet dry off quickly and dry your clothes as well. Seek medical attention if you have been exposed to the disease and tell the doctor your suspicions, as bilharzia in the early stages can be confused with malaria or typhoid.

If you cannot get medical help immediately, Niridazole is the recommended treatment. The recommended adult dosage is 750 mg (1½ tablets) taken twice daily for a week. Children aged between eight and 12 years should be given 500 mg (one tablet) twice daily for a week.

Prickly Heat & Fungus You can sweat profusely in tropical Vietnam; the sweat can't evaporate when the air itself is already moist, and before long you'll be dripping in it. Prickly heat is a common problem for people from temperate climates. Small red blisters appear on the skin where your sweat glands have been unable to cope with the amount of sweat you're generating. The problem is exacerbated because the sweat fails to evaporate. To prevent or cure it, wear clothes which are light and leave an air space between the material and the skin; don't wear synthetic clothing since it can't absorb the sweat; dry well after bathing and use calamine lotion or a zinc-oxide-based talcum powder. Anything that makes you sweat more – exercise, tea, coffee, alcohol – only makes the condition worse. You can also keep your skin dry with air-conditioning, electric fans or a trip to the cool mountains.

Fungal infections also occur more frequently in this sort of climate – travellers sometimes get patches of infection on the inside of the thigh. It itches like hell but is easy to clear up with an anti-fungal cream and powder.

Fungal ear infections usually result from swimming or washing in unclean water – Aquaear drops, available over-the-counter in Australia, are a preventative to be used before you enter or wash in the water. Some travellers carry a broad-spectrum antibiotic like Septrim to cure fungal infections. This is not a bad idea, although antibiotics can lower your resistance to other infections.

Athlete's foot is also a fungal infection, usually occuring between the toes. Wearing open-toed sandals will often solve the problem without further treatment because this permits the sweat to evaporate. It also helps to clean between the toes with a warm soapy water and an old toothbrush.

Worms – Roundworm, Threadworm & Hookworm In warmer climates where hygiene standards are low there are many forms of worm infestation. Some are spread by infected meat, some by infected fish, some by infected water, and others by faecally infected earth or food.

If you get roundworm, threadworm or hookworm, treatment is straightforward. Mebendazole (a generic name which is marketed under many different labels) is most effective – you just take one pill which is good for three months. Children under six months old, nursing mothers and pregnant women should not take it without first consulting a doctor.

Ascaris or roundworm is the most common worm infestation that plagues foreigners. The eggs are usually ingested through vegetables that have been grown using human faeces as manure, and which have not been properly washed; the eggs hatch in the stomach and then the larvae burrow through the intestines, enter the bloodstream and make their way through the liver to the heart, from where they work their way up to the lungs and the windpipe. They are then coughed up, swallowed and deposited in the intestines where they mature and grow up to from 20 to 35 cm (eight to 14 inches) long. The most common symptoms of adult roundworm infestation are abdominal discomfort increasing to acute pain due to intestinal blockage.

Threadworm eggs, when swallowed, hatch in the stomach. The worms enter the intestine where they grow and mate; the mature female worms make their way through the bowel to the anus where the depositing of their sticky eggs causes intense itching. One way to diagnose the presence of worms is to stretch a piece of adhesive tape over a flat stick, with the sticky area on the outside, and press it into the area around the anus. If there is an infestation you may be able to see worms and eggs on the tape – the mature worms look like little strands of cotton thread about 1.3 cm (half an inch) long.

Hookworms can be picked up by walking around in bare feet, in soil littered with infected faeces. The eggs hatch in the soil and then the larvae enter the bloodstream by burrowing through the skin. Following much the same internal route as the roundworm, they reach the intestine and hook onto the lining. By feeding on the host's blood, hookworms can grow up to 1.3 cm (half an inch) long. The most common result of hookworm infestation is anaemia, although they can also do damage to the organs they come into contact with. The best prevention is to wear shoes unless on the beach. Even with shoes on, if you walk through muddy water there is a chance of getting it. Hookworms can also be absorbed by drinking infected water or eating uncooked and unwashed vegetables.

Cuts, Bites & Stings

Snakes We speak here not of Vietnamese police, but of legless animals that crawl around on their bellies and make hissing noises. Vietnam has several poisonous snakes, the most famous being the cobra. There are many other poisonous species. *All* sea snakes are poisonous and are readily identified by their flat tails.

Fortunately, even poisonous snakes tend to be shy. Most snakebite victims are people who accidentally step on a snake. Be careful about walking through tropical areas with a lot of underbrush. Wearing boots gives a little more protection than running shoes.

Should you be so unfortunate as to get bitten, try to remain calm (sounds easier than it really is) and not run around. The conventional wisdom is to rest and allow the poison to be absorbed slowly. Tying a rag or towel around the limb to apply pressure slows down the poison, but the use of tourniquets is not advisable because it can cut off circulation and cause gangrene. Cutting the skin and sucking out the poison has also been widely discredited. Immersion in cold water is also considered useless.

Treatment in a hospital with an antivenin would be ideal. However, getting the victim to a hospital is only half the battle – you will also need to identify the snake. In this particular case, it might be worthwhile to kill the snake and take its body along, but don't attempt that if it means getting bitten again. Try to transport the victim on a makeshift stretcher.

All this may sound discouraging, but the simple fact is that there is very little first-aid treatment you can give which will do much good. Fortunately, snakebite is rare and the vast majority of victims survive even without medical treatment.

Sea Creatures Local advice is the best way of avoiding contact with these sea creatures with their stinging tentacles. Jellyfish generally get nastier the closer one gets to the equator and some species are potentially fatal, but stings from most jellyfish are simply rather painful. Dousing in vinegar will de-activate any stingers which have not 'fired'. Calamine lotion, antihistamines and analgesics may reduce the reaction and relieve the pain.

Other nasty sea creatures which can live in Vietnam's tropical coastal areas include sting rays and stonefish – be careful where you put your feet.

Wasps & Bees Wasps, which are common in the tropics, are a more serious hazard than snakes because they are more aggressive and will chase humans when stirred up. They won't attack unless they feel threatened, but if they do attack, they usually do so en masse. This is not just uncomfortable, it can be fatal. If you're out hiking and see a wasp nest, the best advice is to move away quietly. A few brainless people like to see how skilful they are at throwing rocks at wasp nests – this is not recommended. Should you be attacked, the only sensible thing to do is run like hell.

It would take perhaps 100 wasp or bee stings to kill a normal adult, but a single sting can be fatal to someone who is allergic. In fact, death from wasp and bee stings is more common than death from snakebite. People who are allergic to wasp and bee stings are also allergic to bites by red ants. If you happen to have this sort of allergy, you'd be wise to throw an antihistamine such as epinephrine into your first-aid kit. Epinephrine is most effective when injected, but taking it in pill form is better than nothing.

Agent Orange

Scientists have yet to assemble conclusive evidence of a link between the residues of chemicals used by the USA during the war and spontaneous abortions, stillbirths, birth defects and other human health problems. But almost all health professionals in Vietnam, faced with an abnormally high incidence of diseases known to be caused by dioxin and other chemicals found in the defoliant Agent Orange, are absolutely certain that such a link exists. Tests have determined that the soil of southern Vietnam has one of the highest levels of dioxin in the world whereas northern Vietnam, which was not defoliated, has one of the lowest levels of dioxin in the world. And statistics show that the rate of abnormal births is about four times as high in the south as in the north.

It is not clear what level of risk a visitor to Vietnam – especially a woman who is pregnant or soon-to-be-so – may face from these chemicals as a result of exposure to the air, water and food of the south. The risks of short-term low-level exposure are probably negligible. But because the effects are potentially devastating, women – especially those in the early months of pregnancy – may want to consider either postponing their visit or travelling only in the north. Or they may want to try to limit their intake of food and liquid to things unlikely to contain chemical residues, such as food grown in the north, imported tinned food, canned drinks, granola bars, etc. Bread made with foreign

grain would be ideal if you could be sure it wasn't Soviet wheat grown near Chernobyl...

Traditional Medicine

There are a number of traditional medical treatments practised in Vietnam. Herbal medicine, much of it imported from China, is widely available and sometimes surprisingly effective. The Cholon district of Ho Chi Minh City is probably the best all around place in Vietnam to go looking for herbal treatments. As with Western medicine, it's best not to experiment yourself but to see a doctor. Traditional medicine doctors, also mostly ethnic-Chinese, can be readily found wherever a large Chinese community exists.

If you visit a traditional Chinese-Vietnamese doctor, you might be surprised by what he or she discovers about your body. For example, the doctor will almost certainly take your pulse and then may tell you that you have a slippery pulse or perhaps a thready pulse. Traditional doctors have identified more than 30 different kinds of pulses. A pulse could be empty, prison, leisurely, bowstring, irregular or even regularly irregular. The doctor may then examine your tongue to see if it is slippery, dry, pale, greasy, has a thick coating or maybe no coating at all. The doctor, having discovered that you have wet heat, as evidenced by a slippery pulse and a red greasy tongue, will prescribe the proper herbs for your condition.

One traditional treatment is called moxibustion. Various types of herbs, rolled into what looks like a ball of fluffy cotton, are held just near the skin and ignited. A slight variation of this method is to place the herb on a slice of ginger and then ignite it. The idea is to apply the maximum amount of heat possible without burning the patient. This heat treatment is supposed to be good for such diseases as arthritis.

Another technique employs suction cups made of bamboo placed on the patient's skin. A burning piece of alcohol-soaked cotton is briefly put inside the cup to drive out the air before it is applied. As the cup cools, a partial vacuum is produced, leaving a nasty-looking but harmless red circular mark on the skin. The mark goes away in a few days.

The rather horrible-looking red marks seen on the necks of Vietnamese (especially in the Mekong Delta region) are not from some disease. Rather, they are the result of the cure. The marks are made by pinching the skin or scraping it vigorously with a coin or spoon. This is supposed to bring blood to the surface – and indeed it does – producing nasty looking welts that eventually heal. This is a treatment for the common cold, fatigue, headaches and other ailments. Whether the cure hurts less than the disease is something one can only judge from experience.

Can you cure people by sticking needles into them? The adherents of acupuncture say you can, and they have some solid evidence to back them up. For example, some major surgical operations have been performed using acupuncture as the only anesthetic (this works best on the head). In this case, a small electric current (from batteries) is passed through the needles.

Getting stuck with needles might not sound pleasant, but if done properly it doesn't hurt. Knowing just where to insert the needle is crucial. Acupuncturists have identified more than 2000 insertion points, but only about 150 are commonly used. The exact mechanism by which acupuncture works is not fully understood. Practitioners talk of energy channels or meridians which connect the needle insertion point to the particular organ, gland or joint being treated. The acupuncture point is sometimes quite far from the area of the body being treated.

Nonsterile acupuncture needles pose a genuine health risk in this era of the AIDS epidemic. You'd be wise to purchase your own if you wish to try this treatment.

Women's Health
Gynaecological Problems Poor diet, lowered resistance due to the use of antibiotics for stomach upsets and even contraceptive pills can lead to vaginal infections when travelling in hot climates. Keeping the genital area clean, and wearing skirts or loose-fitting trousers and cotton underwear will help to prevent infections.

Yeast infections, characterised by a rash, itch and discharge, can be treated with a vinegar or even lemon-juice douche or with yoghurt. Nystatin suppositories are the usual medical prescription. Trichomonas is a more serious infection; symptoms are a discharge and a burning sensation when urinating. Male sexual partners must also be treated, and if a vinegar-water douche is not effective medical attention should be sought. Flagyl is the prescribed drug.

Pregnancy Most miscarriages occur during the first three months of pregnancy, so this is the most risky time to travel. The last three months should also be spent within reasonable distance of good medical care, as quite serious problems can develop at this time. Pregnant women should avoid alcohol and all unnecessary medication, but vaccinations should still be taken where possible. Additional care should be taken to prevent illness and particular attention should be paid to diet and nutrition.

WOMEN TRAVELLERS
Like Thailand and other predominantly Buddhist countries, Vietnam is, in general, relatively free of serious hassles for women travellers. An important exception seems to be in or around cheap hotels where prostitution is a major part of the business.

The scarcity of public toilets seems to be a greater problem for women than for men. Vietnamese males can often be seen urinating in public, but this seems to be socially unacceptable for women. It is not very clear how Vietnamese women handle this situation.

DANGERS & ANNOYANCES
Undetonated Explosives
Four armies expended untold energy and resources for over three decades mining, booby-trapping, rocketing, strafing, mortaring, bombing and bombarding wide areas of Vietnam. When the fighting stopped most of this ordnance remained exactly where it had

landed or been laid; American estimates at the time placed the quantity of unexploded ordnance at 150,000 tonnes. After the war only small areas were effectively cleared of mines and other explosives.

Since 1975, many thousands of Vietnamese have been maimed or killed by this leftover ordnance while clearing land for cultivation or ploughing their fields. While cities, cultivated areas and well-travelled rural roads and paths are safe for travel, straying away from these areas could land you in the middle of a minefield which, though known to the locals, may be completely unmarked.

Never touch any rockets, artillery shells, mortars, mines or other relics of the war you may come across. Such objects can remain lethal for decades. In Europe, people are still sometimes injured by ordnance left over from WW II and even WW I, and every few years you read about city blocks in London or Rotterdam being evacuated after an old bomb is discovered in someone's backyard.

Especially dangerous are white phosphorus artillery shells (known to the Americans as 'Willy Peter'), whose active ingredient does not deteriorate as quickly as do explosives. Upon contact with the air the white phosphorus contained in the shells ignites and burns intensely; if any of it gets on your body it will eat all the way through your hand, leg or torso unless scooped out with a razor blade – imagine that. This stuff terrifies even scrap-metal scavengers. If you want to find out more about it, just ask the doctors at any provincial hospital in an area that saw heavy fighting.

And don't climb inside bomb craters – you never know what undetonated explosive device is at the bottom. Remember, one bomb can ruin your whole day.

Theft

Although the amount pinched by snatch thieves and pickpockets pales in comparison to what is raked in by high-ranking kleptocra's, it's the street crime that most worries travellers.

Vietnamese are convinced that their cities are very dangerous and full of criminals. Before reunification street crime was rampant in the South, especially in Saigon. Motorbike-borne thieves would speed down major thoroughfares, ripping pedestrians' watches off their wrists. Pickpocketing and confidence tricks were also common. After the fall of Saigon, a few bold criminals even swindled the newly arrived North Vietnamese troops. When a few such outlaws were summarily shot street crime almost disappeared overnight.

When the Vietnamese withdrawal from Cambodia was completed in 1989, the government accelerated its programme to cut military expenditures by discharging tens of thousands of soldiers from the army. Joining an already oversaturated job market without marketable skills and without government assistance in finding employment, many have been unable to earn a living. Angry that while they were in Cambodia most Vietnamese their age were building their lives, some have turned to crime. Crime rates – especially for break-ins and robberies – have risen precipitously all over the country in the past couple of years. The criminals have not overlooked the lucrative tourism sector.

The street crime for which Saigon and Cholon were infamous before 1975 has recently been making a comeback. Foreigners have occasionally reported having their eyeglasses snatched from their heads (keep yours on a cord to avoid this) and expensive pens plucked from their pockets by drive-by thieves on motorbikes. Pickpocketing – often involving kids, women with babies and even newspaper vendors – is also becoming a serious problem, especially in Ho Chi Minh City.

The street kids, no matter how cute and convincing, are quick with their hands. Watch it! They are *very* persistent indeed and often need to be physically shooed away like animals. If they can touch you, they can pickpocket you. Especially watch out for the 'under the newspaper' scam.

While changing money is usually safe in shops it is extremely inadvisable to change money on the street, especially in Ho Chi Minh City. And you should never leave your luggage unattended for even a moment.

Despite all this, you should not be overly paranoid. Although crime certainly exists and you need to be aware of it, theft in Vietnam does not seem to be any worse than elsewhere in the Third World. Don't assume that everyone's a thief – most Vietnamese are very poor but reasonably honest.

Violence

Unlike in some Western cities, recreational homicide is not a popular sport in Vietnam. Though someone took a pot shot at an obnoxious American journalist at Cu Chi a few years ago, the only other cases we know of physical attacks on foreigners have been against Americans who were mistaken for Russians! One traveller reported that he was assaulted twice in Haiphong by Vietnamese toughs shouting angrily *Lien Xo! Lien Xo!* (Soviet! Soviet!).

In general, violence against foreigners is extremely rare. Vietnamese thieves prefer to pick your pocket or grab your bag and then run away – knives, guns, sticks and other weapons are almost never used. However, you should take care in remote parts of the Central Highlands (where army deserters are said to hide out) and if you travel between towns alone at night by bicycle or motorbike. There are rumours that in areas with localised food shortages hungry people sometimes take to stopping and robbing vehicles, even tourist cars.

Beggars

Just as you're about to dig into the scrumptious Vietnamese meal you've ordered, you feel someone gently tugging on your shirtsleeve. You turn around to deal with this latest 'annoyance' only to find it's a boney eight-year-old boy holding his three-year-old sister in his arms. The little girl has a distended stomach, her palm is stretched out to you and her hungry eyes fixed on your plate of steaming chicken, vegetables and rice.

This is the face of poverty. How do you

deal with these situations? If you're like most of us, not very well. On occasion, we've given food to a small group of beggars and watched in horror as they fought over it. Give or refuse as you wish, and spare a moment to think of just how lucky you are.

The Police

Vietnam has the best police force that money can buy. This might sound overly cynical, but it seems to be true. Almost every Vietnamese will tell you that it does no good whatsoever to report thefts to the police unless, of course, you are willing to pay the police for their assistance.

Even worse is that many police are little more than criminals themselves. There have been numerous cases of travellers being arbitrarily stopped by the police (or soldiers) to 'check their papers', some discrepancy is noted and an on-the-spot 'fine' is demanded. It's often possible to talk your way out of these situations or have the 'fine' reduced. During the research of this edition, Robert Storey was stopped while trying to leave Ho Chi Minh City, his passport checked, no discrepancy was found but the police demanded a fine anyway. The 'fine' was eventually negotiated down from US$20 to US$1.50, and needless to say, no receipt was issued. During the research of the first edition, author Daniel Robinson was detained by the police in Hanoi and then expelled from the country, because he was taking notes (an obvious act of espionage).

There have been some genuine horror stories, though fortunately, these are occurring less frequently. The US State Department issued the following travel advisory which – though somewhat outdated and aimed at American citizens – should be contemplated by all foreign travellers who visit Vietnam:

An increasing number of Americans travel to Vietnam. Most have no problems. However, Vietnamese authorities have detained a few Americans and other foreigners without charges or for activities that would not be considered crimes in the United States. Some of those detained have been held incommunicado for months without any contact with US authorities or their families. There have been cases where release from confinement was contingent on the payment of a large fine.

Travellers should arrive with a proper visa. Once in country, visitors should comply with conditions of entry, including place and duration of stay. Visitors can also reduce risks of detention by avoiding involvement in politics or unsanctioned religious activities while in Vietnam and by declining to carry papers that are political or of unknown content.

The Vietnamese security apparatus may place American visitors under surveillance simply because they are foreign. Visitors who fail to keep their documentation fully in order or who engage in activities defined suspicious may be detained, along with their Vietnamese contacts, relatives and friends. The Vietnamese authorities do not always inform the US government of arrests, nor can they be counted on to provide access to American citizens under detention.

To be fair, the problem of police corruption is not unique to Vietnam. The problems which plague many Third World police forces – very low pay, low morale and low education – exist elsewhere. The main problem is that the Vietnamese police seem to have almost unlimited power and they know it, and there seems to be no attempt to punish police who are openly corrupt unless they attempt to extort money out of someone who is politically powerful or well connected.

On the positive side, we can say that things have improved now that many countries have restored diplomatic relations with Vietnam. The local police are reluctant to arrest a foreigner knowing that it will likely mean getting involved with a foreign embassy and creating an international incident which could get the powerful Foreign Ministry in Hanoi involved.

If you do have some problems with the police, you might spare a thought for the Vietnamese people, who cannot complain to their embassy or leave the country. Now that the economy is improving, the police have discovered other sources of revenue besides robbing foreigners (ie extorting bribes from Vietnamese businesses). The prostitution business has proven particularly lucrative.

Drugs

During the Vietnam War, US troops were known to partake in large quantities of noxious weeds, hashish and stronger recreational chemicals. After 1975, the loss of American customers plus the communists' sophisticated police state apparatus and the country's extreme poverty suppressed domestic demand for drugs. However, the recent influx of foreign tourists along with economic progress has revived the drug trade. Besides domestic production, many drugs are smuggled in through Cambodia to Ho Chi Minh City, Vietnam's biggest consumer market.

Needless to say, the drug trade has its ugly side. There are many local heroin addicts in Ho Chi Minh City. In addition, there is corruption, and this can effect foreigners. The police are in a good position to extort money from the drug dealers, who in turn have good incentive to turn in Western customers – this satisfies the police who can extort huge fines from foreigners. You should also be aware that there are many plainclothes police in Vietnam – just because you don't see them doesn't mean they aren't there.

The drug export market has also been doing well, and Vietnam's reputation is such that customs officials at your next destination might vigorously search your luggage. In short, drug use in Vietnam is still a perilous activity and taking home samples is also a high-risk activity.

Cockroaches

While some travellers are amused by the antics of cockroaches, at least some people find them very disturbing. Vietnamese cockroaches are well fed and can grow to amazingly large size; some travellers refer to them as the 'Viet Cong'. Cockroach-infested hotel rooms are the norm in Vietnam, especially at the budget end of the scale.

Cockroaches are actually relatively easy to deal with if you come prepared. One way is to launch a chemical blitzkrieg against these beasties with insecticide, though such nerve-gas attacks might pose a hazard to your own health.

Boric acid (a white powder) is deadly poison to cockroaches if they so much as inhale the dust. This chemical is also very poisonous to humans if taken internally, but is harmless externally (mixed with water, boric acid is often used as eyewash). When checking into a hotel room, sprinkling some boric acid powder under the bed (not in the bed!), in the corners, on the washroom floor and along other likely cockroach routes, will have the desired effect. At first you might think there are more cockroaches than ever because the poison drives them out into the open, but after a few hours your room will be cockroach-free.

Boric acid can be purchased easily and cheaply in almost any pharmacy, both inside and outside Vietnam. Try to keep it in a reasonably sturdy container (not a plastic bag) – small, plastic jars are useful for this purpose. Some hazards: it's dangerous to keep around children, and some travellers report being harassed by Customs because of boric acid's physical resemblance to cocaine!

Rats

Even cockroach enthusiasts are generally reluctant to share a hotel room with rats. If you encounter rats in Vietnam, they are not likely to be the cute, fluffy white creatures forced to smoke cigarettes and drink Diet Coke in Western medical experiments. Rather, they are the grey, decidedly less friendly variety.

Avoiding nocturnal visits by these creatures is fairly simple; don't keep any food in your hotel room.

Noise

One thing that can be insidiously draining on your energy during a trip to Vietnam is noise. At night, there is often a competing cacophony from motorbikes, dance halls, cafes, video parlours, restaurants and so on; if your hotel is situated near any of the above (and it's unlikely to be in a totally noise-free zone), sleep may be difficult. In some places, such as Nha Trang, even the small carts of ice cream and snack vendors have a booming, distorted portable cassette player attached.

Fortunately, most of the noise subsides around 10 or 11 pm, as few clubs stay open much later than that. Unfortunately, though, the Vietnamese are very early risers; most people are up and about from around 5 am onwards. This not only means that traffic noise starts early, but that you're likely to be woken up by the crackle of cafe speakers, followed by very loud (and often atrocious) local or foreign music. It's worth trying to get a hotel room at the back, so the effect of street noise is diminished (especially in Ho Chi Minh City with its motorcycle 'raceways'). Other than that, perhaps you could consider bringing a set of earplugs.

WORK

From 1975 to about 1990, Vietnam's foreign workers were basically technical specialists and military advisors from Eastern Europe and the now-defunct Soviet Union. The declining fortunes of the Eastern Bloc has caused most of these advisors to be withdrawn.

Vietnam's opening to the West has raised speculation about work opportunities. Unfortunately, such opportunities are still decidedly limited. Most of the Westerners living in Vietnam either work for official foreign organisations such as the United Nations and embassies, or else have been hired by private foreign companies attempting to set up joint-venture operations. Some Western journalists and photographers manage to make a living in Vietnam by selling their stories and pictures to Western news organisations.

While many Vietnamese young people are genuinely interested in learning English, as far as we know, government schools in Vietnam are not hiring any foreign teachers. Certainly one reason for this is a lack of money with which to pay foreigners. However, another reason seems to be the government's paranoia; Westerners might pollute the students' minds with bourgeois foreign ideas.

However, there is a budding free market

tutoring. Ho Chi Minh City's ...veaux riches (there aren't many) have a practical reason for studying English – namely, to do business with Western countries. And there are a few fledgling private academies which now teach English to those with the ability to pay. A scant few foreigners have managed to tap into this market for teaching English to upper-crust families, but pay is pretty dismal at around US$1.25 per hour. On the other hand, this is over 10 times what most Ho Chi Minh City residents earn. While this is no way to get rich, it is one way to visit Vietnam on a shoestring.

Attitudes will probably change in the not-too-distant future and foreigners should be able to find employment in Vietnamese universities. However, if and when this happens, don't expect to make any money from teaching English. As in China, Mongolia and other reforming communist countries, foreign teachers are likely to be hired as volunteers with salaries set at the subsistence level. Nevertheless, this is one way to experience life in a foreign country and get to know the local people.

When the USA re-establishes diplomatic relations with Vietnam, US citizens might be able to find volunteer work with the US Peace Corps. Citizens of the UK might want to contact the British Consul to find out about similar opportunities. Organisations like the International Red Cross might also be able to advise you.

ACTIVITIES
Swimming & Snorkelling
With 3260 km of mostly tropical coastline, Vietnam would seem like Asia's answer to Queensland or the Spanish Riviera. Indeed, there are some excellent beaches, though not quite as many as you'd expect. Part of the reason is that the southern part of the country (which has the best tropical climate and highest population) is dominated by the huge Mekong Delta. While this region is lush, green and lovely, it's also very muddy and the beaches tend to be mangrove swamps. One of the few beach areas in this region is

Ha Tien, right on the Cambodian border and facing the Gulf of Thailand.

The southernmost good beach on the east coast is Vung Tau, a very popular place just north of the Mekong Delta and very close to Ho Chi Minh City. Without a doubt, Nha Trang has emerged as Vietnam's premier beach resort in part because of its year-round lovely weather. Heading north towards Danang are numerous other good beaches, mostly undeveloped, but the weather becomes more seasonal – May to July is the best time, while during the winter powerful rip tides make swimming dangerous. North of Hué, the weather becomes truly awful with frequent storms and typhoons. But in the far north near Haiphong, summers are usually fine and the beaches often crowded.

Most Vietnamese people love the beach but have a respectful fear of the sea – they like to wade up to their knees but seldom dive in and go for a proper swim. Where you are most likely to see Vietnamese actually swimming is in rivers and public swimming pools. Surfing and windsurfing have not caught on yet, but it seems only a matter of time. It is possible to hire snorkelling gear and scuba equipment at most beach resorts. One might shudder at the possibility, but we may be witnessing another Kuta Beach in the making.

Gambling
After being banned by the Communists for 14 years, gambling, that most bourgeois capitalist activity, is staging a comeback. Horse racing is once again popular in Saigon (see the Ho Chi Minh City chapter). Slot machines have popped up in pubs and nightclubs – these are now legal as 'entertainment machines'.

You can easily avoid the horse racing and slot machines if you don't want to play, but you'll have a hard time escaping the state lottery. Touts selling lottery tickets will approach you anytime and anywhere, and they are usually *very* persistent.

While your chances of winning are miniscule, hitting the jackpot in the state lottery can make you a dong multimillionaire. The smallest denomination lottery ticket is 1000d (less than US$0.10) while the largest prize is 25 million dong (somewhat less than US$2500).

The official state lottery has to compete against an illegal numbers game *(danh de)* reputed to offer better odds. Two of the most popular forms of illegal gambling are dominoes *(tu sat)* and cock fighting. Some of the ethnic Chinese living in the Cholon district of Ho Chi Minh City are said 'to be keen mahjong players.

The government has been discussing opening up-market gambling casinos to help foreigners part with their spare hard currency.

Golf

The Vietnam International Club in Ho Chi Minh City was under construction at the time of this writing. This is to be a joint-venture operation between a Taiwanese investor and the ever-enterprising Saigon Tourist. Other clubs are either under construction or already operating in Song Be Province, Vung Tau and Hanoi.

Language Courses

If you'd like to learn to speak Vietnamese, courses are now being offered in Ho Chi Minh City and the prices charged are not unreasonable.

The courses are conducted by the Asia-Pacific Research Centre (☎ 352020, 352021, 358149), Ho Chi Minh City University of Education, 280 An Duong Vuong St, District 5, Ho Chi Minh City. The Saigon Tourist can also provide you with information about these language courses.

The rates currently being charged are as follows (prices in US dollars):

Duration	Sessions	Price
two weeks	12	$40
four weeks	50	$150
four weeks	80	$200
eight weeks	100	$300
16 weeks	150	$450
16 weeks	200	$600

Applicants who are foreign university students are offered a 25% reduction of the foregoing fees. For an additional (also reasonable) fee, the university can arrange your accommodation and visa extensions.

HIGHLIGHTS

Vietnam offers tremendous variety and can suit many different tastes – it's difficult to say just what places should be on the top of your list. But if we had to choose, certainly Dalat -- with its parklike setting, waterfalls, ethnic minorities and cool mountain climate – would rate high priority. Beach lovers will almost certainly want to check out Nha Trang. The splendid rock formations, sea cliffs and grottoes of Halong Bay could easily rate as one of the wonders of the world. The islands around Vinh Long give perhaps the best glimpse of rural Mekong Delta life. For those willing to endure a rugged (and somewhat expensive) jeep trip, Dien Bien Phu offers spectacular scenery in one of Vietnam's most wild and remote areas.

History and architecture buffs will be attracted to Hué and Hoi An. For those fascinated by the Vietnam War and all its implications, what better place to pursue the topic than the old Demilitarised Zone (DMZ)?

Finally, one should not forget the cities. Freewheeling Saigon with its dilapidated colonial elegance, outstanding food and bustling nightlife is a laboratory for Vietnam's economic reforms. Hanoi, with its monuments, parks, lakes and tree-lined boulevards, is the beguiling seat of power in a country trying to figure out which direction to head.

ACCOMMODATION

There are now regulations requiring hotels and guest houses to maintain certain standards before they can be approved to receive foreign guests (you'd never know it by some of the dumps around). So it is possible that you will front up to what seems like a perfectly serviceable hotel and be refused a room even if the place is empty. In that case, there is little point arguing; if the government (the police) says 'no foreigners', it means 'no'. Hotel owners aren't going to risk 're-education' just to rent you a room, though they may advise you of other places which can accept foreigners.

Regulations require hotels to hold the identity cards of domestic guests for the duration of their stay (a system borrowed from the Soviets). For foreigners, it's usual to hold the visa, but not the passport. In many cases (but not all), the hotel registers guests with the local police. It is at this point that most travellers encounter problems with the police if their papers are not in order: for a brief period, a specific individual (a hotel clerk, a police official) has personal responsibility to make sure that you are supposed to be there.

At most hotels, you will not be requested to pay in advance, but remember that they've got your visa. Before you depart, it is usual for the staff to check your room to make sure that you don't have any kleptomaniac tendencies (are the towels and TV set still there?).

Camping

Perhaps because so many millions of Vietnamese spent much of the war years living in tents (either as soldiers or refugees), camping is not the popular pastime it is the West. Even in Dalat, where youth groups often come for out-of-doors holidays, very little proper equipment can be hired. For more information on camping in the Dalat area, see the Central Highlands chapter.

Dormitories

While there are dormitories (nha tro) all around Vietnam (especially at railway stations), these are now officially off limits to foreigners. Considering the very high risk of being robbed while you sleep, it doesn't really make much sense to stay in a dormitory to save money.

Hotels

Until 1989 'capitalist' tourists were allowed to stay in only a few large tourist-class hotels that required payment in US dollars cash. These days, all sorts of options are available,

ranging from almost-international-standard hotels in Ho Chi Minh City to district-level official guesthouses without electricity. The particulars of what is available are listed under each city and town in the Places to Stay section.

Most hotels are government owned, but there is an increasing number of private hotels. These are usually called 'mini-hotels'.

Official policy is to insist that 'capitalist tourists' pay double what Vietnamese pay, but even so, the prices are still reasonable, ranging from US$4 to US$15 a night for low-end accommodation. However, prices tend to be higher in the north simply because old-style attitudes towards 'rich capitalists' still prevails.

A few hotels might try to charge the foreigners' price for your Vietnamese guide and/or driver as long as they know that you're paying the bill. This is not on – if they stay in a separate room, they should be charged like any local tourist. Don't accept this nonsense from anyone.

There has also been a tendency for some hotels serving the domestic market to prepare exorbitant price lists for presentation to the first hapless foreigners to show up at the front desk. Other establishments, however, have realised that reasonable prices bring more tourists, who bring in badly needed cash. The point is, some of the 'bottom end' places may become 'mid-range' and vice versa, so do not pass up a place simply because once upon a time (the day we were there) they were not the best deal around. Again, expect more problems in the north.

The best hotels in Ho Chi Minh City and Hanoi can be booked out weeks in advance. The need for more world-class hotel rooms has not been lost on hawk-eyed investors, and Ho Chi Minh City and Hanoi are continually abuzz with rumours of new hotel deals. The rumour that the bankrupt floating hotel from Australia's Great Barrier Reef would come to the Saigon River turned out to be true. Will Saigon's Holiday Inn be finished on schedule (or ever)? Will Club Med's much-heralded beach resort actually be built? Stay tuned...

During the festival of Tet (New Year), which usually falls in late January or early February, Vietnam's hotels are packed with domestic tourists and Overseas Vietnamese visiting relatives. Tet is a wonderful time to see Vietnam at its most festive, but before, during and after the week-long festivities it is extremely difficult to find accommodation at any price.

Vietnam Tourism may tell you that you can only stay in their dollar-priced hotels – don't listen to them. Smaller hotels (most run by the various echelons of provincial and municipal government, state companies, government ministries and even private entrepreneurs) are aware of the benefits of admitting foreign guests.

Many such places have yet to set their prices for 'capitalist' tourists. Some of those that have have unwittingly priced themselves out of the market, and others will take their sudden popularity with Western travellers as a cue to raise their rates. As market forces become a major factor in pricing (with different sectors of the centralised economy competing for tourist dong) hotel managers will learn, by trial and error, what the market will bear and tariffs will stabilise.

In hotels for domestic travellers Westerners are ofte: steered towards the most expensive room available. If you prefer something simpler, quickly look around for a posted price list and point good-naturedly to the prices. At this point, younger travellers might try producing documentation of their status as a stu lent – the more impressively official-looking the better – which can also serve to establish that you are younger than they think. Explain that you are not rich and a cheaper room may suddenly become available.

The Vietnamese seem to be absolutely obsessed with air-conditioning which has become a big prestige item. If you travel with Vietnam Tourism guides, don't be surprised if they insist on an air-con room (which costs three times as much a a room with fan) and then complain the next morning that they couldn't sleep because the room was too cold.

For some reason, practically no hotels in Vietnam have screens on the windows. Maybe the cold air from the air-conditioning is supposed to drive the insects away.

It is a good idea to keep all hotel receipts, especially if you are staying for more than a few days. Confusion, sometimes intentional, often arises over how many days you have paid for and how much you still owe. This is especially true of cheaper places with chaotic bookkeeping, since one shift at the front desk has no clue about what people from other shifts have and have not done.

The following are some of the more common hotel names and their translations:

Bong Sen	lotus
Cuu Long	nine dragons
Doc Lap	independence
Ha Long	descending dragon
Hoa Binh	pence
Huong Sen	lotus fragrance
Huu Nghi	friendship
Thang Long	ascending dragon
Thong Nhat	reunification
Tu Do	freedom

Hotel Security Hotel security can be a problem. Even though there may be a guard on each floor, the guards usually have keys to your room. Supposedly, they are responsible if anything gets stolen, but reports from travellers indicate that this often means nothing. The worst problem seems to be in hotels with 'number names' like 'Khach San 44', etc. These places are often owned by the police or military – if your Walkman gets stolen here, you're likely to see a policeman the next day walking around wearing it.

Privately run or joint-venture hotels are *usually* better – the owners don't want trouble with the authorities. Don't leave cameras, passports and other valuables in your room. Many hotel rooms come equipped with a closet which can be locked – if so, use it. If your room or the hotel's front desk has a safe, you can make use of it. A few hotels have a place where you can attach a

Toilets

The issue of toilets and what to do with used toilet paper has caused some concern. As one traveller wrote:

We are still not sure about the toilet paper...in two hotels they have been angry with us for flushing down the paper in the toilet. In other places it seems quite OK though.

In general, if you see a wastepaper basket next to the toilet, that is where you should throw the toilet paper. The problem is that in many hotels, the sewage system cannot handle toilet paper. This is especially true in old hotels where the antiquated plumbing system was designed in the pre-toilet paper era. Also, in rural areas there is no sewage treatment plant – the waste empties into an underground septic tank and toilet paper will really create a mess in there. For the sake of international relations, be considerate and throw the paper in the wastepaper basket.

Toilet paper is seldom provided in the toilets at bus and railway stations or in other public buildings, though hotels usually have it. You'd be wise to keep a stash of your own with you at all times while travelling around.

If you're wondering what poor Vietnamese do when they can't afford toilet paper (many actually cannot), the answer is simple; they use water and the left hand. There is often a bucket and water scoop next to the toilet for just such a purpose. Those who have been to other parts of South-East Asia should be well familiar with the procedure.

And while we're on this subject, another thing you need to be mentally prepared for is squat toilets. For the uninitiated, a squat toilet has no seat for you to sit on while reading the morning newspaper; it's a hole in the floor. The only way to flush it is to fill the conveniently placed bucket with water and pour it into the hole. While it takes some practice to get proficient at balancing yourself over a squat toilet, at least you don't need to worry if the toilet seat is clean. Furthermore, experts who study such things (scatologists?) claim that the squatting position is better for your digestive system.

Better hotels will have the more familiar Western-style sit-down toilets, but squat toilets still exist in cheaper hotels and in public places like restaurants, bus stations, etc. ■

padlock to the outside of the door rather than a lock built into the door itself. At such hotels you will be provided with a padlock, but you'd be wise to bring your own which means that you'll have the only key (don't lose it!).

Rental

It's possible to arrange to stay in the homes of local people, but the family has to report all foreign visitors to their homes – even relatives – to the local police.

Renting a medium-sized house in Ho Chi Minh City costs about US$15 per month for a Vietnamese family. Foreigners can rent cheaply directly from a family or landlord, but it's wise to report to the police that you are paying a bundle even if you are paying a pittance. The authorities are not happy with foreigners getting off cheaply.

FOOD

One of the delights of visiting Vietnam is the amazing cuisine – there are said to be nearly 500 different traditional Vietnamese dishes – which is, in general, superbly prepared and very reasonably priced. The Vietnamese are particularly fond of seafood, but they do equally well at preparing chicken, beef, pork and vegetable dishes. Regional specialities are mentioned at the beginning of the Places to Eat listing in each section.

The proper way to eat Vietnamese food is to take rice from the large shared dish and put it in your rice bowl. Using your chopsticks, take meat, fish or vegetables from the serving dishes and add them to your rice. Then, holding the rice bowl near your mouth, use your chop sticks to eat. Leaving the rice bowl on the table and conveying your food, precariously perched between chop sticks, all the way from the table to your mouth strikes Vietnamese as odd, though they will be more amused than offended. When not eating, it is acceptable to set your chopsticks on flat across the top of your rice bowl. Sticking your chopsticks vertically into a rice bowl and leaving them there is very offensive (a classic Buddhist death sign).

The meat of some snakes and forest animals, prepared according to traditional recipes, is considered a delicacy by those who can afford it. Special restaurants around the country cater to this market, offering the fresh meat of such animals as cobras, deer, porcupines, bats, turtles, wild pigs and pangolins (scaly animals similar to anteaters). Often, the animals to be eaten are kept alive in cages inside the restaurant until ordered by a customer. A one-metre cobra weighing about one kg costs US$20. Whole cobras pickled in large glass jars with special Chinese spices are another favourite.

Vegetarian Food

Because Buddhist monks of the Mahayana tradition are strict vegetarians (at least they are supposed to be), Vietnamese vegetarian cooking (an chay) has a long history and is an integral part of Vietnamese cuisine. In general, the focus of vegetarian cuisine in Vietnam has been on reproducing traditional dishes prepared with meat, chicken, seafood or egg without including these ingredients. Instead, tofu, mushrooms and raw, dried, cooked and fermented vegetables are used. Because it does not include many expensive ingredients, vegetarian food is unbelievably cheap.

On days when there is a full or sliver moon (the beginning and middle days of the lunar month), many Vietnamese and Chinese do not eat meat, chicken, seafood or eggs – or even nuoc mam (fermented fish sauce). On such days, some food stalls, especially in the marketplaces, serve vegetarian meals. To find out when the next sliver or full moon will be, consult any Vietnamese calendar.

Places to Eat

You'll never have to look very far for food in Vietnam – restaurants of one sort or another seem to be in every nook and cranny. There are a wide variety of places to eat, including curb-side food stands, road-side food stalls, high-volume government-run eateries catering to locals, Chinese restaurants, Western-style cafes, hotel restaurants (which are usually quite good though more expensive than most restaurants), pastry shops, restaurants serving traditional (rather than everyday) Vietnamese dishes, and restaurants that specialise in the exotic (cobra, etc).

Most places can rustle up something Western (such as a steak with chips) if you're desperate. For some inexplicable reason, tour groups are often served Western food unless the participants specifically request a Vietnamese menu. Occasionally, the Western food is truly awful – Vietnamese hamburgers are not an outstanding success, and the peanut butter (with crunchy sugar granules) is so sweet it can turn your teeth inside out.

Unless you eat in exclusive hotels or aristocratic restaurants, food is very cheap. At the bottom of the barrel are street stalls where meals cost around US$0.20. Very casual restaurants with bamboo and cardboard walls have meals in the range of US$0.30 to US$0.50. Most decent restaurants can fill your stomach for US$1 to US$4. However, in classy restaurants (like Maxim's in Saigon) be aware that the small dishes of snacks which appear on the table cost money if you indulge (and are charged per person!). And in many restaurants, the fresh hand towels might be charged too – say 'no thanks' if you object to paying US$0.10 for a hand wipe. Check out the bill very carefully:

Overcharging seems to be standard practice when more than one person orders food or when many items are listed on the bill. I would say a good 50% of the time we were initially overcharged. After going over the menu and bill item by item and correcting with a pencil each problem and showing we didn't use the wash clothes or eat the appetiser nuts, the waitresses or waiters usually shamelessly and unapologetically accepted our corrections.

Rice and soup stalls along highways can be identified by signs reading 'Com Pho'.

Your best bet for a late meal (after 8.30 pm) is usually a hotel restaurant.

To get the bill (check), politely catch the attention of the waiter or waitress and write in the air as if with a pen on an imaginary piece of paper.

Condiments

Nuoc mam (pronounced something like 'nuke mom') is a type of fermented fish sauce – instantly identifiable by its distinctive smell – without which no Vietnamese meal is complete. Though nuoc mam is to Vietnamese cuisine what soy sauce is to Japanese food, many hotel restaurants do not automatically serve it to foreigners, knowing that the odour may drive away their Western customers. Nuoc mam actually isn't bad once you get used to it, and some foreigners even go home with a few bottles in their luggage. The sauce is made by fermenting highly salted fish in large ceramic vats for four to 12 months.

If nuoc mam isn't strong enough for you, try mam tom, a powerful shrimp sauce which American soldiers sometimes called 'Viet Cong tear gas'.

Salt with chilli and lemon juice is often served as a condiment and most Westerners seem to like it.

On the other hand, monosodium glutamate (msg) gets mixed reviews from foreigners. It's salty and tasty, but some people have reported allergic reactions (the face gets all flushed and hot). Others just don't like the sodium (also found in ordinary table salt) which can raise the blood pressure in sensitive individuals. While msg is used all over Vietnam, food in the north is positively buried in it. Some useful terms:

msg
   mì chính (in the north)
   bột ngọt (in the south)
fish sauce
   nước mắm
shrimp sauce
   mắm tôm

Snacks

Vietnamese spring rolls are called cha gio (pronounced 'chow yau') in the south and nem Sai Gon or nem ran in the north. They are made of rice paper filled with minced pork, crab, vermicelli, moc nhi (a kind of edible fungus), onion, mushroom and eggs and then fried until the rice paper turns a crispy brown. Nem rau are vegetable spring rolls.

Banh cuon is a steamed rice pancake into which minced pork and moc nhi is rolled. It is served with a special sauce made from watered-down nuoc mam, vinegar, sugar, pepper, clove and garlic.

Oc nhoi is snail meat, pork, chopped green onion, nuoc mam and pepper rolled up in ginger leaves and cooked in snail shells.

Gio is lean pork seasoned and then pounded into paste before being packed into banana leaves and boiled.

Cha is pork paste fried in fat or broiled over hot coals. Cha que is cha prepared with cinnamon.

One thing you'll undoubtedly find for sale at street stalls everywhere is betelnut. This is not a food – swallow it and you'll be sorry! The betelnut is in fact the seed of the the betel palm (beautiful trees, by the way) and is meant to be chewed. The seed is usually sold with a slit in it, mixed with lime and wrapped in a leaf. Like tobacco, it's strong stuff that you first can barely tolerate but eventually get addicted to. The first time you bite into betelnut, your whole face gets hot – chewers say it gives them a buzz. Like chewing tobacco, betelnut causes excessive salivation – the result is that betel chewers must constantly spit. The disgusting reddish-brown stains you see on sidewalks are not blood but betel-saliva juice. Years of constant chewing causes the teeth to become stained progressively browner, eventually becoming nearly black. ■

Chao tom is grilled sugar cane rolled in spiced shrimp paste.

Dua chua is bean sprout salad that tastes vaguely like Korean kimchi.

There are a number of Western-style snack foods. Excellent French bread is available everywhere fresh daily, especially in the morning. Imported French cheese spread can be bought from street stalls for around US$1.50 per box and sometimes salami is also available.

Soups & Noodles

Pho is the Vietnamese name for the noodle soup that is eaten at all hours of the day but is a special favourite for breakfast. It is prepared by quickly boiling noodles and placing them into a bowl along with greens (shallots, parsley) and shredded beef, chicken or pork. A broth made with boiled bones, prawns, ginger and nuoc mam is then poured into the bowl. Some people take their pho with chilli sauce or lemon.

Lau is fish and vegetable soup served in a bowl resembling a samovar with the top cut off. Live coals in the centre keep it hot.

Mien luoi is vermicelli soup with eel seasoned with mushrooms, shallots, fried eggs and chicken.

Bun thang is rice noodles and shredded chicken with fried egg and prawns on top. It is served with broth made by boiling chicken, dried prawns and pig bones.

Xup rau is vegetable soup.

Canh khi hoa is a bitter soup said to be especially good for the health of people who have spent a lot of time in the sun.

The noodles served with Vietnamese soups are of three types: white, rice noodles *(banh pho)* clear noodles made from rice mixed with manioc powder *(mien)*, and yellow, wheat noodles *(mi)*. Many noodle soups are available either with broth *(nuoc leo)* or without *(kho, literally 'dry')*.

Main Dishes

The staple of Vietnamese cuisine is plain white rice dressed up with a plethora of vegetables, meat, fish and spices.

On menus, dishes are usually listed according to their main ingredient. For instance, all the chicken dishes appear together, as do all the beef dishes, and so on.

Cha ca is filleted fish slices broiled over charcoal. It is often served with noodles, green salad, roasted peanuts and a sauce made from nuoc mam, lemon and a special volatile oil.

Ech tam bot ran is frog meat soaked in a thin batter and fried in oil. It is usually served with a sauce made of watered-down nuoc mam, vinegar and pepper.

Rau xao hon hop is fried vegetables.

Bo bay mon are sugar-beef dishes.

Com tay cam is rice with mushrooms, chicken and finely sliced pork flavoured with ginger.

Some useful words to know include the following:

vegetables
   rau
vegetarian person
   người ăn chay
vegetarian restaurant
   tiệm cơm chay
white rice
   cơm trắng
bread
   bánh mì
butter
   bơ
boiled egg
   trứng luộc
fried egg
   trứng chiên (south), *trứng rán* (north)
cheese
   pho mát, pho mai

Cooking Methods

boiled
   luộc
boiled chicken
   gà luộc
broiled
   nướng

fried
   chiên (south), *rán* (north)
fried rice
   cơm chiên
steamed
   chưng (south), *hấp* (north)

Meat & Fish

beef
   thịt bò
chicken
   thịt gà
crab
   cua
crayfish
   tôm hùm
eel
   lươn
fish
   cá
frog
   ếch
oyster
   sò
shrimp
   tôm

Exotic Fare

bat
   con dơi
cobra
   rắn hổ mang
gecko
   con kỳ nhông, kỳ đà
goat
   con dê
pangolin
   con trút, con tê tê
porcupine
   con nhím
python
   con trăn
small hornless deer
   nai tơ
turtle
   con rùa
venison
   thịt nai
wild pig
   heo rừng

Desserts

Sweets *(do ngot)* and desserts *(do trang mieng)* you are likely to have an opportunity to sample include the following:

Banh chung, a traditional Tet favourite, is a square cake made from sticky rice and filled with beans, onion and pork and boiled in leaves for 10 hours.

Banh deo is a cake made of dried sticky rice flour mixed with a boiled sugar solution. It is filled with candied fruit, sesame seeds, fat, etc.

Banh dau xanh is mung bean cake. Served with hot tea it 'melts on your tongue'.

Mut (candied fruit or vegetables) is made with carrot, coconut, cumquat, gourd, ginger root, lotus seeds, tomato, etc.

Banh bao is a filled Chinese pastry that can most easily be described as looking like a woman's breast, complete with a reddish dot on top. Inside the sweet, doughy exterior is meat, onions and vegetables. *Banh bao* is often eaten dunked in soy sauce.

Banh it nhan dau, a traditional Vietnamese treat, is a gooey pastry made of pulverised sticky rice, beans and sugar. It is steamed (and sold) in a banana leaf folded into a triangular pyramid. You often see banh it nhan dau on sale at Mekong Delta ferry crossings. *Banh it nhan dua* is a variation made with coconut instead of beans.

Ice cream *(kem)* was introduced to Vietnam on a large scale by the Americans, who made ensuring a reliable supply of the stuff a top wartime priority. The US Army hired two American companies, Foremost Dairy and Meadowgold Dairies, to build dozens of ice cream factories all around the country. Inevitably, local people developed a taste for their product. Even 15 years after bona fide Foremost products ceased to be available in the Socialist Republic, the company's orange-and-white logo was prominently on display in shops selling ice cream. Recently, however, the government has been making an effort to purge the country of signs advertising foreign companies which no longer do business in Vietnam.

Ice cream served in a baby coconut *(kem dua* or *kem trai dua)* deliciously mixes ice cream, candied fruit and the jelly-like meat of young coconut.

Ice cream stalls usually sell little jars or plastic cups of sweetened frozen yoghurt (*yaourt*).

A number of sweet soups and local pastries are listed under Places to Eat in the Hué chapter.

Fruit

Fruit (*qua* or *trai*) is available in Vietnam all year round, but many of the country's most interesting specialities have short seasons. Vietnamese bananas will fool you – the green bananas sold in the marketplace are usually ripe enough to eat, and in fact taste better than the yellow ones.

Some of Vietnam's fruits include the following:

apple
bom, táo

apricot
lê

avocado
trái bơ

banana
trái chuối

coconut
trái dừa

custard apple
mãng cầu, quả na

durian
trái sầu riêng

grapes
nho

green dragon fruit
trái thanh long

guava
trái ổi

jackfruit
trái mít

jujube (Chinese date)
trái táo ta

khaki (resembles tomato)
hồng xiêm

lemon
chanh

longan
trái nhãn

lychee
trái vải

mandarin orange
trái quít

mangosteen
trái măng cụt

orange
trái cam

papaya
trái đu đủ

peach
trái đào

pineapple
trái khom, trái dứa

plum
mận, mơ

pomelo
trái bưởi, trái đôi

rambutan
chôm chôm

starfruit
trái khế

strawberry
trái dâu

tangerine
trái quít

three-seed cherry
trái sê ri

water apple
roi đường

watermelon
dưa hấu

Avocado is often eaten in a glass with ice and sweetened with either sugar or condensed milk.

Cinnamon apple is also known in English as custard apple, sugar apple and sweetsop. It is ripe when very soft and the area around the stem turns blackish.

Mature coconuts are eaten only by children or as jam. For snacking, Vietnamese prefer the soft jelly-like meat and fresher milk of young coconuts.

DRINKS
Nonalcoholic Drinks
Coffee Vietnamese coffee is fine stuff. Rather than instant coffee, the Vietnamese prefer to brew it right at the table, French style – a dripper with coffee grounds is over the cup and hot water poured in. If you prefer ice coffee, the same method is applied but with a glass of ice under the dripper.

Both the drippers and packaged coffee are favourite items with tourists looking for things to buy and take home.

Tea Vietnamese tea is cheap but disappointing – perhaps the best stuff is exported. Excellent Chinese tea is available but considerably more expensive. If you can't live without good tea, you'd better bring your own.

Mineral Water The selection of mineral water *(nuoc suoi)* has been expanding rapidly ever since the Vietnamese realised that foreigners were willing to pay good money for water sealed in plastic bottles.

Imported mineral water (from Indonesia) is now available for about US$1 per bottle. The Vietnamese brands are cheaper but quality varies. The Vietnamese-produced Vinh Hao carbonated mineral water is outstanding, especially when served with a bit of ice, lemon and sugar.

Coconut Milk There is nothing more refreshing on a hot day than fresh coconut milk *(nuoc dua)*, perhaps sweetened with a bit of sugar. Coconut milk is as hygienic and safe to drink as the vessel it is served in is clean. The Vietnamese believe that coconut milk, like hot milk in Western culture, makes you tired. Athletes, for instance, never drink it before a competition.

The coconuts grown around the Ha Tien area in the Mekong Delta are a special variety with very tasty milk and delicious coconut flesh.

Soft Drinks Tri Beco is a domestic soft-drink manufacturer producing strawberry, lychee and other fruity, flavoured carbonated drinks. It's not overly sweet, which means it does a better job at quenching your thirst than some of the sugary imported brands. Tri Beco Coca (cola) is a bit watery compared to the Western stuff but not bad.

Lemon soda *(so-da chanh)* is popular. An excellent domestic soft drink with a pleasant fruit flavour is called *nuoc khoang kim boi*; one bottle costs US$0.20.

Imported (smuggled?) Coca-Cola and Sprite in cans is widely available and costs slightly less than US$1.

Alcohol
Beer Vietnam has some of the world's cheapest prices for imported beers. Cans of Heineken, San Miguel, Tiger, Old Milwaukee, etc are available in hotels for US$1 and in the marketplaces sometimes for US$0.50.

Saigon Export (do they really export it?), Saigon Lager and 333 cost about ⅔ the price as the imported brands in cans and half that in bottles. Bottles of inferior Hanoi and Halida beers are available in the north for about the same price. Nameless regional beers, though watery and often flat, are available in bottles for a bit less than the name brands. On tap, they go for as little as US$0.10 per glass. One traveller described such 'no-label beers' as being a cross between light beer and iced tea.

Wine Vietnam produces over 50 varieties of wine *(ruou)*, many of them made from rice. The cheapest rice wines are used for cooking, not drinking, as you will find out to your displeasure if you drink them.

Hard Liquor Alcoholic beverages *(ruou manh)* from China are very cheap though vile. Russian vodka is one of the few things the former USSR has left to export. Locally produced Hanoi Vodka is also available.

Cobra blood is used to make a special alcoholic cocktail which is supposed to serve as an aphrodisiac.

Some useful terms for ordering Vietnamese drinks include the following:

water
  nước
boiled water
  nước sôi
ice
  nước đá
drinking water
  nước uống
cold water
  nước lạnh
mineral water
  nước suối
carbonated water
  nước sô-đa
lemon soda
  sô-đa chanh
orange soda
  sô-đa cam
tea
  nước trà (south), *nước chè* (north)
coffee
  cà phê
coffee with milk
  cà phê sữa
iced coffee
  cà phê đá
iced coffee & milk
  cà phê sữa đá
sugar
  đường
condensed milk
  sữa đặc
coconut milk
  nước dừa
yoghurt
  dao-ua
beer
  bia
glass
  cái ly
bottle
  cái chai

TOBACCO

Vietnamese men smoke like chimneys. The women almost never smoke, and for a woman to do so in public would indicate to most Vietnamese men that she's a prostitute.

As poor as Vietnam is, many men seem willing to spend their last dong on expensive imported cigarettes, especially American cigarettes. There are some dirt cheap home-grown brands like Dien Bien Phu (US$0.06) and Dalat (US$0.08), or the 'premium' brand Cholon filter cigarettes (US$0.20). Cheaper still is to buy tobacco and roll your own, but only a few older Vietnamese men do this – young people consider it terribly primitive.

Recently there has been a problem with counterfeit 'imported' cigarettes which look like the real thing, but smokers claim they can easily taste the difference.

Pipe tobacco and cigars also exist but have not proven popular, so if this is something you need, bring your own supply.

ENTERTAINMENT
Cinemas

Movie theatres are common in nearly all major towns and cities. Many urban maps have cinemas *(rap* in Vietnamese) marked with a special symbol.

Films from the former Eastern Bloc are fading fast, being replaced with Western movies which are either subtitled or dubbed. Vietnam now produces its own kungfu movies rather than importing all from China, Hong Kong and Taiwan. Love stories also are popular, but Vietnamese censors take a dim view of nudity and sex – murder and mayhem is OK.

Discos

Vietnam is one of the few places left where a major component of the nightlife is still ballroom dancing. Of course, these *soirées dansantes* have become more and more like discos in recent years, and the guests are likely to be affluent young people dressed in jeans and copies of the latest designer bootlegs from Bangkok, but the principle is the same. A place where dancing takes place is called a *vu truong* in Vietnamese; to dance is *khieu vu*.

After reunification, ballrooms and discos were denounced as imperialist dens of iniquity and were shut down by the authorities. Since around 1990 they have reopened, though certain forms of dancing (like Brazil's erotic dance, the lambada) remained banned. Young people unable to afford a night on the town often create impromptu discos with tape players and pirated rock music cassettes from the West. There are now even modern dance classes at public schools.

Karaoke

Some say it causes brain damage. Others say it's used by the government for brainwashing. Whatever it does, we do know that it originated in Japan and is rapidly spreading. And now karaoke has invaded Vietnam.

For those who haven't experienced karaoke, it's simply a system where you are supposed to sing along with a video. The words to the song are flashed on the bottom of the screen (a number of languages are possible) and participants are supplied with a microphone. Really fancy karaoke bars have superb audio systems and big screen video, but no matter how good the equipment, it's not going to sound any better than the ability of the singer. And with a few exceptions, it usually sounds awful.

While it has not proven quite so popular with Westerners, karaoke is taking over Asia. At the moment, karaoke bars are permitted in hotels and restaurants but the Vietnamese government doesn't allow them elsewhere. To find karaoke, look for signs advertising 'KTV' ('Karaoke TV', the Japanese answer to MTV).

Pubs

During the Vietnam War, pubs staffed with legions of prostitutes were a major form of R&R ('rest & relaxation') for American soldiers. After reunification, the pubs were shut down and the prostitutes were compelled to find other employment, like stoop labour in the rice paddies.

The pubs are back, at least in Saigon. Though these tend to be male-oriented businesses, there are a few places where women might feel comfortable having a drink. Such respectable pubs tend to be in the big tourist hotels. As time goes on, it's likely that some entrepreneurs will open places similar to British-style pubs with darts, food, live music and so on. Right now, such businesses are in their infancy.

Video Games

What the USA couldn't achieve with bombs and bullets is now being accomplished with a new, secret weapon. Video games are taking over Vietnam (though karaoke is giving it stiff competition). Never mind that people don't have enough to eat – almost everyone from well-heeled cadres to cyclo drivers and street beggars has a portable, hand-held video game. It's not unusual to see motorcycle drivers playing these games whenever they stop at traffic lights – some even try it while they're driving. We can only hope that these evil machines are banned from the cockpits of Vietnam Airlines flights.

For those who want the full effects of sound and colour, video-game parlours are just starting to spring up. Just how the government will cope with this latest imperialist assault upon the mental health of the Vietnamese people remains to be seen.

Video Parlours

Vietnam's opening to the outside world is creating massive headaches for the country's censors. Despite their best efforts, customs agents haven't been able to hold back the flood tide of video tapes which are smuggled into Vietnam. The pirating of video tapes has become big business and the tapes are sold or rented all over the country. Kung fu movies from Hong Kong and pornography from the West and Japan are much in demand. Ditto for the latest MTV (music &

TV) tapes. Video movies about the Vietnam War are also enthusiastically sought after – some popular war movies include *Rambo, Apocalypse Now, Full Metal Jacket, Platoon, The Deer Hunter, Good Morning Vietnam, Born on the 4th of July* and *Air America*.

Obviously, most Vietnamese cannot afford video equipment, but that hardly matters. Budding entrepreneurs have set up instant mini-theatres consisting of a video cassette recorder (VCR), a few chairs and curtains to keep out nonpaying onlookers. The admission price is very low, on the order of US$0.20. Some of these video parlours provide food and beverage services.

Spectator Sports
Football (soccer) is number one with spectators. Tennis has considerable snob appeal – trendy Vietnamese like to both watch and play. The Vietnamese are incredibly skilled at shuttlecock. Other favourites include volleyball and ping-pong.

THINGS TO BUY
Handicrafts
Handicrafts available for purchase as souvenirs include lacquerware items (see Folk Crafts in the Facts about the Country chapter for details on how they are made), mother-of-pearl inlay, ceramics (including enormous elephants), colourful embroidered items (hangings, tablecloths, pillow cases, pyjamas and robes), greeting cards with silk paintings on the front, wood-block prints, oil paintings, watercolours, blinds made of hanging bamboo beads (many travellers like the replica of the Mona Lisa), reed mats (rushes are called *coi* in the north, *lac* in the south), Chinese-style carpets, jewellery and leatherwork.

Objects made of ivory and tortoiseshell are on sale everywhere. Please remember that purchasing them directly contributes to the extinction of the world's endangered populations of elephants and sea turtles. And if that's not enough of an incentive to buy other souvenirs, maybe this is: ivory purchased in Vietnam might be confiscated by

Lacquerware

customs officials when you get home anyway.

Clothing
Ao dais are a popular item, especially for women. Ready-made ao dais cost about US$10 to US$20, while custom-tailored sets are notably more. Prices vary by the store and material used. If you want to buy custom-made clothing for your friends, you'll need their measurements; neck diameter, breast, waist, hip and length (from waist to hem). As a general rule, you get best results when you're right there and get measured by the tailor or seamstress.

Women all over the country wear conical hats, in part to keep the sun off their faces (though they also function like umbrellas in the rain). If you hold a well-made conical hat up to the light, you'll be able to see that between the layers of straw material are fine paper cuts. The best quality conical hats are produced in the Hué area.

Sandals are a practical item to take home, and cheap at around US$3.50. Finding large sizes to fit Western feet can be a problem, though. Make sure they are very comfortable before you purchase them – some tend to be poorly made and will give you blisters.

Stamps
Postage stamps already set in a collector's book are readily available near the GPO in major cities or at some hotel gift shops and bookstores. You can even find stamps from the now-extinct South Vietnamese regime.

Music
Saigon has an astounding collection of audio tapes for sale. Most are Vietnamese hits, and

there are also the latest Chinese-language music tapes from Hong Kong and Taiwan (mostly soft rock). Hard rock from the West is not as popular, but there is a small and devoted core of avant-garde types who like it. Heavy metal tapes (mostly pirated) are available in the markets.

Old Cars

Assuming you are an automobile collector and have sufficient funds to support such an expensive habit, Vietnam is a worthwhile place to check out. During the war Saigon had a large population of resident US technical advisors, business people, journalists, diplomats, CIA agents, etc, many of whom bought imported American and European cars for personal use. When South Vietnam suddenly collapsed in 1975, the Americans had to flee abruptly, abandoning their vehicles in the process.

Ironically, Vietnam's severe poverty means that automobile owners take good care of their vehicles since replacements are unaffordable. So if you're in the market for a 1965 Ford Mustang, an Austin-Healey convertible or an old De Soto, this is the place to look. Automobiles easily exceed the 20 kg luggage weight limit imposed by Vietnam Airlines, so you'll have to make arrangements to ship the vehicle home by sea freight, unless you want to attempt a land crossing into Cambodia. Good luck.

US Government Restrictions

The rules may change, but at present US citizens and residents should take into account restrictions that allow only US$100 worth of Vietnamese goods to be brought into the USA as accompanied baggage. The Treasury Department has had this information printed in every US passport under 'Treasury'. Such goods cannot be sent by mail, must be for personal use only and cannot be resold. It is permitted to take advantage of this allowance once every six months. Single copies of Vietnamese publications are not included in the US$100 limit.

Receipts should be kept to document any goods purchased in Vietnam and those receipts should be available for US Customs officials when entry is made into the USA.

Getting There & Away

AIR

The only practicable way into Vietnam for Western travellers (except those coming from Cambodia) is by air. Regularly scheduled air services presently linking Ho Chi Minh City and Hanoi with points outside the country are listed in the following paragraphs under the 'Direct Flights' section. In most cases, there is a return flight out of Vietnam on the same day as each flight into the country arrives.

Warning

The Immigration Police in Hanoi's airport continue to cause headaches for travellers. In years past, it was a common practice to simply arrest departing foreign passengers for no apparent reason and 'fine' them thousands of US dollars for arbitrary violations of some unwritten statute. Mercifully, this practice seems to have stopped, largely due to protests by Western embassies.

However, a new scam began in 1992 and might still be going when you visit. Arriving foreigners who have a visa are being told that their visa is not valid because their 'sponsor' did not submit the necessary paperwork and therefore they are arriving illegally. (Your travel agent is supposed to be your 'sponsor'.) In this case, the foreigners in question cannot leave the airport, will be forced to spend a night at the Airport Hotel and then will be booted out of the country on the next available flight.

Conveniently, it just so happens that a representative from some travel agency is right there and will gladly agree to be your sponsor and sign your arrival card for a 'modest fee' (US$50 is usual). If you don't have the cash on hand, they will hold your passport, camera or some other collateral until you can cash your travellers' cheques at the bank. The travel agents might also require that you spend at least one night in their guesthouse (US$20 or so) and that you

use their taxi (perhaps another US$20) to get from the airport to the city.

Whether or not you fall into this trap may depend on a number of factors – who is on duty when you arrive, the type of visa you have (tourist, business) and your nationality (Westerners are especially targeted). The Immigration Police are definitely involved in the scam. The company which is raking in most of the cash is the East-Asia Company (EA Co) at 23 Hoa Ma St in Hanoi.

Considering all this, you should either have a visa in hand or else fly to Ho Chi Minh City rather than Hanoi. At the present time there appears to be no problem exiting the country via Hanoi. It might be worth noting that in 1991, the same scam was occuring at Ho Chi Minh City's airport (the 'modest fee' was US$90 at that time) but this particular form of extortion seems to have stopped in the south.

Vietnam Airlines

Vietnam's flag carrier is the government-owned Vietnam Airlines (Hang Khong Viet Nam). Long noted for shoddy service and unsafe aircraft, Vietnam Airlines has been working hard recently to spruce up its battered image. The standards of food and customer service are still lacking, but safety has improved because ageing Russian-built Tupolev aircraft are being replaced with much safer French-built Airbuses (at least on international routes). Vietnam Airlines originally wanted to purchase or lease American-made Boeings, but the US government (under the administration of former president George Bush) forbade Boeing and other American companies from doing any business with Vietnam. Although the Vietnamese could have bought the Boeings through third parties, they decided to shop elsewhere – the French must have laughed all the way to the bank.

Almost all flights into and out of Vietnam are joint operations between Vietnam Airlines and foreign carriers. The air ticket you purchase might have the words 'Vietnam Airlines' printed on it, but you could find yourself flying on, for example, Cathay Pacific or THAI.

Refunds for tickets to Vietnam are possible but there is a US$40 cancellation charge and getting your money back – especially from Vietnam Airlines – could take several months. If you intend to fly into Ho Chi Minh City and fly out by way of Hanoi (or vice versa), you should get this specified on your ticket along with any other stopoffs. It is possible to get the airlines to allow a change of departure points after arrival in Vietnam; for example, a Ho Chi Minh City-Bangkok return ticket can be endorsed for a Hanoi-Bangkok return flight for a US$10 surcharge, but such a ticket will be of no use at all if you choose to stop over in Vientiane (Laos).

The 20-kg checked-luggage weight limit is strictly enforced, especially on Vietnam Airlines. On flights out of Vietnam, they can prevent you from leaving unless you pay the steep overweight fee.

At all Vietnam Airlines offices which book international flights, there is a computer link-up with the SITA international reservations system.

It is extremely difficult to get reservations for flights to or from Vietnam around Tet (the Lunar New Year), which can fall around late January to mid-February. If you will be in Vietnam during this period (which is a favourite time for family visits by Overseas Vietnamese) make reservations well in advance or you may find yourself marooned in Bangkok on the way in or stranded in Ho Chi Minh City on the way out. Travellers have reported that ticket scalpers and corrupt airline officials will come up with a seat (or jump you to the head of the waiting list queue) during Tet for a 'service charge' of US$100 or so.

Be aware that Vietnam is not the only country to celebrate the Lunar New Year – it's also *the* major holiday in Singapore, Hong Kong, Macau, China, Taiwan, Korea and Japan, and is also celebrated by the sizeable Chinese minorities in Thailand and Malaysia. People from these countries hit the road at that time, with the result that airlines, trains and hotels are booked solid all over East Asia. The chaos begins about a week before the Lunar New Year and lasts until two weeks after it.

There are almost no discounts on flights going directly to Vietnam. Some travel agents booking flights to Vietnam offer a package deal with the visa and air ticket combined at a slight discount, but the savings isn't likely to be huge. Still, it's better than nothing.

The lack of discounts reflects the lack of cut-throat competition. Vietnam Airlines decides the official price, and all the airlines which have cooperative agreements with Vietnam Airlines must follow. Fortunately, the prices charged by Vietnam Airlines are not outrageous for the distances flown, though no doubt it would be cheaper if the airlines indulged in a cut-throat capitalist-style price war.

To give Vietnam Airlines some needed competition, the newly formed Pacific Airlines has been authorised to fly the same international and domestic routes as Vietnam Airlines. Right now, Pacific Airlines has a very limited flight schedule, but that is likely to increase in the future. In most cases, Pacific Airlines charges the exact same prices as Vietnam Airlines, but there is competition for who has better standards of service. Recently, Pacific Airlines has experimented with limited promotional discounts on the ridiculously expensive Taipei-Ho Chi Minh City route, perhaps a sign of price wars to come. Pacific Airlines has obtained a number of American-made Boeings and McDonnell-Douglas aircraft.

A few airlines do charter flights on demand to Vietnam (Korea's Asiana Airlines, for example) – such flights might offer discount ticket possibilities.

Vietnam Airlines Representative Offices
Australia

61 Todman Ave, Kensington, Sydney 2023, NSW (☎ (02) 3138943; fax (61-2) 6632505)

Cambodia
    73, 214 Rd, Phnom Penh (☎ 24588)
China
    CITS, 179 Huanshi Rd, 510010, Guangzhou
    (☎ (020) 677881, 666276, 666279, 677941; telex
    44450 CITS-CN; fax (86-20) 3330791)
Hong Kong
    Star House, Room 1522, 3 Salisbury Rd,
    Tsimshatsui, Kowloon, Hong Kong (☎ 7352382;
    fax (852) 7352372)
Laos
    141 Samsenthai Rd, Vientiane (☎ 4799)
Malaysia
    2.46-2. 49 2nd floor, Wisma Stephens, 88 Jalan
    Raja Chulan 50200, Kuala Lumpur (☎ (03)
    2443076; telex MA 20328; fax (60-3) 2429342)
Philippines
    120 Ground floor, Anson, Arcade Building,
    Manila (☎ 874878; fax 8125670)
Singapore
    50 Cucaden Rd, HLP House No 07-01, Singa-
    pore 1024 (☎ 2356277; fax (65) 7361662)
Taiwan
    3rd floor, 99 Sungchiang Rd, Taipei (☎ (02)
    5061449, 5156165; fax (886-2) 5156169)
Thailand
    578-580 Ploenchit Rd, Bangkok (☎ 2514242,
    2515439, 2553978; fax 2523895, 2553978)

Direct Flights to Vietnam

There are two ways to approach your travel arrangements to Vietnam; either take a direct flight from your home country (or wherever you happen to be at the moment you are reading this), or else make a special trip to Bangkok and do all your visa and air ticket arrangements from there. This latter option is the most popular, even though it means spending up to a week in Bangkok.

The following paragraphs discuss the direct approach. A later section covers Vietnam via Bangkok. Countries are listed here in alphabetical order:

To/From Australia Qantas and Vietnam Airlines offer joint service from Ho Chi Minh City to both Melbourne and Sydney. The flights are currently being offered only twice monthly, but this is likely to increase. The one-way air fare is A$1800, but there are round-trip excursion (90 days) fares for as low as A$1350. Ethnic-Vietnamese living in Australia are known to have the inside scoop on ticket discounts.

To/From Cambodia There are daily flights between Phnom Penh and Ho Chi Minh City (US$55 one way; US$100 return) on either Cambodia Airlines or Vietnam Airlines. There are flights between Phnom Penh and Hanoi (US$157 one way, US$314 return) every Monday. There is a US$5 airport tax to fly out of Cambodia. To obtain a Cambodian visa in Vietnam see the Visas & Embassies section in the Facts for the Visitor chapter.

To/From China China Southern Airlines flies jointly with Vietnam Airlines between Ho Chi Minh City and Guangzhou (Canton) via Hanoi, using Soviet-built Tupolev 134 aircraft which are due to retire soon. The Guangzhou-Hanoi flight takes 1½ hours; Guangzhou-Ho Chi Minh City (US$270 one way) takes 4½ hours. There are two flights weekly.

The Beijing-Hanoi flight on China Southern Airlines now stops at Nanning (capital of China's Guangxi Province) en route – you can board or exit the plane there. Unfortunately, this flight is a favourite of traders ('smugglers' as far as the authorities are concerned). This not only makes it difficult to get a ticket, but travellers arriving in Hanoi on this flight have reported vigorous baggage searches and numerous customs hassles. Going the other way, arrival in Nanning *might* be a little bit smoother, but don't count on it – Chinese customs agents are diligently on the lookout for drugs, and if you look like 'the type', expect a thorough going over.

To/From France Vietnam Airlines cooperates with Air France. Flights between Paris and Ho Chi Minh City (usually via Dubai) depart on Wednesday and Saturday. The flight takes about 18 hours and there are four flights weekly.

Pacific Airlines also flies the Ho Chi Minh-Paris route. The cheapest fare is US$940 one way, or US$1800 return.

To/From Germany Germany's Lufthansa and Vietnam Airlines offer joint service between Frankfurt and Ho Chi Minh City. There are two flights weekly, and flying time is at least 14½ hours. The air fare is US$1270 for a round-trip three-month excursion ticket.

To/From Hong Kong Next to Bangkok, Hong Kong is the second most popular point for departures to Vietnam. However, there is still no Vietnamese consulate in Hong Kong, so getting a visa requires four days. If you haven't done so before, you can make good use of the waiting time exploring nearby Macau and Guangzhou (Canton), China.

Hong Kong's flag carrier, Cathay Pacific, and Vietnam Airlines offer joint service daily between Hong Kong and Ho Chi Minh City (US$293 one way; US$558 return). There are also direct Hong Kong-Hanoi flights twice weekly (US$266 one way; US$503 return). The most popular ticket allows you to fly from Hong Kong to Ho Chi Minh City and return from Hanoi to Hong Kong; this ticket costs US$535. Obtaining a Vietnamese visa in Hong Kong costs about US$70.

A travel agent in Hong Kong specialising in discount air tickets and customised tours to Vietnam is Phoenix Services, (☎ 7227378; fax 852-3698884) in Room B, 6th floor, Milton Mansion, 96 Nathan Rd, Tsimshatsui, Kowloon. They offer a package deal – round-trip air fare plus visa and registration for US$525. Many travellers have had good things to say about this place.

To/From Indonesia A Garuda flight connects Jakarta with Ho Chi Minh City twice weekly. A Jakarta-Ho Chi Minh City ticket is US$437 each way. Round-trip excursion fares (good for 30 days) cost from US$705. Keep your eyes open for additional flights from Denpasar in Bali which should be coming soon.

To/From Japan At the time of this writing, Japan Airlines (JAL) was running charters to Ho Chi Minh City while waiting for approval to begin regularly scheduled flights.

To/From Korea Korean Air flies twice

monthly between Seoul and Ho Chi Minh City for US$624 one way. Asiana Airlines does charter flights to Vietnam as demand warrants.

It is possible to use Seoul as a transit point and continue on to the USA.

To/From Laos Lao Aviation and Vietnam Airlines offer joint service between Vientiane and Hanoi on Thursday and Sunday (50 minutes). The fare is US$80. There are flights between Vientiane and Ho Chi Minh City on Sunday. To obtain a Laotian visa in Vietnam see the Visas & Embassies section in the Facts for the Visitor chapter.

Visit Laos for free? It can be done if you are exiting Vietnam by air from Hanoi. An air ticket from Hanoi to Vientiane costs US$80; a Laos transit visa costs US$15, land transport (airport to hotel to boat) is US$5, the boat across the Mekong is US$1 and a train from Nong Khai to Bangkok costs US$16. The total is US$117, and compared to a straight Hanoi-Bangkok air ticket (US$160) you save US$43 – more than enough for food, shopping and other miscellaneous expenses! ■

To/From Malaysia Malaysian Airline System (MAS) and Vietnam Airlines have joint service from Kuala Lumpur to Ho Chi Minh City three times weekly. The one-way fare is US$221; round trip costs US$335.

To/From the Philippines Philippine Airlines and Vietnam Airlines fly from Manila to Ho Chi Minh City twice weekly, then continue to Danang and Hanoi. The air fare is US$280 one way or US$560 return.

To/From Russia Aeroflot flies Ilyushin IL86s and IL62s from Moscow to Hanoi and Ho Chi Minh City with numerous stopoffs along the way. The whole hopscotch across Asia takes 21 to 24 hours. Given the declining fortunes of Russia, the schedule remains uncertain; flights are becoming less frequent.

To/From Singapore Singapore Airlines and Vietnam Airlines offer joint service to Ho Chi Minh City five times weekly. Most of the flights continue onwards to Danang and Hanoi. A one-way ticket costs US$258; round-trip tickets are exactly double.

Cassidy Aviation (☎ 3387708; fax (65) 3391000), 122 Middle Rd, 08-03 Midlink Plaza, Singapore 0718, operates charters to Vietnam at discount prices.

There is no Vietnamese embassy in Singapore, so unless you pick up a visa somewhere else (the nearest Vietnamese consulate is in Kuala Lumpur), make your visa arrangement far enough in advance to catch your flight.

To/From Taiwan Taiwan's Mandarin Airlines offers joint service with Vietnam Airlines between Taipei and Ho Chi Minh City. The one-way air fare is an outrageous US$800; round-trip costs US$968. The ticket is valid for one year from date of purchase. There is a special excursion air fare of US$880, but this ticket is valid for 30 days only.

Vietnam's Pacific Airlines is currently offering a great promotional air fare; Ho Chi Minh City-Taipei for US$320 one way or US$620 return.

Visas arranged in Taiwan take about two weeks – travel agents make all the arrangements. The Vietnamese government has talked about opening a representative office in Taipei to speed up the visa process – this would make sense, since the Taiwanese are the biggest foreign investors in Vietnam and Taiwanese tour groups are noted for their free-spending habits.

A travel agent in Taiwan which has specialised in Vietnam tours is Hongyi Travel (☎ (02) 5059212, 5039862; fax (886-2) 5023763), 6th floor, Room 602, 185 Sungchiang Rd, Taipei.

To/From Thailand Bangkok, only 80 minutes flying time from Ho Chi Minh City,

has emerged as the main port of embarkation for air travel to Vietnam.

Thai Airways International (THAI), Air France, Pacific Airlines and Vietnam Airlines offer Bangkok-Ho Chi Minh City service for US$140 one way; round-trip tickets cost exactly double.

There are daily flights from Bangkok to Ho Chi Minh City, and some of the flights continue on to Danang. There are also direct Bangkok-Hanoi flights (US$170 one way; US$338 round trip).

To/From the USA At the time of this writing the US government was still prohibiting US carriers from flying to Vietnam without special permission. Such permission has been granted to US airlines flying Vietnamese refugees to the USA under the Orderly Departure Program. There is keen interest amongst US carriers to begin regularly scheduled flights – keep your eyes open for changes which should be coming soon.

The most direct way for Americans to fly to Vietnam is to transit Hong Kong for a few hours. Some travel agents in the USA offer a package deal – US$1150 for a visa plus a Los Angeles (or San Francisco) to Ho Chi Minh City round-trip ticket with a brief stopoff in Hong Kong.

Vietnam via Bangkok

First get yourself to Bangkok, from where you can arrange onward travel to Vietnam. This option costs you slightly more travel time but offers all sorts of discount ticket possibilities.

There are good reasons for Bangkok's popularity as the jumping-off point for Vietnam. For one thing, air tickets from Bangkok to Vietnam are relatively cheap. You can also live fairly cheaply in Bangkok while waiting for your visa and air ticket, which in any case is only four or five days. There are enough things to see and do in the Bangkok area to keep you amused during the waiting period. Not surprisingly, backpackers with more time than money usually choose this option.

When you're looking for bargain fares to Bangkok, you have to go to a travel agent rather than directly to the airline which can only sell fares by the book. Travel agents often hesitate to sell you the cheapest ticket available, not necessarily because they want to cheat you, but because many budget tickets come with lots of restrictions which you may find inconvenient. If you want the cheapest ticket, be sure to tell this to the travel agent and then ask what restrictions, if any, apply.

There are plenty of discount tickets which are valid for 12 months, allowing multiple stopovers with open dates. These tickets allow for a great deal of flexibility.

APEX (Advance Purchase Excursion) tickets are sold at a discount but will lock you into a rigid schedule. Such tickets must be purchased two or three weeks ahead of departure, do not permit stopovers and may have minimum and maximum stays as well as fixed departure and return dates. Unless you definitely must return at a certain time, it's best to purchase APEX tickets on a one-way basis only. There are stiff cancellation fees if you decide not to use your APEX ticket.

Round-the-World (RTW) tickets are usually offered by an airline or combination of airlines, and let you take your time (six months to a year) moving from point to point on their routes for the price of one ticket. The main restriction is that you have to keep moving in the same direction; a drawback is that because you are usually booking individual flights as you go, and can't switch carriers, you can get caught out by flight availabilities, and have to spend more or less time in a place than you want.

Some airlines offer student discounts on their tickets of up to 25% to student card holders. Besides having an International Student Identity Card (ISIC), an official-looking letter from the school is also required by some airlines. Many airlines also require you to be age 26 or younger to qualify for a discount. These discounts are generally only available on ordinary economy-class fares. You wouldn't get one, for instance, on an APEX or a RTW ticket since these are already discounted.

Frequent flyer deals were pioneered in the USA but have now spread to other countries. The way it works is that you fly frequently with one airline, and eventually you accumulate enough mileage to qualify for a free ticket or some other goodies. First, you must apply to the airline for a frequent flyer account number (some airlines will issue these on the spot or by telephone if you call their head office). A few airlines still require that you have a mailing address in the USA or Canada, but most now don't care where you live.

Every time you buy an air ticket and/or check in for your flight, you must inform the clerk of your frequent flyer account number, or else you won't get credit. Save your tickets and boarding passes, since it's not uncommon for the airlines to fail to give proper credit. You should receive monthly statements by post informing you how much mileage you've accumulated. Once you've accumulated sufficient mileage to qualify for freebies, you are supposed to receive vouchers by mail. Many airlines have 'black-out periods', or times when you cannot fly for free (Christmas and Tet are good examples).

The worst thing about frequent-flyer programs is that these tend to lock you into one airline, and that airline may not always have the cheapest fares or most convenient flight schedule.

Airlines usually carry babies up to two years of age at 10% of the relevant adult fare, a few may carry them free of charge. Reputable international airlines usually provide nappies (diapers), tissues, talcum and all the other paraphernalia needed to keep babies clean, dry and half-happy. For children between the ages of four and 12 the fare on international flights is usually 50% of the regular fare or 67% of a discounted fare. These days most fares are likely to be discounted.

Some discount possibilities for getting to Bangkok from the following countries:

To/From Australia Australia is not a cheap

place to fly out of, and air fares between Australia and Asia are absurdly expensive considering the distances flown. However, there are a few ways of cutting the costs.

Among the cheapest regular tickets available in Australia are APEX tickets. The cost depends on your departure date from Australia. The year is divided into 'peak' (expensive), 'shoulder' (less expensive) and 'low' (relatively inexpensive) seasons; peak season is December to January.

It's possible to get reductions on the cost of APEX and other fares by going to the student travel offices and/or some of the travel agents in Australia that specialise in discounting.

If you book through such an agent, the APEX fares from Melbourne to Bangkok are around A$500 one way and A$900 return, flying with Cathay Pacific. Discount fares from Melbourne to Bangkok are around A$1000 one way and A$1500 return, flying with Thai International.

The weekend travel sections of papers like *The Age* (Melbourne) or the *Sydney Morning Herald* are good sources of travel information. Also look at *Student Traveller*, a free newspaper published by Student Travel Australia (STA), the Australian-based student travel organisation which now has offices worldwide. STA has offices all around Australia (check your phone directory) and you definitely do not have to be a student to use them.

Also well worth trying is the Flight Shop (☎ (03) 6700477), 386 Little Bourke St, Melbourne. They also have branches under the name of the Flight Centre in Sydney (☎ (02) 2332296) and Brisbane (☎ (07) 2299958).

To/From Canada Getting discount tickets in Canada is much the same as in the USA – go to the travel agents and shop around until you find a good deal.

CUTS is Canada's national student bureau and has offices in a number of Canadian cities including Vancouver, Edmonton, Toronto and Ottawa – you don't necessarily have to be a student. There are a number of

good agents in Vancouver for cheap tickets; CP-Air are particularly good for fares to Thailand.

To/From Europe The Netherlands, Brussels and Antwerp are good places for buying discount air tickets. In Antwerp, WATS has been recommended. In Zurich, try SOF Travel and Sindbad. In Geneva, try Stohl Travel. In the Netherlands, NBBS is a reputable agency. Some of the best deals going to Bangkok are with Eastern European airlines.

To/From New Zealand Air New Zealand flies from Auckland to Bangkok. In peak season a return excursion ticket costs around NZ$1850, and in low season it's NZ$1650. You have to pay for your ticket at least 21 days in advance.

A minimum of six days must be spent overseas, not that this is any problem if you're heading to Vietnam.

To/From the UK Air-ticket discounting is a long-running business in the UK and it's wide open. The various agents advertise their fares and there is nothing under-the-counter about it at all. To find out what's going, there are a number of magazines in Britain which have good information about flights and agents. These include: *Trailfinder*, free from the Trailfinders Travel Centre in Earls Court; and *Time Out* or *City Limits*, London weekly entertainment guides widely available in the UK.

Discount tickets are almost exclusively available in London. You won't find your friendly travel agent out in the country offering cheap deals. The danger with discounted tickets in Britain is that some of the 'bucket shops' (as ticket-discounters are known) are unsound. Sometimes the backstairs over-the-shop travel agents fold up and disappear after you've handed over the money and before you've received the tickets. Get the tickets before you hand over the cash.

Two reliable London bucket shops are Trailfinders, in Earls Court, and the Student Travel Association, with several offices. Tickets from London to Hong Kong are often far cheaper than to Bangkok, but check current prices.

Flights from London and Manchester to East Asian destinations are cheapest on THAI, Singapore Airlines, Malaysian (MAS) and Cathay Pacific. These airlines do not charge extra if passengers want to stop over en route, and in fact offer stopover packages which encourage it. There are also direct flights on Lüfthansa and Air France – both are significantly more expensive than the forementioned Asian-based carriers.

To/From the USA The cheapest low-season one-way/return San Francisco-Bangkok ticket costs US$600/1100.

There are some very good open tickets which remain valid for six months or one year (opt for the latter), but don't lock you into any fixed dates of departure and allow multiple stopoffs. For example, there are cheap tickets between the US west coast and Bangkok with stopoffs in Japan, Korea and/or Taiwan for very little extra money – the departure dates can be changed and you have one year to complete the journey. However, be careful during the peak season (summer and Tet) because seats will be hard to come by unless reserved months in advance.

It is possible to fly from the USA to Vietnam with a quick transit stop in a third country for a change of aircraft. Korean Air, for example, will fly you Los Angeles-Ho Chi Minh City with a brief stop in Seoul. You can check your luggage all the way through to Vietnam and do not need to go through Korean customs or immigration. Currently, Korean Air offers this service twice monthly.

Usually, and not surprisingly, the cheapest fare to whatever country is offered by a bucket shop owned by someone of that particular ethnic origin. San Francisco is the bucket shop capital of America, though some good deals can be found in Los Angeles, New York and other cities. Bucket shops can be found through the Yellow Pages or the major daily newspapers. Those listed in both Roman and Oriental scripts are invariably discounters. A more direct way is to wander around San Francisco's Chinatown where most of the shops are – especially in the Clay St and Waverly Place area. Many of these are staffed by recent arrivals from Hong Kong and Taiwan who speak little English. Enquiries are best made in person. One place popular with budget travellers is Wahlock Travel in the Bank of America Building on Stockton St.

It's not advisable to send money (even checks) through the post unless the agent is very well established – some travellers have reported being ripped off by fly-by-night mail order ticket agents. Nor is it wise to hand over the full amount to Shady Deal Travel Services unless they can give you the ticket straight away – most US travel agencies have computers that can spit out the ticket on the spot.

Council Travel is the largest student travel organisation, and, though you don't have to be a student to use them, they do have specially discounted student tickets. Council Travel has an extensive network in all major US cities and is listed in the telephone book. There are also Student Travel Network offices which are associated with STA.

One of the cheapest and most reliable travel agents on the west coast is Overseas Tours (☎ (800) 3238777 in California, (800) 2275988 elsewhere), 475 El Camino Real, Room 206, Millbrae, CA 94030. Another good agent is Gateway Travel (☎ (214) 9602000, (800) 4411183), 4201 Spring Valley Rd, Suite 104, Dallas, TX 75244 – they seem to be trustworthy for mail-order tickets.

LAND

To/From Cambodia

The only frontier crossing between Cambodia and Vietnam which is open to Westerners is at Moc Bai, which connects Vietnam's Tay Ninh Province with Cambodia's Svay Rieng Province. Other border crossings which *might* open to foreigners in the future include the crossing between Kep in Kampot Province and Ha Tien in Kien Giang Province; between Kandal Province and Chau Doc in An Giang Province (by Mekong River ferry); and between Ratanakiri Province and Chu Nghe in Gia Lai Province, 65 km west of Pleiku.

Buses run every day between Phnom Penh and Ho Chi Minh City (via Moc Bai). The cost is US$3 to US$4 depending on bus size. In Vietnam, departures are from the Phnom Penh Bus Garage at 155 Nguyen Hue Blvd, Saigon, adjacent to the Rex Hotel. You are supposed to obtain a travel permit for the journey from Saigon to the Cambodian border (but only if you get off the bus and wander around because you are not supposed to be there – be careful about taking photos). In addition, you will need a Cambodian visa (which takes seven working days to process) and a re-entry visa for Vietnam if you are going back to Vietnam rather than flying on to a third country.

Foreigners making the crossing at Moc Bai have reported attempts by Vietnamese customs agents to solicit bribes.

The corrupt customs guards at the Moc Bai border crossing (Vietnamese side that is; the Cambodians were far more easy-going) held our bus for no reason for four long hot hours. Meanwhile, all of the innocent-looking Vietnamese women who posed as tourists were smuggling suitcases full of cigarettes, toothpaste, booze, etc and paying the guards off. The eight of us foreign devils who didn't want to play that game were the reason for the delay.

Vehicles belonging to nongovernmental organisations (NGOs) working in Cambodia are always going back and forth between Phnom Penh and Ho Chi Minh City via Moc Bai. The only land route from Phnom Penh to Cambodia's north-eastern province of Ratanakiri is through Vietnam.

The Cambodian Foreign Ministry will drive you to Phnom Penh in a beautiful new Japanese car for US$300 – enquire at the Cambodian Consulate in Ho Chi Minh City if interested. You can also book cars from Saigon Tourist, but it's cheaper at private travel agencies.

To/From Laos

The land crossings between Laos and Vietnam are presently closed to foreigners.

If/when both Laos and Vietnam open up more to tourism, it should be possible to drive between the southern Lao province of Savannakhet and central Vietnam via the border crossing at Lao Bao, which is on National Highway 9, 80 km west of Dong Ha. For more information on Lao Bao and nearby Khe Sanh, see the DMZ & Vicinity chapter.

To/From Thailand

Thailand does not have a land border with Vietnam, but it is possible to go across the Thai-Cambodian border and then onwards to Vietnam. There are ambitious plans to open up the Thai-Cambodian border to tourism. Unfortunately, at the moment it's still very difficult to make the crossing, but it is possible. Here's how:

The only open border crossing is at Aranyaprathet (Thailand) and Poipet (Cambodia), which is near the Bangkok-Phnom Penh railway line. Unfortunately, the rail line is still not functioning so you have to go by road.

First you need a visa. At the time of this writing there was no Cambodian Embassy in Bangkok (this could change), so the only way is to contact the Foreign Ministry in Phnom Penh by fax (or phone if you need clear instructions), give them the information they need and then you can pick up the visa at the border. Currently, the Foreign Ministry's international telephone number in Phnom Penh is (855) 23-26-133, 23-26-144; fax (873-1) 770102. Note that there is a different country code for the fax number.

The information they want is: your name; birth place; birth date; nationality; sex; intended date of entry and departure; point of entry; means of transport; address during the visit; passport number; place of issue; date of issue; expiry date; if you have children under the age of 13 who will travel with you; if you have any relatives in Cambodia (if yes, then their name, birth date and address); your occupation; place of employment; permanent address; purpose of visit (tourism!); point of exit; means of transport at exit; organisations and persons to be visited; whether you have visited Cambodia before (if so, date of visit, duration of stay, purpose of visit and places visited).

Submit all this information to the fax machine along with a photocopy of your passport. Your visa will be ready to pick up at the border when you enter Cambodia, at which time they will ask you for a US$20 fee and five passport-type photos. Allow 10 days for the visa process.

Next, you need to obtain permission from the Thai

Supreme Command to leave the country and cross the border at Aranyaprathet. The Thai Supreme Command can be found in the Ministry of Foreign Affairs near the Royal Palace in Bangkok.

Once across the border, cars will be there and drivers willing to take you to Phnom Penh for US$60. The second leg of the journey from Phnom Penh to Saigon will cost US$150 by car, US$55 by air or US$4 by bus. A Vietnamese visa can be obtained in Phnom Penh but these are usually only valid for three days! Much better to get it in Bangkok.

When Laos' relations with Thailand get sorted out and the Vietnamese relax their restrictions, t should be possible to go overland from Ubon Ratchathani to central Vietnam via Savannakhet Province and the Lao Bao border crossing.

To/From China

Vietnam's land border with China was closed for many years as a result of the 1979 Chinese invasion. The border is now at least partially reopened. Citizens of Vietnam and China can readily obtain visas to cross the border at Dong Dang (20 km north of Lang Son in north-east Vietnam). The nearest major Chinese city to this border crossing is Nanning, capital of Guangxi Province. Vietnamese and Chinese traders can regularly be seen crossing this border, hauling tremendous quantities of 'personal luggage' in the hopes of avoiding import taxes. However, they are often intercepted by customs, who joyously rip open their luggage with knives and extort 'fines' or confiscate the goods.

For foreigners, the situation is improving fast. At the present time, foreigners can exit Vietnam by this route with few problems, but there are some bureaucratic hurdles to clear. Since Vietnamese visas show both the authorised point of entry and exit, the visa must show Lang Son as the exit point if you want to take this route. If your visa shows a different exit point, it is possible to get it changed in Hanoi or Ho Chi Minh City at the Foreign Ministry office – this does not seem to be difficult. Furthermore, a travel permit for Lang Son is required – these can be obtained by travel agencies in Hanoi.

While you should be able to manage exiting Vietnam to China overland, going the other way is much less certain. You will need a Vietnamese visa marked 'Huu Nghi Quan' ('Friendship Gate') – obtaining these seems to be hit or miss. Some travel agencies in Hong Kong seem to be able to get these if they have the right connections, but most say it is impossible. Some travellers who have managed to get the requisite stamp on their visa have found that the Vietnamese border guards are uncooperative – they may claim the visa is 'not valid'. On the other hand, travellers have shown up at this border with a visa valid only for Hanoi entry but were permitted to cross! As elsewhere in Vietnam, the only thing that is certain is that nothing is certain.

It seems that the best way to handle border guards is to exercise patience – sitting down with them for five or six hours while sharing cigarettes (and sometimes booze) has been known to do the trick. Getting visibly angry does not seem to work – indeed, this will almost certainly prove counterproductive. However, no method is guaranteed to work, and until things lighten up a bit, you'll just have to take your chances if you want to enter Vietnam by this route. The biggest problem with being turned back is that once you've had your visa stamped on the Chinese side, you are not supposed to re-enter China without a new visa. You can prepare for this only by having a multiple-entry or dual-entry Chinese visa, but these are more expensive.

Full details about exiting Vietnam to China overland are included in the last chapter of this book (The North) under the Lang Son section.

Before 1979, an 851 km metre-gauge railway, inaugurated in 1910, linked Hanoi with Kunming in Yunnan Province, crossing the border at Lao Cai in north-west Vietnam. So far, this border crossing is still closed and there is no word yet on when it might be reopened.

It may someday be possible (as it was just before WW II) to take trains all the way from Moscow to Beijing, then to Hong Kong,

Hanoi and Ho Chi Minh City and, after travelling by road to Phnom Penh, from there by rail to Bangkok, Kuala Lumpur and Singapore!

SEA

Amongst fed-up Vietnamese nationals, unauthorised departure by sea has been very popular since 1975. Since about 1990, the numbers of boat people fleeing the country has been considerably reduced by the Orderly Departure Programme and the opening of the Chinese border which provides a much safer and easier route.

For foreign tourists, there seem to be no options as yet to arrive or depart legally by sea. There is some talk of allowing luxury cruisers to dock at Vietnamese ports. Major port facilities in Vietnam include Haiphong, Danang, Vung Tau and Ho Chi Minh City – all frequent ports of call for freighters especially from Singapore, Taiwan and Thailand.

Yachts and fishing boats that have shown up without authorisation in Vietnamese territorial waters have been seized and their crews imprisoned   sometimes for many months – until a satisfactory payment in hard currency gets delivered to the aggrieved authorities.

TOURS

The simplest way to get into Vietnam is to purchase a package tour in Bangkok. Package tours are sold by a variety of agencies in Bangkok and elsewhere, but in Vietnam all the tours, which usually follow one of a dozen or so set itineraries, are run by the omnipresent government tourism authorities, Vietnam Tourism and Saigon Tourist. The tours, which include round-trip air fare, are not a total rip-off given what you get (tourist-class accommodation, food, transport, a guide, etc) but then again they're not inexpensive: they range in price from about US$480 for a three-day Saigon 'shopping tour' to over US$1,000 for a week-long trip that includes flying all around the country. Doing the same things on your own

can cost as little as US$10-15 a day (not including air fare).

Most agencies impose a surcharge for tours run for less than *two* people. In other words, a small group can purchase a virtually private tour. If you deal with a travel agent who deals directly with Vietnam, it should be possible to arrange for your itinerary to deviate significantly from the usual packages, but make sure to get any special arrangements *in writing* and to confirm them as soon as you arrive in Vietnam.

Companies in Bangkok selling their own versions of the standard tours often farm out the sale of their offerings to other travel agencies. The price may be pretty much the same if you purchase a tour on Khao San Rd rather than at one of the places listed in this section (most of which are in the vicinity of the Vietnamese Embassy), but you'll be dealing with people less knowledgeable about the ins and outs of travel to Vietnam. And arranging the tour and visa may take much longer – up to a week rather than a day or two.

Agencies in Bangkok offering tours to Vietnam include:

Air People Tour & Travel Co Ltd
    2nd Floor, Regent House Bldg, 183 Rajdamri Rd, Bangkok 10500 (☎ 2543921/2/3/4/5; telex 82419 APT TH; fax (662) 2553750)
Diethelm Travel
    Kian Gwan Building II, 140/1 Wireless Rd, Bangkok 10500 (☎ 2559150/60/70; telex 81183, 21763, 22700, 22701 DIETRAV TH; fax (662) 2560248/9). Diethelm tends to be much more expensive than other agencies.
Exotissimo Travel (Bolsa Travelmart)
    21/17 Sukhumvit Soi 4, Bangkok 10110 (☎ 2535240/1, 2552747; telex 20479 ASIAN TH; fax 2547683)
Lam Son International Ltd
    23/1 Sukhumvit Soi 4 (Soi Nana Tai), Bangkok 10110 (☎ 2556692/3/4/5, 2522340; fax 2558859)
Namthai Travel
    Bangkok (☎ 2159003/10, 2157339; telex 22663 NAMTHAI TH; fax (662) 2156240)
Red Carpet Service & Tour
    459 New Rama 6 Rd, Phayathai, Bangkok 10400 (☎ 2159951, 2153331; fax (662) 2153331)
Thaninee Trading Company
    1131/343 Terddumri Rd, Dusit, Bangkok 10300

(☎ 2431794, 2432601, 2433245; telex 87411 TANINEE TH; fax (662) 2430676)

Viet Tour Holidays (The Crescendo Co Ltd)
1717 Lard-Prao Rd, Samsennok, Huay-Kwang, Bangkok 10310 (☎ 5113272; telex ALLENTR 84561 TH; fax 5113357)

Vikamla Tours (same office as Lam Son International)
Room 401, Nana Condo, 23/11 Sukhumvit Soi 4 (Soi Nana Tai), Bangkok 10110 (☎ 2522340, 2558859; telex 22586 VIKAMLA TH)

Agencies in Australia and New Zealand offering tours to Vietnam include:

Orbitours
Suite 7, 7th floor, Dymock's Bldg, 428 George St, Sydney (GPO Box 3309), 2000 (☎ (02) 2217322; fax (02) 2217425)
183 Elizabeth St, Melbourne, Vic 3000 (☎ (03) 6707071)
(They can also be contacted in the USA on (☎ (1-800) 2355895); Canada (☎ (1-800) 6650809); and the UK (☎ (0800) 89-2006)

Prima Holidays Ltd
1st floor, 277 Flinders Lane, Melbourne, Vic 3000 (☎ (03) 6544211; fax (03) 6547204)

Vietnam Ventures
1st floor, 92 Victoria St, Richmond, Vic 3121 (☎ (03) 4280385; fax (03) 4287005)

Destinations
2nd floor, Premier Bldg, 4 Durham St, Auckland, New Zealand (☎ (09) 390464)

In North America you might try contacting:

California
Budgetours International, 8907 Westminster Ave, Garden Grove, CA 92644 (☎ (714) 2216539, 6378229, 8952528)
Tour Connections, 8907 Westminster Ave, Garden Grove, CA 92644 (☎ (213) 4657315, (714) 8952839)

New York
Mekong Travel, 151 First Ave, Suite 172, New York, NY 10003 (☎ (212) 4201586)

Pennsylvania
US-Indochina Reconciliation Project, 5808 Green St, Philadelphia, PA 19144 (☎ (215) 8484200, Compuserve: 71001,714)

Quebec
Club Voyages Berri, 1650 Berri, Suite 8, Montreal, Quebec H2L 4E6 (☎ (514) 9826168/9; telex 05561074; fax (514) 9820820)
New Asia Tours (Tour Nouvelle Asie), 1063 Blvd St Laurent, Montreal, Quebec H2Z 1J6 (☎ (514) 8740266; telex 3959341 (Asia); fax (514) 8740251)

Que Viet Tours, 1063 Blvd St Laurent, Montreal, Quebec H2Z 1J6 (☎ (514) 3933211; telex 4959321 (Asia); fax (514) 8740251)

In Europe, agencies booking tours to Vietnam include:

Austria
View Travel, Sankt Voitgasse 9, A-1130 Vienna (☎ (222) 8218532)

France
Hit Voyages, 21 Rue des Bernardins, 75005 Paris (☎ 43 54 17 17)
Pacific Holidays, 34 Ave du Général Leclerc, 75014 Paris (☎ 45 41 52 58)
International Tourisme, 26 Blvd St Marcel, 75005 Paris (☎ 45 87 07 70)

Germany
Indoculture Tours (Indoculture Reisedienst GmbH), Bismarckplatz 1 D-7000 Stuttgart 1 (☎ 0711/61 705758)
Saratours, Sallstr 21 D-3000, Hannover 1 (☎ (0511) 282353)

Switzerland
Exotissimo, 8 Ave du Mail, 1205 Geneva (☎ (22) 81.21.66; telex 421358 EXOT CH; fax (022) 81 21 71)
Artou, 8 Rue de Rive, 1204 Geneva
Nayak, Steinengrabes 42, CH-4001 Basel (☎ (061) 224343)

UK
Regent Holidays (UK) Ltd, 15 John St, Bristol BS1 2HR (☎ (0272) 211711; fax (0272) 254866; telex 444606 REGENTG)

In East Asia, companies offering tours to Vietnam include:

Hong Kong
Chu & Associates, Unit E, 5/F, 8 Thomson Rd, Hong Kong (☎ 5278828/41)
Vietnam Tours & Trading Company, Room 302, Loader Commercial Bldg, 54 Hillwood Rd, TST (☎ 3682493, 3676663)
Traveller Services Ltd, Metropole Bldg, 57 Peking Rd, Tsimshatsui, Kowloon (☎ 674127)
Phoenix Services Agency, Room B, 6/F, Milton Mansion, 96 Nathan Rd, Tsimshatsui, Kowloon (☎ 7227378; telex 3167 PHNXHK)
Cathay Pacific Airlines, Ground floor, Swire House, 9-25 Chater Rd, Central (☎ 7477888)

Japan
Japan-Soviet Travel Service, 5th Floor, Daihachi-Tanaka Bldg 5-1, Gobancho Chiyoda-Ku, Tokyo (☎ (03) 32384101)
Sai Travel Service, 2F Suzuki Daini Bldg 4-12-4, Shinbashi Minato-Ku, Tokyo

Philippines
Impex International, Suite 201, Centrum Bldg, 104 Perea St, Lagaspi Village, Makati (☎ 8134865/66/67)

Visits by US Vietnam Veterans

A growing number of US veterans of the Vietnam War are deciding to visit Vietnam. Many psychologists who deal with the long-term effects of the war believe that 'going back' to Vietnam can help groups of veterans confront the root causes of post-traumatic stress disorder (PTSD). For more information on group trips to Vietnam by veterans (and other veterans' issues), contact:

The William Joiner Center
    University of Massachusetts at Boston, Boston, MA 02125 (☎ (617) 929-7865)
US-Indochina Reconciliation Project
    5808 Greene St, Philadelphia, PA 19144 (☎ (215) 848-4200; telex 254830 USIN UR; Compuserve: 71001,714)

LEAVING VIETNAM

Be aware that Vietnamese visas specify from which point(s) – usually Ho Chi Minh City's Tan Son Nhat Airport or Hanoi's Noi Bai Airport – you are permitted to leave the country. If you intend to exit from some place not listed on your visa (such as to Cambodia via Moc Bai or China via Dong Bang), make sure to have the Ho Chi Minh City or Hanoi office of the Foreign Ministry add the additional border crossing to your visa. The service charge for making this change is currently US$1.

Except at peak holiday times, it's not too difficult to get a flight out of the country, but it's wise to book your departure at least a few days in advance.

If you bought an air ticket with a definite departure date, it's essential to reconfirm after you've arrived in Vietnam or your seat will likely be given away to somebody else.

Travellers have reported things being pilfered from their luggage on departure:

Security of checked luggage at the Ho Chi Minh City airport continues to be a concern: I had a Walkman removed from the bottom of a duffle bag. I recommend any checked baggage contain only clothing.

Harry Hunter

Duty-Free Shopping

Although you can pig out on the usual chocolate-coated macadamia nuts or drown your sorrows in a bottle of duty-free XO, we suggest you check out the Vietnamese-made goods at the airport. At least in Ho Chi Minh's Tan Son Nhat Airport, there's a reasonably good collection of crafts, edibles, T-shirts and the like. Furthermore, the duty-free shops at Vietnam's international airports offer something extraordinary – reasonable prices! This comes as a surprise, especially if you're familiar with the Japanese-run duty-free shops in places like Hong Kong and Los Angeles (where 'duty-free' means 'three times as expensive').

If you've got a nicotine habit, you can also get a duty-free fix at the airport, but prices for smuggled cigarettes on the streets of Ho Chi Minh City are nearly the same.

Departure Tax

The departure tax at all international airports is US$6. Although change can be given, it's best not to show up with nothing but a US$100 bill.

Getting Around

AIR

All air travel within Vietnam is handled by Vietnam Airlines and Pacific Airlines. Flights fill up fast (some flights are literally standing room only) so reservations should be made at least several days before departure. Many provincial destinations are included as a stopover on Hanoi-Ho Chi Minh City flights; there will be a Ho Chi Minh City-Hué-Hanoi run on one day of the week and a Hanoi-Hué-Ho Chi Minh City flight on another. In a given city, reservations can be made only for travel originating in that city. In Ho Chi Minh City, for instance, you can book a flight to Danang but cannot – unless you cable ahead – make reservations from Danang to Hanoi. The baggage weight limit on all domestic flights is 20 kg and this is strictly enforced.

The international and domestic booking offices of Vietnam Airlines are at separate locations in most cities. While the international booking offices are not generally crowded, the domestic booking offices tend to be an unruly mass of elbows and hands – no one stands in line. You will have little choice but to dive headlong into the vortex if you want to book a seat. Do not forget to bring either your passport or visa – you will need one or the other to buy an air ticket.

Reservations and ticketing is something you usually take care of yourself – no travel agents have computer terminals in their office to book air tickets. Of course, for a sufficient service charge, most travel agents will send someone down to the Vietnam Airlines office to battle the queues for you.

'Capitalist tourists' must pay for airline tickets with US dollars. Vietnam Airlines does not usually accept other hard currencies or travellers' cheques; both must be exchanged at a bank before you can buy a ticket. (Vietnam Airlines will accept travellers' cheques but only after a long bureaucratic wrangle and deduction of a large commission.)

On international routes, Vietnam Airlines has retired all of the Soviet-built aircraft. Unfortunately, it's a different matter within the country. The all-Soviet line-up of domestic aircraft includes the 70-seat Tupolev 134 jet (Tu134), the 45-passenger prop-powered Antonov An24, the 32-passenger three jet-engined YAK40 and assorted helicopters.

Vietnam Airlines has suffered a bad reputation in the past. Basically, the problem has been old equipment, a lack of spare parts and lack of funds to set things right. Fortunately, Vietnam's recently improved economy has also meant recently improved safety. Now that the Tupolevs have been retired from international service, the best of the bunch have been put on domestic routes. Unfortunately, problems still occur, especially with smaller aircraft; on 14 November 1992, a

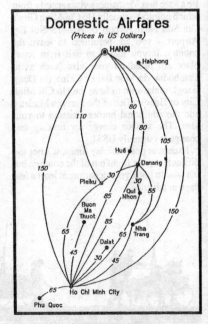

Domestic Airfares
(Prices in US Dollars)

HANOI
Haiphong
80
110
80
105
Huè
150
Danang
30
Pleiku
30
85
Qui Nhon
55
Buon Ma Thuot
150
85
65
Nha Trang
Dalat
65
45
30
45
Ho Chi Minh City
65
Phu Quoc

146

Domestic Air Services

From	To	Schedule	Price
Danang	Hanoi	Daily	US$80
Danang	Ho Chi Minh City	Daily	US$85
Danang	Nha Trang	Tue, Fri	US$55
Danang	Pleiku	Tue, Fri	US$30
Danang	Qui NhonThu,	Sun	US$30
Hanoi	Danang	Daily	US$80
Hanoi	Ho Chi MinhCity	Daily	US$150
Hanoi	Hué	Tue, Fri	US$80
Hanoi	Nha Trang	Thu, Sun	US$105
Hanoi	Pleiku	Tue, Fri	US$110
Ho Chi Minh City	Buon Ma Thuot	Mon, Wed, Sat	US$45
Ho Chi Minh City	Dalat	Mon, Wed, Sat	US$30
Ho Chi Minh City	Danang	Daily	US$85
Ho Chi Minh City	Haiphong	Daily except Thu	US$150
Ho Chi Minh City	Hanoi	Daily	US$150
Ho Chi Minh City	Hué	Tue, Fri, Sun	US$85
Ho Chi Minh City	Nha Trang	Daily except Mon	US$45
Ho Chi Minh City	Phu Quoc	Wed, Sat	US$65
Ho Chi Minh City	Pleiku	Mon, Thu	US$65
Ho Chi Minh City	Qui Nhon	Thu, Sun	US$65

YAK40 crashed near Nha Trang killing 22 Vietnamese and nine foreigners.

While Vietnam Airlines is trying to rid itself of the legacy of Soviet planes, upstart Pacific Airlines has managed to lease or buy US-made Boeings and McDonnell-Douglas aircraft to fly domestic routes. Since US companies cannot have direct financial dealings with Vietnam, it is assumed the aircraft were purchased or leased through third parties.

Charter flights on both planes and helicopters are possible. For information on arranging such private excursions, contact Vietnam Tourism. The price tag is likely to be in the thousands of US dollars.

Flights between Hanoi and Ho Chi Minh City do not fly over Laos and Cambodia even though this route would be shorter. Apparently, the Vietnamese do not want to pay for flyover rights.

All aircraft return to their point of origin the same day, so the domestic air schedule above covers all possible routes both coming and going.

BUS

The good news is that Vietnam has an extensive network of dirt-cheap buses and other passenger vehicles which reaches virtually every corner of the country.

The bad news is that buses tend to be slow, crowded, uncomfortable and unreliable. Almost all Vietnamese buses suffer from frequent breakdowns (many have been in service for two to four decades, and spare parts are home-made). The seats, often benches, are tiny and offer almost no leg room, let alone space for luggage (but most Vietnamese bring plenty of luggage anyway). You can purchase two tickets which, theoretically, entitles you to two seats – but you might have to defend your turf when the bus gets packed to overflowing! Chronic overcrowding is the norm (overloaded buses are often pulled over by the police but let go in exchange for a bribe). Many buses are literally standing room only – if you drop dead, you'll never hit the floor until the bus arrives at its destination. After an eight-hour ride, one foreigner put it succinctly when she said, 'I feel like a million dong'.

It's fair to say that riding the buses will give you ample opportunity to have 'personal contact' with the Vietnamese people. If you're looking to meet locals, what better way than to have a few sitting on your lap!

I enjoyed the bus riding scene, the scenery and the conversations (gesturing) with people. Although I'd rate the conditions as terrible, the riding community suffered, slept and ate together.

Figuring out the bus system is anything but easy. Many cities have several bus stations between which responsibilities are divided according to the location of the destination (whether it is north or south of the city) and the type of service being offered (local or intercity express or non-express).

Most intercity buses depart in the early morning. Often, half-a-dozen vehicles to the same destination will leave at the same time, usually around 5.30 am. A few overnight runs have begun since curfew regulations were relaxed in early 1989 but people are not yet in the habit of travelling all night long. Short-distance buses – which, like service taxis, depart when full (ie jam-packed with people and luggage) – often operate throughout the day, but don't count on anything leaving after about 4 pm.

Classes

The appellation 'express' *(toc hanh)* is applied rather loosely in Vietnam. Genuine express buses are considerably faster than local buses, which drop off and pick up peasants and their produce at each cluster of houses along the highway. But many express buses are the same decrepit vehicles used on local runs except that as they limp along the road – kept rolling by the sheer ingenuity and willpower of the driver/mechanic and the assistant – they stop a bit less frequently. A good rule of thumb is that local buses average 15 to 25 km/h over the course of a journey. Express buses rarely exceed an average speed of 35 km/h. Real express runs – the minibus from Ho Chi Minh City to Vung Tau, for instance – can average 50 km/h or more.

However slow they may be, express buses do offer certain advantages. At ferries, they are usually given priority (as are cadre vehicles), which can save an hour or more at each crossing. And since they are marginally more expensive than regular buses, people lugging large parcels around the country to make a few dong reselling something are likely to consider their time and comfort less valuable than the cash.

Reservations

Buses normally leave early in the morning, so it's a wise practice to show up at the bus station the day before departure and purchase a ticket.

Costs

Negligible. Depending on class, figure around US$0.01 per km.

TRAIN

The 2600-km Vietnamese railway system (Duong Sat Viet Nam) runs along the coast between Ho Chi Minh City and Hanoi and links the capital with Haiphong and points north. While sometimes even slower than buses, the trains offer a more relaxing way to get around. Large-bodied Westerners will find that the trains offer a bit more leg and body room than the jam-packed buses. And dilapidated as the tracks, rolling stock and engines may appear, the trains are more reliable than the country's ancient bus fleet.

One key factor to take into account when deciding whether to go by train or bus should be the hour at which the train gets to where you want to go – trying to find a place to stay at 3 am is likely to be very frustrating.

Even the fastest trains in Vietnam are extremely slow, averaging 30 km/h and slowing to five or 10 km/h in some sections. The quickest rail journey between Hanoi and Ho Chi Minh City takes 42 hours at an average speed of 41 km/h. The slowest through trains take 48 hours averaging 34 km/h.

Then there are local trains which do not make the complete journey, but only cover part of the route like Ho Chi Minh City to Nha Trang. These local trains at times crawl along at 15 km/h. There are several reasons for the excruciating slowness. First of all, the track network is metre-gauge (except for 300 km in the north). Second, much of the track system is in poor condition, in part because of inadequate post-reunification repair of Viet Cong sabotage in the south and US bombing in the north. And third, there is only one track running between Ho Chi Minh City and Hanoi. Trains can pass each other only at those few points where a siding has been constructed. Each time trains go by each other, one of them has to stop on the pre-arranged sidetrack and wait for the

oncoming train to arrive. If one is late, so is the other, and subsequent trains going in both directions may also be delayed.

Petty crime is a problem on Vietnamese trains. While there don't seem to be organised pack-napping gangs as there are in India, the Vietnamese seem convinced that the young men and boys you see hanging out in the stations and on trains have only larceny

The Hanoi-Saigon Railway

Construction of the 1729 km Hanoi-Saigon railway – the Transindochinois – was begun in 1899 (under Governor-General Paul Doumer) and completed in 1936. In the late 1930s, the trip from Hanoi to Saigon took 40 hours and 20 minutes at an average speed of 43 km/h. During WW II, the Japanese made extensive use of the rail system, resulting in Viet Minh sabotage on the ground and US bombing from the air. After the war, efforts were made to repair the Transindochinois, major parts of which were either damaged or overgrown.

During the Franco-Vietminh War, the Viet Minh engaged in massive sabotage against the rail system. Sometimes, they would pry up and carry off several km of track in a single night. In response, the French introduced in 1948 two armoured trains equipped with turret-mounted cannon, anti-aircraft machine guns, grenade launchers and mortars (similar trains are used in Cambodia today on the Phnom Penh-Battambang line). During this period, the Viet Minh managed to put into service 300 km of track in an area wholly under their control (between Ninh Hoa and Danang), a fact to which the French responded with sabotage of their own.

In the late 1950s, the South, with US funding, reconstructed the track between Saigon and Hué, a distance of 1041 km. But between 1961 and 1964 alone, there were 795 VC attacks on the rail system, forcing the abandonment of large sections of track (including the Dalat spur). A major reconstruction effort was carried out between 1967 and 1969 and three sections of track were put back into operation: one in the immediate vicinity of Saigon, another between Nha Trang and Qui Nhon and a third between Danang and Hué.

By 1960, the North had repaired 1000 km of track, mostly between Hanoi and China. During the US air war against the North, the northern rail network was repeatedly bombed. Even now – almost two decades since the end of US bombing – clusters of bomb craters can be seen around virtually every rail bridge and train station in the north.

After reunification, the government immediately set about re-establishing the Hanoi-Saigon rail link as a symbol of Vietnamese unity. By the time the Reunification (Thong Nhat) Express trains were inaugurated on 31 December 1976, 1334 bridges, 27 tunnels, 158 stations and 1370 shunts (switches) had been repaired.

The Vietnamese railway system still has some steam engines in service, but these are rapidly being retired. Some (models such as the Pacific and Mikado) date from the colonial period while others were purchased over the years from Poland. In 1962, one steam engine was even built in Vietnam. The new diesel-powered engines include the French-built Alsthom, the Belgian BN/Cockerill and assorted American military, Czech and Indian equipment. The system's 4000 train wagons include 600 passenger cars from the French period. There is a staff of 70,000. There is a major railway repair yard at Thap Cham (near Phan Rang) which it may be possible to visit.

Recently, Ofermat (the French agency responsible for cooperation in the field of railway transport) began exploring the possibility of assisting Vietnam upgrade the Hanoi-Ho Chi Minh City line. And rumour has it that the Franco-Belgian group Compagnie Internationale des Wagons-Lits et du Tourisme is considering operating trains in Vietnam as it does in Egypt and elsewhere. Although the project to build a rail link with Laos has been shelved, the possibility of someday reopening the entire 84-km Thap Cham-Dalat line (44 km of which is a rack (cog) railway, or crémaillère) is being looked into. Recently, a five-km stretch has been reopened as a tourist attraction. ∎

on their minds. To protect your belongings, always keep your backpack or suitcase near you and lock or tie it to something, especially at night. If you must leave your pack for a moment, ask someone who looks responsible to keep an eye on it.

Thieves have become proficient at grabbing packs through the windows as trains pull out of stations. However, some trains are so slow that travellers have been known to jump off the train, run down the thief, recover the pack and hop back on board again!

There is supposedly a 20-kg limit for luggage carried on Vietnamese trains. Enforcement isn't real strict, but if you have too much stuff you might have to send it in the freight car (on the same train) and pay a small extra charge. This is a hassle that you'll probably want to avoid. Bicycles can also be sent in the freight car – this is a common practice.

Eating is no problem – there are vendors in every railway station who board the train and practically stuff food, drinks, cigarettes and lottery tickets into your pockets. However, the food that is supplied by the railway company (for free, as part of the cost of the ticket for some long journeys) is usually inedible, and possibly even a threat to your health. It's not a bad idea to stock up in the local market before taking a long trip.

Schedules

Odd-numbered trains travel southward; even-numbered trains travel northward. The Reunification Express trains go between Ho Chi Minh City and Hanoi. Local rail services connect various cities along the coast. Hanoi is linked with Haiphong and points between the capital and the Chinese border.

At the time of this writing, there were two trains daily departing Saigon and continuing all the way to Hanoi. The first departs Saigon Station daily at 7.30 am, arriving in Hanoi 48 hours later at 7.30 am. The second train departs Saigon on Monday, Wednesday and Saturday at 2.30 pm and arrives in Hanoi 42 hours later at 8.30 am. Another train departs Saigon Tuesday, Thursday, Friday and Sunday at 3 pm, arriving in Hanoi 48 hours later at 3 pm.

In addition, there are local trains. One train departs Saigon daily at 4.50 pm and arrives in Nha Trang at 5.05 am. There is a local train to Hué departing Saigon every other day at 9.15 am. And there is a local train to Qui Nhon, departing Saigon every other day at 9.50 am.

The train schedule changes so frequently (about every six months) that there's little point in reproducing the whole thing here. But the table should give you some idea of what to expect. The train schedule is posted at major stations and you can copy it down. There is also a limited schedule (express trains only) printed in English and available from the Saigon Railway Station.

Various local trains run between cities along the coast. They are incredibly slow, partly because other trains are given priority in both equipment and switching and partly because most of them stop at every one-horse town on the way. Most offer only very basic hard-seat cars.

Three rail lines link Hanoi with the other parts of northern Vietnam. One takes you east to the port city of Haiphong. A second heads north-east to Lang Son and Nanning, China. A third goes north-west to Pho Lu (which is 30 km short of Lao Cai) and Kunming, China. Train service to China was discontinued in 1979.

Classes

There are five classes of train travel in Vietnam: hard-seat, soft-seat, hard-berth, soft-berth and super-berth. Since it's the only thing the vast majority of Vietnamese can afford, hard-seat is usually packed. Hard-seat is tolerable for day travel, but overnight it can be even less comfortable than the bus, where at least you are hemmed in and thus propped upright. However, hard-seat is educational, and will give you some idea of the determined entrepreneurial spirit of the Vietnamese:

The train was a zoo. The hard-seat coach I was in had a centre aisle with benches on both sides arranged to face each other at a distance that allowed the knees of Vietnamese travellers to just miss each other. The other annoyance was that the constant traffic up and down the aisle required me to be continually moving my legs to unblock the path and allow the people to pass. Vendors of water and tea passed back and forth with ridiculous frequency. Constantly calling out their wares, they navigated the cluttered aisles in search of thirsty travellers whereby they would fill an aluminium Coke can that had had its top removed, leaving a jagged and rusted maw from which to drink. I preferred to purchase bottled water and carry it with me.

Both the marathon train rides I took stopped about once an hour. During these stops the train cars would be besieged both from the exterior by vendors attempting to sell their goods to you through the open window and from the interior by the more persistent who would add to the already crowded aisles (now filled with people getting on and off with their baggage). The variety of items to be purchased now ranged from whole cooked chickens to pieces of sugar cane to gnaw on.

The truly daring would climb onto the top of the train while it was stopped and then once we had started again and they believed it was safe, they would climb down and crawl through the open windows while the train was cruising along at its stately 40 to 50 km per hour. They would then have someone above pass them their food and/or drink and we would now have more sellers to cope with. The unfortunate were the passengers whose window this new entrepreneur had decided to enter from. They would have to deal with a clambering soul who would come pouncing across the unsuspecting riders' laps. These travelling salespeople also had to deal with the train conductors who carried electric shocking devices which they

would use on someone that they caught sneaking on board. Often our aisle would fill with vendors who were being chased from one end to the other. When the conductor got too close, everyone would head for the windows paying little heed to the passengers they had to hastily crawl over in order to get to the windows and freedom.

On one winding bit of track, I leaned out the window and got a good look at the roof of the train. I saw about 30 people of all ages and genders milling about with their goods trying to find out from their comrades already in the train where the conductors were and which was the best window to climb back into.

David Fisher

Hard-berth has three tiers of beds (six beds per compartment). Because the Vietnamese don't seem to like climbing up, the upper berth is cheapest, followed by the middle berth and finally the lower berth. The best bunk is the one in the middle because the bottom berth is invaded by seatless travellers during the day. There is no door to separate the compartment from the corridor.

Soft-seat carriages have vinyl-covered seats, rather than the uncomfortable benches of hard-seat.

Soft-berth has two tiers (four beds per compartment) and all bunks are priced the same. These compartments have a door. Super-berth compartments have two beds in a room with a door.

Station	Distance from Saigon	Hard Seat	Soft Seat	High Berth	Mid Berth	Low Berth	Soft Berth	Super Berth
Muong Man	175 km	$7	$8	$10	$11	$12	$13	$14
Thap Cham	319 km	$10	$12	$17	$18	$20	$22	$23
Nha Trang	411 km	$13	$15	$21	$23	$25	$27	$29
Tuy Hoa	529 km	$16	$18	$26	$29	$32	$34	$37
Dieu Tri	631 km	$18	$21	$31	$34	$37	$40	$44
Quang Ngai	798 km	$22	$26	$38	$42	$46	$50	$54
Danang	935 km	$27	$32	$46	$50	$55	$60	$64
Hué	1038 km	$29	$35	$50	$55	$61	$66	$71
Dong Ha	1104 km	$31	$37	$53	$59	$64	$70	$75
Dong Hoi	1204 km	$34	$40	$58	$64	$70	$76	$82
Vinh	1407 km	$40	$47	$68	$75	$82	$89	$96
Thanh Hoa	1551 km	$43	$51	$74	$82	$90	$98	$105
Ninh Binh	1612 km	$45	$53	$77	$85	$93	$101	$109
Nam Dinh	1639 km	$45	$54	$78	$86	$95	$103	$111
Hanoi	1726 km	$48	$56	$82	$91	$99	$108	$117

Reservations

As with all forms of transport in Vietnam, the supply of train seats is insufficient to meet demand. Reservations for all trips – even short ones – should be made at least one day in advance. For sleeping berths, you may have to book passage three or more days before the date of travel. Bring your passport, visa when buying train tickets. Though such documents are rarely checked at bus stations, train personnel may ask to have a look at them.

In any given city, reservations can be made only for travel originating in that city. In Nha Trang, for instance, you can reserve a place to Danang but cannot book passage from Danang to Hué. For this reason – and because train stations are often far from the part of town with the hotels in it – it is a good idea to make reservations for onward travel as soon as you arrive in a city (provided the ticket office is open). Local information on rail services, train station hours, etc is provided in the Getting There & Away listing under each city.

If you are unable to make reservations in advance, try showing up at the station half-an-hour before departure time. Station staff may make some sort of provision for you (after payment of an appropriate 'tip'), but be aware that because you are their guest, that provision may be the conductor's ordering some hapless Vietnamese to give up his or her seat.

If you are travelling with a bicycle (for which there is a small surcharge), it may only be possible to get it out of checked baggage at certain stations.

Costs

One disadvantage of rail travel is that officially, foreigners and Overseas Vietnamese are supposed to pay a surcharge of around 400% over and above what Vietnamese pay. It works out to about US$100 for a Saigon-Hanoi ticket in a hard-sleeper compartment. This is compared to US$150 to fly the same route.

Foreigners are expected to pay in US dollars cash only. Some foreigners have managed to pay local dong prices, but this is getting harder to do unless you have an Asian face. Even with Asian features, you are supposed to show an ID when the ticket is purchased, though a Vietnamese could buy the ticket for you. The ticket clearly indicates whether you paid in dollars or dong, and the name of the purchaser is also written on the ticket. Most conductors will enforce the rules – if you have blond hair and a big nose, don't think that you're going to fool the conductors into believing you're Vietnamese, even if you do wear a conical hat.

One advantage the train has over flying is that tickets are priced by multiplying the length of the trip (in km) by the tariff for the class you are travelling in. In other words, you are not penalised for breaking your journey. At least that's the theory – in practice, a short run is charged higher only because all ticket prices must be rounded off to the even dollar (and always rounded upwards, never downwards). If you were paying in dong, it would work out exactly.

You might also combine train travel with cheaper modes of transport, taking the train only for the most scenic sections of your

Station	Distance from Saigon	Soft Seat	High Berth	Mid Berth	Low Berth	Soft Berth	Super Berth
Nha Trang	411 km	$17	$23	$25	$27	$29	$31
Dieu Tri	631 km	$25	$34	$37	$40	$44	$47
Danang	935 km	$36	$50	$55	$60	$64	$69
Hué	1038 km	$40	$55	$61	$66	$71	$76
Dong Hoi	1204 km	$46	$64	$70	$76	$82	$88
Vinh	1407 km	$53	$74	$81	$88	$95	$102
Hanoi	1726 km	$64	$90	$98	$107	$116	$124

journey (say, between Danang and Hué), or only when the train schedule fits the times you wish to depart and arrive (you wouldn't want to arrive in Nam Dinh at 2 am no matter how cheap the ticket was).

The actual price you pay for a ticket depends on which train you take – the fastest trains are the most expensive. The table on page 151 has prices (in US dollars) for the Reunification Express trains taking 48 hours to make the Saigon-Hanoi run.

The fastest and most expensive Reunification Express train takes 42 hours to complete the Saigon-Hanoi run. Prices are listed in the table on page 152.

CAR

In Vietnam, traffic drives on the right-hand side of the road (usually). The police are known to be strict, though for a fee they may decide to forgive your transgressions.

Overall, the Vietnamese intercity road network of two-lane highways is fairly good, especially in the south (thanks to huge US war-time infrastructure investments). Though maintenance has been spotty and potholes are a problem in some places, highway travel is fast if you have a serviceable vehicle (a big *if*). On intercity roads, honking at all pedestrians (to warn them of your approach) is considered a basic element of safe driving.

Black-market petrol *(xang)* is sold – along with oil *(dau)* – in soft drink bottles at little stalls along city streets and intercity highways. You'll also see plenty of old petrol stations in the former South Vietnam bearing the signs of US companies long departed, like Caltex and Texaco.

If travelling long distance by car, it's often necessary to find a hotel with a garage or fenced-in compound (many hotels are so equipped). There are also commercial non-hotel garages. Leaving an unattended car parked out on the street overnight is not wise.

Rental

Drive-them-yourself rental cars have yet to

make their debut in the Socialist Republic, but cars with drivers can be hired from a variety of sources. For details on exactly what is available, see each city's Getting There & Away and Getting Around sections.

Ho Chi Minh City has an especially wide selection of government bodies, state companies and private concerns that hire out vehicles. Vietnam Tourism will hire out new Japanese cars with drivers for US$0.33 per km (with a minimum per-day charge). The same service is offered by various competing agencies, including many provincial tourism authorities and newly formed private companies.

For a seven-day trip (Saigon to Dalat, Nha Trang, Qui Nhon, Danang and Hué) we paid US$360. We flew on to Hanoi and the driver went back to Saigon. We were quoted over US$700 for the same trip by the government tourist agencies. Four French tourists we met paid US$560 but for 16 days and continuing north to Hanoi.

Tony & Maureen Wheeler

It is also possible to hire out a van – these can hold approximately eight to 12 persons. One advantage of vans is that they have high-clearance, a consideration on some of the dismal unsurfaced roads. With the exception of Russian-built or really old vehicles, most are equipped with air-conditioning. Since air-conditioned cars often cost more to rent, you might make your preferences known early when negotiating a price. Also, it's been our experience that not having an air-conditioner can be an advantage – Vietnamese drivers usually insist on keeping the air-conditioner at full-blast all day, even if it means wearing a winter coat in the tropical heat.

Most drivers refuse to drive after dark in rural areas because the unlit highways often have huge potholes, occasional collapsed bridges and lots of bicycles and pedestrians who seem oblivious to the traffic.

Almost all cars are equipped with a cassette tape player. Bring some music tapes or buy them from the local markets, and hope your driver, guide and fellow passengers have the same taste in music as you do!

MOPED & MOTORCYCLE

Mopeds and motorcycles are a popular form of transport among people, especially in the south, but increasingly in the north too. Potholes make intercity travel – especially at night – a risky proposition. And during the monsoon season, motorbike travel can be rather wet. Fortunately, rainsuits and ponchos are available at shops almost everywhere.

A moped is any motor-driven two-wheeled vehicle up to 50 cc. Over 50 cc is a motorcycle. In Vietnam, no driver's licence is needed to drive a moped, while to drive a motorcycle, you will need an international driver's licence endorsed for motorcycle operation.

Travellers availing themselves of two-wheeled motorised transport should be aware that Vietnam does not have an emergency rescue system or even a proper ambulance network – if something happens to you out on the road, you could be many hours from even rudimentary medical treatment.

Safety standards are not very high, and it's wise to drive during daylight hours only. Many Vietnamese drivers do suicidal things like driving at night with the headlights turned off – they believe that this saves petrol (it doesn't).

Only the very cheapest 'eggshell' motorcycle helmets are sold in Vietnam, and even then only at a handful of sports shops in Ho Chi Minh City (most of which are on Cach Mang Thang Tam St between Ben Thanh Market and the Immigration Police Office). You might consider purchasing a slightly battered US Army helmet – the bullet holes provide ventilation.

The roads are in poor condition and punctured tyres a common occurance, but tyre-patch stalls are ubiquitous. For motorcycles, this should cost around US$0.20 to US$0.30.

Rental

Renting a motorbike is now possible at some travel agencies in Ho Chi Minh City. It seems only a matter of time before this business spreads to Hanoi, Danang, Dalat and elsewhere.

The cost depends on the engine size. Renting a 50cc moped (the most popular model) is cheap at around US$5 to US$10 per day, usually with unlimited mileage. Large displacement bikes start from US$10 and there might be a distance charge in addition to the daily fee.

BICYCLE

By far the best way to get around Vietnam's towns and cities is to do as the locals do: ride a bicycle. During rush hours, urban thoroughfares approach gridlock as rushing streams of cyclists force their way through intersections without the benefit of traffic lights. Riders are always crashing into each other and getting knocked down, but because bicycle traffic is so heavy, they are rarely going fast enough to be injured. Westerners on bicycles are often greeted enthusiastically by locals who may never have seen a foreigner pedalling around before.

Vietnam is also a good place for intercity cycling: much of the country is flat or only moderately hilly, the major roads are of a serviceable standard (especially those built by the Americans in the south, many of which have wide shoulders) and the shortage of vehicles makes for relatively light traffic. Bicycles can be transported around the country on the top of buses or in train baggage compartments.

Groups of Western cyclists have begun touring Vietnam. The flat lands of the Mekong Delta region are one logical place for long-distance riding. The entire coastal route is also feasible, though some stretches of road are hilly and riddled with potholes. For more information on cycling tours to Vietnam, contact Saigon Tours or Que Viet Tours (☎ (514) 3933211) in Montreal.

You will not find 10-speed bikes or mountain bikes in Vietnam, so you must bring one if you plan to travel long distance by pedal power. Mountain bikes are definitely preferred – the occasional big pothole or unsealed road can be rough on a set of delicate rims. Basic cycling safety equipment is also not available in Vietnam, so such items as helmets, front and rear reflectors, leg reflectors and rear-view mirrors should be brought along. Another useful accessory to buy abroad is a pocket-size inner tube repair kit.

Hotels and some travel agencies are starting to get into the business of renting bicycles. The cost for this is around US$1 per day or US$0.20 per hour.

There are innumerable roadside bicycle repair stands in every city and town in Vietnam. Usually, they consist of no more than a pump, an upturned military helmet and a metal ammunition box filled with oily bolts and a few wrenches. In the south, the men who run these repair stands are mostly South Vietnamese Army veterans who are denied other opportunities to make a living.

Pumping up a tyre costs US$0.02. Fixing a punctured inner tube should cost between US$0.10 to US$0.20 depending on the size of the patch, the time of day and the presence of competition. The mechanics employ a brilliant system that allows them to patch inner tubes without removing the wheel from the frame or even taking the tyre off the rim. The tyre and inner tube are taken half off the rim and the exposed inner tube is partially pumped up and wetted. As the air drains out of the hole bubbles, which are easily visible and audible, are formed in the water. After the tyre is dried and sanded, rubber cement is used to glue on a patch.

The major cities have bicycle parking lots – usually just a roped-off section of sidewalk – which charge US$0.10 to guard your bike (bicycle theft is a major problem). When you pull up, a number will be chalked on the seat or stapled to the handlebars and you'll be handed a reclaim chit. Without it, getting your wheels back may be a real hassle, especially if you come back after the workers have changed shifts.

Many travellers buy a cheap bicycle, use it during their visit, and at the end either sell it or give it to a Vietnamese friend. Locally produced bicycles are available starting at

about US$25 but are of truly inferior quality. A decent one-speed Chinese-made bicycle costs about US$75. A locally assembled three-speed bike made with imported (Chinese, Japanese and Taiwanese) parts costs about US$100. Older bikes used French parts but these are no longer being sold.

All Vietnamese-made bicycles have the same mixte frame, but the various models are equipped with different accessories. The best of the lot is the 'Corporate' (is that an appropriate name for a good socialist bicycle?), which goes for US$35. The 'Saigon' costs US$25. The bottom-of-the-line 'Huu Nghi' will set you back US$20.

The Vietnamese-made frame is serviceable but the locally produced moving parts (including brakes, the crank shaft, pedals and gears as well as tyre inner tubes) should be avoided unless you want to spend as much time haggling with bicycle mechanics as you would have with cyclo drivers if you hadn't bought the bicycle in the first place.

The simplest place to buy a domestic bicycle is at government stores, but watch out for misaligned wheels, improperly assembled brakes, crooked bolts and worn threadings. In general, private shops provide superior assembly work.

Vietnamese-made bicycles are absolutely the worst I have ever seen. Two weeks after I bought my shiny new 'Corporate' bicycle, the bearings on the 'Forever' crankshaft brand began grinding horribly and thereafter required frequent adjustments. Two weeks later, one of the pedals suddenly snapped off. The brakes barely functioned from the first and were only marginally better than having no brakes at all (though it was comforting to think of them as brakes). One of the tyres blew out at least once every two days. According to newspaper reports, the state-run bicycle-making company is going broke: under the new economic policies, the company is now responsible for the huge stocks of unsold bicycles that are accumulating in warehouses because no one will buy them.

Daniel Robinson

Information on bicycle stores is listed under Bicycle in the Getting Around sections of Ho Chi Minh City, Danang, Hanoi, etc.

HITCHING

Westerners have reported great success at hitching in Vietnam. In fact, the whole system of passenger transport in Vietnam is premised on people standing along the highways and flagging down buses or trucks. To get a bus, truck or other vehicle to stop, stretch out your arm and gesture towards the ground with your whole hand. Drivers will expect to be paid for picking you up. Some Western travellers have had their offers to pay refused, but don't count on this. As long as you look like a foreigner (to many Vietnamese, foreigner = money) you rarely wait for more than a few passenger vehicles to pass before one stops.

One of the advantages of going from Hanoi to Saigon is that most people are doing just the opposite. Many folks pay for car rides heading north, so it's relatively easy to catch an empty car going south. I'd got to larger hotels, met the driver the night before and made a private deal (not with the driver's boss). I also tried standing by the roadside and flagging cars down. Some drivers knew what was going on and knew exactly how much to charge. But on certain stretches of highway, traffic of passenger vehicles was light indeed. The best advice in such cases is to start out early.

Ivan Kasimoff

The engines of most older trucks are equipped with an ingenious gravity-powered heat-dissipation system. When the vehicle's original radiator rusted out and became worthless, a drum was attached to the roof of the cab and connected to the engine by a hose routed via the driver's window, where a stopcock was installed to allow him to control the flow. Cold water in the rooftop drum slowly drains into the engine; hot water squirts out the side of the truck from a little nozzle. When the drum is empty, the truck stops at any of the numerous water-filling stations that line major highways.

Licence Plates

You can learn a great deal about a vehicle by examining its licence plate. Whether you are in a confusing bus station looking for the right bus or hitchhiking and wish to avoid accidentally flagging down an army truck,

the following information should prove useful.

First, there are the several types of licence plates. Vehicles with white numbers on a green field are owned by the government. Vehicles operated by cooperatives or private concerns have black numbers on white. Diplomatic cars have the letters NG in red over green numbers on a white field. Other cars owned by foreigners begin with the letters NN and are green-on-white. Military plates have white numerals on red.

The first two numerals on a number plate are the two-digit code assigned to the vehicle's province of origin. Because the vast majority of vehicles in the country are controlled at the provincial level and used to link a given province with other parts of the country, there is usually a 50-50 chance that the vehicle is headed towards its home territory.

The two-digit number codes for most provinces (listed more or less north to south) are as follows:

13	Ha Bac
15	Greater Haiphong
17	Thai Binh
18	Nam Ha & Ninh Binh
20	Bac Thai
21	Lao Cai & Yen Bai
28	Hoa Binh
29	Greater Hanoi
36	Thanh Hoa
37	Nghe An
38	Ha Tinh
39/40	Quang Binh, Quang Tri & Thua Thien-Hué
43	Quang Nam-Danang
44	Quang Ngai & Binh Dinh
45	Phu Yen & Khanh Hoa
46	Kon Tum
47	Dac Lac
48	Binh Thuan
49	Lam Dong
50	Ho Chi Minh City (government)
51/55	Ho Chi Minh City (private)
60	Dong Nai
61	Song Be
62	Long An
63	Tien Giang
64	Vinh Long
65	Cantho

WALKING

You aren't likely to do much long-distance walking in the steamy tropical lowlands which are dominated by dense vegetation, but some spots in the central highlands and the far north offer hiking possibilities. The biggest hazard is likely to be the police – check to make sure that you aren't entering a prohibited area.

One thing to be aware of in the south is that in equatorial regions, there is very little twilight – night comes on suddenly without warning. Therefore, you can't readily judge how many hours of daylight remain unless you have a watch. Pay attention to how long you'll need to get back to civilisation – otherwise, be prepared for an impromptu camping trip.

If you'd rather run, not walk, it's interesting to note that long-distance running has made its debut in Vietnam. At the end of the '80s, someone actually ran from Hanoi to Danang. No wonder the Vietnamese think that foreigners are mad.

BOAT

Vietnam has an enormous number of rivers that are at least partly navigable, the most important of which are the multibranched Mekong River in the south and the Red River and its tributaries in the north. Both deltas are crisscrossed with waterways which can be crossed by boat. Vessels of all sorts can be hired in most riverine and seaside towns. For more information, see the Getting There & Away sections of Ho Chi Minh City, the Mekong Delta cities and Hoi An; the Getting Around sections of Nha Trang and Hué; and Halong Bay.

Some of the smaller rivercraft can only accommodate three or four people. Whenever you take such a small boat, it's wise to keep your camera in a plastic bag when not actually in use so as to protect it from being splashed by water.

LOCAL TRANSPORT

Bus

Vietnam has some of the worst local inner-city bus transport in Asia. There is a bare-bones bus system in Hanoi and Ho Chi Minh City, but in general, this is not a practical way to get around. Fortunately, there are many other options.

Taxi

Western-style taxis with meters are just beginning to make their appearance in Ho Chi Minh City. In most cases, the only option is to rent a car.

For sightseeing trips just around the Saigon or Hanoi areas, a car with driver can also be rented by the day or by the hour (renting by the day is cheaper). For definition purposes, a 'day' is eight hours or less with a total distance travelled of less than 100 km. Based on this formula, a car costs US$25 per day (or US$4 per hour) for a Russian-built vehicle; US$35 per day (US$5 per hour) for a small Japanese car; US$40 per day (US$6 per hour) for a larger late-model Japanese car; US$64 per day (US$8 per hour) for a limousine.

For details on exactly what is available in each city, see the Getting There & Away and

Getting Around sections of each chapter. Ho Chi Minh City is particularly rich in options.

Cyclo

The cyclo or pedicab *(xich lo)*, short for the French *cyclo-pousse*, is the best invention since sliced bread. Cyclos offer an easy, cheap and aesthetic way to get around Vietnam's confusing, sprawling cities. Riding in one of these clever contraptions will also give you the moral superiority that comes with knowing you are being kind to the environment – certainly kinder than all those drivers on whining, smoke-spewing motorbikes.

Groups of cyclo drivers always hang out near major hotels and markets, and quite a number of them speak at least a bit of English (in the south, many of the cyclo drivers are former South Vietnamese Army soldiers). The ones who speak English charge a little more than the ones who don't, but avoiding the language problem may be worth the minor added expense (we're talking peanuts). To make sure the driver understands where you want to go, it's useful to bring a city map with you, though some drivers cannot read maps either.

Fares are very cheap, but only if you bargain: the drivers know that US$1 or its dong equivalent is nothing to most Westerners. If the cyclo drivers waiting outside the hotel want too much, flag down someone else less used to spendthrift tourists. Settle on a fare *before* going anywhere or you're likely to be asked for some outrageous quantity of dong at the trip's end.

Average price is around US$0.10 to US$0.20 per km (towards the upper end of this price scale in Saigon). Hanoi fares are cheaper. Have your money counted out and ready before getting on a cyclo. It also pays to have the exact money – drivers will sometimes claim they cannot make change for a 5000d note.

Cyclos are cheaper if you charter one for the day. A typical price might be US$4 for six to eight hours. If this works out well, don't be surprised if the driver comes around your hotel the next morning to see if you want to hire him again.

Xe Lam

Xe Lams are tiny three-wheeled trucks used for short-haul passenger and freight transport (similar to the Indonesian *bajaj*). They tend to have whining two-stroke 'lawn mower' engines with no mufflers, and emit copious quantities of blue exhaust smoke, but they get the job done.

Honda Om

The *Honda om* is an ordinary motorbike on which you ride seated behind the driver. Getting around this way with luggage is quite a challenge. There is no set procedure for finding a driver willing to transport you somewhere. You can either try to flag someone down (most drivers can always use a bit of extra cash) or ask a Vietnamese to find a Honda om for you. The fare is a bit more than a cyclo for short trips and about the same as a cyclo for longer distances.

Walking

If you don't want to wind up like a bug on a windshield, you need to pay attention to a few pedestrian survival rules, especially in motorbike-crazed Saigon. Foreigners frequently make the mistake of thinking that the best way to cross a busy Vietnamese street is to run quickly across it. Sometimes this works and sometimes it doesn't. Most Saigonese cross the street slowly – very slowly – giving the motorbike drivers sufficient time to judge your position so they can pass to either side of you. They will *not* stop or even slow down, but they *will* try to avoid hitting you. Just don't make any sudden moves. Good luck.

Mekong Delta Special

Two forms of transport used mostly in the Mekong Delta are the *xe dap loi*, a wagon pulled by a bicycle, and the *xe Honda loi*, a wagon pulled by a motorbike.

TOURS

If you decide to rent a car with driver and guide, you'll have the opportunity to design your own itinerary for what amounts to a private tour for you and your companions. Seeing the country this way is almost like individual travel except that you'll have to decide where to go in advance.

The cost varies considerably. On the high end are tours booked through government travel agencies like Saigon Tourist and Vietnam Tourism. A tour booked with these agencies is about US$50 to US$60 a day for one person (and less each for two or more people because transport and lodging costs can be shared). Students receive a 15% discount, which they are more likely to get if they have an official-looking letter from their university registrar to show.

This price includes accommodation at a tourist-class hotel (which costs at least US$25 per night for a single anyway, though hotels for domestic tourists cost a tenth of that), a guide who will accompany you everywhere, a local guide in each province you visit, a driver and a car. Insist that your guides are fluent in a language you know well. The cost of the car is computed on a per-km basis. At present, Vietnam Tourism cars, usually new imports from Japan, are billed at US$0.33 per km.

When you settle on your itinerary, make sure to get a written copy from Vietnam Tourism. If you later find that your guide feels like deviating from what you paid for, that piece of paper is your most effective leverage. If your guide asks for the itinerary, keep the original and give him or her a photocopy, as there have been reports of guides taking tourists' itineraries and then running the tour their way.

> Our guide was incredibly stubborn and arrogant, always thinking that he knew more than us. Whenever we tried to tell him something, he suddenly developed a hearing problem. But whenever he wasn't sure about something (like the location of a hotel, the name of a temple, etc), he asked to borrow our Lonely Planet book!
>
> **Robert Storey**

A tour booked with Vietnam Tourism, Saigon Tourist or any travel agent will likely be more expensive if you book it outside of Vietnam. However, large groups booking far in advance usually do get a discount.

Do-It-Yourself Tours

It's entirely possible to round up a small group of budget travellers, hire a guide and private car and arrange your own tour for much less than a travel agency would charge you.

Guides A good guide can be your translator, travelling companion and can save you as much money as he or she is costing you (by helping you pay local prices and by keeping you out of trouble with the police). A bad guide can ruin your trip. Interview your guide thoroughly before starting out – make sure that this is someone you can travel with. Agree on the price before beginning the journey; for a private guide, US$5 per day is a typical rate (this might increase in future) and it's proper to throw in a bonus at the end of your trip if your guide proved particularly helpful and saved you money.

A guide hired from a government-owned travel agency will cost you US$15 per day, of which perhaps only US$1 actually goes into the guide's pocket. With private guides, you are also responsible for their travel expenses – with a guide hired from the government, you need to ask. If you can gather up a small group of travellers, the cost of hiring a guide can be shared amongst all of you. If you are travelling solo, your guide may be able to drive you around on a motorbike but you should pay for the petrol and parking fees.

For the writing of this second edition, we found an able guide at the Sinh Café in Saigon. The best time to look for guides seems to be in the morning – visit the cafes around 8 or 9 am.

For trips in and around big cities like Saigon and Hanoi, you will often find women working as guides. Very few women are employed as guides on long-distance trips.

Ho Chi Minh City
Thành Phố Hồ Chí Minh

Ho Chi Minh City (population four million) covers an area of 2029 sq km stretching from the South China Sea almost to the Cambodian border. Its land is overwhelmingly rural (93%), dotted with villages and groups of houses set amidst rice paddies. Nevertheless, this rural area holds only about 25% of Ho Chi Minh City's population.

The downtown section of Ho Chi Minh City, now officially called District 1, is still known as Saigon. Many people use the name 'Saigon' and 'Ho Chi Minh City' interchangeably, but 'Ho Chi Minh City' is politically correct while 'Saigon' is what most local residents prefer. Whatever you wish to call it, this is the neighbourhood most visited by Western travellers.

To the west of downtown is District 5, the huge Chinese neighbourhood called Cholon which some people will tell you means Chinatown. In fact, Cholon means Big Market, a good indication of the importance the Chinese have traditionally played in Vietnam's economy. However, Cholon is not quite as Chinese as it used to be, largely thanks to the anticapitalist anti-Chinese campaign of 1978-79 which caused many ethnic Chinese to flee the country, taking with them their money and entrepreneurial skills. With Vietnam's recent opening to the outside world, many of these refugees are returning (with foreign passports) to explore investment possibilities, and Cholon's hotels are once again packed with Chinese-speaking business people.

Along with surrounding areas, Saigon and Cholon constitute the industrial and commercial heart of Vietnam, accounting for 30% of Vietnam's manufacturing output and 25% of its retail trade. It is to Ho Chi Minh City that the vast majority of foreign business people come to invest and trade. It is to Ho Chi Minh City that ambitious young people and bureaucrats – from the north and

south – gravitate to make a go of it. And it is here that the economic changes sweeping Vietnam – and their social implications – are most evident.

Saigon, Cholon and the immediately surrounding areas have a population of about three million – easily Vietnam's most densely populated area (the average density in the city is 21,500 per sq km). The huge numbers of people and their obvious industriousness give Ho Chi Minh City a bustling, dynamic, vital atmosphere. The streets, where much of the city's life takes place, are lined with stores, shops, stalls, stands-on-wheels and vendors with their wares spread out on the sidewalk selling everything from soup to sophisticated electronics.

While their rural compatriots are working from dawn to dusk in the country's rice paddies, Ho Chi Minh City's residents are working just as hard at the pursuits of urban people: selling vegetables, buying necessities, cutting business deals, commuting. There is something exhilarating about it all, something reassuring about being surrounded by living evidence of the tenacious will of human beings to survive and improve their lot.

Saigon's neoclassical and international-style buildings (and nearby sidewalk kiosks selling French rolls and croissants) give certain neighbourhoods a vaguely French atmosphere.

Other sections of the city are obviously American, at least in architecture. If you've ever wanted to visit (or revisit) a small American city of the 1960s, Saigon's US-era buildings, which have not been completely redecorated every five years like those in the USA, may be the closest you'll ever get. There are places in Ho Chi Minh City where miniskirts and bell-bottom polyester leisure suits would blend in perfectly with the rest of the decor.

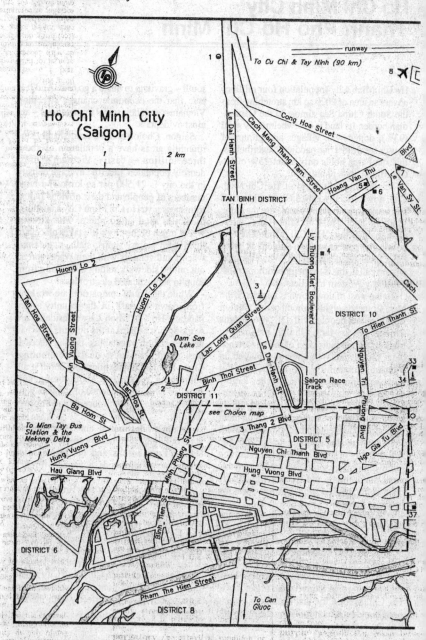

Ho Chi Minh City
(Saigon)

0   1   2 km

runway

To Cu Chi & Tay Ninh (90 km)

1

8 ✈

Cong Hoa Street

Cach Mang Thang Tam Street

Hoang Van Thu

Blvd

Le Van Sy St.

5

6

7

TAN BINH DISTRICT

Le Dai Hanh Street

Ly Thuong Kiet Boulevard

4

Cach

Huong Lo 2

Huong Lo 14

3

DISTRICT 10

To Hien Thanh St

Tan Hoa Street

An Vuong Street

Lac Long Quan Street

Le Dai Hanh St.

Nguyen Tri Phuong Blvd

Dam Sen
Lake

2

Binh Thoi Street

Saigon Race
Track

33

34

DISTRICT 11

see Cholon map

Ba Hom St

3 Thang 2 Blvd

DISTRICT 5

Ngo Gia Tu Blvd

To Mien Tay Bus
Station & the
Mekong Delta

Hung Vuong Blvd

Nguyen Chi Thanh Blvd

Hau Giang Blvd

Hung Vuong Blvd

37

Minh Phung St.

Binh Tien St

DISTRICT 6

Pham The Hien Street

To Can
Giuoc

DISTRICT 8

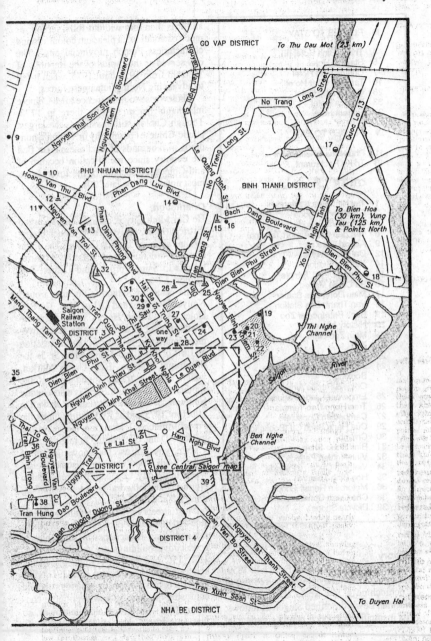

■ **PLACES TO STAY**

4 Thanh Binh Hotel (II)
5 Star Hill Hotel
6-7 Chains First Hotel
10 Tan Son Nhat Hotel
28 Que Huong Hotel
33 Ky Hoa Hotel
37 Regent Hotel

▼ **PLACES TO EAT**

11 Phu Nhuan Restaurant
13 Tri Ky Restaurant

OTHER

1 Tay Ninh Bus Station
2 Giac Vien Pagoda
3 Giac Lam Pagoda
8 Tan Son Nhat Airport Terminal
9 Airport Gate
12 Dai Giac Pagoda
14 Xe Lam Station
15 Le Van Duyet Temple
16 Ba Chieu Market
17 Mien Dong Bus Station
18 Van Thanh Bus Station
19 Back Entrance of Zoo
20 History Museum
21 Main Zoo Gate
22 Zoo
23 Military Museum
24 Vietnam Airlines Domestic Booking Office & Pacific Airlines
25 Emperor of Jade Pagoda
26 Tran Hung Dao Temple
27 Cambodian Consulate
29 Cua Hang Sach Cu (Bookshop)
30 Church
31 Binh Soup Shop
32 Vinh Nghien Pagoda
34 Vietnam Quoc Tu Pagoda
35 Hoa Binh Theatre
36 Motorbike Repair Shops
38 Cho Quan Church
39 Bicycle Shops

History

Saigon was captured by the French in 1859, becoming the capital of the French colony of Cochinchina a few years later. In 1950, Norman Lewis described Saigon as follows: 'its inspiration has been purely commercial and it is therefore without folly, fervour or much ostentation...a pleasant, colourless and characterless French provincial city'. The city served as the capital of the Republic of Vietnam from 1956 until 1975, when it fell to advancing North Vietnamese forces.

Cholon rose to prominence after Chinese merchants began settling there in 1778. Though Cholon still constitutes the largest ethnic-Chinese community in Vietnam, hundreds of thousands of Cholonese have fled the country since reunification because of anti-Chinese persecution by the government, most notably in the late '70s.

Orientation

Ho Chi Minh City is divided into 12 urban districts (*quan,* derived from French *quartier*) and six rural districts (*huyen*). The urban districts are numbered. District 1 corresponds to Saigon proper and District 5 is Cholon.

The centre of Saigon is the area around Nguyen Hue Blvd and Le Loi Blvd. The Rex Hotel (Ben Thanh Hotel), which is at the intersection of these two streets, is a convenient landmark. Nearby, at the intersection of Le Loi Blvd and Dong Khoi St, is the Municipal Theatre. Ben Thanh Market, which fronts a traffic roundabout at the southern end of Le Loi Blvd, is also a handy landmark. Dong Khoi St (known as Tu Do St before 1975 and as Rue Catinat under the French) stretches 1.1 km from the waterfront to Notre Dame Cathedral. On maps lacking a scale, you can use the known length of Dong Khoi St to estimate distances elsewhere in the city. Le Duan Blvd runs behind Notre Dame Cathedral between Reunification Hall and the Zoo.

Most streets have even numbers on one side and odd numbers on the other, but there are confusing exceptions. In some places, consecutive buildings are numbered 15A, 15B, 15C and so forth, while elsewhere, consecutive addresses read 15D, 17D, 19D, etc. Often, two numbering systems – the old confusing one and the new even-more-confusing one – are in use simultaneously, so that an address may read '1743/697'. In some cases (such as Lac Long Quan St, where Giac Lam Pagoda is located) several streets, numbered separately, have been run together under one name so that as you walk along, the numbers go from one into the hundreds (or thousands) and then start over again.

For fans of Graham Greene's 1954 novel *The Quiet American*, Rue Catinat is now Dong Khoi St; Blvd Charner has become Nguyen Hue Blvd; Blvd Bonnard is now known as Le Loi Blvd; Place François Garnier is at the intersection of Le Loi and Nguyen Hue boulevards; Blvd de la Somme is now Ham Nghi Blvd; Avenue Galliéni has become Tran Hung Dao Blvd; Quai de la Marne is now called Ben Van Don St; and Rue D'Ormay has become Mac Thi Buoi St.

Information

Tourist Office Saigon Tourist (Cong Ty Du Lich Thanh Pho Ho Chi Minh) is Ho Chi Minh City's official government-run travel agency. Saigon Tourist owns 60 hotels and numerous high-class restaurants in Ho Chi Minh City, plus a car-rental agency and tourist traps like the International Tourist Club, Vietnam International Golf Club and the Chu Chi Tunnel site, to name a few.

The way Saigon Tourist got so big is simple; the hotels and restaurants were 'liberated' from their former capitalist (mostly ethnic-Chinese) owners after 1975, most of whom subsequently fled the country. To be fair, Saigon Tourist has in the past few years been wisely investing much of the profits back into new hotels and tourist theme parks like the Binh Quoi Tourist Village. The company keeps growing bigger – if Vietnam ever establishes a stock market, Saigon Tourist shares will be blue chip.

Saigon Tourist has two offices in Ho Chi Minh City, each with a different function. The most important for visitors is Saigon Tourist Travel Service (☎ 230100, 295834, 298129; telex 812745 SGTOUR-VT; fax (84-8) 224987) at 49 Le Thanh Ton St (corner Dong Khoi St). Perhaps they are overworked, underpaid or just sick of tourists, but we have found the staff at this office

to be cordial but cold – they lack the friendly Vietnamese smile which is so common elsewhere.

The main administrative office of Saigon Tourist (☎ 295000, 295534; telex 812745 SGTOUR-VT; fax (84-8) 291026) is at 39 Le Thanh Ton St. This would be the office to contact for establishing business relationships (like cooperative joint tours with a foreign travel agency, etc).

Saigon Tourist charges the standard government rate of US$0.33 per km for car rentals. This place also offers trips to Cambodia, for which 'capitalist tourists' are asked to pay US$1000 for a four-day tour to Angkor Wat. Much more reasonable are the various city tours which are popular even with some budget travellers.

Vietnam Tourism (Tong Cong Ty Du Lich Viet Nam; ☎ 291276; telex 811295 DULIVN-VT; fax (84-8) 290775) is at 69-71 Nguyen Hue Blvd. This is the government's main tourist agency and is open from 7.30 to 11.30 am and 1 to 4.30 pm Monday to Saturday. The staff of Vietnam Tourism are even less enthusiastic than those at Saigon Tourist – they have little interest in individual travellers, at least not until you wave a wad of money in front of them. Their job is to provide package tours, but if you push them the staff may grudgingly reveal information about visa extensions. Like Saigon Tourist, Vietnam Tourism is anxious to book pricey Cambodia tours.

Travel Agencies There are plenty of other travel agencies in Ho Chi Minh City, both government and private, which can provide cars, book air tickets and extend your visa. Some of these places charge the same as Saigon Tourist and Vietnam Tourism, while others are much cheaper. Competition between these agencies is keen – the price war has turned into a price bloodbath – and you can often undercut Saigon Tourist's tariffs by 50% if you shop around. Some agencies which have been recommended by travellers for low prices and good service include: Ann Tourist, Cam On Tour, CESAIS Lam Son Travel, Easiway, Sinh Café, Oscan

Enterprises, Phoenix Services and Peace Tours.

However, no matter what recommendations you get, always compare prices before you put down the cash – management can change so good places can go bad and bad places can suddenly improve. No doubt that new travel agencies will be opening up, but at the time of this writing the line-up included:

An Giang Tourist
(Cong Ty Du Lich An Giang) 52 An Binh, District 5 (☎ 353324)
Ann Tourist
58 Ton That Tung, District 1 (☎ 323866; fax (84-8) 298540)
Ben Thanh Tourist
(Khoi Cong Ty Du Lich Ben Thanh) 86 Ly Tu Trong, District 1 (☎ 291616)
Ben Tre Tourist
(Cong Ty Du Lich Ben Tre) 36 Vo Van Tan, District 3 (☎ 222031)
Binh Duong Tourist
(Dai Dien Du Lich Song Be) 281 Cach Mang Thang 8, Tan Binh District (☎ 231015)
Cam On Tour
62 Hai Ba Trung St, District 1 (☎ 222166; fax (84-8) 298540)
CESAIS Lam Son Travel
9 Lam Son Square (behind the Municipal Theatre), District 1
CESAIS Tourism Service Centre
(Trung Tam Dich Vu Du Lich CESAIS) 17 Pham Ngoc Thach, District 3 (☎ 296750)
Cholon Tourism Service
(Cong Ty Dich Vu Du Lich Cho Lon) 192-194 Su Van Hanh, District 5 (☎ 557100)
Cuu Long Tourist
(Cong Ty Du Lich Cuu Long) 45 Dinh Tien Hoang, District 1 (☎ 293990)
Dong Nai Tourist
(Du Lich Dong Nai) 178 Tran Hung Dao, District 1 (☎ 222467)
Dong Thap Tourist
(Cong Ty Dich Vu Du Lich Dong Thap) 16/1A Le Hong Phong, District 10 (☎ 355826)
Easiway
(Pham Bac Hoa & Christine Hong) 34 Pham Ngoc Thach, District 3 (☎ 231337)
Forsevico
(also Kathy's Ceramic Shop) No 6 Kiosque, Nguyen Hue, District 1 (☎ 299111 ext 798; fax (84-8) 290194)
Haco Tourist
64 Nguyen Cong Tru, District 1 (☎ 293409)

Kim Café
Pham Ngu Lao St (next to Hoang Vu Hotel), District 1
Lam Dong Tourist
(Dai Dien Cong Ty Du Lich Lam Dong) 470 Ngo Gia Tu, District 10 (☎ 350973)
Oil Services Company (OSC)
(Chi Nhanh OSC Thanh Pho Ho Chi Minh) 65 Nam Ky Khoi Nghia, District 1 (☎ 296658)
Oscan Enterprises
2D Pham Ngoc Thach St, District 3 (☎ 231191, fax (84-8) 231024)
Peace Tours
(Cong Ty Du Lich Hoa Binh) 60 Vo Van Tan, District 3 (☎ 298707)
Phoenix Services
199 Nam Ay Khoi Nghai, District 3 (☎ 396143)
Phu Yen Tourist
(Cong Ty Du Lich Phu Yen) 46 Cach Mang Thang 8, District 3 (☎ 645680)
Railroad Tourism Service Company
(Cong Ty Du Lich Duong Sat) 10 Bis Ky Dong, District 3 (☎ 291274)
Sinh Café
6 Pham Ngu Lao St (opposite Prince Hotel), District 1
Vietnam Youth Tourism Service Center II
(Trung Tam Du Lich Thanh Nien VN Co So 2) 31 Cao Thang, District 3 (☎ 390704)
Vung Tau Tourist
(Cong Ty Dich Vu Du Lich Vung Tau) 191 Nam Ky Khoi Nghia, District 3 (☎ 222204)
VYC Tourism Center
(Khoi Trung Tam Dich Vu Du Lich VYC) 180 Nguyen Cu Trinh, District 1 (☎ 323643)
Youth Tourist Centre
06 Mac Dinh Chi St, District 1 (☎ 290345)

Money There is a bank at the airport which gives an excellent exchange rate. The only problem is that the staff works banker's hours, which means it's closed when at least half of the flights arrive. For this reason, you'd be wise to have sufficient US dollar notes in small denominations to get yourself into the city.

Vietcombank (☎ 4252831; fax 4259224), also known as the Bank for Foreign Trade of Vietnam (Ngan Hang Ngoai Thuong Viet Nam), is at 29 Ben Chuong Duong St on the corner of Nguyen Thi Minh Khai St (Pasteur St), two blocks south of Ham Nghi Blvd. It is open from 7 to 11.30 am and 1.30 to 3.30 pm daily except Saturday afternoons and the last day of the month. Here you can change

US dollars cash, other major hard currencies and travellers' cheques at the official rate. Besides US dollars, hard currencies which are currently acceptable (but this could change) include Australian dollars, British pounds sterling, Canadian dollars, Deutchmarks, French francs, Hong Kong dollars, Japanese yen, Singapore dollars, Swiss francs and Thai baht. Travellers' cheques denominated in US dollars can be changed for a 1½% commission. Bring your passport (or a photocopy of it) for identification.

Vietcombank does cash advances for holders of MasterCard. If you need a cash advance against a Visa card, the place to go is Banque Française du Commerce Extérieur, 10 Ham Nghi St. Of course, the situation could change and perhaps by the time you read this, Vietcombank will also provide this service.

Incombank HCM (☎ 290491) has plans to change foreign currencies. The service windows are on the ground floor of a 10-storey building at 79A Ham Nghi Blvd, District 1.

Currently, the only foreign bank authorised to handle foreign currency transactions (cash, not travellers' cheques) is Banque Indovina, a joint-venture between Indonesia's Summa group and Vietnam's Bank for Industry & Trade.

There are a number of other foreign banks with representative offices in Saigon. These banks do not handle foreign exchange (though they might in the future) and are mostly geared towards trying to set up loans for foreign joint-venture companies. For whatever it's worth, Saigon's foreign banks include:

Banque Française du Commerce Extérieur
    10 Ham Nghi St, District 1 (☎ 294144; telex 811563 BFCE; fax (84-8) 299126)
Banque Indosuez
    4 Dong Khoi, District 1 (☎ 295048; telex 812688 INDOS; fax (84-8) 296065)
Banque Indovina
    36 Ton That Dam, District 1 (☎ 230130; telex 811515 IVB, fax (84-8) 230131)

Banque Nationale de Paris
    4 Dong Khoi, District 1 (☎ 299504; telex 812693 BNP; fax (84-8) 299486)
Crédit Lyonnais
    17 Ton Duc Thang, District 1 (☎ 299226; telex 812742 CRED; fax (84-8) 296465)
Standard Chartered Bank
    134 Dong Khoi St, District 1 (☎ 298335; telex 811411 SCBHCM; fax (84-8) 298426)

You can get the bank rate at the officially sanctioned exchange windows in the jewellery shops at 71c Dong Khoi St (☎ 291522) and 112 Nguyen Hue Blvd (☎ 225693). For a rate that is about 5% below the bank rate, try the *bureau de change* at the top of the escalators on the 2nd floor of the Saigon Intershop (101 Nam Ky Khoi Nghia St, just off Le Loi Blvd).

All the major tourist hotels can change money quickly, easily, legally and well after business hours. The catch is that they offer rates around 5% lower than the bank rate.

To find a shopkeeper willing to trade dong for dollars on the black market, ask around discreetly. The men who accost you on the street offering great rates are con artists.

Post & Telecommunications Saigon's French-style General Post Office (Buu Dien Thanh Pho Ho Chi Minh; ☎ 296644, fax 298540), with its glass canopy and iron frame, is at 2 Cong Xa Paris, right next to Notre Dame Cathedral. The structure was built between 1886 and 1891 and is still the largest post office in Vietnam. Under the benevolent gaze of Ho Chi Minh, you will be charged exorbitant rates for whatever international telecommunications services you require. The staff at the information desk (☎ 296555, 299615), which is to the left as you enter the building, speak English. Postal services are available daily from 7.30 am to 7.30 pm. Pens, envelopes, aerograms and postcards are on sale at the counter to the right of the entrance and outside the GPO along Nguyen Du St.

DHL Worldwide Express (☎ 296203, 290446; fax (84) 298540/1), which offers express document and parcel delivery, has a

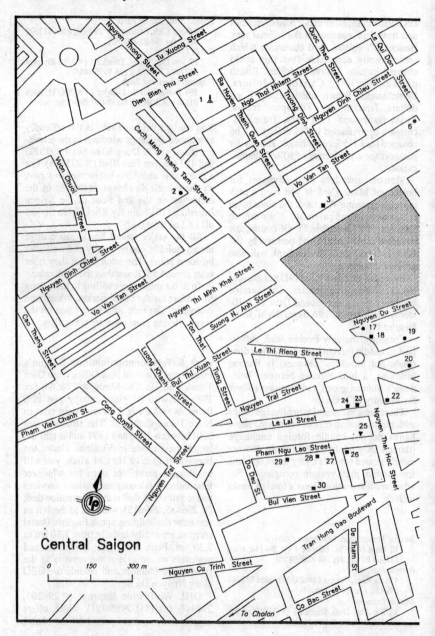

Central Saigon

0   150   300 m

To Cholon

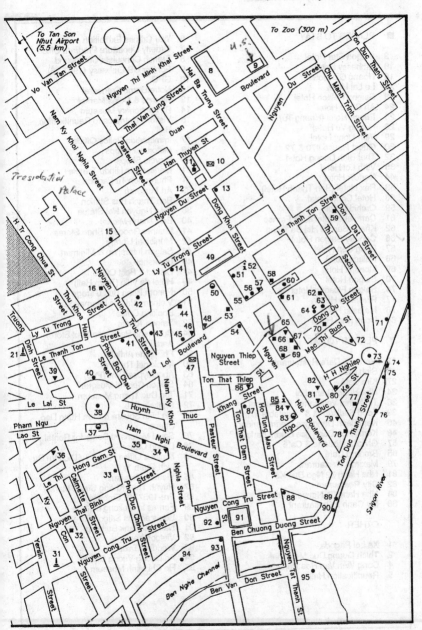

■ PLACES TO STAY

3   Saigon Star Hotel
16 Embassy Hotel
18 Hoang Gia Hotel
22 Le Lai Hotel
23 Saigon Palace Hotel
24 Ah Chau Hotel
26 Prince Hotel (Hoang Tu)
28 Hoang Vu Hotel
29 Vien Dong Hotel
30 Guest House #70 & 72
32 Thai Binh Duong Hotel
35 Vinh Loi Hotel
44 Norfolk Hotel
53 Rex Hotel (Ben Thanh Hotel)
58 Hotel Continental
59 Orchid Hotel
61 Caravelle Hotel & Air France
62 Khach San 69 Hai Ba Trung
66 Century Saigon Hotel
67 Bong Sen Hotel
68 Palace Hotel
69 Mondial Hotel
70 Saigon Hotel
74 Saigon Floating Hotel
77 Riverside Hotel
78 Majestic Hotel
80 Dong Khoi Hotel

▼ PLACES TO EAT

12 Madame Dai's Restaurant
25 Sinh Café
27 Kim Café
34 Nha Hang Thang Loi
36 Tin Nghia Vegetarian Restaurant
39 Food Stalls/Fruit & Vegetable Market
46 Kem Bach Dang (ice cream parlour)
48 Kem Bach Dang (ice cream parlour)
57 Givral Pâtisserie & Café
65 Brodard Café
79 Maxim's Restaurant
81 Nha Hang 32 Ngo Duc Ke
82 City Restaurant
84 Nha Hang 51 Nguyen Hue
86 My Canh 2 Restaurant

OTHER

1   Xa Loi Pagoda
2   Thich Quang Duc Memorial
4   Cong Vien Van Hoa Park
5   Reunification Hall

6   War Crimes Exhibition
7   Orderly Departure Program Office
8   French Consulate Compound
9   Former US Embassy (1967-75)
10 GPO
11 Notre Dame Cathedral
13 Stamps & Coins Market
14 Revolutionary Museum
15 Visitors' Entrance to Reunification Hall
17 Immigration Police Office
19 Motorbike Shops
20 Bicycle Shops
21 Mariamman Hindu Temple
31 Phung Son Tu Pagoda
33 Art Museum
37 Ben Thanh Bus Station
38 Tran Nguyen Hai Statue
40 Ben Thanh Market
41 Leather Goods & Shoe Stores
42 Municipal Library
43 Saigon Intershop & Minimart
45 Bookshop
47 District 1 Post Office
49 Hôtel de Ville (Town Hall)
50 Phnom Penh Bus Garage
51 Vietnam Airlines International Booking Office
52 Saigon Tourist
54 Cua Hang Bach Hoa (Tax Store)
55 Aeroflot
56 Philippine Airlines
60 Municipal Theatre
63 Apocalypse Now (Pub)
64 Saigon Central Mosque
71 Ton Duc Thang Museum
72 Shake's Pub
73 Me Linh Square & Tran Hung Dao Statue
75 Small Motorised Boats for Rental
76 Dining Cruise
83 Minibus Office (Cong Ty Dich Vu Du Lich Quan 1)
85 Vietnam Tourism
87 Huynh Thuc Khang Street Market
88 Pre-1967 US Embassy
89 Ferries to Mekong Delta
90 Boats across Saigon River
91 National Bank Building
92 Vietcombank
93 Wedding Taxis
94 An Duong Vuong Statue
95 Ho Chi Minh Museum

desk to the right and up the short flight of stairs as you enter the GPO. It is open from 7.30 to 11.45 am and 1 to 4.30 pm Monday to Saturday. The DHL business office (☎ 296203, 244268; telex 811214 DHLSGN-VT) is at 253 Hoang Van Thu, Tan Binh District. For rates, see the Post & Telecommunications section in the Facts for the Visitor chapter.

Postal, telex, telegram and fax services are available at counters run by the post office at the hotels Caravelle, Le Lai, Majestic, Palace and Rex.

The District 1 post office (☎ 299086), which serves downtown Saigon, is on Le Loi Blvd near its intersection with Nguyen Thi Minh Khai St (Pasteur St).

In Ho Chi Minh City, the following special phone numbers are available but don't be surprised if the person answering only speaks Vietnamese:

Ambulance	15
Directory Enquiries	16
Directory Information	108
Emergency	296485
Fire Brigade	14
International Calls	00 & 110
Interprovincial Calls	01 & 101
Police	13
Telex Service	296738
Traffic Police	296449

Foreign Consulates The addresses and telephone numbers of Ho Chi Minh City's consulates are as follows:

Cambodia
    43 Phung Khac Khoan St (☎ 292751, 292744)
Cuba
    23 Phung Khac Khoan St, District 1 (☎ 297350, 297351)
Czech
    176 Nguyen Van Thu St, District 1 (☎ 291475, 298277)
France
    102 Hai Ba Trung St, District 1 (☎ 297231, 297235)
Germany
    126 Nguyen Dinh Chieu St, District 3 (☎ 291967, 224385)

Hungary
    22 Phung Khac Khoan St, District 1 (☎ 290130, 292410)
India
    49 Tran Quoc Thao St (☎ 294498, 294495)
Japan
    55 Ngo Thoi Nhiem St, District 3 (☎ 291341)
Laos
    181 Hai Ba Trung St, District 3 (☎ 297667)
Malaysia
    53 Nguyen Dinh Chieu St, District 3 (☎ 299023)
Poland
    2 Tran Cao Van St, District 1 (☎ 290114)
Russia
    40 Ba Huyen Thanh Quan St, District 3 (☎ 292936, 292937)
Thailand
    77 Tran Quoc Thao St, District 3

Bookshops Most books sold in Saigon are in Vietnamese, but if you're looking to pick up Vietnamese dictionaries, language-study books and the like, this is the place to get them. The best area to look is along the north side of Le Loi Blvd between the Rex Hotel and Nam Ky Khoi Nghia St (near Kem Bach Dang ice cream parlour), where there's a collection of book and stationery shops selling maps, books and a wide range of items.

The Foreign Languages Bookstore (☎ 224670) is at 185 Dong Khoi St. It has a limited selection of used books in English and some antiquarian books that might interest the collector. It is open from 7.30 to 11.15 am and 1.30 to 5 pm.

For novels in English, French or German, try Cua Hang Sach Cu in District 3 at 142B Vo Thi Sau St, which is just off of Hai Ba Trung St. It has things you'd never expect to find in Vietnam, such as copies of *Mad* magazine from the 1960s!

Xunhasaba (☎ 292900), which is an acronym for State Enterprise for Export & Import of Books & Periodicals, has an outlet at 82 Dong Du St (near the Saigon Central Mosque). This place is a gold mine of unusual books, some of which come from the former East Bloc countries.

Cua Hang Mua Ban Sach Cu is a second-hand bookstore near the Van Canh Hotel at 4-6 Dang Thi Nhu St. Sach Tong Hop (☎ 291491) at 40 Ngo Duc Ke St, off

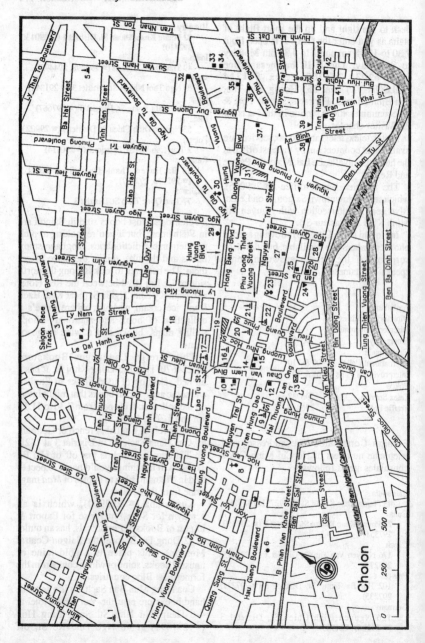

■ PLACES TO STAY

3   Phu Tho Hotel
4   Goldstar Hotel
10   Thu Do Hotel
11   Truong Thanh Hotel
12   Phuong Huong (Phenix) Hotel
14   Song Kim Hotel
15   Trung Mai Hotel
25   Arc En Ciel Hotel
26   Tan Dan Hotel
27   Bat Dat Hotel
28   Phu Do 1 Hotel
32   Dong Khanh 5 Hotel
33   Cholon Hotel
34   Cholon Tourist Mini-Hotel
36   Andong Hotel
37   Cathay Hotel
38   Dong Khanh Hotel
40   Hoa Binh Hotel
41   Tokyo Hotel
42   Hanh Long Hotel

▼ PLACES TO EAT

24   My Le Hoa Restaurant
39   Tiem Com Chay Phat Huu Duyen
     (Vegetarian Restaurant)

     OTHER

1   Phung Son Pagoda
2   Khanh Van Nam Vien Pagoda
5   An Quang Pagoda
6   Binh Tay Market
7   Cholon Bus Station
8   Cha Tam Church
9   Ong Bon Pagoda
13   Post Office
16   Quan Am Pagoda
17   Phuoc An Hoi Quan Pagoda
18   Cho Ray Hospital
19   Electronics Market
20   Thien Hau Pagoda
21   Nghia An Hoi Quan Pagoda
22   Tam Son Hoi Quan Pagoda
23   Cholon Mosque
29   Taxi Stand at Pham Ngoc Thach
30   Nha Sau Church
31   Consumer Goods Market
35   Andong Market

Libraries The address of the Municipal Library is 34 Ly Tu Trong St. Nearby at 69 Ly Tu Trong St is the General Sciences Library with a total of 500 seats in its reading rooms.

Maps Maps of Ho Chi Minh City and other Vietnamese cities are sold in downtown Saigon at sidewalk stands along Dong Khoi St, along Le Loi Blvd between Dong Khoi St and Nguyen Hue Blvd, and on Nguyen Hue Blvd between Le Loi Blvd and the Palace Hotel. These stalls have the best selection of maps in Vietnam; almost all the maps sold here are impossible to find anywhere else in the country. If you think you will need any maps later in your trip, this is the place to get them. Maps of Ho Chi Minh City may also be on sale at the Rex Hotel gift shop.

If you are interested in the pre-1975 names of Ho Chi Minh City's streets, the map with the dark blue border and the inset of Ho Chi Minh City in the lower right-hand corner has an index of old and new names on the back. *Ten Truoc 1975* means 'Name before 1975'.

Photography For film and other photographic needs, there are a number of stores along Nguyen Hue Blvd. There is a large photo shop at 118-120 Dong Khoi St. The latest Japanese-made one-hour colour developing equipment has been installed in stores at 66A Nguyen Hue Blvd and 110-112 Dong Khoi St and in the Eden Colour Photo Centre at 4 Le Loi Blvd.

Emergency Cho Ray Hospital (Benh Vien Cho Ray; ☎ 254137, 258074; 1000 beds), one of the best medical facilities in Vietnam, is at 201B Nguyen Chi Thanh Blvd, District 5 (Cholon). There is a section for foreigners on the 10th floor. About a third of the 200 doctors speak English. You might also try Nhi Dong 2 Hospital (Grall Hospital) on Ly Tu Trong St opposite the Franco-Vietnamese Cultural Centre.

High-ranking cadres enjoy access to Thong Nhat Hospital, a modern five-storey building on the corner of Ly Thuong Kiet

Nguyen Hue Blvd, has a few old English and French books along with postage stamps and some Soviet publications.

Blvd and Cach Mang Thang Tam St in the Tan Binh district.

There are hundreds of pharmacies *(nha thuoc)* around the city. One of the largest is Hieu Thuoc Dong Khoi, conveniently located downtown at 201 Dong Khoi St. The pharmacists speak English and French. It is open from 7.30 am to noon and 1.30 to 5 pm. Another pharmacy in Saigon you might try is at 105 Nguyen Hue Blvd; it is open from 8 to 11.30 am and 2 to 6 pm.

Police The best advice we can give about the police is to avoid them, especially late at night:

I would advise people going to Vietnam to make a photocopy of their passport and visa and keep them on hand while your real ones should be in a money belt or stored safely somewhere. Reason being that if the police or soldiers get a hold of them, you won't see them again or you'll pay dearly to 'buy them back'.

One woman I met was confronted by two cops late at night in Saigon and they insisted she pay US$20 for some fabricated law she broke like insulting the flag. She refused and didn't get her passport back (which of course they had asked to see) until she coughed up some dollars.

The next evening around midnight, I was on the way back to my hotel in a cyclo when two cops waved us over and demanded my 'papers'. I gave them the photocopies and told them they were all I had with me, and after a valiant effort to extort US$10 for riding in a cyclo without a licence, they let me go without paying anything. I told them (nicely!) they could keep the papers and there was nothing they could do but shoot me with the AK-47 one of them was carrying. Anyway, carry copies in any case.

Travel Permits & Visas For what it's worth (and it's not worth much), the Immigration Police Office (Phong Quan Ly Nguoi Nuoc Ngoai; ☎ 392221) is at 161 Nguyen Du St, corner of Cach Mang Thang Tam St; it's open from 8 to 11 am and 1 to 4 pm.

Hotels and travel agencies can arrange visa extensions – shop around for the best price but figure on around US$20 for 15 days. For more information, see the Visas & Embassies section of the Facts for the Visitor chapter.

Useful Organisations The Saigon branch of the Chamber of Commerce & Industry of Vietnam (Chi Nhanh Phong Thuong Mai Va Cng Nghiep or Vietcochamber (☎ 230331, 230339; telex 811215 CHAMMER-HCM; fax (84-8) 294472) is at 171 Vo Thi Sau St, District 3.

IMC (Investment & Management Consulting Corporation; ☎ 299062) offers various business services to investors and business people. The External Affairs Office of the Foreign Ministry (So Ngoai Vu; ☎ 223032, 224311) is at 6 Thai Van Lung St.

Aid Organisations Vietnam needs all the help it can get, and there are a number of international aid organisations filling that role. While most officially have their Vietnam branch headquarters in Hanoi, most maintain more staff in Ho Chi Minh City (which makes one wonder just where Vietnam's capital really is). They are:

FAO
    (UN Food & Agriculture Organisation; TC Luong Thuc Va Nong Nghiep) 2 Phung Khac Khoan St, District 1 (☎ 290781)
ICRC
    (International Committee of the Red Cross; UB Chu Thap Do Quoc Te) 79 Ba Huyen Thanh Quan St, District 3 (☎ 222965)
UNDP
    (UN Development Programme; Chuong Trinh Cua LHQ Ve Phat Trien) 2 Phung Khac Khoan St, District 1 (☎ 295821, 295865)
UNHCR
    (UN High Commission for Refugees; Cao Uy LHQ Ve Nguoi Ti Nan) 257 Hoang Van Thu St, Tan Binh District (☎ 445895, 445896)
UNICEF
    (UN Children's Fund; Quy Nhi Dong LHQ) Room 309, Majestic Hotel, 1 Dong Khoi St, District 1 (☎ 2991006)

Commercial Delegations A few countries maintain commercial delegations in Ho Chi Minh City. Amongst the most important are:

Australia
    Austrade, 4 Dong Khoi St, District 1 (☎ 299387)

France
    75 Tran Quoc Thao St, District 3 (☎ 296056)
Italy
    Room 226, Ben Thanh Hotel (☎ 292185, 292186)

Places of Worship – Ho Chi Minh City

The following places of worship are on the Ho Chi Minh City map.

Giac Lam Pagoda Giac Lam Pagoda dates from 1744 and is believed to be the oldest pagoda in Ho Chi Minh City. Because the last reconstruction here was in 1900, the architecture, layout and ornamentation remain almost unaltered by the modernist renovations that have transformed so many other religious structures in Vietnam. Ten monks live at this Vietnamese Buddhist pagoda, which also incorporates aspects of Taoism and Confucianism. It is well worth the trip out here from downtown Saigon.

Giac Lam Pagoda is about three km from Cholon at 118 Lac Long Quan St in Tan Binh District. Beware: the numbering on Lac Long Quan St is extremely confused, starting over from one several times and at one point jumping to four digits. In many places, odd and even numbers are on the same side of the street.

The best way to get to Giac Lam Pagoda is to take Nguyen Chi Thanh Blvd or 3 Thang 2 Blvd to Le Dai Hanh St. Go north-westward on Le Dai Hanh St and turn right onto Lac Long Quan St. Walk 100 metres; the pagoda gate will be on your left. It is open to visitors from 6 am to 9 pm.

To the right of the gate to the pagoda compound are the ornate tombs of venerated monks. The *bo de* (bodhi, or pipal) tree in the front garden was the gift of a monk from Sri Lanka. Next to the tree is a regular feature of Vietnamese Buddhist temples, a gleaming white statue of Quan The Am Bo Tat (Avalokiteçvara; Guanyin in Chinese, the Goddess of Mercy) standing on a lotus blossom, symbol of purity.

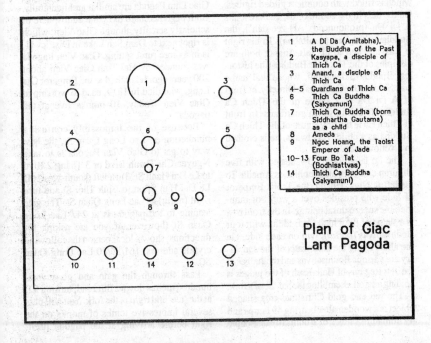

1	A Di Da (Amitabha), the Buddha of the Past
2	Kasyape, a disciple of Thich Ca
3	Anand, a disciple of Thich Ca
4–5	Guardians of Thich Ca
6	Thich Ca Buddha (Sakyamuni)
7	Thich Ca Buddha (born Siddhartha Gautama) as a child
8	Ameda
9	Ngoc Hoang, the Taoist Emperor of Jade
10–13	Four Bo Tat (Bodhisattvas)
14	Thich Ca Buddha (Sakyamuni)

Plan of Giac Lam Pagoda

The roofline of the main building is decorated both inside and outside with unusual blue and white porcelain plates. Through the main entrance is a reception hall lined with funeral tablets and photos of the deceased. Roughly in the centre of the hall, near an old French chandelier, is a figure of 18-armed Chuan De, another form of the Goddess of Mercy. Note the carved hardwood columns, which bear gilded Vietnamese inscriptions written in nom characters, a form of writing in use before the adoption of the Latin-based quoc ngu alphabet. The wall to the left is covered with portraits of great monks from previous generations. Monks' names and biographical information about them are recorded on the vertical red tablets in gold nom characters. A box for donations sits nearby. Shoes should be removed when passing from the rough red floor tiles to the smaller, white-black-grey tiles.

On the other side of the wall from the monks' funeral tablets is the main sanctuary, which is filled with countless gilded figures. On the dais in the centre of the back row sits A Di Da (pronounced 'AH-zee-dah'), the Buddha of the Past (Amitabha). To his right is Kasyape and to his left Anand; both are disciples of the Thich Ca Buddha (the historical Buddha Sakyamuni, whose real name was Siddhartha Gautama). Directly in front of A Di Da is a statue of the Thich Ca Buddha, flanked by two guardians. In front of Thich Ca is the tiny figure of the Thich Ca Buddha as a child. As always, he is clothed in a yellow robe.

The fat laughing fellow, seated with five children climbing all over him, is Ameda. To his left is Ngoc Hoang, the Taoist Emperor of Jade who presides over a world of innumerable supernatural beings. In the front row is a statue of the Thich Ca Buddha with four Bodhisattvas (bo tat), two on each side. On the altars along the side walls of the sanctuary are various Bodhisattvas and the Judges of the Ten Regions of Hell. Each of the judges is holding a scroll resembling the handle of a fork.

The red and gold Christmas-tree shaped object is a wooden altar bearing 49 lamps and 49 miniature statues of Bodhisattvas. People pray for sick relatives or ask for happiness by contributing kerosene for use in the lamps. Petitioners' names and those of ill family members are written on slips of paper, which are attached to the branches of the 'tree'.

The frame of the large bronze bell in the corner looks like a university bulletin board because petitioners have attached to it lists of names: the names of people seeking happiness and the names of the sick and the dead, placed there by their relatives. It is believed that when the bell is rung, the sound will resonate to the heavens above and the underground heavens below, carrying with it the attached supplications.

Prayers here consist of chanting to the accompaniment of drums, bells and gongs and follow a traditional rite seldom performed these days. Prayers are held daily from 4 to 5 am, 11 am to noon, 4 to 5 pm and 7 to 9 pm.

Giac Vien Pagoda Giac Vien Pagoda and Giac Lam Pagoda are similar architecturally. Both pagodas share the same atmosphere of scholarly serenity, though Giac Vien, which is right next to Dam Sen Lake in District 11, is in a more rural setting. Giac Vien Pagoda was founded by Hai Tinh Giac Vien about 200 years ago. It is said that the Emperor Gia Long, who died in 1819, used to worship at Giac Vien. Today, 10 monks live at the pagoda.

Because of the impossibly confusing numbering on Lac Long Quan St, the best way to get to Giac Vien Pagoda is to take Nguyen Chi Thanh Blvd or 3 Thang 2 Blvd to Le Dai Hanh St. Turn left (south-west) off Le Dai Han St on to Binh Thoi St and turn right (north) at Lac Long Quan St. The gate leading to the pagoda is at 247 Lac Long Quan St (however, if you are asking for directions, show a local person the following cryptic address: 161/35/20 Lac Long Quan St).

Pass through the gate and go several hundred metres down a dirt road, turning left at the 'tee' and right at the fork. You will pass several impressive tombs of monks on the right before arriving at the pagoda itself.

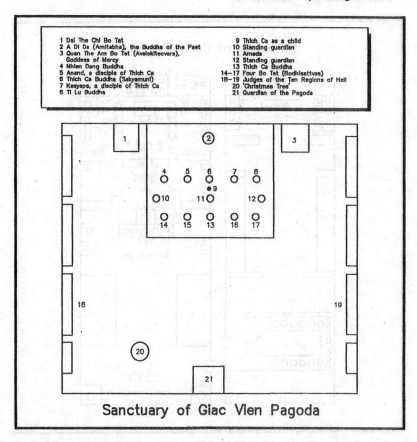

1 Dai The Chi Bo Tat
2 A Di Da (Amitabha), the Buddha of the Past
3 Quan The Am Bo Tat (Avalokitecvara), Goddess of Mercy
4 Nhien Dang Buddha
5 Anand, a disciple of Thich Ca
6 Thich Ca Buddha (Sakyamuni)
7 Kasyape, a disciple of Thich Ca
8 Ti Lu Buddha
9 Thich Ca as a child
10 Standing guardian
11 Ameda
12 Standing guardian
13 Thich Ca Buddha
14–17 Four Bo Tat (Bodhisattvas)
18–19 Judges of the Ten Regions of Hell
20 'Christmas Tree'
21 Guardian of the Pagoda

Sanctuary of Giac Vien Pagoda

Giac Vien Pagoda is open from 7 am to 7 pm but come before dark as the electricity is often out.

As you enter the pagoda, the first chamber is lined with funeral tablets. At the back of the second chamber is a statue of the pagoda's founder, Hai Tinh Giac Vien, holding a horse-tail swatch. Nearby portraits are of his successors as head monk and disciples. A donation box sits to the left of the statue. Opposite Hai Tinh Giac Vien is a representation of 18-armed Chuan De, a form of the Goddess of Mercy, who is flanked by two guardians.

The main sanctuary is on the other side of the wall behind Hai Tinh Giac Vien. A Di Da, the Buddha of the Past, is at the back of the dais. Directly in front of him is the Thich Ca Buddha (Sakyamuni), flanked by Thich Ca's disciples Anand (on the left) and Kasyape (on the right). To the right of Kasyape is the Ti Lu Buddha; to the left of Anand is the Nhien Dang Buddha. At the foot of the Thich Ca Buddha is a small figure of Thich Ca (Siddhartha Gautama) as a child. Fat, laughing Ameda is seated with children climbing all over him; far on either side of him are guardians, standing. In the front row of the

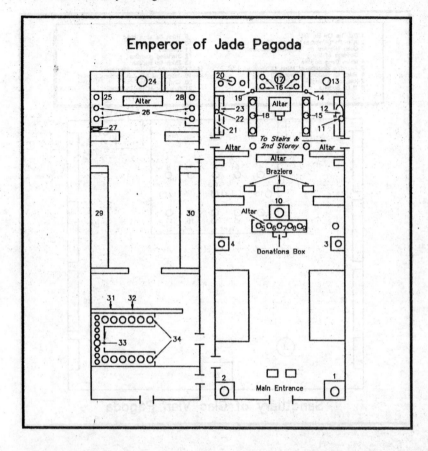

Emperor of Jade Pagoda

dais is Thich Ca with two Bodhisattvas on each side.

In front of the dais is a fantastic brass incense basin with fierce dragon heads emerging from each side. On the altar to the left of the dais is Dai The Chi Bo Tat; on the altar to the right is Quan The Am Bo Tat (Avalokiteçvara), the Goddess of Mercy. The Guardian of the Pagoda is against the wall opposite the dais. Nearby is a 'Christmas tree' similar to the one in Giac Lam Pagoda. Lining the side walls are the Judges of the Ten Regions of Hell (holding scrolls) and 18 Bodhisattvas.

Prayers are held daily from 4 to 5 am, 8 to 10 am, 2 to 3 pm, 4 to 5 pm and 7 to 9 pm.

Emperor of Jade Pagoda The Emperor of Jade Pagoda (known in Vietnamese as Phuoc Hai Tu and Chua Ngoc Hoang), built in 1909 by the Cantonese (Quang Dong) Congregation, is truly a gem of a Chinese temple. It is one of the most spectacularly colourful pagodas in Ho Chi Minh City, filled with statues of phantasmal divinities and grotesque heroes. The pungent smoke of burning joss sticks fills the air, obscuring exquisite wood carvings decorated with

1	Mon Quan, the God of the Gate	15	Nam Tao, God of the Southern Polar Star and God of Happiness
2	Tho Than (Tho Dia), the God of the Land	16	Tu Dai Kim Cuong, the 'Four Big Diamonds'
3	The general who defeated the Green Dragon	17	Ngoc Hoang, the Emperor of Jade
4	The general who defeated the White Tiger	18	Bac Dau, God of the Northern Polar Star and God of Longevity
5	Phat Mau Chuan De, mother of the five Buddhas of the cardinal directions	19	Goddess of the Moon
		20	Ong Bac De, a reincarnation of the Emperor of Jade
6	Dia Tang Vuong Bo Tat, the King of Hell	21	Thien Loi's guards (upper step)
7	Di Lac Buddha (Maitreya), the Buddha of the Future	22	Thien Loi, the God of Lightning
		23	Ong Bac De's military comanders (lower step)
8	Quan The Am Bo Tat (Avalokiteçvara), the Goddess of Mercy	24	Thanh Hoang, the Chief of Hell
		25	Am Quan, the God of Yin
9	Thich Ca Buddha (Sakyamuni; in a bas-relief portrait)	26	Thuong Thien Phat Ac
		27	Thanh Hoang's red horse
10	Duoc Su Buddha (Nhu Lai Budha; in glass case)	28	Duong Quan, the God of Yang
		29-30	Panels of the Hall of the Ten Hells
11	Dai Minh Vuong Quang (on the back of a phoenix)	31	Dia Tang Vuong Bo Tat, the King of Hell
12	The Tien Nhan (God-Persons)	32	Quan Am Thi Kinh, the Guardian Spirit of Mother and Child
13	Phat Mau Chuan De, mother of the five Buddhas of the cardinal directions	33	Kim Hoa Thanh Mau, the Chief of All Women
14	God of the Sun	34	Figurines of 12 Women

gilded Chinese characters. The roof is covered with elaborate tilework. The statues, which represent characters from both the Buddhist and Taoist traditions, are made of reinforced papier mâché.

The Emperor of Jade Pagoda is at 73 Mai Thi Luu St in a part of Ho Chi Minh City known as Da Kao (or Da Cao). To get there, go to 20 Dien Bien Phu St and walk half a block north-westward (to the left as you head out of Saigon towards Thi Nghe Channel).

As you enter the main doors of the building Mon Quan, the God of the Gate, stands to the right in an elaborately carved wooden case. Opposite him, in a similar case, is Tho Than (Tho Dia), the God of the Land. Straight on is an altar on which are placed, from left to right, figures of: Phat Mau Chuan De, mother of the five Buddhas of the cardinal directions; Dia Tang Vuong Bo Tat (Ksitigartha), the King of Hell; the Di Lac Buddha (Maitreya), the Buddha of the Future; Quan The Am Bo Tat, the Goddess

of Mercy; and a bas-relief portrait of the Thich Ca Buddha (Sakyamuni). Behind the altar, in a glass case, is the Duoc Su Buddha, also known as the Nhu Lai Buddha. The figure is said to be made of sandalwood.

To either side of the altar, against the walls, are two especially fierce and menacing figures. On the right (as you face the altar) is a four-metre-high statue of the general who defeated the Green Dragon. He is stepping on the vanquished dragon. On the left is the general who defeated the White Tiger, which is also getting stepped on.

The Taoist Emperor of Jade, Ngoc Hoang, presides over the main sanctuary, draped in luxurious robes. He is flanked by the 'Four Big Diamonds' (Tu Dai Kim Cuong), his four guardians, so named because they are said to be as hard as diamonds. In front of the Emperor of Jade stand six figures, three to each side. On the left is Bac Dau, the Taoist God of the Northern Polar Star and God of Longevity, flanked by his two guardians; and on the right is Nam Tao, the Taoist God of the Southern Polar Star and God of Happiness, also flanked by two guardians.

In the case to the right of the Emperor of Jade is 18-armed Phat Mau Chuan De, mother of the five Buddhas of the north, south, east, west and centre. Two faces, affixed to her head behind each ear, look to either side. On the wall to the right of Phat Mau Chuan De, at a height of about four metres, is Dai Minh Vuong Quang, who was reincarnated as Sakyamuni, riding on the back of a phoenix. Below are the Tien Nhan, literally the 'god-persons'.

In the case to the left of the Emperor of Jade sits Ong Bac De, a reincarnation of the Emperor of Jade, holding a sword. One of his feet is resting on a turtle while the other rests on a snake. On the wall to the left of Ong Bac De, about four metres off the ground, is Thien Loi, the God of Lightning, who slays evil people. Below Thien Loi are the military commanders of Ong Bac De (on the lower step) and Thien Loi's guardians (on the upper step). At the top of the two carved pillars that separate the three alcoves are the Goddess of the Moon (on the left) and the God of the Sun (on the right).

Out the door on the left-hand side of the Emperor of Jade's chamber is another room. The semi-enclosed area to the right (as you enter) is presided over by Thanh Hoang, the Chief of Hell; to the left is his red horse. Of the six figures lining the walls, the two closest to Thanh Hoang are Am Quan, the God of Yin (on the left) and Duong Quan, the God of Yang (on the right). The other four figures, the Thuong Thien Phat Ac, are gods who dispense punishments for evil acts and rewards for good deeds. Thanh Hoang faces in the direction of the famous Hall of the Ten Hells. The carved wooden panels lining the walls graphically depict the varied torments awaiting evil people in each of the 10 regions of hell. At the top of each panel is one of the Ten Judges of Hell examining a book in which the deeds of the deceased are inscribed.

On the wall opposite Thanh Hoang is a bas-relief wood panel depicting Quan Am Thi Kinh, the Guardian Spirit of Mother and Child, standing on a lotus blossom, symbol of purity. Unjustly turned out of her home by her husband, Quan Am Thi Kinh disguised herself as a monk and went to live in a pagoda, where a young woman accused her of fathering her child. She accepted the blame – and the responsibility that went along with it – and again found herself out on the streets, this time with her 'son'. Much later, about to die, she returned to the monastery to confess her secret. When the Emperor of China heard of her story, he declared her the Guardian Spirit of Mother & Child.

It is believed that she has the power to bestow male offspring on those who fervently believe in her. On the panel, Quan Am Thi Kinh is shown holding her 'son'. To her left is Long Nu, a very young buddha who is her protector. To Quan Am Thi Kinh's right is Thien Tai, her guardian spirit, who knew the real story all along. Above her left shoulder is a bird bearing prayer beads.

To the right of the panel of Quan Am Thi Kinh is a panel depicting Dia Tang Vuong Bo Tat, the King of Hell.

On the other side of the wall is a fascinating little room in which the ceramic figures of 12 women, overrun with children and wearing colourful clothes, sit in two rows of six. Each of the women exemplifies a human characteristic, either good or bad (as in the case of the woman drinking alcohol from a jug). Each figure represents one year in the 12-year Chinese calendar. Presiding over the room is Kim Hoa Thanh Mau, the Chief of All Women.

To the right of the main chamber, stairs lead up to a 2nd-floor sanctuary and balcony.

Dai Giac Pagoda This Vietnamese Buddhist pagoda is built in a style characteristic of pagodas constructed during the 1960s. In the courtyard, under the unfinished 10-level red-pink tower inlaid with porcelain chards, is an artificial cave made of volcanic rocks in which there is a gilded statue of the Goddess of Mercy. In the main sanctuary, the 2½-metre gilt Buddha has a green neon halo,

Top: Bai Dau Beach, Vung Tau·(RS)
Bottom: Inside the tunnels of Cu Chi (DR)

Top: Caodai Great Temple, Tay Ninh (RS)
Left: Inside the Caodai Great Temple, Tay Ninh (RS)
Right: Nui Ba Den (Black Lady Mountain) (RS)

while below, a smaller white reclining Buddha (in a glass case) has a blue neon halo. Dai Giac Pagoda is at 112 Nguyen Van Troi St, 1.5 km towards the city centre from the gate to the airport.

Vinh Nghiem Pagoda Vinh Nghiem Pagoda, inaugurated in 1971, is noteworthy for its vast sanctuary and eight-storey tower, each level of which contains a statue of the Buddha. It was built with help from the Japan-Vietnam Friendship Association, which explains the presence of Japanese elements in its architecture. At the base of the tower (which is open only on holidays) is a store selling Buddhist ritual objects. Behind the sanctuary is a three-storey tower which serves as a repository for carefully labelled ceramic urns containing the ashes of people who have been cremated. The pagoda is in District 3 at 339 Nam Ky Khoi Nghia St and is open from 7.30 to 11.30 am and 2 to 6 pm daily.

Le Van Duyet Temple This temple is dedicated to Marshal Le Van Duyet (pronounced 'Lee Van Zyet'), who is buried here with his wife. The Marshal, who lived from 1763 to 1831, was a southern Vietnamese general and viceroy who helped put down the Tay Son Rebellion and reunify Vietnam. When the Nguyen Dynasty came to power in 1802, he was elevated by Emperor Gia Long to the rank of marshal. Le Van Duyet fell into disfavour with Gia Long's successor, Minh Mang, who tried him posthumously and desecrated his grave. Emperor Thieu Tri, who succeeded Minh Mang, restored the tomb, fulfilling a prophesy of its destruction and restoration. Le Van Duyet was considered a great national hero in the South before 1975 but is disliked by the Communists because of his involvement in the expansion of French influence.

Le Van Duyet Temple is three km from the centre of Saigon in the Gia Dinh area at 131 Dinh Tien Hoang St (near where Phan Dang Luu Blvd becomes Bach Dang Blvd).

The temple itself was renovated in 1937 and has a distinctly modern feel to it. Since 1975, the government has done little to keep it from becoming dilapidated. Among the items on display are a portrait of Le Van Duyet, some of his personal effects (including European-style crystal goblets) and other antiques. There are two wonderful life-size horses on either side of the entrance to the third and last chamber, which is kept locked.

During celebrations of Tet and the 30th day of the 7th lunar month (anniversary of Le Van Duyet's death), the tomb is thronged with pilgrims. Vietnamese used to come here to take oaths of good faith if they could not afford the services of a court of justice. The tropical fish are on sale to visitors. The caged birds are bought by pilgrims and freed to earn merit. The birds are often recaptured (and liberated again).

Tran Hung Dao Temple This small temple is dedicated to Tran Hung Dao, a Vietnamese national hero who in 1287 vanquished an invasion force, said to have numbered 300,000 men, which had been dispatched by the Mongol emperor Kublai Khan. The temple is at 36 Vo Thi Sau St, a block northeast of the telecommunications dishes that are between Dien Bien Phu St and Vo Thi Sau St.

The public park between the antenna dishes and Hai Ba Trung St was built in 1983 on the site of the Massiges Cemetery, burial place of French soldiers and settlers. The remains of French military personnel were exhumed and repatriated to France. Another site no longer in existence is the tomb of the 18th-century French missionary and diplomat, Pigneau de Béhaine, Bishop of Adran, which was completely destroyed after reunification.

The temple is open every weekday from 6 to 11 am and 2 to 6 pm.

Cho Quan Church Cho Quan Church, built by the French about 100 years ago, is one of the largest churches in Ho Chi Minh City. This is the only church we've seen in the city where the figure of Jesus on the altar has a neon halo. The view from the belfry is worth the steep climb. The church is at 133 Tran

Binh Trong St (between Tran Hung Dao Blvd and Nguyen Trai St), and is open daily from 4 to 7 am and 3 to 6 pm and Sundays from 4 to 9 am and 1.30 to 6 pm. Sunday masses are held at 5, 6 , and 7 am and at 5 pm.

Places of Worship – Central Saigon

The following places are on the Central Saigon map.

Notre Dame Cathedral Notre Dame Cathedral, built between 1877 and 1883, is set in the heart of Saigon's government quarter. The cathedral faces down Dong Khoi St. Its neo-Romanesque form and two 40-metre-high square towers, tipped with iron spires, dominate the city's skyline. In front of the cathedral (in the centre of the square bounded by the GPO) is a statue of the Virgin Mary. If the front gates are locked try the door on the side of the building that faces Reunification Hall.

There are several other interesting French-era churches around Saigon, including one at 289 Hai Ba Trung St.

Xa Loi Pagoda Xa Loi Vietnamese Buddhist Pagoda, built in 1956, is famed as the repository of a sacred relic of the Buddha. In August 1963, truckloads of armed men under the command of President Ngo Dinh Diem's brother, Ngo Dinh Nhu, attacked Xa Loi Pagoda, which had become a centre of opposition to the Diem government. The pagoda was ransacked and 400 monks and nuns, including the country's 80-year-old Buddhist patriarch, were arrested. This raid and others elsewhere helped solidify opposition among Buddhists to the Diem regime, a crucial factor in the US decision to support the coup against Diem. This pagoda was also the site of several self-immolations by monks protesting against the Diem regime and the war.

Thich Quang Duc was a monk from Hué who travelled to Saigon and publicly burned himself to death in June 1963 to protest the policies of President Ngo Dinh Diem. A famous photograph of his act was printed on the front pages of newspapers around the world. His death soon inspired a number of other self-immolations.

Many Westerners were shocked less by the suicides than by the reaction of Tran Le Xuan (Madame Nhu, the president's notorious sister-in-law), who happily proclaimed the self-immolations a 'barbecue party' and said 'Let them burn, and we shall clap our hands'. Her statements greatly added to the already substantial public disgust with Diem's regime; the US press labelled Madame Nhu the 'Iron Butterfly' and 'Dragon Lady'. In November, both President Diem and his brother Ngo Dinh Nhu (Madame Nhu's husband) were assassinated by Diem's own military. Madame Nhu was outside the country at the time (fortunate for her) and was last reported to be living in Rome.

The Thich Quang Duc Memorial (Dai Ky Niem Thuong Toa Thich Quang Duc) is at the intersection of Nguyen Dinh Chieu and Cach Mang Thang Tam streets, just around the corner from the Xa Loi Pagoda.

Women enter the main hall of Xa Loi Pagoda by the staircase on the right as you come in the gate; men use the stairs on the left. The walls of the sanctuary are adorned with paintings depicting the Buddha's life.

Xa Loi Pagoda is in District 3 at 89 Ba Huyen Thanh Quan St, near Dien Bien Phu St. It is open daily from 7 to 11 am and from 2 to 5 pm. A monk preaches every Sunday morning from 8 to 10 am. On days of the full moon and new moon, special prayers are held from 7 to 9 am and from 7 to 8 pm.

Phung Son Tu Pagoda Phung Son Tu Pagoda, built by the Fujian Congregation in the mid-1940s, is more typical of Ho Chi Minh City's Chinese pagodas than is the Emperor of Jade Pagoda. The interior is often hung with huge incense spirals that burn for hours. Worshippers include both ethnic-Chinese and ethnic-Vietnamese. Phung Son Tu Pagoda is dedicated to Ong Bon, Guardian Spirit of Happiness & Virtue, whose statue is behind the main altar in the sanctuary. On the right-hand side of the main hall is the multi-armed Buddhist Goddess of Mercy. This pagoda is only one km from downtown Saigon at 338 Nguyen Cong Tru St.

Mariamman Hindu Temple Mariamman Hindu Temple, the only Hindu temple still in use in Ho Chi Minh City, is a little piece of southern India in the centre of Saigon. Though there are only 50 to 60 Hindus in Ho Chi Minh City – all of them Tamils – this temple, known in Vietnamese as Chua Ba Mariamman, is also considered sacred by many ethnic-Vietnamese and ethnic-Chinese. Indeed, it is reputed to have miraculous powers. The temple was built at the end of the 19th century and dedicated to the Hindu goddess Mariamman.

The lion to the left of the entrance used to be carried around Saigon in a street procession every autumn. In the shrine in the middle of the temple are Mariamman flanked by her guardians, Maduraiveeran (to her left) and Pechiamman (to her right). In front of the figure of Mariamman are two lingams. Favourite offerings placed nearby include joss sticks, jasmine flowers, lilies and gladioli. The wooden stairs, on the left as you enter the building, lead to the roof, where you'll find two colourful towers covered with innumerable figures of lions, goddesses and guardians.

After reunification, the government took over the temple and turned part of it into a factory for joss sticks. Another section was occupied by a company producing seafood for export – the seafood was dried in the sun on the roof. The whole temple is to be returned to the local Hindu community.

Mariamman Temple is only three blocks from Ben Thanh Market at 45 Truong Dinh St. It is open from 7 am to 7 pm daily. Take off your shoes before stepping onto the slightly raised platform.

Saigon Central Mosque Built by South Indian Muslims in 1935 on the site of an earlier mosque, the Saigon Central Mosque is an immaculately clean and well-kept island of calm in the middle of bustling downtown Saigon. In front of the sparkling white and blue structure at 66 Dong Du St, with its four nonfunctional minarets, is a pool for ritual ablutions (washing), required by Islamic law before prayers. As with any mosque, take off your shoes before entering the sanctuary.

The simplicity of the mosque is in marked contrast to the exuberance of Chinese temple decorations and the rows of figures, facing elaborate ritual objects, in Buddhist pagodas. Islamic law strictly forbids using human or animal figures for decoration.

Only half-a-dozen Indian Muslims remain in Saigon; most of the community fled in 1975. As a result, prayers – held five times a day – are sparsely attended except on Fridays, when several dozen worshippers (including many non-Indian Muslims) are present. The mass emigration also deprived the local Muslim community of much of its spiritual leadership, and very few Muslims knowledgeable in their tradition and Arabic, the language of the Koran, remain.

There are 12 other mosques serving the 5000 or so Muslims in Ho Chi Minh City.

Places of Worship – Cholon
The following places are on the Cholon map.

An Quang Pagoda The An Quang Pagoda gained some notoriety during the Vietnam War as the home of Thich Tri Quang, a politically powerful monk who led protests against the South Vietnamese government in 1963 and 1966. When the war ended, you would have expected the Communists to be grateful. Instead, he was first placed under house arrest and later thrown in solitary confinement for 16 months. Thich Tri Quang was eventually released and is said to still be living at An Quang Pagoda.

The An Quang Pagoda is on Su Van Hanh St near the intersection with Ba Hat St, District 10.

Tam Son Hoi Quan Pagoda This pagoda, known to the Vietnamese as Chua Ba Chua, was built by the Fujian Congregation in the 19th century and retains unmodified most of its original rich ornamentation. The pagoda is dedicated to Me Sanh, the Goddess of Fertility. Both men and women – but more of the latter – come here to pray for children. Tam Son Hoi Quan Pagoda is at 118 Trieu

Quang Phuc St, which is very near 370 Tran Hung Dao B Blvd.

To the right of the covered courtyard is the deified general Quan Cong (in Chinese: Guangong) with a long black beard; he is flanked by two guardians, the mandarin general Chau Xuong on the left (holding a weapon) and the administrative mandarin Quan Binh on the right. Next to Chau Xuong is Quan Cong's sacred red horse.

Behind the main altar (directly across the courtyard from the entrance) is the goddess Thien Hau, Goddess of the Sea and Protector of Fisherfolk and Sailors. To the right is an ornate case in which Me Sanh (the Goddess of Fertility; in white) sits surrounded by her daughters. In the case to the left of Thien Hau is Ong Bon, Guardian Spirit of Happiness & Virtue. In front of Thien Hau is Quan The Am Bo Tat (also known as Avolokiteçvara), the Goddess of Mercy, enclosed in glass.

Across the courtyard from Quan Cong is a small room containing ossuary jars (in which the ashes of the deceased are reposited) and memorials in which the dead are represented by their photographs. Next to this chamber is a small room containing the papier mâché head of a dragon of the type used by the Fujian Congregation for dragon dancing. There is a photograph of a dragon dance on the wall between Quan Cong's red horse and Me Sanh.

Thien Hau Pagoda Thien Hau Pagoda (also known as Ba Mieu, Pho Mieu and Chua Ba) was built by the Cantonese Congregation in the early 19th century. Of late it has become something of a showcase for tours operated by Saigon Tourist and Vietnam Tourism, which may explain the recent extensive renovations. This pagoda is one of the most active in Cholon.

The pagoda is dedicated to Thien Hau (also known as Tuc Goi La Ba), the Chinese Goddess of the Sea who protects fisherfolk, sailors, merchants and anyone else who travels by sea. It is said that Thien Hau can travel over the oceans on a mat and ride the clouds to wherever she pleases. Her mobility

allows her to save people in trouble on the high seas.

Thien Hau is very popular in Hong Kong (where she's called Tin Hau) and in Taiwan (where her name is Matsu). This might explain why Thien Hau Pagoda is included on so many tour group agendas (tourists from both those places are known for their free-spending habits).

Though there are guardians to either side of the entrance, it is said that the real protectors of the pagoda are the two land turtles who live here. There are intricate ceramic friezes above the roofline of the interior courtyard. Near the huge braziers are two miniature wooden structures in which a small figure of Thien Hau is paraded around each year on the 23rd day of the 3rd lunar month. On the main dais are three figures of Thien Hau, one behind the other, each flanked by two servants or guardians. To the left of the dais is a bed for Thien Hau. To the right is a scale-model boat and on the far right is the Goddess Long Mau, Protector of Mothers & Newborns.

Thien Hau Pagoda is at 710 Nguyen Trai St and is open from 6 am to 5.30 pm.

Nghia An Hoi Quan Pagoda Nghia An Hoi Quan Pagoda, built by the Chaozhou Chinese Congregation, is noteworthy for its gilded woodwork. There is a carved wooden boat over the entrance and inside, to the left of the doorway, is an enormous representation of Quan Cong's red horse with its groom. To the right of the entrance is an elaborate altar in which a bearded Ong Bon, Guardian Spirit of Happiness & Virtue, stands holding a stick. Behind the main altar are three glass cases. In the centre is Quan Cong (Chinese: Kuan Kung) to either side are his assistants, the general Chau Xuong (on the left) and the administrative mandarin Quan Binh (on the right). To the right of Quan Binh is an especially elaborate case for Thien Hau, Goddess of the Sea & Protector of Fisherfolk & Sailors.

Nghia An Hoi Quan Pagoda is at 678 Nguyen Trai St (not far from Thien Hau Pagoda) and is open from 4 am to 6 pm.

Cholon Mosque The clean lines and lack of ornamentation of the Cholon Mosque are in stark contrast to nearby Chinese and Vietnamese pagodas. In the courtyard is a pool for ritual ablutions. Note the tile *mihrab* (the niche in the wall indicating the direction of prayer, which is towards Mecca). The mosque was built by Tamil Muslims in 1932. Since 1975, the mosque has served the Malaysian and Indonesian Muslim communities.

Cholon Mosque is at 641 Nguyen Trai St and is open all day Friday and at prayer times on other days.

Quan Am Pagoda Quan Am Pagoda, at 12 Lao Tu St one block off Chau Van Liem Blvd, was founded in 1816 by the Fujian Congregation. The temple is named for Quan The Am Bo Tat, the Goddess of Mercy.

This is the most active pagoda in Cholon and the Chinese influence is obvious. The roof is decorated with fantastic scenes, rendered in ceramic, from traditional Chinese plays and stories. The tableaux include ships, houses, people and several ferocious dragons. The front doors are decorated with very old gold and lacquer panels. On the walls of the porch are murals in slight relief picturing scenes of China from the time of Quan Cong. There are elaborate wooden carvings on roof supports above the porch.

Behind the main altar is A Pho, the Holy Mother Celestial Empress, gilded and in rich raiment. In front of her, in a glass case, are three painted statues of Thich Ca Buddha (Sakyamuni), a standing gold Quan The Am Bo Tat (Avalokiteçvara, Goddess of Mercy), a seated laughing Ameda, and, to the far left, a gold figure of Dia Tang Vuong Bo Tat (the King of Hell).

In the courtyard behind the main sanctuary, in the pink tile altar, is another figure of A Pho. Quan The Am Bo Tat, dressed in white embroidered robes, stands nearby. To the left of the pink altar is her richly ornamented bed. To the right of the pink altar is Quan Cong flanked by his guardians, the general Chau Xuong (on the left) and the

administrative mandarin Quan Binh (on the right). To the far right, in front of another pink altar, is the black-faced judge Bao Cong.

Phuoc An Hoi Quan Pagoda Phuoc An Hoi Quan Pagoda, built in 1902 by the Fujian Congregation, is one of the most beautifully ornamented pagodas in Ho Chi Minh City. Of special interest are the many small porcelain figures, the elaborate brass ritual objects, and the fine wood carvings on the altars, walls, columns and hanging lanterns. From outside the building you can see the ceramic scenes, each containing innumerable small figurines, which decorate the roof. Phuoc An Hoi Quan Pagoda is at 184 Hung Vuong Blvd (near the intersection of Thuan Kieu St).

To the left of the entrance is a life-size figure of the sacred horse of Quan Cong. Before leaving on a journey, people make offerings to the horse. They then pet the horse's mane before ringing the bell around its neck. Behind the main altar, with its stone and brass incense braziers, is Quan Cong (Chinese: Kuan Kung), to whom the pagoda is dedicated. Behind the altar to the left is Ong Bon, Guardian Spirit of Happiness and Virtue, and two servants. The altar to the right is occupied by representations of Buddhist (rather than Taoist) personages. In the glass case are a plaster Thich Ca Buddha (Sakyamuni) and two figures of the Goddess of Mercy, one made of porcelain and the other cast in brass.

Ong Bon Pagoda Ong Bon Pagoda (also known as Chua Ong Bon and Nhi Phu Hoi Quan) was built by the Fujian Congregation and is dedicated to Ong Bon, Guardian Spirit of Happiness & Virtue. The wooden altar is intricately carved and gilded. Ong Bon Pagoda is at 264 Hai Thuong Lai Ong Blvd, which runs parallel to Tran Hung Dao B Blvd, and is open from 5 am to 5 pm.

As you enter the pagoda, there is a room to the right of the open-air courtyard. In it, behind the table, is a figure of Quan The Am

Bo Tat (Goddess of Mercy) in a glass case. Above the case is the head of a Thich Ca Buddha (Sakyamuni).

Directly across the courtyard from the pagoda entrance, against the wall, is Ong Bon, to whom people come to pray for general happiness and relief from financial difficulties. He faces a fine carved wooden altar. On the walls of this chamber are two rather indistinct murals of five tigers (to the left) and two dragons (to the right).

In the area on the other side of the wall with the mural of the dragons is a furnace for burning paper representations of the wealth people wish to bestow upon deceased family members. Diagonally opposite is Quan Cong flanked by his guardians Chau Xuong (to his right) and Quan Binh (to his left).

Ha Chuong Hoi Quan Pagoda Ha Chuong Hoi Quan Pagoda at 802 Nguyen Trai St is a typical Fujian pagoda. It is dedicated to Thien Hau Thanh Mau, Goddess of the Sea and protectress of all who travel the seas, who was born in Fujian. The four carved stone pillars, wrapped in painted dragons, were made in China and brought to Vietnam by boat. There are interesting murals to either side of the main altar. Note the ceramic relief scenes on the roof.

Cha Tam Church It is in Cha Tam Church that President Ngo Dinh Diem and his brother Ngo Dinh Nhu took refuge on 2 November 1963 after fleeing the Presidential Palace during a coup attempt. When their efforts to contact loyal military officers (of whom there were almost none) failed, Diem and Nhu agreed to surrender unconditionally and revealed where they were hiding.

The coup leaders sent an M-113 armoured personnel carrier to the church to pick them up (Diem seemed disappointed that a limousine befitting his rank had not been dispatched) and the two were taken into custody. But before the vehicle arrived in Saigon, the soldiers in the APC killed Diem and Nhu by shooting them at point-blank range and then repeatedly stabbing their bodies.

When news of the death of the brothers was broadcast on the radio, Saigon exploded into rejoicing. Portraits of the two were torn up and political prisoners, many of whom had been tortured, were set free. The city's nightclubs, closed because of the Ngos' conservative Catholic beliefs, reopened. Three weeks later, US president John F Kennedy was assassinated. Since Kennedy's administration supported the coup against Diem, some conspiracy theorists have speculated that Kennedy was killed by Diem's family in retaliation. Then again, there are theories that Kennedy was murdered by the Russians, the Cubans, left-wing radicals, right-wing radicals, the CIA and the Mafia.

Cha Tam Church, built around the turn of the century, is an attractive white and pastel-yellow structure. The statue in the tower is of François Xavier Tam Assou (1855-1934), a Chinese-born vicar apostolic of Saigon. (A vicar apostolic is a delegate of the pope who administers an ecclesiastical district in a missionary region.) Today, the church has a very active congregation of 3000 ethnic-Vietnamese and 2000 ethnic-Chinese.

Vietnamese-language masses are held daily from 5.30 to 6 am and on Sundays from 5.30 to 6.30 am, 8.30 to 9.30 am and 3.45 to 4.45 pm. Chinese-language masses are held from 5.30 to 6 pm every day and from 7 to 8 am and 5 to 6 pm on Sundays. Cha Tam Church is at 25 Hoc Lac St, at the western end of Tran Hung Dao B Blvd.

Khanh Van Nam Vien Pagoda Built between 1939 and 1942 by the Cantonese, Khanh Van Nam Vien Pagoda is said to be the only Taoist pagoda in all of Vietnam. This statement needs to be qualified since most Chinese practice a mixture of Taoism and Buddhism, rather than one or the other exclusively. The number of 'true' Taoists in Ho Chi Minh City is said to number only 4000, though you can take this figure with a grain of salt since most of the true Taoists are probably Buddhists too.

The pagoda is open from 6.30 am to 5.30

pm every day and prayers are held from 8 to 9 am daily. To get there, turn off Nguyen Thi Nho St (which runs perpendicular to Hung Vuong Blvd) between numbers 269B and 271B; the address is 46/5 Lo Sieu St.

A few metres from the door is a statue of Hoang Linh Quan, chief guardian of the pagoda. There is a Yin & Yang symbol on the platform on which the incense braziers sit. Behind the main altar are four figures: Quan Cong (on the right) and Lu Tung Pan (on the left) represent Taoism; between the two of them is Van Xuong representing Confucianism; and behind Van Xuong is Quan The Am Bo Tat (Avalokiteçvara), the Buddhist Goddess of Mercy.

In front of these figures is a glass case containing seven gods and one goddess, all of which are made of porcelain. In the altars to either side of the four figures are Hoa De (on the left), a famous doctor during the Han Dynasty, and Huynh Dai Tien (on the right), a disciple of the founder of Taoism, Laotze.

Upstairs is a 150-cm-high statue of the founder of Taoism, Laotze (Vietnamese: Thai Thuong Lao Quan). Behind his head is a halo consisting of a round mirror with fluorescent lighting around the edge.

To the left of Laotze are two stone plaques with instructions for inhalation and exhalation exercises. A schematic drawing represents the human organs as a scene from rural China. The diaphragm, agent of inhalation, is at the bottom. The stomach is represented by a peasant ploughing with a water buffalo. The kidney is marked by four Yin & Yang symbols, the liver is shown as a grove of trees, and the heart is represented by a circle with a peasant standing in it, above which is a constellation. The tall pagoda represents the throat, and the broken rainbow is the mouth. At the top are mountains and a seated figure representing the brain and the imagination, respectively. The 80-year-old chief monk says that he has practised these exercises for the past 17 years and hasn't been sick a day.

The pagoda operates a home at 46/14 Lo Sieu St for 30 elderly people who have no families. Each of the old folk, most of whom

are women, have their own wood stove made of brick and can cook for themselves. Next door, also run by the pagoda, is a free medical clinic which offers Chinese herbal medicines (which are stored in the wooden drawers) and acupuncture treatments to the community. Before reunification, the pagoda ran (also free of charge) the school across the street.

Phung Son Pagoda Phung Son Pagoda (also known as Phung Son Tu and Chua Go) is extremely rich in statuary made of hammered copper, bronze, wood and ceramic. Some are gilded while others, beautifully carved, are painted. This Vietnamese Buddhist pagoda was built between 1802 and 1820 on the site of structures from the Oc-Eo (Funan) period, which was contemporaneous with the early centuries of Christianity. In 1988, a Soviet archaeological team carried out a preliminary excavation and found the foundations of Funanese buildings, but work was stopped pending authorisation for a full-scale dig.

Phung Son Pagoda is in District 11 at 1408 3 Thang 2 Blvd, near its intersection with Hung Vuong Blvd. Prayers are held three times a day from 4 to 5 am, 4 to 5 pm and 6 to 7 pm. The main entrances are kept locked most of the time because of problems with theft but the side entrance (which is to the left as you approach the building) is open from 5 am to 7 pm.

Once upon a time, it was decided that Phung Son Pagoda should be moved to a different site. The pagoda's ritual objects – bells, drums, statues – were loaded onto the back of a white elephant for transport to the new location, but the elephant slipped because of the great weight and all the precious objects fell into a nearby pond. This event was interpreted as an omen that the pagoda should remain at its original location. All the articles were retrieved except for the bell, which locals say was heard ringing whenever there was a full or new moon until about a century ago.

The main dais, with its many levels, is

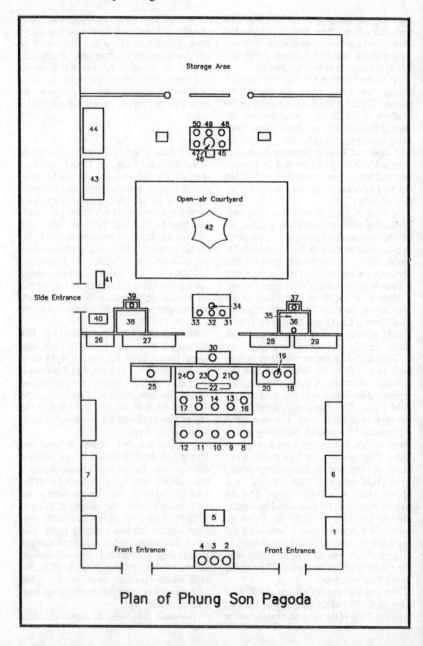

Plan of Phung Son Pagoda

1	Dia Tang Vuong Bo Tat, the Chief of Hell	30	Memorial Tablets, portraits of ancestor monks
2	A guardian	31	Thich Ca Buddha (Sakyamuni)
3	Guardian of the Pagoda	32	Standing Bronze Thich Ca Buddha from Thailand
4	Tieu Dien, a guardian		
5	Donations box	33	Thich Ca Buddha
6-7	Judges of the Ten Regions of Hell	34	Ameda, fat and smiling, with six kids
8	Pho Hien Bo Tat	35	Rosewood platform, used as table and for sleeping
9	Dai The Chi Bo Tat		
10	A Di Da Buddha (Amitabha), Buddha of the Past	36	Sandalwood statue of Long Vuong (Dragon King)
11	Quan The Am Bo Tat (Avalokiteçvara), Goddess of Mercy	37	Statue of Head Monk Hue Thanh, who succeeded Hue Minh
12	Van Thu Bo Tat	38	Rosewood platform, used as table and for sleeping
13	Dai The Chi Bo Tat		
14	A Di Da Buddha	39	Statue of Hue Minh, founder of this pagoda
15	Quan The Am Bo Tat		
16-17	Guardians	40	Desk with old photos of monks under glass
18	Thien Tai		
19	Quan The Am Bo Tat	41	Desk with old paper money displayed under glass
20	Lang Nu		
21	Dai The Chi Bo Tat	42	Minature mountain made of volcanic rocks
22	Statuettes of Quan The Am Bo Tat, her guardians and Thich Ca Buddha as a child	43-44	Rosewood platforms, used as tables and for sleeping
23	A Di Da Buddha (Amitabha), Buddha of the Past	45	Guardian
		46	18-armed Chuan De
24	Quan The Am Bo Tat (Avalokiteçvara), Goddess of Mercy	47	Guardian
		48	Dai The Chi Bo Tat
25	Boddhi Dharma	49	A Di Da Buddha
26-29	Memorial Tablets, portraits of ancestor monks	50	Quan The Am Bo Tat

dominated by a gilded A Di Da Buddha, the Buddha of the Past, seated under a canopy flanked by long mobiles resembling human forms without heads. A Di Da is flanked by Quan The Am Bo Tat, the Goddess of Mercy, (on the left) and Dai The Chi Bo Tat (on the right). To the left of the main dais is an altar with a statue of Boddhi Dharma, the founder of Zen Buddhism who brought Buddhism from India to China. The statue, which is made of Chinese ceramic, has a face with Indian features.

As you walk from the main sanctuary to the room with the open-air courtyard in the middle, you come to an altar with four statues on it, including a standing bronze Thich Ca Buddha of Thai origin. To the right is an altar on which there is a glass case containing a statue made of sandalwood. The statue is claimed to be Long Vuong (Dragon

King) who brings rain. Around the pagoda building are a number of interesting monks' tombs.

Museums

War Crimes Exhibition Once known as the 'Museum of American War Crimes', the name has been changed so as not to offend the sensibilities of American tourists. However, the pamphlet handed out at reception pulls no punches; it's entitled 'Some Pictures of US Imperialist's Aggressive War Crimes in Vietnam'.

Whatever the current name, this has become the most popular museum in Saigon with Western tourists. Many of the atrocities documented in the museum were well publicised in the West, but it is one thing for US antiwar activists to protest against Pentagon policies and quite another for the victims of US actions to tell their own story. But no matter what side of the political fence you stand on, the museum is well worth a visit – if for no other reason than to get a sobering reminder that war is anything but glorious.

In the yard of the museum, US armoured vehicles, artillery pieces, bombs and infantry weapons are on display. There is also a guillotine which the French used to deal with 'troublemakers'. Many of the photographs illustrating US atrocities are from US sources, including a picture of a suspected VC being pushed from a helicopter because he refused to 'cooperate'. There is a model of the notorious tiger cages used by the South Vietnamese military to house VC prisoners on Con Son Island. In an adjacent room are exhibits detailing 'counter-revolutionary war crimes' committed by saboteurs within Vietnam after the 1975 liberation. The counter-revolutionaries are portrayed as being allied with both US and Chinese imperialists.

The War Crimes Exhibition (☎ 290325) is housed in the former US Information Service building at 28 Vo Van Tan St (the intersection with Le Qui Don St). Opening hours are from 8 to 11.30 am and 2 to 5 pm Tuesday to Sunday.

Revolutionary Museum Housed in a white neoclassical structure built in 1886 and once known as Gia Long Palace, the Revolutionary Museum (Bao Tang Cach Mang; ☎ 299741) displays artefacts from the various periods of the communist struggle for power in Vietnam. The photographs of anti-colonial activists executed by the French appear out of place in the gilded 19th-century ballrooms, but then again, the contrast helps you get a feel for the immense power and self-confident complacency of colonial France. There are photos of Vietnamese peace demonstrators in Saigon demanding that US troops get out, and a dramatic suicidal photo of Thich Quang Duc, the monk who set himself on fire to protest the policies of President Ngo Dinh Diem.

The information plaques are in Vietnam-

ese only, but some of the exhibits include documents in French or English and many others are self-explanatory if you know a bit of Vietnamese history. Some of the guides speak English – consider leaving them a tip if they work hard for it.

The exhibition begins in the first room on the left (as you enter the building), which covers the period from 1859 to 1940. Upstairs, two more rooms are currently open. In the room to the left, is a *ghe* (a long, narrow rowboat) with a false bottom in which arms were smuggled. The weight of the contraband caused the boat to sit as low in the water as would any ordinary ghe. Nearby is a small diorama of the Cu Chi tunnels. The adjoining room has examples of infantry weapons used by the VC and various captured South Vietnamese and American medals, hats and plaques. A map shows Communist advances during the dramatic collapse of South Vietnam in early 1975. There are also photographs of the 'liberation' of Saigon.

Deep underneath the building is a network of reinforced concrete bunkers and fortified corridors. The system, branches of which stretch all the way to Reunification Hall, included living areas, a kitchen and a large meeting hall. In 1963, President Diem and his brother hid here immediately before fleeing to a Cholon church where they were captured (and, shortly thereafter, murdered). The network is not yet open to the public because most of the tunnels are flooded, but if you bring a torch, a museum guard may show you around a bit.

In the garden behind the museum is a Soviet tank, an American Huey UH-1 helicopter and an anti-aircraft gun. In the garden fronting Nam Ky Khoi Nghia St is some more military hardware, including the American-built F-5E jet used by a renegade South Vietnamese Air Force pilot to bomb the Presidential Palace (now Reunification Hall) on 8 April 1975.

The Revolutionary Museum is at 65 Ly Tu Trong St (corner Nam Ky Khoi Nghia St), which is one block south-east of Reunification Hall. It is open from 8 to 11.30 am and

2 to 4.30 pm Tuesday to Sunday. The museum offices are at 114 Nam Ky Khoi Nghia St. Admission is free.

History Museum The History Museum (Bao Tang Lich Su; ☎ 298146), built in 1929 by the Société des Études Indochinoises and once the National Museum of the Republic of Vietnam, is just inside the main entrance to the Zoo, on Nguyen Binh Khiem St. The museum has an excellent collection of artefacts illustrating the evolution of the cultures of Vietnam, from the Bronze Age Dong Son civilisation (13th century BC to 1st century AD), to the Oc-Eo (Funan) civilisation (1st to 6th centuries AD), to the Chams, Khmers and Vietnamese. At the back of the building on the 3rd floor is a research library (☎ 290268; open Monday to Saturday) with numerous books on Indochina from the French period.

The museum is open from 8 to 11.30 am and 1 to 4 pm, Tuesday to Sunday.

Ho Chi Minh Museum The Ho Chi Minh Museum (Bao Tang Ho Chi Minh; ☎ 291060) is in the old customs house (nicknamed the 'Dragon House') at 1 Nguyen Tat Thanh St just across Ben Nghe Channel from the quayside end of Ham Nghi Blvd. The tie between Ho Chi Minh and the museum building is tenuous: 21-year-old Ho, having signed on as a stoker and galley-boy on a French freighter, left Vietnam from here in 1911, beginning 30 years of exile in France, the Soviet Union, China and elsewhere.

The museum houses many of Ho's personal effects, including some of his clothing (he was a man of informal dress), sandals, his beloved American-made Zenith radio and other memorabilia. The explanatory signs in the museum are in Vietnamese, but if you know a bit about Uncle Ho (Bac Ho), you should be able to follow most of the photographs and exhibits. For a brief biography of Ho (1890-1969), see the entry on his mausoleum in the Hanoi chapter.

The museum is open on Tuesday, Wednesday, Thursday and Saturday from 8 to 11.30 am and 2 to 6 pm; on Sundays, it stays open until 8 pm. The museum is closed on Mondays and Fridays.

Military Museum The Military Museum is just across Nguyen Binh Khiem St (corner Le Duan Blvd) from the main gate of the Zoo. US, Chinese and Soviet war materiel is on display, including a Cessna A-37 of the South Vietnamese Air Force and a US-built F-5E Tiger with the 20-mm nose gun still loaded. The tank on display is one of the tanks which broke into the grounds of what is now Reunification Hall on 30 April 1975.

Art Museum To see Revolutionary painting and sculpture alongside artefacts from the Oc-Eo (Funan) civilisation, try the Art Museum (Bao Tang My Thuat; ☎ 222577) at 97A Pho Duc Chinh St in central Saigon. It is open from 7.30 am to 4.30 pm Tuesday to Sunday.

Ton Duc Thang Museum This small, rarely visited museum (Bao Tang Ton Duc Thang; ☎ 294651) is dedicated to Ton Duc Thang, Ho Chi Minh's successor as President of Vietnam, who was born in Long Xuyen, An Giang Province in 1888. He died in office in 1980. Photos illustrate his role in the Vietnamese Revolution, including the time he spent imprisoned on Con Dao Island. The explanations are in Vietnamese only.

The museum is along the waterfront at 5 Ton Duc Thang St, half a block north of the Tran Hung Dao statue at the foot of Hai Ba Trung St. It is open Tuesday to Sunday from 8 to 11 am and 2 to 6 pm.

Binh Soup Shop
It might seem strange to introduce a restaurant in the sightseeing section of this book rather than the Places to Eat section, but there is more to this shop than just the soup. The Binh Soup Shop was the secret headquarters of the Viet Cong in Saigon. It was from here that the VC planned the attack on the US Embassy and other places in Saigon during the Tet offensive of 1968. One has to wonder how many American soldiers must have

eaten here, unaware that the waiters, waitresses and cooks were VC infiltrators.

The Binh Soup Shop is at 9 Ly Chinh Thang St, District 3. By the way, the soup isn't bad.

Markets

See the Things to Buy section at the end of this chapter for information on Ho Chi Minh's bustling indoor markets. Even if you don't want to buy anything, these are a sight not to be missed.

Reunification Hall

It was towards this building – then known as Independence Hall or the Presidential Palace – that the first Communist tanks in Saigon rushed on the morning of 30 April 1975. After crashing through the wrought iron gates in a dramatic scene recorded by photojournalists and shown around the world, a soldier ran into the building and up the stairs to unfurl a Viet Cong flag from the 4th-floor balcony. In an ornate 2nd-floor reception chamber, General Minh, who had become head of state only 43 hours before, waited with his improvised cabinet. 'I have been waiting since early this morning to transfer power to you', Minh said to the VC officer who entered the room. 'There is no question of your transferring power', replied the officer, 'you cannot give up what you do not have'.

Reunification Hall (Hoi Truong Thong Nhat) is one of the most fascinating things to see in Saigon, both because of its striking modern architecture and because of the eerie feeling you get, as you walk through the deserted halls, that from here ruled arrogant men wielding immense power who nevertheless became history's losers. The building, once the symbol of the Southern government, is preserved exactly as it was on 30 April 1975, the day that the Republic of Vietnam, which hundreds of thousands of Vietnamese and 58,183 Americans died trying to save, ceased to exist.

Reunification Hall is open for visitors from 7.30 to 10.30 am and 12.30 to 3.30 pm daily except Sunday afternoons and when official receptions or meetings are taking place. The present office and entrance is at 106 Nguyen Du St (☎ 290629). The entrance fee for foreigners is US$3.25. Groups can make reservations in person or by phone and this is supposed to be done a day in advance to be sure a guide is available. If you just show up you will be let in but it's not certain you'll have a guide, which is needed to see the entire building. Unfortunately, many of the guides only speak Vietnamese so you may need to supply your own interpreter unless you've made previous arrangements.

In 1868 a residence for the French Governor General of Cochinchina was built on this site. The present structure was designed by Paris-trained Vietnamese architect Ngo Viet Thu and completed in 1966. The building, both inside and out, is an outstanding example of 1960s architecture; it is much more interesting up close than you would expect from the street. Reunification Hall has an airy and open atmosphere and its spacious chambers are tastefully decorated with the finest modern Vietnamese art and craft. In its grandeur, the building feels worthy of a head of state.

The ground-floor room with the boat-shaped table was used for conferences. Upstairs, in the Presidential Receiving Room (the one with the red chairs in it, called in Vietnamese Phu Dau Rong, or the Dragon's Head Room), South Vietnam's president used to receive foreign delegations. The president sat behind the desk; the chairs with dragons carved into the arms were used by his assistants. The chair facing the desk was reserved for foreign ambassadors. Next door is a meeting room. The room with gold-coloured chairs and curtains was used by the vice president.

In the back of the structure is the area in which the president lived. Check out the model boats, horse-tails and severed elephants' feet. On the 3rd floor there is a card-playing room with a bar, a movie-screening chamber and a heliport. The 4th floor was used for dancing.

Former US Embassies

There are actually two former US embassies in Saigon: the one from whose roof the famous chaotic helicopter-evacuation took place as the Communists took over the city in April 1975; and the building used before that one was built.

The older former US Embassy (Dai Su Quan My Truoc 1967) is an ugly fortress-like concrete structure at 39 Ham Nghi Blvd (corner Ho Tung Mau St). In 1967, the building was bombed by the VC. It now serves as a dormitory for young people studying banking.

The newer structure (Dai Su Quan My Tu 1967-75) – from which US policy was conducted during the last eight years of the Republic of Vietnam – is on the corner of Le Duan Blvd and Mac Dinh Chi St in the middle of what was (and still is) a neighbourhood of key government buildings. The main building, once the chancery, is encased in a concrete shield intended to protect it from bomb blasts as well as rocket and shell fire. There are round concrete pillboxes, protected with anti-grenade screens, at each corner of the compound.

The embassy building, which became a symbol of the overwhelming American presence in South Vietnam, was finished just in time to almost get taken over in the 1968 Tet offensive. On TV, 50 million Americans watched chaotic scenes of dazed US soldiers and diplomats firing at the VC commando team which had attacked the embassy, leaving the grounds littered with US and Vietnamese dead. These images were devastating to US home-front support for the war.

The ignominious end of three decades of US involvement in Vietnam, also shown around the globe on TV, took place on the roof of the US embassy chancery building. As the last defences of Saigon fell to the North Vietnamese Army and the city's capture became imminent, the Americans, as unprepared for the speed of the collapse of the South as everyone else (including the North Vietnamese), were forced to implement emergency evacuation plans. Thousands of Vietnamese desperate to escape the country (many of them had worked for the Americans and had been promised to be evacuated) congregated around the embassy and tried to get inside; US marine guards forced them back. Overhead, American helicopters (carrying both Americans and Vietnamese) shuttled to aircraft carriers waiting offshore. In the pre-dawn darkness of 30 April 1975, with most of the city already in Communist hands, US Ambassador Graham Martin, carrying the embassy's flag, climbed onto the roof of the building and boarded a helicopter. The end.

The compound is now occupied by the government-owned Oil Exploration Corporation. Present policy is to forbid visitors from entering the grounds. Much of the building, designed for use with powerful air-conditioning equipment, is not in use because the elaborate cooling system is broken.

Hôtel de Ville

Saigon's gingerbread Hôtel de Ville (City Hall), one of the city's most prominent landmarks, was built between 1901 and 1908 after years of the sort of architectural controversy peculiar to the French. Situated at the north-western end of Nguyen Hue Blvd and facing towards the river, the white-on-pastel-yellow Hôtel de Ville, with its ornate façade and elegant interior lit with crystal chandeliers, is now the somewhat incongruous home of the Ho Chi Minh City People's Committee. The building is not normally open to tourists, but it is possible to obtain permission to visit the interior – ask at the office (☎ 290739) signposted as Phong Hanh Chanh and Phong So 2 in the wing of the building opposite 77 Le Thanh Ton St. The office and the whole People's Committee Building is closed on Sundays.

For gecko fans: at night, the exterior of the Hôtel de Ville is usually covered with thousands of geckos feasting on insects.

French Colonial Architecture

Many of the buildings in Cholon are a distinctive mix of Chinese and French styles.

Van Long Catholic church

Some of the most interesting structures in Cholon are to be found along Hung Vuong Blvd.

Zoo & Botanical Garden

The Zoo and Botanical Garden (Thao Cam Vien) are a delightful place for a relaxing stroll under giant tropical trees which thrive amidst the lakes, lawns and carefully tended flower beds. The zoo facilities are a bit run-down but they are being repaired, and the animals, which include elephants, crocodiles and big cats, look well fed. Many of the cages are fairly spacious outdoor enclosures. The Botanical Garden, founded in 1864, was one of the first projects undertaken by the French after they established Cochinchina as a colony. It was once one of the finest such gardens in Asia.

The main gate of the Zoo is on Nguyen Binh Khiem St at the intersection of Le Duan Blvd. There is another entrance on Nguyen Thi Minh Khai St near the bridge over Thi Nghe Channel.

The History Museum is next to the main gate. The rickety amusement park rides around the gardens have not worked for years, but children (and adults, of course) are occasionally entertained by water-puppet shows performed on a small island in one of the lakes.

There is a basic outdoor restaurant next to the History Museum. Ice cream and fresh French rolls are sold at a few places around the park. Outside the main gate (along Nguyen Binh Khiem St) there are numerous food stalls selling rice dishes, soup and drinks.

Parks

Cong Vien Van Hoa Park Next to the old Cercle Sportif, an elite sporting club during the French period, the bench-lined walks of Cong Vien Van Hoa Park are shaded with avenues of enormous tropical trees.

This place is still an active sports centre although now you don't have to be French to visit. There are 11 tennis courts, a swimming pool and club house which have a grand colonial feel about them. It's worth a look for the pool alone. There are Roman-style baths with a coffee shop overlooking the colonnaded pool.

The tennis courts are available for hire at a reasonable fee. Hourly tickets are on sale for use of the pool and you can even buy a bathing costume on the grounds if you don't have one. The antique dressing rooms are quaint but there are no lockers! Other facilities include a gymnasium, table tennis, weight lifting, wrestling mats and ballroom dancing classes.

Cong Vien Van Hoa Park is adjacent to Reunification Hall. There are entrances across from 115 Nguyen Du St and on Nguyen Thi Minh Khai St.

Ho Ky Hoa Park Ho Ky Hoa Park, whose name means Lake & Gardens, is a children's amusement park in District 10 just off 3 Thang 2 Blvd. It is near the Hoa Binh Theatre and behind Vietnam Quoc Tu Pagoda. There are paddleboats, rowboats and sailboats for hire. Fishing is allowed in the lakes and a small swimming pool is open to the public for part of the year. The cafes are open year-round and there are also two arcades of Japanese video games. Within the park boundaries is a rather expensive hotel. Ho Ky Hoa Park is open from 7 am to 9.30 pm daily and is crowded on Sundays.

Binh Quoi Tourist Village Built on a small peninsula in the Saigon River, the Binh Quoi Tourist Village (Lang Du Lich Binh Quoi; ☎ 991833, 293444) is a slick tourist trap operated by Saigon Tourist. So far, it has not been a big hit with foreign visitors, but city-weary Saigon residents seem to like it. The 'village' is essentially a park featuring boat rides, water-puppet shows, a restaurant, swimming pool, tennis courts, camping ground, guesthouse and amusements for the kids. The park puts in a plug for Vietnam's ethnic minorities by staging traditional-style minority weddings accompanied by music.

On Tuesday and Saturday evenings from 5 to 10 pm, there is a traditional music performance and boat rides along the river. This might be worthwhile doing.

Binh Quoi Tourist Village is eight km north from downtown Saigon in the Binh Thanh district. The Official address is 1147 Xo Viet Nghe Tinh St. You can get there by cyclo or taxi.

Orchid Farm

The Artex Saigon Orchid Farm is the largest in Vietnam, with 50,000 plants representing 1000 varieties. It is primarily a commercial concern but visitors are welcome to stop by to relax in the luxurious garden. This is a great place to sit sipping a cold drink, shaded by coconut palms and bamboo and surrounded by acres of orchids.

The farm, founded in 1970, uses revenues from the sale of orchid flowers for its oper-

ating budget but makes its real profit selling orchid plants, which take six years to mature and are thus very expensive. In addition to varieties imported from overseas, the farm has a collection of orchids native to Vietnam. Ask to see the orange-yellow Cattleya orchid variety called Richard Nixon; they have another variety named for Joseph Stalin. The best time of year for a visit is the sunny season. The blooms are at their height during January and February.

For reservations, which should be made a day or two in advance, call the English-speaking owner, Tran Kim Khu, at his home (☎ 240124) in Saigon. Or you can stop by Kiosk Number 2 on Nguyen Hue Blvd, which is run by the same family.

The Artex Saigon Orchid Farm is 15 km from Saigon in Thu Duc District, a rural part of Ho Chi Minh City, on the way to Bien Hoa. The official address is 5/81 Xa Lo Vong Dai, but this highway is better known as 'Xa Lo Dai Han', the 'Korean Highway', because it was built during the war by Koreans. At 'Km 14' on Xa Lo Dai Han there is a two-storey police post. Turn left (if heading out of Saigon toward Bien Hoa), continue 300 metres, and turn left again.

Saigon Race Track

When South Vietnam was liberated in 1975, one of Hanoi's policies was to ban debauched capitalistic pastimes such as gambling. Horse race tracks – mostly found in the Saigon area – were shut down. However, the government's need for hard cash has caused a rethink. The Saigon Race Track (Cau Lac Bo TDTT; ☎ 551205), which dates back to around 1900, was permitted to reopen in 1989.

Much of the credit for the reopening goes to Philip Chow, a Chinese-Vietnamese businessman who fled to Hong Kong as a youth but returned to Vietnam in 1987 after the government promised to launch capitalist-style reforms. After getting the race track up and running through his own hard work, Mr Chow was rewarded for his efforts by being sacked from his position. Government officials, sensing the opportunity to line their own pockets, saw no reason to keep an entrepreneur on the payroll.

Mr Chow has not given up his ambition to run a race track; he has approached the government with a proposal to reopen the Duc Hoa Thung Race Track, 45 km from Saigon. Realising that this could draw some of the business away from their own state-run monopoly, government officials have adamantly refused.

Like the state lottery, the race track is extremely lucrative. But grumbling about just where the money is going has been coupled with widespread allegations about the drugging of horses. The minimum legal age for jockeys is 14 years; most look like they are about 10.

The overwhelming majority of gamblers are Vietnamese though there is no rule prohibiting foreigners. The maximum legal bet is currently US$2. High rollers can win a million dong (about US$92). Races are held four times a week but this might be increased in the future.

The Saigon Race Track is in District 11 at 2 Le Dai Hanh St.

Vietnam International Golf Club

This place was only in the early stages of construction at the time of this writing. This Taiwan-Vietnam joint-venture project is another hoped-for cash cow, brought to you by Saigon Tourist. When finished, the club (Cau Lac Bo Gon Quoc Te Viet Nam; ☎ 390367, 391680) will be at Lam Vien Park in the Thu Duc District, about 20km east of central Ho Chi Minh. Membership will range from US$5000 to US$60,000.

There is another golf course nearing completion at Song Bé, 20 km north of Ho Chi Minh City. The Song Be club will have memberships available at US$20,000 for foreigners and US$15,000 for Vietnamese. The whole resort, including hotel, swimming pool and tennis courts, should be completed by 1995.

The recent proliferation of golf courses in Vietnam is ironic in view of the fact that the communists formerly declared golf to be a 'bourgeois practice'; in 1975, after the fall of South Vietnam, golf was banned and all courses were shut down.

Places to Stay

Ho Chi Minh City has quite a few large hotels and many more smaller places, ranging from the luxurious Saigon Floating Hotel to truly grungy dives in Cholon available by the hour. Prostitution is supposedly banned in government-owned hotels (unless the army or police run the hotel), creating an enormous opportunity for the new privately owned 'mini-hotels'. Mini-hotels are concentrated in District 3.

Tourist-class hotels require payment in US dollars. By international standards, the prices set by the government for the best hotels in Ho Chi Minh City are not unreasonable, though one night in any of these places would bankrupt a Vietnamese.

Not all hotels in the city are permitted to serve 'capitalist tourists'. While there are some really grotty dumps that will take foreigners, the tendency is to force foreigners up-market. However, it is still entirely possible to find a hotel room for US$5. Hotels seem to be opening in Ho Chi Minh City at the rate of one per month – ask other travellers for the latest low-down on the places currently welcoming foreigners.

Cholon is a gold mine of cheap hotels and is likely to remain so despite the recent renovations of several places in the area. Cholon is Ho Chi Minh City at its most crowded and bustling, but if you don't mind the occasional commute to central Saigon, staying in Cholon is certainly worth considering, especially if you enjoy visiting Chinese pagodas. There are half-a-dozen hotels along Chau Van Liem Blvd and quite a few others along Tran Hung Dao B Blvd and Tran Hung Dao Blvd. Few Westerners stay in this part of the city, but heaps of travellers from Taiwan, Hong Kong and Singapore prefer Cholon because they can get around easily speaking Chinese. Cholon also seems to be popular with business travellers from Malaysia, Indonesia and India.

The oldest of Ho Chi Minh City's hotels were built early in the century under the

French, the newest in the early 1970s to accommodate US military officials, Western business people and war correspondents. Some of the latter seem to have learned most of what they knew about Vietnam over drinks at hotel bars.

When the city surrendered in 1975 North Vietnamese soldiers, fresh from years in the field after having grown up in the spartan North, were billeted in the emptied high-rise hotels. There is an oft-told story about several such soldiers who managed to scrape together enough money to buy fish and produce at the market. To keep their purchases fresh, they put them in the Western-style toilet, an appliance completely foreign to them. Then, out of curiosity, one of the soldiers flushed the toilet and the fish and vegetables disappeared. They were outraged by this perfidious imperialist booby trap and bitterly cursed those responsible. We can't swear that this incident actually took place (or that it happened only once), but we do know that a great deal of damage was done to Saigon's hotels after reunification and that bathroom fixtures were especially targeted. Some of this damage is only just now being repaired.

Places to Stay – bottom end

Touts from private hotels hang around the airport looking for business. If you haven't got a clear idea of where you want to stay, you can at least talk to them. Cyclo drivers just outside the airport can also find you accommodation to suit any budget.

District 1 (Central Saigon) Pham Ngu Lao St has emerged as Saigon's main centre for budget travellers. The *Hoang Vu Hotel* (☎ 396522, 396552; 161 rooms) at 265A Pham Ngu Lao St is extremely popular with backpackers. Prices for singles/doubles/triples with fan only are US$6/8/10.

The Hoang Vu fills up quickly and much of the overflow winds up staying in the nearby *Prince Hotel (Hoang Tu* in Vietnamese) at 193 Pham Ngu Lao St. Unfortunately, many travellers have reported theft of valuables from their rooms in the Prince. Some

travellers even claim they have had some things stolen while they slept! If you must stay in the Prince Hotel, lock your door with your own padlock, not the ones they hand out to travellers, and don't leave your camera, money or Walkman in your room when you go out. You can try reporting these thefts to the police, but all they'll probably do is fine you. The hotel is government-owned and seems to have little interest in dealing with the problem.

If you want to stay at the Prince, rooms are US$6 to US$8 with fan and US$10 to US$12 with air-con. The cheaper rooms are on the upper floors because there is no lift. We also give thumbs down to the adjoining Prince Restaurant – poor food and shoddy service.

The extremely popular *Vien Dong Hotel*, 275A Pham Ngu Lao St (☎ 393001, 392941) has double rooms with fan for US$7 to US$12 per night.

Nearby on Bui Vien St are two very clean and very safe private hotels, *Guest House 70* and *Guest House 72*; both charge US$5 to US$6 for a room with fan or US$8 for air-conditioning.

The *Khach San 69 Hai Ba Trung* (☎ 291513; 18 rooms) is, as its name suggests, at 69 Hai Ba Trung St. This small, pleasant place is conveniently near the centre. Triples with ceiling fans cost US$10. Air-con pushes the tariff to US$15 while 'special' double rooms cost US$20.

The *Dong Khoi Hotel* (☎ 294046, 230163; 34 rooms), is a grand old French-era building with renovation potential. For foreigners and overseas Vietnamese, spacious air-con suites with 4.5-metre-high ceilings and French windows overlooking Dong Khoi St cost US$10. The management is friendly and building security is good. The Dong Khoi Hotel is at 12 Ngo Duc Ke St (corner with Dong Khoi St).

The *A Chau Hotel* (☎ 331571; 39 rooms) is at 12 Le Lai St, 50 metres from the fancy Le Lai Hotel. Single rooms, which is all they have, cost US$5 with fan and US$10 with air-con.

District 5 (Cholon) The *Phuong Huong*

Hotel (☎ 551888; fax (84-8) 552228; 70 rooms) is in an eight-storey building at 411 Tran Hung Dao B Blvd. Also known as the Phenix Hotel, this place is just off Chau Van Liem Blvd in the middle of downtown Cholon. Rooms for foreigners cost US$10 to US$20.

Just up Chau Van Liem Blvd at 111-117 is the *Truong Thanh Hotel* (☎ 556044; 81 rooms). None of the rooms have air-con, but the hotel provides 'other services', namely prostitution. Singles/doubles cost US$4/5, other services not included.

Half a block away, at 125 Chau Van Liem Blvd, is the *Thu Do Hotel* (☎ 559102; 70 rooms). It looks very much like a dump, but like the neighbouring Truong Thanh Hotel, offers 'extra services'. Rooms with fan are US$4 while air-con rooms cost US$8.

Across the street from the Phuong Huong Hotel, the *Song Kim Hotel* (☎ 559773; 33 rooms) is at 84-86 Chau Van Liem Blvd. It's a grungy and somewhat disreputable establishment with doubles for US$5 with fan or US$8 with air-con. Reception is up a flight of stairs. You can do better than this for marginally more money.

The *Trung Mai Hotel* (☎ 552101, 554067; 142 rooms) is a six-storey establishment at 785 Nguyen Trai St, just off Chau Van Liem Blvd. It's definitely a 'lower end' hotel but should be OK for the night. Singles/doubles with fan cost US$5/6 while air-con rooms are US$_11.

The *Bat Dat Hotel* (☎ 555817, 555843; 117 rooms) is an excellent place to stay at 238-244 Tran Hung Dao B Blvd (near the pricier Arc En Ciel Hotel). Rooms with fan only cost US$5 for a single, while air-con ups the damage to US$11. The large restaurant on the ground floor is excellent and specialises in Chinese food.

The *Phu Do 1 Hotel* (☎ 556821; 40 rooms) is two blocks from Tran Hung Dao B Blvd on Ngo Quyen St. The official street address is 634-640 Ben Ham Tu St. Doubles here cost from US$15 to US$20.

The *Tan Dan Hotel* (☎ 555711) is at 17-19 Tan Da St very close to the up-market Arc En Ciel Hotel. This place is a bit tacky and

not overly friendly, but room prices are reasonable at US$8 to US$12.

The *Hoa Binh Hotel* (☎ 355133; 35 rooms) is a seven-floor building at 1115 Tran Hung Dao Blvd. The building is a bit tattered around the edges but is otherwise OK. Like most places in Cholon, most of the guests are from Taiwan, Hong Kong and Singapore. Double rooms with air-con and refrigerator cost US$12 to US$15.

The five-storey *Dong Khanh Hotel* (☎ 357177; 45 rooms) is at 2 Tran Hung Dao B Blvd. Once known as a budget hotel, at the time of this writing the hotel was under renovation and room prices are anticipated to escalate.

The *Hanh Long Hotel* (☎ 350251; 51 rooms) at 1025-1029 Tran Hung Dao Blvd was another former cheapie under renovation at the time of this writing.

The *Cathay Hotel* (Khach San Quoc Thai; ☎ 351657), 41 Nguyen Duy Duong St, gets some of the overflow of budget travellers who can't find room at the Prince, Vien Dong or Hoang Vu hotels. The hotel isn't special but will do for the night. As a fringe benefit, the street is pleasantly shaded by trees. Rooms with private bath and fan go for US$3 to US$4.

The *Dong Khanh 5 Hotel* (☎ 250632; 16 rooms) is on the edge of Cholon at 1 Nguyen Chi Thanh Blvd. Singles/doubles cost US$5/7. Reception is upstairs. The ground-floor restaurant is one of the city's worst.

Places to Stay – middle & top end

District 1 (Central Saigon) The *Saigon Hotel* (☎ 299734; 100 rooms) is at 47 Dong Du St, across the street from the Saigon Central Mosque. This used to be a backpackers hang-out but the hotel has had a facelift recently and singles/doubles have now risen to US$15/22 to US$28/36.

The *Thai Binh Duong Hotel* (☎ 322674) at 92 and 107 Ky Con St is a good middle-priced place with air-con rooms from US$15 to US$20.

The *Vinh Loi Hotel* (☎ 230272; telex 811317 HOTVL-VT; fax (84-8) 230776; 38 rooms), 129-133 Ham Nghi Blvd, is also known as the Champagne Hotel. Singles/doubles with fan go for US$20/26 while air-con sets you back US$24/30, breakfast included. There is a restaurant on the 1st floor.

The *Orchid Hotel* (☎ 231809; fax (84-8) 231811) is a relatively small place at 29A Don Dat St. The hotel has its own restaurant, coffee shop and karaoke lounge. Room prices start at US$40.

The *Bong Sen Hotel* (☎ 291516; telex 811273 HOTBS-VT; fax (84-8) 299744; 134 rooms) at 117-119 Dong Khoi St offers air-con singles/doubles for US$22/32 to US$55/72 (plus 10% service). Formerly called the Miramar Hotel, the Bong Sen is also signposted as the Lotus Hotel, which is a translation of its Vietnamese name. There is a restaurant on the 8th floor.

The *Huong Sen Hotel* (☎ 291415; telex 811273 HOTBS-VT; fax (84-8) 298076; 50 rooms) is at 70 Dong Khoi St. Once known as the Astor Hotel, it's now an annexe of the nearby Bong Sen Hotel. This place charges US$29/39 to US$44/54 (plus 10% service) for singles/doubles with air-con and hot water. The in-house restaurant is on the 6th floor.

The *Hoang Gia Hotel* (☎ 294846; fax (84-8) 225346) is at 12D Cach Mang Thang Tam St, around the corner from the Immigration Police Office. Recently refurbished, singles/doubles now go for US$30/40. The hotel has a respectable restaurant.

The *Le Lai Hotel* (☎ 291246; telex 811500 HOTLL-VT; fax (84-8) 290282; 52 rooms) at 76 Le Lai St is one of Saigon's fanciest. Singles/doubles/triples range from US$22/29/36 to US$68/81/94. The telecommunications and postal desk in the lobby is open from 7 to 11 am and from noon to 3 pm daily except Sunday. An exchange counter in the lobby offers the bank rate. There are restaurants on the 2nd and 3rd floors.

The *Embassy Hotel* (☎ 291430; telex 813024 HOTEM-VT; fax (84-8) 231978) is a medium-size place at 35 Nguyen Trung Truc St, not far from Reunification Hall. Recently renovated, the hotel has its own restaurant, karaoke bar and live music in the

evening. Double rooms go for US$70 to US$120.

The classiest hotel in the city is unquestionably the venerable *Hotel Continental* (☎ 294456; telex 811344 HOCONT-VT; fax (84-8) 290936; 87 rooms), setting for much of the action in Graham Greene's novel *The Quiet American*. Just across the street from the Municipal Theatre at 132-134 Dong Khoi St, the hotel dates from the turn of the century and in the late '80s underwent a US$2.6 million renovation. The Continental, now run by Saigon Tourist, charges US$66 to US$132 for singles and US$88 to US$154 for doubles (including breakfast and fruit). Budget travellers may still be able to afford a cold glass of Saigon Export on the terrace, known as the 'Continental Shelf' to war journalists.

Another preferred hotel in town is the *Rex Hotel* (Khach San Ben Thanh; ☎ 292186; telex 811201 HOTBT-VT; fax (84-8) 291469; 206 rooms). Its ambience of mellowed kitsch dates from the time it served as a hotel for US military officers. The Rex is at 141 Nguyen Hue Blvd (corner Le Loi Blvd). Singles cost from US$59 to US$165; doubles are priced between US$71 and US$198. The Rex has, among other amenities, computerised billing, a large gift shop, a tailor, a unisex beauty parlour, photocopy machines, a postal counter with fax and telex services, a massage service, acupuncture, a swimming pool on the 6th floor, an excellent restaurant on the 5th floor, a coffee shop on the ground floor and a beautiful view from the large 5th-floor veranda, which is decorated with caged birds and potted bushes shaped like animals. The Rex is almost always booked up and reservations are advised. At the end of the day, the Rex is a good though not cheap place to enjoy a sunset beer.

The five-star *Saigon Floating Hotel* (☎ 290783; telex VT812614 HOTL-VT; fax (84-8) 290784, PO Box 752; 200 rooms) was towed to the Saigon River from Australia's Great Barrier Reef (where it had gone spectacularly bankrupt) in 1989. Amenities offered by the Saigon Floating Hotel, which is moored at 1A Me Linh Square (on Ton Duc Thang St near the Tran Hung Dao Statue), include two restaurants, saunas, a gym, a tennis court, a swimming pool, meeting rooms, audio-visual equipment and a business centre (open 15 hours a day) with international telecommunications links, secretarial services, interpreters and personal computers. The small air-con rooms, which cost between US$175 and US$375, are wired for satellite TV reception.

Another favourite is the *Caravelle Hotel* (Khach San Doc Lap; ☎ 293704; telex 811259 HOTDL-VT; fax (84-8) 299902; 112 rooms), at 19-23 Lam Son Square (across the street from the Municipal Theatre). Once owned by the Catholic Diocese of Saigon, the Caravelle is Saigon's most-French hotel, and this heritage is alive and well in the rude reception English-speakers may encounter (and in the form of the Air France office on the ground floor). Singles/doubles with air-con cost from US$41/57 to US$125/151, but if it helps they throw in a free breakfast and basket of fruit. There are postal and telecommunications facilities in the lobby. The hotel features two restaurants, one of which serves Japanese food. There is dancing nightly on the 10th floor. The hotel also boasts massage services and a sauna.

The *Majestic Hotel* (Khach San Cuu Long; ☎ 295515; telex 812615 HOTCL-VT; fax (84-8) 291470; 115 rooms). Located along the Saigon River at 1 Dong Khoi St, it was once the city's most elegant and prestigious hotel. Singles/doubles with breakfast range from US$35/47 to US$120/140, and Visa, MasterCard and JCB cards are accepted. Postal and telecommunications services are available in the lobby. There are restaurants on the street level and the 5th floor.

The *Palace Hotel* (Khach San Huu Nghi; ☎ 222316; telex 811208 HOTHN-VT; fax (84-8) 299872; 130 rooms) is at 56-64 Nguyen Hue Blvd. This hotel, whose Vietnamese name means Friendship, occupies the second-tallest building in the city, and the views from the 14th floor restaurant

and 15th-floor terrace are superb. Singles/doubles cost from US$35/48 to US$88/108 with breakfast included. The Palace has telex and fax facilities, an imported-food shop, a dance hall, the Bamboo Bar and a small swimming pool on the 16th floor.

The *Saigon New World Hotel* (☎ 295134; telex 811403 NW-HSGN-VT; fax 295318) is under construction next to the Le Lai Hotel at 76 Le Lai St. When finished, it should be among the fanciest in the city.

The *Norfolk Hotel* (☎ 295368; fax (84-8) 293415) is at 117 Le Thanh Ton. All rooms in this Australian joint-venture hotel boast STAR satellite TV and a minibar. Singles/doubles cost US$70/85 to US$140/155, which includes breakfast.

The *Century Saigon Hotel* (☎ 293416; telex 811328; fax (84-8) 292732; 109 rooms), 68A Nguyen Hue Ave, is a Hong Kong joint-venture. Singles/doubles go for US$76/96 to US$475 (plus 10%). You can book rooms from Century International offices abroad: Hong Kong (☎ 5988888); Australia (☎ (008) 021211 or (02) 2615334); USA (☎ (808) 9559718).

The *Riverside Hotel* (☎ 224038; 30 rooms) is at 18 Ton Duc Thang St, very close to the Saigon Floating Hotel. This old colonial building has been renovated and now features a good restaurant and bar. Singles/doubles cost US$30/37 to US$40/47 with breakfast included.

The *Mondial Hotel* is at 117-119 Dong Choi St, adjacent to the Bong Sen Hotel. Singles/doubles start from US$35/50 and range up to US$65/80.

District 3 (North-Central Area) The *Que Huong Hotel* (☎ 294227; telex 811345 HOTQH-VT; fax (84-8) 290919; 48 rooms) – also known as the Liberty Hotel – is two blocks from the French Consulate at 167 Hai Ba Trung St. Singles/doubles are priced from US$20/30 to US$30/40.

The *Saigon Star Hotel* (☎ 230260; telex 812777 SSH-VT; fax (84-8) 230255), 204 Nguyen Thi Minh Khai St (PO Box 605), is a new place. The hotel features the Venus Disco from 8 pm until 1 am, plus the Terrace

Coffee Shop and Violetta Cocktail Lounge. Singles/doubles cost a mere US$80/95 a night.

Tan Binh District (Airport Area) The *Tan Son Nhat Hotel* (☎ 241079; 25 rooms) at 200 Hoang Van Thu Blvd has some of the nicest rooms in all of Ho Chi Minh City. This place was built as a guesthouse for top South Vietnamese government officials. In 1975, the North Vietnamese Army inherited it along with the nearby headquarters of the South Vietnamese Army. Recently, the entrepreneurial spirit sweeping the south has infected even the army, which, hoping to earn a bit of extra cash, renovated this place for use as a hotel.

The rooms are all doubles and cost US$25, US$30 and US$44 with breakfast included. All rooms have very high ceilings, air-con, refrigerators, hot water and the finest in imported bathroom fixtures, all in vintage early '70s style. A ground-floor room used by South Vietnamese Prime Minister Tran Thien Khiem has been preserved exactly as it was in 1975, plastic fruit and all. There is a small swimming pool out the back.

The *Chains First Hotel* (Khach San De Nhat; ☎ 441199; telex 811558 HOTTB-VT; fax (84-8) 444282; 132 rooms), 201/3 Hoang Viet St, boasts a coffee shop, gift shop, tennis courts, a sauna, massage services, three restaurants, a swimming pool, business centre and free airport shuttle service. Formerly, this place was known as the Tan Binh Hotel, and some locals still call it by that name. Rooms with air-con and fridge cost from US$65 to US$125 with breakfast and fruit thrown in. Air-con singles/doubles in the main building go for US$20/24 to US$33/38. A suite for four costs US$55. Rooms with fans in a building across the street from reception cost between US$8 for a single and US$15 for four persons.

Just next to the Chains First Hotel is the considerably cheaper *Star Hill Hotel* (☎ 443625) which has air-conditioned doubles for US$20.

To get there, turn off Hoang Van Thu Blvd

opposite number 312 and go straight (south) for one block.

The *Thanh Binh Hotel* (☎ 440984, 440599; 35 rooms) is a mediocre establishment at 315 Hoang Van Thu Blvd. Doubles (which is all they have) cost between US$15 (with fan) to US$25. The ground-floor restaurant is dismal. Because there are two hotels with this name, we call this the Thanh Binh Hotel I (not its official name). The other we'll call *Thanh Binh Hotel II* (☎ 642643) which is on Ly Thuong Kiet Blvd, costs US$15 and is a little better than the other Thanh Binh Hotel.

District 5 (Cholon) The *Arc En Ciel Hotel* (Khach San Thien Hong; ☎ 552869; telex 811330 HOTTH-VT; fax (84-8) 550332; 90 rooms) is also known as the Rainbow Hotel. It used to be a cheapie but has been fully renovated and now charges renovated prices. Single/double rooms with air-con cost from US$33/38 to US$55/66. The hotel is at 52-56 Tan Da St (corner Tran Hung Dao B Blvd).

The *Regent Hotel* (☎ 353548; telex 811417 LEAPRO-VT; fax (84-8) 357094), 700 Tran Hung Dao Blvd (see Ho Chi Minh City map), is also called the Hotel 700. The Regent is a joint-venture between Vietnam Union and three Thai companies, and facilities are excellent. Single/double standard rooms cost US$34/38, deluxe rooms are US$40/45 and suites go for US$60/65.

The five-storey *Tokyo Hotel* (Khach San Dong Kinh; ☎ 357032; fax (84-8) 352505; 93 rooms), 106-108 Tran Tuan Khai St, has seen a bit of renovation and now looks very nice. Double rooms with air-con, telephone and refridgerator cost US$25 to US$27. The hotel boasts a gift shop, restaurant, dance hall and karaoke bar.

The *Cholon Hotel* (☎ 357058) at 170-174 Su Van Hanh St is a mid-range hotel which is very popular with Taiwanese. The desk clerks speak both English and Chinese, not to mention Vietnamese. Squeaky-clean singles/doubles cost US$22/32. The hotel has its own restaurant.

Right next door is the privately owned

Cholon Tourist Mini-Hotel (☎ 257089; telex 811461 CHOMEX-VT; fax (84-8) 255375) at 192-194 Su Van Hanh St. Like its neighbour, the hotel caters to Taiwanese but accepts anybody. Singles/doubles cost US$24/28.

The *Andong Hotel* (☎ 352001) is at 9 An Duong Vuong Blvd right at the intersection with Tran Phu Blvd. It's a new place and all rooms feature hot water, telephone, air-con and refrigerator. Doubles cost US$28 and US$38.

District 10 (North-West Area) The *Ky Hoa Hotel* is next to the amusement park by the same name. It's a bit remote from the centre, but convenient if you like ferris wheels. Rooms in Building A go for US$70 to US$90. Cheaper accommodation in Building B costs from US$45 to US$60.

District 11 (West Area About one km north of central Cholon is the *Phu Tho Hotel* (☎ 551309; fax (84-8) 551255) at 527 3 Thang 2 Blvd (see Cholon map). Singles/doubles with air-con, a fridge and hot water cost US$25/30, US$39/44, US$35/40 and US$40/45. There is a huge restaurant on the lowest three floors with built-in karaoke facilities.

The *Goldstar Hotel* (☎ 551646; fax (84-8) 551644), 174-176 Le Dai Hanh St, is a new and spotlessly clean place. All rooms have private bath, refrigerator and air-con, and the upper floors give a good view of the race track. Double rooms cost US$40. For a room with twin beds the tariff rises to US$50 to US$60.

Places to Eat
There are three categories of restaurants in Ho Chi Minh City; government owned, privately owned and cooperative. These are often hard to tell apart except when the bill comes; prices tend to be slightly lower in government-owned establishments, in part because private businesses are heavily taxed. The quality of both the food and service tends to be better in private establishments. There have been disturbing reports recently

of the government leasing out old, dilapidated restaurants and letting the new private tenants fix up the place with their own money; then the lease suddenly gets cancelled and the government takes it over again.

Not surprisingly, Chinese food is a speciality in Cholon. Both Vietnamese and Western food predominate in central Saigon.

Restaurant in Vietnamese is 'nha hang'; it usually appears on signs preceding the name of the establishment.

Food Stalls The cheapest food available in Saigon is sold on the streets. In the mornings, pho, a tasty soup made of noodles, bean sprouts, scallions and pork, chicken or beef is sold from tiny sidewalk stands that disappear by 11 am. A serving costs about US$0.20. Late at night, food stands appear on the sidewalk of Nguyen Hue Blvd just south of the Rex Hotel and at other locations downtown.

Pho is available all day long at *Pho Hien Hanoi*, a soup shop in the heart of Saigon at 50 Dong Khoi St. A large bowl of delicious beef pho costs US$0.50. *Pho Tien* soup shop is on Dong Du St next to the Saigon Hotel. There is another pho shop at 99 Nguyen Hue Blvd.

Sandwiches with a French look and a very Vietnamese taste are sold by street vendors. Fresh French *petits pains* (rolls) are stuffed with something resembling pâté (don't ask) and cucumbers and seasoned with soy sauce. A sandwich costs between US$0.20 and US$0.50, depending on what is in it and whether you get overcharged. Sandwiches filled with imported French soft cheese cost a bit more.

Just west of the Central Market (Ben Thanh Market) is a cluster of food stalls. Mobile food stands often set up shop in the vicinity of numbers 178 and 264 Dien Bien Phu St.

Everyday Vietnamese In Saigon, there are a number of government-run restaurants that cater to locals and offer pre-prepared Vietnamese food at very reasonable prices.

Most are open at lunch time and dinner time only and are usually crowded. The waiter will assume that everyone in your party will eat some of each of the dishes ordered, so portion size (and price) will be adjusted accordingly. Don't show up just before closing time and expect a complete selection of dishes.

Nha Hang 51 Nguyen Hue at 51 Nguyen Hue Blvd serves superior Vietnamese food at very reasonable prices. It is open from 10.30 am to 2 pm and 4 to 7 pm. *Nha Hang 32 Ngo Duc Ke*, just off Nguyen Hue Blvd at 32 Ngo Duc Ke St, is almost as good. A meal for three, including inferior beer on tap, will cost you about US$2. It is open from 10.15 am to 2 pm and 4.15 to 8 pm.

Near the Ben Thanh Market, *Nha Hang Kim Son* at 68 Le Loi Blvd (☎ 296204) serves excellent Vietnamese food. A meal here costs the equivalent of US$1 to US$3. In this vicinity, you might also try *Nha Hang Thang Loi* (☎ 298474), also known as Victory Restaurant, at 55 Ham Nghi Blvd (corner Nam Ky Khoi Nghia St). The fare includes European and Vietnamese dishes.

Traditional Vietnamese Traditional Vietnamese food is the speciality of a cluster of restaurants on Nguyen Cu Trinh St, which is about 1.5 km from Ben Thanh Market towards Cholon along Tran Hung Dao Blvd. The restaurants here include: *Com Viet Nam 85* at 85 Nguyen Cu Trinh; *Com Viet Nam Thanh Son* at 113 Nguyen Cu Trinh; *Tiem Com Phuoc Thanh* at 125 Nguyen Cu Trinh; and *Tiem Com Lam Vien* at 131 Nguyen Cu Trinh.

A number of restaurants in Ho Chi Minh City cater to fans of more exotic traditional Vietnamese specialities such as cobra, python, bat, turtle, porcupine, pangolin, wild pig, turtle dove and venison (deer). Among them are the following:

Nha Hang 5 Me Linh is two blocks from Nguyen Hue Blvd, near the statue of Tran Hung Dao and the Saigon Floating Hotel. It is open from 10 am to 9 pm. All the traditional specialities, including cobra, are served here in an informal, covered patio.

The *My Canh 2 Restaurant* is at 125 Ho Tung Mau St (corner Ton That Thiep St), just off Nguyen Hue Blvd; it is open from 10.30 am to 10 pm.

The *Tri Ky Restaurant* (☎ 240968) is about four km north-west of central Saigon in a converted villa at 82 Tran Huy Lieu St (just around the corner from the mosque at 5 Nguyen Van Troi St). Most meals at this fancy place (white tablecloths, etc) cost US$1.50 to US$4, but a medium-size cobra may cost US$8 to US$10. It is open from 10 am to 10 pm. Less than a km north-west of Tri Ky is the huge *Phu Nhuan Restaurant* (☎ 240183; 700 seats), built in 1985 in the style of the mid-60s. It is at 8 Truong Quoc Dung St (corner Nguyen Van Troi), opposite the Dai Giac Pagoda.

Out near the airport, you might try the upscale restaurant of *Nha Khach Viet Kieu* (Overseas Vietnamese Guest House) at 311 Nguyen Van Troi St; it is open from 8 am to 10 pm. This is one of the nicest restaurants in the city, but because it caters to Overseas Vietnamese the prices are a bit high; meals can be ordered in small or large portions and cost from US$2 to US$5. In the evening, there is live Vietnamese and Western music.

Chinese Cholon being a Chinese neighbourhood, not surprisingly there are some excellent Chinese restaurants. The *My Le Hoa Restaurant* opposite the Tan Dan Hotel dishes up moderately priced Chinese meals.

Cafes For light Western-style meals or something to drink, there are a number of cafes often featuring clean food at dirt-cheap prices. A popular hang-out for budget travellers staying at the Prince and Hoang Vu hotels is the *Sinh Café*, 6 Pham Ngu Lao St. This is a very good place to meet people and get travel information. The cafe also arranges low-priced tours and can introduce you to English-speaking Vietnamese guides.

The *Kim Café*, 199 Pham Ngu Lao St, provides similar service and similar prices, but there have been a number of travellers reporting serious problems with the tours (driver, guide and car disappearing during the night!). However, the cafe's food is OK and it's still a good place to meet people. It's also worth noting that there are two Kim Cafés; one Kim Café is almost next door to the Sinh Café, but this is not the popular one with budget travellers – the popular one is a sidewalk cafe on the opposite side of the road between the Vien Dong and Hoang Vu hotels.

Nha Hang 95 Dong Khoi, formerly the Imperial Bar, is on the corner of Mac Thi Buoi St at 95 Dong Khoi St; it is open from 5.30 am to 9.30 pm. The old name, worked in wrought metal, is still partly visible above the windows. Nha Hang 95 retains some of its French-era charm and is an ideal place to watch Saigon bustle by while sipping something cold, like soda water with lemon or the weak beer on tap. Both the Vietnamese and European dishes are decent. The steak & chips can be recommended. An English menu is available.

The *Hotel Continental* has a coffee shop whose large picture windows overlook Lam Son Square.

The government-owned *Givral Pâtisserie & Café* at 169 Dong Khoi St (across the street from the Hotel Continental) has the best selection of cakes and pastries in the city. The cafe section offers home-made ice cream and yoghurt as well as a limited selection of Western food. The house speciality is ice cream served in a baby coconut *(kem trai dua)*. Check your bill here carefully! Givral, which is open from 7 am to 11 pm, is the perfect place to grab a snack after an evening at the Municipal Theatre, across the street. A second *Givral Pâtisserie* is at 141 Dien Bien Phu St.

Another good source of cakes and the like, including elephant ears and banana cake, is the *Cua Hang Ban Banh & Kem* (☎ 324673) at 11 Nguyen Thiep St (between Nguyen Hue Blvd and Dong Khoi St near Brodard Café); it is open from 7 am to 9 pm. Out the front, a red neon sign encased in a metal screen reads 'Pâtisserie Glace'.

The *Brodard Café* (☎ 225837), also

known as *Nha Hang Dong Khoi*, is a favourite with trendy, young, well-off Saigonese who come here in groups to eat to the accompaniment of taped Western pop music. Despite recent renovations, the decor is still vintage 1960s. This place is known for Vietnamese and French food (they are much better at the former than the latter). Prices are mid-range. Brodard is at 131 Dong Khoi St (corner Nguyen Thiep St).

Restaurants Without a doubt, the best restaurant in Saigon (and probably all of Indochina) is *Maxim's* (☎ 296676) at 13-17 Dong Khoi St (next to the Majestic Hotel); it is open from 4 to 9.30 pm. This is *the* place for power dining. The French and Chinese menu is truly voluminous, with meals ranging from US$5 (for Chinese food) to an arm and a leg (abalone for US$12). There is live Western classical music nightly from 7 pm.

A number of enthralled backpackers have reported that this place is absolutely not to be missed. The Chinese food has received rave reviews; the onion soup and filet mignon have gotten the thumbs down from many despite being pricier. Reservations are necessary for dinners on weekends. You can pay in dong, dollars or by credit card.

Near Maxim's, at 63 Dong Khoi St, is the very trendy and pricey *City Restaurant*.

Hotel Restaurants Many hotel restaurants offer Vietnamese and Western food at very reasonable prices, and a good, solid meal can be had for the equivalent of US$2 to US$5. After 9 pm, very few restaurants other than those in hotels are likely to be open.

An excellent place to relax from a day in the noise and bustle of Saigon is the restaurant on the 5th floor of the *Rex Hotel*, presided over by a fine Mona Lisa done in hanging beads. The food is usually excellent, the waiters in black bow ties are highly professional, the place is well lighted for reading, and meals begin at US$2. During dinner, live Western classical music is performed. The fish Normandie is excellent, as is the *cha gio* (spring rolls). Don't bother coming in shorts: such attire is considered inappropriate and you won't get in. The bar out on the veranda is less formal and has a view of the city centre.

The 9th-floor restaurant at the *Caravelle Hotel*, with its white tablecloths and crisp, starched napkins, is open from 6 am to 10 pm and serves one of the best breakfasts in town. There is live music during dinner and lunch.

Chez Guido Ristorante is an Italian pizza restaurant on the ground floor of the Hotel Continental. This is a joint-venture operation between Saigon Tourist and a gentleman from Italy by the name of Guido.

The *Nihon Basi* (☎ 292185) is a Japanese restaurant in the Rex Hotel which charges Japanese prices. *Kiku* (☎ 293704) is another Japanese restaurant in the Caravelle Hotel, and is also not particularly cheap.

The 15th-floor restaurant at the *Palace Hotel* affords one of the finest panoramic views in the city. There is also a decent restaurant at the *Majestic Hotel*. It can be reached via the Art Gallery Thang Long at 70 Nguyen Hue Blvd and is open from 2 to 10 pm. The Saigon Floating Hotel has two 'international standard' restaurants, the *Oriental Court* and *The Veranda*.

The *International Tourist Club* (☎ 295134) is in the Le Lai Hotel at 76 Le Lai St, District 1. This place has a dinner buffet from 6 until 10 pm and costs US$5. The club is also proud of its 'state-of-the-art' karaoke system.

The *Bong Sen Hotel* (☎ 291516), 117-119 Dong Khoi St, is known for its classy and expensive Vietnamese restaurant.

In Cholon, the *Bat Dat Hotel* at 238-244 Tran Hung Dao B Blvd has a large restaurant on the ground floor. The *Phu Tho Hotel* at 527, 3 Thang 2 Blvd has a restaurant occupying the lower three floors of the building.

Madame Dai's *La Bibliothèque de Madame Dai* is a Saigon institution – at least with Westerners (the Vietnamese find the atmosphere peculiar). Run by Madame Nguyen Phuoc Dai, a lawyer and former vice-chairperson of the South Vietnamese National Assembly, Madame Dai's is an intimate little restaurant consisting of half a dozen small tables set in her old law library, which is lined with dusty French legal tomes. The food, French or Vietnamese, is not spectacular, but the real attraction of the place is the cultured ambience. Though she is fluent in English, conversation with Madame Dai is in French as befits the atmosphere, and unless your French is impeccable your talk with her will be brief. Maybe she prefers it that way.

A dinner with beer costs US$10 to US$12. Reservations should be made at least a day in advance. Madame Dai's is in an unmarked building not far from Notre Dame Cathedral at 84A Nguyen Du St. If the gate is locked, pull the bell cord.

Vegetarian The ethnic-Vietnamese owners of the *Tin Nghia Vegetarian Restaurant* are strict Buddhists. This small, simple little establishment, which is about 200 metres from Ben Thanh Market at 9 Tran Hung Dao Blvd, serves an assortment of delicious traditional Vietnamese foods prepared without meat, chicken, fish or egg. Instead, tofu, mushrooms and vegetables are used. The prices here are incredibly cheap: meals cost less than US$1. It is open from 7 am to 8 pm daily.

In Cholon, *Tiem Com Chay Thien Phat Duyen* is a small Chinese vegetarian restaurant about one km east of Chau Van Liem Blvd at 509 Nguyen Trai St. *Tiem Com Chay Phat Huu Duyen*, also Chinese, is at 952 Tran Hung Dao Blvd (corner An Binh St, where Tran Hung Dao B Blvd begins); it is open from 7 am to 10 pm. Across An Binh St at 3 Tran Hung Dao B Blvd is another Chinese place, *Tiem Com Chay Van Phat Duyen*, which is open from 7 am to 9 pm.

On the first and 15th days of the lunar month, food stalls around the city – especially in the markets – serve vegetarian versions of non-vegetarian Vietnamese dishes.

Fast Food Given all that delicious Vietnamese and Chinese food available for low prices, it seems almost like a sin to seek out hamburgers and fried chicken. However, if you're going into fast-food withdrawals and need a fix before you can get back to Hong Kong or Bangkok, there are a couple of restaurants to try. One is *California Fried Chicken* (☎ 297354) at 68 Hai Ba Trung St, District 1 – the hamburgers are OK but the French fries are awful. Takeaway fast food is available at *Donald* (no relation to Mac), Kiosk 46, Nguyen Hue Blvd, District 1.

Ice Cream The best ice cream (kem) in Ho Chi Minh City is served at the two shops called *Kem Bach Dang* (☎ 292707), which are on Le Loi Blvd on either side of Nguyen Thi Minh Khai St. Kem Bach Dang 2 is at 28 Le Loi Blvd. Both are under the same management and serve ice cream, hot and cold drinks and cakes for very reasonable prices. A US$0.50 speciality is ice cream served in a baby coconut with candied fruit on top (kem trai dua).

Dozens of little ice cream and yoghurt (yaourt) places line Dien Bien Phu St between numbers 125 and 187.

Bars Two pokey bars serving hot and cold beverages and ice cream in an ambience of semi-darkness are *Café 46* at 46 Nguyen Hue Blvd and *Café 50* at 50 Nguyen Hue Blvd. The tables in these places have just enough room for 1½ people. There is another quiet, dark place at 8 Nguyen Thiep St (near Brossard Café).

If you want to sit at intimate little tables with red lights on them and watch music videos, try the *Hoan Khiem* (☎ 225753), also known as the My Man Bar (yes, the name *is* in English), at 27 Ngo Duc Ke St.

Dining Cruise The *Du Lich Tren Song* (Tourist Ferry Boat), which docks on the waterfront near the Majestic Hotel, is Saigon's version of Paris' *bateaux mouches*. Twice a day, this restaurant-on-a-barge is towed along the Saigon River by a tugboat, giving diners a leisurely view of rural Ho Chi Minh City. The lunch cruise (11 am to 2 pm) costs US$1; the evening cruises (at 6.30 and 9.30 pm) costs US$1.50 and includes a live band. These prices do not cover the food

(which is mediocre) or drinks. Tickets are sold at 14 Ton Duc Thang St.

Do-It-Yourself Simple meals can easily be assembled from fruits, vegetables, French bread and other basics sold in the city's markets. The widest selection of vegetables in the city is at Ben Thanh Market in Saigon and Binh Tay Market in Cholon. Plenty of this stuff is available in the little street market opposite the Tran Nguyen Hai statue, but make sure you do not get short-weighed or overcharged. Fruit vendors can be found all over the city, such as along Tran Hung Dao B Blvd in Cholon near the Bat Dat Hotel.

The best bread bakery in town is, according to many Saigonese, Nhu Lan Bakery at 66 Ham Nghi Blvd. You can buy oven-fresh bread here from morning till night. Fresh eggs are sold in the pastry shop of Givral Pâtisserie & Café at 169 Dong Khoi St. Imported 'luxury' foods – soft cheese, tinned meats, sardines, real chocolate, alcoholic beverages – are available at various shops around the city, including a group of stores and stalls between numbers 48 and 76 Ham Nghi Blvd in Saigon. In Cholon, luxury goods are sold on the odd side of the 100 block of Nguyen Tri Phuong Blvd.

Find yourself daydreaming about Kellogg's Frosties, Pringle's potato chips, Twining's tea or Campbell's soup? If you have an insatiable craving for plastic foods, by far the best place to go in Ho Chi Minh City is the Minimart (☎ 298189, extension 44) on the 2nd floor of the Saigon Intershop, which is at 101 Nam Ky Khoi Nghia St (just off of Le Loi Blvd). If this ultimate symbol of Western capitalism looks like it was transported lock, stock and barrel from Singapore, that's because it was. To enjoy the proffered delights, you must pay in US dollars. The Minimart is open from 9 am to 6 pm daily.

Entertainment
Sunday Night Live Downtown Saigon is *the* place to be on Sunday and holiday nights. The streets are jam-packed with young Saigonese, in couples and groups, cruising

the town on bicycles and motorbikes, out to see and be seen. The mass of slowly moving humanity is so thick on Dong Khoi St that you can hardly get across the street, even on foot. It is utter chaos at intersections, where eight, 10 or more lanes of two-wheeled vehicles intersect without the benefit of traffic lights.

Near the Municipal Theatre, fashionably dressed young people take a break from cruising around to watch the endless procession, lining up along the street next to their cycles. The air is electric with the glances of lovers and animated conversations among friends. It is a sight not to be missed.

Municipal Theatre The Municipal Theatre (Nha Hat Thanh Pho; ☎ 291249, 291584) is on Dong Khoi St between the Caravelle Hotel and the Continental Hotel. It was built in 1899 for use as a theatre but later served as the heavily fortified home of the South Vietnamese National Assembly.

Each week, the theatre offers a different programme, which may be Eastern European-style gymnastics, nightclub music or traditional Vietnamese theatre. There are performances at 8 pm nightly. Refreshments are sold during intermission; public toilets are in the basement.

Hoa Binh Theatre The huge Hoa Binh Theatre complex (Nha Hat Hoa Binh, or the Peace Theatre) in District 10 often has several performances taking place simultaneously in its various halls, the largest of which seats 2400 people. The complex is at 14, 3 Thang 2 Blvd (next to the Vietnam Quoc Tu Pagoda). The ticket office (☎ 655199) is open from 7.30 am until the end of the evening show.

Evening performances, which begin at 7.30 pm, are usually held once or twice a week. Shows range from traditional and modern Vietnamese plays to Western pop music and circus acts. On Sunday mornings, there are marionette shows for children at 9 am in the 400-seat hall, and well-known Vietnamese pop singers begin performances in the large hall at 8.30 and 11 am.

Films are screened all day every day beginning at 8.30 am. Most of the films – from the Socialist countries, France, Hong Kong and the USA (Disney productions are a favourite) – are live-dubbed (someone reads a translation of the script over the PA system), leaving the original soundtrack at least partly audible. A weekly schedule of screenings is posted outside the building next to the ticket counter. Films cost US$0.20 (US$0.30 for a double feature).

The disco on the ground floor is open Tuesday to Sunday from 8 to 11 pm. Admission is US$1.25.

Conservatory of Music Both traditional Vietnamese and Western classical music are performed publicly at the Conservatory of Music (Nhac Vien Thanh Pho Ho Chi Minh; ☎ 396646), which is near Reunification Hall at 112 Nguyen Du St. Concerts are held at 7.30 pm each Monday and Friday evening during the two annual concert seasons, from March to May and from October to December. Tickets cost about US$0.25.

Students aged seven to 16 attend the Conservatory, which performs all the functions of a public school in addition to providing instruction in music. The music teachers here were trained in France, Britain and the USA as well as the former Eastern Bloc. The school is free but most of the students come from well-off families because only the well-to-do can afford musical instruments. There are two other conservatories of music in Vietnam, one in Hanoi and the other in Hué.

Binh Quoi Tourist Village On Tuesday and Saturday evenings from 5 to 10 pm, there is a traditional music performance and boat rides along the river. Binh Quoi Tourist Village is eight km from downtown Saigon in the Binh Thanh district. The address is 1147 Xo Viet Nghe Tinh St.

Pubs At the moment, the most popular pub in Saigon with the avant-garde crowd is *Apocalypse Now* on Dong Du St opposite the Saigon Hotel. This place seems to attract a crowd of very mixed backgrounds – prostitutes and drug dealers along with clean-cut types who wouldn't touch anything stronger than mom's apple pie.

Just next door to Apocalypse Now is *Good Morning Vietnam*. Two newly opened places in the same neighbourhood are the *Cyclo Bar* and *B.475* (Before '75).

Shake's Pub is named after Shakespeare and appeals to the more well-dressed business traveller set than the 'shorts & thongs' backpacker. This place serves pub food (fish & chips, steak & kidney pie, etc) in addition to the beer. Shake's is on Me Linh Square (near the Saigon River).

Dancing & Discos There is dancing with a live band at the *Rex Hotel* nightly from 7.30 to 11 pm; admission is US$2. At the *Caravelle Hotel*, where admission is US$2.50, there is dancing on the 10th floor every night from 8 to 11 pm. At the *Majestic Hotel*, dancing is held every night from 7 to 11 pm; the cover charge is US$2. The *Palace Hotel* has dancing every night from 8 to 11 pm. You might also try the *Down Under Discotheque* at the Saigon Floating Hotel.

There is a good band at *Saigon Dancing* on the 3rd floor of the Saigon Intershop, which is at 101 Nam Ky Khoi Nghia St; the entrance fee is US$2. At the *Hoa Binh Theatre* (☎ 255199), which is at 14 3 Thang 2 Blvd, the disco on the ground floor is open Tuesday to Sunday from 8 to 11 pm; admission is US$1.25.

The *Volvo Dance Hall* is a Chinese-oriented disco inside the Arc En Ciel Hotel at 52-56 Tan Da St in Cholon. This disco is a joint venture between Saigon Tourist and Golden Desire Company of Hong Kong.

Shuttlecock Vietnamese are extremely skilled at shuttlecock *(da cau)*. It can be amazing to watch even if you don't play. Competitions take place regularly in front of a church called Nha Thoi in District 6.

Slot Machines The *International Tourist Club* (☎ 295134) in the Le Lai Hotel at 76 Le Lai St, District 1, is reputed to be the classiest slot machine venue in town. Other

hotels are planning to get on the bandwagon shortly. Already, many Vietnamese bars have installed the one-armed bandits. The machines must use tokens since there are no dong coins.

Cinemas Many Saigon maps have cinemas *(rap* in Vietnamese) marked with a special symbol. There are several cinemas downtown, including the *Rex Cinema* (☎ 292185) at 141 Nguyen Hue Blvd (next door to the Rex Hotel); another on Le Loi Blvd a block towards Ben Thanh Market from the Rex Hotel; and a third, *Rap Mang Non*, on Dong Khoi St 100 metres up from the Municipal Theatre. *Rap Dong Khoi* is at 163 Dong Khoi St.

Culture Clubs These are really geared towards the domestic audience, but you might have some interest in seeing what sort of culture the government produces for the masses. Some venues for Vietnamese cultural entertainment include the Youth House of Culture at 4 Pham Ngoc Thach St; the Children's House of Culture at 4 Tu Xuong St; and the Workers' Club at 55B Xo Viet Nghe Tinh.

Things to Buy
Souvenirs In the last few years the free market in tourist junk has been booming – you can pick up a useful item like a lacquered turtle with a clock in its stomach or a ceramic Buddha that whistles the national anthem. And even if you're not the sort of person who needs a wind-up mechanical monkey that plays the cymbals, keep looking – Saigon is a good shopping city and there is sure to be something that catches your eye.

Typical souvenir handicrafts are sold at innumerable shops in central Saigon, especially along Dong Khoi St. Many of these places also offer overpriced fake antiques.

Not surprisingly, Saigon Tourist is also trying to milk this market; the Saigon Tourist Art Gallery (☎ 293444) is at 55 Dong Khoi St.

One of the larger stores in this business is

Culturimex (☎ 292574, 292896) at 50 Dong Khoi St, which sells ceramics, wood carvings, hand-painted greeting cards, copies of antiquities and other items you'd expect to find in a shop with a name like Culturimex.

Artexport (☎ 294494), 159 Dong Khoi St, does much the same business as the foregoing.

The Saigon Lacquerwares Factory (☎ 294183), at 139 Hai Ba Trung St (near the French Consulate), is the sort of place to which bus loads of tourists are brought to do their souvenir shopping. The selection of lacquerware, ceramics, etc is large but prices are high. The Saigon Intershop at 101 Nam Ky Khoi Nghia St also sells handicrafts.

Oil paintings, watercolours and paintings on silk can be bought at Phuong Tranh Art Arcade, 151 Dong Du St (opposite the Caravelle Hotel). There is another art gallery, Thang Long, at 70 Nguyen Hue Blvd (next to the Century Saigon Hotel).

The Ho Chi Minh City Association of Fine Arts (☎ 230025), 218 Nguyen Thi Minh Khai, District 1, is where aspiring young artists display their latest works. Typical prices for paintings are in the US$30 to US$50 range, but the artists may ask 10 times that.

Women's ao dais (pronounced, in the south, 'ow-yai'), the flowing silk blouse slit up the sides and worn over pantaloons, are tailored at a store on Dong Khoi St one block towards Notre Dame Cathedral from the Municipal Theatre. For embroidered items, try Mai Anh at 91 Mac Thi Buoi St (across from the Palace Hotel).

The Rex Hotel gift shop, like other hotel shops, has souvenirs and other items at moderate prices set by its owner – you guessed it – Saigon Tourist.

Lac Long's, a shop at 143 Le Thanh Ton St (two blocks from the Hotel de Ville), sells fine exotic leathers and much more. This store is run by a gregarious ethnic-Chinese businessman known among socialist and capitalist travellers alike for his interesting connections. Nearby shops (around 121 Le Thanh Ton St) sell high-quality leather boots, sandals and shoes.

War Surplus Market For real and fake US, Chinese and Russian military surplus, the place to go is Dan Sinh Market at 104 Nguyen Cong Tru St (next to Phung Son Tu Pagoda). The front part of the market is filled with stalls selling automobiles and motorbikes, but directly behind the pagoda building you can find out what happened to at least a part of the hundreds of billions of dollars the USA spent losing the Vietnam War.

Stall after stall sells everything from gas masks and field stretchers to rain gear and mosquito nets. You can also find canteens, duffel bags, ponchos and boots, a lot of it brand-new. Much of the stuff here is newer than you'd guess: enterprising back-alley tailors have made it look just like US government issue. Anyone planning on spending time in Lebanon or New York City should consider picking up a second-hand flak jacket (demand has slumped since the war, and the prices are very competitive). On the other hand, exorbitant overcharging of foreigners looking for a poignant souvenir is common.

Tax Department Store The biggest department store in Ho Chi Minh City, Cua Hang Bach Hoa, is on the corner of Le Loi Blvd and Nguyen Hue Blvd. Built as the Grands Magasins Charner six decades ago, this three-storey emporium, which for years was run by the government and had a pathetic selection of goods, has been 'privatised', and floor space is now rented to individual shopowners. Items for sale include consumer electronics, blank and pirated cassette tapes, locally produced bicycles and parts, domestic alcoholic beverages, stationery, little globes of the world labelled in Vietnamese, sports equipment, cheap jewellery and clothing made of synthetic fibres.

Stamps & Coins As you face the main entrance of the GPO, just off to your right is a collection of stalls selling all manner of goods, including excellent stamp collections, foreign coins and banknotes. You can even find old stuff from the former South

Vietnamese regime. Prices are low: about US$2 will get you a decent set of late-model stamps already mounted in a book, but the older and rarer collections cost more.

Many bookshops and antique shops along Dong Khoi St sell overpriced French Indochinese coins and banknotes and packets of Vietnamese stamps.

Street Markets The street market which runs along Huynh Thuc Khang and Ton That Dam Sts sells everything. The area used to be known as the Electronics Black Market until early 1989, when it was legalised. It's now generally called the Huynh Thuc Khang Street Market though it doesn't have an official name.

You can still buy electronic goods of all sorts – from mosquito zappers to video cassette players – but the market has expanded enormously to include clothing, washing detergent, lacquerware, condoms, pirated cassettes, posters of Ho Chi Minh, posters of Michael Jackson, posters of Mickey Mouse, smuggled bottles of Johnny Walker, Chinese-made 'Swiss' Army knives and just about anything else to satisfy your material needs.

All along Nguyen Hue Blvd you can buy 'Saigon' T-shirts in white or numerous colours. Prices are around US$2.50 if you bargain, but the price also depends on the quality and complexity of the design.

Similar items are available in Cholon in the stores around 261 An Duong Vuong Blvd, which is also signposted as Hong Bang Blvd.

Indoor Markets Ho Chi Minh City has a number of incredibly huge indoor markets selling all manner of goods. They are some of the best places to pick up the conical hats and ao dais for which Vietnam is famous.

Ben Thanh Market Ben Thanh Market (Cho Ben Thanh) and the surrounding streets are one of the city's liveliest, most bustling marketplaces. Everything commonly eaten, worn or used by the average resident of Saigon is available here: vegetables, fruits,

meat, spices, biscuits, sweets, tobacco, clothing, hats, household items, hardware and so forth. The legendary slogan of US country stores applies equally well here: 'If we don't have it, you don't need it'. Nearby, food stalls sell inexpensive meals.

Ben Thanh Market is 700 metres southwest of the Rex Hotel at the intersection of Le Loi Blvd, Ham Nghi Blvd, Tran Hung Dao Blvd and Le Lai St. Known to the French as the Halles Centrales, it was built in 1914 of reinforced concrete and covers an area of 11 sq km; the central cupola is 28 metres in diameter. The main entrance, with its belfry and clock, has become a symbol of Saigon.

Opposite the belfry, in the centre of the traffic roundabout, is an equestrian statue of Tran Nguyen Hai, the first person in Vietnam to use courier pigeons. At the base, on a pillar, is a small white bust of Quach Thi Trang, a Buddhist woman killed during antigovernment protests in 1963.

Food seller

Binh Tay Market Binh Tay Market (Cho Binh Tay) is Cholon's main marketplace. Actually, it's technically not in Cholon proper, but about one block away in District 6 (Cholon is District 5). Much of the business here is wholesale. Binh Tay Market is on Hau Giang Blvd. It is about one km south-west of Chau Van Liem Blvd.

Andong Market Cholon's other indoor market, Andong, is very close to the intersection of Tran Phu and An Duong Vuong boulevards. This market is four-storeys tall and is packed with shops. The 1st floor has heaps of clothing – imported designer jeans from Hong Kong, the latest pumps from Paris, Vietnamese ao dais – and everything else imaginable. The basement is a gourmet's delight of small restaurants – a perfect place to pig out on a shoestring.

Toiletries The best selection of Western shampoos, soaps, diapers, sanitary napkins and the like can be bought at the Minimart on the 2nd floor of the Saigon Intershop, which is at 101 Nam Ky Khoi Nghia St (just off Le Loi Blvd); it is open from 9 am to 6 pm daily. The semi-legal black market and hotel gift shops have a limited selection of such items too.

Miscellaneous There are numerous tailors' shops in Cholon and several in downtown Saigon; the Rex and Century Saigon hotels each have in-house tailors.

There are several reliable photocopying places in the centre strip of Nguyen Hue Blvd just outside the Century Saigon Hotel. Photocopying is dirt-cheap and machines are now widely available in most parts of Vietnam.

No bureaucracy, Communist or otherwise, can exist without the official stamps and seals that provide the *raison d'être* for legions of clerks. To fill this need, the artisans at the shop at 39 Dong Khoi St make reasonably priced brass and rubber stamps entirely by hand. Letters and numbers – backwards, of course – are carved out of a block of brass or a chunk of rubber using a hammer and a tiny chisel.

Stationery is sold next to the GPO and on the even side of Le Loi Blvd between street numbers 30 and 60.

Getting There & Away

There is an occasional scam in operation at the airport, whereby the Immigration authorities try to cut down your visa when you arrive from 30 to two days. This is because of the revenue taken from them due to abolition of the former Registration stamp system (which every traveller had to pay for).

Be sure to ask for a full month on your visa and insist on it at the airport.

Air Vietnam Airlines has direct international flights between Ho Chi Minh City and Bangkok, Dubai, Frankfurt, Guangzhou (Canton), Hong Kong, Kuala Lumpur, Manila, Melbourne, Paris, Phnom Penh, Singapore, Sydney and Taipei. In addition, there are regularly scheduled 'charters' on foreign carriers to Jakarta, Moscow and Seoul.

Vietnam Airlines has separate offices for international and domestic booking. Unfortunately, the domestic booking is inconveniently located nearly two km from the centre of Saigon. Pacific Airlines books domestic and international flights at one office. Major foreign carriers also maintain their own offices. Vietnam Airlines also acts as sales agent for Lao Aviation (Hang Khong Lao), Cambodia Airlines (Hang Khong Cam Bot) and Korean Air (Hang Khong Trieu Tien). The complete list of airline offices is as follows:

Aeroflot (Hang Khong Nga), 4H Le Loi, District 1 (☎ 293489)
Air France (Hang Khong Phap), 130 Dong Khoi (Caravelle Hotel), District 1 (☎ 290982)
Cathay Pacific (Hang Khong Ca-thay Pa-ci-fic), 49 Le Thanh Ton, District 1 (☎ 223272)
China Southern Airlines (Hang Khong Nam Trung Hoa), Pham Hong Thai, 52B District 1 (☎ 291172)
Garuda Indonesia (Hang Khong In-do-ne-xia), Room 67 & 68, Tan Son Nhat Airport (☎ 442696)
Lufthansa (Hang Khong CHLB Duc), Tan Son Nhat Airport (☎ 440101)

Malaysian Airline System (Hang Khong Ma-lay-sia), 116 Nguyen Hue, District 1 (☎ 230695)

Pacific Airlines (Hang Khong Pa-ci fic), 76D Le Thanh Ton, District 1 (☎ 222614)

Philippine Airlines (Hang Khong Phi-lip-pin), 4A Le Loi, District 1 (☎ 292113)

Singapore Airlines (Hang Khong Sin-ga-po), 6 Le Loi, District 1 (☎ 231583)

Thai Airways International (Hang Khong Thai Lan), Room 7 & 8, Tan Son Nhat Airport (☎ 446235)

Vietnam Airlines – domestic (Phong ve Quoc noi Hang Khong Vietnam), 27B Nguyen Dinh Chieu (☎ 299980)

Vietnam Airlines – international (Phong ve Quoc Te Hang Khong Vietnam), 116 Nguyen Hue, District 1 (☎ 292118)

It is essential to reconfirm all reservations for flights out of the country. For more information on international air transport to and from Vietnam, see the Getting There & Away chapter.

Domestic flights from Ho Chi Minh City on Vietnam Airlines with one-way ticket prices are as follows:

Destination	Schedule	Price
Buon Ma Thuot	Mon, Wed, Sat	US$45
Dalat	Mon, Wed, Sat	US$30
Danang	Daily	US$85
Haiphong	Daily except Thu	US$150
Hanoi	Daily	US$150
Hué	Tue, Fri, Sun	US$85
Nha Trang	Daily except Mon	US$45
Phu Quoc	Wed, Sat	US$65
Pleiku	Mon, Thu	US$65
Qui Nhon	Thu, Sun	US$65

Pacific Airlines flies from Ho Chi Minh City to Haiphong on Wednesdays and to Hanoi on Mondays and Fridays. The one-way fare to either destinations is US$150. For more information on domestic air transport, see the Getting Around chapter.

All checked baggage coming into Vietnam is x-rayed upon arrival for contraband electronic equipment. The primitive x-ray equipment in use will destroy any film in your checked baggage, so keep your film and camera in your carry-on. Visitors have reported pilfering from checked luggage, especially when leaving the country (the baggage handlers don't even leave a 'thank you' note).

Tan Son Nhat Airport (it was previously spelled Tan Son Nhut by southerners, but the northerners had the final say) was one of the three busiest airports in the world during the late 1960s. The runways are still lined with lichen-covered mortar-proof aircraft revetments and other military structures, some still showing war damage. The sagging aluminium hulks of US-built transport planes sit next to ageing Soviet helicopters and jets of the Vietnamese Air Force. The complex of the US Military Assistance Command (MACV), also known as 'Pentagon East', was blown up by the Americans on 29 April 1975, hours before Saigon surrendered to North Vietnamese troops.

Bus – Mien Tay Station Intercity buses depart from and arrive at a variety of stations around Ho Chi Minh City. Almost all buses to points south of Ho Chi Minh City leave from the enormous Mien Tay Bus Station (Ben Xe Mien Tay; ☎ 255955), which is about 10 km west of Saigon in An Lac, a part of Binh Chanh District (Huyen Binh Chanh) of Greater Ho Chi Minh City. To get there, take Hau Giang Blvd or Hung Vuong Blvd west from Cholon and then continue past where these thoroughfares merge. As you head out of the city, Mien Tay Bus Station is on the left, opposite 130 Quoc Lo 4. There are buses from central Saigon to Mien Tay Bus Station from the Ben Thanh Bus Station (at the end of Ham Nghi Blvd near Ben Thanh Market). Express *(toc hanh)* buses are not quite as slow as regular buses.

Mien Tay Bus Station links Ho Chi Minh City with the southern provinces of An Giang, Ben Tre, Cantho, Dong Thap, Kien Giang, Long An, Minh Hai, Tay Ninh, Tien Giang and Vinh Long.

Express buses and minibuses from Mien Tay Bus Station serve Bac Lieu (six hours), Camau (12 hours; US$2.75), Cantho (3½ hours; US$1.35), Chau Doc (six hours), Long Xuyen (five hours) and Rach Gia (six to seven hours; US$2.25).

These buses, which receive priority treatment at ferry crossings, all depart twice a day: at 4.30 am and at 3 pm. Tickets are sold from 3.30 am for the early buses and from noon for the afternoon runs. Express bus tickets are also on sale at 121 Chau Van Liem Blvd in Cholon; 142 Hung Vuong Blvd west of Cholon; and at 638 Le Hong Phong St in District 10.

The following cities are served by non-express bus service from the Mien Tay Bus Station:

An Phu, Mytho, Bac Lieu, Ngoc Hien, Ben Tre, O Mon, Binh Minh Ferry, Phung Hiep, Camau (10 hrs), Rach Gia, Cang Long, Sa Dec, Cantho (five hrs), Soc Trang, Cao Lanh, Tam Binh, Cau Ke, Tam Nong, Cau Ngang, Tan Chau, Chau Doc, Tan Hiep, Chau Phu, Tay Ninh, Cho Moi, Thanh Tri, Duyen Hai, Thoai Son, Ha Tien, Thot Not, Ho Phong, Tieu Can, Hong Ngu, Tinh Bien, Long An, Tra Vinh, Long My, Thu Thua, Long Phu, Vam Cong, Long Xuyen, Vi Thanh, Moc Hoa, Vinh Chau, My Thuan, Vinh Long, My Xuyen.

Tickets for non-express buses are sold from 3.30 am to 4 pm at counters marked according to the province of destination. Non-express buses also leave from platforms arranged by province. At present, buses depart during daylight hours only. To guarantee a seat, you can make reservations a day in advance by asking a Vietnamese-speaker to phone the station office (☎ 255955).

Bus – Mien Dong Station Buses to places north of Ho Chi Minh City leave from Mien Dong Bus Station (Ben Xe Mien Dong; ☎ 294056), which is in Binh Thanh District about five km from downtown Saigon on Quoc Lo 13 (National Highway 13). Quoc Lo 13 is the continuation of Xo Viet Nghe Tinh St. The station is just under two km north of the intersection of Xo Viet Nghe Tinh St and Dien Bien Phu St. The station's main gate is opposite 78 Quoc Lo 13 (according to the new numbering) and next to 229 Quoc Lo 13 (according to the old numbering). To get there, you can take a bus from Ben Thanh Bus Station near Den Thanh

Market. A cyclo from the city centre should cost about US$1.25.

There is express service from Mien Dong Bus Station to Buon Ma Thuot (15 hrs), Dalat (7½ hrs; US$1.65), Danang (26 hrs), Haiphong (53 hrs), Hanoi (49 hrs), Hué (29 hrs), Nam Dinh (47 hrs), Nha Trang (11 hrs), Pleiku (22 hrs), Quang Ngai (24 hrs), Qui Nhon (17 hrs), Tuy Hoa (12 hrs), Vinh (42 hrs) and Vung Tau (2½ hrs).

All the express buses leave daily between 5 and 5.30 am. To Nha Trang, there is also a daily bus at 5 pm. To buy express tickets, turn left as you enter the main gate of the station (which is on Quoc Lo 13) and go all the way to the end to a blue and white one-storey building. Tickets are sold between 4 am and 4 pm in the room marked Quay Ban Ve Xe Toc Hanh (Express Bus Ticket Counter). To make express bus reservations by telephone, have a Vietnamese-speaker call (☎ 294056).

Non-express buses from Mien Dong Bus Station serve:

Bao Loc, Lam Ha, Baria, Long Khanh, Ben Cat, Madagoui, Binh Long, Nha Trang, Bu Dang, Phan Rang, Buon Ma Thuot, Phan Ri, Cam Ranh, Phan Thiet, Dai Te, Phu Tuc, Dalat, Phuong Lam, Danang, Pleiku, Di Linh, Quang Ngai, Don Duong, Qui Nhon, Dong Xoai, Tan Dinh, Duc Linh, Tan Phu, Duc Trong, Tanh Linh, Gia Nghia, Tay Son, Ham Tan, Thu Dau Mot, Ham Thuan Nam, Tuy Hoa, Hué, Tuy Phong, Kien Duc, Vung Tau, Xuyen Moc.

Many of the non-express buses leave around 5.30 am. Tickets for short trips can be bought before departure. For long-distance buses, tickets should be purchased a day in advance. The ticket windows, open from 5 am until the last seat on the last bus of the day is sold, are in a large open shed with a corrugated iron roof across from the express bus ticket counter. Tickets for many buses that leave from the Mien Dong Bus Station can also be purchased at the Mien Tay Bus Station in An Lac.

There are a number of restaurants just outside the station along Quoc Lo 13.

Bus – Other Stations Buses to Tay Ninh, Cu Chi and points north-east of Ho Chi Minh

City depart from the Tay Ninh Bus Station (Ben Xe Tay Ninh), which is in Tan Binh District. To get there, head all the way out Cach Mang Thang Tam St. The station is about one km past where Cach Mang Thang Tam St merges with Le Dai Hanh St.

Vehicles departing from Van Thanh Bus Station (Ben Xe Van Thanh; ☎ 294839) serve destinations within a few hours of Ho Chi Minh City, mostly in Song Be and Dong Nai provinces. Van Thanh Bus Station is in Binh Thanh District about 1.5 km east of the intersection of Dien Bien Phu St and Xo Viet Nghe Tinh St at 72 Dien Bien Phu St. As you head out of Saigon, go past where the numbers on Dien Bien Phu St climb up into the 600s. A cyclo ride from central Saigon should cost US$0.75.

An assortment of decrepit US vans, Daihatsu Hijets and Citroën Traction 15s leave Van Thanh Bus Station for Baria, Cho Lau, Ham Tan, Long Dien, Long Hai, Phu Cuong, Phu Giao, parts of Song Be Province, Vung Tau and Xuan Loc. Xe Lams go to Tay Ninh Bus Station in Tan Binh District. Vehicles leave when full. Van Thanh Bus Station is open from 6 am to about 6 pm.

Minibuses Cong Ty Dich Vu Du Lich Quan 1 (☎ 290541) at 39 Nguyen Hue Blvd offers the fastest transport in town to Vung Tau. Express minibuses (tiny Isuzu vans), whose standard complement is 20 passengers plus the driver, depart from 6 am to 5 pm on the hour. Fifty-seat buses leave daily for Dalat (seven hours) at 4.15 am and Nha Trang (10 hours) at 4 am and 4 pm.

The office is open from 7 am to 7 pm. Making reservations the day before you would like to travel is advisable. Tickets for these runs are also sold at 7 Ky Con St in District 1; at Nha Van Hoa Phuong Tan Dinh at 124 Tran Quang Khai St in Da Cao, part of District 1; and at 75 Pham Dinh Ho St in District 6.

Bus – To Cambodia Daily buses to Phnom Penh, Cambodia, leave from the Phnom Penh Bus Garage (☎ 293754) at 155 Nguyen

Hue Blvd, adjacent to the Rex Hotel. Look for the sign in Khmer and Vietnamese. A one-way ticket costs US$3 to US$4 depending on bus size. Vietnamese can book four-day tours to Cambodia here. If you already have a Cambodian visa, this is by far the cheapest way to get to Phnom Penh. It may be possible to hire a car for the drive to Phnom Penh at the Mien Tay Bus Station in An Lac (☎ 255955).

The Cambodian Foreign Ministry will drive you to Phnom Penh in a beautiful new Japanese car for US$300 – enquire at the Cambodian Consulate if interested. You can also book cars from Saigon Tourist and Vietnam Tourism, but it's likely to be cheaper at private travel agencies.

Train Saigon Railway Station (Ga Sai Gon; ☎ 245585) is in District 3 at 1 Nguyen Thong St. Trains from here serve cities along the coast north of Ho Chi Minh City. The ticket office is open from 7.15 to 11 am and 1 to 3 pm daily. Dong prices for foreigners' tickets are computed at a disadvantageous rate.

To get to the railway station, turn off Cach Mang Thang Tam St next to number 132/9. Go down the alley for about 100 metres and then follow the railway tracks to the left. Or you can go to the roundabout at the intersection of Cach Mang Tang Tam St and 3 Thang 2 Blvd and follow the disused railway tracks a few hundred metres. The tracks run down the middle of the alleyway that begins next to 252/1B Ly Chinh Thang St. A cyclo ride from the city centre to the station should cost US$0.50. The railway station is closed from noon until 1 pm for lunch.

The Reunification (Thong Nhat) Express trains connect Ho Chi Minh City with all the major towns along the coast from Phan Rang-Thap Cham to Hanoi. Schedules change, but at the time of this writing, there were two trains reunifying the country daily. The first departs Saigon daily at 7.30 am, arriving in Hanoi 48 hours later at 7.30 am. The second train departs Saigon on Monday, Wednesday and Saturday at 2.30 pm and arrives in Hanoi 42 hours later at 8.30 am. Another train departs Saigon Tuesday,

Thursday, Friday and Sunday at 3 pm, arriving in Hanoi 48 hours later at 3 pm.

There are also local trains. One train departs Saigon daily at 4.50 pm and arrives in Nha Trang at 5.05 am. There is a local train to Hué departing Saigon every other day at 9.15 am. And there is a local train to Qui Nhon, departing Saigon every other day at 9.50 am.

Car Private drivers hang out in front of the Mondial Hotel. They ask about US$40 for a trip to Tay Ninh in an air-conditioned car.

Saigon Tourist Car Rental Company (☎ 295925; telex 812745 SGTOUR-VT; fax (84-8) 224987), 34 Ton Duc Thang St, charges US$0.33 per km. Ditto for Vietnam Tourism.

Cong Ty Dich Vu Du Lich Quan 1 (☎ 290541) at 39 Nguyen Hue Blvd hires cars for intercity runs at US$0.20 per km (without air-con) and US$0.30 per km (with air-con). Trung Tam Du Lich Thanh Nien Viet Nam (the Youth Tourism Centre), which is next door at 44 Ngo Duc Ke St, has competitively priced vehicles as well. You can also try Vicarrent (Xi Nghiep Vicarrent; ☎ 290415) at 20 Nguyen Cong Tru, District 1.

Cars with drivers can also be hired at the Phnom Penh Bus Garage (☎ 230754), 155 Nguyen Hue Blvd next to the Rex Hotel.

Cars (and for larger groups, buses) can be arranged through the Mien Tay Bus Station (☎ 255955) in An Lac. Reservations should be made two to seven days in advance.

Major hotels can also arrange for cars; they charge US$30 to US$35 per day for distances under 100 km.

Boat Passenger and goods ferries to the Mekong Delta depart from a dock (☎ 297892) at the river end of Ham Nghi Blvd. There is daily service to the provinces of An Giang and Vinh Long and to the towns of Ben Tre (eight hours), Camau (30 hours; once every four days), Mytho (six hours; departs at 11 am) and Tan Chau. Buy your tickets on the boat. Simple food may be available on board. Be aware that these ancient vessels lack the most elementary safety gear, such as life jackets.

Getting Around

To/From the Airport Ho Chi Minh City's Tan Son Nhat International Airport is seven km from the centre of Saigon. The taxis for hire outside the customs hall will try to grossly overcharge, so bargain hard (a fair price into town is about US$5 to US$7). Cyclos (pedicabs) can be hailed outside the gate to the airport, which is a few hundred metres from the terminal building. A ride to central Saigon should cost about US$1. You might also try to flag down a motorbike and hitch a ride seated behind the driver; this should cost about the same as a cyclo.

To get to the airport, try hiring a taxi at one of the taxi stands listed in the Taxi section. This will certainly prove cheaper than the US$20 limousine service available at the front desk of the Rex Hotel. If you take a cyclo or motorbike to Tan Son Nhat, you may have to walk from the airport gate to the terminal. Private cars can bring you into the airport but must drop you off at the domestic terminal, only a one-minute walk from the international terminal. There is a public bus from downtown Saigon.

Bus Forgive the computer jargon, but Ho Chi Minh City's bus system is not 'user-friendly'. Indeed, it might be described as 'user-hostile'.

There is only limited local public transport. No decent bus map is available and bus stops are mostly unmarked. Very few of the locals use the bus system – usually only if they cannot afford a cyclo.

There are several bus lines linking Saigon and Cholon. Perhaps the most convenient begins on Nguyen Hue Blvd near the river. The red-and-white Czech-built Karosa coaches leave from here, turn left onto Le Loi Blvd, pass Ben Thanh Market, continue south-west on Tran Hung Dao Blvd, and turn left on Chau Van Liem Blvd in Cholon for one block. They then turn right onto Hai Thuong Lan Ong Blvd near the Cholon post office and continue on to Binh Tay Market.

There is a major depot for local buses on Le Lai St, a few blocks west of Nguyen Thai Hoc St.

Ben Thanh Bus Terminal, which is on the other side of the roundabout from Ben Thanh Market, offers transport to other parts of Ho Chi Minh City, including Mien Tay Bus Station in An Lac, Ba Queo, Binh Tay Market in Cholon, Binh Phuoc, Binh Trieu (near the railway station), Nha Be, Phu Lam, Phu Xuan, Quang Trung (the exhibition ground) and Tam Hiep (near Bien Hoa). This part of Saigon is infamous for its many pickpockets, razor artists and lowlifes.

Taxi Metered taxis do not cruise the streets, but they can be hired from Vinataxi Limited (☎ 222990). Just call and one will be dispatched to wherever you are. These taxis operate from 6 until 2 am, but you must pay in US dollars!

Saigon Taxi (☎ 297545, 298805, 296624) is at 27B Nguyen Dinh Chieu in the same building as the Domestic Booking Office of Vietnam Airlines. If there is no meter, agree on the fare first. Another place to try is SATAXI (☎ 298016), 75 Ham Nghi, District 1.

There is a taxi stand on Le Loi Blvd in front of the Rex Hotel. There is another taxi stand along the median strip in the middle of Ham Nghi Blvd by number 54. Again, check if there is a meter; if not, set the fare before starting out.

In Cholon, there are always a few ancient Renault 4 taxis sitting next to the entrance to the Pham Ngoc Thach Hospital at 120 Hung Vuong Blvd. They are there to transport sick people too ill to walk or ride in a cyclo, but healthy people who can pay are also welcome to use them. These Renault 4s break down frequently and are not recommended for travel outside the city.

Xe Lam Xe Lams (tiny three-wheeled trucks formerly called Lambrettas) leave from a parking lot opposite 54 Le Lai St. There is another Xe Lam station on Phan Dang Luu Blvd.

Car If, in this age of compact and subcompact automobiles, you have ever wondered how it was that US teenagers of the 1950s were supposed to have been sexually initiated in the back seat of a car, experiencing Ho Chi Minh City's boat-like 'wedding taxis' will put to rest forever your logistical confusion. These huge US cars date from the late '50s and early '60s, and many come complete with tail fins and impressive chrome fenders. They are now used mostly to add a touch of class to Vietnamese weddings, but they can also be hired for excursions in and around Ho Chi Minh City.

Hop Tac Xa Xe Du-Lich (Tourist Car Corporation; ☎ 290600), opposite Vietcombank and across the street from 43 Ben Chuong Duong St (corner Nam Ky Khoi Nghia St), is easy to spot: dozens of the old classics are lined up next to the dispatcher's booth. Make reservations the day before your departure. Always specify exactly where you want to go and the times you expect to depart and return *before* you sign anything or hand over any money. The usual deposit is between one-quarter and one-third of the total; the balance should be paid at the end of the trip.

Motorbike If you're brave, you can rent a motorbike and really earn your 'I Survived Saigon' T-shirt. Many say that this is the fastest and easiest way to get around Ho Chi Minh City, and that's probably true as long as you don't crash into anything.

There is a shop on Le Thanh Ton St between Vietnam Airlines International Booking Office and Saigon Tourist which rents motorbikes. Another place renting motorbikes is Ky Hoa Tourism (☎ 653456), 16 February 3rd Ave, District 10. Sinh Café has motorbikes for US$4 per day or US$7 with a guide.

For motorbike repairs, also try the area around the intersection of Hung Vuong Blvd and Tran Binh Trong St.

A 50cc motorbike can be rented for US$5 to US$10 per day. Before renting one, make sure it's rideable.

Cyclo Cyclos (pedicabs) can be hailed along

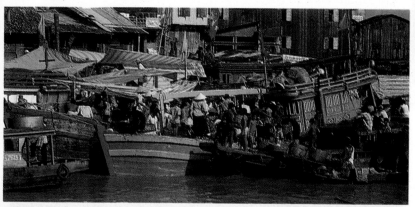

Top: Boat Habour, Mytho (RI)
Middle: Rice Fields, Ha Tien (RS)
Bottom: Duong Beach, Ha Tien (RS)

Top: Pagoda, Sam Mountain (RS)
Left: Scooter, Mekong Delta (MF)
Right: Rice Fields, Mekong Delta (TA)

major thoroughfares almost any time of the day or night. In Ho Chi Minh City, many of the drivers are former South Vietnamese Army soldiers, and quite a few of them know at least a bit of English. Each of them has a story of war, 're-education' and poverty to tell.

Many of the cyclo drivers are unwilling to go right into the city centre because the police have fined them in the past. Such drivers might drop you off one or two blocks away from the Rex Hotel and ask you to walk the last short distance. Many travellers have gotten angry at their cyclo drivers for this, but try to have some sympathy – a small fine could just about bankrupt them. Remember that when they get shaken down by the police, they can't call their embassy to complain.

Short hops around the city centre should cost about US$0.50; central Saigon to central Cholon costs about US$0.90. Settle on a price beforehand and have exact change ready.

Honda Om A quick (if precarious) way around town is to ride on the back of a motorbike (Honda om). You can either try to flag someone down (most drivers can always use a bit of extra cash) or ask a Vietnamese to find a Honda om for you. The accepted rate is comparable to what cyclos charge.

Bicycle A bicycle is a good, slow way to get around the city and see things. Bikes can be rented from a number of places; the Prince Hotel (☎ 322657) at 187 Pham Ngu Lao St; Sinh Café, 6 Pham Ngu Lao St; from a stand opposite the Rex Hotel; SGT Travel Service (☎ 298914), 49 Le Thanh Ton St; The Youth Centre (☎ 294345), 1 Pham Ngoc Thach; Eden Tourist Office (☎ 295417), 114 Nguyen Hue.

The best place in Ho Chi Minh City to buy a decent (ie 'imported') bicycle is at the shops around 288 Le Thanh Ton St (corner Cach Mang Thang Tam St). You can also buy bike components: Czech and French frames, Chinese derailleurs, headlamps, etc. A

decent bicycle with foreign components costs about US$100. In Cholon, you might try the bicycle shops on Ngo Gia Tu Blvd just south-west of Ly Thai To Blvd (near An Quang Pagoda). In District 4 there are bicycle parts shops along Nguyen Tat Thanh St just south of the Ho Chi Minh Museum.

For cheap and poorly assembled domestic bicycles and parts, try the ground floor of Cua Hang Bach Hoa, the department store on the corner of Nguyen Hue Blvd and Le Loi Blvd. Vikotrade Company at 35 Le Loi Blvd (across the street from the Rex Hotel) also has locally made components.

For on-the-spot bicycle repairs, look for an upturned army helmet and a hand pump sitting next to the curb. There is a cluster of bicycle repair shops around 23 Phan Dang Luu Blvd.

Bicycle parking lots in Ho Chi Minh City are usually just roped- off sections of a sidewalk. For US$0.10 you can leave your bicycle knowing that it will be there when you get back (bicycle theft is a big problem). When you pull up, your bicycle will have a number written on the seat in chalk or stapled to the handlebars. You will be given a reclaim chit (don't lose it!). If you come back and your bicycle is gone, the parking lot is supposedly required to replace it.

Boat To see Ho Chi Minh City from the Saigon River, you can easily hire a motorised five-metre boat near Me Linh Square (at the river end of Hai Ba Trung St, next to the Saigon Floating Hotel). The price should be US$2 to US$5 per hour. Interesting destinations for short trips include Cholon (along Ben Nghe Channel) and the zoo (along Thi Nghe Channel).

We hired a small boat with driver and female guide for US$5 for an hour for two people and were able to go up the Cholon Channel and see life on the waterfront. The bridges are too low for regular tourist craft. It was extremely interesting to see how these stilt-house dwellers live. We were told that already when the water level is low 'pirate boys' board the boats demanding money, but we had no problems. We were able to take many interesting photographs.

Ferries across the Saigon River leave from a dock at Me Linh Square. They run every half hour or so from 4.30 am to 10.30 pm. Small boats to the other bank of the Saigon River leave from the end of Ham Nghi Blvd, but to get one you have to brave a gauntlet of greedy boat owners.

There are boat cruises at the Binh Quoi Tourist Village, eight km from downtown Saigon in the Binh Thanh district. The smaller boats have 16 seats and cost US$1 per person for a one-hour trip. The larger boats have 100 seats and cost US$0.40 per person, but only leave when full (unless you want to charter the boat for US$40 per hour!).

Around Ho Chi Minh City

CU CHI TUNNELS
CỦ CHI ĐỊA ĐẠO;
ĐƯỜNG HẦM CỦ CHI

The tunnel network of Cu Chi District, now part of Greater Ho Chi Minh City, became legendary during the 1960s for its role in facilitating Viet Cong control of a large rural area only 30 to 40 km from Saigon. At its height, the tunnel system stretched from the South Vietnamese capital to the Cambodian border; in the district of Cu Chi alone, there were over 200 km of tunnels. The network, parts of which were several stories deep, included innumerable trap doors, specially constructed living areas, storage facilities, weapons factories, field hospitals, command centres and kitchens.

The tunnels made possible communiction and coordination between VC-controlled enclaves isolated from each other by South Vietnamese and American land and air operations. They also allowed the guerrillas to mount surprise attacks wherever the tunnels went – even within the perimeters of American bases – and to disappear into hidden trapdoors without a trace. After ground operations against the tunnels claimed large numbers of casualties and proved ineffective, the Americans resorted to massive firepower, eventually turning Cu Chi's 420 sq km into what Tom Mangold and John Penycate have called 'the most bombed, shelled, gassed, defoliated and generally devastated area in the history of warfare'.

Today, Cu Chi has become a pilgrimage site for Vietnamese schoolchildren and Party cadres. Parts of this remarkable tunnel network – enlarged and upgraded versions of the real thing – are open to the public. The unadulterated tunnels, though not actually closed to tourists, are hard to get to and are rarely visited.

For those who wish, there is the opportunity to fire an M-16, AK-47 or Russian carbine rifle at the tunnel site. This costs US$1 per bullet but may be the only opportunity you'll ever get. It's recommended that you wear hearing protection.

History

The tunnels of Cu Chi were built over a period of 2½ decades beginning in the late 1940s. They were the improvised response of a poorly equipped peasant army to its enemy's high-tech ordnance, helicopters, artillery, bombers and chemical weapons.

The Viet Minh built the first dugouts and tunnels in the hard, red earth of Cu Chi – ideal for the construction of tunnels – during the war against the French. The excavations were used mostly for communication between villages and to evade French army sweeps of the area.

When the National Liberation Front (Viet Cong) insurgency began in earnest around 1960, the old Viet Minh tunnels were repaired and new extensions excavated. Within a few years the system assumed enormous strategic importance, and most of Cu Chi District and nearby areas came under firm Viet Cong control. In addition, Cu Chi was used as a base for infiltrating intelligence agents and sabotage teams into Saigon itself. The stunning attacks in the South Vietnamese capital itself during the 1968 Tet Offensive were planned and launched from Cu Chi.

In early 1963, the Diem government implemented the botched 'strategic hamlet' programme under which fortified encampments, surrounded by rows of sharp bamboo spikes, were built to house people relocated from Communist-controlled areas. The first 'strategic hamlet' was in Ben Cat District, next door to Cu Chi. Not only was the programme carried out with incredible incompetence and cruelty, alienating the peasantry, but the VC launched a major (successful) effort to defeat it – the VC was able to tunnel into the hamlets and control them from within. By the end of 1963, the first showpiece hamlet had been overrun.

The series of setbacks and defeats suffered by the South Vietnamese government forces in the Cu Chi area helped make a complete Viet Cong victory by the end of 1965 seem a distinct possibility. Indeed, in the early months of that year, the guerrillas boldly held a victory parade in the middle of Cu Chi town. VC strength in and around Cu Chi was one of the reasons the Johnson administration decided to involve American combat troops in the war.

To deal with the threat posed by VC control of an area so near the South Vietnamese capital, one of the Americans' first actions was to establish a large base camp in Cu Chi District. Unknowingly, they built it right on top of an existing tunnel network. It took months for the 25th Division to figure out why they kept getting shot at in their tents at night.

The Americans and Australians tried to 'pacify' the area around Cu Chi that came to be known as the 'Iron Triangle' by a variety of methods. They launched large-scale ground operations involving tens of thousands of troops but failed to locate the tunnels. To deny the VC cover and supplies, rice paddies were defoliated, huge swathes of jungle bulldozed and villages evacuated and razed. The Americans also sprayed chemical defoliants on the area from the air and then, a few months later, ignited the tinder-dry vegetation with gasoline and napalm. But the intense heat interacted with the wet tropical air in such a way as to create cloudbursts that extinguished the fires. The VC remained safe and sound in their tunnels.

When the Americans began using Alsatians trained to use their keen sense of smell to locate trapdoors and guerrillas, the VC put out pepper to distract the dogs. They also began washing with American toilet soap, which gave off a scent the canines identified as friendly. Captured American uniforms, which had the familiar smell of bodies nourished on American-style food, were put out to confuse the dogs further. Most importantly, the dogs were not able to spot booby traps. So many dogs were killed or maimed that their horrified army handlers refused to send them into the tunnels; so the US Army began sending down men instead. These 'tunnel rats', who were often involved in underground fire fights, sustained appallingly high casualty rates.

The Americans declared Cu Chi a free-strike zone: minimal authorisation was needed to shoot at anything in the area, random artillery was fired into the area at night and pilots were told to drop unused bombs and napalm there before returning to base. But the Viet Cong stayed put. Finally, in the late 1960s, the Americans carpet-bombed the whole area with B-52s, destroying most of the tunnels along with everything else around. But it was too late; the USA was already on its way out of the war. The tunnels had served their purpose.

The Viet Cong guerrillas serving in the tunnels lived in extremely difficult conditions and suffered horrific casualties. Only about 6000 of the 16,000 cadres who fought in the tunnels survived the war. In addition, uncounted thousands of civilians in the area, relatives of many of the guerrillas, were killed. Their tenacity despite the bombings, the pressures of living underground for weeks and months at a time and the deaths of countless friends and comrades is difficult to comprehend.

The villages of Cu Chi have been presented with numerous honorific awards, decorations and citations by the government, and many have been declared 'heroic villages'. Since 1975, new hamlets have been established and the population of the area has more than doubled to 200,000, but chemical defoliants remain in the soil and water and crop yields are still poor.

For more details, you might want to take a look at *The Tunnels of Cu Chi* by Tom Mangold & John Penycate (Random House, New York, 1985).

The Tunnels

Over the years the VC, learning by trial and error, developed simple but effective techniques to make their tunnels difficult to detect or disable. Wooden trapdoors were camouflaged with earth and branches; some were booby-trapped. Hidden underwater entrances from rivers were constructed. To cook, they used 'Dien Bien Phu kitchens', which exhausted the smoke through vents many metres away from the cooking site. Trapdoors were installed throughout the network to prevent tear gas, smoke or water from moving from one part of the system to another. Some sections were even equipped with electric lighting.

The small, renovated section of the tunnel system now open to visitors is near the village of Ben Dinh. In one of the classrooms of the visitors' centre, a large map shows the extent of the network (the area shown is in the north-western corner of Greater Ho Chi Minh City). The tunnels are marked in red. Viet Cong bases are shown in light grey. The light blue lines are rivers (the Saigon River is at the top). Fortified villages held by South Vietnamese and American forces are marked in grey. Blue dots represent the American and South Vietnamese military posts that were supposed to ensure the security of nearby villages. The dark blue area in the centre is the base of the American 25th Infantry Division. Most pre-arranged tours do not take you to this former base, but it is not off limits and if you have your own guide and driver you can easily arrange a visit.

To the right of the large map are two cross-section diagrams of the tunnels. The bottom diagram is a reproduction of one used by General William Westmoreland, the commander of American forces in Vietnam from 1964 to 1968. For once, the Americans seemed to have had their intelligence information right (though the tunnels did not pass under rivers nor did the guerrillas wear headgear underground).

The section of the tunnel system presently open to visitors is a few hundred metres south of the visitors' centre. It snakes up and down through various chambers along its 50 metre length. The unlit tunnels are about 1.2 metres high and 80 cm across. A knocked-out M-48 tank and a bomb crater are near the exit, which is in a reafforested eucalyptus grove.

Entry to the tunnel site, which is now controlled by Saigon Tourist, costs US$2 for foreigners but is free for Vietnamese nationals.

Organised Tours
Organised tours run by Saigon Tourist and Vietnam Tourism often visit Cu Chi but these are a bit pricey. Most private travel agents can arrange it more cheaply.

Getting There & Away
Cu Chi is a district which covers a large area, parts of which are as close as 30 km to Saigon. The actual tunnels that exist now are at Ben Duoc, 75 km from the city.

Bus Buses from Ho Chi Minh City to Tay Ninh leave from the Tay Ninh Bus Station (Ben Xe Tay Ninh) in Tan Binh District and Mien Tay Bus Station in An Lac. All buses to Tay Ninh pass though Cu Chi town, but getting from the town of Cu Chi to the tunnels by public transport is difficult.

Taxi Hiring a taxi (or 'marriage taxi') in Saigon and just driving out to Cu Chi is not all that expensive, especially if the cost is split by several people. If you want to visit the 'real' tunnels rather than those open to the public, make this clear to your driver before you cut a deal. A non-English speaking guide can be hired at the visitors' centre. For details on hiring vehicles in Saigon, see the Getting There & Away and Getting Around sections in the Ho Chi Minh City chapter.

A visit to the Cu Chi tunnel complex can easily be combined with a stop at the headquarters of the Caodai sect in Tay Ninh. A taxi for an all-day excursion to both should cost about US$40.

TAY NINH
TÂY NINH
Tay Ninh town (population 26,000), capital of Tay Ninh Province, serves as the headquarters of one of Vietnam's most interesting indigenous religions, Caodaism. The Caodai Great Temple at the sect's Holy See is one of the most striking structures in all of Asia

Built between 1933 and 1955, it is a rococo extravaganza combining the architectural idiosyncrasies of a French church, a Chinese pagoda, the Tiger Balm Gardens and Madame Tussaud's Wax Museum.

Tay Ninh Province, which is north-west of Ho Chi Minh City, is bordered by Cambodia on three sides. The area's dominant geographic feature is Nui Ba Den (Black Lady Mountain), which towers 850 metres above the surrounding plains. Tay Ninh Province's eastern border is formed by the Saigon River. The Vam Co River flows from Cambodia through the western part of the province.

Because of the once-vaunted political and military power of the Caodai, this region was the scene of prolonged heavy fighting during the Franco-Vietminh War. Tay Ninh Province served as a major terminus of the Ho Chi Minh Trail during the Vietnam War. In 1969, the VC captured Tay Ninh town and held it for several days.

During the period of tension between Cambodia and Vietnam in the late-1970s, the Khmer Rouge launched a number of cross-border raids into Tay Ninh Province during which horrific atrocities were committed against the civilian population.

The Cao Dai Religion

Caodaism (Dai Dao Tam Ky Pho Do) is the product of an attempt to create the ideal religion through the fusion of the secular and religious philosophies of the East and West. The result is a colourful and eclectic potpourri that includes bits and pieces of most of the religious philosophies known in Vietnam during the early 20th century: Buddhism, Confucianism, Taoism, Hinduism, native Vietnamese spiritism, Christianity and Islam.

The term 'Cao Dai', which literally means 'high tower or palace', is used to refer to God. The religion is called 'Caodaism'; its adherents are the 'Caodais'. The hierarchy of the sect, whose priesthood is non-professional, is partly based on the structure of the Roman Catholic Church.

History Caodaism was founded by the mystic Ngo Minh Chieu (also known as Ngo Van Chieu; born 1878), a civil servant who once served as district chief of Phu Quoc Island. He was widely read in Eastern and Western religious works and became active in seances, at which his presence was said to greatly improve the quality of communication with the spirits. Around 1919 he began to receive a series of revelations from Cao Dai in which the tenets of Caodai doctrine were set forth.

Caodaism was officially founded as a religion in a ceremony held in 1926. Within a year, the group had 26,000 followers. Many of the sect's early followers were Vietnamese members of the French colonial administration. By the mid-1950s, one in eight southern Vietnamese was a Caodai, and the sect was famous worldwide for its imaginative garishness. But in 1954, British author Graham Green, who had once considered converting to Caodaism, wrote in *The Times* of London: 'What on my first two visits has seemed gay and bizarre (was) now like a game that had gone on too long'.

By the mid-50s, the Caodai had established a virtually independent feudal state in Tay Ninh Province, and they retained enormous influence in the affairs of Tay Ninh Province for the next two decades. They also played a significant political and military role in South Vietnam from 1926 to 1956, when most of the 25,000 strong Caodai army, which had been given support by the Japanese and later the French, was incorporated into the South Vietnamese Army. During the Franco-Viet Minh War, Caodai munitions factories specialised in making mortar tubes out of automobile exhaust pipes.

Because they had refused to support the Viet Cong during the Vietnam War – and despite the fact that they had been barely tolerated by the Saigon government – the Caodai feared the worst after reunification. Indeed, all Caodai lands were confiscated by the new Communist government and four members of the sect were executed in 1979, but in 1985, the Holy See and some 400 temples were returned to Caodai control.

Caodaism is strongest in Tay Ninh Province and the Mekong Delta, but Caodai temples can be found throughout southern and central Vietnam. Today, there are an estimated two million followers of Caodaism.

Philosophy Much of Caodai doctrine is drawn from Mahayana Buddhism mixed with Taoist and Confucian elements (Vietnam's 'Triple Religion'). Caodai ethics are based on the Buddhist ideal of 'the good person' but incorporate traditional Vietnamese taboos and sanctions as well.

The ultimate goal of the disciple of Caodaism is to escape the cycle of reincarnation. This can be achieved by the performance of certain human duties, including first and foremost following the prohibitions against killing, lying, luxurious living, sensuality and stealing.

The main tenets of Caodaism include believing in one God, the existence of the soul and the use of mediums to communicate with the spiritual world. Caodai practices include priestly celibacy, vegetarianism, communications with spirits through seances, reverence for the dead, maintenance of the cult of ancestors, fervent proselytising and sessions of meditative self-cultivation.

Following the Chinese duality of Yin and Yang, there are two principal deities, the Mother Goddess, who is female, and God, who is male. There is a debate among the Caodai as to which deity was the primary source of creation.

According to Caodaism, history is divided into three major periods of divine revelation. During the first period, God's truth was revealed to humanity through Laotze and figures associated with Buddhism, Confucianism and Taoism. The human agents of revelation during the second period were Buddha (Sakyamuni), Mohammed, Confucius, Jesus and Moses. The Caodai believe that their messages were corrupted because of the human frailty of the messengers and their disciples. They also believe that these revelations were limited in scope, intended to be applicable only during a specific age to

the people of the area in which the messengers lived.

Caodaism sees itself as the product of the 'Third Alliance Between God and Man', the third and final revelation. Disciples believe that Caodaism avoids the failures of the first two periods because it is based on divine truth as communicated through spirits, which serve as messengers of salvation and instructors of doctrine. Spirits who have been in touch with the Caodai include deceased Caodai leaders, patriots, heroes, philosophers, poets, political leaders and warriors as well as ordinary people. Among the contacted spirits who lived as Westerners are Joan of Arc, René Descartes, William Shakespeare (who hasn't been heard from since 1935), Victor Hugo, Louis Pasteur and Vladimir Ilyich Lenin. Because of his frequent appearances to Caodai mediums at the Phnom Penh mission, Victor Hugo was posthumously named the chief spirit of foreign missionary works.

Communication with the spirits is carried on in Vietnamese, Chinese, French and English. The methods of receiving messages from the spirits illustrate the influence of both East Asian and Western spiritism on Caodai seance rites. Sometimes, a medium holds a pen or Chinese calligraphy brush. In the 1920s, a 66-cm-long wooden staff known as a *corbeille à bec* was used. Medium(s) held one end while a crayon attached to the other wrote out the spirits'

Caodai Great Temple

messages. The Caodai also use what is known as *pneumatographie*, in which a blank slip of paper is sealed in an envelope and hung above the altar. When the envelope is taken down, there is a message on the paper.

Most of the sacred literature of Caodaism consists of messages communicated to Caodai leaders during seances held between 1925 and 1929. Since 1927, only the official seances held at Tay Ninh have been considered reliable and divinely ordained by the Caodai hierarchy, though dissident groups continued to hold seances which produced communications contradicting accepted doctrine.

The Caodai consider vegetarianism to be of service to humankind because it does not involve harming fellow beings during the process of their spiritual evolution. They also see vegetarianism as a form of self-purification. There are several different vegetarian regimens followed by Caodai disciples. The least rigourous involves eating vegetarian food six days a month. Priests must be full-time vegetarians.

The clergy (except at the highest levels) is open to both men and women, though when male and female officials of equal rank are serving in the same area, male clergy are in charge. Female officials wear white robes and are addressed with the title *Huong*, which means 'perfume'. Male clergy are addressed as *Thanh*, which means 'pure'. Caodai temples are constructed so that male and female disciples enter on opposite sides; women worship on the left, men on the right.

All Caodai temples observe four daily ceremonies, which are held at 6 am, noon, 6 pm and midnight. These rituals, during which dignitaries wear ceremonial dress and hats, include offerings of incense, tea, alcohol, fruit and flowers. All Caodai altars have above them the 'divine eye', which became the religion's official symbol after Ngo Minh Chieu saw it in a vision he had while on Phu Quoc Island.

Information

Tourist Office Tay Ninh Tourist (Cong Ty Du Lich Tay Ninh; ☎ 2376, 2383, 2538) is at 1A Dai Lo 30/4. This is the official tourist agency for Tay Ninh Province.

Warning! The police in Tay Ninh have acquired a bad reputation for avarice – even the locals are afraid of them. Although foreigners are not supposed to need a travel permit for visiting Tay Ninh unless they spend the night, day travellers have been arrested and fined for not having such a permit. So to play safe, perhaps you'd better get one.

One Canadian who wandered into the local market was arrested and fined US$50 even though he had a travel permit!

Caodai Holy See

The Caodai Holy See, founded in 1926, is four km east of Tay Ninh in the village of Long Hoa. Guests should wear modest and respectful attire (no shorts or tank tops). The complex includes the Great Temple, administrative offices, residences for officials and adepts, and a hospital of traditional Vietnamese herbal medicine to which people from all over the south travel for treatment. After reunification, the government 'borrowed' parts of the complex for its own use (and perhaps to keep an eye on the sect).

Prayers are conducted in the Great Temple every day at 6 am, noon, 6 pm and midnight. Only a few hundred priests participate in weekday prayers, but on festivals several thousand priests, dressed in special white garments, may attend. The Caodai clergy have no objection to you photographing temple objects, but you cannot photograph people without their permission, which is seldom granted.

Above the front portico of the Great Temple is the 'divine eye', the supreme symbol of Caodaism. Americans often comment that it looks as if it were copied from the back of a US$1 bill. Lay women enter the Great Temple through a door at the base of the tower on the left. Once inside, they walk around the outside of the colonnaded hall in a clockwise direction. Men enter on the right and circumambulate the hall in a counter-clockwise direction. Shoes must be removed upon entering the building. The area in the centre of the sanctuary (between the pillars) is reserved for Caodai priests.

A mural in the front entry hall depicts the three signatories of the 'Third Alliance Between God and Man'. The Chinese statesman and revolutionary leader Dr Sun Yat Sen (1866-1925) holds an inkstone while Vietnamese poet Nguyen Binh Khiem (1492-1587) and Victor Hugo (1802-85), French poet and author, write 'God and Humanity' and 'Love and Justice' in Chinese and French. Victor Hugo uses a quill pen; Nguyen Binh Khiem writes with a brush. Nearby signs in English, French and German each give a slightly different version of the fundamentals of Caodaism.

The Great Temple is built on nine levels which represent the nine steps to heaven. Each level is marked by a pair of columns. At the far end of the sanctuary, eight plaster columns entwined with multicoloured dragons support a dome representing – as does the rest of the ceiling – the heavens. Under the dome is a giant star-speckled blue globe with the 'divine eye' on it.

The largest of the seven chairs in front of the globe is reserved for the Caodai pope, a position that has remained unfilled since 1933. The next three chairs are for the three men responsible for the religion's law books. The remaining chairs are for the leaders of the three branches of Caodaism, which are represented by the colours yellow, blue and red.

On both sides of the area between the columns are two pulpits similar in design to the *minbars* found in mosques. During festivals, the pulpits are used by officials to address the assembled worshippers. The upstairs balconies are used if there is an overflow crowd downstairs.

Long Hoa Market

Long Hoa Market is several km south of the Caodai Holy See complex. Open every day from 5 am to about 6 pm, this large market sells meat, food staples, clothing and pretty much everything else you would expect to find in a rural marketplace. Before reunification, the Caodai sect had the right to collect taxes from the merchants here.

Places to Stay

In the town of Tay Ninh, there are a couple of hotels a few hundred metres east and then north of the triple-arch bridge.

Places to Eat

Nha Hang Diem Thuy (☎ 27318), at 30/4 St, is an outstanding restaurant with low prices. Giant crayfish *(tom can)* are one of their specialities and, though not cheap, cost only one-third of what you'd pay in Saigon.

Nha Hang So 1 (Restaurant Number 1) is on the western side of the river near the old triple-arch concrete bridge. Prices here are also very low.

Getting There & Away

Bus Buses from Ho Chi Minh City to Tay Ninh leave from the Tay Ninh Bus Station (Ben Xe Tay Ninh) in Tan Binh District and Mien Tay Bus Station in An Lac.

Tay Ninh is 96 km from Ho Chi Minh City on National Highway 22 (Quoc Lo 22). The road passes through Trang Bang, where a famous news photo of a young naked girl, severely burned, screaming and running, was taken during an American napalm attack. There are several Caodai temples along National Route 22 including one, under construction in 1975, that was heavily damaged by the Viet Cong.

Taxi The easiest way to get to Tay Ninh is by taxi or 'marriage taxi', perhaps on a day trip that includes a stop in Cu Chi. An all-day round trip by marriage taxi should cost about US$40. No special permit is required for Cu Chi if you return to Saigon to sleep, but it might be wise to get one for Tay Ninh because of the avarice of the Tay Ninh police.

AROUND TAY NINH

Nui Ba Den

Núi Bà Đen

Nui Ba Den (Black Lady Mountain), 15 km

north-east of Tay Ninh town, rises 850 metres above the rice paddies of the surrounding countryside. Over the centuries, Nui Ba Den has served as a shrine for various peoples of the area, including the Khmer, Chams, Vietnamese and Chinese. There are several cave-temples on the mountain. The summits of Nui Ba Den are much cooler than the rest of Tay Ninh Province, most of which is only a few dozen metres above sea level.

Nui Ba Den was used as a staging ground by both the Viet Minh and the Viet Cong and was the scene of fierce fighting during the French and American wars. At one time, there was a US Army fire base and relay station at the summit of the mountain, which was defoliated and heavily bombed by American aircraft.

The name Black Lady Mountain is derived from the legend of Huong, a young woman who married her true love despite the advances of a wealthy mandarin. While her husband was away doing military service, she would visit a magical statue of Buddha at the summit of the mountain. One day, Huong was attacked by kidnappers but, preferring death to dishonour, threw herself off a cliff. She reappeared in the visions of a monk living on the mountain, who told her story.

The hike from the base of the mountain to the main temple complex and back takes about 1½ hour. Although steep in parts, it's not a difficult walk – plenty of old women in sandals make the journey to worship at the temple. Around the temple complex are a few stands selling snacks and drinks.

If you need more exercise, a walk to the summit of the peak and back takes about six hours.

VUNG TAU
VŨNG TÀU

Vung Tau, known under the French as Cap Saint Jacques (it was so named by Portuguese mariners in honour of their patron saint), is a beach resort on the South China Sea, 128 km south-east of Saigon. Vung Tau's beaches are not Vietnam's nicest by any stretch of the imagination, but they are easily reached from Ho Chi Minh City and have thus been a favourite of the Saigonese since French colonists first began coming here around 1890. Seaside areas near Vung Tau are dotted with the villas of the pre-1975 elite, now converted to guesthouses and villas for the post-1975 elite.

In addition to sunning on the seashore and sipping sodas in nearby cafes, visitors to this city of 100,000 can cycle around or climb up the Vung Tau Peninsula's two mountains. There are also a number of interesting religious sites around town, including several pagodas and a huge standing figure of Jesus blessing the South China Sea.

Vung Tau was once the headquarters of Vietsovpetro, a joint Soviet-Vietnamese company that operated oil rigs about 60 km offshore. Soviet expats used to live in a large compound bordering Front Beach occupying the desirable neighbourhood in the city. The Russian Compound (whose entrances were, until 1989, sealed by roadblocks) was the area between Quang Trung St, Hoang Dieu St, Le Loi Blvd and Bacu St. Perhaps because of the strategic importance of oil exploration, Vung Tau was once famous for its elaborate secret police apparatus. With the collapse of the Soviet Union and waning Russian influence, the compound fences have come down and the area has given way to new hotels catering to well-heeled Western tourists.

The local fishing fleet is quite active, though many Vietnamese fleeing their homeland by sea set sail from Vung Tau, taking many of the town's fishing trawlers with them. Vietnamese navy boats on patrol offshore ensure that the rest of the fleet comes home each day.

Vung Tau has been competing with Saigon to become the sex capital of Vietnam – massage parlours are as ubiquitous as Vietnamese fish sauce. Despite claims of innocence and virginal purity by government officials, high-ranking cadres are said to be the most frequent customers, though all with hard currency are welcome. The local clinics have noticed an embarassing increase in 'social diseases'. The entire massage trade in

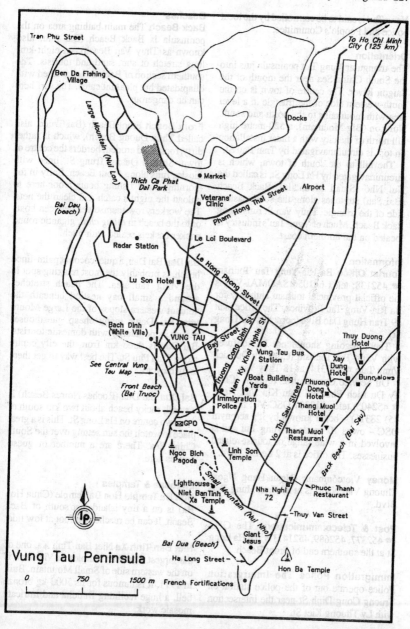

Vung Tau Peninsula

0   750   1500 m

Vung Tau is said to be controlled by the local police and People's Committee.

Orientation

The triangular Vung Tau peninsula juts into the South China Sea near the mouth of the Saigon River. The centre of town is on the south-western side of the triangle in a level area with mountains to the north and south. Nui Lon (Big Mountain), a 520-metre-high hill north of the city with a radar installation on top, is circumnavigated by Tran Phu St.

The hill to the south of town, which is circumnavigated by Ha Long St, is called the Nui Nho (Small Mountain). Back Beach (Bai Sau) stretches along the south-eastern side of the triangle. Thuy Van St runs along Back Beach. Much of Vung Tau's industry is located on the northern coast.

Information

Tourist Office Ba Ria-Vung Tau Tourism (☎ 452138; telex 641056 SAOMAI-VT) is the official provincial tourism authority for Ba Ria-Vung Tau Province. The office is at 59 Tran Hung Dao Blvd (corner Ly Tu Trong St).

The foregoing should not be confused with Vung Tau Tourism (Cong Ty Du Lich Vung Tau; ☎ 452314) at 18 Thuy Van.

Oil Service Company & Tourism (Cong Ty Du Lich Phuc Vu Dau Khi Viet Nam; ☎ 452405; telex 812307 OSC-VT; fax (84-45) 28311) – better known by it's acronym OSC – owns 10 hotels in Vung Tau and is involved in a wide range of tourist-related businesses. The office is at 2 Le Loi Blvd.

Money Vietcombank (Ngan Hang Ngoai Thuong Viet Nam) is at 27 Tran Hung Dao Blvd.

Post & Telecommunications The GPO (☎ 452377, 452689, 452141) is at 4 Ha Long St at the southern end of Front Beach.

Immigration Police The Immigration Police operate out of the police station on Truong Cong Dinh St near the intersection with Ly Thuong Kiet St.

Beaches

Back Beach The main bathing area on the peninsula is Back Beach (Bai Sau, also known as Thuy Van Beach), an eight-km-long stretch of sun, sand and tourists. The southern section of Back Beach is lined with dilapidated but pleasant cafes. The surf here can be dangerous.

Front Beach Front Beach (Bai Truoc, also called Thuy Duong Beach), which is rather dirty, rocky and eroded, borders the centre of town. Shaded Quang Trung St, lined with kiosks, runs along Front Beach. Early in the morning, local fishing boats moor here to unload the night's catch and clean the nets. The workers row themselves between boats or to the beach in *thung chai*, gigantic round wicker baskets sealed with pitch.

Bai Dau Bai Dau, a quiet coconut palm-lined beach, is probably the most relaxing spot in the Vung Tau area. The beach stretches around a small bay nestled beneath the verdant western slopes of the Large Mountain. Bai Dau's many cheap guesthouses reflect its popularity with domestic tourists. Bai Dau is three km from the city centre along Tran Phu St. The best way to get there is by bicycle.

Bai Dua Bai Dua (Roches Noires Beach) is a small, rocky beach about two km south of the town centre on Ha Long St. This is a great place to watch the sun setting over the South China Sea. There are a number of guest-houses here.

Pagodas & Temples

Hon Ba Temple Hon Ba Temple (Chua Hon Ba) is on a tiny island just south of Back Beach. It can be reached on foot at low tide.

Niet Ban Tinh Xa Niet Ban Tinh Xa, one of the largest Buddhist temples in Vietnam, is on the western side of Small Mountain. Built in 1971, it is famous for its 5000-kg bronze bell, a huge reclining Buddha and intricate mosaic work.

Thich Ca Phat Dai Park

Thich Ca Phat Dai, a must-see site for domestic tourists, is a hillside park of monumental Buddhist statuary built in the early 1960s. Inside the main gate and to the right is a row of small souvenir kiosks selling, among other things, inexpensive items made of seashells and coral. Above the kiosks, shaded paths lead to several large white cement Buddhas, a giant lotus blossom and many smaller figures of people and animals. A couple of pathside refreshment stalls sell cold drinks. There are several restaurants near the main gate.

Thich Ca Phat Dai, which is open from 6 am to 6 pm, is on the eastern side of the Large Mountain at 25 Tran Phu St. To get there from the town centre, take Le Loi Blvd north almost to the end and turn left onto Tran Phu St.

Lighthouse

The 360° view of the entire hammerhead-shaped peninsula from the lighthouse *(hai dang)* is truly spectacular, especially at sunset. The lighthouse, which is atop Small Mountain 197 metres above sea level, was built in 1910. The concrete passage from the tower to the building next to it was constructed by the French because of Viet Minh attacks. A 1939 French guidebook warns visitors that photography is not permitted from here, and unfortunately this is still the case half-a-century and four regimes later.

The narrow paved road up Small Mountain to the lighthouse intersects Ha Long St 150 metres south-west of the GPO. The grade is quite mild and could even be bicycled. There is also a dirt road (which gets muddy during the wet season) to the lighthouse from near Back Beach.

Giant Jesus

An enormous Rio de Janeiro-style figure of Jesus (Thanh Gioc) with arms outstretched gazes across the South China Sea from the southern end of Small Mountain. The figure, 30 metres high, was constructed in 1974 on the site of a lighthouse built by the French a century before. The Giant Jesus can be reached on foot by a path that heads up the hill from a point just south of Back Beach. The path circles around to approach the figure from the back.

Bach Dinh

Bach Dinh, the White Villa (Villa Blanche), is a former royal residence set amidst frangipanis and bougainvilleas on a lushly forested hillside overlooking the sea. It is an ideal place to sit, relax and contemplate.

Bach Dinh was built in the 19th century as a summer palace for governor Paul Doumer. Vietnamese King Thanh Thai was kept here in 1909 under house arrest before being shipped off to the French island of Reunion to perform hard prison labour. In the late 1960s to the early '70s, the building was a part-time playground for South Vietnamese President Thieu.

The mansion itself is emphatically French in its ornamentation, which includes colourful mosaics and Roman-style busts set into the exterior walls. Inside, there is an exhibit of old Chinese (Qing Dynasty) pottery salvaged from an 18th century shipwreck near Con Dao Island. There are also lots of 'new antiques' on sale in the villa's gift shop.

The main entrance to the park surrounding Bach Dinh is just north of Front Beach at 12 Tran Phu St. It is open from 6 am to 9 pm. The admission price is US$1.20 for foreigners. If you want to take photos it will cost you an additional US$0.20, and to use a video the 'service charge' is US$1.20.

There are a couple of cafes near the main gate though they seem to do less than robust business.

Veterans' Clinic

The Veterans' Clinic (☎ 457348, 452573), officially called the Huu Nghi (Friendship) Clinic, was built in early 1989 by a group of American veterans of the Vietnam war working alongside war vets from the other side. Its construction marked a milestone in post-1975 cooperation between Americans and Vietnamese. Though the California-based Veterans' Vietnam Restoration Project, which initiated and funded the undertaking, was shamelessly overcharged by the local People's Committee, the clinic was completed and is now used for both obstetrics and general medicine. Hundreds of babies are delivered here each year. The clinic also welcomes sick travellers with hard currency.

The Veterans' Clinic is 1.5 km north of the centre of town. To get there, go 100 metres down an alley across the street from 99 Le Loi Blvd. The clinic entrance, marked by a plaque, is on the right.

Boat-Building Yards

New wooden fishing craft are built at a location which, oddly enough, is over a km from the nearest water. The boat yards are on Nam Ky Khoi Nghia St, 500 metres south of Vung Tau Bus Station.

Golf Course

A Taiwanese joint-venture is constructing a golf course in Vung Tau. It is not known when it will be open.

Small Mountain Circuit

The six-km circuit around Small Mountain (Nui Nho), known to the French as *le tour de la Petite Corniche*, begins at the GPO and continues on Ha Long St along the rocky coastline. A road leads up the hill to the lighthouse, 150 metres south of the GPO.

Ha Long St passes Ngoc Bich Pagoda (which is built in the style of Hanoi's famous One Pillar Pagoda), Bai Dua Beach and a number of villas before reaching the tip of the Vung Tau peninsula. The promontory here, reached through a traditional gate, was once guarded by French naval guns whose reinforced concrete emplacements remain, slowly crumbling in the salt air.

Phan Boi Chau St goes from the southern end of Back Beach into town along the eastern base of Small Mountain, passing century-old Linh Son Temple which contains a Buddha of pre-Angkorian Khmer origin.

Large Mountain Circuit

The 10-km circuit around the Large Moun-

tain (Nui Lon) passes seaside villas, Bai Dau Beach, the homes of poor families living in old French fortifications, and a number of quarries where boulders blown out of the hillside by dynamite are made into gravel by workers using sledgehammers. Blasting sometimes closes the road for a few hours. At the northern tip of the Large Mountain is Ben Da fishing village with its large church; from here a road leads up and along the spine of the hill to the old radar installation *(rada)*.

On the eastern side of the Large Mountain, which faces tidal marshes and the giant cranes of the Vietsovpetro docks, is Thich Ca Phat Dai statuary park.

Places to Stay

The Vung Tau peninsula has quite a number of hotels and guesthouses both in town and at Back Beach, Bai Dau and Bai Dua. During holidays, Vung Tau's hotels are usually booked out.

Front Beach This part of town is definitely moving up-market. If you need a really dirt-cheap place to stay, take a look at Bai Dau.

The *Lu Son Hotel* (☎ 452576; 65 rooms) is a large, airy place a bit north of town at 27 Le Loi Blvd. It's rather far from the beach, and for this reason it's somewhat cheaper than many other places in Vung Tau of similar standard. Double rooms with private bath and air-con cost US$10.

The *Sao Mai Hotel* (☎ 452462, 452248; 22 rooms) at 89 Tran Hung Dao Blvd is run by the Oil Service Company. Double rooms with air-con cost US$10 to US$15. It's a pleasant-looking place and good value.

The *Song Huong Hotel* (☎ 452491; 24 rooms) is at 10 Truong Vinh Ky St. This was once a dormitory for Russian experts and still looks it. Single rooms with shared bath cost US$12 and are not worth it. Doubles with private bath go for US$20. Overall, poor value.

The *Rang Dong Hotel* (☎ 452133; 125 rooms) is at 5 Duy Tan St just off Le Loi Blvd. This large place was also once a dormitory for Soviet experts and looks worse for the wear. Rooms are reasonably priced at

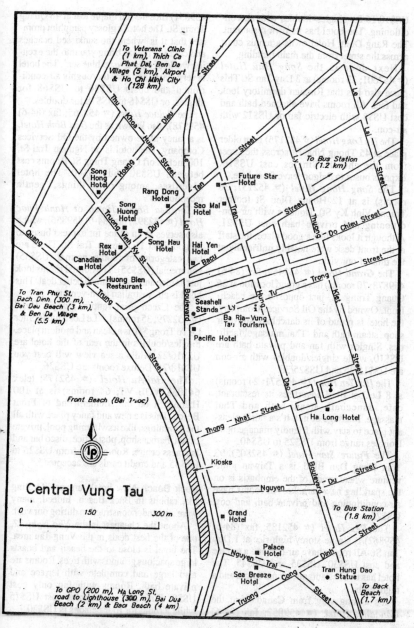

Central Vung Tau

0   150   300 m

US$10/16 for singles/doubles with air-conditioning. The hotel has its own restaurant. The Rang Dong Hotel owns a tennis court across the street from the main building.

Next door is the *Song Hau Hotel* (☎ 452601; 23 rooms) at 3 Duy Tan St. This place also has that Russian dormitory look and feel. All rooms have attached bath and cost US$8 with electric fan or US$12 with air-con.

The *Ha Long Hotel* (☎ 452175) is an older place at 45 Thong Nhat St across the street from the church. Singles cost US$10. Express buses to Saigon leave from here.

The *Song Hong Hotel* (☎ 452137; 36 rooms) is at 12 Hoang Dieu St (corner Truong Vinh Ky St). Doubles with air-conditioning and private bath cost US$21. Although it looks like a good place, the staff at the front desk were notably unfriendly at the time of our visit.

The *Grand Hotel* (☎ 452469; fax (84-6) 459878; 70 rooms) has a grand location at 26 Quang Trung St, just opposite the beachfront. Owned by the Oil Services Company, the hotel is proud of its dancehall, souvenir shop, steam bath and 'Thai massage' facilities. Singles with fan and private bath are US$10, while singles/doubles with air-con are US$15/25 and US$25/30.

The *Hai Yen Hotel* (☎ 452571; 24 rooms) at 8 Le Loi Blvd advertises its restaurant, cafe, dancehall, steam bath and Thai massage. Massage or not, it's a fairly pleasant place to stay with friendly management. Doubles range from US$25 to US$40.

The *Future Star Hotel* (☎ 452805), 93 Tran Hung Dao Blvd, is a Taiwan joint-venture where much of the emphasis is on the sparkling new karaoke. All rooms have air-conditioning and private bath and cost US$25.

The *Rex Hotel* (☎ 452135; fax (84-6) 459862) is a nine-storey high-rise at 1 Duy Tan St. All rooms have air-con and a terrace and cost US$30, US$35 and US$45. The hotel has two restaurants, tennis courts and a night club.

It's a long way from Canada, but the *Canadian Hotel* (☎ 459852; fax (84-6) 459851) flies the red maple leaf at 48 Quang Trung St. The hotel's glossy pamphlet promises that it is 'where the sunkissed beaches and cool sea breeze bring you into the exciting world of deep crystal blue sea'. The hotel is very classy and very thoroughly air-conditioned and costs US$36 to US$68 for singles, or US$46 to US$78 for doubles.

The *Palace Hotel* (☎ 452265; fax (84-6) 459878), also known as the *Hoa Binh Hotel*, is a fancy place owned by the Oil Services Company. The hotel is on Nguyen Trai St, 100 metres off Quang Trung St. Rooms cost between US$30 and US$60. The hotel advertises, among other things, 'gentle receptionists'.

The *Sea Breeze Hotel*, or *Hanh Phoc Hotel* (☎ 452392; fax (84-6) 459856), which also serves as an office for express buses to Saigon, is at 11 Nguyen Trai St. There are two categories of rooms, normal (US$35) and special (US$55). The normal rooms look just as nice and seem a much better deal. This hotel is an Australian joint-venture.

The Czech joint-venture *Pacific Hotel* (☎ 452279; 35 rooms), 4 Le Loi Blvd (corner Ly Tu Trong St), is a clean and modern place. Singles/doubles in the rear of the hotel are US$16/22, while a sea view will cost you US$18/24. Deluxe rooms are US$26.

The *Hai-Au Hotel* (☎ 452178; telex 641058 VOB-VT; 64 rooms) is at 100 Halong St on the southern end of Front Beach. This is a new and fancy place with all the trimmings, like a swimming pool, private beach, barber shop, post office, disco bar and business centre. Rooms cost from US$25 to US$45 and credit cards are accepted.

Back Beach New hotels are proliferating like rabbits in Back Beach. Indeed, many were still under construction during our visit.

About the cheapest is the *Nha Nghi 72*, one of the best deals in the Vung Tau area. The hotel is close to the beach and boasts large spacious grounds with trees. Rooms are also large and complete with terrace and private bath. Rooms with fan only cost US$8. With air-con, doubles cost US$15 while a room for four persons is US$20.

The Oil Service Company's *Thang Muoi Hotel* (☎ 452665, 452645; 93 rooms) is at 4-6 Thuy Van St. This is one of the older places in Back Beach but also one of the most beautiful. The Thanh Muoi's single-storey buildings are set on quiet, spacious grounds with trees. The beach is just across the street. Doubles cost between US$15 and US$30. The hotel's restaurant is air-conditioned.

The *Thuy Duong Hotel* (☎ 452635) is a new and attractive place on Thuy Van St. Also known as the Weeping Willow Hotel, all rooms have air-con and hot water and cost between US$15 and US$30.

Another new place is the *Xay Dung Hotel* at the northern end of Back Beach. Rooms in the main hotel cost US$15 to US$30. The hotel also rents bungalows nestled in a grove of casuarina trees at the north-eastern end of Thuy Van St. Each of the 21 steel-roofed bungalows costs US$15 with a fan and US$25 with air-con.

The *Phuong Dong Hotel* (☎ 452593; 54 rooms) at 2 Thuy Van is one of the most impressive hotels in the Vung Tau. It was built to cater mostly the Hong Kongers, Taiwanese and Singaporeans, as evidenced by the massive karaoke facilities. Rooms cost US$25 to US$40.

We found a wonderful family in Back Beach on the beach side of the street before the Thuong Muoi Restaurant. They run a small hotel and you will find them by their small sign saying 'English/French spoken here'. The entrance to their hotel is right before the sign and their English was very good.
Terri Ruyter

Bai Dau There are dozens of guesthouses *(nha nghi)* in former private villas along Bai Dau. This is the cheapest neighbourhood in the Vung Tau area. This is not because it's an unattractive place (indeed, Bai Dau is very relaxing), but the lack of a white-sand beach and other tourist amusements makes this a relative backwater, with low prices to match.

Most of the guesthouses have rooms with fans and communal bathrooms and cost US$5 or less, but several up-market places have now added air-con and private baths. A few of the guesthouses do meals, but most

don't. However, there are plentiful cheap restaurants offering fine sea views.

Nha Nghi My Tho, with its rooftop terrace overlooking the beach, is at 47 Tran Phu St. A light, airy room with beach view will cost you US$5. Rooms are equipped with a ceiling fan.

Nha Nghi 128 is at 128 Tran Phu St. Rooms for four cost US$5. It's rather dilapidated looking.

Nha Hang 96 is a restaurant but also one of the largest hotels in Bai Dau. Construction Company Number One runs this three-storey place. A room with air-con and private bath costs US$7. Unfortunately, it is not right on the waterfront.

Nha Nghi 29 is right on the sea front. It's a large good-looking place and can be recommended. Rooms with air-con cost US$15.

Nha Nghi Doan 28 is at 126 Tran Phu St. It's also a large hotel with air-con rooms and private bath. Doubles cost US$15.

Nha Nghi DK 142 also has relatively high-standard air-con rooms with private bath for US$15..

Bai Dua Among the villas-turned-guesthouses at Bai Dua are *Nha Nghi 50 Ha Long* at 50 Ha Long St, *Nha Nghi Dro* at 88B Ha Long St and, at 48 Ha Long St, *Nha Nghi 48 Ha Long*, which charges foreigners US$20 for a triple with air-con. Their cheapest double goes for US$15.

Places to Eat
For excellent seafood, try *Huong Bien Restaurant*, which is along Front Beach at 47 Quang Trung St. There are several places to eat nearby and quite a few more along Tran Hung Dao Blvd. Hotels with decent restaurants include the *Palace* and the *Grand*.

At the southern end of Back Beach is the excellent *Phuoc Thanh Restaurant*, which does a mean salad and splendid sea food, yet charges low prices. The largest restaurant along Back Beach is the *Thang Muoi Restaurant* (☎ 452515) at 7-9 Thuy Van St.

At Bai Dau, you might try the seaside restaurant run by An Giang Tourism at 41

Tran Phu St, which is across the street from 114 Tran Phu St.

At Bai Dua, there are restaurants at 88 Ha Long St and 126 Ha Long St.

Things to Buy

Colourful seashells and various items made out of shells (purses, plant hangers, necklaces, etc) can be bought for US$0.10 and up at the intersection of Le Loi Blvd and Ly Tu Trong St (across the street from the Pacific Hotel). Other souvenir shops are located along Front Beach and at the Thich Ca Phat Dai statuary park.

The government Tourist Shop at the intersection of Le Loi Blvd and Quang Trung St and other such shops in major hotels carry imported goods.

Getting There & Away

Air There are (sometimes) chartered helicopter flights available from Vung Tau to the Con Dao Islands.

Bus Buses to Vung Tau from Ho Chi Minh City leave from the Mien Dong Bus Station and the Van Thanh Bus Station. Express minibuses depart from Cong Ty Dich Vu Du Lich Quan 1 (☎ 90541) at 39 Nguyen Hue Blvd every hour between 5 am and 6 pm; the 128 km trip takes two hours.

Vung Tau Bus Station (Ben Xe Khach Vung Tau) is about 1.5 km from the city centre at 52 Nam Ky Khoi Nghia St. To get there from Front Beach, take either Bacu St or Truong Cong Dinh St to Le Hong Phong St. Turn right and then turn right again onto Nam Ky Khoi Nghia St. There are non-express buses from here to Baria, Bien Hoa, Saigon, Long Khanh, Mytho and Tay Ninh. An express bus to Ho Chi Minh City leaves at 6 am, 9 am and 3 pm.

Express buses and minibuses to Ho Chi Minh City also depart from the Ha Long Hotel (near the church) and the Hanh Phuoc Hotel (across the street from the Palace Hotel). The last bus of the day from the Hanh Phuoc Hotel departs in the mid-to-late afternoon; tickets should be purchased a day in advance at the reception desk.

Taxi For a day-trip to Vung Tau, you might consider hiring a taxi or 'marriage taxi'. Information on hiring vehicles in Saigon appears in the Getting There & Away section of the Ho Chi Minh City chapter.

Boat It may be possible to get from Vung Tau to the Con Dao Archipelago by boat, but don't count on it.

Yachters who have shown up in Vung Tau without the necessary authorisations have been imprisoned and had their boats seized.

Getting Around

The best way to get around the Vung Tau peninsula is by bicycle. These are available for hire from some hotels for around US$1 per day.

CON DAO ISLANDS
CÔN ĐẢO

The Con Dao Archipelago is a group of 14 islands and islets 180 km (97 nautical miles) south of Vung Tau. The largest island in the group, whose total land area is 20 sq km, is partly forested Con Son Island, which is ringed with bays, bathing beaches and coral reefs. Con Son Island is also known by its Europeanised Malay name, Poulo Condore (Pulau Kundur), which means Island of the Squashes. Local products include teak and pine wood from the islands' forests, fruits (cashews, grapes, coconuts and mangoes), pearls, sea turtles, lobster and coral.

Occupied at various times by the Khmers, Malays and Vietnamese, Con Son also served as an early base for European commercial ventures in the region. The British East India Company maintained a fortified trading post here from 1702 to 1705, an experiment which ended when the English on the island were massacred in a revolt by the Makassar soldiers they had recruited on the Indonesian island of Sulawesi.

Under the French, Con Son was used as a prison for opponents of French colonialism, earning a fearsome reputation for the routine mistreatment and torture of prisoners. In 1954, the prison was taken over by the South Vietnamese Government, which continued

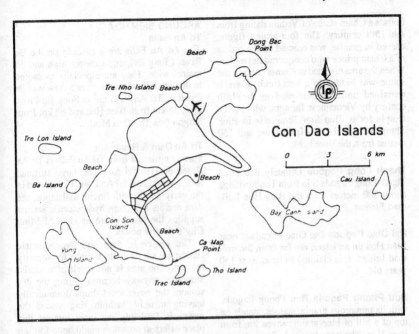

Con Dao Islands

Dong Bac Point
Beach
Tre Nho Island Beach
Tre Lon Island
Beach
Ba Island
Beach
Con Son Island
Vung Island
Beach
Ca Map Point
Trac Island
Tho Island
Cau Island
Bay Canh Island

0   3   6 km

to take advantage of its remoteness to hold opponents of the government (including students) in horrifying conditions. The island's Revolutionary Museum has exhibits on Vietnamese resistance to the French, Communist opposition to the Republic of Vietnam, and the treatment of political prisoners held on the island. A ditch in which Communist Party members were dunked in cow's urine is open to the public.

There has been talk of building a casino and giving Con Dao duty-free status. At the present time, Con Dao sees few foreign visitors other than the occasional tour group interested in the island's history as a horrific prison.

Getting There & Away
Air Vietnam Airlines flies chartered helicopters from Vung Tau to Con Son Island.

Boat The 215-km boat trip from Vung Tau takes 12 hours.

BIEN HOA
BIÊN HÒA
Bien Hoa (population 175,000), known as a centre of pottery and porcelain making, is on the east bank of the Dong Hai River 32 km north of Ho Chi Minh City. The city was founded by Chinese refugees and immigrants in the 1680s.

Bien Hoa has the distinction of being the place to claim the very first US casualties in the Vietnam War – in July 1959, two American soldiers were killed here during a VC raid. In the next decade, they were to be joined by over 58,000 of their fellow citizens. When the Vietnam War really got cooking in the mid-1960s, Bien Hoa was the site of a huge American airfield and headquarters base. It's now the capital of Dong Nai Province.

Pagodas & Temples
Buu Son Temple The most famous religious site in Bien Hoa is Buu Son Temple, which

houses a Cham statue of Vishnu dating from the 15th century. The four-armed figure, carved in granite, was erected on the orders of a Cham prince who conquered the region. When the area reverted to Khmer control, the statue was hidden in a tree trunk where it remained until rediscovered in the 18th century by Vietnamese farmers, who built a temple for it. Buu Son Temple is in Binh Thuoc village, 1.5 km from town and 150 metres from the river bank.

Thanh Long Pagoda Ornately decorated Thanh Long Pagoda is in Binh Thuoc village about 300 metres from the Bien Hoa Railroad Station.

Dai Giac Pagoda Dai Giac Pagoda is near Bien Hoa on an island not far from the railroad bridge. It is claimed to be at least 150 years old.

Buu Phong Pagoda Buu Phong Pagoda, with its numerous granite statues, stands on top of a hill of blue granite seven km from Bien Hoa. The pagoda was built on the site of an earlier Cham or Khmer temple on the orders of Emperor Gia Long.

Getting There & Away

There is a four-lane super highway from Ho Chi Minh City to Bien Hoa (a distance of 32 km) constructed with American aid between 1958 and 1961. Most of the trains heading north from Ho Chi Min City stop at Bien Hoa.

AROUND BIEN HOA
Tri An Falls

The Tri An Falls are a cascade on the Be River (Song Be), eight metres high and 30 metres wide. They are especially awesome in the late fall, when the river's flow is at its greatest. Tri An Falls are in Song Be Province, 36 km from Bien Hoa and 68 km from Saigon (via Thu Dau Mot).

Tri An Dam & Reservoir

Further upstream from Tri An Falls is Tri An Reservoir (Ho Tri An). This large artificial lake is created by Tri An Dam. Completed in the early 1980s with Soviet assistance, the dam and its adjoining hydroelectric station supplies the lion's share of Ho Chi Minh City's electric power.

The reservoir, dam and hydroelectric station are off limits to tourists for security reasons. The area is not much of a tourist attraction anyway because during the dry season, the water level drops dramatically leaving an ugly 'bathtub' ring around the reservoir. Probably the main interest this place offers to outsiders could be to foreign investors – the hydroelectric station is severely overtaxed by the surging demand for electricity and the Vietnamese are reportedly looking for foreign partners to provide some sort of solution. Should you happen to be in the electrical engineering business, the Vietnamese would probably like to hear from you.

If you are seriously contemplating a visit to Tri An Dam and Reservoir, be sure that you have official permission.

Mekong Delta
Đồng Bằng Cửu Long

Pancake flat but lusciously green and beautiful, the Mekong Delta is the southernmost region of Vietnam. It was formed by sediment deposited by the Mekong River, a process which continues today; silt deposits extend the delta's shoreline at the mouths of the river by as much as 79 metres per year.

The land of the Mekong Delta is renowned for its richness; almost half of the region's total land area is under cultivation. The area is known as Vietnam's 'breadbasket', producing enough rice to feed the south and central parts of the country as well as some of the north. Other food products from the delta include coconut, sugar cane, various fruits and fish. Although this area is primarily rural, it is one of the most densely populated regions in Vietnam – nearly every hectare is intensively farmed. An exception are the sparsely inhabited mangrove swamps around Camau in Minh Hai Province where the land is not very productive.

The Mekong River, one of the great rivers of the world, is known to the Vietnamese as Song Cuu Long, River of the Nine Dragons. The Mekong originates high in the Tibetan plateau, flowing 4500 km through China, between Myanmar and Laos, through Laos, along the Lao-Thai border, and through Cambodia and Vietnam on its way to the South China Sea. At Phnom Penh, the Mekong splits into two main branches: the Hau Giang (the Lower River, also called the Bassac River), which flows via Chau Doc, Long Xuyen and Cantho to the sea; and the Tien Giang (Upper River), which splits into several branches at Vinh Long and empties into the sea at six points.

The level of the Mekong begins to rise around the end of May and reaches its highest point in September; its flow ranges from 1900 to 38,000 cubic metres per second depending on the season. A tributary of the river which empties into the Mekong at Phnom Penh drains Cambodia's Tonlé Sap Lake. When the Mekong is at flood stage, this tributary reverses its flow and drains *into* Tonlé Sap, thereby reducing the danger of serious flooding in the Mekong Delta.

The Mekong Delta was once part of the Khmer kingdom and was the last region of modern-day Vietnam to be annexed and settled by the Vietnamese. The Cambodians, mindful that they controlled the area until the 18th century, still call the delta 'Lower Cambodia'. Most of the inhabitants of the Mekong Delta are ethnic-Vietnamese, but there are significant populations of ethnic-Chinese and Khmer as well as a few Chams.

MYTHO
MỸ THO

Mytho, the capital of Tien Giang Province, is a quiet city of 90,000 easily reached from Ho Chi Minh City yet very near some of the most beautiful rural areas of the Mekong Delta. The city can be visited as a day trip from Ho Chi Minh City; its hotels, restaurants and transport facilities can also be used as a base for exploring Tien Giang Province and the neighbouring island province of Ben Tre.

Mytho was founded in the 1680s by Chinese refugees fleeing Taiwan for political reasons. The economy of the area is based on fishing and the cultivation of rice, coconuts, bananas, mangoes, longans and citrus fruit.

Orientation

Mytho, which sprawls along the bank of the northernmost branch of the Mekong River, is laid out in a fairly regular grid pattern. The bus station, Ben Xe Khach Tien Giang, is several km west of town. Coming from the station, you enter Mytho on Ap Bac St. Ap Bac St turns into Nguyen Trai St, which is oriented west-east. The main north-south

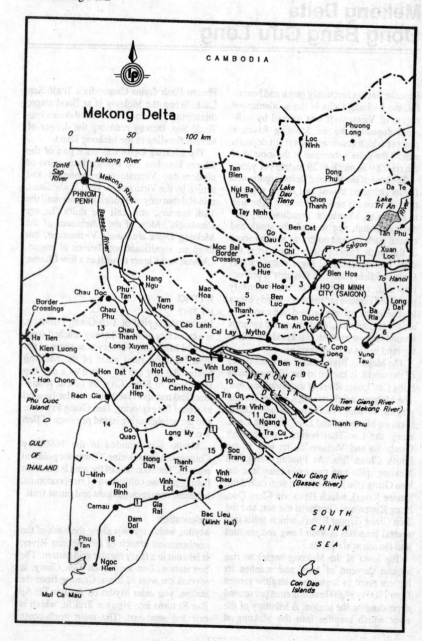

Mekong Delta

CAMBODIA

Mekong River

Tonlé Sap River

Mekong River

PHNOM PENH

0   50   100 km

Bassac River

Phuong Long

Loc Ninh

Tan Bien

Dong Phu

Da Te

Lake Dau Tieng

Chon Thanh

Lake Tri An

Da Te River

Nui Ba Den

Tay Ninh

Ben Cat

Tan Phu

Go Dau

Cu Chi

Saigon

Xuan Loc

Moc Bai Border Crossing

Duc Hue

Bien Hoa

To Hanoi

Hang Ngu

Mac Hoa

Duc Hoa

HO CHI MINH CITY (SAIGON)

Long Dat

Chau Doc

Phu Tan

Tam Nong

Ben Luc

Ba Ria

Border Crossings

Chau Phu

Tan Thanh

Can Duoc

Ha Tien

Chau Thanh

Cao Lanh

Cai Lay

Tan An

Mytho

Cong Dong

Kien Luong

Long Xuyen

Vung Tau

Hon Chong

Thot Not

Sa Dec

Vinh Long

Ben Tre

MEKONG

Phu Quoc Island

Hon Dat

O Mon

Cantho

Tra On

DELTA

Tien Giang River (Upper Mekong River)

Rach Gia

Tan Hlep

Tra Vinh

Cau Ngang

Go Quao

Long My

Tra Cu

Thanh Phu

GULF OF THAILAND

Hong Dan

Thanh Tri

Soc Trang

Vinh Chau

Hau Giang River (Bassac River)

U-Minh

Thoi Binh

Vinh Loi

SOUTH CHINA SEA

Camau

Gia Rai

Bac Lieu (Minh Hai)

Dam Doi

Phu Tan

Ngoc Hien

Con Dao Islands

Mui Ca Mau

1	Song Be
2	Dong Nai
3	Ho Chi Minh City
4	Tay Ninh
5	Long An
6	Ba Ria-Vung Tau
7	Tien Giang
8	Dong Thap
9	Ben Tre
10	Vinh Long
11	Tra Vinh
12	Cantho
13	An Giang
14	Kien Giang
15	Soc Trang
16	Minh Hai

thoroughfare in town (and the widest street in the city) is Hung Vuong Blvd.

Information

Tourist Office Tien Giang Tourism (Cong Ty Du Lich Tien Giang; ☎ 72154, 72105) is the official tourism authority for Tien Giang Province. The office is on the northern edge of the city at 66 Hung Vuong Blvd and is open Monday to Saturday.

Ben Tre Tourism (Cong Ty Du Lich Ben Tre; ☎ 2197, 2392) is the provincial tourism authority for Ben Tre Province. The office is at 65 Dong Khoi St in Ben Tre.

Island of the Coconut Monk

Until his imprisonment by the Communists for anti-government activities and the consequent dispersion of his flock, the Coconut Monk (Ong Dao Dua) led a small community on Phung Island (Con Phung), a few km from Mytho. In its heyday, the island was dominated by a fantastic open-air sanctuary that looked like a cross between a cheaply built copy of Disneyland and the Tiger Balm Gardens of Singapore. The dragon-enwrapped columns and the multiplatformed tower with its huge metal globe must have once been brightly painted, but these days the whole place is faded, rickety and silent. With a bit of imagination though, you can picture how it all must have appeared as the Coconut

Monk presided over his congregation, flanked by elephant tusks and seated on a richly ornamented throne.

The Coconut Monk, so named because it is said that he once ate only coconuts for three years, was born Nguyen Thanh Nam (though he later adopted Western name order, preferring to be called Nam Nguyen Thanh) in 1909 in what is now Ben Tre Province. He studied chemistry and physics in France at Lyons, Caen and Rouen from 1928 until 1935, when he returned to Vietnam, married and had a daughter.

In 1945 the Coconut Monk left his family to pursue a monastic life. For three years, he sat on a stone slab under a flagpole and meditated day and night. He was repeatedly imprisoned by successive South Vietnamese governments, which were infuriated by his philosophy of bringing about the country's reunification through peaceful means.

The Coconut Monk founded a religion, Tinh Do Cu Si, which was a mixture of Buddhism and Christianity. Representations of Jesus and the Buddha appeared together, as did the Virgin Mary and eminent Buddhist women. He employed both the cross and Buddhist symbols.

The best way to get from Mytho to Phung Island is to hire a motorised wooden boat, which should cost US$3 per hour. Larger boats are available for slightly more. The trip takes about 20 minutes. The Coconut Monk's complex is visible from the car ferry that runs from near Mytho to Ben Tre Province. The plaques on the 3½-metre-high porcelain jar (created in 1972) tell all about the Coconut Monk.

Mytho Church & Bishopric

Mytho Church, a solid pastel-yellow building at 32 Hung Vuong Blvd (corner Nguyen Trai St), was built about a century ago. The stone plaques set in the church walls express *merci* and *cam on* to Fatima and other figures.

Today, two priests, two sisters and several assistants minister to much of Mytho's Catholic population of 7000. The church is open to visitors every day from 4.30 to 6.30 am

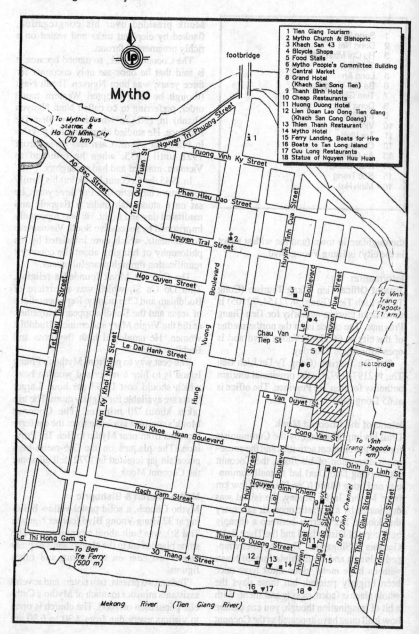

Mytho

To Mytho Bus
Station &
Ho Chi Minh City
(70 km)

footbridge

1 Tien Giang Tourism
2 Mytho Church & Bishopric
3 Khach San 43
4 Bicycle Shops
5 Food Stalls
6 Mytho People's Committee Building
7 Central Market
8 Grand Hotel
  (Khach San Song Tien)
9 Thanh Binh Hotel
10 Cheap Restaurants
11 Huong Duong Hotel
12 Lien Doan Lao Dong Tien Giang
  (Khach San Cong Doang)
13 Thien Thanh Restaurant
14 Mytho Hotel
15 Ferry Landing, Boats for Hire
16 Boats to Tan Long Island
17 Cuu Long Restaurants
18 Statue of Nguyen Huu Huan

Ap Bac Street

Nguyen Tri Phuong Street

Truong Vinh Ky Street

Tran Quoc Tuan St

Phan Hieu Dao Street

Nguyen Trai Street

Huynh Tinh Cua Street

Le Loi Boulevard

Nguyen Hue Street

To Vinh
Trang
Pagoda
(1 km)

Ngo Quyen Street

Le Dai Hanh Street

Tet Mau Than Street

Nam Ky Khoi Nghia Street

Hung Vuong Boulevard

Chau Van
Tiep St

footbridge

Le Van Duyet St

Thu Khoa Huan Boulevard

Ly Cong Van St

To Vinh
Trang
Pagoda
(1 km)

Rach Gam Street

Dinh Bo Linh St

Nguyen Binh Khiem St

Do Huu Trac Street

Le Loi Boulevard

Bao Dinh Channel

Le Thi Hong Gam St

Thien Ho Duong Street

Huyen Toai St

Trung Trac Street

Phan Thanh Gian Street

Trinh Hoai Duc Street

To Ben
Tre Ferry
(500 m)

30 Thang 4 Street

12   13   14

16   17   18

Mekong   River   (Tien Giang River)

and 2.30 to 6.30 pm. Daily masses are held at 5 am and 5 pm. On Sunday, there are masses at 5 am, 7 am and 5 pm and catechism classes in the late afternoon.

Mytho Central Market

Mytho Central Market is an area of town along Trung Trac St and Nguyen Hue St that is closed to traffic. The streets are filled with stalls selling everything from fresh food (along Trung Trac St) and bulk tobacco to boat propellers.

Tan Long Island

The well-known longan (nhan) orchards of Tan Long Island are a five-minute boat trip from the dock at the southern end of Le Loi Blvd. The lush, palm-fringed shores of the island are lined with wooden fishing boats similar to those used by the 'boat people' to flee the country. Some of the residents of the island are shipwrights.

Chinese District

The Chinese district is around Phan Thanh Gian St on the eastern bank of the Bao Dinh Channel.

Snake Farm

There is a snake farm at Dong Tam, which is about 10 km from Mytho towards Vinh Long.

Vinh Trang Pagoda

Vinh Trang Pagoda, which is often visited by organised tour groups, is an eclectic tourist trap in which sacred Buddhist ritual objects have become one element in a pathetic little amusement park which also includes a repainted US Air Force Cessna and an unhappy zoo. At least the animals, if not healthy, are alive; the sanctuary is spiritless and utterly devoid of life, with unused ritual objects, some holding long-extinguished joss sticks, placed about unlovingly. The only thing worth seeing here is a partly three-dimensional portrait of Ho Chi Minh with real hairs making up his beard placed on a altar. Are people supposed to come and worship Ho Chi Minh? Pity the tourist for whom this is the only Buddhist pagoda he or she sees.

Vinh Trang Pagoda is about one km from the city centre at 60A Nguyen Trung Truc St. To get there, take the bridge across the river (at Nguyen Trai St) and continue for about a km. The entrance to the sanctuary is on the right-hand side of the building as you approach it from the ornate gate.

Quan Thanh Pagoda

This Chinese pagoda, built by the Fujian and Chaozhou congregations, was being repaired for tourists. All the figures, most of which are made of plaster, have been repainted. Quan Cong is behind the main altar. Quan Thanh Pagoda is between Dinh Bo Linh St and Vinh Trang Pagoda at 3/9 Nguyen Trung Truc St.

Places to Stay

The Thanh Binh Hotel (four rooms) at 44 Nguyen Binh Khiem St is a dilapidated dump which amazingly still accepts foreigners. The tariff is US$3 for doubles without fans or attached bath.

Most budget travellers now stay at the Lien Doan Lao Dong Tien Giang (☎ 72166), also known as Khach San Cong Doang. Baths and toilets are outside and there is no air-conditioning, but rooms are cheap at US$4 and the good river view makes up for the lack of amenities. It's also reasonably clean. The hotel is on the corner of 30 Thang 4 St and Le Loi Blvd.

The five-storey Huong Duong Hotel (☎ 72011; 20 rooms) at 33 Trung Trac St has doubles with ceiling fans and attached bath for US$8. Air-con doubles cost US$10 and US$12. Overall, not bad.

The Khach San 43 (☎ 72126; 24 rooms) is a clean, modern and airy place at 43 Ngo Quyen St. Triple rooms with fan and attached bath cost US$6 while a double with air-con costs US$7.

The eight-storey Grand Hotel (☎ 72009; 35 rooms), also known as the Khach San Song Tien, is the largest in town. A double room with electric fan and attached bath costs US$5. Air-con makes it US$12 and

US$15. If you also want a hot water shower, the cost is US$18.

The run-down *Mytho Hotel* (24 rooms) at 67 30 Thang 4 St used to accept foreigners but no longer does. This place has a good river view and definite renovation potential, so it is possible that foreigners will be allowed in the future.

Places to Eat
Mytho is known for a special vermicelli soup, *hu tieu My Tho*, which is richly garnished with fresh and dried seafood, pork, chicken and fresh herbs. It is served either with broth or dry (with broth on the side).

Thien Thanh Restaurant is at 65, 30 Thang 4 St. Across the street, next to the Tan Long Island ferry dock, is *Cuu Long Restaurant* which has excellent river views. There are numerous excellent small and cheap restaurants along Trung Trac St between the statue of Nguyen Huu Huan (a 19th century anti-colonial fighter) on 30 Thang 4 St and the Thu Khoa Huan Blvd bridge.

The *Grand Hotel* also has a decent restaurant. *Khach San 43* also has a restaurant.

Getting There & Away
Bus Mytho is served by non-express buses leaving Ho Chi Minh City from Mien Tay Bus Station in An Lac.

The Mytho Bus Station (Ben Xe Khach Tien Giang; ☎ 3359) is several km west of town; it is open from 4 am to about 5 pm. To get there from the city centre, take Ap Bac St westward and continue on to National Highway 1.

Buses to Ho Chi Minh City leave when full from the early morning until about 5 pm; the trip takes 1½ hours. There is daily bus service to Cantho (five hours; departures at 4 am and 9 pm), Chau Doc (leaves at 4 am), Phu Hoa (departs at 6 pm), Tay Ninh (six hours; departs at 5 am) and Vung Tau (five hours; leaves at 5 am). There are also buses to Ba Beo, Bac My Thuan, Cai Be, Cai Lay, Go Cong Dong, Go Cong Tay, Hau My Bac, Phu My, Tan An and Vinh Kim. There is no express bus service from Mytho.

Car By car, the drive from Ho Chi Minh City to Mytho on National Highway 1 (Quoc Lo 1) takes about 90 minutes.

Road distances from Mytho are 16 km to Ben Tre, 104 km to Cantho, 70 km to Ho Chi Minh City and 66 km to Vinh Long.

Boat A passenger ferry to Mytho leaves Ho Chi Minh City daily at 11 am from the dock at the end of Ham Nghi Blvd; the trip should take about six hours if you're lucky.

The Rach Mieu car ferry to Ben Tre Province leaves from a station (Ben Pha Rach Mieu) about one km west of the city centre near 2/10A Le Thi Hong Gam St (Le Thi Hong Gam St is the western continuation of 30 Thang 4 St). The ferry operates from 4 am to 10 pm and runs at least once an hour. Ten-person trucks shuttle between the ferry terminal and the bus station.

Getting Around
Motorised seven-metre boats can be hired at an unmarked ferry landing on Trung Trac St at the eastern end of Thien Ho Duong St; ferry boats to points across the river also dock here. Wooden rowboats to Tan Long Island leave from the pier at the southern end of Le Loi St next to Cuu Long Restaurant. The prices get jacked up for foreigners, but typically a four-hour boat trip costs around US$2.

VINH LONG
VĨNH LONG
Vinh Long, the capital of Vinh Long Province, is a medium-sized town along the banks of the Mekong River about midway between Mytho and Cantho.

Information
Tourist Office Vinh Long Tourist (Cong Ty Du Lich Vinh Long; ☎ 22494, 22357) is at 1 Duong 1/5.

Mekong River Islands
What makes a trip to Vinh Long so worthwhile is not the town itself, but the beautiful small islands in the river. The islands are

totally given over to agriculture, especially the raising of tropical fruits which are shipped to markets in Ho Chi Minh City.

A trip to the islands requires that you charter a boat. Small motorboats can be had for about US$1 per hour. Some of the more popular islands to visit include Binh Hoa Phuoc and An Binh Island, but there are many others. It would be wise to bring an English-speaking Vietnamese guide with you to get the full benefit out of the trip.

Places to Stay
Most travellers coming to Vinh Long overnight in the *Cuu Long Hotel*, which costs US$15 for a double with air-con.

Getting There & Away
Bus Buses to Vinh Long leave Ho Chi Minh City from Mien Tay Bus Station in An Lac. Non-express buses take four hours.

Car Vinh Long is just off National Highway 1, 66 km from Mytho, 98 km from Cantho and 136 km from Ho Chi Minh City.

Boat It is possible to go from Vinh Long all the way to Chau Doc, but you should have a Vietnamese guide if you want to attempt this. If you go to Chau Doc, you'll probably have to stop off at Long Xuyen along the way to get a travel permit (see the Chau Doc and Long Xuyen sections for details).

SA DEC
SA ĐÉC
Sa Dec is famous in Vietnam for the many nurseries cultivating flowers, which are picked almost daily and transported fresh to shops in Ho Chi Minh City.

You're welcome to have a look around, but not to pick any flowers unless you plan on buying them. Photography is certainly permitted – indeed, the flower farmers are very used to it.

Sa Dec is also visited by Ho Chi Minh aficionados. Uncle Ho's father lived here and you can visit his grave site if you wish.

Information
Tourist Office Dong Thap Tourist (Cong Ty Du Lich Dong Thap; ☎ 61430, 61432) is the official tourism authority for Dong Thap Province. The office is at 108/5A Hung Vuong in Sa Dec. Dong Thap Tourist operates two hotels.

Getting There & Away
Sa Dec is in Dong Thap Province, midway between Vinh Long and Long Xuyen.

CANTHO
CẦN THƠ
Cantho (population 150,000), capital of Cantho Province, is the political, economic, cultural and transportation centre of the Mekong Delta. This friendly, bustling city is connected to most other population centres in the Mekong Delta by a system of rivers and canals. Rice-husking mills are a major local industry.

Orientation
Nguyen Trai St links Cantho's bus station, north-west of the centre, with Hoa Binh Blvd, a wide avenue with a centre strip. Hoa Binh Blvd becomes 30 Thang 4 Blvd at Nguyen An Ninh St. Hai Ba Trung St runs along the Cantho River waterfront. Phan Dinh Phung St, the main commercial thoroughfare, is two blocks inland from Hai Ba Trung St.

Information
Tourist Office Cantho Tourism (Cong Ty Du Lich Can Tho; ☎ 21804, fax (84-71) 22719) is the provincial tourism authority; the office is at 27 Chau Van Liem St.

Money Vietcombank (Ngan Hang Ngoai Thuong Viet Nam; ☎ 20445) is at 2 Ngo Gia Tu St.

Post & Telecommunications The GPO is a five-storey building at the intersection of Hoa Binh Blvd and Ngo Quyen St.

Emergency The general hospital is on the

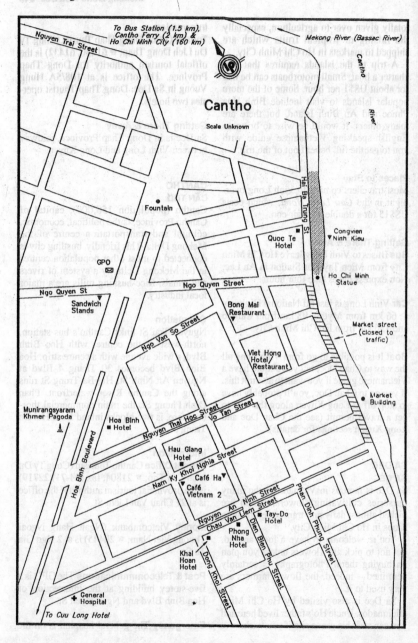

To Bus Station (1.5 km),
Cantho Ferry (2 km) &
Ho Chi Minh City (160 km)

Mekong River (Bassac River)

Cantho

Cantho River

Nguyen Trai Street

Scale Unknown

Fountain

Hai Ba Trung St

Quoc Te
Hotel

Congvien
Ninh Kieu

GPO

Ngo Quyen Street

Ho Chi Minh
Statue

Ngo Quyen St

Sandwich
Stands

Bong Mai
Restaurant

Market street
(closed to
traffic)

Ngo Van So Street

Viet Hong
Hotel/
Restaurant

Market
Building

Munirangsyaram
Khmer Pagoda

Nguyen Thai Hoc Street

Vo Tan Street

Hoa Binh Boulevard

Hoa Binh
Hotel

Hau Giang
Hotel

Nam Ky Khoi Nghia Street

Café Ha

Café
Vietnam 2

Nguyen An Ninh Street

Phan Dinh Phung Street

Tay-Do
Hotel

Nguyen Van Liem Street

Chau Van Liem

Dien Bien Phu Street

Phong
Nha
Hotel

Khai
Hoan
Hotel

Dong Khoi Street

General
Hospital

To Cuu Long Hotel

corner of Chau Van Liem St and Hoa Binh Blvd.

Munirangsyaram Pagoda

The ornamentation of Munirangsyaram Pagoda at 36 Hoa Binh Blvd is typical of Khmer Hinayana Buddhist pagodas, lacking the multiple Bodhisattvas and Taoist spirits common in Vietnamese Mahayana pagodas. In the upstairs sanctuary, a 1½-metre-high representation of Siddhartha Gautama, the historical Buddha, sits under a *potthe* (bodhi) tree. Built in 1946, Munirangsyaram Pagoda serves the Khmer community of Cantho, which numbers about 2000. The two Khmer monks, one in his 70s and the other in his 20s, hold prayers at 5 am and 6 pm every day.

Quan Thanh De Pagoda

This small Chinese pagoda, also known as Minh Huong Hoi Quan, was built by the Cantonese Congregation about 70 years ago. Cantho previously had a large ethnic-Chinese population, but most fled after the anti-Chinese persecutions of 1978-79.

Quan Thanh De Pagoda is on Le Minh Ngu On St between Nguyen Hue B St and Nguyen Trai St and is open from 5 am to 8 pm. On the main dais are Quan Cong and his guardians, the general Chau Xuong and the administrative mandarin Quan Binh. To the left of the dais is Ong Bon, Guardian Spirit of Happiness and Virtue. Thien Hau, the Goddess of the Sea, is to the other side of the dais.

Central Market

The Central Market is strung out along Hai Ba Trung St. The main market building is at the intersection of Hai Ba Trung St and Nam Ky Khoi Nghia St.

University of Cantho

Cantho University, founded in 1966, is on 30 Thang 4 Blvd.

Nearby Rural Areas

Rural areas of Cantho Province, renowned for their durian, mangosteen and orange orchards, can easily be reached from Cantho by boat or bicycle.

Boat Rides

The most interesting thing to do in Cantho is take a boat ride. The cost for this is very reasonable, around US$1.50 per hour for a small paddle boat which can carry two or three passengers. You won't have to look hard for the boats – they will be looking for you. Just wander by the docks across from the Quoc Te Hotel and you'll have plenty of offers. Most of the boats are operated by women. Bring your camera, though also keep it in a plastic bag when you're not actually shooting because it's easy to get splashed by the wake of motorised boats.

Places to Stay

The *Quoc Te Hotel* (☎ 22079; 32 rooms) at 12 Hai Ba Trung St is along the Cantho River and is the most pleasant place in town. Rooms with fan and private bath start at US$8, while a double with TV, fridge and air-con costs US$25. On weekends the karaoke bar is in full operation.

The six-storey *Hau Giang Hotel* (☎ 21851; 32 rooms) at 34 Nam Ky Khoi Nghia St is also very pleasant and popular with foreigners – even the lobby has air-conditioning. Singles/doubles with fan only go for US$8/10 while air-con rooms start at US$12/14 and escalate up to US$28/32.

The *Hoa Binh Hotel* (☎ 20536) at 5 Hoa Binh St is a reasonably well-appointed place which also tries to milk the foreign market. A small single room with fan and private bath costs US$8 while air-con doubles are US$12 and US$14. A triple air-con room costs US$21.

Moving down-market, the *Viet Hong Hotel* (☎ 25831) at 55 Phan Dinh Phung St has singles/doubles with air-con and private bath for US$5/7. It's nothing fancy, but acceptable. The hotel also has a decent restaurant.

The *Tay Do Hotel* (☎ 35265) on Chau Van Liem St is the cheapest place in town which is currently accepting foreigners. Room prices are just US$3 to US$4 per night.

The *Khai Hoan Hotel* (☎ 35261) at 83 Chau Van Liem St sometimes accepts foreigners and sometimes not. Probably if you're badly dressed they'll accept you, but if you look like someone with class, you'll be referred to a 'decent hotel'. Rooms cost US$5.

The *Phong Nha Hotel* (☎ 35466) at 79 Chau Van Liem St is also one of those places that sometimes accepts foreigners and sometimes not. Rooms are priced the same as at the Khai Hoan Hotel.

The *Cuu Long Hotel* is on the south side of town at 52 Quang Trung St. Rooms with fan cost US$4.50, or US$6 with air-con.

Other hotels in Cantho which sometimes (but not usually) accept foreigners include: the *Hao Hoa Hotel* (☎ 35407) at 6 Lu Gia St; the *Huy Hoang Hotel* (☎ 35403) at 35 Ngo Duc Ke St; the *Phuoc Thanh Hotel* (☎ 35406) at 5 Phan Dang Luu St; the *Thuy Tien Hotel* (☎ 35412) at 6 Tran Phu St; and the *Tuy Quang Lau Hotel* (☎ 35402) at 33 Chau Van Liem St.

Places to Eat

Along the Cantho River waterfront there are several restaurants serving Mekong Delta specialities such as fish, snake, frog and turtle.

The *Bong Mai Restaurant* is at 19-23 Phan Dinh Phung St.

The *Quoc Te Hotel* (☎ 22079) operates two restaurants, both with English menus but limited English-speaking ability by the staff.

There are a number of restaurants that cater to a local clientele along Nam Ky Khoi Nghia St, between Phan Dinh Phung St and Dien Bien Phu St. Mobile stands selling soup and French-roll sandwiches are often set up on Hoa Binh Blvd near the GPO.

Congvien Ninh Kieu is a waterside cafe across the street from the Quoc Te Hotel.

Café Ha, across the street from 1 Dien Bien Phu St, is a favourite hang-out of young local men. Surrounded by posters of has-been rock groups from the 1960s, they listen to country & western music while sipping beers. Just around the corner and opposite the Hau Giang Hotel is *Café Vietnam 2*, a small but cozy place with decent food.

Getting There & Away

Bus Buses to Cantho leave Ho Chi Minh City from Mien Tay Bus Station in An Lac. Non-express buses take five hours; the express bus, which has priority at ferry crossings, takes about 3½ hours.

The main bus station in Cantho is several km out of town at the intersection of Nguyen Trai St and Tran Phu St. There is another bus depot near the intersection of 30 Thang 4 Blvd and Mau Than St.

Car By car, the ride from Ho Chi Minh City to Cantho along National Highway 1 usually takes about four hours. There are two ferry crossings between Ho Chi Minh City and Cantho, the first at Vinh Long and the second at Cantho itself. The Cantho ferry runs from 4 to 2 am. Fruit, soft drinks and other food are sold where vehicles wait for the ferries.

To get from Hoa Binh Blvd in Cantho to the ferry crossing, take Nguyen Trai St to the bus station and turn right onto Tran Phu St.

Road distances from Cantho are as follows:

Camau	179 km
Chau Doc	117 km
Ho Chi Minh City	168 km
Long Xuyen	62 km
Mytho	104 km
Rach Gia	116 km
Sa Dec	51 km
Soc Trang	63 km
Vinh Long	34 km

Getting Around

An interesting innovation seen in Cantho is motorised cyclos – few other places in Vietnam have them.

LONG XUYEN
LONG XUYÊN

Long Xuyen, the capital of An Giang Province, has a population of about 100,000. It was once a stronghold of the Hoa Hao sect, founded in 1939, which emphasises simplicity in worship and does not believe in temples or intermediaries between humans and the Supreme Being. Until 1956, the Hoa Hao had an army and constituted a major military force in this region.

Orientation

Tran Hung Dao St runs north from the bus station and then continues on towards Chau Doc. Nguyen Hue St and Hai Ba Trung St, which are perpendicular to each other, are both wide, divided avenues.

Information

Tourist Office The office of An Giang Tourist Company (☎ 52086) – the government-owned official tourist authority for An Giang Province – is at 83.85 Nguyen Hue B St.

Tourism Services Company (Xi Nghiep Dich Vu Du Lich; ☎ 52277) at 93 Nguyen Trai St runs tours to Cambodia and may be able to provide other services, such as car rental.

Post & Telecommunications The GPO is at 11 Ngo Gia Tu St.

Travel Permit If you are going to stay in Chau Doc more than one night, then you need to get a permit from the Immigration Police in Long Xuyen. If you fail to do this, hotels in Chau Doc will only permit you to stay one night and then you'll have to leave town. The Immigration Police Office in Long Xuyen is right next to the Xuan Phuong Hotel on Hung Vuong St.

Long Xuyen Catholic Church

Long Xuyen Catholic Church, an impressive modern structure with a 50-metre-high bell tower, is one of the largest churches in the Mekong Delta. It was constructed between 1966 and 1973 and can seat 1000 worshippers. The church is on the triangular block created by Tran Hung Dao St, Hung Vuong St and Nguyen Hue A St and is open for visitors from 4 am to 8 pm. Masses are held daily from 4.30 to 5.30 am and 6 to 7 pm; on Sunday, there are masses from 5 to 6.30 am, 3.30 to 5 pm and 6 to 7.30 pm.

Long Xuyen Protestant Church

Long Xuyen Protestant Church is a small, modern structure at 4 Hung Vuong St. Prayers are held on Sundays from 10 am to noon.

Cho Moi District

Cho Moi District, across the river from Long Xuyen, is known for its rich groves of banana, durian, guava, jackfruit, longan, mango, mangosteen and plum. The women here are said to be the most beautiful in the Mekong Delta. Cho Moi District can be reached by ferry from the Cho Moi (An Hoa) Ferry Terminal at the foot of Nguyen Hue St.

Places to Stay

The *Binh Dan Hotel* (12 rooms), 12 Nguyen An Ninh St, is a basic dump and centre for prostitution. You enter the hotel through a long, dark corridor. If none of this deters you, rooms are very cheap at US$2.50.

The *Phat Thanh Hotel* (14 rooms) is on the same block at 2 Nguyen An Ninh St. It's also very basic but better than the Binh Dan Hotel. Rooms with fan and private bath are US$3 and US$3.50.

The *Thien Huong Hotel* (nine rooms) is nearby at 4 Nguyen An Ninh St. Like the preceding, it's also very basic but cheap at US$2.50 for a double with electric fan.

The *Kim Tinh Hotel* (☎ 53137) at 39-41-43 Nguyen Trai St is a reasonably good budget hotel. Double rooms with fan cost US$4.50.

Song Hau Hotel (☎ 52979; 26 rooms) is at 10 Hai Ba Trung St. Rooms here are decent and still moderately priced at US$7 with electric fan and US$9 with air-con.

The *Thai Binh Hotel* (☎ 52184, 52345; 24 rooms) is at 12 Nguyen Hue A St. Living conditions here are not bad. A double with fan costs US$6 and air-con rooms are US$8.

The *Xuan Phuong Hotel* (☎ 52041), at the corner of Nguyen Trai and Hung Vuong Sts, is also pleasant enough. Double rooms with air-con cost US$10 or US$12, while a room for four people is US$15.

The *An Giang Hotel* (☎ 52297; 16 rooms)

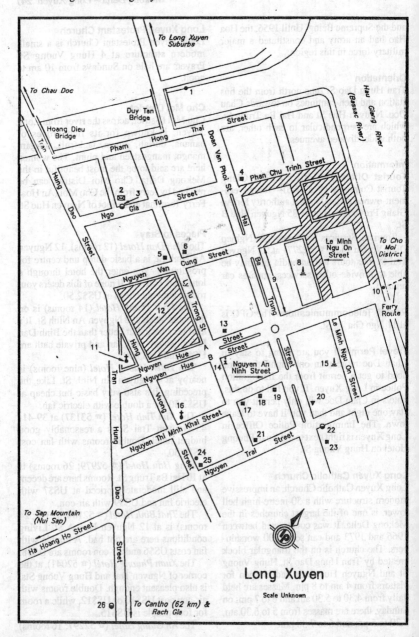

To Long Xuyen
Suburbs

To Chau Doc

Duy Tan
Bridge

Hoang Dieu
Bridge

Hau Giang River
(Bassac River)

1

Thai   Street

Doan Van Phoi St.

Hong

Pham

Street

Tran

Hung

Dao   Street

Ngo   Gia   Tu   Street

2 3

Phan Chu Trinh Street

4

Hai   Street

7

5   6

Cung   Street

Nguyen   Van

Le Minh
Ngu On
Street

8

Ly Tu Trong St.

Da   Street

9

Trung   Street

To Cho
Moi
District

Ferry
Route

10

12

Hung

Tran

11

13

Street

A

Nguyen   Hue

B

14   Nguyen An
Ninh Street

Le Minh Ngu On Street

15

Nguyen   Hue

Vuong

16

17   18   19

20

Nguyen Thi Minh Khai Street

21

Street

22

23

24

25

Trai   Street

Nguyen

Street

Dao

Street

Hung

To Sap Mountain
(Nui Sap)

Ha Hoang Ho Street

26

To Cantho (62 km) &
Rach Gia

Long Xuyen

Scale Unknown

■ PLACES TO STAY

4 An Giang Hotel
5 Long Xuyen Hotel
6 Mekong Hotel (Khach San Cuu Long)
13 Thai Binh Hotel
17 Binh Dan Hotel
18 Thien Huong Hotel
19 Phat Thanh Hotel
21 Kim Tinh Hotel/Restaurant
23 Song Hau Hotel
25 Xuan Phuong Hotel

▼ PLACES TO EAT

9 Small Restaurants
20 Long Xuyen Restaurant

OTHER

1 Long Xuyen Ferry Terminal
2 GPO
3 Express Bus Office
7 Long Xuyen Market
8 Dinh Than Long Xuyen (Temple)
10 Cho Moi (An Hoa) Ferry Terminal
11 Long Xuyen Catholic Church
12 Consumer Goods Market
14 An Giang Tourist Company
15 Quan Thanh De Pagoda
16 Long Xuyen Protestant Church
22 Express Bus Office
24 Immigration Police
26 Long Xuyen Bus Station

at 40 Hai Ba Trung St is not bad at all. Rooms with air-con cost US$12.

The *Long Xuyen Hotel* (☎ 52927; 37 rooms), run by An Giang Tourism, is at 17 Nguyen Van Cung St. This is a relatively up-market place though there are a few cheaper rooms with electric fan for US$10. Air-con rooms range from US$13 to US$18.

The *Mekong Hotel* (Khach San Cuu Long; ☎ 52365; 24 rooms) at 15 Nguyen Van Cung St is the most expensive in town with double rooms costing from US$18 to US$22.

Places to Eat

Long Xuyen is known for its flavourful rice.

The *Long Xuyen Restaurant*, a large place

which serves both Chinese and Western dishes and specialises in seafood, is near the corner of Nguyen Trai St and Hai Ba Trung St.

The *Kim Tinh Hotel/Restaurant* serves excellent Vietnamese food and is very cheap. The *Xuan Phuong Hotel* also has a pleasant restaurant. There are also restaurants in the hotels *An Giang, Cuu Long, Long Xuyen, Song Hau* and *Thai Binh*.

Getting There & Away

Bus Buses from Ho Chi Minh City to Long Xuyen leave from the Mien Tay Bus Station in An Lac.

Long Xuyen Bus Station (Ben Xe Long Xuyen; ☎ 52125) is at the southern end of town opposite 96/3B Tran Hung Dao St. There are buses from Long Xuyen to Camau, Cantho, Chau Doc, Ha Tien, Ho Chi Minh City and Rach Gia (three hours). An express bus to Ho Chi Minh City leaves Long Xuyen Bus Station every day at 4 am.

Express buses also leave from several other places around town. The express bus office at 225/4 Nguyen Trai St (☎ 52238) is open from 7 am to 5 pm and offers daily service to Ho Chi Minh City at 3 am. The bus office at 11 Ngo Gia Tu St (in front of the GPO), open from 8 am to 5 pm, sends an 18-seat minibus to Ho Chi Minh City at 2 am each morning. The Tourist Services Company (Xi Nghiep Dich Vu Du Lich; ☎ 52277) at 93 Nguyen Trai St runs an express bus to Ho Chi Minh City every day at 4 am; bus tickets are sold from 7 am to 9 pm.

Car Long Xuyen is 62 km from Cantho, 126 km from Mytho and 189 km from Ho Chi Minh City.

Boat To get to the Long Xuyen Ferry Terminal from Pham Hong Thai St, cross Duy Tan Bridge and turn right. Passenger ferries leave from here to Cho Vam, Dong Tien, Hong Ngu, Kien Luong, Lai Vung, Rach Gia, Sa Dec and Tan Chau.

There may be a ferry service to An Giang

Province from Saigon; check at the ferry dock at the river end of Ham Nghi Blvd.

Getting Around

The best way to get around Long Xuyen is to take a *xe dap loi* (a wagon pulled by a bicycle) or a *xe Honda loi* (a wagon pulled by a motorbike).

Car ferries from Long Xuyen to Cho Moi District (across the river) leave from the Cho Moi (An Hoa) Ferry Terminal near 17/4 Nguyen Hue B St every half hour from 4 am to 6.30 pm.

CHAU DOC
CHÂU ĐỐC

Chau Doc (population 40,000) is a riverine commercial centre not far from the Cambodian border. The city was once known for its pirogue (dugout canoe) races. Chau Doc has sizeable Chinese, Cham and Khmer communities.

Orientation

Chau Doc stretches along the bank of the Hau Giang River. The road closest to the water bears several names and is called (from north to south) Tran Hung Dao St, Gia Long St, Le Loi St and Lien Tinh Lo 10. Lien Tinh Lo 10 leads to Long Xuyen.

Information

Post Office The GPO (☎ 94550) is on the corner of Bao Ho Thoai St and Gia Long St.

Travel Permit If you want to spend more than one night in Chau Doc, you need to get a special permit from the immigration police in Long Xuyen.

The police in Chau Doc are bad news – even the locals are afraid of them. If you go to Sam Mountain, don't do any hiking off the main road or you might get arrested and fined!

Chau Phu Temple

Chau Phu Temple (Dinh Than Chau Phu), at the corner of Bao Ho Thoai St and Gia Long St, was built in 1926 to worship Thoai Ngoc

1	Con Tien Ferry Terminal
2	Khach San 44
3	Chau Doc Hotel & Bong Mai Restaurant
4	Fresh Food Market
5	Consumer Goods Market
6	Chau Doc Market & Restaurants
7	Express Bus Office
8	Hong Phat Restaurant
9	Lam Hung Ky Restaurant
10	Tan Tai Hotel
11	Thai Binh Hotel
12	My Loc Hotel
13	Chau Phu Temple
14	GPO
15	Cheap Restaurant
16	Hang Chau Hotel
17	Chau Giang Ferry Terminal

Hau (1761-1829), who is buried at Sam Mountain. The structure is decorated with both Vietnamese and Chinese motifs. Inside are funeral tablets bearing the names of the deceased and biographical information about them.

Chau Doc Church

This small Catholic church, constructed in 1920, is across the street from 459 Lien Tinh Lo 10 and is not far from FB Phu Hiep Ferry Terminal. There are masses every day at 5 am and 5 pm; on Sunday, masses are held at 7 am and 4 pm.

Chau Giang Mosque

The domed and arched Chau Giang Mosque, which serves the local Cham Muslim community, is in Chau Giang District. To get there, take the car ferry from Chau Giang Ferry Terminal in Chau Doc across the Hau Giang River. From the landing, go away from the river for 30 metres, turn left, and walk 50 metres.

Floating Houses

These houses, whose floats consist of empty metal drums, provide both a place to live and a livelihood for their residents. Under each house fish are raised in suspended metal nets: the fish flourish in their natural river habitat,

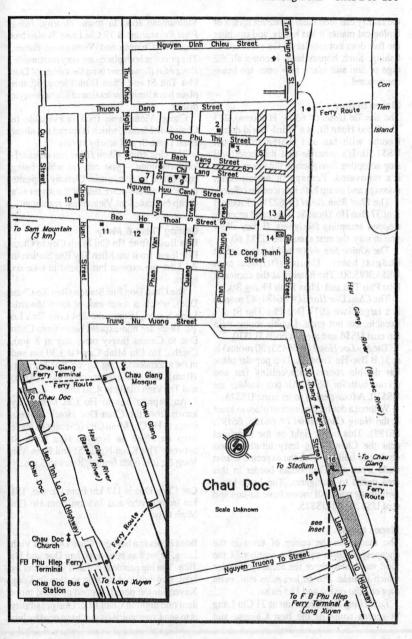

Nguyen Dinh Chieu Street

Tran Hung Dao St

Con
Tien
Island

Ferry Route

1

4

Thu Khoa

Thuong

Dang

Le

Street

Nghia

Doc

Phu

Thu

Street

2

Street

3

5

Bach

Dang

Street

Doc Phu Thu

6

Chi

Street

Lang

7

8

9

Nguyen

Huu

Canh

Street

Street

Thu Khoa

Vang

Street

10

Bao

Ho

Thoai

Street

13

To Sam Mountain
(3 km)

11

12

Van

Trung

Street

Phung

Dinh

Le Cong Thanh
Street

14

Gia Long Street

Hau Giang River (Bassac River)

Phan

Quang

Street

Trung Nu Vuong Street

30 Thang 4 Park

Le Loi Street

Chau Doc

Scale Unknown

To Stadium

15

16

17

To Chau
Giang

Ferry
Route

see
inset

Lien Tinh Lo 10 (Highway)

Nguyen Truong To Street

To F B Phu Hiep
Ferry Terminal &
Long Xuyen

Inset:

Chau Giang
Ferry Terminal

Chau Giang
Mosque

Ferry Route

To Chau Doc

Chau Giang

Hau Giang River
(Bassac River)

Chau Doc

Lien Tinh Lo 10 (Highway)

Chau Doc

Chau Doc
Church

FB Phu Hiep Ferry
Terminal

Chau Doc Bus
Station

Ferry Route

To Long Xuyen

the family can feed them whatever scraps of biological matter it has handy, and catching the fish does not require all the exertions of fishing. Such houses have become all the rage of late and many new ones are being constructed.

Places to Stay

The *Tan Tai Hotel* (☎ 6563; 11 rooms), 273 Thu Khoa Huan St, is a Third-World dump. Rooms with fan and shared toilet cost US$1.50. It's possible that this hotel will stop accepting foreigners in the future unless it's renovated. Perhaps in anticipation, massage and steam bath services are offered.

The *Thai Binh Hotel* (☎ 6221; 15 rooms) is at 37 Bao Ho Thoai St. This hotel recently stopped accepting foreigners. If they allow you to stay, the cost should be US$1.60.

The *Khach San 44* (☎ 66540) is a decent budget hotel. Doubles/triples cost US$4.30/5.50. The hotel is at the corner of Doc Phu Thu and Phan Dinh Phung Sts.

The *Chau Doc Hotel* (☎ 66484; 42 rooms) is a large place at 17 Doc Phu Thu St. It's liveable, but not great. Double rooms with fan cost US$6 and air-con costs US$10.

The *My Loc Hotel* (☎ 66455; 20 rooms) is at 51 B Bao Ho Thoai St. This popular place has double rooms with ceiling fan and private bath for US$8. Air-con doubles are US$10. A four-person room costs US$15.

Without a doubt, the fanciest place in town is the *Hang Chau Hotel* (☎ 66196, 66197, 66198). This hotel, right on the riverfront near the Chau Giang ferry terminal, was obviously built to catch the expected tourist trade when the Cambodian border in this area opens to foreigners. The hotel has a swimming pool. All rooms have air-con and cost US$20 and US$25.

Places to Eat

The market in the centre of town is the cheapest place to eat and a number of the food stalls here serve the local specialities which include: *kho ca loc*, *mam thai*, *mam ruot ca*, *kho ca tra* and *kho ca su*.

Lam Hung Ky Restaurant at 71 Chi Lang St serves some of the best Chinese and Vietnamese food in town. Nearby, *Hong Phat Restaurant* at 79 Chi Lang St also has excellent Chinese and Vietnamese dishes. The prices at both places are very reasonable. *Bong Mai Restaurant* is on the corner of Doc Phu Thu St and Phan Dinh Phung St; this place has a limited selection of Western-style dishes.

Cheap Vietnamese food is available in Chau Doc Market, which is spread out along Bach Dang St and nearby streets:

The chic *Hang Chau Hotel* has an excellent restaurant – you can eat while being entertained by live music. Directly opposite the hotel on the other side of the street is a cheap but excellent Vietnamese restaurant.

Getting There & Away

Bus Buses from Ho Chi Minh City to Chau Doc leave from the Mien Tay Bus Station in An Lac; the express bus is said to take six hours.

The Chau Doc Bus Station (Ben Xe Chau Doc), which is south-east of town towards Long Xuyen, is opposite 214 Lien Tinh Lo 10. There are non-express buses from Chau Doc to Camau (every other day at 8 am), Cantho, Ho Chi Minh City (at 3.30 am and in the afternoon), Long Xuyen, Soc Trang (at 10 am), Tien Giang (every other day at 5 am) and Tra Vinh (daily at 4.30 am).

An express bus to Ho Chi Minh City leaves from the Chau Doc Hotel. Express buses to Ho Chi Minh City (overnight) leave from an office on Nguyen Huu Canh St between Thu Khoa Nghia St and Phan Van Vang St; it is open from 7.30 am to 5 pm.

Car Chau Doc is 117 km from Cantho, 181 km from Mytho and 245 km from Ho Chi Minh City.

Boat Boats run between Chau Doc and Vinh Long, as well as between Chau Doc and Ha Tien. The big problem is that if you travel by boat, you will not be able to stop in Long Xuyen for the permit needed to spend more than one night in Chau Doc. One possibility is to send your guide (if you have one) by bus

Top: Fishing Village, Mieu Island (GB)
Left: Cham Towers near Nha Trang (OT)
Right: Island off Nha Trang (GB)

Left: Giant Seated Budda, Nha Trang (TW)
Right: Island off Nha Trang (GB)
Bottom: Nha Trang (RS)

to Long Xuyen to get the permit for you and then meet up again in Chau Doc.

Getting Around
Land Transport The main forms of land transport in Chau Doc are the xe dap loi and the xe Honda loi.

Boat Boats to Chau Giang District (across the Hau Giang River) leave from two docks: vehicle ferries depart from Chau Giang Ferry Terminal (Ben Pha Chau Giang), which is opposite 419 Le Loi St; smaller, more frequent boats leave from F B Phu Hiep Ferry Terminal (Ben Pha FB Phu Hiep). To get there from the centre of town, head southeast along Gia Long St (which turns into Le Loi St) and turn left at 349 Lien Tinh Lo 10. Take an immediate right and continue on for 200 metres. The prices of both ferries double at night.

Vehicle ferries to Con Tien Island depart from the Con Tien Ferry Terminal (Ben Pha Con Tien), which is off Gia Long St at the river end of Thuong Dang Le St; prices are double at night.

AROUND CHAU DOC
Tan Chau District
Tan Chau District is famous all over southern Vietnam for its traditional industry, silk making. The area is also known for its wealth, which is apparent in the proliferation of TV antennas and the widespread ownership of luxury goods (eg electric fans, high-quality cloth) imported from Thailand via Cambodia. The marketplace in Tan Chau

has a selection of competitively priced Thai and Cambodian goods.

To get to Tan Chau District from Chau Doc, take a boat across the Hau Giang River from the FB Phu Hiep Ferry Terminal. Then catch a ride on the back of a Honda om for the 18-km trip from Chau Giang District to Tan Chau District.

Sam Mountain
There are dozens of pagodas and temples, many of them set in caves, around Sam Mountain (Nui Sam), which is about three km south-west of Chau Doc out Bao Ho Thoai St. The Chinese influence is obvious, and this is a favourite spot for ethnic-Chinese pilgrims from Ho Chi Minh City and ethnic-Chinese tourists from Hong Kong and Taiwan.

Tay An Pagoda Tay An Pagoda (Chua Tay An), on the left as you arrive at Sam Mountain, is renowned for the fine carving of its hundreds of religious figures, most of which are made of wood. Aspects of the building's architecture reflect Hindu and Islamic influences. The first chief monk of Tay An Pagoda, which was founded in 1847, came from Giac Lam Pagoda in Ho Chi Minh City. Tay An Pagoda was last rebuilt in 1958.

The main gate is of traditional Vietnamese design. Above the bi-level roof there are figures of lions and two dragons fighting for possession of pearls, chrysanthemums, apricot trees and lotus blossoms. Nearby is a statue of Quan Am Thi Kinh, the Guardian Spirit of Mother & Child (for her legend, see the section on the Emperor of Jade Pagoda in the Ho Chi Minh City chapter).

In front of the pagoda are statues of a black elephant with two tusks and a white elephant with six tusks. Around the pagoda there are various monks' tombs.

Temple of Lady Chua Xu The Temple of Lady Chua Xu (Mieu Ba Chua Xu), founded in the 1820s, stands facing Sam Mountain

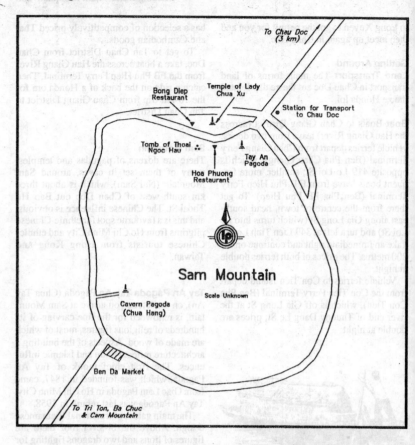

not far from Tay An Pagoda. The first building here was made of bamboo and leaves; the last reconstruction took place in 1972.

According to legend, the statue of Lady Chua Xu used to stand at the summit of Sam Mountain. In the early 19th century, Siamese troops invaded the area and, impressed with the statue, decided to take it back to Thailand with them. But as they carried the statue down the hill, it became heavier and heavier, and they were forced to abandon it by the side of the path.

One day, villagers out cutting wood came hereupon the statue and decided to bring it

back to their village in order to build a temple for it; but it weighed too much for them to budge. Suddenly, there appeared a girl who, possessed by a spirit, declared herself to be Lady Chua Xu. She announced that 40 virgins were to be brought and that they would be able to transport the statue down the mountainside. The 40 virgins were summoned and carried the statue down the slope, but when they reached the plain, it became too heavy and they had to set it down. The people concluded that the site where the virgins halted had been selected by Lady Chua Xu for the construction of a temple, and it is at that place that the Temple of Lady Chua Xu stands to this day.

Another story relates that the wife of Thoai Ngoc Hau, builder of the Vinh Te Canal, swore to erect a temple when the canal, whose construction claimed many lives, was completed. She died before being able to carry through on her oath, but Thoai Ngoc Hau implemented her plans by building the Temple of Lady Chua Xu.

The temple's most important festival is held from the 23rd to the 26th of the fouth lunar month. During this time, pilgrims flock here, sleeping on mats in the large rooms of the two-storey rest house next to the temple; they are charged only US$0.05 a night.

Tomb of Thoai Ngoc Hau Thoai Ngoc Hau (1761-1829) was a high-ranking official who served the Nguyen Lords and, later, the Nguyen Dynasty. In early 1829, Thoai Ngoc Hau ordered that a tomb be constructed for himself at the foot of Sam Mountain. The site he chose is not far from Tay An Pagoda.

The steps are made of red 'beehive' (*da ong*) stone brought from the eastern part of southern Vietnam. In the middle of the platform is the tomb of Thoai Ngoc Hau and those of his wives, Chau Thi Te and Truong Thi Miet. Nearby are several dozen other tombs where officials who served under Thoai Ngoc Hau are buried.

Cavern Pagoda The Cavern Pagoda (Chua Hang, also known as Phuoc Dien Tu) is about halfway up the western side of Sam Mountain. The lower part of the pagoda includes monks' quarters and two hexagonal tombs in which the founder of the pagoda, a female tailor named Le Thi Tho, and a former head monk, Thich Hue Thien, are buried.

The upper section consists of two parts: the main sanctuary, in which there are statues of A Di Da (the Buddha of the Past) and Thich Ca Buddha (Sakyamuni); and the cavern. At the back of the cave, which is behind the sanctuary building, is a shrine dedicated to Quan The Am Bo Tat (the Goddess of Mercy).

According to legend, Le Thi Tho came from Tay An Pagoda to this site half a century ago to lead a quiet, meditative life. When she arrived, she found two enormous snakes, one white and the other dark green. Le Thi Tho soon converted the snakes, who thereafter led pious lives. Upon her death, the snakes disappeared.

Places to Eat For tasty Vietnamese specialities (including cobra and turtle) try *Hoa Phuong Restaurant* between Tay An Pagoda and the tomb of Thoai Ngoc Hau. This place has a huge garden. *Bong Diep Restaurant* is across from the Tomb of Thoai Ngoc Hau; the selection here is similar to Hoa Phuong Restaurant but the food is not as good.

RACH GIA
RACH GIÁ

Rach Gia, the capital of Kien Giang Province, is a relaxing port-city on the Gulf of Thailand. The population of about 120,000 includes significant numbers of ethnic-Chinese and Khmers. The economy of the area is based on fishing and agriculture. The Rach Gia area was once famous as the source of large feathers used to make ceremonial fans for the Imperial Court.

Orientation
To get into town from the bus station, head north on Nguyen Trung Truc St, which becomes Le Loi St when you cross the channel. The heart of the city, where most of the hotels and restaurants are found, is between Le Loi St and Tran Phu St on the island.

Information
Tourist Office Kien Giang Tourist (Cong Ty Du Lich Kien Giang; ☎ 62081, 63824) – the provincial tourism authority – is at 12 Ly Tu Trong St. The Tourism Management Office (Phong Dieu Hanh Du Lich; ☎ 63669) is at 50 Nguyen Hung Son St.

Money Vietcombank (Ngan Hang Ngoai

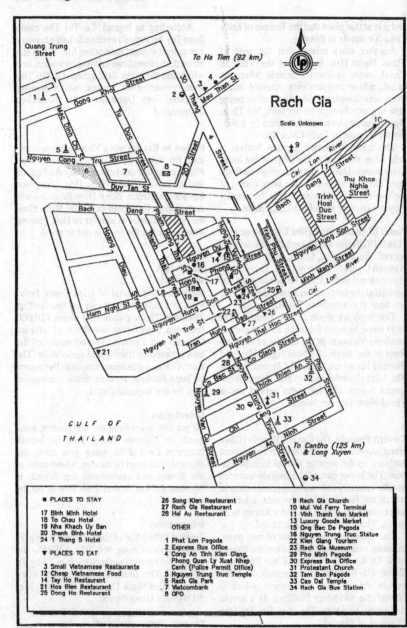

Rach Gia

Scale Unknown

To Ha Tien (92 km)

CULF OF THAILAND

To Cantho (125 km) & Long Xuyen

■ **PLACES TO STAY**

17 Binh Minh Hotel
18 To Chau Hotel
19 Nha Khach Uy Ban
20 Thanh Binh Hotel
24 1 Thang 5 Hotel

▼ **PLACES TO EAT**

3 Small Vietnamese Restaurants
12 Cheap Vietnamese Food
14 Tay Ho Restaurant
21 Hoa Bien Restaurant
25 Dong Ho Restaurant

26 Song Kien Restaurant
27 Rach Gia Restaurant
28 Hai Au Restaurant

OTHER

1 Phat Lon Pagoda
2 Express Bus Office
4 Cong An Tinh Kien Giang, Phong Quan Ly Xuat Nhap Canh (Police Permit Office)
5 Nguyen Trung Truc Temple
6 Rach Gia Park
7 Vietcombank
8 GPO

9 Rach Gia Church
10 Mui Voi Ferry Terminal
11 Vinh Thanh Van Market
13 Luxury Goods Market
15 Ong Bac De Pagoda
16 Nguyen Trung Truc Statue
22 Kien Giang Tourism
23 Rach Gia Museum
29 Pho Minh Pagoda
30 Express Bus Office
31 Protestant Church
32 Tam Bao Pagoda
33 Cao Dai Temple
34 Rach Gia Bus Station

Thuong Viet Nam) is at 2 Duy Tan, next to the GPO.

Post & Telecommunications The GPO is across the channel from the intersection of Tu Duc St and Bach Dang St.

Travel Permit If you want to overnight in Ha Tien (even just one night), you *must* get a travel permit from the police in Rach Gia. This is very important! The official excuse for requiring the permit is that 'Ha Tien is near the Cambodian border'. The real reason is to squeeze US$3 out of you for another worthless piece of paper.

The place where you get the permit is a mouthful: 'Cong An Tinh Kien Giang, Phong Quan Ly Xuat Nhap Canh'. The address is 69 Mau Than St. It's an obscure building but can be readily identified by two stars. The permit can be issued in five minutes.

Pagodas & Temples
Nguyen Trung Truc Temple This temple is dedicated to Nguyen Trung Truc, a leader of the Vietnamese resistance campaign of the 1860s against the newly arrived French. Among other exploits, he led the raid that resulted in the burning of the French warship *Espérance*. Despite repeated attempts to capture him, Nguyen Trung Truc continued to fight until 1868, when the French took his mother and a number of civilians hostage and threatened to kill them if he did not surrender. Nguyen Trung Truc turned himself in and was executed by the French in the marketplace of Rach Gia on 27 October 1868.

The first temple structure was a simple building with a thatched roof; over the years it has been enlarged and rebuilt several times. The last reconstruction took place between 1964 and 1970. In the centre of the main hall on an altar is a portrait of Nguyen Trung Truc.

Nguyen Trung Truc Temple is at 18 Nguyen Cong Tru St and is open from 7 am to 6 pm.

Phat Lon Pagoda This large Cambodian Hinayana Buddhist pagoda, whose name means Big Buddha, was founded about two centuries ago. Though all of the three dozen monks who live here are ethnic-Khmers, ethnic-Vietnamese also frequent the pagoda. Prayers are held daily from 4 to 6 am and from 5 to 7 pm. The pagoda, off Quang Trung St, is open from 4 am to 5 pm during the seventh, eighth and ninth lunar months (the summer season) but guests are welcome year-round.

Inside the sanctuary *(vihara)*, the figures of Sakyamuni, the historical Buddha, all wear Cambodian and Thai-style pointed hats. Around the exterior of the main hall are eight small altars. The two towers near the main entrance are used to cremate the bodies of deceased monks. Near the pagoda are the tombs of about two dozen monks.

Ong Bac De Pagoda Ong Bac De Pagoda, in the centre of town at 14 Nguyen Du St, was built by Rach Gia's Chinese community about a century ago. On the central altar is a statue of Ong Bac De, a reincarnation of the Emperor of Jade. To the left is Ong Bon, Guardian Spirit of Happiness and Virtue; to the right is Quan Cong (in Chinese, Kuan Kung).

Pho Minh Pagoda Two Buddhist nuns live at Pho Minh Pagoda, which is at the corner of Co Bac St and Nguyen Van Cu St. This small pagoda was built in 1967 and contains a large Thai-style Thich Ca Buddha (Sakyamuni) donated in 1971 by a Buddhist organisation in Thailand. Nearby is a Vietnamese-style Thich Ca Buddha. The nuns live in a building behind the main hall. The pagoda is open to visitors from 6 am to 10 pm; prayers are held daily from 3.30 to 4.30 am and 6.30 to 7.30 pm.

Tam Bao Pagoda Tam Bao Pagoda, which dates from the early 19th century, is near the corner of Thich Thien An St and Tran Phu St; it was last rebuilt in 1913. The garden contains numerous trees sculpted as dragons, deer and other animals. The pagoda is open from 6 am to 8 pm; prayers are held from 4.30 to 5.30 am and 5.30 to 6.30 pm.

Cao Dai Temple There is a small Cao Dai Temple, constructed in 1969, at 189 Nguyen Trung Truc St, which is not far from Rach Gia Bus Station.

Churches
Rach Gia Church Rach Gia Church (Nha Tho Chanh Toa Rach Gia), a red brick structure built in 1918, is in Vinh Thanh Van subdistrict, across the channel from Vinh Thanh Van Market. Weekday masses are held from 5 to 6 am and 5 to 6 pm; Sunday masses are from 5 to 6 am, 7 to 8 am, 4 to 5 pm and 5 to 6 pm.

Protestant Church Services are held every Sunday from 10 am to noon at the Protestant Church, built in 1972, which is at 133 Nguyen Trung Truc St.

Rach Gia Museum
The refurbished Rach Gia Museum is at 21 Nguyen Van Troi St.

Vinh Thanh Van Market
Vinh Thanh Van Market, Rach Gia's main market area, stretches along Bach Dang St, Trinh Hoai Duc St and Thu Khoa Nghia St east of Tran Phu St.

The luxury goods market is between Hoang Hoa Tham St and Pham Hong Thai St.

Places to Stay
The *Nha Khach Uy Ban* (☎ 63237; 12 rooms) is a very basic but cheap hotel at 31 Nguyen Hung Son St. Singles/doubles with fan and shared bath cost US$1.30/1.50. OK for the desperate.

The *Thanh Binh Hotel* (☎ 63053; nine rooms) is an OK place though nothing to write home about. All rooms have fan and private bath. Singles/doubles cost US$6/8. The hotel is at 11 Ly Tu Trong St.

Somewhat better is the *Binh Minh Hotel* (☎ 62154; 15 rooms) at 48 Pham Hong Thai St. Double rooms with fan cost US$6 and

US$8 while air-conditioned rooms are US$10 and US$15.

The comfortable *1 Thang 5 Hotel* (☎ 62103; 26 rooms) is at 39 Nguyen Hung Son St. This place is also known as Khach San 1.5. Singles/doubles with fan and shared bath are US$5/7. With air-con and private bath, doubles/triples are US$10/15.

The *To Chau Hotel* (☎ 63718; 31 rooms), the best in town, is at 4F Le Loi St (next to the Thang Loi Cinema). If you're arriving by car, your driver will much appreciate the fact that the hotel has a garage. All rooms are air-conditioned and have private bath. Prices range from US$10 to US$20.

Places to Eat
Rach Gia is known for its seafood, dried cuttlefish, ca thieu (dried fish slices), nuoc mam (fish sauce) and black pepper.

For deer, turtle, cobra, eel, frog and cuttlefish (as well as more conventional fare), try the *Hoa Bien Restaurant*, which is on the water at the western end of Nguyen Hung Son St. There is no sandy beach here, but the restaurant sets up lawn chairs for their customers to admire the view.

The *Tay Ho Restaurant* at 16 Nguyen Du St serves good Chinese and Vietnamese food. The *Dong Ho Restaurant* at 124 Tran Phu St has Chinese, Vietnamese and Western dishes. Other places you might try are the *Rach Gia Restaurant*, on the water at the intersection of Ly Tu Trong St and Tran Hung Dao St, and the *Song Kien Restaurant*, which is a block away at the intersection of Tran Hung Dao St and Hung Vuong St. The *Hai Au Restaurant* is at the corner of Nguyen Trung Truc St and Nguyen Van Cu St.

Cheap, tasty Vietnamese food is sold along Hung Vuong St between Bach Dang St and Le Hong Phong St. There are several small Vietnamese restaurants on Mau Thanh St near the intersection of 30 Thanh 4 St.

There are restaurants in the *To Chau Hotel*, *Binh Minh Hotel* and the *1 Thang 5 Hotel*.

Getting There & Away
Air Rach Gia has an airport, but at the time

of writing there were no regularly scheduled flights. Vietnam Airlines has contemplated the possibility of chartered flights.

Bus Buses from Ho Chi Minh City to Rach Gia leave from the Mien Tay Bus Station in An Lac; the express bus takes six to seven hours. An express minibus from Ho Chi Minh City to Rach Gia departs from an office (☎ 93318) at 83 Cach Mang Thang Tam St (half a block from the Immigration Police Office) once every three days; the trip, which begins at 4 am, costs US$2.25.

The Rach Gia Bus Station (Ben Xe Kien Giang; ☎ 3430, 2185) is south of the city on Nguyen Trung Truc St (towards Long Xuyen and Cantho). Non-express buses link Rach Gia with Cantho, Dong Thap (departs once a day at 7 am), Ha Tien, Ho Chi Minh City and Long Xuyen. There are daily express buses to Ho Chi Minh City (departs 4.30 am) and Ha Tien (leaves 2.30 am). Bus services to rural areas near Rach Gia operate between 3.30 am and 4.30 pm. Destinations include Duong Xuong, Giong Rieng, Go Quao, Hon Chong, Kien Luong, Soc Xoai, Tan Hiep, Tri Ton and Vinh Thuan.

There is an express bus office at 33, 30 Thang 4 St offering daily express service to Cantho (departs 5 am), Ha Tien (leaves 4.30 am) and Ho Chi Minh City (departs 3.45 am). Another express bus to Ho Chi Minh City leaves every morning at 4 am from Trung Tam Du Lich Thanh Nien, which is at 78 Nguyen Trung Truc St.

Car Rach Gia is 92 km from Ha Tien, 125 km from Cantho and 248 km from Ho Chi Minh City.

Boat Mui Voi Ferry Terminal (*mui* means nose and *voi* means elephant – so named because of the shape of the island) is at the north-eastern end of Bach Dang St. Boats from here make daily trips to Chau Doc (at 5.30 pm), Long Xuyen (at 12.30 pm) and Tan Chau (at 4.30 pm).

Getting Around
The main forms of ground transport in Rach Gia are cyclos and xe dap lois.

AROUND RACH GIA
Ancient City of Oc-Eo
Oc-Eo was a major trading city during the 1st to 6th centuries AD, when this area (along with the rest of southern Vietnam, much of southern Cambodia and the Malay Peninsula) was ruled by the Indianised empire of Funan. Much of what is known about Funan, which reached its height in the 5th century AD, comes from contemporary Chinese sources (eg the accounts of Chinese emissaries and travellers) and the archaeological excavations at Oc-Eo, which have uncovered evidence of significant contact between Oc-Eo and what is now Thailand, Malaysia, Indonesia, Persia and even the Roman Empire.

An elaborate system of canals around Oc-Eo was used for both irrigation and transportation, prompting Chinese travellers of the time to write about 'sailing across Funan' on their way to the Malay peninsula. Most of the buildings of Oc-Eo were built on piles, and pieces of these structures indicate the high degree of refinement achieved by Funanese civilisation. Artefacts found at Oc-Eo are on display in Ho Chi Minh City at the History Museum and the Art Museum and in Hanoi at the History Museum.

The remains of Oc-Eo are not far from Rach Gia. The site itself, a hill 11 km inland littered with potsherds and shells, is near Vong The village, which can be reached by jeep from Hue Duc village, a distance of about eight km. Oc-Eo is most easily accessible during the dry season. Special permission may be required to visit; for more information, contact Kien Giang Tourist.

HA TIEN
HÀ TIÊN
Ha Tien (population 80,000) is on the Gulf of Thailand eight km from the Cambodian border. The area, famous for its nearby white-sand beaches and fishing villages, is also known for its production of seafood,

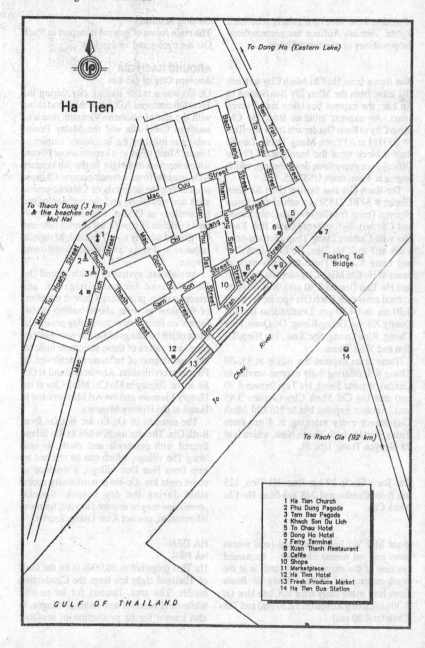

Ha Tien

To Dong Ho (Eastern Lake)

To Thach Dong (3 km)
& the beaches of
Mui Nai

Floating Toll
Bridge

Chau River

To Rach Gia (92 km)

GULF OF THAILAND

1 Ha Tien Church
2 Phu Dung Pagoda
3 Tam Bao Pagoda
4 Khach San Du Lich
5 To Chau Hotel
6 Dong Ho Hotel
7 Ferry Terminal
8 Xuan Thanh Restaurant
9 Cafés
10 Shops
11 Marketplace
12 Ha Tien Hotel
13 Fresh Produce Market
14 Ha Tien Bus Station

black pepper and items made from the shells of sea turtles. All around the area are lovely, towering limestone formations that give this place a very different appearance from the rest of the Mekong Delta region. The rock formations support a network of caves, many of which have been turned into cave temples. Plantations of black-pepper trees cling to the hillsides in places where it's not too steep. On a clear day, Phu Quoc Island is visible across the water to the west.

Ha Tien was a province of Cambodia until 1708 when, in the face of attacks by the Thais, the Khmer-appointed governor, a Chinese immigrant named Mac Cuu, turned to the Vietnamese for protection and assistance. Mac Cuu thereafter governed this area as a fiefdom under the protection of the Nguyen Lords. He was succeeded as ruler by his son, Mac Thien Tu. During the 18th century, the area was invaded and pillaged several times by the Thais. Rach Gia and the southern tip of the Mekong Delta came under direct Nguyen rule in 1798.

During the rule of the genocidal Khmer Rouge regime in Cambodia (1975-79), Khmer Rouge forces repeatedly attacked Vietnamese territory and massacred hundreds of civilians. The entire populations of Ha Tien and nearby villages – tens of thousands of people – fled their homes. During this period, areas north of Ha Tien (along the Cambodian border) were sown with mines and booby-traps which have yet to be cleared.

Orientation

The main drag is Ben Tran Hau St, which runs along the To Chau River; it turns northward just north-east of the floating toll bridge. The city's fresh produce market and general marketplace are between Ben Tran Hau St and the To Chau River. Few of Ha Tien's buildings are numbered.

Information

Travel Permit If you want to overnight in Ha Tien, you must get a travel permit from the police in Rach Gia. See the Rach Gia section for details.

Pagodas & Temples

Tombs of the Family of Mac Cuu The Tombs of the Family of Mac Cuu (Lang Mac Cuu) are on a low ridge not far from town. They are known locally simply as Nui Lang, the Hill of the Tombs. Several dozen relatives of Mac Cuu, Chinese émigré and 18th-century ruler of this area, are buried here in traditional Chinese tombs decorated with figures of dragons, phoenixes, lions and guardians.

The largest tomb is that of Mac Cuu himself; it was constructed in 1809 on the orders of Emperor Gia Long and is decorated with finely carved figures of Thanh Long (the Green Dragon) and Bach Ho (the White Tiger). The tomb of Mac Cuu's first wife is flanked by dragons and phoenixes. At the bottom of the ridge is a shrine dedicated to the Mac family.

Tam Bao Pagoda Tam Bao Pagoda, also known as Sac Tu Tam Bao Tu, was founded by Mac Cuu in 1730. It is now home to seven Buddhist nuns. In front of the pagoda is a statue of Quan The Am Bo Tat (the Goddess of Mercy) standing on a lotus blossom in the middle of a pond. Inside the sanctuary, the largest statue on the dais is of A Di Da Buddha, the Buddha of the Past. It is made of bronze but has been painted. Outside the building are the tombs of 16 monks.

Near Tam Bao Pagoda is a section of the city wall dating from the early 18th century.

Tam Bao Pagoda is at 328 Phuong Thanh St and is open from 7 am to 9 pm; prayers are held from 8 to 9 am and 2 to 3 pm. From the 15th day of the fourth lunar month to the 15th day of the seventh lunar month (roughly from May to August) prayers are held six times a day.

Phu Dung Pagoda Phu Dung Pagoda, also called Phu Cu Am Tu, was founded in the mid-18th century by Mac Cuu's second wife, Nguyen Thi Xuan. It is now home to one monk.

In the middle of the main hall is a peculiar statue of nine dragons embracing newly born Thich Ca Buddha (Sakyamuni, born Siddhartha Gautama). The most interesting statue on the main dais is a bronze Thich Ca Buddha brought from China; it is kept in a glass case. On the hillside behind the main hall are the tombs of Nguyen Thi Xuan and one of her female servants; nearby are four monks' tombs.

Behind the main hall is a small temple, Dien Ngoc Hoang, dedicated to the Taoist Emperor of Jade. The figures inside are of Ngoc Hoang flanked by Nam Tao, the Taoist God of the Southern Polar Star and the God of Happiness (on the right) and Bac Dao, the Taoist God of the Northern Polar Star and the God of Longevity (on the left). The statues are made of papier mâché moulded over bamboo frames.

Phu Dung Pagoda is open from 6 am to 10 pm; prayers are held from 4 to 5 am and 7 to 8 pm. To get to Phu Dung Pagoda, turn off Phuong Thanh St next to number 374.

Thach Dong

Thach Dong, the Stone Cavern, also known as Chua Thanh Van, is a subterranean Vietnamese Buddhist temple 3.5 km from town on Mac Tu Hoang St.

To the left of the entrance is the Stele of Hatred (Bia Cam Thu) commemorating the massacre of 130 people here by the forces of Khmer Rouge leader Pol Pot on 14 March 1979.

Several chambers of the grotto contain funerary tablets and altars to Ngoc Hoang (the Emperor of Jade), Quan The Am Bo Tat (the Goddess of Mercy) and the two Buddhist monks who founded the temples of Thach Dong. The wind creates extraordinary sounds as it blows through the grotto's passageways. Openings in several branches of the cave afford views of nearby Cambodia.

Dong Ho

Dong Ho (dong means east; ho means lake) is in fact not a lake at all but an inlet of the sea. The 'lake' is just east of Ha Tien on Ben Tran Hau St, and bound to the east by a chain of granite hills known at the Ngu Ho (five tigers) and to the west by hills known as To Chan. Dong Ho is said to be most beautiful on nights when there is a full or almost-full moon. According to legend, it is on such nights that fairies dance here in the moonlight.

Ha Tien Market

Ha Tien has an excellent market along the To Chau River. It's well worth your while to stop in here – many of the goods are imported (smuggled?) from Thailand and Cambodia, and prices are lower than you can find in Ho Chi Minh City. Cigarette smuggling is a particularly big business.

Places to Stay

The To Chau Hotel (with eight rooms) on To Chau St is the cheapest in town with rooms for US$1.80. You get what you pay for – the bath and toilet are outside and many rooms lack ceiling fans.

The Dong Ho Hotel (☎ 52141; 18 rooms) is simple but acceptable. Rooms cost US$5. The bath is attached but the toilet is outside the rooms. The hotel is near the floating bridge at the corner of Ben Tran Hau St and To Chau St.

The Ha Tien Hotel is at the corner of Ben Tran Hau St and Phuong Thanh St. At the time of this writing, only cadres and other persons of note were being permitted to stay here.

Most foreigners stay at the Khach San Du Lich (☎ 8644) on Mac Thien Tich St. Large, echo chamber rooms cost US$10 and can sleep up to four persons. This is the only place in town where rooms have an attached bath and toilet. There are good ceiling fans but no air-conditioning.

Places to Eat

Ha Tien's speciality is an unusual variety of coconut which grows only in this area. Restaurants all around the Ha Tien area serve the coconut milk in a glass with ice, sugar and strips of coconut meat.

The Xuan Thanh Restaurant is opposite the market at the corner of Ben Tran Hau and Tham Tuong Sanh Sts. This place has best food in town and the most salubrious surroundings.

There is a whole collection of small cafes

on Ben Tran Hau St adjacent to the floating bridge. These places can do the usual noodle and rice dishes.

The *Khach San Du Lich* has a basic restaurant but it is not especially recommended.

Getting There & Away

Bus Buses from Ho Chi Minh City to Ha Tien leave from the Mien Tay Bus Station in An Lac; the trip takes nine to 10 hours.

Ha Tien Bus Station (Ben Xe Ha Tien) is on the other side of the floating toll bridge from the centre of town. Buses leave from here to An Giang Province, Cantho (at 5.50 am and 9.10 am), Vinh Long Province, Ho Chi Minh City (at 2 am) and Rach Gia (five times a day). The bus trip from Rach Gia to Ha Tien takes about five hours.

Car Ha Tien is 92 km from Rach Gia, 95 km from Chau Doc, 206 km from Cantho, 338 km from Ho Chi Minh City and 225 km from Phnom Penh (via Kampot). The road between Rach Gia and Ha Tien is in a dismal state of repair. Travelling along this route you pass the largest cement factory in Vietnam at Kien Luong – too bad some of that cement isn't being used to repair the road.

Boat Passenger ferries dock at the Ferry Terminal, which is not far from the To Chau Hotel next to the floating bridge. Daily ferries depart for Chau Doc at 6 am and for Tinh Bien (Cambodian border) at 11 am and noon. You can travel by boat all the way from Ho Chi Minh City to Ha Tien with a change of boats in Chau Doc, but it's a long journey and the boats are anything but luxurious.

It may be possible to travel between Rach Gia and Ha Tien by scheduled or chartered boat; for more information, ask around each town's quay.

Getting Around

The tolls for the floating bridge across the To Chau River are US$0.03 for a person, half

that for a bicycle and US$0.50 for a motorbike.

The main form of local transport is the xe dap loi.

AROUND HA TIEN

Beaches Near Town

The beaches in this part of Vietnam face the Gulf of Thailand. The water is incredibly warm and calm, like a placid lake. They're good for bathing and diving but hopeless for surfing.

Mui Nai (Stag's Head Peninsula) is four km west of Ha Tien; it is said to resemble the head of a stag with its mouth pointing upward. On top is a lighthouse; there are sand beaches on both sides of the peninsula. Mui Nai is accessible by road from both the town of Ha Tien and from Thach Dong.

No Beach (Bai No), lined with coconut palms, is several km west of Ha Tien near a fishing village. Bang Beach (Bai Bang) is a long stretch of dark sand shaded by *bang* trees.

Mo So Grotto

About 17 km towards Rach Gia from Ha Tien and three km from the road, Mo So Grotto consists of three large rooms and a labyrinth of tunnels. The cave is accessible on foot during the dry season and by small boat during the wet season. Visitors should have torches (flashlights) and a local guide.

Hang Tien Grotto

Hang Tien Grotto, 25 km towards Rach Gia from Ha Tien, served as a hide-out for Nguyen Anh (later Emperor Gia Long) in 1784, when he was being pursued by the Tay Son Rebels. His fighters found zinc coins buried here, a discovery which gave the cave its name, which means Coin Grotto. Hang Tien Grotto is accessible by boat.

Chua Hang Grotto & Duong Beach

Chua Hang Grotto is entered through a Buddhist temple set against the base of the hill. The temple is called Hai Son Tu (Sea Mountain Temple). Visitors light joss sticks and offer prayers here before entering the grotto itself, whose entrance is behind the altar. Inside is a plaster statue of Quan The Am Bo Tat (the Goddess of Mercy). The thick stalactites are hollow and resonate like bells when tapped.

From Chua Hang Grotto, you can see Father & Son Isle (Hon Phu Tu) several hundred metres offshore; it is said to be shaped like a father embracing his son. The island, a column of stone, is perched on a 'foot' worn away by the pounding of the waves; the foot is most fully exposed at low tide.

Duong Beach (Bai Duong), next to Chua Hang Grotto, is one of the nicest beaches in the Ha Tien area. It is known for its *duong* trees, white sand, clear water and absence of underwater rocks. The beach is bounded by the Hon Trem peninsula.

Places to Stay There is a reasonably comfortable hotel about one km from Duong Beach called *Nha Nghi Binh An*. It's a very quiet place in a large compound surrounded by a wall with gardens inside. Rooms have private bath and electric fan, but no air-conditioning, and cost US$4 per night. There is no electricity after 10 pm.

Places to Eat There are food stalls just by the entrance of Chua Hang Grotto. For a few dollars, you can point to one of their live chickens which will be summarily executed and barbecued right on the spot.

This is also a good place to sample the delicious Ha Tien coconuts which only grow is this part of Vietnam.

Getting There & Away Chua Hang Grotto and Duong Beach are about 32 km toward Rach Gia from Ha Tien. To get here, you may have to hire a car or motorbike – expect a rough ride over a dirt road.

Hon Giang Island

Hon Giang Island, which is about 15 km from Ha Tien and can be reached by small boat, has a lovely, secluded beach. There are numerous other islands off the coast between Rach Gia and the Cambodian border. Some local people make a living gathering precious salangane or swifts' nests (the most important ingredient of that famous Chinese delicacy, bird's nest soup) on the islands' rocky cliffs.

PHU QUOC ISLAND
ĐẢO PHÚ QUỐC

Mountainous and forested Phu Quoc Island (population 18,000) is in the Gulf of Thailand, 45 km west of Ha Tien and 15 km south of the coast of Cambodia. The tear-shaped island, which is 48 km long and has an area of 1320 sq km, is governed as a district of Kien Giang Province. The island's fishing

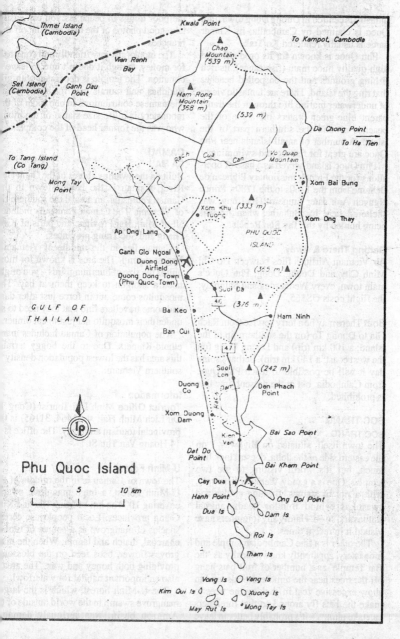

Phu Quoc Island

GULF OF THAILAND

Thmei Island (Cambodia)

Kwala Point

To Kampot, Cambodia

Vien Renh Bay

Set Island (Cambodia)

Ganh Dau Point

Chao Mountain (539 m)

Ham Rong Mountain (368 m)

(539 m)

Da Chong Point

To Ha Tien

To Tang Island (Co Tang)

Rach Cua Can

Vo Quap Mountain

Mong Tay Point

Xom Bai Bung

Xom Khu Tuong

(333 m)

Xom Ong Thay

PHU QUOC ISLAND

Ap Ong Lang

Ganh Gio Ngoai

Duong Dong Airfield

Duong Dong Town (Phu Quoc Town)

(365 m)

Suoi Da

46

(376 m)

Ba Keo

Ham Ninh

Ban Cui

47

Suoi Lon

Dam

(242 m)

Duong Co

Den Phach Point

Xom Duong Dam

Rach

Kien Van

Bai Sao Point

Dat Do Point

Bai Kham Point

Cay Dua

Hanh Point

Ong Doi Point

Dua Is

Dam Is

Roi Is

Tham Is

Vong Is

Vang Is

Kim Qui Is

Xuong Is

May Rut Is

Mong Tay Is

0   5   10 km

industry is centred in Duong Dong town. Phu Quoc is claimed by Cambodia; its Khmer name is usually rendered Ko Tral.

Phu Quoc is known for its production of high-quality nuoc mam (fish sauce), its rich fishing grounds and the unspoiled beaches that ring the island. There are fantastic views of underwater marine life through the transparent blue-green waters off some of the beaches around the southern part of the island. A number of small islands near Phu Quoc are great for fishing and swimming.

Phu Quoc Island served as a base of operations for the French missionary Pigneau de Behaine from the 1760s to the 1780s. Prince Nguyen Anh, later Emperor Gia Long, was sheltered here by Behaine when he was being hunted by the Tay Son Rebels.

Getting There & Away

Air Vietnam Airlines flies between Ho Chi Minh City and Duong Dong, Phu Quoc's main town, every Wednesday and Saturday; the flight costs US$65.

Boat There may be a ferry service from Rach Gia to Duong To (on the southern tip of the island; a 100 km trip) and Duong Dong (on the west coast; a 140 km trip). Perhaps some day it will be possible to reach Phu Quoc from Cambodia, but at the present time this is prohibited.

SOC TRANG
SÓC TRĂNG

The town itself, situated on Highway 1 on the eastern side of the delta, doesn't look like much, but it's worth visiting to see two temples. One is a gaudy Vietnamese temple, with a riot of statues, flashing circles and swastikas behind Buddha heads, animal statues and so on. Hardly any foreigners have visited it in recent times.

The other is a fine Cambodian temple and monastery, apparently known locally as 'the Bat Temple' as a number of fruit bats hang off the trees near the temple. Locals tend to show excessive zeal in shaking the trees to make the bats fly around so that foreigners can take photos – it's probably better to leave the poor things in peace, as you can easily take good photos of the bats hanging off the branches.

The monks are very friendly and don't ask for money, though it doesn't hurt to leave a donation. The temple is decorated with gil Buddhas, and murals paid for by Overseas Vietnamese contributors. In one room of the monastery is a life-size statue of the monk who was the former head of the complex.

CAMAU
CÀ MAU

Built on the swampy shores of the Ganh Hao River, Camau is the largest town in the Camau Peninsula, an area at the southern tip of Vietnam. The Camau Peninsula includes all of Minh Hai Province and parts of Kien Giang and Soc Trang provinces.

Camau lies in the middle of Vietnam's largest swamp. The area is known for mosquitos the size of hummingbirds – you might need a shotgun to keep them at bay. The mosquitos come out in force just after dark and some travellers find that they need to sit under their mosquito net just to eat dinner.

The population of Camau includes many ethnic-Khmers. Due to the boggy terrain this area has the lowest population density in southern Vietnam.

Information

Tourist Office Minh Hai Tourist (Cong Ty Du Lich Minh Hai; ☎ 31464, 31165) is the provincial tourism authority. The office is at 14 Hoang Van Thu St.

U-Minh Forest

The town of Camau is in the middle of the U-Minh Forest, a huge mangrove swamp covering 1000 sq km of Minh Hai and Kien Giang provinces. Local people use certain species of mangrove as a source of timber, charcoal, thatch and tannin. When the mangroves flower, bees feed on the blossom providing both honey and wax. The area also an important habitat for waterfowl.

The U-Minh Forest, which is the largest mangrove swamp in the world outside of the Amazon basin, was seriously damaged during the Vietnam War by American aerial defoliation. Despite replanting efforts, 20% of Camau's tidal mangrove forests are still a wasteland of rotting stumps protruding from the murky waters. What Agent Orange started, the locals are finishing – the mangrove forests are being further reduced by clearing for shrimp-raising ponds, charcoal making and wood chipping.

There are supposed to be several 'bird parks' somewhere outside Camau; that is, patches of untouched forest with large populations of wild birds. According to some travellers, however, even locals in the small villages along the network of river channels are unsure of the exact location of these 'parks' and patches of pristine forest are not easy to find.

Zoo

Camau has a zoo, with a poorly maintained collection of miserable animals. In the grounds of the zoo, along with a few noisy cafes, is a 'botanic garden', which looks rather like a half-acre patch of weeds. In short, there is nothing particularly inviting to see or do here.

Places to Stay

Most of the hotels that are allowed to have foreigners (some don't have the necessary permit) are in a strip along Phan Ngoc Hien St. To judge by the young women loitering around the lobby of many of the hotels, even the US$50 a night ones, most of these establishments double as brothels.

One that is definitely a brothel is the *Khach San Sao Mai*, on the corner of Phan Ngoc Hien & Duong Ly Bon Sts. Rooms are pretty grotty, some to the point of being uninhabitable. They cost from US$6.50 for a windowless, grubby single, with common bathroom (which is not only unsafe for women but indescribably filthy), to US$7.50 for a marginally acceptable double, with its own cold-water bathroom and non-flushing Western toilet. Although the Sao Mai has a 'restaurant', it serves no food, only beer for brothel patrons. One traveller reported that their room had the 'mother of all black spiderwebs' in one corner.

Most of the rest of the hotels are in the US$25-plus league; the most luxurious being the *Phuong Nam Hotel*, on the corner of Phan Ngoc Hien & Pham Dinh Phong Sts. It costs from US$30 to US$50 for singles/doubles.

Places to Eat

There is a cluster of small roadside restaurants on Ly Bon St, at the entrance to the market. They are very cheap and the food is OK, but nothing special.

Getting There & Away

Bus Buses from Ho Chi Minh City to Camau leave from Mien Tay Bus Station in An Lac. The trip takes 12 hours by regular bus and 10 hours by express bus.

Car Camau is 179 km from Cantho and 348 km from Ho Chi Minh City. The road is in dismal condition. A high-clearance vehicle like a van is much preferred on this road to a low late-model luxury car.

Boat Boats run between Camau and Ho Chi Minh City approximately once every four days. The trip takes 30 hours.

Getting Around

Camau has plenty of cyclos, motorbikes and xe dap lois, so getting around on land is no problem. There are also plenty of water taxis along the river at the back of the market. For longer trips upriver, larger longboats collect at a cluster of jetties just outside the market area. You can either join the throngs of passengers going downriver or hire the whole boat for about US$5 an hour.

Central Highlands
Cao Nguyên Miền Trung

The Central Highlands cover the southern part of the Truong Son Mountain Range (Annamite Cordillera) and include the provinces of Lam Dong, Dac Lac (Dak Lak), Gia Lai and Kon Tum. The region, which is home to many ethno-linguistic minority groups (Montagnards), is renowned for its cool climate, beautiful mountain scenery and innumerable streams, lakes and waterfalls.

Though the population of the Central Highlands is only about two million, the area has always been considered strategically important. During the Vietnam War, considerable fighting took place around Buon Ma Thuot, Pleiku and Kontum.

With the exception of Lam Dong Province (in which Dalat is located), the Central Highlands was, until recently, closed to foreigners. Even Westerners with legitimate business in the area were arrested and sent back to Ho Chi Minh City. This extreme sensitivity stemmed partly from the limited nature of central government control of remote areas, as well as a concern that secret 're-education camps' (rumoured to be hidden in the region) would be discovered and publicised.

The situation has changed. Most of the Central Highlands is open to foreigners now. However, there is one glaring exception: citizens of the USA are still prohibited from visiting any part of the Central Highlands except Lam Dong Province (Dalat area). The reason given for this policy has to do with alleged continuing US support for an organisation called FULRO.

Vietnam is still accusing FULRO supporters in the USA of channelling weapons and money to the guerrillas; this is the main reason why Vietnam prohibits US citizens from visiting the Central Highlands. The US government denies that FULRO is receiving

---

FULRO – Still Fighting the War

FULRO (Front Unifié de Lutte des Races Opprimées, or the United Front for the Struggle of the Oppressed Races), is a continuing thorn in the side for the Vietnamese government. FULRO is a band of well-organised guerrillas who were supported by France and later by America, Thailand and China. FULRO's recruits come mainly from Montagnards who feel threatened by Hanoi's policies of: 1) populating the highlands with ethnic-Vietnamese settlers, especially in New Economic Zones (NEZs); 2) encouraging the replacement of traditional slash-and-burn agriculture with sedentary farming; 3) promoting Vietnamese language and culture (Vietnamisation); 4) forcibly introducing Communist economic structures (collectivisation, etc); and 5) Communist religious oppression (most Montagnards are Christians).

When the Communists took over in 1975, FULRO's fighters numbered around 10,000. In just four years, over 8000 were killed or captured. Some were killed by the Khmer Rouge when they crossed into Cambodia. Ironically, when Vietnam invaded Cambodia in 1979 to battle the Khmer Rouge, FULRO benefited – the Khmer Rouge started supplying FULRO with weapons and ammunition.

At the time of this writing, FULRO was largely a spent force, with most of its guerrilla bands either dead, captured, living abroad or having given up the fight. However, in 1992, a band of several hundred FULRO adherents was found to be still living in the remote north-eastern corner of Cambodia (Ratanakiri Province) and conducting raids across the border into Vietnam. With the settlement of the Cambodian civil war, all armed factions in that country are supposed to lay down their weapons, and this would include FULRO. However, devoted FULRO guerrillas say they would rather die than concede a Vietnamese victory, and so the insurgency continues even though it is ineffective. ■

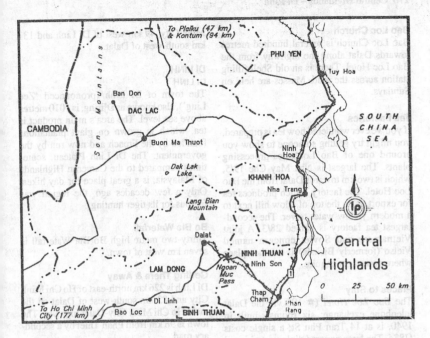

any American assistance. Former FULRO guerrillas living in the USA also say they are no longer supporting the war because they realise it's a lost cause, and have urged their compatriots in Vietnam to cease fighting, apply for refugee status and emigrate abroad. In the meantime, it could be said that for some people, the Vietnam War is still not over.

BAO LOC
BẢO LỘC
The town of Bao Loc (also known as B'Lao; elevation 850 metres) is a convenient place to break the trip between Ho Chi Minh City and Dalat. National Highway 20 is called Tran Phu St as it passes through town. Tea, mulberry leaves (for the silkworm industry) and silk are the major local industries.

For a while after reunification, this area was placed under an 8 pm to dawn curfew because of the FULRO insurgency.

Bay Tung Falls
The trail to the Bay Tung Falls (Thac Bay Tung, which means Seven Steps) begins seven km towards Ho Chi Minh City from the Bao Loc Hotel along National Highway 20 (and three km from the Dai Lao Bridge over the Dai Binh River). The trailhead is in Ap Dai Lao, a hamlet in the village of Xa Loc Chau, behind a refreshments shop run by Ba Hai. The shop is on the right as you travel towards Ho Chi Minh City.

Suoi Mo (the Stream of Dreaming) is 400 metres west of Ba Hai's place along a path that passes among wood and thatch houses set amidst tea bushes, coffee trees and banana and pineapple plants. The path veers left at the stream and becomes torturously slippery as it makes its way along the bamboo and fern-lined bank. The first cascade is about 100 metres straight ahead. Several of the pools along Suoi Mo are swimmable but the water is of uncertain purity.

Bao Loc Church

Bao Loc Church is several hundred metres towards Dalat along the highway from the Bao Loc Hotel. There is an old Shell filling station across the road. Masses are held on Sundays.

Tea Factories

If you've ever wondered how tea is prepared, you might try getting someone to show you around one of Bao Loc's tea-processing plants. The largest is Nha May Che 19/5, which is two km towards Dalat from the Bao Loc Hotel. The factory, which produces tea for export, is on the top of a low hill next to a modern yellow water tower. The second-largest tea factory is named 28/3. A joint Vietnamese and Soviet concern named Vietso (formerly Bisinée) is another place where you might enquire.

Places to Stay

The *Bao Loc Hotel* (☎ 105 via the Dalat telephone exchange; six rooms), built in 1940, is at 14 Tran Phu St; a single costs US$4. The large covered dining area is used to screen videos every evening from 6.30 to 9 pm.

Places to Eat

Local products, sold in shops along Tran Phu St, include avocados, strawberries, jams and honey. Buy a French roll or two and you've got a meal.

The restaurant of the *Bao Loc Hotel* serves Vietnamese food, including dishes featuring venison; European-style food can be special-ordered. There is a restaurant called *Nha Hang 28/3* on National Highway 20 about two km towards Ho Chi Minh City from the Bao Loc Hotel. Other places to eat are strung out along Tran Phu St (National Highway 20) in both directions from the hotel.

Getting There & Away

Bus The bus station is two km from the Bao Loc Hotel.

Car Bao Loc is 177 km north-east of Ho Chi Minh City, 49 km west of Di Linh and 131 km south-west of Dalat.

DI LINH
DI LINH

The town of Di Linh (pronounced 'Zee Ling'), also known as Djiring, is 1010 metres above sea level. The area's main product is tea, which is grown on giant plantations founded by the French and now run by the government. The Di Linh Plateau, sometimes compared to the Cameron Highlands of Malaysia, is a great place for day hikes. Only a few decades ago, the region was famous for its tiger hunting.

Bo Bla Waterfall

Thirty-two metre high Bo Bla Waterfall is seven km west of town.

Getting There & Away

Di Linh is 226 km north-east of Ho Chi Minh City and 82 km south-west of Dalat on the main Ho Chi Minh City-Dalat highway. The town is 96 km from Phan Thiet by a secondary road.

WATERFALLS
Pongour Falls

Pongour Falls, the largest in the Dalat area, is about 55 km towards Ho Chi Minh City from Dalat and seven km off the highway. During the rainy season, the falls form a full semicircle.

Gougah Falls

Gougah Falls is approximately 40 km from Dalat towards Ho Chi Minh City. It is only 500 metres from the highway and is easily accessible.

Lien Khang Falls

At Lien Khang Falls, the Dan Nhim River, 100 metre wide at this point, drops 15 metres over an outcrop of volcanic rock. The site, which can be seen from the highway, is 35 km towards Ho Chi Minh City from Dalat. Lien Khang Falls is not far from Lien Khang airport.

DAN NHIM LAKE
HỒ ĐAN NHIM

Dan Nhim Lake (elevation 1042 metres) was created by a dam built between 1962 and 1964 by the Japanese as part of its war reparations. The huge Dan Nhim hydroelectric project supplies electricity to much of the south.

The surface of the lake (which is often used by Ho Chi Minh City movie studios for filming romantic lakeside scenes) is 9.3 sq km.

The power station is at the western edge of the coastal plain. Water drawn from Dan Nhim Lake gathers speed as it rushes almost a vertical km down from Ngoan Muc Pass in two enormous pipes.

It is said that the forested hills around Dan Nhim Lake are fine for hiking, and that there is good fishing in the area. Unfortunately, you aren't likely to get a chance to find out. Although it was once open to the public, the government now apparently fears that foreign spies and saboteurs are lurking behind every backpack – the whole Dan Nhim Lake area is currently off limits to foreigners. We are including this information here in the hopes that someday the government's paranoia will be ameliorated by the possibilities of earning tourist dollars, and that Dan Nhim Lake will be opened to visitors.

Places to Stay

There is a hotel in Ninh Son, though currently foreigners cannot use it.

Getting There & Away

Dan Nhim Lake is about 38 km from Dalat in the Don Duong District of Lam Dong Province. As you head towards Phan Rang, the dam is about a km to the left of the Dalat-Phan Rang highway. The power station is at the base of Ngoan Muc Pass near the town of Ninh Son.

NGOAN MUC PASS
ĐÈO NGOAN MỤC

Ngoan Muc Pass (altitude 980 metres), known to the French as Bellevue Pass, is about five km towards Phan Rang from Dan Nhim Lake and 64 km west of Phan Rang. On a clear day, you can see all the way across the coastal plain to the Pacific Ocean, an aerial distance of 55 km. As the highway winds down the mountain in a series of switchbacks, it passes under the two gargantuan water pipes – still guarded by armed troops in concrete fortifications – which link Dan Nhim Lake with the hydroelectric power station. To the south of the road (to the right as you face the ocean) you can see the steep tracks of the *crémaillère* (cog railway) linking Thap Cham with Dalat (see the Dalat section for details).

Sites of interest at the top of Ngoan Muc Pass include a waterfall next to the highway, pine forests and the old Bellevue Railway Station.

Dalat
Đà Lạt

Dalat (elevation: 1475 metres), which is situated in a temperate region dotted with lakes and waterfalls and surrounded by evergreen forests, is the most delightful city in all of Vietnam. That it was once called *Le Petit Paris* is a great compliment to the capital of France. Not surprisingly, Dalat is a favourite honeymooning spot.

Local industries include growing garden vegetables and flowers which are sold all over southern Vietnam. But the biggest contribution to the economy of Dalat is tourism (over 300,000 domestic tourists visit every year plus an increasing number of foreigners). The downside is that the Dalat authorities are trying to create circus-style 'tourist attractions', complete with sailboats, mini-zoos, balloons for the kiddies and Vietnamese dressed as bunny rabbits.

The Dalat area was once famous for its big-game hunting, and a 1950s brochure boasted that 'a two-hour drive from the town leads to several game-rich areas abounding in deer, roes, peacocks, pheasants, wild boar,

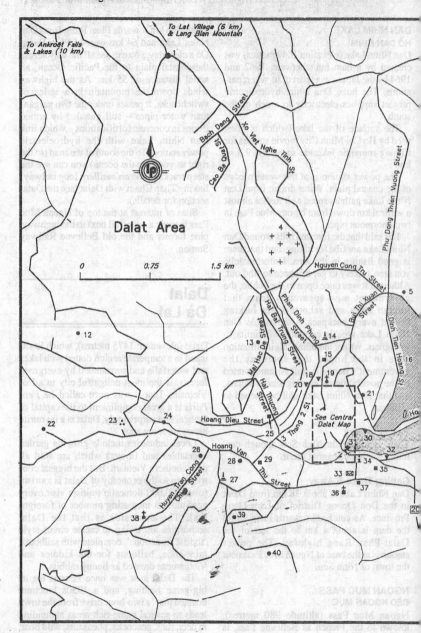

To Lat Village (6 km)
& Lang Bian Mountain

To Ankroët Falls
& Lakes (10 km)

Bach Dang Street

Cao Ba Quat St

Xo Viet Nghe Tinh St

Phu Dong Thien Vuong Street

Dalat Area

0   0.75   1.5 km

Nguyen Cong Tru Street

Bui Thi Xuan Street

Dinh Tien Hoang St.

Phan Dinh Phung Street

Mai Hac De Street

Hai Ba Trung Street

Hai Thuong Street

Hoang Dieu Street

3 Thang 2 St

Thu Street

Hoang Van

Huyen Tran Cong Chua Street

See Central
Dalat Map

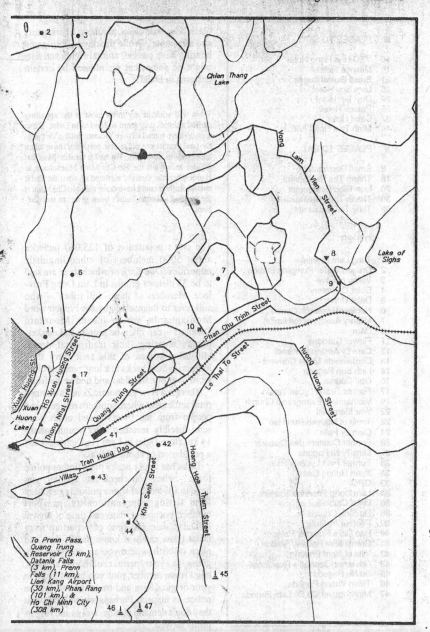

To Prenn Pass,
Quang Trung
Reservoir (5 km),
Datania Falls
(3 km), Prenn
Falls (11 km),
Lien Kang Airport
(30 km), Phan Rang
(101 km), &
Ho Chi Minh City
(308 km)

■ PLACES TO STAY

10 VYC Hoa Hong Hotel
15 Mimosa Hotel
21 Small Guesthouses
25 Lam Son Hotel
29 Duy Tan Hotel
35 Palace Hotel
37 Dalat Hotel
44 Minh Tam Hotel (Villas)

▼ PLACES TO EAT

8   Small Restaurants
18 Thanh The Restaurant
20 Lien Hiep Restaurant
30 Thanh Thuy Restaurant
32 Thuy Ta Restaurant

OTHER

1   Tung Lam Hamlet .
2   Dragon Water-Pumping Station
3   Valley of Love
4   Dalat Cemetery
5   Dalat University
6   Nuclear Research Centre
7   Military Academy (off limits)
9   Dam
11 Flower Gardens
12 Cam Ly Airstrip (unused)
13 Domaine de Marie Convent
14 Linh Son Pagoda
16 Golf Course
17 Former Grand Lycée Yersin
19 Vietnamese Evangelical Church
22 War Memorial
23 Tomb of Nguyen Huu Hao
24 Cam Ly Falls
26 Former Couvent des Oiseaux
27 Lam Ty Ni Pagoda
28 Former Petit Lycée Yersin
31 Xuan Huong Dam
33 GPO
34 Lam Dong Province Tourism
36 Dalat Cathedral
38 Du Sinh Church
39 Pasteur Institute
40 Bao Dai's Summer Palace
41 Crémaillère Railway Station
42 Villa of Nam Phuong
43 Governor-General's Residence
45 Su Nu Pagoda
46 Thien Vuong Pagoda
47 Minh Nguyet Cu Sy Lam Pagoda

black bear, wild caws, panthers, tigers, gaurs and elephants'. While the days of big-game hunting have passed, animal rights activists might be somewhat nonplussed by certain customs in Dalat:

What will stick in my mind most is the appalling stuffed animals they seem so fond of in Dalat. These seem to have spread all over Vietnam but the Vietnamese (and the citizens of Dalat in particular) have taken taxidermy to new lows. We had a terrible fit of the giggles as we left the Ho Chi Minh Mausoleum in Hanoi when the thought surfaced of what the Dalat animal stuffers could have done with Ho Chi Minh if the stuffing contract hadn't been given to the Russians.

The city's population of 125,000 includes about 5000 members of ethno-linguistic minorities *(Dan Toc)*, of which there are said to be 33 distinct groups in Lam Dong Province. Members of these 'hill tribes' – who still refer to themselves by the French word Montagnards, which means Mountain Dwellers – can often be seen in the marketplaces wearing their traditional dress. Hill-tribe women of this area carry their infants on their backs in a long piece of cloth worn over one shoulder and tied in the front.

There is a New Economic Zone (a planned rural settlement where southern refugees and people from the overcrowded north were semi-forcibly resettled after reunification) 14 km from Dalat in Lam Ha District; it has a population of about 10,000.

Dalat has a very nosey plainclothes police force – when you check into a hotel, you have to fill out and sign a police registration form listing your nationality, passport number, occuption, date and time of arrival in Dalat, date and time of departure from Dalat (how can you know that?), date and place of birth, where you are coming from, going to, your permanent home address, hotel room number, plus you have to turn in your original visa and travel permit for the police to inspect. Perhaps we're lucky that they don't demand photos, x-rays and fingerprints as well.

History

The site of Dalat was 'discovered' in 1897 by Dr Alexandre Yersin (1863-1943), a protégé of Louis Pasteur who was the first person to identify the plague bacillus. The city itself was established in 1912 and quickly became popular with Europeans as a cool retreat from the sweltering heat of the coastal plains and the Mekong Delta. In the local Lat language, Da Lat means the River of the Lat Tribe.

During the Vietnam War Dalat was, by the tacit agreement of all parties concerned, largely spared the ravages of war. Indeed, it seems that while South Vietnamese Army officers were being trained at the city's Military Academy and affluent officials of the Saigon regime were relaxing in their villas, VC cadres were doing the same thing not far away in *their* villas. Dalat fell to North Vietnamese forces without a fight on 3 April 1975. There is no problem with left-over mines and ordnance in the Dalat area.

Climate

Dalat is often called the City of Eternal Spring. The average maximum daily temperature is a cool 24°C; the average minimum daily temperature is 15°C. The dry season runs from December to March. Even during the rainy season, which lasts more or less from April to November, it is sunny most of the time.

Orientation

Dalat's sights are very spread out. The city centre is around Rap 3/4 cinema (named for the date on which Dalat was 'liberated' in 1975), which is up the hill from the Central Market. Xuan Huong Lake is 500 metres south-east of the Central Market.

Information

Tourist Office The headquarters of Lam Dong Tourism (Cong Ty Du Lich Lam Dong; ☎ 2125, 2034) is along the lake just over the bridge out of town. This organisation is the government-owned provincial tourism authority. In spite of this fact, the staff seems efficient, is eager to promote foreign tourism to Dalat and can help with getting a travel permit to other parts of Lam Dong Province.

Lam Dong Tourism is well aware of the importance of preserving Dalat's unique charm and is working on a programme to ensure that the city is well served by development, most of which is likely to be funded by investors from abroad. Lam Dong Tourism operates 12 hotels in Dalat.

Lam Dong Youth Tourism Company (Hiep Hoi Du Lich; ☎ 2136, 2318) runs sightseeing excursions and camping trips in and around Dalat for groups of Vietnamese young people. This private concern has an office at 7 Hoa Binh Square. The Youth Tourism Company, which has guides who speak English, French and Russian, is planning to introduce trekking expeditions lasting several days or longer that will include camping with the Chill, Koho and Lat minority peoples.

The cost depends on the size of the group, the transport required and food expenses. Reservations should be made at least five days in advance. The company has only a limited supply of camping equipment for hire so participants should bring their own warm clothing, medical supplies, rain gear, sleeping bags and backpacks; the company does have nylon tents.

Money Dollars can be changed at the usual hotel rate in the Palace Hotel.

Post & Telecommunications The GPO is across the street from the Dalat Hotel at 14 Tran Phu St. In addition to postal services, the GPO has international telegraph, telex, telephone and fax facilities.

Xuan Huong Lake

Xuan Huong Lake in the centre of Dalat was created in 1919 by a dam. It is named after a 17th century Vietnamese poet known for her daring attacks on the hypocrisy of social conventions and the foibles of scholars, monks, mandarins, feudal lords and kings. The lake is circumnavigated by a strollable path.

Paddleboats that look like giant swans can

be rented near Thanh Thuy Restaurant, which is 200 metres north-east of the dam. A golf course, which is being refurbished, occupies 50 hectares on the northern side of the lake near the Flower Gardens. The majestic hilltop Palace Hotel overlooks Xuan Huong Lake from the south.

Crémaillère Railway
About 500 metres to the east of Xuan Huong Lake is a railway station, and though you aren't likely to arrive in Dalat by train, the station is worth a visit. The crémaillère (cog railway) linked Dalat and Thap Cham (Phan Rang) from 1928 to 1964 – it was closed in 1964 because of repeated Viet Cong attacks. The line has now been partially repaired and is operated as a tourist attraction. You can't get to anywhere useful (like Ho Chi Minh City) on this train, but you can ride five km down the tracks to the suburbs of Dalat and back again. The fee for this journey is US$2 for the round trip.

House with 100 Roofs
This bizarre architectural curiosity is not one of the usual touristy sights, but attracts a small crowd of devoted avant-garde enthusiasts. It's hard to describe this place – the designers call it 'the house in the forest and the forest in the house'.

The House with 100 Roofs is near the Thanh Thuy Restaurant, which is on the lakefront about 200 metres along Nguyen Thai Hoc St from the Xuan Huong Dam.

French District
The area between Rap 3/4 cinema and Phan Dinh Phung St hasn't changed in decades. If, in the year 1934, someone had evacuated a provincial town in France and repopulated it with Vietnamese, this is what it would have looked like 20 years later. This is a delightful area for walking around.

Central Market
Dalat's Central Market, built in 1958, is at the northern end of Nguyen Thi Minh Khai St. The finest, freshest vegetables in Vietnam (as well as cut flowers and the usual mer-

chandise) are available here. There are dozens of food stalls in the roofed-over section behind the main building.

Governor-General's Residence
The old French Governor-General's Residence (Dinh Toan Quyen, or Dinh 2; ☎ 2093), now used as a guesthouse and for official receptions, is a dignified building of modernist design built in 1933. The original style of furnishing has been retained in most of the structure's 25 rooms. Shoes must be taken off at the front door.

The Governor-General's Residence is about two km east of the centre of town up the hill from the intersection of Tran Hung Dao St and Khoi Nghia Bac Son St; it is open to the public from 7 to 11 am and 1.30 to 4 pm. Entrance tickets are sold at an outbuilding (once the servants' quarters) several hundred metres from the residence itself. They may try to charge extra if you want to take photographs inside the building.

Guests can stay in the upstairs bedroom suites, with their balconies and huge bathrooms, for US$30 per person per night; for details, contact Lam Dong Tourism.

Bao Dai's Summer Palace
Emperor Bao Dai's Summer Palace (Biet Dien Quoc Truong, or Dinh 3) is a tan, 25-room villa constructed in 1933. The decor has not changed in decades except for the addition of Ho Chi Minh's portrait over the fireplace. The palace, filled with artefacts from decades and governments past, is extremely interesting.

The engraved glass map of Vietnam was given to Emperor Bao Dai (born 1913; reigned 1926-45; he has lived in France since the mid '50s) in 1942 by Vietnamese students in France. In Bao Dai's office, the life-size white bust above the bookcase is of Bao Dai himself; the smaller gold and brown busts are of his father, Emperor Khai Dinh. Note the heavy brass royal seal (on the right) and military seal (on the left). The photographs over the fireplace are of (from left to right) Bao Dai, his eldest son Bao Long (in uniform) and Empress Nam Phuong, who died in 1963.

Upstairs are the royal living quarters. The room of Bao Long, who now lives in England, is decorated in yellow, the royal colour. The huge semicircular couch was used by the Emperor and Empress for family meetings, during which their three daughters were seated in the yellow chairs and their two sons in the pink chairs. Check out the ancient tan Rouathermique infra-red sauna machine near the top of the stairs.

Bao Dai's Summer Palace is set in a pine grove 500 metres south-east of the Pasteur Institute, which is on Le Hong Phong St two km south-west of the city centre. The palace is open to the public from 7 to 11 am and 1.30 to 4 pm. Shoes must be removed at the door.

Tourists can stay here for US$30 per person per night; for more information, contact Lam Dong Tourism.

Flower Gardens

The Dalat Flower Gardens (Vuon Hoa Dalat; ☎ 2151) were established in 1966 by the South Vietnamese Agriculture Service and renovated in 1985. Flowers represented include hydrangeas, fuchsias and orchids (hoa lan). Most of the latter are in special shaded buildings off to the right from the entrance. The orchids are grown in blocks of coconut palm trunk and in terracotta pots with lots of ventilation holes.

Several monkeys live in cages on the grounds of the Flower Gardens – Japanese tourists like posing for photos with the animals; Vietnamese tourists enjoy tormenting the monkeys by throwing rocks and lit cigarettes, but some of the monkeys have learned to throw them back.

Near the gate you can buy cu ly, reddish-brown animal-shaped pieces of fern stems whose fibres are used to stop bleeding in traditional medicine.

The Flower Gardens front Xuan Huong Lake at 2 Phu Dong Thien Vuong St, which leads from the lake to Dalat University; they are open from 7.30 am to 4 pm. Ticket sales are suspended for a while around noon.

Dalat University

Dalat University (☎ 2246) was founded as a Catholic university in 1957 by Hué Archbishop Ngo Dinh Thuc, older brother of President Ngo Dinh Diem (assassinated in 1963), with the help of Cardinal Spelman of New York. The university, which was closed in 1975 and reopened two years later, has

1200 students from south-central Vietnam. The students live in off-campus boarding houses. The university library contains 10,000 books, including some in English and other Western languages. The US-Indochina Reconciliation Project of Philadelphia, Pennsylvania, USA, is interested in holding summer programmes in intensive Vietnamese language study here.

Dalat University is at 1 Phu Dong Thien Vuong St (corner Dinh Tien Hoang St). The 38-hectare campus can easily be identified by the red-star-topped triangular tower, which once held aloft a cross. Permission for foreigners to visit the university can be arranged if you ring them up (☎ 2246).

Nuclear Research Centre

Dalat's Nuclear Research Centre uses its American-built Triga Mark II reactor for radioactive medicine to train scientists and to analyse samples collected for geological and agricultural research. The centre, financed under the US Atoms for Peace programme, was formally dedicated in 1963 by President Ngo Dinh Diem (who was assassinated four days later) and US Ambassador Henry Cabot Lodge. In 1975, as the South was collapsing, the USA spirited away the reactor's nuclear fuel elements; the centre was reopened in 1984.

The Nuclear Research Centre, with its tall, thin chimney, can easily be seen from the Palace Hotel as well as from the Dragon Water-Pumping Station.

Former Petit Lycée Yersin

The former Petit Lycée Yersin at 1 Hoang Van Thu St is now a cultural centre (☎ 2511) run by the provincial government. Lessons in electric and acoustic guitar, piano, violin, clarinet, saxophone, etc are held here, making this a good place to meet local musicians. A new music centre is being established on Tang Bat Ho St.

Valley of Love

Named the Valley of Peace by Emperor Bao Dai, the Valley of Love (Thung Lung Tinh Yeu, or Vallée d'Amour in French), had its name changed in 1972 (the year Da Thien Lake was created) by romantically minded students from Dalat University.

The place has since taken on a carnival atmosphere; tourist buses line up to regurgitate visitors, and boats line up to accommodate them. Paddleboats cost US$0.50 per hour; 15-person canoes cost US$4 an hour; obnoxious noise-making motorboats cost US$5 for a whirlwind tour of the lake.

This is a good place to see the 'Dalat Cowboys' (no relation to the American 'Dallas Cowboys' football team). The 'cowboys' are in fact Vietnamese guides dressed as American cowboys (come back in another year and they'll have the Montagnards dressed up as Indians). The cowboys rent horses to tourists for US$2 to US$4 per hour and can take you on a guided tour around the lake. Refreshments and local delicacies (jams, candied fruits, etc) are on sale at the lookout near where the buses disgorge tourists.

The Valley of Love is five km north of Xuan Huong Lake out Phu Dong Thien Vuong St. The entrance fee is US$0.20.

Cam Ly Falls

Cam Ly Falls, opened as a tourist site in 1911, is one of those must-see spots for domestic visitors. The grassy areas around the 15-metre-high cascades are decorated with stuffed jungle animals which Vietnamese tourists love to be photographed with. Many of the cowboys you see around here aren't guides, but tourists – for a fee you can get dressed as a cowboy and have your photo taken. The waterfall is between numbers 57 and 59 on Hoang Van Thu St; it is open from 7 am to 6 pm.

Tomb of Nguyen Huu Hao

Nguyen Huu Hao, who died in 1939, was the father of Nam Phuong, Bao Dai's wife. He was the richest person in Go Cong District of the Mekong Delta. Nguyen Huu Hao's tomb is on a hilltop 400 metres north-west of Cam Ly Falls.

Dragon Water-Pumping Station

Guarded by a fanciful cement dragon, the Dragon Water-Pumping Station was built in 1977-78. The statue of the Virgin Mary holding baby Jesus and gazing towards Dalat dates from 1974. Thong Nhat Reservoir is on top of the hill just west of the pumping station.

The Dragon Water-Pumping Station is on top of a low rise 500 metres west of the entrance to the Valley of Love.

Pagodas & Churches

Lam Ty Ni Pagoda Lam Ty Ni Pagoda, also known as Quan Am Tu, was founded in 1961. The decorative front gate was constructed by the pagoda's one monk, Vien Thuc, an industrious man who learned English, French, Khmer and Thai at Dalat University. During his 20 years here, he has built flower beds and gardens in several different styles, including a miniature Japanese garden complete with a bridge. Nearby are trellis-shaded paths decorated with hanging plants. Signs list the Chinese name of each garden. Vien Thuc also built much of the pagoda's wooden furniture.

Lam Ty Ni Pagoda is about 500 metres north of the Pasteur Institute at 2 Thien My St. A visit here can easily be combined with a stop at Bao Dai's Summer Palace.

Linh Son Pagoda Linh Son Pagoda was founded in 1938. The giant bell is said to be made of bronze with gold mixed in, its great weight making it too heavy for thieves to carry off. Behind the pagoda are coffee and tea plants tended by the 15 monks, who range in age from 20 to 80, and half-a-dozen novices.

One of the monks here has led a fascinating and tragic life whose peculiar course reflects the vagaries of Vietnam's modern history. Born in 1926 of a Japanese father and a Vietnamese mother, during WW II he was pressed into the service of the Japanese occupation forces as a translator. He got his secondary school degree from a French-language Franciscan convent in 1959 at the age of 35. His interest later turned to American literature, in which he received a masters degree (his thesis was on William Faulkner) from Dalat University in 1975. The monk speaks half-a-dozen East Asian and European languages with fluent precision.

Linh Son Pagoda is about one km from the town centre on Phan Dinh Phung St; the street address is 120 Nguyen Van Troi St.

Dalat Cathedral Dalat Cathedral, which is on Tran Phu St next to the Dalat Hotel, was built between 1931 and 1942 for use by French residents and vacationers. The cross on the spire is 47 metres above the ground. Inside, the stained-glass windows bring a bit of medieval Europe to Dalat. The first church built on this site (in the 1920s) is to the left of the cathedral; it has a light blue arched door.

There are three priests here. Masses are held at 5.30 am and 5.15 pm every day and on Sundays at 5.30 am, 7 am and 4 pm. The parish's three choirs (one for each Sunday mass) practise on Thursdays and Saturdays from 5 to 6 pm.

Vietnamese Evangelical Church Dalat's pink Evangelical Church, the main Protestant church in the city, was built in 1940. Until 1975, it was affiliated with the Christian & Missionary Alliance. The minister here was trained at Nha Trang Bible College.

Since reunification, Vietnam's Protestants have been persecuted even more than have Catholics, in part because many Protestant clergymen were trained by American missionaries. Although religious activities at this church are still restricted by the government, Sunday is a busy day: there is Bible study from 7 to 8 am followed by worship from 8 to 10 am; a youth service is held from 1.30 to 3.30 pm.

Most of the 25,000 Protestants in Lam Dong Province, who are served by over 100 churches, are hill-tribe people. Dalat's Vietnamese Evangelical Church is one of only six churches in the province whose membership is ethnic-Vietnamese.

The Vietnamese Evangelical Church is

300 metres from Rap 3/4 at 72 Nguyen Van Troi St.

Domaine de Marie Convent The pink, tile-roofed structures of the Domaine de Marie Convent (Nha Tho Domaine), constructed between 1940 and 1942, were once home to 300 nuns. Today, the eight remaining nuns support themselves by making ginger candies and by selling the fruit grown in the orchard out the back.

Suzanne Humbert, wife of Admiral Jean Decoux, Vichy-French Governor-General of Indochina from 1940 to 1945, is buried at the base of the outside back wall of the chapel. A benefactress of the chapel, she was killed in an auto accident in 1944.

Masses are held in the large chapel every day at 5.30 am and on Sundays at 5.30 am and 4.15 pm.

The Domaine de Marie Convent is on a hilltop at 6 Ngo Quyen St, which is also called Mai Hac De St.

Du Sinh Church Du Sinh Church was built in 1955 by Catholic refugees from the North. The four-post Sino-Vietnamese-style steeple was constructed at the insistence of a Hué-born priest of royal lineage. The church is on a hilltop with beautiful views in all directions, making this a great place for a picnic.

To get to Du Sinh Church, go 500 metres south-west along Huyen Tran Cong Chua St from the former Couvent des Oiseaux, which is now a teachers' training high school.

Thien Vuong Pagoda Thien Vuong Pagoda, also known simply as Chua Tau (the Chinese pagoda), is popular with domestic tourists, especially ethnic-Chinese. Set on a hilltop amidst pine trees, the pagoda was built by the Chaozhou Chinese Congregation. Tho Da, the monk who initiated the construction of the pagoda in 1958, emigrated to the USA; there are pictures of his 1988 visit on display. The stalls out the front are a good place to buy local candied fruit and preserves.

The pagoda itself consists of three yellow buildings made of wood. In the first building is a gilded wooden statue of Ho Phap, one of

the Buddha's protectors. On the other side of Ho Phap's glass case is a gilded wooden statue of Pho Hien, a helper of A Di Da Buddha (the Buddha of the Past). Shoes should be removed before entering the third building, in which there are three four-metre-high standing Buddhas donated by a British Buddhist and brought from Hong Kong in 1960. Made of gilded sandalwood and weighing 1400 kg each, the figures – said to be the largest sandalwood statues in Vietnam – represent Thich Ca Buddha (Sakyamuni, the historical Buddha; in the centre); Quan The Am Bo Tat (Avalokiteçvara; on the right); and Dai The Chi Bo Tat (an assistant of A Di Da; on the left).

Thien Vuong Pagoda is about five km south-east of the centre of town out Khe Sanh St.

Minh Nguyet Cu Sy Lam Pagoda A second Chinese Buddhist pagoda, Minh Nguyet Cu Sy Lam Pagoda, is reached by a path beginning across the road from the gate of Thien Vuong Pagoda. It was built by the Cantonese Chinese Congregation in 1962. The main sanctuary of the pagoda is a round structure constructed on a platform representing a lotus blossom.

Inside is a painted cement statue of Quan The Am Bo Tat (Avalokiteçvara, the Goddess of Mercy) flanked by two other figures. Shoes should be taken off before entering. Notice the repetition of the lotus motif in the window bars, railings, gateposts, etc. There is a giant red gourd-shaped incense oven near the main sanctuary. The pagoda is open all day long.

Su Nu Pagoda Su Nu Pagoda, also known as Chua Linh Phong, is a Buddhist nunnery built in 1952. The nuns here – who, according to Buddhist regulations, are bald – wear grey or brown robes except when praying, at which time they don saffron raiment. Men are allowed to visit, but only women live here. The nunnery is open all day, but it is considered impolite to come around lunch time, when the nuns sing their prayers a cappella before eating. Across the driveway from the pagoda's buildings and set among tea plants is the grave-marker of Head Nun Thich Nu Dieu Huong.

Su Nu Pagoda is about one km south of Le Thai To St at 72 Hoang Hoa Tham St.

Hiking & Cycling

The best way to enjoy the forests and cultivated countryside around Dalat is either on foot, seated on horseback or pedalling a bicycle.

It's important to be aware that certain areas marked with a 'C' are off limits to foreigners. Some travellers speculate that this is to hide 'secret re-education camps' or to keep you away from bands of 'Montagnard guerrillas', while another story is that there are still armed soldiers who deserted the Vietnamese army and roam the highlands robbing tourists. The government refuses to comment, but perhaps the real reason is to extort some cash from foreigners for travel permits, guides and drivers, or to find an excuse for imposing a 'fine'.

Assuming that you don't run into any of the 'C' signs, some suggested routes include:

- Heading out 3 Thang 4 St, which becomes National Highway 20, to the pine forests of Prenn Pass and Quang Trung Reservoir.
- Going via the Governor-General's Residence out Khe Sanh St to Thien Vuong Pagoda.
- Taking Phu Dong Thien Vuong St from Dalat University to the Valley of Love.
- Going out to Bao Dai's Summer Palace and from there, after stopping at Lam Ty Ni Pagoda, via Thien My St and Huyen Tran Cong Chua St to Du Sinh Church.

Golf

A Hong Kong joint-venture is renovating a golf course in Dalat which was once used by Bao Dai, the last Vietnamese emperor. No further details are available at this stage.

Places to Stay – bottom end

Camping Camping is permitted on the out-of-service golf course, at the Dalat Flower Gardens, in the Valley of Love (Da Thien Lake) area, around Quang Trung Reservoir (Tuyen Lam Lake) and near Datanla and Prenn waterfalls. Locals say that security is not a problem, though this really could just mean it's not a problem if you're Vietnamese. Only limited equipment can be hired locally, so the more of your own you have the better. Sleeping bags, unnecessary in Vietnam's coastal areas, are well worth bringing – the nights are often chilly.

Hotels Because of its popularity with domestic travellers, Dalat has an extensive network of cheap, well-run hotels. Nevertheless, demand is heavy and it is often difficult to find a room after 5 pm, especially on Saturday night. Unless you like icy showers, make sure they have hot water before you check in. If there is a power failure, the hot water will be off too, but in that case some hotels will boil water on a gas stove and give it to you in a bucket. No hotels in Dalat have air-conditioning and it's hard to imagine why anyone would want it!

Two places have emerged in Dalat as unofficial backpacker guesthouses. One is the *Mimosa Hotel* (☎ 2656, 2180), 170 Phan Dinh Phung St. Single rooms start at US$5 while doubles are US$8 and US$10. The hotel has hot water. The friendly manager speaks good English and is an excellent source of information on the area.

The *Cam Do Hotel* on Phan Dinh Phung St is the other notable budget place in town. Rooms with hot water cost US$6 to US$8 per night.

The *Thanh Binh Hotel* (☎ 2394, 2909; 42 rooms) is a good budget hotel right across the street from the main building of the Central Market at 40-42 Nguyen Thi Minh Khai St. Singles/doubles are US$8/15 and the hot water seems to work OK. The attached Chinese restaurant is outstanding.

The *Lang Bian Hotel* (☎ 2419), which was formerly the youth hostel, is about 100 metres from the Central Market on Nguyen Thi Minh Khai St. Fairly shabby singles with common bathroom cost from US$5; similar doubles with own bathroom are US$20.

The *Phu Hoa Hotel* (☎ 2194), 16 Tang Bat Ho St, is an old but still reasonably pleasant

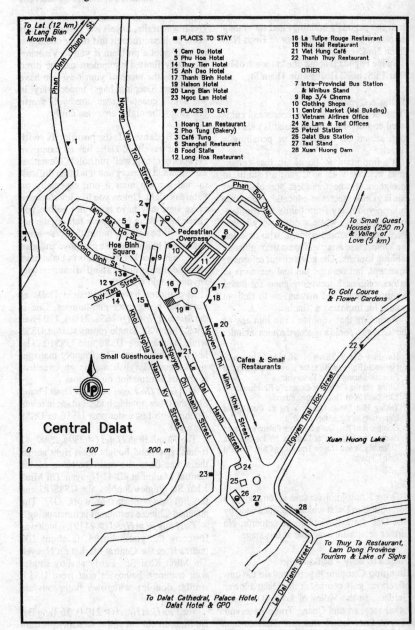

To Lat (12 km)
& Lang Bian
Mountain

Phan Dinh Phung St.

Nguyen Van Troi Street

Phan Boi Chau Street

■ PLACES TO STAY

4 Cam Do Hotel
5 Phu Hoa Hotel
14 Thuy Tien Hotel
15 Anh Dao Hotel
17 Thanh Binh Hotel
19 Haison Hotel
20 Lang Bian Hotel
23 Ngoc Lan Hotel

▼ PLACES TO EAT

1 Hoang Lan Restaurant
2 Pho Tung (Bakery)
3 Café Tung
6 Shanghai Restaurant
8 Food Stalls
12 Long Hoa Restaurant

16 La Tulipe Rouge Restaurant
18 Nhu Hai Restaurant
21 Viet Hung Café
22 Thanh Thuy Restaurant

OTHER

7 Intra-Provincial Bus Station
& Minibus Stand
9 Rap 3/4 Cinema
10 Clothing Shops
11 Central Market (Mai Building)
13 Vietnam Airlines Office
24 Xe Lam & Taxi Offices
25 Petrol Station
26 Dalat Bus Station
27 Taxi Stand
28 Xuan Huong Dam

To Small Guest
Houses (250 m)
& Valley of
Love (5 km)

To Golf Course
& Flower Gardens

Lang Bat Street

Truong Cong Dinh St.

Ho St.

Hoa Binh
Square

Pedestrian
Overpass

Duy Tan Street

Khoi Nghia Nam Ky Street

Le Dai Hanh Street

Nguyen Chi Thanh Street

Nguyen Thi Minh Khai Street

Small Guesthouses

Cafes & Small
Restaurants

Central Dalat

0   100   200 m

Xuan Huong Lake

Nguyen Thai Hoc Street

To Thuy Ta Restaurant,
Lam Dong Province
Tourism & Lake of Sighs

To Dalat Cathedral, Palace Hotel,
Dalat Hotel & GPO

Le Dai Hanh Street

place in the centre. Singles are US$4 and US$5 while doubles are US$10.

The *Thuy Tien Hotel* (☎ 2444; eight rooms) is in the heart of the old French section at the corner of Duy Tan and Khoi Nghia Nam Ky Sts. At US$15 for a double, it's hardly worth it – it looks a bit dumpy despite the up-market price. However, the rooms are relatively large.

The *Ngoc Lan Hotel* (☎ 2136; 25 rooms), a big place overlooking the bus station and the lake, is at 42 Nguyen Chi Thanh St. This old place has good renovation potential, but at present it's not a good deal at US$6/10 for singles/doubles with *cold water*, or US$12/20 for rooms with hot water.

There are small guesthouses along Nguyen Chi Thanh St at numbers 6, 12, 14, 20, 22, 34, 36, 40 and 80.

The *Duy Tan Hotel* (☎ 2216; 26 rooms) at 82 3 Thang 2 St (corner Hoang Van Thu St) is actually quite a bargain if you want to be in a quiet, out of the centre place. Travellers have complained about 'very aggressive cockroaches' here, but the fenced-in car park in front of the hotel makes this place quite popular for people doing car trips. Singles range from US$5 to US$15; doubles from US$8 to US$25; triples from US$24 to US$35.

The *Lam Son Hotel* (☎ 2362; 12 rooms) is about one km west of the centre of town in an old French villa at 5 Hai Thuong St. This large, quiet place is good value if you don't mind the distance from the town centre. All rooms cost US$10 and are equipped with hot water. The management is very friendly.

The *VYC Hoa Hong Hotel* (☎ 2653) on Lu Gia St is a long way from the centre. However, it's a new, modern place built in the finest tradition of American motel architecture. All rooms cost US$15. You can make reservations in Ho Chi Minh City at VYC Tourism Centre (☎ 298707), 180 Nguyen Cu Trinh.

Places to Stay – middle & top end

The *Anh Dao Hotel* (☎ 2384) is up the hill from the Central Market on Nguyen Chi Thanh St; the postal address is 50-52 Khu Hoa Binh Quarter. This is definitely an up-market place with singles/doubles from US$20/25 to US$30/40. Breakfast is included in the tariff.

The *Haison Hotel* (☎ 2379) is a spiffy place at 1 Nguyen Thi Minh Khai St across the roundabout from the Central Market. The hotel advertises its 'elegant and cosy dancing hall' and 'urbane service staff'. Singles range from US$10 to US$35 while doubles are US$15 to US$40. The hotel can also be contacted at the Saigon office (fax (84-8) 92889). This place is often full.

The *Palace Hotel* (☎ 2203; 43 rooms) is a grand old place built between 1916 and 1922. Panoramic views of Xuan Huong Lake can be enjoyed in the hotel's expansive ground-floor public areas, where one can sit in a rattan chair sipping tea or soda while gazing out through a wall of windows. We can't give you the current prices because at the time of our visit the hotel was under renovation. Doubtless it will be more expensive after re-opening, but pre-renovation prices for foreigners were singles/doubles at US$18/23 in 2nd class, US$20/27 in 1st class, US$24/33 for a deluxe room and US$37/45 for a suite. The restaurant should be open from 6.30 to 8.30 am, 11.30 am to 1.30 pm and 6 to 8 pm. There are tennis courts nearby. The hotel's street address is 2 Tran Phu St. The renovated hotel will be a Franco-Vietnamese joint venture.

Another vintage hostelry is the *Dalat Hotel* (☎ 2363; 65 rooms), built in 1907. Though the building, which is at 7 Tran Phu St (opposite the driveway of the Palace Hotel), is a bit run-down there are said to be plans to renovate it. Singles and doubles cost US$20/22/25. There is a billiard room on the ground floor and a restaurant. Probably the worst thing about this place is the staff – they were decidedly unfriendly during our visit.

The *Minh Tam Hotel* (☎ 2447; 17 rooms) is three km out of town at 20A Khe Sanh St. There are nice views from here of the surrounding landscape of pine-forested hills and cultivated valleys. Formerly the magnificent summer palace of Tran Le Xuan (Madame Nhu, the notorious sister-in-law of

President Ngo Dinh Diem), the villa, constructed in 1936, was renovated in 1984. The unfriendly, stuck-up staff seem to have been created in Madame Nhu's image. Nevertheless, this place is a peaceful retreat, or would be were it not for the busloads of domestic tourists continually parading through the flower garden on the hotel's grounds. Double rooms in the main building cost US$40, while villas belonging to the hotel go for US$25.

Many of Dalat's 2500 chalet-style villas can be rented. Prime villas are found along the ridge south of Tran Hung Dao St and Le Thai To St, and there is a whole neighbourhood of villas near the Pasteur Institute (around Le Hong Phong St). If you don't mind the tourists tramping through, you can even stay in the old Governor-General's Residence and Bao Dai's Summer Palace for US$30 per person per night. For more information, enquire at Lam Dong Tourism.

Places to Eat
Local Specialities Dalat is a paradise for lovers of fresh garden vegetables, which are grown locally and sold all over the south. The abundance of just-picked peas, carrots, radishes, tomatoes, cucumbers, avocados, green peppers, lettuce, Chinese cabbage, bean sprouts, beets, green beans, potatoes, corn, bamboo shoots, garlic, spinach, squash and yams makes for meals unavailable anywhere else in the country. Persimmons and cherries are in season from November to January. Avocados are eaten for desert with either sugar or salt and pepper. Apples are known here as *bom* after the French *pomme*. Because of fierce competition in the domestic tourism market, restaurant prices are very reasonable.

The Dalat area is famous for its strawberry jam, dried blackcurrants and candied plums and peaches, all of which can be purchased cheaply around the Central Market. Other local delicacies include avocado ice cream, sweet beans *(mut dao)* and strawberry, blackberry and artichoke extracts (syrups for making drinks). The strawberry extract is great in tea. The region also produces grape,

mulberry and strawberry wines. Artichoke tea, another local speciality, is made from the root of the artichoke plant. Most of these products can be purchased at the central market and at stalls in front of Thien Vuong Pagoda.

Dau hu, a type of pudding, is a Dalat speciality. Made from soymilk, sugar and a bit of ginger, dau hu is sold by itinerant women vendors who walk around carrying a large bowl of the stuff and a small stand suspended from either end of a bamboo pole.

Restaurants The *Shanghai Restaurant* is a privately owned place on the other side of Rap 3/4 cinema from the Central Market; the address is 8 Khu Hoa Binh Quarter. They serve Chinese, Vietnamese and French food from 8 am to 9.30 pm.

The *Long Hoa Restaurant* on Duy Tan St is also very popular with travellers and even cheaper than the Shanghai Restaurant. The *Hoang Lan Restaurant* on Phan Dinh Phung St has excellent food and also attracts many backpackers.

Close to the Shanghai Restaurant is *Pho Tung*, which is not a bad restaurant but also an outstanding bakery. It's hard to resist all those delectable pastries and cakes in the windows – close your eyes as you walk by or else break out some dong and pig out.

If it's fresh Vietnamese vegetables you want, the place to find them is the *Nhu Hai Restaurant* on the traffic circle in front of the Central Market.

The *My Canh Restaurant* is attached to the Thanh Binh Hotel right on the circle in front of the Central Market at 41 Nguyen Thi Minh Khai St. This restaurant serves the best Chinese food in Dalat.

La Tulipe Rouge Restaurant (☎ 2394) is across the square from the main building of the Central Market at 1 Nguyen Thi Minh Khai St; it is open from 6 am to 9 pm. The fare includes Vietnamese, Chinese and European dishes.

There are dozens of food stalls in the covered area behind the main Central Market building. A number of cafes and small restaurants are along Nguyen Thi Minh Khai St between the Central Market and Xuan Huong Lake.

The *Thanh The Restaurant* is at 118 Phan Dinh Phung St (near the Mimosa Hotel). The food is good – too bad the attached hotel is off limits to foreigners. Ditto for the nearby *Lien Hiep Restaurant* at No 147.

The *Thuy Ta Restaurant* (☎ 2268), formerly *La Grenouillère* (roughly translated, The Froggery), is built on piles over the waters of Xuan Huong Lake. The panoramic view from the veranda encompasses almost the whole of the lake's forested coastline. Thuy Ta Restaurant, which is at the tip of a perfectly round island reached by a bridge, is directly below the Palace Hotel; it is open from 6 am to 9 pm and makes a great place for breakfast.

Across the lake is *Thanh Thuy Restaurant* (Cua Hang Thanh Thuy), which is on the water 200 metres along Nguyen Thai Hoc St from the Xuan Huong Dam.

Vegetarian There are three vegetarian food stalls, each signposted *'com chay'* (vegetarian food), in the area of covered food stalls behind the main building of the Central Market. They are right across the street from Nha Khach, a hotel at 27A Nguyen Thi Minh Khai St. All three serve delicious 100% vegetarian food prepared to resemble and taste like traditional Vietnamese meat dishes.

Cafes The *Café Tung* at 6 Khu Hoa Binh St was a famous hang-out of Saigonese intellectuals during the 1950s. Old-timers swear that the place remains exactly as it was when they were young, including the 1950s prices (US$0.10 for coffee). As it did then, Café Tung serves only tea, coffee, hot cocoa, lemon soda and orange soda to the accompaniment of mellow French music. This is a marvellous place to warm up and unwind on a chilly evening.

The *Viet Hung Café* (Kem Viet Hung) specialities are ice cream and iced coffee. The cafe has entrances across from 22 Nguyen Chi Thanh St and on Le Dai Hanh St.

Entertainment
The busy market area near the Intra-Provincial Bus Station is the main entertainment. It's one big buy and sell, but this is one of the best places in Vietnam to pick up clothing at a good price.

The Central Market is the other hot spot in the evening. This is where you can hang out and drink coffee and chat with the locals.

Things to Buy
In the past few years, the Dalat tourist kitsch-junk market has really come into its own. Without any effort at all, you'll be able to find that special something for your loved ones at home – perhaps a battery-powered stuffed koala bear that sings 'Waltzing Matilda' or a lacquered alligator with a light-bulb in its mouth.

In addition to these useful items, Dalat is known for its *kim mao cau tich*, a kind of fern whose fibres are used to stop bleeding in traditional Chinese medicine. The stuff is also known as *cu ly* (animals) because the fibrous matter is sold attached to branches pruned to resemble reddish-brown hairy animals. The tourists from Taiwan and Hong Kong go crazy for this stuff.

The hill tribes of Lam Dong Province make handicrafts for their own use only – but just wait, Saigon Tourist will get them too. Lat products include dyed rush mats and rice baskets that roll up when empty. The Koho and Chill produce the split-bamboo baskets used by all the national minorities in this area to carry things on their backs. The Chill also weave cloth, including the dark blue cotton shawls worn by some Montagnard women.

The hill-tribe people carry water in a hollow gourd with a corn-cob stopper that is sometimes wrapped in a leaf for a tighter fit. A market for such goods has not yet developed so there are no stores in town selling them. If you are interested in Montagnard handicrafts, you might ask around Lat Village, which is 12 km north of Dalat.

Getting There & Away
Air At present there are flights to and from

Ho Chi Minh City on Monday, Wednesday and Saturday (US$30 one way).

Lien Khang Airport is about 30 km south of the city. A taxi should cost less than US$10. The airport is authorised to accept light aircraft which, the provincial government hopes, will be carrying well-heeled visitors from other South-East Asian countries; when the 1500-metre runway is lengthened to 2500 metres, the airport will be able to handle larger aircraft. Cam Ly Airstrip, only three km from the centre of Dalat, is not in use.

The Vietnam Airlines office in Dalat (☎ 2895) is at 5 Truong Cong Dinh St, which is across the street from Rap 3/4 cinema.

Bus Dalat Bus Station (Ben Xe Dalat; ☎ 2077) is next to the petrol station, which is 100 metres towards the Central Market from Xuan Huong Dam; the ticket office is open from 4.30 am to 5.30 pm. There is daily express service from Dalat to Ho Chi Minh City (six to seven hours; US$1.65) and Nha Trang (US$1.47). Express buses also run two or three times a week to Danang (19 hours; US$3.04), Quang Ngai and Qui Nhon. All the express buses, most of which are Czech-built Karosas, depart at 5 am.

Minibuses from Dalat to Nha Trang can be booked at many hotels. It's advised that you purchase more than one ticket as they will otherwise seat six across!

Non-express buses, which depart when full starting at 6 am, link Dalat with:

Bao Loc (B'Lao), Cat Tien, Da Hoai, Da Teh, Danang, Di Linh (Djiring), Don Duong (Darang), Dong Van, Duc Trong, Hanoi (with a change of buses), Ho Chi Minh City (eight to nine hours), Nam Bang, Phan Rang, Phan Thiet, Phu Son, Quang Ngai, Qui Nhon, Tan My.

The Intra-Provincial Bus Station (Ben Xe Khach Noi Thanh) is one block north of Rap 3/4 cinema. Buses departing from here connect Dalat with destinations within Lâm Dong Province, including Bao Loc, Cau Dat, Di Linh (Djiring), Da Thien, Lac Duong, Ta In and Ta Nun. The administrative offices of the Intra-Provincial Bus Station are near the main bus station.

Car From Ho Chi Minh City, taking the inland route via Bao Loc and Di Linh is faster than the coastal route via Ngoan Muc Pass. Parts of the road between Dalat and Phan Rang are in poor condition, so a high-clearance vehicle is preferred though not mandatory. Road distances from Dalat are:

Buon Ma Thuot	396 km
Danang	746 km
Di Linh	82 km
Ho Chi Minh City	308 km
Nha Trang	205 km
Phan Rang	101 km
Phan Thiet	247 km

Getting Around

Taxi Rentable Peugeot 203s – all of them black with white roofs – park on the Central Market side of Xuan Huong Dam (near the bus station) and near Rap 3/4 cinema; it costs only US$10 to rent one for a full day if you just go around the Dalat area. The taxi office is next to the main bus station and is signposted as Xe Taxi Dalat. Automobiles with drivers can also be hired through Lam Dong Tourism.

Xe Lam & Horse Carts There is a Xe Lam and horse-cart station on Nguyen Thi Minh Khai St in front of the Haison Hotel, which is across the roundabout from the main building of the Central Market. The Xe Lam office (Xe Lam Dalat) is next to the petrol station and the bus station.

Motorbike Motorbikes (Honda om), which can carry one passenger in addition to the driver, stop in front of the petrol station next to Dalat Bus Station.

Cyclo Dalat is too hilly for cyclos

AROUND DALAT
Lake of Sighs
The Lake of Sighs (Ho Than Tho) is a natural lake enlarged by a French-built dam; the

forests in the area are hardly Dalat's finest. There are several small restaurants up the hill from the dam. Horses can be hired near the restaurants for US$2 an hour.

According to legend, Mai Nuong and Hoang Tung met here in 1788 while he was hunting and she picking mushrooms. They fell in love and sought their parents' permission to marry. But at that time Vietnam was threatened by a Chinese invasion and Hoang Tung, heeding Emperor Quang Trung's call-to-arms, joined the army without waiting to tell Mai Nuong. Unaware that he was off fighting and afraid that his absence meant that he no longer loved her, Mai Nuong sent word for him to meet her at the lake. When he did not come she was overcome with sorrow and, to prove her love, threw herself into the conveniently located lake and drowned. Thereafter, the lake has been known as the Lake of Sighs.

The Lake of Sighs is six km north-east of the centre of Dalat out Phan Chu Trinh St.

Prenn Pass
The area along National Highway 20 between Dalat and Datanla Waterfall is known as Prenn Pass. The hillsides support mature pine forests while the valleys are used to cultivate vegetables. This is a great area for hiking and horseback riding, but make local enquiries before heading out to be sure that there will be no problems with the police.

Quang Trung Reservoir
Quang Trung Reservoir (Tuyen Lam Lake) is an artificial lake created by a dam in 1980. It is named after Emperor Quang Trung (also known as Nguyen Hue), a leader of the Tay Son Rebellion who is considered a great hero for vanquishing a Chinese invasion force in 1789. The area is being developed for tourism; there are several cafes not far from the dam and paddleboats, rowboats and canoes are for rent nearby. The hillscape around the reservoir is covered with pine trees, most of them newly planted. There is a switchback path up the hill due south-west

of the water intake tower. Minority farmers live and raise crops in the vicinity of the lake.

To get to Quang Trung Reservoir, head out of Dalat on National Route 20. At a point five km from town turn right and continue for two km.

Datanla Falls
The nice thing about Datanla is the short but pleasant walk to get there. The falls are 350 metres from Highway 20 on a path that first passes through a forest of pines and then continues steeply down the hill into a rain forest.

To get to Datanla, turn off Highway 20 about 200 metres past the turn-off to Quang Trung Reservoir; the entrance fee is US$0.10. There is a second entrance to the falls several hundred metres farther down the road.

Prenn Falls
This is one of the largest and most beautiful falls in the Dalat area, but it is also starting to suffer the effects of commercial exploitation.

Prenn Waterfall (elevation 1124 metres) consists of a 15-metre free fall over a wide rock outcrop. A path goes under the outcrop, affording a view of the pool and surrounding rainforest through the curtain of falling water. An ominous sign of possible abominations to come are the 'Dalat Tourist Sailboats' now plying the waters of the tiny pool at the waterfall's base.

After a rainstorm the waterfall becomes a raging brown torrent (deforestation and the consequent soil erosion are responsible for the coffee colour). Refreshments are sold at kiosks near the falls. The park around the falls was dedicated by the Queen of Thailand in 1959.

The entrance to Prenn Falls is near the Prenn Restaurant, which is 13 km from Dalat towards Phan Rang; the entrance fee is US$0.10 but there is a US$0.50 'camera fee'.

Lat Village
The nine hamlets of Lat Village (population 6000), whose name is pronounced 'lak' by

the locals, are about 12 km from Dalat at the base of Lang Bian Mountain. The inhabitants of five of the hamlets are of the Lat ethnic group; the residents of the other four are members of the Chill, Ma and Koho tribes, each of which speaks a different dialect.

Traditionally, Lat houses are built on piles with rough plank walls and a thatch roof. The people of Lat Village eke out a living growing rice, coffee, black beans and sweet potatoes. The villages have 300 hectares of land and produce one rice crop per year. Many residents of Lat have been forced by economic circumstances into the business of producing charcoal, a lowly task often performed by members of Vietnam's minorities. Before 1975, many men from Lat worked with the Americans, as did Montagnards elsewhere in the Central Highlands.

Classes in the village's primary and secondary schools, successors of the École Franco-Koho established in Dalat in 1948, are conducted in Vietnamese rather than the tribal languages. Lat has one Catholic church and one Protestant church. A Koho-language Bible *(Sra Goh)* was published by Protestants in 1971; a Lat-language Bible, prepared by Catholics, appeared the following year. Both Montagnard dialects, which are quite similar to each other, are written in a Latin-based script.

Place's to Eat There are no restaurants in Lat, just a few food stalls.

Getting There & Away There is a serious obstacle to visiting the Lat Village – the Dalat police! It's not illegal to visit the village, it's just that the Dalat municipal government has discovered a way to bilk foreigners of some cash. To visit the village, you must first go to the Immigration Police in Dalat to obtain a permit for US$10. In addition, you cannot take a bus or even use your own car if you have one. Rather, you must rent a car from the Dalat government at a cost of US$15. So the minimum charge for visiting the village is US$25, though you can share the car with other travellers. If you attempt to visit the village on the sly without

a permit, you will almost certainly be stopped by the police and fined!

Several travellers reported being fined US$100 each for visiting the Lat Village without a special permit, a local guide plus an OK from the police. One British girl went there after asking the police and got fined because they simply phoned the outpost to cash her in!

Andreas Hessberger

If these idiotic rules are ever rescinded, you should be able to visit the Lat Village by taking the bus, though this won't be comfortable. A small, usually packed bus makes two daily round trips between Dalat and Lat. The bus departs from Dalat at noon and sometime between 4.30 and 5 pm; it leaves Lat at 7 am and (for the last time of the day) at 12.30 pm.

To get to Lat from Dalat, head north on Xo Viet Nghe Tinh St. At Tung Lam Hamlet there is a fork in the road marked by a shot-up cement street sign. Continue straight on (that is, north-westward) rather than to the left (which leads to Suoi Vang, the Golden Stream, 14 km away). By bicycle, the 12-km trip from Dalat to Lat takes about 40 minutes. On foot, it's a two-hour walk. The road is in poor repair.

Lang Bian Mountain
Lang Bian Mountain (known in Vietnamese as Lam Vien Mountain) has five volcanic peaks ranging in altitude from 2100 to 2400 metres. Of the two highest peaks, the eastern one is known to locals by the woman's name K'Lang; the western one bears a man's name, K'Biang. The upper reaches of the mountain are forested. Only half a century ago, the verdant foothills of Lang Bian Mountain, now defoliated, sheltered wild oxen, deer, boars, elephants, rhinoceros and tigers.

The hike up to the top of Lang Bian Mountain, from where the views are truly spectacular, takes three to four hours from Lat Village. The path begins due north of Lat and is easily recognisable as a red gash in the green mountainside. It is possible to hire young locals as guides.

Top: Scenery around Dalat (RS)
Middle: Bridge at Cam Ly Falls, Dalat (RS)
Bottom: Street Vendors, Dalat (RS)

Top: China Beach, Danang (RM)
Left: Chinese Pagoda, Hoi An (GB)
Right: Street Vendor, China Beach (RS)

Ankroët Falls & Lakes

The two Ankroët Lakes were created as part of a hydroelectric project. The waterfall (Thac Ankroët) is about 15 metres high. The Ankroët Lakes are 18 km north-west of Dalat in an area inhabited by hill tribes.

Remote Highlands

The western region of the Central Highlands along the border with Cambodia and Laos was, until recently, off limits to foreigners. Now it is possible to obtain a travel permit to visit – that is, for every foreign nationality *except* citizens of the USA.

At the present time, not many foreigners at all go to this remote region and the locals are not well equipped to handle tourists, but that will probably change in the future.

Roads in this area are in poor condition, which means you'd be better off travelling by jeep rather than by car. However, flights to Buon Ma Thuot and Pleiku now make this part of Vietnam more accessible.

BUON MA THUOT
BUÔN MA THUỘT

Buon Ma Thuot (or Ban Me Thuot; population 65,000; elevation 451 metres) is the capital of Dac Lac (Dak Lak) Province. A large percentage of the area's population is made up of ethnic minorities. One of the region's main crops is coffee, which is grown on plantations run by German managers who are said to be as imperiously demanding as were their French predecessors. Before WW II, the city was a centre of big-game hunting.

In March 1975, Buon Ma Thuot briefly achieved world fame when North Vietnamese troops (who had been infiltrating via Laos and Cambodia) attacked the city. This proved to be the final battle of the war – President Nguyen Van Thieu ordered a 'strategic withdrawal' from the Highlands which turned into a rout. The ARVN collapsed, and by the end of April the South Vietnamese government surrendered.

The rainy season around Buon Ma Thuot lasts from April to November, though downpours are usually of short duration. Because of its lower elevation, Buon Ma Thuot is warmer and more humid than Dalat.

Information

Dac Lac Tourist (☎ 52322, 52324) – the provincial tourism authority – is at 3 Phan Chu Trinh St. The exchange bank is on Ama Tranglon St.

Hill-Tribe Museum

Displays at the museum feature traditional Montagnard dress as well as agricultural implements, fishing gear, bows and arrows, weaving looms and musical instruments. There are said to be 31 distinct ethnic groups in Dac Lac Province.

The Hill-Tribe Museum is near the Thang Loi Hotel at 1 Me Mai St.

Places to Stay

Buon Ma Thuot's main hotel is the *Thang Loi Hotel* (☎ 2322), which is at 1 Phan Chu Trinh St. Other places in town include the *Hoang Gia Hotel* at 2 Le Hong Phong St and the *Hong Kong Hotel* at 30 Hai Ba Trung St.

Getting There & Away

Air Vietnam Airlines has flights between Buon Ma Thuot and Ho Chi Minh City on Monday, Wednesday and Saturday for US$45.

Bus There is bus service to Buon Ma Thuot from most major towns and cities between Ho Chi Minh City and Hanoi.

Car The road linking the coast with Buon Ma Thuot intersects National Highway 1 at Ninh Hoa, which is 34 km north of Nha Trang. Land distances from Buon Ma Thuot are as follows:

Dalat	396 km
Danang	666 km
Ho Chi Minh City	352 km
Kontum	246 km
Nha Trang	191 km

Ninh Hoa	160 km
Phan Rang	295 km
Pleiku	197 km
Qui Nhon	223 km

AROUND BUON MA THUOT
Drai Sap Falls
Drai Sap Falls, about 12 km from Buon Ma Thuot, is in the middle of a hardwood rainforest.

Tua
The Rhade (or Ede) hamlet of Tua is 13 km from Buon Ma Thuot. The people here make a living raising animals and growing manioc, sweet potatoes and maize.

Rhade society is matrilineal and matrilocal (centred around the household of the wife's family). Extended families live in long-houses, each section of which houses a nuclear family. Each long-house is presided over by a man, often the husband of the senior woman of the family. The property of the extended family is owned and controlled by the oldest woman in the group.

The religion of the Rhade is animistic. In the past century many Rhade have been converted to Catholicism and Protestantism.

Ban Don
The residents of Ban Don village in Ea Sup District, which is 55 km north-west of Buon Ma Thuot, are mostly M'nong, a matrilineal tribe in which the family name is passed down through the female line and children are considered members of their mother's family. Despite feminist theories to the contrary, the M'nong are known for their fiercely belligerent attitude towards other tribes in the area as well as towards ethnic Vietnamese. The M'nong hunt wild elephants using domesticated elephants, dozens of which live in Ban Don.

There is a 13th century Cham tower 36 km north of Ban Don at Ya Liao.

Dac Lac Lake
Dac Lac Lake (Ho Dac Lac) is about 50 km south of Buon Ma Thuot. Emperor Bao Dai built a small palace here.

PLEIKU
PLEI KU
Pleiku (or Playcu; elevation 785 metres) is a market town in the centre of a vast, fertile plateau whose red soil is of volcanic origin. Many of the 35,000 inhabitants of the city,

Drai Sap Falls

which is 785 metres above sea level, are members of ethnic minorities.

In February 1965, the VC shelled a US compound in Pleiku killing eight Americans. Although the USA already had over 23,000 military advisors in Vietnam, their role was supposed to be non-combatant at that time. The attack on Pleiku was used as a justification by then President Johnson to begin a relentless bombing campaign against North Vietnam and the rapid build-up of American troops.

Getting There & Away

Air Vietnam Airlines has flights connecting Pleiku to Ho Chi Minh City on Monday and Thursday (US$65 one way). Flights to/from Hanoi fly on Tuesday and Friday (US$110). Flights to/from Danang are every Tuesday and Friday (US$30).

Bus There is non-express bus service to Pleiku from most coastal cities between Nha Tranh and Danang.

Car Pleiku is linked by road to Buon Ma Thuot, Qui Nhon (via An Khe), Kontum and Cambodia's Ratanakiri Province (via Chu Nghe).

Road distances from Pleiku are 197 km to Buon Ma Thuot, 550 km to Ho Chi Minh City, 424 km to Nha Trang, and 186 km to Qui Nhon.

KONTUM
KON TUM

Kontum (population 35,000; altitude 525 metres) is in a region inhabited primarily by ethnic minority groups, including the Bahnar, Jarai, Rengao and Sedeng.

During the course of a major battle between South Vietnamese forces and the North Vietnamese that took place in and around Kontum in the spring of 1972, the area was devastated by hundreds of US B-52 raids.

Getting There & Away

Bus Buses connect Kontum to Danang, Pleiku and Buon Ma Thuot.

Car Land distances from Kontum are 246 km to Buon Ma Thuot, 896 km to Ho Chi Minh City, 436 km to Nha Trang, 46 km to Pleiku, and 198 km to Qui Nhon.

AROUND KONTUM
Jrai Li Falls

The 42-metre-high Jrai Li Falls (Thac Ya Li) are 22 km south-west of Kontum.

This section covers the littoral provinces of Binh Thuan, Ninh Thuan, Khanh Hoa, Phu Yen, Binh Dinh, Quang Ngai and southern Quang Nam-Danang. The cities, towns, beaches and historical sites in this region, most of which are along National Highway 1, are listed from south to north.

Binh Thuan
Bình Thuân

PHAN THIET
PHAN THIẾT
Phan Thiet (population 76,000) is best known for its nuoc mam (fish sauce) and fishing industry. The population includes descendants of the Chams, who controlled this area until 1692. During the colonial period, the Europeans lived in their own segregated ghetto which stretched along the north bank of the Phan Thiet River, while the Vietnamese, Chams, Southern Chinese, Malays and Indonesians lived along the river's south bank.

Binh Thuan Province (at least north of Phan Thiet) is one of the most arid regions of Vietnam. The nearby plains, which are dominated by rocky, roundish mountains, support a bit of irrigated rice agriculture. The relative dryness seems to help support a large population of flies – Aussies should feel right at home.

Orientation
Phan Thiet is built along both banks of the Phan Thiet River, which is also known as the Ca Ti River and the Muong Man River. National Highway 1 runs right through town; south of the river, it is known as Tran Hung Dao St while north of the river it is called Le Hong Phong St.

Provinces of South-Central Vietnam	
1	Quang Tri
2	Thua Thien-Hué
3	Quang Nam-Danang
4	Kon Tum
5	Quang Ngai
6	Binh Dinh
7	Gia Lai
8	Phu Yen
9	Dac Lac
10	Khanh Hoa
11	Lam Dong
12	Ninh Thuan
13	Binh Thuan
14	Song Be
15	Dong Nai
16	Tay Ninh
17	Long An

Information
Tourist Office The office of Binh Thuan Tourist (Cong Ty Du Lich Binh Thuan; ☎ 22494, 21394, 22894) is at 82 Trung Trac St (corner Tran Hung Dao St), which is just south of the bridge over the Phan Thiet River.

Phan Thiet Beach
To get to Phan Thiet's beachfront, turn east (right if you're heading north) at Victory Monument, an arrow-shaped, concrete tower with victorious cement people at the base.

Fishing Harbour
The river flowing through the centre of town creates a small fishing harbour which is always chock-a-block with boats. It makes for charming photography.

Mui Ne Beach
Mui Ne Beach, famous for its sand dunes, is 22 km east of Phan Thiet near a fishing

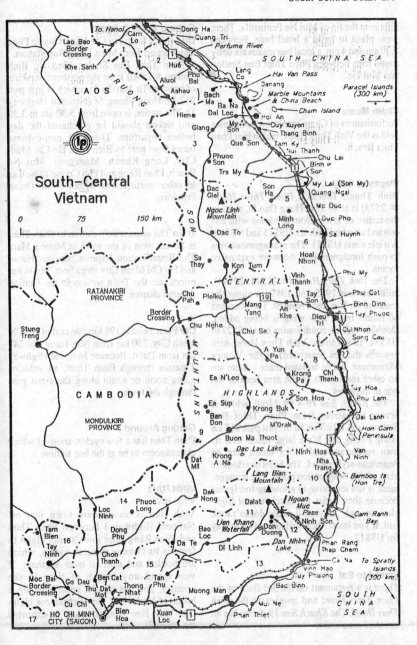

South-Central
Vietnam

0   75   150 km

village at the tip of Mui Ne Peninsula. There were plans to build a hotel here. Between 8.30 am and 4 pm, a local bus makes six daily round trips between **Phan Thiet Bus Station** and Mui Ne.

Cham Music

Performances of Cham music are sometimes held at the Vinh Thuy Hotel, which is at Phan Thiet Beach.

Places to Stay

Binh Thuan Tourist's *Phan Thiet Hotel* (☎ 2573) is at 40 Tran Hung Dao St, right in the centre of town. Double rooms with air-con and attached bath are US$15 and US$18. A triple costs US$21. The management tries to push foreigners into the more expensive rooms.

The *Vinh Thuy Hotel* (☎ 21294, 22394), built between 1985 and 1989, is along the seashore on Ton Tuc Thang St. The hotel has 66 rooms but a new wing is being added. Doubles with air-conditioning cost US$27 to US$34. To get to the Vinh Thuy Hotel, turn towards the sea (eastward) at the Victory Monument. It's an isolated place – there are no other restaurants in the area besides the one in the hotel.

The *Khach San 19-4* (☎ 2460), which is across the street from Phan Thiet Bus Station, is at 1 Tu Van Tu St (just past 217 Le Hong Phong St). It's a large place with its own restaurant and looks much like an American-style motel. The hotel overlooks a vista of salt-evaporation pools. The management is not receptive to allowing foreigners because they insist the hotel 'is not high-class enough', though it really doesn't look bad. If you insist, they will allow you to stay for US$12.

Places to Eat

There is a restaurant on the 3rd floor of the *Phan Thiet Hotel* and another at the *Vinh Thuy Hotel*. The *Khach San 19-4* also has an attached restaurant.

Getting There & Away

Bus Buses from Ho Chi Minh City to Phan Thiet depart from Mien Dong Bus Station.

Phan Thiet Bus Station (Ben Xe Binh Thuan; ☎ 2590) is on the northern outskirts of town at Tu Van Tu St, which is just past 217 Le Hong Phong St (National Highway 1). The station is open from 5.30 am to 3.30 pm; tickets should be purchased the day before departure. There are non-express buses from here to Bien Hoa, Ho Chi Minh City, Long Khanh, Madagoui, Mui Ne Beach, Phan Rang and Phu Cuong as well as to other destinations within Binh Thuan Province.

Train The nearest train station to Phan Thiet is 12 km west of the town at Muong Man. The Reunification Express between Hanoi and Ho Chi Minh City stops here. For ticket prices, see the Train section in the Getting Around chapter.

Car Phan Thiet is 198 km due east of Ho Chi Minh City, 250 km from Nha Trang and 247 km from Dalat. Because National Highway 1 passes through Phan Thiet, all vehicles going north or south along the coast pass through the town.

Getting Around

Phan Thiet has a few cyclos, some of which always seem to be at the bus station.

VINH HAO

VĨNH HẢO

Vinh Hao is an obscure town just off National Highway 1 between Phan Thiet and Phan Rang. The town's only claim to fame is its famous mineral waters, which are bottled and sold all over Vietnam. If you spend any length of time in the country, you are almost certain to sip a bottle of Vinh Hao. The Vietnamese claim that Vinh Hao mineral water is exported (to where?).

Ninh Thuan
Ninh Thuân

CA NA
CA NA

During the 16th century, princes of the Cham royal family would fish and hunt tigers, elephants and rhinoceros here. Today, Ca Na is better known for its turquoise waters, lined with splendid white-sand beaches dotted with huge boulders – it's a beautiful and relaxing spot. The terrain is studded with magnificent prickly pear cacti. Rau Cau Island is visible offshore.

Tra Cang Temple is to the north about midway between Ca Na and Phan Rang, but you have to sidetrack over an abysmal dirt road to reach it. Many ethnic Chinese from Ho Chi Minh City like to visit the temple.

Places to Stay
There are two hotels in town, the *Khach San Hai Son* and *Khach San Ca Na*. We stayed at the latter and had little sleep because of prostitutes banging on the door all night to solicit business. Both hotels are about the same standard, charging US$10 for a large double room with electric fan and a terrace overlooking the sea. Electricity goes off at 10 pm and there are frequent power failures, so keep your torch (flashlight) handy.

Places to Eat
Both hotels have decent restaurants. Between the two hotels is the *Ca Na Restaurant* which also has a good shop selling biscuits, film, toothpaste and other necessities.

Getting There & Away
Bus Many long-haul buses cruising National Highway 1 stop here for a break.

Car Ca Na is 114 km north of Phan Thiet and 32 km south of Phan Rang.

PHAN RANG & THAP CHAM
PHAN RANG VÀ THÁP CHÀM
The twin cities of Phan Rang and Thap Cham

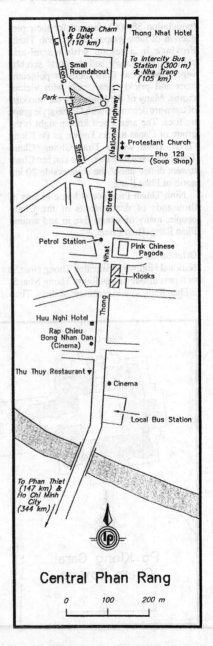

To Thap Cham & Dalat (110 km)

Thong Nhat Hotel

Small Roundabout

To Intercity Bus Station (300 m) & Nha Trang (105 km)

Park

Hong Phong Street

National Highway 1

Protestant Church

Pho 129 (Soup Shop)

Nhat Street

Petrol Station

Pink Chinese Pagoda

Kiosks

Thong Street

Huu Nghi Hotel

Rap Chieu Bong Nhan Dan (Cinema)

Thu Thuy Restaurant

Cinema

Local Bus Station

To Phan Thiet (147 km) & Ho Chi Minh City (344 km)

Central Phan Rang

0   100   200 m

(population 38,000), famous for their production of table grapes, are in Ninh Thuan Province in a region with a semi-arid climate. The sandy soil supports scrubby vegetation; local flora includes poinciana trees and prickly pear cacti with vicious thorns. Many of the houses on the outskirts of town are decorated with Greek-style grape trellises. The area's best known sight is the group of Cham towers known as Po Klong Garai, from which Thap Cham (Cham Tower) derives its name. You can see Cham towers dotted about the countryside 20 km north of Phan Rang.

Ninh Thuan Province is home to tens of thousands of descendants of the Cham people, many of whom live in and around Phan Rang-Thap Cham.

Orientation
National Highway 1 is called Thong Nhat St as it runs through Phan Rang. Thong Nhat St is Phan Rang's main commercial street. Thap Cham is strung out along Highway 20, which heads west from Phan Rang towards Ninh Son and Dalat.

Information
Tourist Office The office of Ninh Thuan Tourist (Cong Ty Du Lich Ninh Thuan; ☎ 2542) is in the Huu Nghi Hotel on Thong Nhat St.

Po Klong Garai Cham Towers
Phan Rang-Thap Cham's most famous landmark is Po Klong Garai, four brick towers constructed at the end of the 13th century during the reign of the Cham monarch Jaya Simhavarman III. The towers, built as Hindu temples, stand on a brick platform at the top of Cho'k Hala, a crumbly granite hill covered with some of the most ornery cacti this side of the Rio Grande.

Over the entrance to the largest tower (the *kalan*, or sanctuary) is a carving of a dancing Shiva with six arms. Note the inscriptions on

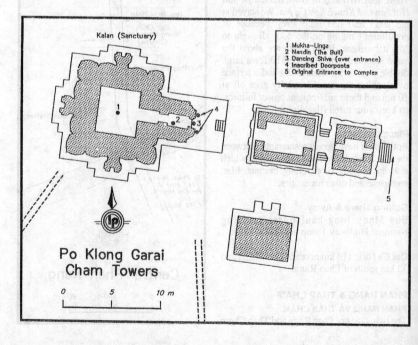

Kalan (Sanctuary)

1 Mukha-Linga
2 Nandin (The Bull)
3 Dancing Shiva (over entrance)
4 Inscribed Doorposts
5 Original Entrance to Complex

Po Klong Garai
Cham Towers

0   5   10 m

the doorposts. Inside the vestibule is a statue of the bull Nandin, symbol of the agricultural productivity of the countryside. To ensure a good crop, farmers would place an offering of fresh greens in front of Nandin's muzzle. Under the main tower is a *mukha-linga*, a linga (a stylised phallus which symbolises maleness and creative power and which represents the Hindu god Shiva) with a painted human face on it. A wooden pyramid has been constructed above the mukha-linga.

Inside the tower opposite the entrance to the kalan you can get a good look at some of the Cham's sophisticated masonry technology. The structure attached to it was originally the main entrance to the complex.

On a nearby hill is a rock with an inscription from the year 1050 commemorating the erection of a linga by a Cham prince.

On the hill directly south of Cho'k Hala there is a concrete water tank built by the Americans in 1965. It is encircled by French pillboxes which were built during the Franco-Viet Minh War to protect the nearby rail yards. To the north of Cho'k Hala you can see the concrete revetments of Thanh Son Airbase, used since 1975 by the Soviet-built MiGs of the Vietnamese Air Force.

Po Klong Garai is several hundred metres north of National Highway 20, at a point seven km towards Dalat from Phan Rang. The towers are on the other side of the tracks from Thap Cham Railroad Station.

Thap Cham Rail Yards

The Thap Cham Rail Yards are 300 metres south-east of Po Klong Garai and across the tracks from the Thap Cham Railway Station. The main function of the yards, which were founded by the French about 80 years ago, is the repair of Vietnamese Railways' ancient one-metre gauge engines and rolling stock. Spare parts are made either by hand or with antique machine tools and metal presses. Each pair of railroad wheels you see lying about weighs 500 kg.

It may be possible to tour the yards, but judging by the small armoury (which includes a 50-calibre machine gun!) kept at the front gate, it seems clear that the area is

deemed to have a certain strategic importance. Indeed, the Vietnamese Communists are well aware of how vital railroads are for national security – that's why they used to go to so much trouble to sabotage them during the Franco-Viet Minh War and the Vietnam War.

The 86-km-long railway from Thap Cham to Dalat operated from 1930 until 1964, when it was closed because of repeated Viet Cong attacks. The line used a crémaillère system in which chains were used to pull the trains up the mountainside at a grade of up to 12 cm per metre. The steepest sections of track are visible at Ngoan Muc Pass (Bellevue Pass) from National Highway 20 (which links Phan Rang with Dalat). There are no plans at present to reopen the Thap Cham-Dalat railway. The oldest engine at the Thap Cham Rail Yards is an inoperable steam engine for the crémaillère manufactured by Machinenfabrik Esselingen in 1929.

Po Ro Me Cham Tower

Po Ro Me Cham Tower (Thap Po Ro Me), among the newest of Vietnam's Cham towers, is about 15 km south of Phan Rang on a rocky hill five km towards the mountains from National Highway 1. The kalan, which is decorated with paintings, is said to have two inscribed doorposts, two stone statues of the bull Nandin, a bas-relief representing a deified king in the form of Shiva and two statues of queens, one of whom has an inscription on her chest. The towers are named after the last ruler of an independent Champa, King Po Ro Me (ruled 1629-51), who died a prisoner of the Vietnamese.

Tuan Tu Hamlet

There is a minaretless Cham mosque, which is closed to visitors, in the Cham hamlet of Tuan Tu (population 1000). This Muslim community is governed by elected religious leaders *(Thay Mun)*, who can easily be identified by their traditional costume, which includes a white robe and an elaborate white turban with red tassels. In keeping with Islamic precepts governing modesty, Cham women often wear head coverings and skirts.

The Chams, like other ethnic minorities in Vietnam, suffer from discrimination and are even poorer than their ethnic-Vietnamese neighbours.

To get to Tuan Tu Hamlet, head south from town along National Highway 1. Go 250 metres south of the large bridge to a small bridge. Cross it and turn left (to the southeast) onto a dirt track. At the market (just past the Buddhist pagoda on the right), turn right and follow the road, part of which is lined with hedgerows of cacti, for about two km, crossing two white concrete footbridges. Ask villagers for directions along the way. Tuan Tu is three km from National Highway 1.

Ninh Chu Beach

Ninh Chu Beach (Bai Tam Ninh Chu) is five km south of Phan Rang.

Places to Stay

The main tourist hotel in Phan Rang is the *Huu Nghi Hotel* (☎ 22606; 20 rooms), also known as the Phan Rang Hotel and also called the Hoa Binh Hotel. Whatever you call it, it's at 354 Thong Nhat St, 150 metres south of the pink pagoda in the market area.

The four-storey *Thong Nhat Hotel* (☎ 2515; 16 rooms) at 164 Thong Nhat St is a modern place with a good restaurant. It's better than the Huu Nghi Hotel but a bit far if you're walking from the bus station. Rooms with electric fan cost US$10 to US$15, or US$20 with air-conditioning.

Places to Eat

A local delicacy is roasted or baked gecko (ky nhong) served with fresh green mango.

The *Thu Thuy Restaurant* is a three-storey eatery on Thong Nhat St. *Nha Hang 426* is across the street from the bus station. *Nha Hang 404* is at 404 Thong Nhat St. For soup, try *Pho 129* at 231 Thong Nhat St (just south of the Protestant church).

Getting There & Away

Bus Buses from Ho Chi Minh City to Phan Rang-Thap Cham depart from Mien Dong Bus Station.

Phan Rang Intercity Bus Station (Ben Xe Phan Rang; ☎ 2031) is on the northern outskirts of town opposite 64 Thong Nhat St. There is bus service from here to Ca Na Beach, Cam Ranh Bay, Dalat, Danang, Don Duong, Ho Chi Minh City, Long Huong, Phan Ri, Phan Thiet, Nha Trang, Nhi Ha, Noi Huyen, Son Hai, Song Dan and Song My.

The Local Bus Station (Ben Xe) is at the southern end of town across the street from 426 Thong Nhat St.

Train The Thap Cham Railroad Station is about six km west of National Highway 1 within sight of Po Klong Garai Cham Towers.

Car Phan Rang is 344 km from Ho Chi Minh City, 147 km from Phan Thiet, 105 km from Nha Trang and 110 km from Dalat.

Khanh Hoa
Khán Hòa

CAM RANH BAY
CAM RANH

Cam Ranh Bay is an excellent natural harbour 56 km north of Phan Rang-Thap Cham. The Russian fleet of Admiral Rodjestvenski used it in 1905 at the end of the Russo-Japanese War as did the Japanese during WW II, when the area was still considered an excellent place for tiger hunting. In the mid-1960s, the Americans constructed a vast base here, including an extensive port, ship-repair facilities and an airstrip.

After reunification, the Russians and their fleet came back, enjoying far better facilities than they had found seven decades before. For a while this became the largest Soviet naval installation outside the USSR.

In 1988, Mikhail Gorbachev offered to abandon the installation if the Americans would do the same with their six bases across the South China Sea in the Philippines. The following year, however, the Vietnamese, evidently annoyed with the Soviets, appeared to offer the Americans renewed use of Cam Ranh Bay. The Soviet presence at Cam Ranh Bay was significantly reduced in 1990 as part of the Kremlin's cost-cutting measures.

With the collapse of the Soviet Union in 1991 and subsequent economic problems, the Russians have vastly cut back on their military facilities. However, at the time of this writing the base was still occupied by the Russian navy though they were supposed to withdraw soon. Despite repeated requests from the Russians, the Vietnamese have refused to grant them permanent rights to the base. Just why the Russians still have any interest at all in Cam Ranh Bay has mystified and worried Western military intelligence experts – perhaps it's just the last hurrah for the Soviet navy.

There are beautiful beaches around Cam Ranh Bay – indeed, Americans stationed here during the war sometimes called it Vietnam's Hawaii. However, as long as this area remains a military base, it isn't likely to develop into a tourist resort. You'll probably have trouble getting a travel permit for Cam Ranh Bay. Some American military veterans have returned to Cam Ranh Bay on organised tours.

Places to Eat
There are some terrific seafood places along National Highway 1 right beside the '63 km to Nha Trang' and '41 km to Phan Rang' marker.

NHA TRANG
NHA TRANG
Nha Trang (population 200,000), the capital of Khanh Hoa Province, has what is probably the nicest municipal beach in all of Vietnam. Club Med hasn't arrived yet, there are still no Monte Carlo-style casinos and only a couple of neon signs. Nevertheless, this area has the potential to become another flashy resort like Thailand's Pattaya Beach (dread the thought), but that will probably take a few more years.

The turquoise waters around Nha Trang are almost transparent, making for excellent fishing, snorkelling and scuba diving. Of late, lots of 'massage' signs have been popping up around town, a sure sign that more visitors are expected.

Nha Trang's dry season, unlike that of Ho Chi Minh City, runs from June to October. The wettest months are October and November, but rain usually falls only at night or in the morning.

The combined fishing fleet of Khanh Hoa Province and neighbouring Phu Yen Province numbers about 10,000 trawlers and junks; they are able to fish during the 250 days of calm seas per year. The area's seafood products include abalone, lobster, prawns, cuttle-fish, mackerel, pomfret, scallops, shrimps, snapper and tuna. Exportable agricultural products from the area include cashew nuts, coconuts, coffee and sesame seeds. Salt production employs 4000 people.

Orientation
Tran Phu Blvd runs along Nha Trang Beach. The centre of Nha Trang is around the Nha Trang Hotel on Thong Nhat St.

Information
Tourist Offices Khanh Hoa Tourist (Cong Ty Du Lich Khanh Hoa; ☎ 22753; telex 581504 HOTHY-VT; fax (84-58) 21912/21092) is the provincial tourism authority. It can provide cars, drivers and guides and may also rent out diving and underwater fishing equipment. Their office is on the 2nd floor of a yellow two-storey building on the grounds of the Hai Yen Hotel. To get there, enter the Hai Yen Hotel through the front entrance (at 40 Tran Phu Blvd) and walk all the way through the main building. Alternatively, you can use the Hai Yen Hotel's back gate at 1 Tran Hung Dao St (next to the Hung Dao Hotel). The office is open from 7 to 11.30 am and 1.30 to 5 pm Monday to Saturday.

Nha Trang Tourism (☎ 21231), which runs various cafes and restaurants around town, has its office in the Hung Dao Hotel at 3 Tran Hung Dao St. Rental cars cost US$0.25 per km with minimum charges of

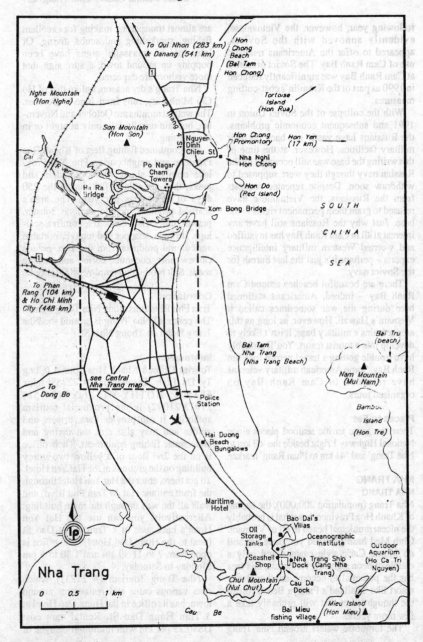

Nha Trang

0   0.5   1 km

US$12.50 for a half day and US$25 for a full day.

Money Vietcombank, also known as the Bank for Foreign Trade (Ngan Hang Ngoai Thuong; ☎ 21054) is at 17 Quang Trung St. It is open from 7 to 11.30 am and 1 to 5 pm Monday to Saturday except Thursday afternoons. Here you can change travellers' cheques for US dollars cash or Vietnamese dong. It is possible to change some other major currencies, but US dollars are preferred.

At the time of this writing, the bank could not do cash advances on major credit cards though this is being considered for the future. They also say they will exchange Vietnamese dong for US dollars (for 5% less than their dong-for-dollars rate) provided you can supply proof of having bought the dong legally.

Post & Telecommunications The GPO (telex 500 GDDB NT) is at 2 Tran Phu Blvd. near the northern end of Nha Trang Beach one block from the Thang Loi Hotel; it is open daily from 6.30 am to 8.30 pm. International telephone calls can be placed via Ho Chi Minh City or Hanoi. The GPO also offers international telex and domestic fax services.

TNT Vietrans (☎ 21043) has international and domestic parcel and document delivery service. For rates, see the Post & Telecommunications section in the Facts for the Visitor chapter.

Emergency An American-built hospital, Bien Vien Tinh (☎ 22175), is on Yersin St.

Po Nagar Cham Towers

The Cham towers of Po Nagar (The Lady of the City) were built between the 7th and 12th centuries on a site used for Hindu worship as early as the 2nd century AD. Today, both ethnic-Chinese and Vietnamese Buddhists

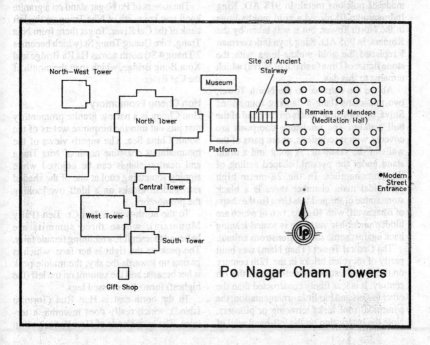

Po Nagar Cham Towers

come to Po Nagar to pray and make offerings according to their respective traditions. Out of deference to the continuing religious significance of this site, shoes should be removed before entering the towers.

There were once seven or eight towers at Po Nagar, four of which remain. All the temples face the east, as did the original entrance to the complex, which is to the right as you ascend the hillock. In centuries past, a person coming to pray passed through the pillared *mandapa* (meditation hall), 10 of whose pillars can still be seen, before proceeding up the staircase to the towers.

The 23-metre-high North Tower (Thap Chinh), with its terraced pyramidal roof, vaulted interior masonry and vestibule, is a superb example of Cham architecture. It was built in 817 AD by Pangro, a minister of King Harivarman I, 43 years after the temples here were sacked and burned by Malay corsairs who probably came from Srivijaya on Sumatra. The raiders also carried off a linga made of precious metal. In 918 AD, King Indravarman III placed a gold mukha-linga in the North Tower, but it was taken by the Khmers. In 965 AD, King Jaya Indravarman I replaced the gold mukha-linga with the stone figure of Uma (a shakti of Shiva) which remains to this day.

Above the entrance to the North Tower, two musicians flank a dancing four-armed Shiva, one of whose feet is on the head of the bull Nandin. The sandstone doorposts are covered with inscriptions, as are parts of the walls of the vestibule. A gong and a drum stand under the pyramid-shaped ceiling of the antechamber. In the 28-metre-high pyramidal main chamber there is a black stone statue of the goddess Uma (in the shape of Bhagavati) with 10 arms, two of which are hidden under her vest; she is seated leaning back against some sort of monstrous animal.

The Central Tower (Thap Nam) was built partly of recycled bricks in the 12th century on the site of a structure dating from the 7th century. It is less finely constructed than the other towers and has little ornamentation; the pyramidal roof lacks terracing or pilasters. Note the inscription on the left-hand wall of the vestibule. The interior altars were once covered with silver. There is a linga inside the main chamber.

The South Tower (Mieu Dong Nam), at one time dedicated to Sandhaka (Shiva), now shelters a linga.

The richly ornamented North-West Tower (Thap Tay Bac) was originally dedicated to Ganesha. The pyramid-shaped summit of the roof of the North-West Tower has disappeared.

The West Tower, of which almost nothing remains, was constructed by King Vikrantavarman during the first half of the 9th century.

Near the North Tower is a small museum with a few mediocre examples of Cham stonework; the explanatory signs are in Vietnamese only. At one time there was a small temple on this site. If you are heading north, be sure to visit the Cham Museum in Danang, which has the finest collection of Cham statuary.

The towers of Po Nagar stand on a granite knoll two km north of Nha Trang on the left bank of the Cai River. To get there from Nha Trang, take Quang Trung St (which becomes 2 Thang 4 St) north across Ha Ra Bridge and Xom Bong Bridge, which span the mouth of the Cai River.

Hon Chong Promontory

Hon Chong is a narrow granite promontory that juts out into the turquoise waters of the South China Sea. The superb views of the mountainous coastline north of Nha Trang and nearby islands can be enjoyed while sipping something cool at one of the shaded refreshment kiosks on a bluff overlooking the promontory.

To the north-west is Nui Co Tien (Fairy Mountain), whose three summits are believed to resemble a reclining female fairy. The peak on the right is her face, which is gazing up towards the sky; the middle peak is her breasts; and the summit on the left (the highest) forms her crossed legs.

To the north-east is Hon Rua (Tortoise Island), which really does resemble a tortoise. The two islands of Hon Yen are off in the distance to the east. A bit south of Hon Chong (that is, towards Nha Trang) and a few dozen metres from the beach is tiny Hon Do (Red Island), which has a Buddhist temple on top.

There is a gargantuan handprint on the massive boulder balanced at the tip of the promontory. According to local legend, it was made by a drunk male giant fairy when he fell down upon spying a female fairy bathing nude at Bai Tien (Fairy Beach), which is the point of land closest to Hon Rua. Despite the force of his fall, the giant managed to get up and eventually catch the fairy. The two began a life together but soon the gods intervened and punished the male fairy, sending him off to a 're-education camp' (this is evidently a post-1975 version of the story) for an indefinite sentence.

The love-sick female fairy waited patiently for her husband to come back, but after a very long time, despairing that he might never return, she lay down in sorrow and turned into Nui Co Tien (Fairy Mountain). When the giant male fairy finally returned and saw what had become of his wife, he prostrated himself in grief next to the boulder with his handprint on it. He, too, turned to stone and can be seen to this day.

Hon Chong is 3.5 km from central Nha Trang. To get there from Po Nagar, head north on 2 Thang 4 St for 400 metres. Just before 15 2 Thang 4 St, turn right onto Nguyen Dinh Chieu St and follow the road for about 700 metres. If you prefer to travel to Hon Chong by Xe Lam, catch one heading to Dong De at the Dam Market Xe Lam Station.

Beaches

Nha Trang Beach Coconut palms provide shelter for both bathers and strollers along most of Nha Trang's six km of beachfront. Three clusters of refreshment stalls sell drinks and light food. The water is usually remarkably clear.

Hon Chong Beach Hon Chong Beach (Bai Tam Hon Chong) is a series of beaches that begin just north of Hon Chong Promontory;

fishers live here among the coconut palms. Behind the beaches are steep mountains whose lower reaches support crops that include mangoes and bananas.

Pasteur Institute

Nha Trang's Pasteur Institute was founded in 1895 by Dr Alexandre Yersin (1863-1943), who was – from among the tens of thousands of colonists who spent time in Vietnam – probably the Frenchman most beloved by the Vietnamese. Born in Sweden of French parents, Dr Yersin came to Vietnam in 1889 after working under Louis Pasteur in Paris. He spent the next four years travelling throughout the Central Highlands and recording his observations. During this period he came upon the site of what is now Dalat and recommended to the government that a hill station be established there. In 1894, in Hong Kong, he discovered the rat-borne microbe that causes bubonic plague. Dr Yersin was the first to introduce rubber and quinine-producing trees to Vietnam.

Today, the Pasteur Institute in Nha Trang coordinates vaccination and hygiene programmes for the country's southern coastal region. Despite its minuscule budget and antiquated equipment (the labs look much as they did half a century ago), the Institute produces vaccines (eg rabies, diphtheria, pertussis, typhoid) and tries to carry out research in microbiology, virology and epidemiology. Vietnam's two other Pasteur Institutes are in Ho Chi Minh City and Dalat.

Dr Yersin's library and office are now a museum; items on display include laboratory equipment (such as his astronomical instruments) and some of his personal effects. There is a picture of Dr Yersin above the door to the veranda. The model boat was given to him by local fishers with whom he spent a great deal of time. The Institute library, which is across the landing from the museum, houses many of Dr Yersin's books as well as modern scientific journals. At his request, Dr Yersin is buried near Nha Trang.

To find someone to show you the museum (Vien Bao Tang), ask around in the main building (a mauve-coloured two-storey structure) during working hours (except at lunchtime). The museum is on the 2nd floor of the back wing of the main building. To get there, go up the stairs near the sign that reads Thu Vien (Library).

Long Son Pagoda

Long Son Pagoda (also known as Tinh Hoi Khanh Hoa Pagoda and An Nam Phat Hoc Hoi Pagoda), a sight popular with domestic tourists, is about 500 metres west of the railroad station opposite 15, 23 Thang 10 St. The pagoda, now home to nine monks, was founded in the late 19th century and has been rebuilt several times over the years. The entrance and roofs are decorated with mosaic dragons made of glass and bits of ceramic tile. The main sanctuary is an attractive hall adorned with modern interpretations of traditional motifs. Note the ferocious nose hairs on the colourful dragons which are wrapped around the pillars on either side of the main altar.

At the top of the hill behind the pagoda is the huge white Buddha, seated on a lotus blossom, which is visible from all over the city. There are great views of Nha Trang and nearby rural areas from the platform around the 14-metre-high figure, which was built in 1963. As you approach the pagoda from the street, the 152 stone steps up the hill to the Buddha begin to the right of the structure.

Nha Trang Cathedral

Nha Trang Cathedral, built in French Gothic style and complete with medieval-looking stained glass windows, stands on a small hill overlooking the railway station. It was constructed of simple cement blocks between 1928 and 1933. Today, the Cathedral is the seat of the bishop of Nha Trang. In 1988, a Catholic cemetery not far from the church was disinterred to make room for a new building for the railway station. The ashes were brought to the Cathedral and reburied in cavities behind the wall of plaques lining the ramp up the hill.

Masses are held daily at 5 am and 4.30 pm and on Sundays at 5 am, 7 am and 4.30 pm. If the main gate on Thai Nguyen St is closed,

■ PLACES TO STAY

6	Thang Loi Hotel
10	Viet Ngu Hotel
11	Nha Trang Hotel 2
12	Nha Trang Hotel
22	Thong Nhat Hotel
25	Nha Khach 24
27	Hung Dao Hotel
29	Vien Dong Hotel
30	Hai Yen Hotel
33	Nha Khach 44

▼ PLACES TO EAT

4	Lac Canh Restaurant
5	Nha Hang 33 Le Loi
13	Binh Minh Restaurant
14	Restaurants Lys
16	Ngoc Lau Restaurant
17	Ice Cream Shops
31	Cafes

OTHER

1	Short-Haul Bus Station
2	Dam Market Xe Lam Station
3	Dam Market
7	GPO
8	Giant Seated Buddha
9	Long Son Pagoda
15	Vietcombank
18	Stadium
19	Youth Tourism Express Bus Office
20	Pasteur Institute & Yersin Museum
21	Bien Vien Tinh (Hospital)
23	Nha Trang Station
24	Nha Trang Cathedral
26	Church
28	Express Bus Station
32	War Memorial Obelisk
34	Lien Tinh Bus Station
35	Nha Trang Ship Chandler Company

go up the ramp opposite 17 Nguyen Trai St to the back of the building.

Oceanographic Institute

The Oceanographic Institute (Vien Nghiem Cuu Bien; ☎ 22536), founded in 1923, has an aquarium (ho ca) and specimen room

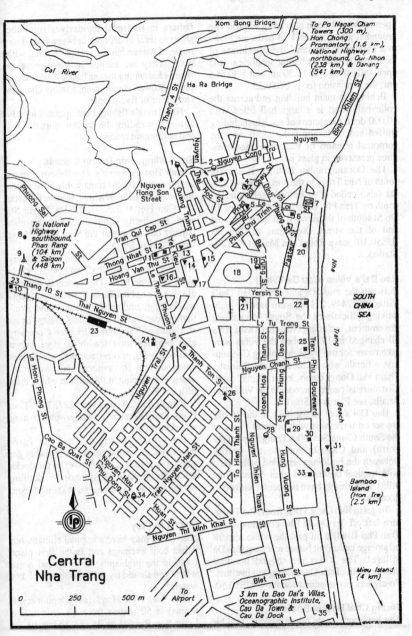

Central
Nha Trang

0   250   500 m

To National
Highway 1
southbound,
Phan Rang
(104 km)
& Saigon
(448 km)

To Po Nagar Cham
Towers (300 m),
Hon Chong
Promantory (1.6 km),
National Highway 1
northbound, Qui Nhon
(238 km) & Danang
(541 km)

Xom Bong Bridge

Cai River

Ha Ra Bridge

Nguyen
Hong Son
Street

Nguyen Cong Tru

SOUTH
CHINA
SEA

Yersin St

Ly Tu Trong St

Nguyen Chanh St

Nha
Trang
Beach

Bamboo
Island
(Hon Tre)
(2.5 km)

Mieu Island
(4 km)

To
Airport

3 km to Bao Dai's Villas,
Oceanographic Institute,
Cau Da Town &
Cau Da Dock

Biet   Thu St

open to the public; it also has a library. The ground-floor aquarium's 23 tanks are home to a variety of colourful live specimens of local marine life, including seahorses. It is open daily from 7 to 11.30 am and 1.30 to 5 pm; the admission fee is US$0.25.

Behind the main building and across the volleyball court is a large hall filled with 60,000 dead specimens of sea life including stuffed sea birds and fish, corals and the corporeal remains of various marine creatures preserved in glass jars.

The Oceanographic Institute is six km south of Nha Trang in the port village of Cau Da (also called Cau Be). To get there, go south on Tran Phu Blvd (which becomes Tu Do St south of the airport) all the way to the end of the street. Xe Lams to Cau Da (US$0.10) leave from Dam Market Xe Lam Station.

Bao Dai's Villas (Cau Da Villas)

Between the mid-50s and 1975, Bao Dai's Villas (☎ 22449, 21124) were used by high-ranking officials of the South Vietnamese government, including President Thieu. This all changed in 1975, when the villas were taken over for use by high-ranking Communist officials who included Prime Minister Pham Van Dong. Today, low-ranking 'capitalist tourists' can rent a room in the Villas (for details, see Places to Stay).

Bao Dai's five villas, built in the 1920s, are set on three hills with brilliant views of the South China Sea, Nha Trang Bay (to the north) and Cau Da port (to the south). Between the buildings are wind paths lined with tropical bushes and trees. Most of the villas' furnishings have not been changed in decades.

To get to Bao Dai's Villas from Nha Trang, turn left off Tu Do St (the continuation of Tran Phu Blvd) a bit past the white cement oil storage tanks (but before reaching Cau Da village). The Villas are several hundred metres north of the Oceanographic Institute. Foreigners pay an admission fee of US$0.50.

Thung Chai Basket Boats

The two-metre-wide round baskets used by fishers to transport themselves from the shore to their boats (and between boats) are made of woven bamboo strips covered with pitch. They are known in Vietnamese as *thung chai (thung* means basket, *chai* means pitch). Rowed standing up, a thung chai can carry four or five people.

Nha Trang's fishing fleet operates mostly at night, spending the days in port for rest and equipment repair.

Snorkelling, Skin Diving & Boats

Khanh Hoa Province's 71 offshore islands are renowned for the remarkably clear water surrounding them. Maritime Recovery (Truc Vot Cuu Ho; ☎ 22327), 2A Da Tuong St, rents out diving equipment. You can also contact this agency at the Vien Dong Hotel (see Places to Stay).

The Nha Trang Ship Chandler Company (Cong Ty Tau Bien Nha Trang; ☎ 21195) is at 74 Tran Phu Blvd. This concern, which is also known as Nha Trang Ship Chanco, rents snorkelling, underwater fishing and skin-diving gear and hires out cars, buses, boats and guides. The Ship Chandler Company also supplies food for ships, does minor marine repairs, runs restaurants and provides entertainment for sailors, including massages and dancing at the villa in which their office is located.

Khanh Hoa Tourist (☎ 22753; 1 Tran Hung Dao St) rents out underwater fishing and skin-diving gear.

Boats can be hired from the forementioned concerns, but you'll probably get a better deal (but at higher risk) on the docks at Cau Da (see Getting Around). Snorkelling equipment can be purchased at Dam Market.

Places to Stay

Nha Trang may have a tropical climate, but it has cool evenings and is the first place (outside the highlands) as you head north where you should try to find a hotel with hot water.

The *Viet Ngu Hotel* (no telephone; 20 rooms) is 50 metres from the entrance to Long Son Pagoda at 25, 23 Thang 10 St;

doubles cost US$6 with fan. It's an old and tattered place a long way from the beach but only half a km from the railway station.

The *Vien Dong Hotel*, 1 Tran Hung Dao St, is a new place that's attracting a lot of travellers. The hotel has a swimming pool, bicycle rentals and diving gear for hire. Clean rooms on the 4th floor with fan and hot-water bathroom cost only US$10; air-con rooms are US$16 to US$25. According to the Vien Dong's pamphlet, 'weapons and objects with offensive smell should be kept at the reception desk'.

The tourist-class *Thang Loi Hotel* (☎ 22241), which resembles an American-style motel, is 100 metres from the beach at 4 Pasteur St, one of the few streets in Vietnam to retain its French name. Singles/doubles with fan are US$5/10; with air-con and hot water they're US$20/24; a room with refrigerator and bathtub will set you back US$25/30 and a 'special room' is US$30/35.

The *Thong Nhat Hotel* (☎ 22966) is at 18 Tran Phu Blvd. It's a beautiful place just across the street from the beach. Singles/doubles/triples with electric fan are US$7/10/15; with air-con and hot water it's US$17 to US$25.

The *Nha Khach 24* (☎ 22671; 83 rooms) is a government-owned beachside place at 24 Tran Phu Blvd. Built in the finest tradition of Soviet concrete box architecture, the building fortunately looks much better on the inside than it does on the outside. Rooms cost US$10 to US$35. However, this place is popular with cadres attending 'meetings' at government expense and is often full.

The *Nha Khach 44* is a large place with a beach view. Like the Nha Khach 24, this hotel looks like a former Communist Party headquarters. Rooms with fan are US$10; with air-con, US$18 to US$42.

The *Hai Yen Hotel* (☎ 22828, 22974; 107 rooms), whose name means Sea Swift, faces the beach at 40 Tran Phu Blvd. This place has a restaurant and dance hall, and amongst the Vietnamese, it's the most famous in Nha Trang and often full. Single/double rooms with fan are US$7/10; air-con rooms are

US$15/20 to US$30/40. The Khanh Hoa Tourist office is around the back.

The *Maritime Hotel* (☎ 21969, 21970; fax 22903; 60 rooms), 34 Tran Phu Blvd (southern end of Nha Trang) caters to an up-market clientele. There are three categories of rooms costing US$25, US$35 and US$50. The beach views from the upper floors are impressive.

The *Hung Dao Hotel* (☎ 22246; 27 rooms) is at 3 Tran Hung Dao St, next to the Vien Dong Hotel. If not full, it's a relative bargain for the good location at US$6/7 for singles/doubles with fan.

The *Hai Duong Beach Bungalows* (☎ 21150; 20 bungalows) are on Tran Phu Blvd a few hundred metres south of one of the gates to the airport. The steep-roofed bungalows, which are often booked up, are in a grove of casuarina trees right along the beach; each has two beds and costs US$15 a night. The bungalows are becoming a bit dilapidated – if you're staying here during the rainy season, make sure the roof doesn't leak. The Hai Duong complex includes a volleyball court and a restaurant.

The *Nha Trang Hotel* (☎ 22347, 22224; 74 rooms) is a seven-storey building at 133 Thong Nhat St. It's a fine-looking hotel, the only drawback being its relatively long distance from the beach. Budget rooms with fan cost US$8; air-con puts the price tag at US$10 to US$20.

Just down the block is the *Nha Trang Hotel II* (☎ 22956), 21 Le Thanh Phuong St. This is a new and clean place. The cheaper double rooms with fan are US$8 and US$12; air-con costs US$15.

The *Bao Dai's Villas* (☎ 22449, 21124), also known as Cau Da Villas, are near Cau Da on the coast six km south of Nha Trang. This is some of the classiest accommodation in the area. For US$27 to US$35 per night, you can sleep in a spacious double room with high ceilings and huge bathrooms where Vietnam's ruling elite has rested itself since the days of French rule. The villas have been renovated and new air-conditioning units have been installed along with the ceiling fans. The restaurant in an adjoining villa has good food at low prices. To get to Bao Dai's Villas from Nha Trang, go south on Tran Phu Blvd and turn left just past the white cement oil storage tanks.

The *Nha Nghi Hon Chong* (☎ 22188; 48 rooms) on Nguyen Dinh Chieu St is at the summit of a hillock 150 metres from Hon Chong Promontory. Housed in the buildings of what was, before 1975, the American-supported Protestant Theological Seminary, Nha Nghi Hon Chong no longer accepts foreigners because it's too run-down. There are some hopes for renovating it in the future. There is a huge on-site dining hall.

Places to Eat

Beach Area The restaurant at the *Hai Yen Hotel* is open from 5 am to midnight. The *Thong Nhat Hotel* also has a restaurant.

There are three clusters of cafes, serving mostly refreshments, along the beach. They are across Tran Phu Blvd from the Thong Nhat Hotel (18 Tran Phu Blvd), the Hai Yen Hotel (40 Tran Phu Blvd) and the Ship Chandler Company office (74 Tran Phu Blvd). At the cluster opposite the Hai Yen Hotel is an unnamed cafe where Hanh conjures up the most delicious seafood salads at incredibly cheap prices.

Central Area One of the best restaurants in town is the *Lac Canh Restaurant*, which is a block east of Dam Market at 11 Hang Ca St. Beef, squid, giant shrimps, lobsters and the like are grilled right at your table.

The *Restaurant Lys* at 117A Hoang Van Thu St is a big, bright and energetic place with an English menu. There's also great seafood at the *Ngoc Lau Restaurant* at 37 Le Thanh Phuong St.

The *Nha Hang 33 Le Loi* at 33 Le Loi St (corner Nguyen Du St) is opposite the main gate to Dam Market. The *Nha Hang 31 Le Loi* is next door.

There is a vegetarian restaurant, *Quay Hang Com Chay*, in the covered semi-circular food pavilion north-east of the main building of Dam Market. The restaurant is right across from stall number 117 (as indicated by the little blue tags with red numbers on them

displayed on each of the stalls that encircle the main market building). The food is made of beans and vegetables and is prepared to look and taste like popular meat dishes.

The *Binh Minh Restaurant*, founded in 1953, is at 64 Hoang Van Thu St (corner Yet Kieu St) in the downtown area; their Vietnamese dishes are excellent. There are several cafes and restaurants in the vicinity of the Nha Trang Hotel.

For ice cream, try the shops around 52 Quang Trung St (corner Le Thanh Ton St).

Dragon Fruit

Nha Trang is best known for its excellent seafood, but a really exotic treat is green dragon fruit *(thanh long)*. This fruit, which is the size and shape of a small pineapple and has an almost-smooth magenta skin, grows only in the Nha Trang area. Its delicious white meat is speckled with black seeds and tastes a bit like kiwifruit. Green dragon fruit grows on a kind of creeping cactus – said to resemble a green dragon – that climbs up the trunks and branches of trees and flourishes on parched hillsides that get very little water. Thanh long is in season from May to September and can be purchased at Dam Market. It is also exported to Ho Chi Minh City and even abroad (it now fetches a high price in Taiwan), but only in Nha Trang is this fruit cheap and fresh. Locals often make a refreshing drink out of crushed green dragon fruit, ice, sugar and sweetened condensed milk. They also use it to make jam. ■

Things to Buy

There are a number of shops selling beautiful seashells (and items made from seashells) near the Oceanographic Institute in Cau Da village. As a brochure of Nha Trang Tourism put it, 'Before leaving Nha Trang, tourists had better call at Cau Da to get some souvenirs of the sea...for their dears at home'. Inexpensive guitars are on sale at 24 Hai Ba Trung St (corner Phan Chu Trinh St). The Hai Yen Hotel has a small gift shop.

Getting There & Away

Air Vietnam Airlines has flights connecting

Nha Trang with Ho Chi Minh City daily except Monday (US$45 one way). There are flights to/from Hanoi every Thursday and Sunday (US$105). Flights to/from Danang fly on Tuesday and Friday (US$55).

Vietnam Airlines' Nha Trang office (☎ 21147) is at 74 Tran Phu St.

Bus Express and regular buses from Ho Chi Minh City to Nha Trang depart from Mien Dong Bus Station. By express bus, the trip takes 11 to 12 hours.

Lien Tinh Bus Station (Ben Xe Lien Tinh; ☎ 22192), Nha Trang's main intercity bus terminal, is opposite 212 Ngo Gia Tu St. Non-express buses from Lien Tinh Bus Station go to:

Bao Loc, Bien Hoa (11 hours), Buon Ma Thuot (six hours), Dalat (six hours; US$1.50), Danang (14 hours; US$3), Di Linh, Ho Chi Minh City (12 hours), Phan Rang (2½ hours), Pleiku (10 hours), Quang Ngai, Qui Nhon (seven hours).

Express buses leave from two different stations. The Youth Tourism Express Bus Office (Du Lich Thanh Nien; ☎ 22010) is just off Yersin St at 6 Hoang Hoa Tham St; tickets are sold daily from 4 am to 6 pm. There are buses from here to:

Buon Ma Thuot (daily at 5 am, the trip takes 5 hours); Dalat (Tuesday, Thursday and Saturday, 5 am, 5 hours); Danang (Monday, Wednesday and Friday, 5 am, 3 hours); Ho Chi Minh City (daily, 5 am and 4.30 pm, 11 hours).

The Express Bus Station (Tram Xe Toc Hanh; ☎ 22397, 22884) is about 150 metres from the Hung Dao Hotel at 46 Le Thanh Ton St; the ticket office is open every day from 6 am to 4.30 pm. Tickets for early morning buses must be purchased one to three days before departure. Tickets for most buses leaving from the Express Bus Station are also sold at Lien Tinh Bus Station. Buses depart at 5 am (unless otherwise indicated) to:

Buon Ma Thuot (5.30 am; five hours), Dalat (five hours), Danang (13 hours), Hanoi (40 hours), Ho Chi Minh City (5 am & 4.30 pm; 12 hours), Hué (15 hours), Quang Binh, Quang Ngai (10 hours), Qui Nhon (six hours), Vinh (35 hours).

The Short-Haul Bus Station (Ben Xe Noi Tinh; ☎ 22191) is opposite 111, 2 Thang 4 St. Aged Renault and DeSoto omnibuses depart from here to Cam Ranh, Nhieu Giang, Ninh Hoa, Tuy Hoa, Tu Bong, Song Cau, Song Hinh, Tay Son and Van Gia.

Train The Nha Trang Railway Station (Ga Nha Trang; ☎ 22113), overlooked by the nearby cathedral, is across the street from 26 Thai Nguyen St; the ticket office is open between 7 am and 2 pm only.

This station has a separate 'Waiting Room for Foreigners & Overseas Vietnamese'. This is on the left-hand side of the main hall and has air-conditioning, fans, comfortable seats and a clean Western-style toilet – a great little oasis.

Nha Trang is well served by both express trains connecting Hanoi and Ho Chi Minh City, and a daily local train between Ho Chi Minh City and Nha Trang. For ticket prices, see the Train section in the Getting Around chapter.

Car Road distances from Nha Trang are: 205 km to Buon Ma Thuot, 541 km to Danang, 448 km to Ho Chi Minh City, 104 km to Phan Rang, 424 km to Pleiku, 412 km to Quang Ngai, and 238 km to Qui Nhon.

A series of roughly parallel roads head inland from near Nha Trang, linking Vietnam's deltas and coastal regions with the Central Highlands.

Getting Around

Xe Lam Dam Market Xe Lam Station (Ben Xe Lam Cho Dam) is on Nguyen Hong Son St near the corner of Nguyen Thai Hoc St. It is due north of the main building of Dam Market, which is a round modern structure several stories high. Xe Lams from Dam Market Xe Lam Station go to: Cau Da (or Cau Be, also known as Chut), where the Oceanographic Institute and the fishing boat dock are; Dong De (near Hon Chong); and

Thanh (take this one to get to Dien Khanh Citadel).

Bicycle All major hotels have bicycle rentals. The cost is US$1 per day or US$0.20 per hour.

Boat The best place in the Nha Trang area to hire boats is the fishing-boat dock at Cau Da (Ben Do Cau Da), which is six km due south of Nha Trang. Motorised seven-metre boats cost US$9 per hour; a round trip to Mieu Island costs about US$5. Boats with a 50-person capacity cost US$10 for the round trip to Mieu Island. Small boats rowed standing up can be hired here as well. It may also be possible to hire boats a few hundred metres away at the larger Nha Trang Ship Dock (Cang Nha Trang).

Tourist boats can be rented from both Khanh Hoa Tourist and the Ship Chandler Company (see earlier for details).

Two enterprising women, Mama Linh and Mama Hanh, run all-day boat trips from Cau Da for US$5 to US$7 (depending on numbers). The trip typically includes stops for snorkelling and swimming on offshore islands, a visit to a fishing village and a good seafood lunch. They will also drive you to and from the dock if you wish. You don't need to search very hard to meet these women; if you spend a little time one evening in the cafes across the road from the Hai Yen Hotel, they'll find you.

Ferries to Tri Nguyen village on Mieu Island depart from Cau Da when full; the fare is US$0.10.

The Vien Dong Hotel advertises a 'traditional junk cruise' along the coast of Vietnam. It's hard to imagine anyone paying the price asked; US$60 per person (!) for an eight-hour cruise, US$48 for six hours or US$25 for three hours. Nice but overpriced.

AROUND NHA TRANG
Mieu Island

Mieu Island (Tri Nguyen Island) is touted in tourist literature as the site of an 'outdoor aquarium' (Ho Ca Tri Nguyen). In fact, the 'aquarium' is an important fish-breeding farm where over 40 species of fish, crustaceans and other marine creatures are raised in three separate compartments. There is a cafe built on stilts over the water. Ask around for canoe rentals.

The main village on Mieu Island is Tri Nguyen. Bai Soai is a gravel beach on the far side of Mieu Island from Cau Da.

Getting There & Away If you have lots of money and little time, you can book an expensive tourist boat with Khanh Hoa Tourist or the Ship Chandler Company. Impoverished and less hurried travellers might catch one of the regular ferries that go to Tri Nguyen village from Cau Da Dock, which is a few hundred metres south of the Oceanographic Institute.

Bamboo Island (Hon Tre)

Bamboo Island (Hon Tre), several km from the southern part of Nha Trang Beach, is the largest island in the Nha Trang area. Tru Beach (Bai Tru) is at the northern end of the island. Ebony Island (Hon Mun), just south of Bamboo Island, is known for its snorkelling. To get to either island, you'll probably have to hire a boat.

Hon Yen

Hon Yen (Salangane Island) is the name of two lump-shaped islands visible in the distance from Nha Trang Beach. Hon Yen and other islands off Khanh Hoa Province are the source of Vietnam's finest salangane (swift) nests. The nests are used in birds' nest soup as well as in traditional medicine, and are considered an aphrodisiac. It is said that Emperor Minh Mang, who ruled Vietnam from 1820 to 1840, derived his extraordinary virility from the consumption of salangane nests.

The nests, which the salanganes build out of their silk-like salivary secretions, are semi-oval and about five to eight cm in diameter. They are usually harvested twice a year. Red nests are the most highly prized. Annual production in Khanh Hoa and Phu Yen provinces is about 1000 kg. At present, salangane nests fetch US$2000 per kg in the international marketplace!

There is a small, secluded beach at Hon Yen. The 17-km trip out to the islands takes three to four hours by small boat.

Dien Khanh Citadel

Dien Khanh Citadel dates from the 17th century Trinh Dynasty. It was rebuilt by Prince Nguyen Anh (later Emperor Gia Long) in 1793 during his successful offensive against the Tay Son Rebels. Only a few sections of the walls and gates are extant. Dien Khanh Citadel is 11 km west of Nha Trang near the villages of Dien Toan and Dien Thanh. The best way to get to Dien Khanh Citadel is to take a Xe Lam to Thanh from Dam Market Xe Lam Station.

Ba Ho Falls

Ba Ho Falls, with its three waterfalls and three pools, is in a forested area 19 km north of Nha Trang and about one km from the road; it is a great place for a picnic. Ba Ho Falls is near Ninh Ich Xa in Vinh Xuong District and not far from Phu Huu village. To get there, take the bus to Ninh Hoa from the Short-Haul Bus Station.

DAI LANH
ĐẠI LÃNH

Semicircular, casuarina-shaded Dai Lanh beach is 83 km north of Nha Trang and 153 km south of Qui Nhon on National Highway 1. At the southern end of the beach is a vast sand-dune causeway; it connects the mainland to Hon Gom, a mountainous peninsula almost 30 km in length. The main village on Hon Gom is Dam Mon (known to the French as Port Dayot), which is on a sheltered bay facing the island of Hon Lon.

At the northern end of Dai Lanh Beach is Dai Lanh Promontory (Mui Dai Lanh), named Cap Varella by the French.

Places to Stay & Eat

There is a four-storey half-completed tourist hotel just off National Highway 1, a few hundred metres south of town. Apparently, construction has been abandoned and the decaying structure is totally overgrown with weeds – makes an interesting photo. Perhaps a foreign investor will rescue the project, but if so it better happen soon before the whole thing topples over.

Just south of the abandoned hotel shell is the *Dai Lanh Restaurant*, the fanciest place in town. There are also at least a dozen small family-owned restaurants in Dai Lanh.

Getting There & Away

Dai Lanh Beach runs along National Highway 1, so any vehicle travelling along the coast between Nha Trang and Tuy Hoa (or Qui Nhon) will get you there.

Phu Yen
Phú Yên

TUY HOA
TUY HÒA

Tuy Hoa, the capital of Phu Yen Province, is a nondescript little town on the coast between Dai Lanh Beach and Qui Nhon. The highway crosses a huge river on the south side of town. The river is navigable and justifies Tuy Hoa's existence – there isn't much else to the place, not even a good beach.

The main interest of Tuy Hoa to travellers is that it has good accommodation, which could be useful if you get a late start heading north or south along National Highway 1.

Information

Tourist Office Phu Yen Tourist (Cong Ty Du Lich Phu Yen; ☎ 23353) is the provincial tourist office, and can be found at 137 Le Thanh Ton.

Places to Stay

The *Huong Sen Hotel* and attached restaurant is a large fancy place near the centre of town.

Binh Dinh
Bình Định

QUI NHON
QUI NHƠN

Qui Nhon (or Quy Nhon; population 188,000) is the capital of Binh Dinh Province and one of Vietnam's more active second-string seaports. The beaches in the immediate vicinity of the city are nothing to write home about and the city itself is a bit dingy, but Qui Nhon is a convenient and not unpleasant place to break the long journey from Nha Trang to Danang. By provincial standards, Qui Nhon is a hopping, happening place on Sunday nights. There are some Cham towers along National Highway 1 about 10 km north of the Qui Nhon turn-off.

During the Vietnam War there was considerable South Vietnamese, American, Viet Cong and South Korean military activity in the Qui Nhon area, and refugees dislocated by the fighting and counter-insurgency programmes built whole slums of tin and thatch shacks around the city. During this period, the mayor of Qui Nhon, hoping to cash in on the presence of American troops, turned his official residence into a 'massage parlour'.

Orientation

Qui Nhon is on an east-west oriented peninsula shaped like the nose of an anteater. The tip of the nose (the port area) is closed to the public. The Municipal Beach is on the peninsula's southern coast. The streets around Lon Market constitute Qui Nhon's downtown.

From the Municipal Beach, Cu Lao Xanh Island is visible offshore. Due east of the beach (to the left as you face the water) you can see, in the distance, an oversize statue of Tran Hung Dao erected on a promontory overlooking the fishing village of Hai Minh.

Information

Tourist Office Binh Dinh Tourism (Cong Ty Du Lich Binh Dinh; ☎ 22524, 22206, 22329) is at 10 Nguyen Hue St, just west of the Quy

■	PLACES TO STAY
1	Viet Cuong Hotel
5	Thanh Binh Hotel
6	Dong Phuong Hotel
8	Saigon Hotel
9	Peace Hotel
11	Olympic Hotel & Vu Hung Restaurant
12	Nha Khach Huu Nghi
18	Hotel Mini Hai Ha
23	Quy Nhon Tourist Hotel

▼	PLACES TO EAT
3	Pho 350 (Soup Shop)
4	Soup Shops
10	Ngoc Lien Restaurant
21	Cau Tin

	OTHER
2	Qui Nhon Bus Station
7	Short-Haul Transport Station
13	Long Khanh Pagoda
14	Foreign Trade Bank (Vietcombank)
15	Lon Market
16	Church
17	GPO
19	War Memorial
20	Express Bus Station
22	Binh Dinh Tourism
24	Zoo

Nhon Tourist Hotel. The office is poorly organised and lacks trained guides; their few translators don't have a clue about the province's history or natural sites. Give them a miss unless you must hire a car.

Money The Foreign Trade Bank (Ngan Hang Ngoai Thuong), otherwise known as Vietcombank (☎ 2408), is at 148 Le Loi St (corner Tran Hung Dao St).

Post & Telecommunications The GPO is in the south-western part of town at the corner of Hai Ba Trung St and Tran Phu St; it is open daily from 6 am to 8 pm. International telephone calls can be placed from here; telegraph services are available. There is a small post office at the corner of Phan

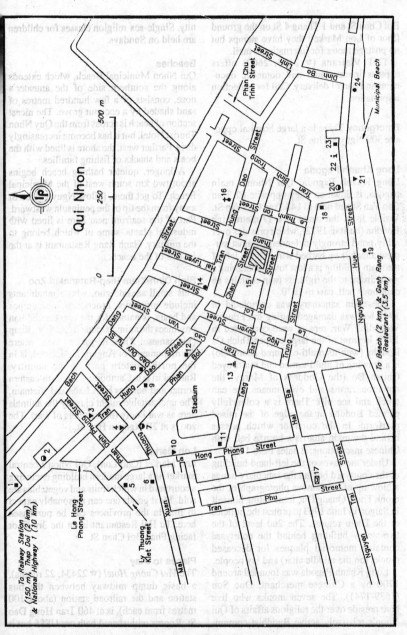

Qui Nhon

0   250   500 m

To Railway Station
(150 m) &
National Highway 1 (10 km)

To Beach (2 km) & Ganh Rang
Restaurant (3.5 km)

Municipal Beach

Phan Chu
Trinh Street

Dinh Bo
Linh Street

Trong
Dieu Street

Dao
Duy Tu Street

Le Thanh Ton Street

Hung
Vuong Street

Tran
Thang Street

Hai Ly Yen Street

Van
Dang Street

Bach
Dang Street

Dao
Duy Tu St

Cao
Ba Bui Street

Chieu
Nguyen Street

Ho
Nguyen Street

Bat
Ngo Street

Trung
Tran Street

Ha
Ba Street

Dinh
Phung Street

Tran
Hung Street

Phan
Bui Street

Le Hong Phong Street

Xuan
Mai Street

Tran
Phu Street

Nguyen
Tri Street

Nguyen
Hue Street

Ly Thuong
Kiet Street

Stadium

Boi Chau St and 1 Thang 4 St on the ground floor of Lon Market; they have stamps but no postage meter for international mail.

TNT Vietrans (☎ 2193, 2600) offers express international and domestic document and parcel delivery. Call for collection information.

Emergency There is a large hospital opposite 309 Nguyen Hue St.

Long Khanh Pagoda

Long Khanh Pagoda, Qui Nhon's main pagoda, is down an alley opposite 62 Tran Cao Van St and next to 143 Tran Cao Van St. Visible from the street is a 17-metre-high Buddha (built in 1972), which presides over a lily pond strongly defended (against surprise attack?) by barbed wire. To the left of the main building is a low tower sheltering a giant drum; to the right, its twin contains an enormous bell, cast in 1970.

The main sanctuary was completed in 1946 but was damaged during the Franco-Viet Minh War; repairs were completed in 1957. In front of the large copper Thich Ca Buddha (with its multi-coloured neon halo) is a drawing of multi-armed and multi-eyed Chuan De (the Goddess of Mercy; the numerous arms and eyes means she can touch and see all). There is a colourfully painted Buddha at the edge of the raised platform. In the corridor which passes behind the main altar is a bronze bell with Chinese inscriptions; it dates from 1805.

Under the eaves of the left-hand building of the courtyard behind the sanctuary hangs a blow-up of the famous photograph of the monk Thich Quang Duc immolating himself in Saigon in June 1963 to protest the policies of the Diem regime. The 2nd level of the two-storey building behind the courtyard contains memorial plaques for deceased monks (on the middle altar) and lay people.

Long Khanh Pagoda was founded around 1700 by a Chinese merchant, Duc Son (1679-1741). The seven monks who live here preside over the religious affairs of Qui Nhon's relatively active Buddhist community. Single-sex religion classes for children are held on Sundays.

Beaches

Qui Nhon Municipal Beach, which extends along the southern side of the anteater's nose, consists of a few hundred metres of sand shaded by a coconut grove. The nicest section of beach is across from the Quy Nhon Tourist Hotel, but it has become increasingly dirty. Farther west, the shore is lined with the boats and shacks of fishing families.

A longer, quieter bathing beach begins about two km south-west of the Municipal Beach. To get there, follow Nguyen Hue St away from the tip of the peninsula westward. Part of the seafront near here is lined with industrial plants, some of which belong to the military. Ganh Rang Restaurant is at the far end of the beach.

Binh Dinh-Xiem Riep-Ratanakiri Zoo

This small seaside zoo, whose inhabitants include monkeys, crocodiles, porcupines and bears, is named for the two Cambodian provinces the animals came from. Siem Reap (Vietnamese: *Xiem Riep*) Province, where the monuments of Angkor are located, is in the north-western part of the country. Ratanakiri is in Cambodia's far north-eastern corner and borders both Laos and Vietnam. The uncharitable might classify the animals here as war booty (or prisoners of war). The zoo is at 2B Nguyen Hue St.

Lon Market

Lon Market (Cho Lon), Qui Nhon's central market, is a large modern building enclosing a courtyard in which fruits and vegetables are sold. Most goods one can reasonably expect to find in the provinces can be purchased here. Tu Hai Restaurant is on the 3rd floor facing Phan Boi Chau St.

Places to Stay

The *Viet Cuong Hotel* (☎ 22434; 22 rooms), a basic dump midway between the bus station and the railroad station (about 100 metres from each), is at 460 Tran Hung Dao St. Rooms with shared bath are US$5 but it is possible that this place will not be accepting foreigners in the near future.

The *Thanh Binh Hotel* (☎ 22041; 80 rooms) is 300 metres from the bus station at 17 Ly Thuong Kiet St. This place, which belongs to the Provincial People's Committee, is frequented by government officials and so is ridiculously overpriced for foreigners at US$20 per room – certainly not worth it.

The *Nha Khach Huu Nghi* (☎ 22152; 22 rooms) at 210 Phan Boi Chau St is a bit grimy but remains popular due to the low price; US$5 for a double with private bath. There is a restaurant on the ground floor.

The modern *Dong Phuong Hotel* (☎ 22915; 20 rooms) at 39-41 Mai Xuan Thuong St (near the corner of Le Hong Phong St) is the best deal in town. Singles/doubles are US$8/12. There's a good restaurant on the ground floor.

The *Peace Hotel* (Khach San Hoa Binh; ☎ 22900; 64 rooms) is opposite 266 Tran Hung Dao St. At US$12, it's a reasonable place to stay.

The *Olympic Hotel* (Khach San Lien Doanh; ☎ 22375; 23 rooms) takes its name from the adjacent stadium. Singles start at US$10. The entrance is opposite 167 Le Hong Phong St (corner Tang Bat Ho St). The Vu Hung Restaurant is upstairs.

The *Saigon Hotel* is a new, chic place obviously meant to catch the tourist traffic doing the Saigon-Hanoi sightseeing route. All rooms cost US$20. The Saigon Hotel is on the corner of Tran Hung Dao and Dao Duy Tu Sts.

The *Quy Nhon Tourist Hotel* (Khach San Du Lich Quy Nhon; ☎ 22401, 22329; 47 rooms) is right on Qui Nhon Municipal Beach at 8 Nguyen Hue St. The rooms and common areas are grimy and dimly lit. The only thing this place has going for it is its proximity to the beach, which is partially offset by its distance from the centre of town. Prices are geared to the tourist traffic; singles/doubles are US$22/26 and a suite costs US$34. The restaurant serves dismal food.

Just around the corner from the Quy Nhon

Tourist Hotel is the privately run *Hotel Mini Hai Ha* (☎ 21295), at the corner of Tran Binh Trong and Hai Ba Trung Sts. It's small, clean and often full. The price of US$20 seems steep for this standard of accommodation.

Places to Eat

There are only a handful of proper restaurants in Qui Nhon. One of the best is the *Vu Hung Restaurant* (☎ 22375, 22908), which is on the roof of the Olympic Hotel. The entrance is opposite 167 Le Hong Phong St (corner Tang Bat Ho St).

The *Huu Nghi Restaurant* is on the ground floor of Nha Khach Huu Nghi at 210 Phan Boi Chau St. They have quite a variety of Vietnamese food and some good Western dishes (stuffed crab, onion soup) as well.

The *Dong Phuong Restaurant* at 39-41 Mai Xuan Thuong St is on the ground floor of the Dong Phuong Hotel; it is open from 6 am to 11 pm. They have a rather limited menu of Vietnamese food and only a few Western dishes.

The *Tu Hai Restaurant* (☎ 22582) is on the 3rd floor of Lon Market (on the side overlooking Phan Boi Chau St); it is open from 6.30 am to 10 pm. The management is friendly and the menu is in English, but the food is indifferently prepared. Nearby Bien Sanh Dancing, an enterprise run as part of Tu Hai Restaurant, offers dancing with a live band from 8 to 10 pm every Tuesday, Thursday and Saturday night.

For tasty food at rock-bottom prices, try the *Ngoc Lien Restaurant*, a favourite with Qui Nhonians, at 288 Le Hong Phong St. There are several other homey restaurants in the immediate vicinity.

The *Ganh Rang Restaurant* is 3.5 km west of town along Nguyen Hue St. Built on pylons and set among palms, this privately run restaurant is right on the water at a site said to have been a favourite of Bao Dai's wife.

Getting There & Away

Air Vietnam Airlines flights link Ho Chi Minh City with Qui Nhon every every Thursday and Sunday (US$65 one way).

There are also flights to/from Danang every Thursday and Sunday (US$30).

Phu Cat Airport is 36 km north of Qui Nhon. For airline passengers, transport to and from Phu Cat is provided by Vietnam Airlines. Small trucks to Phu Cat depart from the Short-Haul Transport Station.

In Qui Nhon, the Vietnam Airlines booking office (☎ 22953) is near the Thanh Binh Hotel in the building next to 30 Nguyen Thai Hoc St. Tickets must be purchased at least two days in advance.

Bus Qui Nhon Bus Station (Ben Xe Khach Qui Nhon; ☎ 22246) is opposite 543 Tran Hung Dao St (across from where Le Hong Phong St hits Tran Hung Dao St). The non-express ticket windows are open from 5 am to 4 pm; the express ticket window (Khach Di Xe Toc Hanh), which is in the fenced-in enclosure next to the non-express windows, is open from 4 am to 4 pm. Tickets should be purchased the day before departure.

Express buses, all of which leave at 5 am, go to Buon Ma Thuot, Dalat, Danang, Hanoi, Ho Chi Minh City, Hué, Nha Trang, Quang Tri and Vinh.

Non-express buses leave from here to:

An Khe, An Lao (at 6 am), Bong Son (6 am), Buon Ma Thuot (5 am; the trip takes 8 hours), Cam Ranh, Dalat (6 am; 10 hrs), Danang (6 am; 6 hrs), Hanoi (5 am; 39 hrs), Ho Chi Minh City (5 am; 16 hrs), Hoi An (6 am), Hué (6 am,) Kontum (8 am; 11 hrs), Nha Trang (5 am; 5½ hrs), Phu My (6 am), Pleiku (6 am; 6 hrs), Quang Ngai (6 am; 5 hrs), Tam Quan (6 am), Tuy Hoa, Van Canh, Vinh Thanh (6 am).

The Express Bus Station (☎ 22172) is 100 metres from the Quy Nhon Tourist Hotel at 14 Nguyen Hue St. There are express buses from here to Buon Ma Thuot, Dalat, Danang, Dong Hoi, Hanoi, Ho Chi Minh City, Hué, Nha Trang, Ninh Binh, Quang Tri, Thanh Hoa and Vinh. All buses depart at 5 am. The ticket window (Phong Ban Ve Xe Toc Hanh Cac Tuyen Duong) is open from 6.30 to 11 am and 1.30 to 5 pm.

Vehicles to places within a 50-km radius of Qui Nhon depart from the Short-Haul Transport Station (Ben Xe 1 Thang 4), which

is at the intersection of Phan Boi Chau St and Mai Xuan Thuong St (near 280 Phan Boi Chau St and 60 Mai Xuan Thuong St). Tickets are sold in a kerbside wood and corrugated iron kiosk. Small trucks leave from here to Binh Dinh (six km from Cha Ban), Dap Da, Dieu Tri (the railway station), Phu Cat (the airport), Tay Son (vehicles from Tay Son go to within about five km of the Quang Trung Museum), Tuy Phuoc and Vinh Thanh.

Train The city of Qui Nhon is poorly served by rail. Qui Nhon Railway Station (Ga Qui Nhon; ☎ 22036) is at the end of a 10-km spur line off the main north-south track. The station is 70 metres from Tran Hung Dao St on Hoang Hoa Tham St, which intersects Tran Hung Dao St between numbers 661 and 663.

Only two very slow local trains stop at Qui Nhon Railway Station. Train DS departs for points south at 9.45 am on even days of the month (its northward-bound twin leaves Ho Chi Minh City on odd days of the month); the trip all the way to Ho Chi Minh City takes 24 hours. Northward-bound 172 leaves at 5 am daily, arriving in Danang about 13 hours later.

The nearest the Reunification Express trains get to Qui Nhon is Dieu Tri, 10 km from the city. Tickets for trains departing from Dieu Tri can be purchased at the Qui Nhon Railroad Station, though if you arrive in Dieu Tri by train, your best bet is to purchase an onward ticket before leaving the station. For ticket prices on the Reunification Express trains, see the Train section in the Getting Around chapter.

Before making the journey out to Dieu Tri it's best to check the schedule. Small trucks from Qui Nhon to Dieu Tri leave from the Short-Haul Transport Station.

Car Road distances from Qui Nhon are 677 km to Ho Chi Minh City, 238 km to Nha Trang, 186 km to Pleiku, 198 km to Kontum, 174 km to Quang Ngai, and 303 km to Danang.

Qui Nhon is 10 km off National Highway

1. It is the nearest coastal city to Pleiku, Kontum and the rest of the northern section of the Central Highlands. National Highway 19 to Tay Son and Pleiku heads westward from Binh Dinh, which is 18 km north of Qui Nhon.

There is a border crossing to Cambodia's remote Ratanakiri Province about 250 km due west of Qui Nhon near the village of Chu Nghe. At present, the crossing is used by Vietnamese companies to bring Ratanakiri's forest products to the coast for export. When the Cambodian civil war ends, it may be possible to visit Ratanakiri, which is not accessible by land from Phnom Penh (the bridges are out), from Qui Nhon.

AROUND QUI NHON
Thap Doi

The two Cham towers of Thap Doi have curved pyramidal roofs rather than the terracing typical of Cham architecture. The larger tower, whose four granite doorways are oriented towards the cardinal directions, retains some of its ornate brickwork and remnants of the granite statuary that once graced its summit. The dismembered torsos of Garudas can be seen at the corners of the roofs of both structures.

The upper reaches of the small tower are home to several flourishing trees whose creeping tendrilous roots have forced their way between the bricks, enmeshing parts of the structure in the sort of net-like tangle for which the monuments of Angkor are famous.

Thap Doi is two km towards National Highway 1 from the Qui Nhon Bus Station. To get there, head out of town on Tran Hung Dao St and turn right between street numbers 900 and 906 onto Thap Doi St; the towers are about 100 metres from Tran Hung Dao St.

There are half a dozen or so other groups of Cham structures in the vicinity of Qui Nhon, two of which (Cha Ban and Duong Long) are described below.

Cha Ban

The ruins of the former Cham capital of Cha Ban (also known at various times as Vijaya and Qui Nhon) are 26 km north of Qui Nhon

and five km from Binh Dinh. The city was built within a rectangular wall measuring 1400 metres by 1100 metres. Canh Tien Tower (Tower of Brass) stands in the centre of the enclosure. The tomb of General Vu Tinh is nearby.

Cha Ban, which served as the seat of the royal government of Champa from the year 1000 (after the loss of Indrapura, also known as Dong Duong) until 1471, was attacked and plundered repeatedly by the Vietnamese, Khmers and Chinese. In 1044, the Vietnamese prince Phat Ma occupied the city and carried off a great deal of booty as well as the Cham king's wives, harem and female dancers, musicians and singers. Cha Ban was under the control of a Khmer overseer from 1190 to 1220.

In 1377, the Vietnamese were defeated in an attempt to capture Cha Ban and their king was killed. The Vietnamese Emperor Le Thanh Ton breached the eastern gate of the city in 1471 and captured the Cham king and 50 members of the royal family. During this, the last great battle fought by the Chams, 60,000 Chams were killed and 30,000 more were taken prisoner by the Vietnamese.

During the Tay Son Rebellion, Cha Ban served as the capital of the region of central

Buddhist monk

Vietnam ruled by the eldest of the three Tay Son brothers. It was attacked in 1793 by the forces of Nguyen Anh (later Emperor Gia Long) but the assault failed. In 1799, the forces of Nguyen Anh, under the command of General Vu Tinh, lay siege to the city and captured it. The Tay Son soon re-occupied the port of Thi Nai (modern-day Qui Nhon) and then lay siege to Cha Ban themselves. The siege continued for over a year, and by June 1801, Vu Tinh's provisions were gone. Food was in short supply; all the horses and elephants had long before been eaten. Refusing to consider the ignominy of surrender, Vu Tinh had an octagonal wood tower constructed. He filled it with gunpowder and, arrayed in his ceremonial robes, went inside and blew himself up. Upon hearing the news of the death of his dedicated general, Nguyen Anh wept.

Duong Long Cham Towers
The Duong Long Cham Towers (Thap Duong Long, the Towers of Ivory) are eight km from Cha Ban. The largest of the three brick towers is embellished with granite ornamentation representing nagas (snakes) and elephants. Over the doors are bas-reliefs of women, dancers, standing lions, monsters and various animals. The corners of the structure are formed by enormous dragon heads.

Hoi Van Hot Springs
The famous hot springs of Hoi Van are north of Qui Nhon in Phu Cat District.

Quang Trung Museum
The Quang Trung Museum is dedicated to Nguyen Hue, the second-oldest of the three brothers who led the Tay Son Rebellion, who crowned himself Emperor Quang Trung in 1788. In 1789 (a few months before a Parisian mob stormed the Bastille), Quang Trung led the campaign that overwhelmingly defeated a Chinese invasion force of 200,000 troops near Hanoi. This epic battle is still celebrated as one of the greatest triumphs in Vietnamese history. Quang Trung died in 1792 at the age of 40.

During his reign, Quang Trung was some-thing of a social reformer. He encouraged land reform, revised the system of taxation, improved the army and emphasised education, opening numerous schools and encouraging the development of Vietnamese poetry and literature. Indeed, Communist literature often portrays him as the leader of a peasant revolution whose progressive policies were crushed by the reactionary Nguyen Dynasty, which came to power in 1802 and was overthrown by Ho Chi Minh in 1945.

The Quang Trung Museum is known for its demonstrations of *binh dinh vo*, a traditional martial art that is performed with a bamboo stick. To get there take National Highway 19 towards Pleiku. The museum, which is 48 km from Qui Nhon, is in Tay Son District five km off the highway. The Tay Son area produces a wine made of sticky rice.

Vinh Son Falls
Vinh Son Falls is 18 km off National Highway 19, which links Binh Dinh and Pleiku. To get there, you might try taking a Vinh Thanh-bound truck from the Short-Haul Transport Station in Qui Nhon and changing vehicles in Vinh Thanh.

Quang Ngai
Quảng Ngãi

SA HUYNH
SA HUỲNH
Sa Huynh is a relatively prosperous little seaside town whose beautiful semicircular beach is bordered by rice paddies and coconut palms. The town is also known for its salt marshes and salt evaporation ponds. In the vicinity of Sa Huynh, archaeologists have unearthed remains of the Dong Son Civilisation dating from the 1st century AD.

Places to Stay & Eat
Sa Huynh is a fairly pleasant place to make overnight stop on the road trip between Nha

Trang and Danang, provided the hotel has room. There is only one hotel, the small and quiet *Sa Huynh Hotel* which is right on the beach. Singles/doubles are US$8/10 and all rooms have ceiling fans and attached bath, but don't expect five-star standards.

There is a government-owned restaurant on the hotel grounds but it's seldom open. However, just outside the hotel gate are some small private restaurants which keep long hours.

Getting There & Away
Train Some non-express trains stop at the Sa Huynh Railway Station (Ga Sa Huynh), but it will be slow going.

Car Sa Huynh is on National Highway 1 about 114 km north of Qui Nhon and 60 km south of Quang Ngai.

QUANG NGAI
QUẢNG NGÃI
Quang Ngai, the capital of Quang Ngai Province, is something of a backwater. Built on the south bank of the Tra Khuc River (known for its oversized water-wheels), the city is about 15 km from the coast, which is lined with beautiful beaches. The city and province of Quang Ngai are also known as Quang Nghia; the name is sometimes abbreviated as Quangai.

History
Even before WW II, Quang Ngai was an important centre of resistance to the French. During the Franco-Viet Minh War, the area was a Viet Minh stronghold. In 1962, the South Vietnamese Government introduced its ill-fated strategic hamlet programme to the area. Villagers were forcibly removed from their homes and resettled in fortified hamlets, infuriating and alienating the local population and increasing popular support for the Viet Cong. Some of the bitterest fighting of the Vietnam War took place in Quang Ngai Province.

Son My subdistrict, 14 km from Quang Ngai, was the scene of the infamous My Lai Massacre of 1968, in which hundreds of

civilians were slaughtered by American soldiers. A memorial has been erected on the site of the killings.

As a result of the wars, very few bridges in Quang Ngai Province remain intact. At many river crossings, the rust-streaked concrete pylons of the old French bridges, probably destroyed by the Viet Minh, stand next to the ruins of their replacements, blown up by the VC. As it has for 15 or more years, traffic crosses the river on a third bridge, made of steel girders, of the sort that army engineering corps put up in a pinch.

Orientation
National Highway 1 is called Quang Trung St as it passes through Quang Ngai. The railway station is three km west of town out Phan Boi Chau St.

Information
Tourist Office Quang Ngai Tourism (Cong Ty Du Lich Quang Ngai; ☎ 2665, 3870) is the government's official tourist agency for Quang Ngai Province. The office is in the Song Tra Hotel.

Post & Telecommunications The GPO is 150 metres off Quang Trung St at the corner of Phan Boi Chau and Phan Dinh Phung Sts.

Places to Stay
There are four hotels in Quang Ngai but only one accepts foreigners. The *Song Tra Hotel* is owned by Quang Ngai Tourism and this is where foreigners are forced to stay. The hotel is a monstrous five-storey structure on the northern outskirts of the city next to the bridge over the Tra Khuc River. All rooms for foreigners cost US$25 and are not worth it. The hotel has a restaurant.

Places to Eat
A local speciality is bo gan, bits of beef topped with ground peanuts and eaten on pieces of giant rice crackers.

The restaurant at *Nha Khach Uy Ban Thi*, the government guesthouse, is the only real restaurant in Quang Ngai. The *Tiem An 72 Restaurant* at 72 Nguyen Nghiem St is about

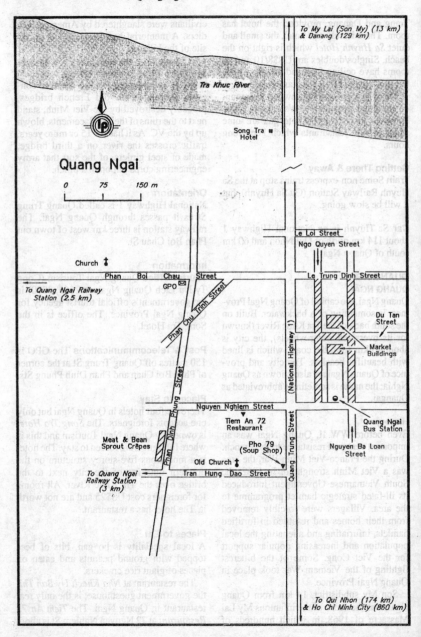

To My Lai (Son My) (13 km)
& Danang (129 km)

Tra Khuc River

Song Tra
Hotel

Quang Ngai

0   75   150 m

Le Loi Street

Ngo Quyen Street

Le Trung Dinh Street

Church ✝

Phan   Boi   Chau   Street

GPO ✉

To Quang Ngai Railway
Station (2.5 km)

Phan Chu Trinh Street

Du Tan
Street

Market
Buildings

Phan Dinh Phung Street

(National Highway 1)

Nguyen Nghiem Street

Tiem An 72
Restaurant

Quang Ngai
Bus Station

Meat & Bean
Sprout Crêpes

Pho 79
(Soup Shop)

Nguyen Ba Loan
Street

Old Church ✝

To Quang Ngai
Railway Station
(3 km)

Tran   Hung   Dao   Street

Quang Trung Street

To Qui Nhon (174 km)
& Ho Chi Minh City (860 km)

150 metres from the bus station. Despite its modern façade, *Nha Hang 155* at 155 Quang Trung St is a place to avoid.

There are cafes at numbers 47, 51 and 53 Phan Boi Chau St (near Hotel Number 2) but they don't have much to eat. Meat and bean sprout crêpes fried over open fires are sold in the evenings on Phan Dinh Phung St between Tran Hung Dao St and Nguyen Nghiem St. *Pho 79* at the corner of Quang Trung St and Tran Hung Dao St has soup.

Getting There & Away

Bus Quang Ngai Bus Station (Ben Xe Khach Quang Ngai) is opposite 32 Nguyen Nghiem St, which is about 100 metres east of Quang Trung St (National Highway 1). Buses from here go to Buon Ma Thuot (and other places in Dac Lac Province), Dalat, Danang, Ho Chi Minh City, Hoi An, Kontum, Pleiku, Nha Trang and Qui Nhon.

There is no express bus from Quang Ngai to Danang. Old Renault buses, which take four hours to cover the 130 km to Danang, begin their daily runs around 6 am.

Train The Quang Ngai Railway Station (Ga Quang Nghia or Ga Quang Ngai) is three km west of the centre of town. To get there, take Phan Boi Chau St west from Quang Trung St (National Highway 1) and continue going in the same direction after the street name changes to Nguyen Chanh St. At 389 Nguyen Chanh St (which you'll come to as Nguyen Chanh St curves left), continue straight on down a side street. The railroad station is at the end of the street.

Reunification Express trains stop at Quang Ngai. For ticket prices, see the Train section in the Getting Around chapter.

Car Road distances from Quang Ngai are 131 km to Danang, 860 km to Ho Chi Minh City, 412 km to Nha Trang, and 174 km to Qui Nhon.

AROUND QUANG NGAI
Son My (My Lai)
Travel Permit You must secure a special travel permit to visit the site of the massacre

at My Lai. The permit costs US$3 and is available from the Immigration Police in Quang Ngai. However, at the present time it is not necessary to rent a vehicle from the local government in order to secure the permit.

Getting There & Away The site of the My Lai Massacre is 14 km from Quang Ngai. To get there from town, head north (towards Danang) on Quang Trung St (National Highway 1) and cross the long bridge over the Tra Khuc River. A few metres from the northern end of the bridge you will come to a triangular concrete stele indicating the way to the Son My Memorial. Turn right (eastward, parallel to the river) on the dirt road and continue for 12 km. The road to Son My passes through particularly beautiful countryside of rice paddies, manioc patches and vegetable gardens shaded by casuarinas and eucalyptus trees.

If you don't have a car, the best way to get to Son My District from Quang Ngai is to hire a motorbike (Honda om) near the bus station or along Quang Trung St.

Bien Khe Ky Beach
Bien Khe Ky Beach (Bai Bien Khe Ky) is a long, secluded beach of fine sand 17 km from Quang Ngai and several km past (east of) the Son My Memorial. The beach stretches for many km along a long, thin casuarina-lined spit of sand separated from the mainland by Song Kinh Giang, a body of water about 150 metres inland from the beach.

As the mass killings in and around Xom Lang were taking place a couple of km to the west, another massacre was committed by Bravo Company just east and south of the bridge across Song Kinh Giang. Huts were indiscriminately fired on and burned, fleeing civilians were gunned down on the sand ridge and as they ran towards the beach, and family bomb shelters were blown up without giving the people in them the chance to escape. Women and children who did manage to run out of the shelters were shot; captured VC suspects were tortured.

This whole incident, in which up to 90

My Lai Massacre

Son My subdistrict was the site of the most horrific war crimes committed by American troops during the Vietnam War. The My Lai Massacre consisted of a series of atrocities carried out all over Son My subdistrict, which is divided into four hamlets, one of which is named My Lai. The largest mass killing took place in Tu Cung Hamlet in Xom Lang sub-hamlet (also known as Thuan Yen sub-hamlet), where the Son My Memorial was later erected.

Son My subdistrict was a known Viet Cong stronghold, and it was widely believed that villagers in the area were providing food and shelter to the VC (if true, the villagers had little choice – the VC was known for taking cruel revenge on those who didn't 'cooperate'). Just whose idea it was to 'teach the villagers a lesson' has never been determined. What is known is that several American soldiers had been killed and wounded in the area in the days preceding the 'search-and-destroy operation' that began on the morning of 16 March 1968. The operation was carried out by Task Force Barker, which consisted of three companies of US Army infantry. At about 7.30 am – after the area around Xom Lang sub-hamlet had been bombarded with artillery and the landing zone raked with rocket and machine gun fire from helicopter gunships – the three platoons of Charlie Company (commanded by Captain Ernest Medina) were landed by helicopter. They encountered no resistance during the 'combat-assault', nor did they come under fire at any time during the entire operation; but as soon as Charlie Company's sweep eastward began, so did the atrocities.

As the soldiers of Lieutenant William Calley's 1st Platoon moved through Xom Lang, they shot and bayonetted fleeing villagers, threw hand grenades into houses and family bomb shelters, slaughtered livestock and burned dwellings. Somewhere between 75 and 150 unarmed local people were rounded up and herded to a ditch, where they were mowed down by machine-gun fire.

In the next few hours, as command helicopters circled overhead and US Navy boats patrolled offshore, the 2nd Platoon (under Lieutenant Stephen Brooks), the 3rd platoon (under Lieutenant Jeffrey La Cross) and the company headquarters group also committed unspeakable crimes. At least half-a-dozen groups of civilians, including women and children, were assembled and executed. Local people fleeing towards Quang Ngai along the road were machine-gunned, and wounded civilians (including young children) were summarily shot. As these massacres were taking place, at least four girls and women were raped or gang-raped by groups of soldiers. In one case, a rapist from 2nd Company is reported to have shoved the muzzle of his assault rifle into the vagina of his victim and pulled the trigger.

One American soldier is reported to have shot himself in the foot to get himself out of the slaughter; he was the only American casualty that day in the entire operation.

Troops who participated were ordered to keep their mouths shut about the whole incident, but several soldiers who were at Son My disobeyed orders and went public with the story after returning to the USA. When the story broke in the newspapers, it had a devastating effect on the military's morale and fuelled further public protests against the war. Unlike WW II veterans who returned home to parades and glory, American soldiers coming home from Vietnam often found themselves ostracised by their fellow citizens and taunted as 'baby killers'.

Action to cover up the atrocities was undertaken at every level of the US Army command, but eventually there were several investigations. Though a number of officers were disciplined, only one, Lieutenant Calley, was court-marshalled and found guilty of the murders of 22 unarmed civilians. He was sentenced to life imprisonment in 1971. He spent three years under house arrest at Fort Benning, Georgia, while appealing his conviction. Calley was paroled in 1974 after the US Supreme Court refused to hear his case. According to newspaper reports, he still lives in Georgia and works as a sales clerk.

Calley's case still causes controversy – many have said that he was made the military's scapegoat because of his low rank, and that officers much higher up ordered the massacres. What is certain is that Calley did not act alone.

The Son My Memorial is set in a park where Xom Lang sub-hamlet once stood. Around it, among the trees and rice paddies, are the graves of some of the victims, buried in family groups. Near the memorial is a worthwhile museum opened in 1992. ∎

civilians may have been killed, was completely covered up, and the charges filed against Bravo Company's commanding officer, 1st Lieutenant Thomas Willingham, were eventually dismissed.

Quang Nam-Danang
Quảng Nam-Đà Nẵng

CHU LAI
CHU LAI

About 30 km north of Quang Ngai, the buildings and concrete aircraft revetments of the huge American base at Chu Lai stretch along several km of sand to the east of National Highway 1. Despite the obvious dangers, collecting and selling scrap metal from old ordnance has become a thriving local industry. During the war, there was a huge shantytown made of packing crates and waste tin from canning factories next to the base. The inhabitants of the shantytown supported themselves by providing services to the Americans: doing laundry, selling soft drinks and engaging in prostitution.

TAM KY
TAM KỲ

Tam Ky is a nondescript town on the highway between Quang Ngai and Danang. The main point of interest are the nearby Cham Towers at Chien Dang (Chien Dang Cham).

Three Cham towers, enclosed by a wall, stand at Chien Dang, which is five km north of Tam Ky, 69 km north of Quang Ngai and 62 km south of Danang. A broken stele here dates from the 13th century reign of King Harivarman. Many of the Cham statues you can see on display at Chien Dang were collected from other parts of the country after the Vietnam War. Many of these statues show signs of war-related damage.

Places to Stay

The *Tam Ky Hotel* (Khach San Tam Ky) is a decent place next to National Highway 1 in the centre of town. This is the only hotel in Tam Ky that accepts foreigners.

HOI AN
HỘI AN

Hoi An is a riverine town 30 km south of Danang. Known as Faifo to early Western traders, it was one of South-East Asia's major international ports during the 17th, 18th and 19th centuries. In its heyday, Hoi An, a contemporary of Macau and Malacca, was an important port of call for Dutch, Portuguese, Chinese, Japanese and other trading vessels. Vietnamese ships and sailors based in Hoi An sailed to Thailand and Indonesia as well as to all sections of Vietnam. Today, parts of Hoi An look exactly as they did a century and a half ago. More than perhaps any other place in Vietnam, Hoi An retains the feel of centuries past, making it the sort of place that grows on you the more you explore it. It's easily possible to do Hoi An as a day trip from Danang, but if you've got the time it's not a bad idea to spend a night in Hoi An and have a couple of days to look around.

History

Recently excavated ceramic fragments from 2200 years ago constitute the earliest evidence of human habitation in the Hoi An area. They are thought to belong to the late-Iron Age Sa Huynh civilisation, which is related to the Dong Son culture of northern Vietnam.

From the 2nd to the 10th century, when this region was the heartland of the Kingdom of Champa – this is when the nearby Cham capital of Simhapura (Tra Kieu) and the temples of Indrapura (Dong Duong) and My Son were built – there was a bustling seaport at Hoi An. Persian and Arab documents from the latter part of the period mention Hoi An as a provisioning stop for trading ships. Archaeologists have uncovered the foundations of numerous Cham towers in the vicinity of Hoi An (the bricks and stones of the towers themselves were reused by later Vietnamese settlers).

In 1307, the Cham king married the

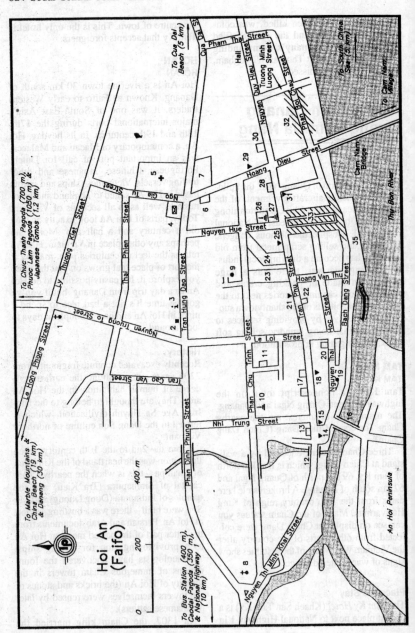

Hoi An
(Faifo)

daughter of a Vietnamese monarch of the Tran Dynasty, presenting Quang Nam Province to the Vietnamese as a gift. When the Cham king died, his successor refused to recognise the deal and fighting broke out; for the next century, chaos reigned. By the 15th century, peace had been restored, allowing normal commerce to resume. During the next four centuries, Chinese, Japanese, Dutch, Portuguese, Spanish, Indian, Filipino, Indonesian, Thai, French, English and American ships called at Hoi An to purchase high-grade silk (for which the area is famous), fabrics, paper, porcelain, tea, sugar, molasses, areca nuts, pepper, Chinese medicines, elephant tusks, beeswax, mother-of-pearl, lacquer, sulphur and lead.

The Chinese and Japanese traders sailed south in the spring, driven by winds out of the north-east. They would stay in Hoi An until the summer, when southerly winds would blow them home. During their four-month sojourn in Hoi An, the merchants rented waterfront houses for use as warehouses and living quarters. Some traders began leaving full-time agents in Hoi An to take care of off-season business affairs. This is how the foreigners' colonies got started. The Japanese ceased coming to Hoi An after 1637, when the Japanese government forbade all contact with the outside world.

Hoi An was the first place in Vietnam to be exposed to Christianity. Among the 17th century missionary visitors was the French priest Alexandre de Rhodes, who devised the Latin-based quoc ngu script for the Vietnamese language.

Hoi An was almost completely destroyed during the Tay Son Rebellion in the 1770s and 1780s but was rebuilt and continued to serve as an important port for foreign trade until the late 19th century, when the Thu Bon River (Cai River), which links Hoi An with the sea, silted up and became too shallow for navigation. During this period Danang (Tourane) began to eclipse Hoi An as a port and centre of commerce. In 1916, a rail line linking Danang with Hoi An was destroyed by a terrible storm; it was never rebuilt.

The French chose Hoi An as an administrative centre. During the American war, Hoi An remained almost completely undamaged.

Hoi An was the site of the first Chinese settlement in southern Vietnam. The town's Chinese congregational assembly halls (hoi quan) still play a special role among southern Vietnam's ethnic-Chinese, some of whom travel to Hoi An from all over the south to participate in congregation-wide celebrations. Today, 1300 of the Hoi An area's present population of about 60,000 are ethnic-Chinese. Relations between ethnic-Vietnamese and ethnic-Chinese in Hoi An are excellent, in part because the Chinese here, unlike their countryfolk elsewhere in the country, have become culturally assimilated to the point that they even speak Vietnamese among themselves.

A number of Hoi An's wooden buildings date from the first part of the 19th century or earlier, giving visitors who have just a bit of imagination the feeling that they have been transported back a couple of centuries to a time when the wharf was crowded with sailing ships, the streets teemed with porters transporting goods to and from warehouses, and traders from a dozen countries haggled in a babble of languages.

Architecture
So far, 844 structures of historical significance have been identified in Hoi An. These structures are of nine types:

- Houses & shops
- Wells
- Family chapels for ancestor worship
- Pagodas
- Vietnamese & Chinese temples
- Bridges
- Communal buildings
- Assembly halls (hoi quan) of various Chinese congregations
- Tombs (Vietnamese, Chinese & Japanese; no original European tombs survive)

Many of Hoi An's older structures exhibit features of traditional architecture rarely seen today. The fronts of some shops which are open during the day to display the wares,

are shuttered at night, as they have been for centuries, by inserting horizontal planks into grooves cut into the columns that support the roof. Some roofs are made of thousands of brick-coloured 'Yin & Yang' roof tiles, so called because of the way the alternating rows of concave and convex tiles fit together. During the rainy season, the lichens and mosses that live on the tiles spring to life, turning entire rooftops bright green.

Many of Hoi An's houses have round pieces of wood with a Yin & Yang symbol in the middle surrounded by a spiral design over the doorway. These 'watchful eyes' (mat cua) are supposed to protect the residents of the house from harm.

Every year during the rainy season, Hoi An has problems with flooding, especially near the waterfront. The greatest flood Hoi An has ever known took place in 1964, when the water reached all the way up to the roof beams of the houses.

Plans are under way to restore Hoi An's historic structures and to preserve the unique character of the city. Assistance is being provided to local authorities by the Archaeological Institute in Hanoi, the Japan-Vietnam Friendship Association and experts from Europe and Japan.

Orientation
Bach Dang St runs along the Thu Bon River, which is also known as the Hoi An River and the Cai River. Many of Hoi An's most interesting sites are along Tran Phu St.

Information
Tourist Office Hoi An Tourism Service Company (☎ 248, 372, 373) is at 6 Tran Hung Dao St and offers tours and information.

Money The bank, which does not yet accept foreign currency, is 50 metres south of the GPO at 2 Hoang Dieu St.

Post & Telecommunications The GPO is across from 11 Tran Hung Dao St (on the north-west corner of Ngo Gia Tu and Tran Hung Dao Sts).

mergency The hospital is opposite the PO at 10 Tran Hung Dao St.

apanese Covered Bridge

he Japanese Covered Bridge (Cau Nhat an, or Lai Vien Kieu) connects 155 Tran hu St with 1 Nguyen Thi Minh Khai St. The irst bridge on this site was constructed in 593 by the Japanese community of Hoi An o link their neighbourhood with the Chinese uarters across the stream. The bridge was rovided with a roof so it could be used as a helter from both the rain and the sun.

The Japanese Covered Bridge is very olidly built, apparently because the original uilders were afraid of earthquakes, which re common in Japan. Over the centuries, the rnamentation of the bridge has remained elatively faithful to the original Japanese lesign, reflecting the Japanese preference or understatement, which contrasts greatly with the Vietnamese and Chinese penchant or wild decoration. The French flattened out he roadway to make it more suitable for their notorcars but the original arched shape was estored during the major renovation work carried out in 1986.

Built into the northern side of the bridge s a small temple, Chua Cau. Over the door s written the name given to the bridge in 1719 to replace the name then in use, which meant the Japanese Bridge. The new name, Lai Vien Kieu (Bridge for Passers-By From Afar), never caught on.

According to legend, there once lived an enormous monster called Cu whose head was in India, its tail in Japan and its body in Vietnam. Whenever the monster moved, terrible disasters, such as floods and earthquakes, befell Vietnam. This bridge was built on the monster's weakest point – its 'Achilles' heel', so to speak – killing it. But the people of Hoi An took pity on the slain monster and built this temple to pray for its soul.

The two entrances to the bridge are guarded by a pair of monkeys on one side and a pair of dogs on the other. According to one story, these animals were popularly revered because many of Japan's emperors were born in years of the dog and monkey. Another tale relates that construction of the bridge was begun in the year of the monkey and finished in the year of the dog.

The steles listing Vietnamese and Chinese contributors to a subsequent restoration of the bridge are written in Chinese characters (chu nho), the nom script not yet having become popular in these parts.

Tan Ky House

The Tan Ky House was built almost two centuries ago as the home of a well-to-do ethnic-Vietnamese merchant. The house has been lovingly preserved and today it looks almost exactly as it did in the early 19th century.

The design of the Tan Ky House shows evidence of the influence Japanese and Chinese styles had on local architecture. Japanese elements include the crabshell-shaped ceiling (in the section immediately before the courtyard), which is supported by three progressively shorter beams one on top of the other. There are similar beams in the salon. Under the crabshell ceiling are carvings of crossed sabres enwrapped by a ribbon of silk. The sabres symbolise force; the silk represents flexibility.

Chinese poems written in inlaid mother-of-pearl are hung from a number of the columns that hold up the roof. The Chinese characters on these 150-year-old panels are formed entirely out of birds gracefully portrayed in various positions of flight.

The courtyard has four functions: to let in light; to provide ventilation; to bring a bit of nature into the home; and to collect rainwater and provide drainage. The stone tiles covering the patio floor were brought from Thanh Hoa Province in north-central Vietnam. The carved wooden balcony supports around the courtyard are decorated with grape leaves, a European import, further evidence of the unique mingling of cultures that took place in Hoi An.

The back of the house, in which several families now live, fronts the river. In olden times, this section of the building was rented out to foreign merchants.

That the house was a place of commerce as well as a residence is indicated by the two pulleys attached to a beam in the storage loft located just inside the front door.

The exterior of the roof is made of tiles; inside, the ceiling consists of wood. This design keeps the house cool in the summer and warm in the winter. The house's floor tiles were brought from near Hanoi.

The Tan Ky House is a private home at 101 Nguyen Thai Hoc St. It is open to visitors for a small fee. The owner, whose family has lived here for six generations, speaks fluent French and English. The house is open every day from 8 am to noon and from 2 to 4.30 pm.

Diep Dong Nguyen House

The Diep Dong Nguyen House was built for a Chinese merchant, an ancestor of the present inhabitants, in the late 19th century. The front room on the ground floor was once a dispensary for Chinese medicines (*thuoc bac*), which were stored in the glass-enclosed cases lining the walls. The owner's private collection of antiques, which includes photographs, porcelain and furniture, is on display upstairs. The objects are not for sale! Two of the chairs were once lent by the family to Emperor Bao Dai.

The house, which is at 80 Nguyen Thai Hoc St (by the new numbering system) and 58 Nguyen Thai Hoc St (by the old system) is open every day from 8 am to noon and from 2 to 4.30 pm.

House at 77 Tran Phu St

This private house, which is across the street from the Nha Hang 92 Tran Phu restaurant, is about three centuries old. There is some especially fine carving on the wooden walls of the rooms around the courtyard, on the roof beams and under the crabshell roof (in the salon next to the courtyard). Note the green ceramic tiles built into the railing around the courtyard balcony. The house is open to visitors for a small fee.

Assembly Hall of the Cantonese Chinese Congregation

The Assembly Hall of the Cantonese Chinese Congregation, founded in 1786, is at 176 Tran Phu St and is open daily from 6 to 7.30 am and from 1 to 5.30 pm. The main altar is dedicated to Quan Cong (Chinese: Guangong). Note the long-handled brass 'fans' to either side of the altar. The lintel and doorposts of the main entrance and a number of the columns supporting the roof are made of single blocks of granite. The other columns were carved out of the durable wood of the jackfruit tree. There are some interesting carvings on the wooden beams that support the roof in front of the main entrance.

Chinese All-Community Assembly Hall

The Chinese All-Community Assembly Hall (Chua Ba), founded in 1773, was used by all five Chinese congregations in Hoi An: Fujian, Cantonese, Hainan, Chaozhou and Hakka. The pavilions off the main courtyard incorporate 19th century French elements.

At present, various parts of the complex are used for the manufacture of hand-tied carpets and hanging blinds made of bamboo beads. The women who work here make between US$7.50 and US$12.50 per month.

The main entrance is on Tran Phu St opposite Hoang Van Thu St, but the only way in these days is around the back at 31 Phan Chu Trinh St.

Assembly Hall of the Fujian Chinese Congregation

The Assembly Hall of the Fujian Chinese Congregation was founded as a place to hold community meetings. Later, it was transformed into a temple for the worship of Thien Hau, Goddess of the Sea and Protector of Fishermen and Sailors, who was born in Fujian Province. The triple gate to the complex was built in 1975.

The mural near the entrance to the main hall on the right-hand wall depicts Thien Hau, her way lit by lantern light, crossing a stormy sea to rescue a foundering ship. On the wall opposite is a mural of the heads of the six Fujian families who fled from China to Hoi An in the 17th century following the overthrow of the Ming Dynasty.

The second-to-last chamber contains a statue of Thien Hau. To either side of the entrance stand red-skinned Thuan Phong Nhi, who can hear for great distances, and green-skinned Thien Ly Nhan, who can see for a 1000 miles. When either sees or hears sailors in distress, they inform Thien Hau, who then sets off to effect a rescue. The replica of a Chinese boat along the right-hand wall is in 1:20 scale. The four sets of triple beams which support the roof are typically Japanese.

The central altar in the last chamber contains seated figures of the heads of the six Fujian families who immigrated to Hoi An in the 17th century. The smaller figures below them represent their successors as clan leaders. In a 30-cm-high glass dome is a figurine of Le Huu Trac, a Vietnamese physician renowned in both Vietnam and China for his curative abilities.

Behind the altar on the left is the God of Prosperity. On the right are three fairies and smaller figures representing the 12 'midwives' *(ba mu)*, each of whom teaches newborns a different skill necessary for the first year of life: smiling, sucking, lying on their stomachs and so forth. Childless couples often come here to pray for offspring. The three groups of figures in this chamber represent the elements most central to life: one's ancestors, one's children and economic wellbeing.

The middle altar of the room to the right of the courtyard commemorates deceased leaders of the Fujian congregation. On either side are lists of contributors, women on the left and men on the right. The wall panels represent the four seasons.

The Assembly Hall of the Fujian Chinese Congregation, which is opposite 35 Tran Phu St, is open from 7.30 am to noon and from 2 to 5.30 pm. It is fairly well lit and can be visited after dark. Shoes should be removed upon mounting the platform just past the naves.

Quan Cong Temple

Quan Cong Temple, also known as Chua Ong, is at 24 Tran Phu St (according to the new numbers) and 168 Tran Phu St (according to the old numbering system). Founded in 1653, this Chinese temple is dedicated to Quan Cong, whose partially gilt statue – made of papier mâché on a wood frame – is in the central altar at the back of the sanctuary. On the left is a statue of General Chau Xuong, one of Quan Cong's guardians, striking a tough-guy pose. On the right is the rather plump administrative mandarin Quan Binh. The life-size white horse recalls a mount ridden by Quan Cong until he was given a red horse of extraordinary endurance, representations of which are common in Chinese pagodas.

Stone plaques on the walls list contributors to the construction and repair of the temple. Check out the carp-shaped rain spouts on the roof surrounding the courtyard. The carp, symbol of patience in Chinese mythology, is a popular symbol in Hoi An.

Shoes should be removed when mounting the platform in front of the statue of Quang Cong.

Hainan Assembly Hall

The Assembly Hall of the Hainan Chinese Congregation was built in 1883 as a memorial to 108 merchants from Hainan Island in southern China who were mistaken for pirates and killed in Quang Nam Province during the reign of Emperor Tu Duc (ruled 1848-83). The elaborate dais contains plaques in their memory. In front of the central altar is a fine gilded wood carving of Chinese court life.

The Hainan Congregation Hall is on the east side of Tran Phu St, near the corner of Hoang Dieu St.

Chaozhou Assembly Hall

The Chaozhou Chinese in Hoi An built their congregational hall in 1776. There is some outstanding woodcarving on the beams, walls and altar. On the doors in front of the altar are carvings of two Chinese girls wearing their hair in the Japanese manner.

The Chaozhou Congregation Hall is across from 157 Nguyen Duy Hieu St (near the corner of Hoang Dieu St).

Truong Family Chapel

The Truong Family Chapel (Nha Tho Toc Truong), founded about two centuries ago, is a shrine dedicated to the ancestors of this ethnic-Chinese family. Some of the memorial plaques were presented by the emperors of Vietnam to honour members of the Truong family who served as local officials and as mandarins at the imperial court. To get there, turn into the alley next to 69 Phan Chu Trinh St.

Gate of Ba Mu Pagoda

Though Ba Mu Pagoda, founded in 1628, was demolished by the South Vietnamese government during the 1960s to make room for a three-storey school building, the gate (Phat Tu) remains standing. Enormous representations of pieces of fruit form part of the wall between the two doorways.

The gate of Ba Mu Pagoda is opposite 68 Phan Chu Trinh St.

Ba Le Well

Water for the preparation of authentic *cao lau* (see Places to Eat) must be drawn from Ba Le Well and no other. The well itself, which is said to date from Cham times, is square in shape. To get there, turn down the alleyway opposite 35 Phan Chu Trinh St. Hang a right before reaching number 45/17.

French Architecture

There is a whole city block of colonnaded French buildings on Phan Boi Chau St between numbers 22 and 73.

Cotton Weaving

Hoi An is known for its production of cotton cloth. All over the city there are cotton mills with rows of fantastic wooden looms that make a rhythmic clackety-clack clackety-clack sound as a whirring cycloidal drive wheel shoots the shuttle back and forth under the watchful eyes of the machine attendant. The elegant technology used in building these domestically produced machines dates from the Industrial Revolution. Indeed, this is what mills in Victorian England must have looked like.

There are cloth mills at numbers 140 and 151 Tran Phu St.

Caodai Pagoda

Serving Hoi An's Caodai community, many of whose members live along the path out to the Japanese tombs, is the small Caodai Pagoda (built 1952) between numbers 64 and 70 Huynh Thuc Khang St (near the bus station). One priest lives here. Sugar and corn are grown in the front yard to raise a bit of extra cash.

Hoi An Church

The only tombs of Europeans in Hoi An are in the yard of the Hoi An Church, which is at the corner of Nguyen Truong To St and Le Hong Phong St. When this modern building was constructed to replace an earlier structure at another site, several 18th century missionaries were reburied here.

Chuc Thanh Pagoda

Chuc Thanh Pagoda is the oldest pagoda in Hoi An. It was founded in 1454 by Minh Hai, a Buddhist monk from China. Among the antique ritual objects still in use are several bells, a stone gong two centuries old and a carp-shaped wooden gong said to be even older. Today, five elderly monks live here.

In the main sanctuary, gilt Chinese characters inscribed on a red roof beam give details of the pagoda's construction. Under a wooden canopy on the central dais sits an A Di Da Buddha flanked by two Thich Ca Buddhas (Sakyamuni). In front of them is a statue of Thich Ca as a boy flanked by his servants.

To get to Chuc Thanh Pagoda, go all the way to the end of Nguyen Truong To St and turn left. Follow the sandy path for 500 metres.

Phuoc Lam Pagoda

Phuoc Lam Pagoda was founded in the mid-17th century. Late in the century, the head monk was An Thiem, a Vietnamese prodigy who became a monk at the age of eight. When he was 18, the king drafted An Thiem's brothers into his army to put down a rebellion. An Thiem volunteered to take the places of the other men in his family and eventually rose to the rank of general. After the war, he returned to the monkhood but felt guilty about the many people he had slain. To atone for his sins, he volunteered to clean the Hoi An Market for a period of 20 years. When the 20 years were up, he was asked to come to Phuoc Lam Pagoda as head monk.

To get to Phuoc Lam Pagoda, continue past Chuc Thanh Pagoda for 350 metres. The path passes by an obelisk erected over the tomb of 13 ethnic-Chinese decapitated by the Japanese during WW II for resistance activities.

Japanese Tombs

The tombstone of the Japanese merchant Yajirobei, who died in 1647, is clearly inscribed with Japanese characters. The stele, which faces north-east towards Japan, is held in place by the tomb's original covering, which is made of an especially hard kind of cement whose ingredients include powdered seashells, the leaves of the *boi loi* tree and cane sugar. Yajirobei may have been a Christian who came to Vietnam to escape persecution in his native land.

To get to Yajirobei's tomb, go north to the end of Nguyen Truong Tu St and follow the sand path around to the left (west) for 40 metres until you get to a fork. The path that continues straight on leads to Chuc Thanh Pagoda, but you should turn right (northward). Keep going for just over one km, turning left (to the north) at the first fork and left (to the north-west) at the second fork. When you arrive at the open fields, keep going until you cross the irrigation channel. Just on the other side of the channel turn right (south-east) onto a raised path. After going for 150 metres, turn left (north-east) into the paddies and walk 100 metres. The tomb, which is on a platform surrounded by a low stone wall, stands surrounded by rice paddies.

The tombstone of a Japanese named Masai, who died in 1629, is a few hundred metres back towards Hoi An. To get there, turn left (south-east) at a point about 100 metres towards town from the edge of the rice fields. The tombstone is on the right-hand side of the trail about 30 metres from the main path.

For help in finding the Japanese tombs, show the locals the following words: *Ma Nhat* (or *Mo Nhat*), which means Japanese tombs.

There are other Japanese tombs in Duy Xuyen District, which is across the delta of the Thu Bon River from Hoi An.

Cua Dai Beach

The fine sands of Cua Dai Beach (Bai Tam Cua Dai) are usually deserted. When there is a full moon, people come here to hang out until late at night. Changing booths are provided; refreshments are sold in the shaded kiosks.

Cham Island is offshore. If it's clear, visible to the north-west are the Marble Mountains and, behind them, the peaks around Hai Van Pass.

Cua Dai Beach is five km east of Hoi An out Cua Dai St, which is the continuation of Tran Hung Dao and Phan Dinh Phung Sts. The road passes shrimp-hatching pools built with Australian assistance. There are plans for a team of Australian submarine archaeologists to excavate sunken ships near here.

Places to Stay

There are several hotels, but the only place authorised to accept foreigners is the *Hoi An Hotel* (☎ 373) at 6 Tran Hung Dao St. This hotel is a grand colonial-style building and was a US Marine base during the Vietnam War. The building has been renovated and sits in a pleasant tree-shaded compound.

Singles/doubles with electric fan cost US$8/10 or US$12/15; with air-conditioning it's US$15/18. The hotel has a restaurant and can arrange permits (US$10) and a car (US$30) for the trip to My Son. However, these arrangements can be made more cheaply in Danang (see the Danang chapter for information on My Son). The hotel's restaurant is known for overcharging – ask the prices before you eat to avoid indigestion later.

Places to Eat

Hoi An's contribution to Vietnamese cuisine is *cao lau*, which consists of doughy flat noodles mixed with croutons, bean sprouts and greens and topped with pork slices. It is mixed with crumbled crispy rice paper immediately before eating. Hoi An is the *only* place genuine cao lau can be made because the water used in the preparation of the authentic article must come from a particular well in town. The best cau lao in Hoi An is served at *Cao Lau Restaurant* at 42 Tran Phu St, which is run by several elderly ladies.

The *Nha Hang 92 Tran Phu* is a restaurant on the ground floor of the Hoi An Town Guest House (Nha Khach Thi Xa Hoi An). The *Nha Hang So Nam* (Restaurant Number 5) is a government-owned place at 5 Hoang Dieu St.

For something to drink, such as a thirst-quenching glass of iced coconut milk (nuoc dua), try one of Hoi An's refreshment shops. The *Coconut Milk Café* is across from the Assembly Hall of the Hainan Chinese Congregation at 7 Tran Phu St. *Café Dong Thi* is at 109 Tran Phu St. Near the Japanese Covered Bridge you'll find the *Nguyen Hue Café* (across from 174 Tran Phu St) and *Café Gia Khat Che*, which is next to 151 Tran Phu St in the old French-era post office building. There are several cafes along Le Loi St near the intersection with Phan Chu Trinh St.

Getting There & Away

Bus Buses from Danang to Hoi An (via the Marble Mountains and China Beach) leave from both the Intercity Bus Station and the Short-Haul Pickup Truck Station, which has more frequent service. The ride takes an hour once the vehicle actually gets going

The Hoi An Bus Station (Ben Quoc Doanh Xe Khach; ☎ 84) is one km west of the centre of town at 74 Huynh Thuc Khang St. Small truck-buses from here go to Dai Loc (Ai Nghia), Danang, Quang Ngai (once a day departing in the early morning), Que Son, Tam Ky and Tra My. Service to Danang begins at 5 am; the last bus to Danang departs in the late afternoon.

Car There are two land routes from Danang to Hoi An. The shortest way is to drive to the Marble Mountains (11 km from Danang) and continue south along the 'Korean Highway' for another 19 km. Alternatively, you can head south from Danang on National Highway 1 and, at a signposted intersection 27 km from the city, turn left (east) for 10 km.

Boat Small motorised ferries leave Hoi An for nearby districts and Cham Island from the Hoang Van Thu Street Dock, which is across from 50 Bach Dang St. The daily boat to Cham Island usually departs between 7 and 8 am. The daily boat to Duy Xuyen leaves at 5 am. There is also frequent service to Cam Kim Island.

Chartered boat trips along the Thu Bon River (the Cai River), the largest in Quang Nam-Danang Province, can be arranged at the Hoang Van Thu Street Dock. It may be possible to take an all-day boat ride from Hoi An all the way to Simhapura (Tra Kieu) and the My Son area.

Getting Around

The best way to get around Hoi An and to surrounding areas is by bicycle. The Hoi An Hotel rents out bicycles for US$1 per day or US$0.10 per hour, but first priority goes to their guests, not travellers passing through.

AROUND HOI AN

Cam Kim Island

The master woodcarvers who in previous centuries produced the fine carvings that graced the homes of Hoi An's merchants and the town's public buildings came from Kim Bong village on Cam Kim Island. These days, some of the villagers build wooden boats. To get there, catch one of the frequent boats from the Hoang Van Thu Street Dock, which is opposite 50 Bach Dang St.

Cham Island

Cham Island (Culao Cham) is in the South China Sea 21 km from Hoi An; by boat, the trip takes about two hours. The island is famous as a source of swifts' nests, which are exported to Hong Kong, Singapore and elsewhere for use in bird's nest soup.

Both foreigners and Vietnamese need authorisation to visit the island because attempts to flee the country have been disguised as excursions to Cham Island. A motorised ferry to Cham Island's two fishing villages departs from the Hoang Van Thu Street Dock at about 7 am; it returns in the afternoon.

You can get a permit for fishing and scuba diving is now also permitted.

ENROUTE TRAM KHAM XE LANG CO (photo of Station kiosk)
765 km (beach)
Khi Va Nam (crescent beach)
PHAN CHAU QUIN +

Danang
Đà Nẵng

The complexes that afflict Hanoi, the nation's capital, and Saigon, itself once a capital city, seem far, far away in Danang (population 400,000), Vietnam's fourth-largest city. Danang's distance from other centres of power, its natural endowments (the port, its proximity to Laos and Thailand) and the high degree of provincial autonomy afforded by Vietnam's political structure allow for considerable local initiative.

Of late, the city has become a leader in implementing economic reforms and has shown itself eager to demonstrate the sort of dynamism and economic pragmatism likely to attract foreign investment. In addition, Danang serves as the main seaport for the southern part of land-locked Laos.

While the city of Danang itself is only of moderate interest to non-business travellers, there are many worthwhile sights in the surrounding area. Among the sites of interest are the Marble Mountains, China Beach (Bai Non Nuoc), the Cham towers at My Son, Ba Na hill station, Hai Van Pass (Col des Nuages) and Lang Co Beach.

History

Danang, known under the French as Tourane, succeeded Hoi An (Faifo) as the most important port in central Vietnam during the 19th century.

In late March 1975 Danang, the second-largest city in South Vietnam, was the scene of utter chaos after Saigon government forces were ordered to abandon Hué and Quang Ngai had fallen to the Communists, cutting South Vietnam in two. Desperate civilians tried to flee the city as soldiers of the disintegrating South Vietnamese Army engaged in an orgy of looting, pillage and rape. On 29 March 1975, two truckloads of Communist guerrillas, more than half of them women, drove into what had been the most heavily defended city in South

Vietnam, and without firing a shot, declared Danang 'liberated'.

Almost the only fighting that took place as Danang fell was between South Vietnamese soldiers and civilians battling for space on flights and ships out of the city. On 27 March, the president of World Airways, Ed Daly, ignoring explicit government orders, sent two 727s from Saigon to Danang to evacuate refugees. When the first plane landed, about a thousand desperate and panicked people mobbed the tarmac. Soldiers fired assault rifles at each other and at the plane as they tried to shove their way through the rear door. As the aircraft taxied down the runway trying to take off, people climbed up into the landing-gear wells and someone threw a hand grenade, damaging the right wing.

Those who managed to fight their way aboard, kicking and punching aside anyone in their way, included over 200 soldiers, mostly members of the elite Black Panthers company. The only civilians on board were two women and one baby – and the baby was there only because it had been thrown aboard by its desperate mother, who was left on the tarmac. Several of the stowaways in the wheel wells couldn't hold on, and as the plane flew southward, TV cameras on the second 727 filmed them falling into the South China Sea.

Orientation

The main east-west artery in the city of Danang is known at various points along its length as Hung Vuong St (in the city centre), Ly Thai To St (near the Central Market) and Dien Bien Phu St (out around the Intercity Bus Station).

Danang is on the western bank of the Han River. Along the eastern bank, which can be reached via the Nguyen Van Troi Bridge, is a long, thin peninsula at the northern tip of which is Nui Son Tra, known as 'Monkey Mountain' to the Americans. It is now a closed military area. To the south, 11 km from the city, are the Marble Mountains. Hai Van Pass overlooks Danang from the north.

The process of bringing the names of Danang's streets in line with the sensitivities of the present government is still going on. The city's distinctive cement street signs date from the French period. Occasionally, one of the new white-on-blue metal plaques falls off, revealing the old French name.

Information

Tourist Offices Danang Tourism (Cong Ty Du Lich Da Nang; ☎ 22112, 21423; telex 515707 DATOUR-VT; fax (84-51) 22854) is the official provincial tourism authority for Quang Nam-Danang Province. The office is at 68 Bach Dang St near the GPO and is open from 7 to 11.30 am and 1 to 4.30 pm Monday to Saturday.

Vietnam Tourism (Tong Cong Ty Du Lich Viet Nam; ☎ 22990, 22999; telex 515735 VITOUR-VT; fax (84-51) 22854) is at 91/1 Nguyen Chi Thanh St.

Money The Foreign Trade Bank, Vietcombank (Ngan Hang Ngoai Thuong Viet Nam; ☎ 22110), is at 46A Le Loi St near the corner of Hai Phong St; it is open from 7.30 to 11.30 am and 1 to 3.30 pm Monday to Saturday except Thursday and Saturday afternoons.

Post & Telecommunications The GPO (☎ 21499; telex 704 PUBLIC DN), which offers telex, telephone and postal services, is next to 46 Bach Dang St (corner of Le Duan St); it is open daily from 6 am to 8.30 pm.

TNT Vietrans (☎ 21685, 22582) offers express domestic and international document and parcel delivery. Call for collection information.

Emergency Hospital C (Benh Vien C; ☎ 22480) is at 35 Hai Phong St.

Useful Organisations Foreigners interested in business, trade or investment in the Danang area would do well to contact the Foreign Economic Relations Department of Quang Nam-Danang Province (☎ 21092) at 136 Ong Ich Khiem St. The dynamic staff are efficient and eager to be of assistance. Indeed, they exemplify this province's pragmatic, pro-business orientation.

Another worthwhile organisation promoting Danang's economic interests is the Chamber of Commerce & Industry, otherwise known as Vietcochamber (☎ 22930; telex 515725 CHAMER). The office is at 172 Bach Dang St.

The offices of the People's Committee of Quang Nam-Danang Province (☎ 21238) are in the French-era city hall at 34 Bach Dang St.

Cham Museum

The best sight in Danang city is the Cham Museum (Bao Tang Cham). The museum was founded in 1915 by the École Française d'Extrême Orient and has the finest collection of Cham sculpture in the world. Many of the sandstone carvings (altars, lingas, garudas, ganeshas and images of Shiva, Brahma and Vishnu) are absolutely stunning; this is the sort of place you can easily visit again and again. It is well worth it to get a knowledgeable guide (a scarce commodity in these parts) to show you around. The Cham Museum is near the intersection of

Cham sculpture, Cham museum

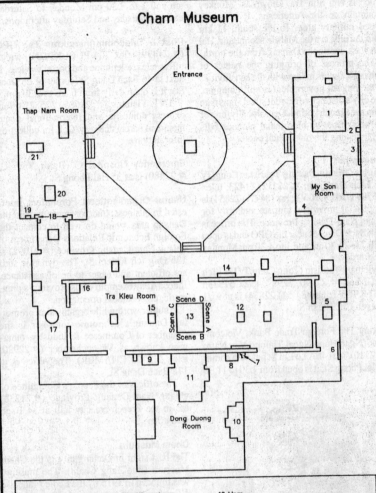

Cham Museum

Entrance

Thap Nam Room

21

20

19 18

My Son Room

1

2

3

4

Tra Kieu Room

16

15

17

14

Scene D
Scene C 13 Scene A
Scene B

12

5

6

9

8 7

11

Dong Duong Room

10

1 My Son Altar; from My Son, 8th–9th century
2 Ganesha (seated elephant); from My Son, 8th–9th century
3 Birthday of Brahma; from My Son, 8th–9th century
4 Polo players; from Thach An, 7th century
5 Altar ornaments; from Khuong My, 10th century
6 The Goddess Sarasvati; from Chanh Lo, 11th century
7 Vishnu, from Tra Kieu, 10th century
8 A deity; from Dong Duong, 9th–10th century
9 A deity; from Dong Duong, 9th–10th century
10 Dong Duong Altar ornaments; from Dong Duong, 9th–10th century
11 Dong Duong Altar; from Dong Duong, 9th–10th century

12 Linga
13 Tra Kieu Altar; from Tra Kieu, 7th century
14 Dancing Shiva; from Phong Le, 10th century
15 Linga
16 Dancing female apsaras; from Quang Nam–Danang Province, 10th century
17 Altar ornaments; from Binh Dinh, 12th–14th century
18 Lions; from Thap Mam, 12th–14th century
19 Shiva; from Thap Mam, 12th–14th century
20 The elephant–lion Gajasimha; from Thap Mam, 12th–14th century
21 The sea monster Makara; from Thap Mam, 12th–14th century

Tran Phu St and Le Dinh Duong St and is open daily from 8 to 11 am and 1 to 5 pm.

A trilingual guidebook to the museum written by its director, Tran Ky Phuong, Vietnam's most eminent scholar of Cham civilisation, gives excellent background on the art of Champa; it also includes some information on the museum's exhibits. The booklet, entitled *Museum of Cham Sculpture – Danang* and *Bao Tang Dieu Khac Cham Da Nang* (Foreign Languages Publishing House, Hanoi, 1987), is usually on sale where you buy your entrance ticket.

Cham art can be divided into two main periods. Before the 10th century, it was very emotionally expressive, reflecting contact with seafaring cultures from Indonesia. From the 10th to the 14th century, as Champa fell into decline because of unending wars with the Vietnamese, Cham art came under Khmer influence and became more formalistic.

The museum's artefacts, which date from the 7th to 15th century, were discovered at Dong Duong (Indrapura), Khuong My, My Son, Tra Kieu (Simhapura), Thap Mam (Binh Dinh) and other sites, mostly in Quang Nam-Danang Province. The rooms in the museum are named after the localities in which the objects displayed in them were discovered.

A recurring image in Cham art is that of Uroja, the 'Mother of the Country', who gave birth to the dynasties that ruled Champa. Uroja, whose name means Woman's Breast in the Cham language, was worshipped in the form of the nipples one often sees in Cham sculpture. Also common is the linga, phallic symbol of Shiva, which came to prominence after Champa's contact with Hinduism. Cham religious beliefs (and thus Cham architecture and sculpture) were influenced by Mahayana Buddhism as early as the 4th century. In addition to its clear Indian elements, Cham art shows Javanese, Khmer and Dai Viet (Vietnamese) influences.

The four scenes carved around the base of the 7th century Tra Kieu Altar tell part of the Ramayana epic in a style influenced by the Amaravati style of South India. Scene A (see diagram), in which 16 characters appear, tells the story of Prince Rama, who broke the sacred bow, Rudra, at the citadel of Videha and thus won from King Janak the right to wed his daughter, Princess Sita. Scene B, which also comprises 16 characters, shows the ambassadors sent by King Janak to Prince Rama's father, King Dasaratha, at Ayodhya. The emissaries inform King Dasaratha of the exploits of his son, present him with gifts, and invite him to Videha to celebrate his son's wedding. In Scene C (which has 18 characters), the royal wedding ceremony (and that of three of Prince Rama's brothers, who marry three of Princess Sita's cousins) is shown. In Scene D, 11 apsaras (heavenly maidens) dance and present flowers to the newlyweds under the guidance of the two gandhara musicians who appear at the beginning of Scene A.

Former US Consulate

After reunification, the former US Consulate building was turned into Danang's Museum of American War Crimes; that's why a Huey helicopter with its door gun still attached is sitting in the courtyard. In 1975, during the chaos that reigned in the days before the Communist takeover, evacuation barges docked right across the street from the consulate. The consulate was later looted, and mobs of Vietnamese – furious at having been 'abandoned' by the Americans – tried to burn it down. Today, the brick structure is considered beyond repair and may be torn down.

The former US Consulate is on the corner of Bach Dang St and Phan Dinh Phung St.

Danang Cathedral

Danang Cathedral (Chinh Toa Da Nang), known to locals as Con Ga Church (the Rooster Church) because of the weathercock on top of the steeple, was built for the city's French residents in 1923. Today, it serves a Catholic community of 4000. The cathedral's architecture is well worth a look, as are the medieval-style stained glass windows of various saints.

Next door to the cathedral are the offices

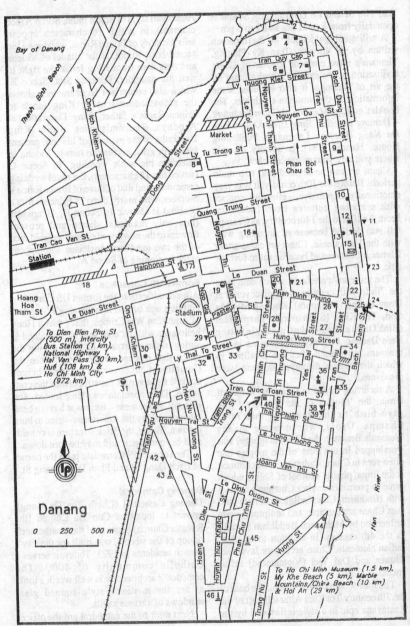

Bay of Danang

Thanh Binh Beach

Ong Ich Khiem St

Tran Quy Cap St

Ly Thuong Kiet Street

Nguyen Chi Thanh St

Le Loi St

Tran Phu Street

Bach Dang Street

Nguyen Du

Market

Ly Tu Trong St

Phan Boi Chau St

Dong Da Street

Quang Trung Street

Nguyen

Tran Cao Van St

Station

Haiphong St

Le Duan Street

Ngo Gia Tu St

Minh

Khai St

Pasteur

St

Phan Dinh Phung

Trinh

Street

Hung Vuong Street

Tran Phu

Bach

Dang St

Hoang
Hoa
Tham St

Le Duan Street

Ong Ich Khiem St

Stadium

Ly Thai To Street

To Dien Bien Phu St
(500 m), Intercity
Bus Station (1 km),
National Highway 1,
Hai Van Pass (30 km),
Huế (108 km) &
Ho Chi Minh City
(972 km)

Phan Chu Trinh Street

Tri Phuong

Yen Bai

Nu

Nguyen Trai

Tran Binh Trong St

Tran Quoc Toan Street

Le Hong Phong St

Vuong St

Thai
Nguyen St

Phien

Hoang Van Thu St

Han River

Nguyen

Le Dinh Duong St

Pham Ngu

Dieu

Huynh Thuc Khang St

Phan Chu Trinh St

Hoang

Trung Nu

Vuong St

Danang

0   250   500 m

To Ho Chi Minh Museum (1.5 km),
My Khe Beach (5 km), Marble
Mountains/China Beach (10 km)
& Hoi An (29 km)

of the diocese of Danang and the Saint Paul Convent. About 100 nuns – who, when praying, wear white habits in the summer and black habits in the winter – live here and at another convent building across the Han River.

Danang Cathedral is on Tran Phu St across from the Hai Au Hotel. If the main gate is locked, try the back entrance, which is opposite 14 Yen Bai St. Masses are held daily at 5 am and 5 pm and on Sundays at 5 am, 6.30 am and 4.30 pm.

Pagodas & Temples
Caodai Temple Danang's main Caodai Temple (Chua Cao Dai), built in 1956 and now home to six priests, is the largest such structure outside of the sect's headquarters in Tay Ninh. There are 50,000 Caodais in Quang Nam-Danang Province, 20,000 in Danang itself. The temple is across the street

from Hospital C (Benh Vien C), which is at 35 Hai Phong St. As at all Caodai temples, prayers are held four times a day at 6 am, noon, 6 pm and midnight.

The left-hand gate to the complex, marked 'Nu Phai', is for women; the right gate, marked 'Nam Phai', is for men. The doors to the sanctuary are also segregated: women to the left, men to the right, and priests of either sex through the central door. Behind the main altar sits an enormous globe with the 'divine eye', symbol of Caodaism, on it.

Hanging from the ceiling in front of the altar is a sign reading 'Van Giao Nhat Ly', which means 'All Religions have the same reason'. Behind the gilded letters is a picture of the founders of five of the world's great religions. From left to right they are: Mohammed; Laotze (wearing blue robes cut in the style of the Greek Orthodox); Jesus (portrayed as he is in French icons); the

■ PLACES TO STAY		
1	Nha Nghi Du Lich Thanh Binh	
3	Dong Da Hotel (Khach San Huu Nghi)	
4	Marble Mountains Hotel (Khach San Ngu Hanh Son)	
5	Danang Hotel	
6	Thu Bon Hotel	
7	Peace Hotel	
8	Hai Van Hotel	
9	Song Han Hotel	
12	Bach Dang Hotel	
32	Thu Do Hotel	
35	Hai Au Hotel	
40	Orient Hotel (Phuong Dong Hotel) ✓	
41	Pacific Hotel (Thai Binh Duong Hotel)	

▼ PLACES TO EAT		
2	Small Cafes	
11	Kim Dinh Restaurant	
14	Thanh Lich Restaurant	
20	Tuoi Hong Café	
21	Phi Lu Restaurant	
23	Seamen's Club (Cafe)	
26	Nha Hang 72	
27	Thanh Huong Restaurant	

29	Chin Den Restaurant	
33	Dac San Restaurant	
37	Ice Cream Cafes	
38	Tiem An Binh Dan Restaurant	
39	Tu Do & Kim Do Restaurants	
42	Quan Chay Vegetarian Restaurant	

OTHER		
10	People's Committee of Quang Nam-Danang Province	
13	Vietnam Airlines Booking Office	
15	GPO	
16	Vietcombank	
17	Caodai Temple	
18	Market	
19	Ancient Renault Buses	
22	Danang Tourism & Tourist Shop	
24	Ferries across the Han River	
25	Former US Consulate	
28	Municipal Theatre	
30	Con Market	
31	Short-Haul Pickup Truck Station	
34	Cho Han (Market)	
36	Danang Cathedral	
43	Phap Lam Pagoda (Chua Tinh Hoi)	
44	Cham Museum	
45	Tam Bao Pagoda	
46	Pho Da Pagoda	

Buddha (who has a distinctly South-East Asian appearance); and Confucius (looking as Chinese as could be).

Portraits of early Caodai leaders, dressed in turbans and white robes, are displayed in the building behind the main sanctuary. Ngo Van Chieu, founder of Caodaism, is shown standing wearing a pointed white turban and a long white robe with blue markings.

Phap Lam Pagoda Phap Lam Pagoda (Chua Phap Lam, also known as Chua Tinh Hoi) is opposite 373 Ong Ich Khiem St (123 Ong Ich Khiem St according to the old numbering). Built in 1936, this pagoda has a brass statue of Dia Tang, the Chief of Hell, near the entrance. Six monks live here. Quan Chay Vegetarian Restaurant is just up the street.

Tam Bao Pagoda The main building of Tam Bao Pagoda (Chua Tam Bao) at 253 Phan Chu Trinh St is topped with a five-tiered tower. Only four monks live at this large pagoda which was built in 1953.

Pho Da Pagoda Pho Da Pagoda (Pho Da Tu), which is across from 293 Phan Chu Trinh St, was built in 1923 in a traditional architectural configuration. Today, about 40 monks, most of them young, live and study here. Local lay people and their children participate actively in the pagoda's lively religious life.

Ho Chi Minh Museum
The Ho Chi Minh Museum (Bao Tang Ho Chi Minh; ☎ 5656) has three sections: a museum of military history in front of which American, Soviet and Chinese weaponry are displayed; a replica of Ho Chi Minh's house in Hanoi (complete with a small lake) in; and, on the other side of the pond from the house, a museum about Uncle Ho.

The museum, which is on Nguyen Van Troi St 250 metres west of Nui Thanh St, is open Tuesday to Sunday from 7 to 11 am and 1 to 4.30 pm.

Tombs of Spanish & French Soldiers
Spanish-led Philippine and French troops attacked Danang in August 1858, ostensibly to end the mistreatment of Vietnamese Catholics and Catholic missionaries by the government of Emperor Tu Duc. The city quickly fell, but the invaders soon had to contend with cholera, dysentery, scurvy, typhus and mysterious fevers. By the summer of 1859, 20 times as many of the invaders had died of illness as had been killed in combat. Many of these soldiers are buried in a chapel (Bai Mo Phap Va Ta Ban Nha) about 15 km from the city. The names of the dead are written on the walls.

To get there, cross Nguyen Van Troi Bridge and turn left onto Ngo Quyen St. Continue north to Tien Sa Port (Cang Tien Sa). The chapel, a white building, stands on the right on a low hill about half a km past the gate of the port.

Beaches
The season for Danang's beaches is from May to July when the sea is most calm. During other times of the year the water is rough and there are usually no lifeguards on duty.

Thanh Binh Beach Thanh Binh Beach is only a couple of km from the centre of Danang. It is often crowded, notwithstanding the fact that the water is not the cleanest. To get there from Con Market, head all the way to the northern end of Ong Ich Khiem St.

My Khe Beach My Khe Beach (Bai Tam My Khe) is about six km by road from downtown Danang. The beach drops off sharply to deep water; the undertow is dangerous, especially in winter.

Many people insist that My Khe was the real China Beach of wartime fame and that the present 'China Beach' is a fake. For more discussion about this see the following Around Danang section.

To get there by car, cross Nguyen Van Troi Bridge and continue straight (eastwards) across the big intersection (instead of turning right (southwards) to the Marble Mountains). If you don't have a car, try hopping on a ferry across the Han River from the foot of Phan Dinh Phung St and catching a ride south-eastward to Nguyen Cong Tru St.

Nam O Beach Nam O Beach is on the Bay of Danang about 15 km from the city towards Hai Van Pass. Vehicles to Nam O depart from the Short-Haul Pickup Truck Station. Kim Lien Railway Station is a few km from the beach.

Places to Stay – bottom end

Danang's ever-entrepreneurial People's Committee has discovered that decent accommodation at fair prices will keep visitors around (and spending money) longer. Towards this end, they have made sure that all sectors of the hotel market in the city are adequately covered.

Danang's ever-entrepreneurial prostitutes are also very much in evidence. At virtually every hotel, single male travellers will almost certainly be approached with an offer for a 'massage where you want it'. It's a wonder the hotel beds are in such good condition, considering how much wear and tear they must get.

The *Nha Nghi Du Lich Thanh Binh* (☎ 21319) at 5 Ong Ich Khiem St is right on Thanh Binh Beach, known for its crowds and polluted water. This place is reserved for Vietnamese workers on organised union vacations but they will rent to foreigners for US$5, US$8 and US$10. Few foreign travellers stay here and you'd probably be better off staying someplace else.

Several large hotels are located, rather inconveniently, in the residential area at the northern tip of the peninsula on which the city of Danang is located. The *Danang Hotel* (☎ 21986; about 100 rooms) at 3 Dong Da St is popular with budget travellers. Singles/doubles with fan cost US$5/6; with air-con, US$6/8 to US$15/20. The building was constructed in the late 1960s to house American military personnel, and some of the prostitutes who hang around here look old enough to have had combat experience.

The Danang Hotel has an acceptable in-house restaurant.

Next door at 7 Dong Da St is the *Dong Da Hotel* (☎ 42216; 68 rooms), also known as *Khach San Huu Nghi*. This is an acceptable alternative to the Danang Hotel. Rooms with fan cost US$6 and with air-con US$8 to US$10. The Dong Da Hotel has its own restaurant called the Nha Hang Festival.

Sandwiched between the Dong Da and Danang hotels is the new *Marble Mountains Hotel* (☎ 23258, 23122), 5 Dong Da St, also known as *Khach San Ngu Hanh Son*. This place is clean and is not a bad deal; all rooms have air-con or fan and hot water and cost from US$5 to US$18.

Just around the corner is the *Thu Bon Hotel* (☎ 21101), 10 Ly Thuong Kiet St. It's not a bad place, but at US$22 for a double, it's overpriced for a hotel of this standard.

A bit closer to the railway station is the *Hai Van Hotel* (☎ 21300; 47 rooms) at 2 Nguyen Thi Minh Khai St. It's an old place but has large rooms, private bath and hot water. All rooms are equipped with both air-conditioners and ceiling fans. The toll is US$5 to US$18.

The *Thu Do Hotel* at 65 Hung Vuong St is also relatively close to the railway station and just a few blocks from Con Market (Cho Con). It's one of the cheapest places in town that accepts foreigners, with rooms at US$3 to US$8 with fan or US$10 with air-con. The staff were friendly during our visit and could speak surprisingly good English. However, this place is a bit run-down.

The *Song Han Hotel* (☎ 22540; telex 215722 CUTB-VT; 30 rooms) is along the Han River at 36 Bach Dang St. It looks better on the inside than it does on the outside, and the staff are very friendly. Among the friendly facilities are a restaurant, dance hall, steam bath and massage service. Singles/doubles are US$12/16 and US$18/21.

The *Thanh Thanh Hotel* is a friendly place but looks dingy. Rooms with fan cost US$6 to US$8, and US$12 with air-conditioning. The hotel is on Phan Chu Trinh St near Tran Quoc Toan St.

The *Pacific Hotel* (☎ 22137, 22921), also called the *Thai Binh Duong Hotel*, is across the street from the much pricier Orient Hotel. It's an old place but not bad. Singles/doubles cost US$7/24 to US$12/30. There is a restaurant on the 7th floor.

Places to Stay – top end

The *Peace Hotel* (☎ 23984; telex 515722 CUTB-VT; fax (84-51) 23161), at 3 Tran Quy Cap St, is also known as the Hoa Binh Hotel. This is a new hotel and all rooms have air-conditioning and hot water. Rooms cost US$20 and US$22, or US$25 with a bathtub. The price includes breakfast.

The *Hai Au Hotel* (☎ 22722; fax (84-51) 24165) opened in early 1989 and for awhile was the fanciest in town. The Hai Au Hotel is conveniently located near the centre of town at 177 Tran Phu St, which is across the street from Danang Cathedral. Single rooms cost US$20; doubles are US$22 to US$30. The hotel has a good restaurant.

The *Bach Dang Hotel* (☎ 23649, 23034; telex 515734 BDHL-VT; fax (84-51) 21659), 50 Bach Dang St, is one of the fanciest places in Danang. Singles/doubles with all the trimmings cost US$25/28, US$28/32 or US$40/45. The hotel has good views of the river.

The *Orient Hotel* (☎ 21266, 22854), also known as the *Phuong Dong Hotel*, 93 Phan Chu Trinh St, is an old but classy place with an elegant wood-panelled lobby. Rooms cost from US$25 to US$40. There is a decent restaurant on the top floor. *First rate food.*

Places to Eat

There are dozens of food stalls behind the main market building in the Con Market, and this is about the cheapest place to eat.

Quan Chay, a vegetarian food stall, serves the usual selection of Vietnamese-style vegetarian dishes prepared to look and taste like meat dishes. The food here is very, very inexpensive. Quan Chay, open daily from 7 am to 4 pm, is half a block from Phap Lam Pagoda and about one km from the city centre. The street address is 484 Ong Ich Khiem St.

Prepared vegetarian food is sold on the first and 15th of each lunar month at *Cho Han*, a vegetable market off Hung Vuong St between Bach Dang St and Tran Phu St.

The *Kim Dinh Restaurant* (☎ 21541), 7 Bach Dang St, is directly opposite the Bach Dang Hotel. The restaurant is suspended over the water on pilings so there are nice views of the Han River.

The best restaurant in Danang is the *Tu Do Restaurant* (☎ 21869) at 172 Tran Phu St, 100 metres from the Hai Au Hotel; it is open from 7 am to 9 pm. The menu is extensive, the service is punctilious and the food is in fact quite good, but some of the prices are a lot higher than you'd reasonably expect to pay. Next door is the *Kim Do*, a slightly fancier place where the food is excellent. Also nearby at 174 Tran Phu St is the *Tiem An Binh Dan Restaurant*, a modest place with reasonable prices.

The *Thanh Huong Restaurant* (☎ 22101) at 40 Hung Vuong St (corner Tran Phu St) is a small, friendly place with a local clientele; it's a good place for morning soup (pho). Avoid the *Nha Hang 72*, an indifferently run greasy spoon at 72 Tran Phu St. The *Dac San Restaurant* at 95 Hung Vuong St is an OK cafe.

A breakfast of fried beef and eggs with fresh French bread and salad is available from 6 to 11 am daily at the *Chin Den Restaurant* (the name means Black Nine), which is near the stadium at 32 Ngo Gia Tu St.

The *Thanh Lich Restaurant*, near the GPO at 42 Bach Dang St, has an extensive menu in English, French and Vietnamese. This place has received good reviews from foreign business people.

The *Phi Lu Restaurant* is a pleasant place, with good Chinese and Vietnamese food. It's located at 106 Nguyen Chi Thanh St, near Phan Dinh Phung St.

For a late-evening drink, head for the extremely popular *Tuoi Hong Caf* t 34 Phan Dinh Phung St (on the corner of Phan Chu Trinh St). It's the music which makes this place so popular with local young people.

Most hotels, even the budget ones, have

restaurants. There are lots of sit-down ice cream shops on Tran Quoc Toan St near the junction with Tran Phu St.

Entertainment

Danang's night life centres around Tran Phu, Hung Vuong, Le Loi and Phan Chu Trinh Sts.

The Municipal Theatre, which offers a wide variety of performances depending on which troupes are in town, is on the corner of Hung Vuong and Le Loi streets. *Hat Tuong*, a form of classical drama, is performed by a provincial troupe that tours all around Quang Nam-Danang Province.

There are a number of cinemas along Tran Phu St near the Vietnam Airlines office. Liberation Day Cinema (Rap 29-3) is on Phan Chu Trinh St near the corner of Tran Quoc Toan St.

Things to Buy

Danang seems particularly well endowed with tailors, many of whom have shops along Hung Vuong St. For a pittance over the cost of the cloth, you can have high-quality shirts, pants, skirts, etc tailored to fit your exact proportions. Cloth is available either from the tailors' stock or at the cloth stalls near the intersection of Hung Vuong and Yen Bai Sts.

Film and photo supplies can be purchased at 86 Phan Chu Trinh St and 136 Hung Vuong St.

Danang's central marketplace, Con Market (Cho Con) is at the intersection of Hung Vuong and Ong Ich Khiem Sts. The front section was built in 1985. Con Market has a huge selection of just about everything sold in Vietnam: household items, ceramics, fresh vegetables, stationary, cutlery, fruit, flowers, polyester clothes, etc.

Getting There & Away

Air During the Vietnam War, Danang had one of the busiest airports in the world. Dozens of American-built cement revetments, some of which are now used to house Vietnamese Air Force MiGs, still line the runways.

The Danang office of Vietnam Airlines

(☎ 21130) is at 35 Tran Phu St. Vietnam Airlines' schedule and one-way fares for domestic flights from Danang is as follows:

Destination	Schedule	Price
Hanoi	daily	US$80
Ho Chi Minh City	daily	US$85
Nha Trang	Tue, Fri	US$55
Pleiku	Tue, Fri	US$30

With high hopes of attracting regular flights from abroad, Danang Airport became Danang International Airport in 1989, joining Tan Son Nhat and Noi Bai as Vietnam's third point of entry by air. There are now international flights from Danang to Bangkok, Hong Kong, Kuala Lumpur, Manila and Paris, but all these flights first stop in Ho Chi Minh City before heading abroad.

Bus The Danang Intercity Bus Station (Ben Xe Khach Da Nang; ☎ 21265) is about three km from the city centre on the thoroughfare known, at various points along its length, as Hung Vuong St, Ly Thai To St and Dien Bien Phu St. The ticket office for express buses is across the street from 200 Dien Bien Phu St; it is open from 7 to 11 am and 1 to 5 pm.

Express bus service is available to Buon Ma Thuot (17 hours), Dalat, Gia Lai, Haiphong, Hanoi (24 hours), Ho Chi Minh City (24 hours), Hong Gai, Lang Son, Nam Dinh and Nha Trang (14 hours; US$3). Tickets for non-express buses to Kontum (5 am departure), Sathay and Vinh (12 hours) are also sold here. All express buses depart at 5 am.

The non-express ticket office is open from 5 am until the late afternoon. There is non-express bus service from Danang Bus Station to:

Ai Nghia, Kham Duc, An Hoa, Kiem Lam, Chu Lai Quang Ngai, Dong Ha, Que Son, Giang, Qui Nhon, Giao Thuy, Tam Ky, Go Noi, Thanh My, Ha Lam, Tien Phuoc, Ha Tan, Tra My, Hoi An, Trao, Hiep Duc, Trung Mang, Hué, Trung Phuoc.

Upon arrival at the Danang Intercity Bus Station, be prepared for aggressive touting by cyclo drivers. A cyclo ride to the city centre should cost about US$0.35.

Ancient Renault buses to Cam Lam, Kim Lien, Mui Bai and Vinh Diem leave from a small local bus station about half a km from the city centre at the corner of Le Duan and Nguyen Thi Minh Khai Sts. The station is in operation from 5 am to about 6 pm.

There is talk about a Bangkok-Vientiane-Danang international bus, but so far it's wishful thinking.

Short-Haul Pickup Truck Station Xe Lams and small passenger trucks to places in the vicinity of Danang leave from the Short-Haul Pickup Truck Station opposite 80 Hung Vuong St, which is about a block west of Con Market (Cho Con). There is service from here to Cam Le, Cau Do, Hoa Khanh, Hoi An (Faifo), Kim Lien, Nam O (there's a beach here), Non Nuoc (the Marble Mountains and China Beach), Phuoc Tuong and Son Cha. The trip to Non Nuoc takes approximately 20 minutes; the ride to Hoi An takes about one hour. Vehicles leave when full (ie when packed with people). The station opens at about 5 am and closes around 5 pm.

Train Danang Train Station (Ga Da Nang) is about 1.5 km from the city centre on Haiphong St at the northern end of Hoang Hoa Tham St. The train ride to Hué is one of the nicest in the country (though driving up and over Hai Van Pass is also spectacular).

Northbound, the quickest ride takes about 3¼ hours to Hué. Local trains take about six hours. Watch your belongings as you pass through the pitch-black tunnels.

Danang is, of course, served by all Reunification Express trains. For ticket prices, see the Train section in the Getting Around chapter.

Car Road distances from Danang are as follows:

Hanoi	764 km
Hué	108 km
Lao Bao (Lao-Vietnam border)	350 km
Nha Trang	541 km
Quang Ngai	130 km
Qui Nhon	303 km
Ho Chi Minh City	972 km
Savannakhet, Laos (Lao-Thai border)	500 km

Getting Around

To/From the Airport By cyclo to Danang's airport only takes about 15 minutes from the centre.

Honda Om Plenty of motorbike guys hang around the small cafes opposite the Marble Mountains Hotel. You can arrange day trips with them to Hoi An, Marble Mountains and China Beach (US$7), My Son (US$10) and other places around Danang. Before you leave you will also probably have to pay about US$1 or so for them to fill up the tank with petrol.

Boat Ferries across the Han River depart from a dock at the foot of Phan Dinh Phung St.

Around Danang

CHINA BEACH
BÃI BIỂN NON NƯỚC

China Beach, made famous in the US TV serial of the same name, stretches for many km north and south of the Marble Mountains. During the Vietnam War, American soldiers were airlifted here for 'rest-and-relaxation' (often including a picnic on the beach) before being returned by helicopter to combat.

Many have insisted that this isn't the real China Beach at all. The place most popular with American soldiers during the war was My Khe Beach five km to the north. The motive behind naming the current beach 'China Beach' seems to be to capitalise on the famous name so as to draw foreign tourists to the government-owned China Beach Hotel. Near the hotel, private vendors flog China Beach baseball caps, wooden carvings

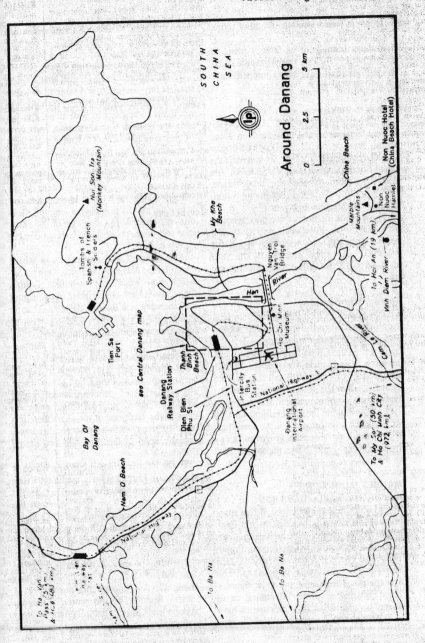

Around Danang

SOUTH CHINA SEA

0   2.5   5 km

Nui Son Tra (Monkey Mountain)

Tombs of Spanish & French Sailors

Tien Sa Port

see Central Danang map

Danang Railway Station

Dien Bien Phu St

Thanh Binh Beach

My Khe Beach

China Beach

Marble Mountains

Non Nuoc Hamlet

Non Nuoc Hotel (China Beach Hotel)

To Hoi An (19 km)

Vinh Diem River

Nguyen Van Troi Bridge

Han River

Ho Chi Minh Museum

Intercity Bus Station

National Highway 1

Danang International Airport

Cam River

To My Son (50 km) & Ho Chi Minh City (972 km)

To Ba Na

To Ba Na

Nam O Beach

Bay Of Danang

National Highway

To Hai Van Pass (5 km) & Hue (108 km)

Ferry Landing

of Buddha, jade bracelets and other tourist paraphernalia.

Perhaps because of its famous name, in December 1992 China Beach was the site of the first international surfing competition to be held in Vietnam.

Places to Stay

The *China Beach Hotel* (☎ 21470, 24145; 100 rooms), also known as the Non Nuoc Hotel, is right on China Beach. Singles/doubles equipped with both air-con and fans cost US$15/18, US$18/22 or US$35/37. You can have a room with a terrace facing the sea. The hotel has two good restaurants – both charge very reasonable prices.

The staff at the hotel's car park seem to have their own little business; when you arrive, you are sold a parking ticket for US$0.20, and when you depart the staff demands an extra dollar for 'watching the car'.

Getting There & Away

Pickup trucks to China Beach (Bai Tam Non Nuoc) depart when full from the Short-Haul Pickup Truck Station in Danang.

To get to the China Beach Hotel by car, motorcycle or bicycle, drive to the Marble Mountains (see next entry) and turn left into Non Nuoc hamlet. Follow the road past the largest Marble Mountain and keep going as it curves around to the right (almost parallel to the beach). Before you hit the sand, turn right towards the casuarina grove (and away from the beach) and follow the road around to the left.

MARBLE MOUNTAINS
NÚI NGŨ HÀNH; NGŨ HÀNH SƠN

The Marble Mountains consist of five stone hillocks, once islands, made of marble. Each is said to represent one of the five elements of the universe and is named accordingly: Thuy Son (water), Moc Son (wood), Hoa Son (fire), Kim So (metal or gold) and Tho Son (earth). The largest and most famous, Thuy Son, has a number of natural caves (*dong*) in which Buddhist sanctuaries have been built over the centuries. When Champa

ruled this area, these same caves were used as Hindu shrines. Thuy Son is a popular pilgrimage site, especially on days of the full and sliver moons and during Tet.

Local children have learned that foreign tourists buy souvenirs and sometimes leave tips for unsolicited guided tours, so you are not likely to begin your visit alone. But the kids are generally good-natured, and some of the caves are difficult to find without their assistance. A torch (flashlight) is useful inside the caves.

Of the two paths leading up Thuy Son, the one closer to the beach (at the end of the village) makes for a better circuit once you get up the top. So unless you want to follow this entry backwards, don't go up the staircase with concrete kiosks and a black cement sign at its base.

At the top of the staircase (from which Cham Island is visible) is a gate, Ong Chon, which is pockmarked with bullets. Behind Ong Chon is Linh Ong Pagoda. As you enter the sanctuary, you'll see on the left a fantastic figure with a huge tongue. To the right of Linh Ong are monks' quarters and a small orchid garden.

Behind Linh Ong and to the left a path leads through two short tunnels to several caverns known as Tang Chon Dong. There are a number of concrete Buddhas and blocks of carved stone of Cham origin in these caves. Near one of the altars there is a flight of steps leading up to another cave, partially open to the sky, with two seated Buddhas in it.

To the left of the small building which is to the left of Linh Ong (ie immediately to the left as you enter Ong Chon gate) is the main path to the rest of Thuy Son. Stairs off the main pathway lead to Vong Hai Da, a viewpoint from which a brilliant panorama of China Beach and the South China Sea is visible.

The stone-paved path continues on to the right and into a canyon. On the left is Van Thong Cave. Opposite the entrance is a cement Buddha behind which a narrow passage leads up to a natural chimney open to the sky.

After you exit the canyon and pass through a battle-scarred masonry gate, a rocky path to the right goes to Linh Nham, a tall chimney-cave with a small altar inside. Nearby, another path leads to Hoa Nghiem, a shallow cave with a Buddha in it. But if you go down the passageway to the left of the Buddha you come to cathedral-like Huyen Khong Cave, lit by an opening to the sky. The entrance to this spectacular chamber is guarded by two administrative mandarins (to the left of the doorway) and two military mandarins (to the right).

Scattered about the cave are Buddhist and Confucian shrines; note the inscriptions carved into the stone walls. On the right a door leads to two stalactites dripping water that local legend says comes from heaven. Actually, only one stalactite drips; the other one supposedly ran dry when Emperor Tu Duc (ruled 1848-83) touched it. During the Vietnam War, this chamber was used by the VC as a field hospital. Inside is a plaque dedicated to the Women's Artillery Group which destroyed 19 US aircraft as they sat at a base below in 1972.

A bit to the left of the battle-scarred masonry gate is Tam Thai Tu, a pagoda restored by Emperor Minh Mang in 1826. A path heading obliquely to the right goes to the monks' residences beyond which are two shrines from which a red dirt path leads to five small pagodas. Before you arrive at the monks' residences, stairs on the left-hand side of the path lead to Vong Giang Dai, which offers a fantastic 180° view of the other Marble Mountains and the surrounding countryside. To get to the stairway down, follow the path straight on from the masonry gate.

Non Nuoc Hamlet

Non Nuoc Hamlet is on the southern side of Thuy Son and is a few hundred metres west of China Beach. The marble carvings made here by skilled (and not-so-skilled) craftspeople would make great gifts if they didn't weigh so much. The town has been spruced up by Danang Tourism.

Getting There & Away

Short-Haul Pickup Truck Pickup trucks to the Marble Mountains (Ngu Hanh Son), Non Nuoc Hamlet and nearby China Beach (Bai Tam Non Nuoc) leave when full from the Short-Haul Pickup Truck Station in Danang. The trip takes about 20 minutes.

Car The 11-km route from Danang to the Marble Mountains passes by the remains of a two-km-long complex of former American military bases; aircraft revetments are still visible.

The Marble Mountains are 19 km north of Hoi An (Faifo) along the 'Korean Highway'.

Boat It is possible to get to the Marble Mountains from Danang by chartered boat. The 8.5-km trip up the Han River and the Vinh Diem River takes about 1¼ hours.

HAI VAN PASS
ĐÈO HẢI VÂN

Hai Van Pass, whose name means Pass of the Ocean Clouds (the French knew it as the Col des Nuages) crosses over a spur of the Truong Son Mountain Range that juts into the South China Sea. About 30 km north of Danang, National Highway 1 climbs to an elevation of 496 metres, passing south of the Ai Van Son peak (altitude 1172 metres). It's an incredibly mountainous stretch of highway with spectacular views. The railway track, with its many tunnels, goes around the peninsula, following the shoreline to avoid the hills. Unfortunately, the buses cannot take this easy route – many break down here.

In the 15th century, Hai Van Pass formed the boundary between Vietnam and the Kingdom of Champa. Until the Vietnam War, the pass was heavily forested. At the top of the Hai Van Pass is an old French fort later used by the South Vietnamese Army and the Americans. The views from near the fortress are quite spectacular. Watch out for the live mortar shells left lying about in the undergrowth!

LANG CO
LĂNG CÔ

Lang Co is a paradisiacal peninsula of palm-shaded sand with a crystal-clear turquoise blue lagoon on one side and many km of beachfront facing the South China Sea on the other. This is one of the most tranquil places in all of Vietnam. There are spectacular views of Lang Co, which is just north of Hai Van Pass, from both National Highway 1 and the train linking Danang and Hué.

Places to Stay

The *Khach San Lang Co* is the only place in town. Rooms cost US$10 and can accommodate up to four people. The hotel is basic but pleasant enough, and all rooms have attached bath. Electricity is only available from 6 until 10 pm, so that's the only time you're going to be able to use the electric fans. The hotel remains open all year round, but it's really only popular (and often full) from May to July.

Getting There & Away

Train Lang Co Railway Station, served by non-express trains, is almost exactly midway between Danang and Hué. However, the railway station is a long way from the hotel.

Car Lang Co is 25 km north of Danang over an extremely mountainous road.

BA NA HILL STATION
TRẠM BÀ NÀ

Ba Na, the 'Dalat of Quang Nam-Danang Province', is a hill station along the crest of Mount Ba Na (or Nui Chua), which rises 1467 metres above the coastal plain. The view in all directions is truly spectacular, and the air is fresh and cool: though it may be 36°C on the coast, the temperature is likely to be between 15° and 26°C at Ba Na. Rain often falls at altitudes of 700 to 1200 metres above sea level, but around the hill station itself the sky is usually clear. Mountain paths in the area lead to a variety of waterfalls and viewpoints.

Ba Na, founded in 1919 for use by French settlers, is not presently in any condition to welcome visitors; but the provincial government has high hopes of making Ba Na once again a magnet for tourists.

By road Ba Na is 48 km west of Danang (as the crow flies, the distance is 27 km). Until WW II, French vacationers travelled the last 20 km by sedan chair!

HO CHI MINH TRAIL
ĐƯỜNG MÒN HỒ CHÍ MINH

Remnants of the Ho Chi Minh Trail can be seen about 60 km west of Danang near the mountain town of Giang. Other areas through which the Ho Chi Minh Trail passed include Hien District and Phuoc Son District. The population of these mountainous parts of Quang Nam-Danang Province includes many Montagnards such as the Katu, some of whom still live as they have for generations.

MY SON
MỸ SƠN

My Son is Vietnam's most important Cham site. During the centuries when Simhapura (Tra Kieu) served as the political capital of Champa, My Son was the site of the most important Cham intellectual and religious centre and may also have served as a burial place for Cham monarchs. My Son is considered to be Champa's counterpart to the grand cities of South-East Asia's other Indian-influenced civilisations: Angkor (Cambodia), Pagan (Myanmar), Ayuthaya (Thailand) and Borobudur (Java).

The monuments are set in a verdant valley surrounded by hills and overlooked by massive Cat's Tooth Mountain (Hon Quap). Clear brooks (in which visitors can take a dip) run between the structures and past nearby coffee plantations. The entrance fee is US$1.25; it is used for upkeep of the site.

My Son became a religious centre under King Bhadravarman in the late 4th century. The site was occupied until the 13th century, the longest period of development of any monument in South-East Asia (by comparison, Angkor's period of development lasted only three centuries, as did that of Pagan). Most of the temples were dedicated to Cham

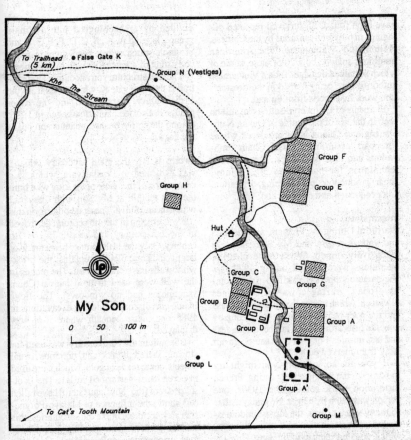

My Son

0   50   100 m

To Cat's Tooth Mountain

kings associated with divinities, especially Shiva, who was regarded as the founder and protector of Champa's dynasties.

Champa's contact with Java was extensive. Cham scholars were sent to Java to study, and there was a great deal of commerce between the two empires; Cham pottery has been found on Java. In the 12th century, the Cham king wed a Javanese wife.

Because some of the ornamentation work at My Son was never finished, archaeologists know that the Chams first built their structures and only then carved decorations into the brickwork. Researchers have yet to

figure out for certain how the Chams managed to get the baked bricks to stick together. According to one theory, they used a paste prepared with a botanical oil indigenous to Central Vietnam. During one period in their history, the summits of some of the towers were covered with a layer of gold.

During the Vietnam War, the vicinity of My Son was completely devastated and depopulated in extended bitter fighting. Finding it a convenient staging ground, Viet Cong guerrillas used My Son as a base; in response the Americans bombed the monuments. Of the 68 structures of which traces have been found, 25 survived repeated pillagings in previous centuries by the Chinese, Khmer and Vietnamese. The American bombings spared about 20 of these, some of which sustained damage. Today, Vietnamese authorities are being helped in their restoration work by experts from Poland.

Elements of Cham civilisation can still be seen in the life of the people of Quang Nam-Danang and Quang Ngai provinces whose forebears assimilated many Cham innovations into their daily lives. These include techniques for pottery-making, fishing, sugar production, rice farming, irrigation, silk production and construction.

Information

Warning! During the Vietnam war, the hills and valleys around the My Son site were extensively mined. When mine clearing operations were carried out in 1977, six Vietnamese sappers were killed in this vicinity. Today, grazing cows are sometimes blown up, which means that as the years pass and the poor beasts locate the mines one by one, the hills around here are becoming less and less unsafe . For your own safety, do *not* stray from marked paths.

If you are so inclined, you might try looking at the bright side: during French restoration work here in the 1930s, one person was eaten by a tiger. Nowadays, after so many years of war, the largest undomesticated animals in the area are wild pigs, which pose no danger to humans. Human-eating animals or mines...it's always something.

Travel Permit Unfortunately, a travel permit is now required to visit My Son. This permit will cost you US$3 but you will also be required to rent a car from the Danang government at a cost of US$20, even if you already have a car. Hopefully, this rule will be quashed eventually when the government realises how much damage it is doing to the tourist industry, but who knows when?

The Site

The monuments of My Son have been divided by archaeologists into 10 main groups, lettered A, A', B, C, D, E, F, G, H and K. Each structure has been given a name consisting of a letter followed by a number.

The first structure you encounter along the trail is the false gate K, which dates from the 11th century. Between K and the other groups is a coffee plantation begun in 1986; among the coffee bushes, peanuts and beans are grown.

Group B B1, the main sanctuary (kalan), was dedicated to Bhadresvara, which is a contraction of the name of the king who built the first temple at My Son with '-esvara,' which means Shiva. The first building on this site was erected in the 4th century, destroyed in the 6th century and rebuilt in the 7th century. Only the 11th century base, made of large sandstone blocks, remains; the brickwork walls have disappeared. The niches in the wall were used to hold lamps (Cham sanctuaries had no windows). The linga inside was discovered during excavations in 1985 one metre beneath where it is now displayed.

B5, built in the 10th century, was used for storing sacred books and precious ritual objects, some made of gold, which were used in ceremonies performed in B1. The boat-shaped roof (the 'bow' and 'stern' have fallen off) shows the influence of Malayo-Polynesian architecture. Unlike the sanctuaries, this building has windows. The fine Cham masonry inside is all original. Over the window on the wall facing B4 is a bas-relief in brick of two elephants under a tree with two birds in it.

The ornamentation on the exterior walls of B4 is an excellent example of a Cham decorative style, typical of the 9th century, said to resemble worms. This style is unlike anything found in other South-East Asian cultures.

B3 has an Indian-influenced pyramidal roof typical of Cham towers. Inside B6 is a bathtub-shaped basin for keeping the sacred water that was poured over the linga in B1; this basin is the only one of its kind of Cham origin known.

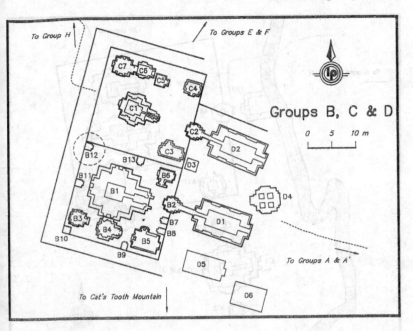

Groups B, C & D

0   5   10 m

To Group H

To Groups E & F

To Groups A & A'

To Cat's Tooth Mountain

B2 is a gate. Around the perimeter of Group B (structures B7 through B13) are small temples dedicated to the gods of the directions of the compass (*dikpalaka*).

Group C The 8th century sanctuary C1 was used to worship Shiva portrayed in human form (rather than in the form of a linga, as in B1). Inside is an altar where a statue of Shiva, now in the Cham Museum in Danang, used to stand. On either side of the stone doorway you can see, bored into the lintel and the floor, the holes in which two wooden doors once swung. Note the motifs, characteristic of the 8th century, carved into the brickwork of the exterior walls.

Group D Building D1, once a mandapa (meditation house), is now used as a store-room. It is slated to become a small museum of Cham sculpture. Objects to be displayed include a large panel of Shiva dancing on a platform above the bull Nandin; to Shiva's

left is Skanda (under a tree), his son Uma, his wife and a worshipper; to Shiva's right is a dancing saint and two musicians under a tree, one with two drums, the other with a flute. The display will also include a finely carved lion – symbol of the power of the king (the lion was believed to be an incarnation of Vishnu and the protector of kings) – whose style belies Javanese influence.

Group A The path from groups B, C and D to Group A leads eastward from near D4.

Group A was almost completely destroyed by US attacks. According to locals, massive A1, considered the most important monu-ment at My Son, remained impervious to aerial bombing and was finally finished off by a helicopter-borne sapper team. All that remains of A1 today is a pile of collapsed brick walls. After the destruction of A1, Philippe Stern, an expert on Cham art and curator of the Guimet Museum in Paris, wrote a letter of protest to President Nixon,

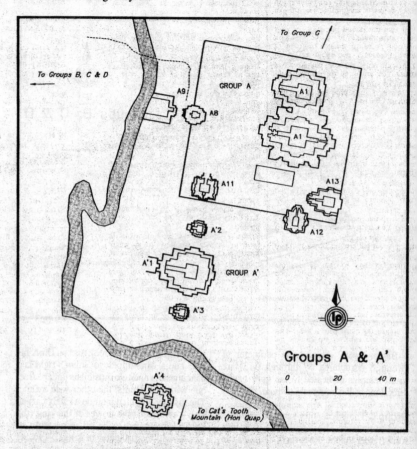

Groups A & A'

0   20   40 m

who ordered US forces to continue killing the Viet Cong but not to do any further damage to Cham monuments.

A1 was the only Cham sanctuary with two doors. One faced the east, direction of the Hindu gods; the other door faced west towards groups B, C and D and the spirits of the ancestor-kings that may have been buried there. Inside A1 is a stone altar pieced back together in 1988. Among the ruins some of the brilliant brickwork, which is of a style typical of the 10th century, is still visible. At the base of A1 on the side facing A10 (which is decorated in 9th century style) is a carving of a worshipping figure, flanked by round columns, with a Javanese *kala-makara* (sea-monster god) above. There may be some connection between the presence of this Javanese motif and the studies in Java of a great 10th century Cham scholar. There are plans to partially restore A1 and A10 as soon as possible.

Other Groups Group A', which dates from the 8th century, is at present overgrown and is thus inaccessible. Group E was built during the 8th to 11th centuries. Group F dates from the 8th century. Group G, which has been damaged by time rather than war, is from the 12th century. There are long-term plans to restore these monuments.

Places to Stay

Unless you have equipment to camp out at My Son, the nearest hotels are in Hoi An and Danang.

Getting There & Away

Bus If the foregoing travel permit and car rental rule is rescinded, you might be able to get to My Son by bus though it won't be easy. There are two daily bus runs between the Danang Intercity Bus Station and Trung Phuoc, departing Danang at 7 am and 1 pm and leaving Trung Phuoc at 7 am and 11 am. Unfortunately, Trung Phuoc is quite a way from the path to My Son. Before trying this, get definite information on exactly how close to My Son the bus will bring you. Note that there is no transport back to Danang in the afternoon.

Car The trailhead to My Son is 60 km from Danang. To get there from Danang, head south on National Highway 1. The turn-off to Hoi An is 27 km south of Danang; at a point 6.8 km south of the turn-off (and two km south of the long bridge over the Thu Bon River), turn right towards Tra Kieu. Buu Chau Hill, on which the Mountain Church sits, is 6.5 km from National Highway 1 on the left. The alleyway leading to Tra Kieu Church and its small museum is 400 metres down the road (past the marketplace).

Twelve km past Tra Kieu (and 8.6 km beyond the Chiem Son Railroad Bridge) is Kim Lam. Turn left here (going straight will lead you to a destroyed bridge). The footpath to the My Son site is on the left-hand side of the road 6.8 km from Kim Lam.

Honda Om It's possible to get to My Son by motorbike; see the Getting Around section under Danang city earlier in this chapter.

Walking It's a bit of a hike (about five km) from the road to My Son. The trail heads south toward Cat's Tooth Mountain (Hon Quap), whose shape does in fact resemble a cat's tooth. When the dirt road is upgraded, vehicles will be able to bring visitors to a point about three km from the monuments.

About two km from the main road the path crosses the Khe The River. If you prefer to cross without swimming, take the detour which goes up the side of the hill to the left. After rejoining the main path, the trail crosses a stream fed by a spring said to have been a favourite stopping place of the famous French archaeologist Henri Parmentier.

Boat If you have lots of time and either hate walking or love boat rides, you might try hiring a small boat (ghe) to take you from Duy Phu hamlet across the Khe The reservoir (Ho Khe The) to where the Khe The River feeds into the reservoir, which is still three km from My Son. Ask the locals for a *ghe den My Son*. The ride takes about 30 minutes.

SIMHAPURA (TRA KIEU)

Simhapura (Tra Kieu), the Lion Citadel, was the first capital city of Champa, serving in that capacity from the 4th to the 8th centuries. Today, nothing remains of the city except the rectangular ramparts. A large number of artefacts, including some of the finest carvings in the Cham Museum in Danang, were found here.

You can get a good view of the city's outlines from the Mountain Church (Nha Tho Nui), which is on the top of Buu Chau Hill in Tra Kieu. This modern open-air structure was built in 1970 to replace an earlier church destroyed by time and war. A Cham tower once stood on this spot. Simhapura is about 500 metres to the south and south-west of the hilltop.

The Mountain Church is 6.5 km from National Highway 1 and 19.5 km from the beginning of the footpath to My Son. Within Tra Kieu, it is 200 metres from the morning market (Cho Tra Kieu) and 550 metres from Tra Kieu Church.

Tra Kieu Church

Tra Kieu Church (Dia So Tra Kieu), which

serves the town's Catholic population of 3000, was built a century ago (though obviously, the border of the semicircular patio, which is made of upturned artillery shells, was added later). The priest here is interested in Cham civilisation and has amassed a collection of Cham artefacts found by local people.

A 2nd-floor room in the building to the right of the church is due to open as a museum in 1990. The round ceramic objects with faces on them, which date from the 8th to the 10th century, were affixed to the ends of tile roofs. The face is that of Kala, the God of Time.

Tra Kieu Church is seven km from National Highway 1 and 19 km from the trail to My Son. It is 150 metres down an alley

opposite the town's clinic of occidental medicine (Quay Thuoc Tay Y), 350 metres from the morning market (Cho Tra Kieu) and 550 metres from the Mountain Church.

INDRAPURA (DONG DUONG)

The Cham religious centre of Indrapura (Dong Duong) was the site of an important Mahayana Buddhist monastery, the Monastery of Lakshmindra-Lokeshvara, founded in 875. Indrapura served as the capital of Champa from 860 to 986, when the capital was transferred to Cha Ban (near Qui Nhon). Tragically, as a result of the devastation wrought by the French and American wars, only part of the gate to Indrapura is extant.

Indrapura is 21 km from My Son as the crow flies and 55 km from Danang.

Hué
Huế

Hué (population 200,000) served as Vietnam's political capital from 1802 to 1945 under the 13 emperors of the Nguyen Dynasty. Traditionally, the city has been one of Vietnam's cultural, religious and educational centres. Today, Hué's main attractions are the splendid tombs of the Nguyen emperors, several notable pagodas and the remains of the Citadel. As locals will tell you repeatedly, the women of Hué are renowned for their beauty. Most of the city's major sights have an admission charge of at least US$3.

History

The citadel-city of Phu Xuan was built on the site of present-day Hué in 1687. In 1744, Phu Xuan became the capital of the southern part of Vietnam, which was under the rule of the Nguyen Lords. The Tay Son Rebels occupied the city from 1786 until 1802, when it fell to Nguyen Anh. He renamed the city Hué and crowned himself Emperor Gia Long, thus founding the Nguyen Dynasty, which ruled the country – at least in name – until 1945. Immediately upon his accession, Gia Long began the decades-long construction of the Citadel, the Imperial City and the Forbidden Purple City.

In 1885, when the advisors of 13-year-old Emperor Ham Nghi objected to French activities in Tonkin, French forces encircled the city. Unwisely, the outnumbered Vietnamese forces launched an attack; the French responded mercilessly. According to a contemporary French account, the French forces took three days to burn the imperial library and remove from the palace every object of value, including everything from gold and silver ornaments to mosquito nets and toothpicks. Ham Nghi fled to Laos but was eventually captured and exiled to Algeria. The French replaced him with the more pliable Dong Khanh, thus ending any pretence of genuine Vietnamese independence.

Hué was the site of the bloodiest battles of the 1968 Tet Offensive and was the only city in South Vietnam to be held by the Communists for more than a few days. While the American command was concentrating its energies on relieving the siege of Khe Sanh, North Vietnamese and VC troops skirted the American stronghold and walked right into Hué, South Vietnam's third-largest city. When the Communists arrived, they hoisted their flag from the Citadel's flag tower, where it flew for the next 25 days; the local South Vietnamese governmental apparatus completely collapsed.

Immediately upon taking Hué, Communist political cadres implemented detailed plans to liquidate Hué's 'uncooperative' elements. Thousands of people were rounded up in extensive house-to-house searches conducted according to lists of names meticulously prepared months in advance. During the 3½ weeks Hué remained under Communist control, approximately 3000 civilians – including merchants, Buddhist monks, Catholic priests, intellectuals and a number of foreigners as well as people with ties to the South Vietnamese government – were summarily shot, clubbed to death or buried alive. The victims were buried in shallow mass graves which were discovered around the city over the course of the next few years.

When South Vietnamese Army units proved unable to dislodge the North Vietnamese and VC forces, General Westmoreland ordered US troops to recapture the city. During the next few weeks, whole neighbourhoods were levelled by VC rockets and American bombs. In 10 days of bitter combat, the VC were slowly forced to retreat from the New City. During the next two weeks, most of the area inside the Citadel (where two-thirds of the population

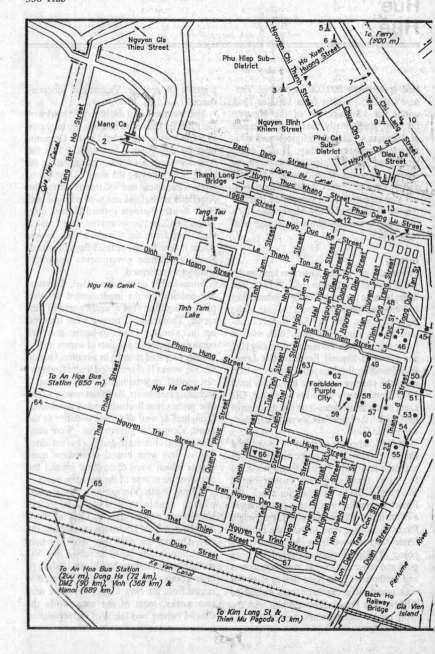

Nguyen Gia Thieu Street

Phu Hiep Sub-District

To Ferry (800 m)

Nguyen Chi Thanh Street

Ho Xuan Huong Street

5

6

Chi Lang Street

3   4

7

8

9   10

Nguyen Binh Khiem Street

Phu Cat Sub-District

Chua Ong St

Nguyen Du St

Dieu De Street

Mang Ca

2

Bach   Dang   Street

Dong   Ba   Canal

11

Thanh Long Bridge

Huynh   Thuc Khang   Street

Qui Hau Canal

Tang Bat Ho Street

196a   Street

Phan Dang Lu Street

13

12

14

Tang Tau Lake

Ngo   Duc   Ke   Street

Le   Thanh   Ton St

Dinh   Tien   Hoang   Street

1

Ngu Ha Canal

Tinh Tam Lake

Tinh   Tam   Street

Nhat   Le   Street

Ngo Si Lien St

Doan Thi Diem Street

Mai Thuc Loan Street

Nguyen Dieu Street

Dang Dung Street

Nguyen Chi Dieu Street

Han   Thuyen   Street

Dinh Cong Trang Street

Le Truc St

Tong Duy Tan St

48

47

46

45

Phung   Hung   Street

Ngu Ha Canal

Tue Tinh Street

Doan Thi   Street

Phan   Dang   Street

63

62

Forbidden Purple City

49

59

58

57

56

Thang 8 Street

50

51

53

54

55

To An Hoa Bus Station (650 m)

Phien   Street

Thai   Phien   Street

Nguyen Trai Street

Phuc   Han   Street

Le Huan   Street

61

60

23

Nguyen   Thien   Thuat   Street

Thach   Han   Street

Trieu Quang   Street

66

Tran Nguyen Han Street

Nho Dang Tran Con St

65

Tran   Nguyen   Dan St

Yet Kieu   Street

Ngo Thoi Nhiem Street

Lon Dang Tran Con St

68

Ton   That   Thiep   Street

Nguyen Cu Trinh Street

Le   Duan   Street

67

Le   Duan   Street

Le Van Canal

Ke Van Canal

To An Hoa Bus Station (200 m), Dong Ha (72 km), DMZ (90 km), Vinh (368 km) & Hanoi (689 km)

To Kim Long St & Thien Mu Pagoda (3 km)

Perfume River

Bach Ho Railway Bridge

Gia Vien Island

64

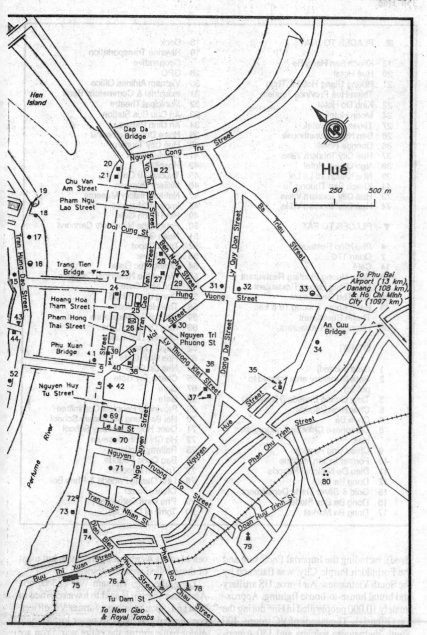

Hen Island

Dap Da Bridge

Nguyen Cong Tru Street

Chu Van Am Street

Pham Ngu Lao Street

Doi Cung St

Trang Tien Bridge

Hoang Hoa Tham Street

Pham Hong Thai Street

Phu Xuan Bridge

Nguyen Huy Tu Street

Perfume River

Le Lai St

Nguyen

Ngo Truong

Tran Thuc Nhan St

Dien Bien

Buu Thi Xuan Street

Tu Dam St

To Nam Giao & Royal Tombs

Nguyen Cong Tru Street

Vo Thi Sau Street

Ben Nghe Street

Ven Street

Hung Vuong Street

Chi Cao

Tran Noi

Ha

Le Loi Street

Ly Thuong Kiet Street

Nguyen Tri Phuong St

Dong Da Street

Nguyen

Hue Street

Ba Trieu Street

Ly Quy Don Street

Phan Chu Trinh Street

Doan Huu Trinh Street

Phan Boi Chau Street

To Phu Bai Airport (13 km), Danang (108 km), & Ho Chi Minh City (1097 km)

An Cuu Bridge

Huế

0   250   500 m

lived), including the Imperial Enclosure and the Forbidden Purple City, was flattened by the South Vietnamese Air Force, US artillery and brutal house-to-house fighting. Approximately 10,000 people died in Hué during the Tet Offensive. Thousands of VC troops, 400 South Vietnamese soldiers and 150 American Marines were among the dead, but most of those killed were civilians.

Long after the Vietnam War ended, one American veteran is said to have returned to Hué and, upon meeting a former VC officer, commented that the USA never lost a single major battle during the entire war: "You are absolutely correct', the former officer agreed, 'but that is irrelevant, is it not?'

Orientation

Hué, 16 km inland from the South China Sea, is bisected by the Perfume River (Huong Giang or Song Huong). Inside the Citadel, which is on the west bank of the river, is the Imperial Enclosure, which surrounds the Forbidden Purple City, former residence of the royal family.

Dong Ba Market is near the eastern corner of the Citadel. Nearby, a commercial district stretches along the Dong Ba Canal. Across the Dong Ba Canal from Dong Ba Market are the subdistricts of Phu Cat and Phu Hiep, known for their Chinese pagodas.

On the right bank of the Perfume River is the New City, once known as the European Quarter. The Imperial Tombs are spread out over a large area to the south of the New City.

Information

Tourist Offices The offices of Thua Thien-Hué Tourism (Cong Ty Du Lich Thua Thien-Hué; ☎ 2369, 2288, 2355) is the government-owned tourism authority for Thua Thien-Hué Province. It's at 30 Le Loi St (the building to the right as you enter the gate of the Huong Giang Hotel). Thua Thien-Hué Tourism can supply guides and cars (including 4WD). Tours of the DMZ, which is in neighbouring Quang Tri Province, can be arranged here. The office is open from 7 to 11.30 am and 1.30 to 5 pm.

Hué City Tourism (Cong Ty Du Lich Thanh Pho Hué; ☎ 3577) is at 18 Le Loi St (corner Ha Noi St). Hué City Tourism runs several tourist villas on Ly Thuong Kiet St and can rent cars and arrange traditional theatre (cai luong) and music performances.

Money Hué's only foreign exchange bank is the Industrial & Commercial Bank (Nhan Hang Cong Thuong; ☎ 3275) at 2A Ly Quy Don St; it's open Monday to Saturday from 7 to 11.30 am and 1.30 to 4 pm. This bank can now change US dollars travellers' cheques into US dollars cash for a 2% commission. You can change foreign hard currencies into dong at the official rate. As of yet, the bank cannot do a cash advance on credit cards.

Post & Telecommunications International postal and telephone services are available at the GPO, 8 Hoang Hoa Tham St; it's open from 6.30 am to 9 pm. International postal, telephone and telex services are available at the 2nd-floor post office (☎ 3093; telex 54154 TWH-VT) in the Huong Giang Hotel (☎ 2122), which is at 51 Le Loi St. The postal windows are supposed to be open from 9 am to 1 pm and 5 to 9 pm.

Emergency Hué General Hospital (Benh Vien Trung Uong Hué; ☎ 2325) is at 16 Le Loi St close to the Phu Xuan Bridge.

Immigration Police Visa extensions can be done at the Immigration Police office on Ben Nghe St. This office seems to be able to handle such matters in about 15 minutes.

Useful Organisations The offices of the Provincial People's Committee are at 14 Le Loi St. The Hué University library is at 18 Le Loi St.

Citadel

Construction of the moated Citadel (Kinh Thanh), whose perimeter is 10 km, was begun in 1804 by Emperor Gia Long on a site chosen by geomancers. The Citadel was originally made of earth, but during the first few decades of the 19th century, tens of thousands of workers laboured to cover the ramparts, built in the style of the French military architect Vauban, with a layer of bricks two metres thick.

The emperor's official functions were carried out in the Imperial Enclosure (Dai Noi, or Hoang Thanh), a citadel-within-the-citadel whose six-metre-high wall is 2.5 km in length. The Imperial Enclosure has four gates, the most famous of which is Ngo Mon Gate. Within the Imperial Enclosure is the Forbidden Purple City (Tu Cam Thanh), which was reserved for the private life of the emperor,

Three sides of the Citadel are straight; the fourth is rounded slightly to follow the curve of the river. The ramparts are encircled by a zig-zag moat 30 metres across and about four metres deep. In the northern corner of the Citadel is Mang Ca fortress, once known as the French Concession, which is still used as a military base. The Citadel has 10 fortified gates, each of which is reached by a bridge across the moat.

Flag Tower The 37-metre-high Flag Tower (Cot Co), also known as the King's Knight, is Vietnam's tallest flagpole. Erected in 1809 and increased in size in 1831, a terrific typhoon (which devastated the whole city of Hué) knocked it down in 1904. The tower was rebuilt in 1915, only to be destroyed again in 1947. It was re-erected in its present form in 1949. During the VC occupation of Hué in 1968, the National Liberation Front flag flew defiantly from the tower for 3½ weeks.

Wide areas within the Citadel are now devoted to agriculture, a legacy of the destruction of 1968.

Nine Holy Cannons Located just inside the Citadel ramparts near the gates to either side of the Flag Tower, the Nine Holy Cannons, symbolic protectors of the Palace and Kingdom, were cast from brass articles captured from the Tay Son Rebels. The cannons, whose casting on the orders of Emperor Gia Long was completed in 1804, were never intended to be fired. Each is five metres long, has a bore of 23 cm and weighs about 10 tonnes. The four cannons near Ngan Gate represent the four seasons; the five cannons next to Quang Duc Gate represent the five elements: metal, wood, water, fire and soil.

Ngo Mon Gate The principle gate to the Imperial Enclosure is Ngo Mon Gate (Noontime Gate), which faces the Flag Tower. It is open from 6.30 am to 5.30 pm; the entrance fee for foreigners is US$3.50.

The central passageway with its yellow doors was reserved for use by the emperor, as was the bridge across the lotus pond.

Everyone else had to use the gates to either side and the paths around the lotus pond.

On top of the gate is Ngu Phung (the Belvedere of the Five Phoenixes), where the emperor appeared on important occasions, notably for the promulgation of the lunar calendar. Emperor Bao Dai ended the Nguyen Dynasty here on 30 August 1945, when he abdicated to a delegation sent by Ho Chi Minh's Provisional Revolutionary Government. The middle section of the roof is covered with yellow tiles; the roofs to either side are green.

Thai Hoa Palace Thai Hoa Palace (the Palace of Supreme Peace), built in 1803 and moved to its present site in 1833, is a spacious hall with an ornate roof of huge timbers supported by 80 carved and lacquered columns. Reached from the Ngo Mon Gate via Trung Dao Bridge, it was used for the emperor's official receptions and other important court ceremonies, such as anniversaries and coronations. During state occasions, the king sat on his elevated throne and received homage from ranks of mandarins. Nine steles divide the bi-level courtyard into areas for officials of each of the nine ranks in the mandarinate; administrative mandarins stood to one side and military mandarins to the other.

Halls of the Mandarins The buildings in which the mandarins prepared for court ceremonies, held in Can Chanh Reception Hall, were restored in 1977. The structures are directly behind Thai Hoa Palace on either side of a courtyard in which there are two gargantuan bronze cauldrons (vac dong) dating from the 17th century.

Nine Dynastic Urns The Nine Dynastic Urns (dinh) were cast in 1835-36. Traditional ornamentation was then chiselled into the sides of the urns, each of which is dedicated to a different Nguyen sovereign. The designs, some of which are of Chinese origin and date back 4000 years, include the sun, the moon, meteors, clouds, mountains, rivers and various landscapes. About two metres in

Left: Imperial City, Hué (TA)
Right: Thien Mu Pagoda, Hué (DR)
Bottom: Unexploded Mortar, Imperial Citadel, Hué (GD)

Top: Rice Farmer, DMZ (MF)
Bottom: Scavenged Battle Zone, DMZ (MF)

height and weighing 1900 to 2600 kg each, the urns symbolise the power and stability of the Nguyen throne. The central urn, which is the largest and most ornate, is dedicated to the founder of the Nguyen Dynasty, Emperor Gia Long.

Forbidden Purple City The Forbidden Purple City (Tu Cam Thanh) was reserved for the personal use of the emperor. The only servants allowed into the compound were eunuchs, who would have no temptation to molest the royal concubines.

The Forbidden Purple City was almost entirely destroyed during the Tet Offensive. The area is now given over to vegetable plots, between which touch-sensitive mimosa plants flourish. The two-storey Library (Thai Binh Lau) has been partially restored. The foundations of the Royal Theatre (Duyen Thi Duong), begun in 1826 and later home of the National Conservatory of Music, can be seen nearby.

Imperial Museum The beautiful hall which houses the Imperial Museum (formerly the Khai Dinh Museum) was built in 1845 and restored when the museum was founded in 1923. The walls are inscribed with poems written in Vietnamese nom characters. The most precious artefacts were lost during the war, but the ceramics, furniture and royal clothing that remain are well worth a look. On the left side of the hall are a royal sedan chair, a gong and a musical instrument consisting of stones hung on a bi-level rack. On the other side of the hall is the equipment for a favourite game of the emperors, the idea of which was to bounce a stick off a wooden platform and into a tall, thin jug.

The building across the street was once a former school for princes and the sons of high-ranking mandarins. Behind the school is the Military Museum, with its usual assortment of American and Soviet-made weapons, including a MiG 17. Nearby is a small natural history exhibit.

The Imperial Museum is open from 6.30 am to 5.30 pm.

Tinh Tam Lake In the middle of Tinh Tam Lake, which is 500 metres north of the Imperial Enclosure, are two islands connected by bridges. The emperors used to come here with their retinues to relax.

Tang Tau Lake An island in Tang Tau Lake, which is a few hundred metres from Tinh Tam Lake, was once the site of a royal library. It is now occupied by a small Hinayana pagoda, Ngoc Huong Pagoda.

Royal Tombs
The tombs *(lang tam)* of the Nguyen Dynasty (1802-1945) are seven to 16 km to the south of Hué. They are open from 6.30 am to 5 pm daily; the entrance fee to each tomb is US$3.

Most of the tomb complexes consist of five parts:

- A Stele Pavilion in which the accomplishments, exploits and virtues of the deceased emperor are engraved on a marble tablet. The testaments were usually written by the dead ruler's successor (though Tu Duc chose to compose his own).
- A temple for the worship of the emperor and empress. In front of each altar, on which the deceased rulers' funerary tablets were placed, is an ornate dais that once held items the emperor used every day: his tea and betelnut trays, cigarette cases, etc, most of which have disappeared.
- A sepulchre, usually inside a square or circular enclosure, where the emperor's remains are buried.
- An Honour Courtyard paved with dark-brown *bat trang* bricks along the sides of which stand stone elephants, horses and civil and military mandarins. The civil mandarins wear square hats and hold the symbol of their authority, an ivory sceptre; the military mandarins wear round hats and hold swords.
- A lotus pond surrounded by frangipani and pine trees. Almost all the tombs, which are in walled compounds, were planned by the Nguyen emperors during their lifetimes. Many of the precious orna-

ments once reposited in the tombs disappeared during the war.

The best way to tour the Royal Tombs is on bicycle. The quiet paved roads between the tombs pass among the solid little homes of peasants; peaceful groves of trees; rice, vegetable, manioc and sugar cane plots; and newly reafforested hills.

Nam Giao Nam Giao (Temple of Heaven) was once the most important religious site in all Vietnam. It was here that every three years, the emperor solemnly offered elaborate sacrifices to the All-Highest Emperor of the August Heaven (Thuong De). The topmost esplanade, which represents Heaven, is round; the middle terrace, representing the Earth, is square, as is the lowest terrace.

After reunification, the provincial government erected – on the site where the sacrificial altar once stood – an obelisk in memory of soldiers killed in the war against the South Vietnamese government and the Americans. There was strong public sentiment in Hué against the obelisk and the Hué Municipal People's Committee proposed tearing down the memorial and erecting another elsewhere, but the weathered and faded column is still there.

Tomb of Dong Khanh Emperor Dong Khanh, nephew and adopted son of Tu Duc, was placed on the throne by the French after they captured his predecessor, Ham Nghi (who had fled after the French sacking of the royal palace in 1885), and exiled him to Algeria. Predictably, Dong Khanh proved docile; he ruled from 1886 until his death two years later.

Dong Khanh's mausoleum, the smallest of the Royal Tombs, was built in 1889. It is seven km from the city.

Tomb of Tu Duc The majestic and serene tomb of Emperor Tu Duc is set amidst frangipani trees and a grove of pines. Tu Duc designed the exquisitely harmonious tomb, which was constructed between 1864 and

1	An Hoa Bus Station
2	Ferry Terminals
3	Hen Island
4	Dong Ba Market
5	Dong Ba Bus Station
6	Trang Tien Bridge
7	Phu Xuan Bridge
8	Imperial Enclosure
9	Flag Tower
10	Bach Ho Railway Bridge
11	Gia Vien Island
12	Thien Mu Pagoda
13	Railway Station
14	Bao Quoc Pagoda
15	An Cuu Bus Station
16	Tu Dam Pagoda
17	Linh Quang Pagoda & Phan Boi Chau's Tomb
18	Duc Duc's Tomb
19	Tam Thai Hill
20	Tra Am Pagoda
21	Ngu Binh Hill
22	Nam Giao
23	Tu Hieu Pagoda
24	Tomb of Dong Khanh
25	Hon Chen Temple
26	Tomb of Tu Duc
27	Truc Lam Pagoda
28	Thien Thai Hill
29	Dong Tranh Hill
30	Tomb of Thieu Tri
31	Ferry
32	Tomb of Khai Dinh
33	Tomb of Minh Mang
34	Vung Hill
35	Tomb of Gia Long

1867, for use both before and after his death. The enormous expense of the tomb and the forced labour used in its construction spawned a coup plot which was discovered and suppressed in 1866.

It is said that Tu Duc, who ruled from 1848 to 1883 (the longest reign of any Nguyen monarch), lived a life of truly imperial luxury: at every meal, 50 chefs prepared 50 dishes served by 50 servants; and his tea was made of drops of dew that had condensed overnight on the leaves of lotus plants. Though Tu Duc had 104 wives and countless concubines, he had no offspring. One theory has it that he became sterile after contracting smallpox.

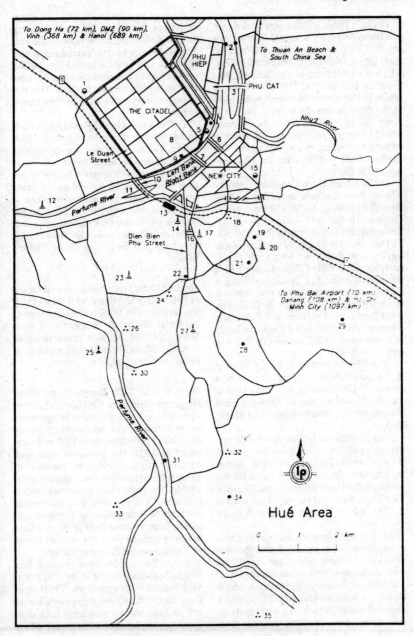

To Dong Ha (72 km), DMZ (90 km), Vinh (368 km) & Hanoi (689 km)

To Thuan An Beach & South China Sea

PHU HIEP

PHU CAT

THE CITADEL

Nhu'Q River

Le Duan Street

Left Bank
Right Bank

NEW CITY

Perfume River

Dien Bien Phu Street

To Phu Bai Airport (10 km), Danang (108 km) & Ho Chi Minh City (1097 km)

Perfume River

Hué Area

0   1   2 km

Tu Duc's Tomb, which is surrounded by a solid octagonal wall, is entered from the east via Vu Khiem Gate. A path paved with bat trang tiles leads to Du Khiem Boat Landing, which is on the shore of Luu Khiem Lake. From the boat landing, Tinh Khiem Island, where Tu Duc used to hunt small game, is off to the right. Across the water to the left is Xung Khiem Pavilion, where the Emperor would sit among the columns with his concubines composing or reciting poetry. The pavilion, built over the water on piles, was restored in 1986.

Across Khiem Cung Courtyard from Du Khiem Boat Landing are steps leading through a gate to Hoa Khiem Temple, where Emperor Tu Duc and Empress Hoang Le Thien Anh are worshipped. Before his death, Tu Duc used Hoa Khiem Temple as a palace, staying here during his long visits to the complex. Hoa Khiem Temple contains a number of interesting items, including a mirror used by the Emperor's concubines; a clock and other objects given to Tu Duc by the French; the Emperor and Empress's funerary tablets; and two thrones, the larger of which was for the Empress (Tu Duc was only 153 cm tall).

Minh Khiem Chamber, to the right behind Hoa Khiem Temple, was built for use as a theatre. Tu Duc's mother, the Queen Mother Tu Du, is worshipped in Luong Khiem Temple, which is directly behind Hoa Khiem Temple.

Back down at the bottom of the stairway, the brick path continues along the shore of the pond to the Honour Courtyard. Across the lake from the Honour Courtyard are the tombs of Tu Duc's adopted son, Emperor Kien Phuc, who ruled for only seven months in 1883, and the Empress Le Thien Anh, Tu Duc's wife.

After walking between the honour guard of elephants, horses and diminutive civil and military mandarins (the stone mandarins were made even shorter than the emperor), you reach the masonry Stele Pavilion, which shelters a massive stone tablet weighing about 20 tonnes. It took four years to transport the stele, the largest in Vietnam, from the area of Thanh Hoa, 500 km to the north. Tu Duc drafted the inscriptions on the stele himself in order to clarify certain aspects of his reign. He freely admitted that he had made mistakes and chose to name his tomb Khiem, which means modest. The two nearby towers symbolise the emperor's power.

Tu Duc's sepulchre, enclosed by a wall, is on the other side of a half-moon-shaped lake. In fact, Tu Duc was never actually interred here, and the site where his remains were buried along with great treasure is not known. Because of the danger of grave robbers, extreme measures were taken to keep the location secret: every one of the 200 servants who buried the king were beheaded.

Tu Duc's Tomb is seven km from Hué on Van Nien hill in Duong Xuan Thuong village.

Tomb of Thieu Tri Construction of the tomb of Thieu Tri, who ruled from 1841 to 1847, was completed in 1848. It is the only one of the Royal Tombs not enclosed by a wall. Thieu Tri's tomb, which is similar in layout to that of Minh Mang (though smaller), is about seven km from Hué.

Tomb of Khai Dinh The gaudy and crumbling tomb of Emperor Khai Dinh, who ruled from 1916 to 1925, is perhaps symptomatic of the decline of Vietnamese culture during the colonial period. Begun in 1920 and completed in 1931, the grandiose reinforced concrete structure makes no pretence of trying to blend in with the surrounding countryside. The architecture, completely unlike that of Hué's other tombs, is an unfortunate synthesis of Vietnamese and European elements. Even the stone faces of the mandarin honour guards are endowed with a mixture of Vietnamese and European features.

After climbing 36 steps between four dragon banisters, you get to the first courtyard, flanked by two pavilions. The Honour Courtyard, with its rows of elephants, horses and civil and military mandarins, is 26 steps further up the hillside. In the centre of the

Honour Courtyard is an octagonal Stele Pavilion.

Up three more flights of stairs is the main building, Thien Dinh, which is divided into three halls. The walls and ceiling are decorated with murals of the 'Four Seasons', the 'Eight Precious Objects', the 'Eight Fairies' and other designs made out of colourful bits of broken porcelain and glass embedded in cement. Under a graceless one-tonne concrete canopy is a gilt bronze statue of Khai Dinh in royal regalia. Behind the statue is the symbol of the sun. The Emperor's remains are interred 18 metres below the statue. Khai Dinh is worshipped in the last hall.

The Tomb of Khai Dinh is 10 km from Hué in Chau Chu village.

Tomb of Minh Mang Perhaps the most majestic of the Royal Tombs is that of Minh Mang, who ruled from 1820 to 1840. Known for the harmonious blending of its architecture with the natural surroundings, the tomb was planned during Minh Mang's lifetime and built between 1841 and 1843 by his successor.

The Honour Courtyard is reached via three gates on the eastern side of the wall: Dai Hong Mon (Great Red Gate; in the centre), Ta Hong Mon (Left Red Gate; on the left) and Huu Hong Mon (Right Red Gate; on the right). Three granite staircases lead from the Honour Courtyard to the square Stele Pavilion, Dinh Vuong. Nearby there once stood an altar on which buffaloes, horses and pigs were sacrificed.

Sung An Temple, dedicated to Minh Mang and his Empress, is reached via three terraces and Hien Duc Gate. On the other side of the temple, three stone bridges span Trung Minh Ho (The Lake of Impeccable Clarity). The central bridge, Cau Trung Dao, constructed of marble, was used only by the emperor. Minh Lau Pavilion stands on the top of three superimposed terraces representing the 'three powers': the heavens, the earth and water. Visible off to the left is the Fresh Air Pavilion; the Angling Pavilion is off to the right.

From a stone bridge across crescent-

Statues at Tomb of Minh Mang

shaped Tan Nguyet Lake (Lake of the New Moon), a monumental staircase with dragon banisters leads to the sepulchre, which is surrounded by a circular wall symbolising the sun. In the middle of the enclosure, reached through a bronze door, is the Emperor's burial place, a mound of earth covered with mature pine trees and dense shrubbery.

The Tomb of Minh Mang, which is on Cam Ke hill in An Bang village, is on the left bank of the Perfume River 12 km from Hué. To get there, take a boat across the river from a point about 1.5 km south-west of Khai Dinh's tomb. Visitors have reported gross overcharging by the boat operator.

Tomb of Gia Long Emperor Gia Long, who founded the Nguyen Dynasty in 1802 and ruled until 1820, ordered the construction of his tomb in 1814. According to the royal annals, the Emperor himself chose the site after scouting the area on elephant-back. The rarely visited tomb, which is presently in a state of ruin, is 14 km from Hué on the left bank of the Perfume River.

Pagodas, Temples & Churches
Thien Mu Pagoda Thien Mu Pagoda (also known as Linh Mu Pagoda), built on a hillock overlooking the Perfume River, is one of the most famous structures in all of Vietnam. Its 21-metre-high octagonal tower, seven-storey Thap Phuoc Duyen, was built by Emperor Thieu Tri in 1844 and has

become the unofficial symbol of Hué. Each of the seven storeys is dedicated to a Buddha who appeared in human form (manushibuddha).

Thien Mu Pagoda was founded in 1601 by the Nguyen Lord Nguyen Hoang, governor of Thuan Hoa Province. According to legend, a Fairy Woman (Thien Mu) appeared to Nguyen Hoang and told him to construct a pagoda here. Over the centuries, the pagoda's buildings have been destroyed and rebuilt several times. Five monks and seven novices now live at the pagoda, which was a hotbed of anti-government protest during the early 1960s.

To the right of the tower is a pavilion containing a stele dating from 1715. It is set on the back of a massive marble turtle, symbol of longevity. To the left of the tower is another six-sided pavilion, this one sheltering an enormous bell, Dai Hong Chung, which was cast in 1710 and weighs 2052 kg; it is said to be audible 10 km away. In the main sanctuary, in a case behind the bronze laughing Buddha, are three statues: A Di Da (pronounced 'AH-zee-dah'), the Buddha of

Thien Mu Pagoda

the Past; Thich Ca (Sakyamuni), the historical Buddha; and Di Lac Buddha, the Buddha of the Future.

Behind the main sanctuary is the Austin motorcar which transported the monk Thich Quang Duc to the site in Saigon of his 1963 self-immolation, which was seen around the world in a famous photograph. Around the back are vegetable gardens in which the monks grow their own food.

Thien Mu Pagoda is on the banks of the Perfume River four km south-west of the Citadel. To get there from Dong Ba Market, head south-west (parallel to the river) on Tran Hung Dao St, which turns into Le Duan St after Phu Xuan Bridge. Cross the railway tracks and keep going on Kim Long St. Thien Mu Pagoda can also be reached by sampan.

Bao Quoc Pagoda Bao Quoc Pagoda was founded in 1670 by a Buddhist monk from China, Giac Phong. It was given its present name, which means Pagoda Which Serves the Country, in 1824 by Emperor Minh Mang, who celebrated his 40th birthday here in 1830. A school for training monks was opened at Bao Quoc Pagoda in 1940. The pagoda was last renovated in 1957.

In the orchid-lined courtyard behind the sanctuary is the cage of a most extraordinary parrot (nhong). The male monks taught the bird, which was born in 1977, to say (with impeccable intonation, of course) 'Thua thay co khach' ('Master, there is a guest') and 'A Di Da Phat '('A Di Da Buddha '). But female visitors also spoke to the bird, and in time it began imitating their higher-pitched voices as well. Now the poor confused creature alternates between male and female renditions of its repertoire of sayings.

The central altar in the main sanctuary contains three identical statues, which represent (from left to right) Di Lac, the Buddha of the Future; Thich Ca, the historical Buddha (Sakyamuni); and A Di Da, the Buddha of the Past. Behind the three figures is a memorial room for deceased monks. Around the main building are monks' tombs, including a three-storey, red-and-grey stupa built for the pagoda's founder.

Bao Quoc Pagoda is on Ham Long Hill in Phuong Duc District. To get there, head south from Le Loi St on Dien Bien Phu St and turn right immediately after crossing the railroad tracks.

Tu Dam Pagoda Tu Dam Pagoda, which is about 600 metres south of Bao Quoc Pagoda at the corner of Dien Bien Phu St and Tu Dam St, is one of Vietnam's best known pagodas. Unfortunately, the present buildings were constructed in 1936 and are of little interest.

Tu Dam Pagoda was founded around 1695 by Minh Hoang Tu Dung, a Chinese monk. It was given its present name by Emperor Thieu Tri in 1841. The Unified Vietnamese Buddhist Association was established at a meeting held here in 1951. During the early 1960s, Tu Dam Pagoda was a major centre of the Buddhist anti-Diem and antiwar movement. In 1968, it was the scene of heavy fighting, scars of which remain.

Today, Tu Dam Pagoda, home to six monks, is the seat of the provincial Buddhist Association. The peculiar bronze Thich Ca Buddha in the sanctuary was cast in Hué in 1966.

Just east of the pagoda down Tu Dam St is Linh Quang Pagoda and the tomb of the scholar and anti-colonialist revolutionary Phan Boi Chau (1867-1940).

Notre Dame Cathedral Notre Dame Cathedral (Dong Chua Cuu The) at 80 Nguyen Hue St is an impressive modern building combining the functional aspects of a European cathedral with traditional Vietnamese elements, including a distinctly Oriental spire. At present, the huge cathedral, which was constructed between 1959 and 1962, has 1600 members. The two French-speaking priests hold daily masses at 5 am and 5 pm and on Sunday at 5 am, 7 am and 5 pm; children's catechism classes are conducted on Sunday mornings. Visitors who find the front gate locked should ring the bell of the yellow building next door.

Phu Cam Cathedral Phu Cam Cathedral, whose construction began in 1963 and was halted in 1975 before completion of the bell tower, is the eighth church built on this site since 1682. The Hué diocese, which is based here, hopes eventually to complete the structure if funds can be found. Phu Cam Cathedral is at 20 Doan Huu Trinh St, which is at the southern end of Nguyen Truong Tu St. Masses are held daily at 5 am and 6.45 pm and on Sundays at 5 am, 7 am, 2 pm and 7 pm.

Phu Cat & Phu Hiep Subdistricts

The island on which Phu Cat & Phu Hiep subdistricts are located can be reached by crossing the Dong Ba Canal near Dong Ba Market. The area is known for its numerous Chinese pagodas and congregational halls, many of which are along Chi Lang St.

Dieu De National Pagoda The entrance to Dieu De National Pagoda (Quoc Tu Dieu De), built under Emperor Thieu Tri (ruled 1841-47), is along Dong Ba Canal at 102 Bach Dang St. It is one of the city's three 'national pagodas' (pagodas that were once under the direct patronage of the Emperor). Dieu De National Pagoda is famous for its four low towers, one to either side of the gate and two flanking the sanctuary. There are bells in two of the towers; the others contain a drum and a stele dedicated to the pagoda's founder.

During the regime of Ngo Dinh Diem (ruled 1955-63) and through the mid-1960s, Dieu De National Pagoda was a stronghold of Buddhist and student opposition to the South Vietnamese government and the war. In 1966, the pagoda was stormed by the police who arrested many monks, Buddhist lay people and students and confiscated the opposition movement's radio equipment. Today, three monks live at the pagoda.

The pavilions on either side of the entrance to the main sanctuary contain the 18 La Ha, whose rank is just below that of Bodhisattva, and the eight Kim Cang, protectors of Buddha. In the back row of the main dais is Thich Ca Buddha (Sakyamuni) flanked by two assistants, Pho Hien Bo Tat (to his right) and Van Thu Bo Tat (to his left).

Former Indian Mosque Hué's Indian Muslim community constructed the mosque at 120 Chi Lang St in 1932. The structure was used as a house of worship until 1975, when the Indian community fled. It is now a private residence.

Chieu Ung Pagoda Chieu Ung Pagoda (Chieu Ung Tu), opposite 138 Chi Lang St, was founded by the Hainan Chinese congregation in the mid-19th century and rebuilt in 1908. It was last repaired in 1940. The sanctuary retains its original ornamentation, which is a bit faded but mercifully unaffected by the third-rate modernistic renovations that have marred other such structures. The pagoda was built as a memorial for 108 Hainan merchants who were mistaken for pirates and killed in Vietnam in 1851.

Hall of the Cantonese Chinese Congregation The Cantonese Chinese Congregational Hall (Chua Quang Dong), founded almost a century ago, is opposite 154 Chi Lang St. Against the right-hand wall is a small altar holding a statue of Confucius (in Vietnamese: Khong Tu) with a gold beard. On the main altar is red-faced Quan Cong (in Chinese: Guangong) flanked by Trung Phi (on the left) and Luu Bi (on the right). On the altar to the left is Laotze with disciples to either side. On the altar to the right is Phat Ba, a female Buddha.

Chua Ba Chua Ba, across the street from 216 Chi Lang St, was founded by the Hainan Chinese Congregation almost a century ago. It was damaged in the 1968 Tet Offensive and was subsequently reconstructed. On the central altar is Thien Hau Thanh Mau, Goddess of the Sea and Protector of Sailors. To the right is a glass case in which Quan Cong sits flanked by his usual companions, the mandarin general Chau Xuong (to his right) and the administrative mandarin Quang Binh (to his left).

Chua Ong Chua Ong, which is opposite 224 Chi Lang St, is a large pagoda founded by the Fujian Chinese Congregation during the reign of Vietnamese Emperor Tu Duc (ruled 1848-83). The building was severely damaged during the 1968 Tet Offensive when an ammunition ship blew up nearby. A gold Buddha sits in a glass case opposite the main doors of the sanctuary. The left-hand altar is dedicated to Thien Hau Thanh Mau, Goddess of the Sea and Protector of Sailors; she is flanked by her two assistants, thousand-eyed Thien Ly Nhan and red-faced Thuan Phong Nhi, who can hear for 1000 miles. On the altar to the right is Quan Cong.

Next door is a pagoda of the Chaozhou Chinese Congregation (Tieu Chau Tu).

Tang Quang Pagoda Tang Quang Pagoda (Tang Quang Tu), which is just down the road from 80 Nguyen Chi Thanh St, is the largest of the three Hinayana (Theravada, or Nam Tong) pagodas in Hué. Built in 1957, it owes its distinctive architecture to Hinayana Buddhism's historical links to Sri Lanka and India (rather than China). The pagoda's Pali name, Sangharansyarama (the Light Coming from the Buddha), is inscribed on the front of the building.

Quoc Hoc Secondary School

Quoc Hoc Secondary School (the Lycée National) is one of the most famous secondary schools in Vietnam. Founded in 1896 and run by Ngo Dinh Kha, the father of South Vietnamese President Ngo Dinh Diem, many of the school's pupils later rose to prominence in both North and South Vietnam. Numbered among Quoc Hoc Secondary School's former students are General Vo Nguyen Giap, strategist of the Viet Minh victory at Dien Bien Phu and North Vietnam's long-serving deputy premier, defence minister and commander-in-chief; Pham Van Dong, North Vietnam's Prime Minister for over a quarter of a century; and Ho Chi Minh himself, who attended the school briefly in 1908.

Next door to Quoc Hoc Secondary School, which is at 10 Le Loi St, is Hai Ba Trung Secondary School.

* AGRIC STUDENT WITH WHOM I SHARED A BEER IN HIS SMALL HOUSE
JUNE 13/94 (RICE FESTIVAL DAY)
(Photo)   DOÀN NGUYỄN THẠCH
01 LÊ LỢI 01
HUE   VIET NAM

Huế – Places to Stay 369

Ho Chi Minh Museum
On display at the Ho Chi Minh Museum (Bao Tang Ho Chi Minh) at 9 Le Loi St are photographs, some of Ho's personal effects and documents relating to his life and accomplishments. The museum is down the block and across the street from Quoc Hoc Secondary School.

Trang Tien Bridge
The Trang Tien Bridge (formerly the Nguyen Hoang Bridge) across the Perfume River was blown up in 1968 and later repaired. The newer Phu Xuan Bridge was built in 1971.

Municipal Theatre
The Municipal Theatre (Nha Van Hoa Trung Tam) is on Huong Vuong St (corner of Ly Quy Don and Dong Da Sts).

Places to Stay – bottom end
The *Nha Khach 18 Le Loi* (☎ 3720) at 18 Le Loi St is run by Hué City Tourism; doubles go for US$6 to US$8. It's a nice place and one of the better deals in the budget range.

A very popular place with budget travellers is the *Ben Nghe Guesthouse* on Ben Nghe St near Tran Cao Van St. Doubles cost US$5 with attached bath and hot water.

The *Khach San Thuong Tu*, 6 Dinh Tien Hoang St, is an old dump but the cheapest place in town. Rooms are just US$3, but in the future it's possible that they will not be permitted to accommodate foreigners.

The *Morin Hotel*, at Le Loi and Hung Vuong Sts, is also one of the cheapest in Hué. Prices are US$3 to US$6 for a double room with electric fan; US$5 to US$10 for a rooms with air-conditioning; and US$12 for a triple room with air-con. The hotel has warm to hot water all day and bike rentals are available. This place has a great atmosphere and has become very popular with travellers.

The *Khach San Hang Be* (☎ 3752) is one of the few places on the west bank of the Perfume River. It fronts Dong Ba Canal at 73 Huynh Thuc Khang St, which is several blocks north-west of Dong Ba Market. At the time of this writing, it was closed for reno-

vation but should be a decent place once it reopens. Unfortunately, prices may rise beyond the budget category.

The *Dongda Hotel* on Ly Thuong Kiet St is just opposite the more expensive Hué City Tourism Villas. Rooms with fan are US$7; with air-conditioning, US$10.

The *Ngo Quyen Hotel* is a large, old, elegant place with that 'seen better days' appearance. A double room with the toilet and bath outside costs US$7; with private bath it's US$10 to US$15. The hotel is just off Ha Noi St.

Places to Stay – middle & top end
The *Kinh Do Hotel* on Vo Thi Sau St is a large place that has just one budget room for US$5 and a few rooms for US$10. Most rooms cost US$20 to US$30.

The *Thuan Hoa Hotel* (☎ 2553, 2576; about 50 rooms), 7 Nguyen Tri Phuong St, has doubles for US$15 to US$30.

Some of most delightful accommodation to be had in Hué are four small houses called the *Hué City Tourism Villas*. These can be found at 11, 16 and 18 Ly Thuong Kiet St and 5 Le Loi St. Run by Hué City Tourism, they each have a homey living room and bedroom. All rooms cost US$20 and can accommodate three persons and meals are prepared on request. There is a fifth villa at 2 Le Loi St which has budget accommodation for US$5, US$6 and US$10, but it is possible that this villa too will be renovated and the price ratcheted upwards.

The *Huong Giang Hotel* (☎ 2122; telex 54155 HOTHGHU-VT; fax (84-54) 3424), 51 Le Loi St, is a grand place on the shore of the Perfume River. Budget rooms are available at US$7 and US$10 per bed; double rooms with air-con are US$38, US$34 and US$55. The Huong Giang is extremely popular and often full.

The *Hué Hotel* (☎ 3391; telex 54154 TWH-VT; fax (84-54) 3394), 49 Le Loi St, is a new large place on the river near the Dap Da Bridge. Singles are US$36 to US$63; doubles cost US$40 to US$70. In this case, you get what you pay for.

Places to Eat

West Bank The *Banh Khoai Thuong Tu* is a few blocks from the Flagpole at 6 Dinh Tien Hoang St; it is open from 7 am to 8 pm. This restaurant, which has the words Lac Thien written in cement on the façade, serves a traditional Hué speciality, banh khoai, which is a crêpe with bean sprouts, shrimp and meat inside. It is eaten with greens, starfruit slices and nuoc leo, a thick brown sauce made with peanuts, sesame seeds and spices. Another Hué speciality available here is bun thit nuong, which is noodles, greens, fruit and fried dried meat eaten with nuoc leo. You might wash down your banh khoai with the mild local beer, '22'.

Just next to the Banh Khoai Thuong Tu is the *Lac Thanh Restaurant*. The food is awesome; see the book travellers have written in for how to order beause the owner, Lac, is mute so everything is done with sign language. However, his daughter, Lan Anh, can speak a bit of English.

Lac, the mute owner of the Lac Thanh Restaurant in Hué, took us by rented motorbike around the DMZ. What a day! He is the best mute tour guide we've ever had – a treat to be with!

Delicious sweet soups (che) made with such ingredients as beans and bananas are served either hot or iced in shops at numbers 10 and 12 Dinh Tien Hoang St.

The *Quan 176* is a small place in Phu Cat subdistrict at 176 Chi Lang St. They serve traditional Hué pastries, including banh nam (a flat cake of rice flour, meat and shrimp fried in a banana leaf), banh loc (a chewy cake made of rice flour and shrimp and baked in a banana leaf) and cha tom (a flat cake made of meat, shrimp and egg).

The *Hang Be Restaurant* (☎ 3752) is on the ground floor of the Khach San Hang Be at 73 Huynh Thuc Khang St. This place gets mixed reviews.

Within the Citadel, the *Huong Sen Restaurant* (☎ 3201) is at 42 Nguyen Trai St (corner of Thach Han St). This 16-sided pavilion, built on pylons in the middle of a lotus pond, is open from 9 am to midnight. This is a great place to enjoy Vietnamese food and kick back at sunset with a Huda beer on ice.

The *Phu Hiep Restaurant* (☎ 3560) in Phu Hiep District is at 19 Ho Xuan Huong St (opposite 53 Nguyen Chi Thanh St).

The *Café* is in an interesting old building at 51 Phan Dang Lu St, a few blocks northeast of Dong Ba Market; they serve only drinks.

East Bank The *Nua Thu Restaurant* (☎ 3929) at 26 Nguyen Tri Phuong St is also a hotel but presently is not permitted to rent rooms to foreigners. However, the restaurant will serve anyone and has excellent food.

The restaurant on the top floor of the *Huong Giang Hotel* at 51 Le Loi St serves Vietnamese, European and vegetarian dishes. The food is excellent and the prices are surprisingly reasonable; around US$5 to US$6 for a large meal for two people.

The *Song Huong Floating Restaurant* is on the bank of the Perfume River just north of the Trang Tien Bridge (near the intersection of Le Loi St and Hung Vuong St). This place is justifiably known for good service, outstanding Vietnamese cuisine and low prices.

The *Nam Song Huong Restaurant* is opposite the GPO at 7 Hoang Hoa Tham St. It is open from 8.30 am to 9 pm. This large, airy place serves excellent soup and egg rolls (this far north they're called nem Sai Gon rather than chia gio).

There is a restaurant in the *Cercle Sportif*, which is on Le Loi St next to the Phu Xuan Bridge. The Cercle Sportif has tennis courts and rents paddle boats.

Vegetarian Vegetarian food, which has a long tradition in Hué, is prepared at pagodas for consumption by the monks. Small groups of visitors might be invited to join the monks for a meal. Stalls in the marketplaces serve vegetarian food on the first and 15th days of the lunar month.

Things to Buy

Hué is known for producing the finest conical hats in Vietnam. The city's speciality are 'poem hats' which, when held up to the light, reveal black cut-out scenes sandwiched between the layers of translucent palm leaves.

Dong Ba Market, which is on the left bank of the Perfume River a few hundred metres north of Trang Tien Bridge, is Hué's main market. It was rebuilt after much of the structure was destroyed by a typhoon in 1986. Nearby are several photography stores. Near the Huong Giang Hotel, film is sold in a shop at 54 Le Loi St.

Gold and silver objects are available at the Gold and Silver Trade Department (Cua Hang My Nghe Vang Bac Hué; ☎ 3949), which is at 55 Tran Hung Dao St.

Getting There & Away
Air The Vietnam Airlines Booking Office (☎ 2249) is at 12 Ha Noi St and is open Monday to Saturday from 7 to 11 am and 1.30 to 5 pm.

There are flights connecting Hué to Ho Chi Minh City (US$85 one way) every Tuesday, Friday and Sunday. There are flights to/from Hanoi (US$80) every Tuesday and Friday.

Bus Hué has three main bus stations, one to destinations south (An Cuu Bus Station), another to destinations north (An Hoa Bus Station) and a short-haul bus station (Dong Ba Bus Station). Fifteen years after reunification, the people of Hué still look to the south for trade and other ties, a fact reflected in the sparseness of traffic passing through the old Demilitarised Zone (DMZ).

Buses to places north of Hué depart from An Hoa Bus Station (Ben Xe An Hoa, or Ben Xe So 1; ☎ 3014), which is at the western tip of the Citadel across from 499 Le Duan St (corner Tang Bat Ho St).

Non-express buses from here go to Aluoi, Ba Don, Dien Sanh, Dong Ha (three hours), Dong Hoi, Hanoi, Hoan Lao, Ho Xa, Khe Sanh (twice daily; seven hours), Ky Anh, Quang Tri, Thanh Khe, Thuong Phong and Vinh

Almost all of the buses depart at 5 or 5.30

am. Tickets for some buses (eg to Aluoi, Ba Don, Dong Hoi, Hanoi, Hoan Lao, Thuong Phong and Vinh) can be purchased at An Cuu Bus Station.

Buses to points south of Hué leave from An Cuu Bus Station (☎ 3817), which is opposite 46 Hung Vuong St (corner Ba Trieu St); the ticket windows are open from 5 to 11 am and 1 to 6 pm.

There is daily (or more frequent) service from here to Buon Ma Thuot, Cau Hai, Danang, Ho Chi Minh City, Khe Tre, Kontum, Nha Trang (once every two days), Pleiku, Qui Nhon, Truoi and Vien Trinh.

Tickets for buses from An Hoa Bus Station to Aluoi, Ba Don, Dong Hoi, Hanoi, Hoan Lao, Thuong Phong and Vinh can be purchased at An Cuu Bus Station.

Vehicles to destinations in the vicinity of Hué depart from Dong Ba Bus Station (Ben Xe Dong Ba; ☎ 3055), which is on the left bank of the Perfume River between Trang Tien Bridge and Dong Ba Market. There are entrances at numbers 85 and 103 Tran Hung Dao St. Signs listing the various destinations mark the spots from which the vehicles depart.

Ancient black Citroën 'Traction' service taxis leave for Dong Ha about every two hours between 5 am and 5 pm. Old Renaults serve La Chu, Phong Loc, Phong Son, Sia, Thuan An Beach and Vu Diem (all of which are in Huong Dien District) between 4 am and 5 pm.

Xe Lams go to An Cuu Bus Station, An Hoa Bus Station, An Lo, Bao Vinh, Cho Dinh, Cho No, Kim Long, La Chu, Phu Bai Airport, Phu Luong, Tay Loc, Thuan An Beach and Van Thanh. Dodge trucks go to Binh Dien, 30 km from Hué.

Train Hué Railway Station (Ga Hué; ☎ 2175) is on the right bank at the south-west end of Le Loi St. The ticket office is open from 6.30 am to 5 pm. There is no accommodation at the station.

The Reunification Express trains stop in Hué. For ticket prices, see the Train section in the Getting Around chapter.

Car Ground distances from Hué are as follows:

Aluoi	60 km
Ben Hai River	94 km
Danang	108 km
Dong Ha	72 km
Dong Hoi	166 km
Hanoi	689 km
Ho Chi Minh City	1097 km
Lao Bao (Lao border)	152 km
Quang Tri	56 km
Savannakhet, Laos (Thai border)	400 km
Vinh	368 km

The road to Aluoi is negotiable only by 4WD. It may soon be possible to reach Hué by land from Thailand via Savannakhet, Lao Bao and Dong Ha.

Hitching To hitch a ride, you might try asking around the truck parking area at 1 Le Duan St (near the left-bank end of Phu Xuan Bridge).

Getting Around

To/From the Airport Hué is served by Phu Bai Airport, once an important American air base, which is 14 km south of the city centre. Xe Lams from Dong Ba Bus Station link Hué with Phu Bai.

Car Cars with drivers can be hired from Hué City Tourism (☎ 3577) and Thua Thien-Hué Tourism (☎ 2369). The offices of Transport Company Number 3 (Cong Ty Van Tai So 3; ☎ 3922, 3622) are on Dien Bien Phu St and at the Nva Thu Hotel (☎ 3929), which the cooperative runs. The Hué City Transport Cooperative (Hop Tac O To) has offices at 1 Le Duan St (near the Citadel-side end of Phu Xuan Bridge) and on Nguyen Thai Hoc St.

Motorbike There is no set place to hire a chauffeur-driven motorbike (Honda om), which is the cheapest motor-driven way to get out to the tombs. Ask around and

someone interested in earning a bit of extra cash will turn up.

Bicycle If it's not raining, the most pleasant way to tour the Hué area is by two-wheeled pedal power. Nha Khach Hué, at 2 Le Loi St, and the Morin Hotel hire out bicycles.

Boat Boat rides down the Perfume River are highly recommended – many restaurants catering to foreigners are starting to arrange these for around US$20 for a boat. Hué Tourism and Thua Thien-Hué Tourism can also arrange river outings.

Many sights in the vicinity of Hué, including Thuan An Beach, Thien Mu Pagoda and several of the Royal Tombs, can be reached by river. You might try hiring a boat behind Dong Ba Market or at the Riverine Transportation Cooperative (Van Tai Gioi Duong Song), whose office is right across Dong Ba Canal from Dong Ba Market. Boats may also be available near Dap Da Bridge, which is a bit east of the Huong Giang Hotel.

AROUND HUÉ
Thuan An Beach

Thuan An Beach (Bai Tam Thuan An), 13 km north-east of Hué, is on a splendid lagoon near the mouth of the Perfume River. Xe Lams and old Renaults from Hué to Thuan An depart from the Dong Ba Bus Station. You might also try hiring a sampan to make the trip by river. At Thuan An, you can stay at the *Tan My Hotel*.

Bach Ma

Bach Ma, a French-era hill station known for its superb weather, is 55 km south-west of Hué. Bach Ma is 1200 metres above sea level but only 20 km from Canh Duong Beach. At present, there are no functioning hotels and the access road is in poor condition. There are plans to redevelop Bach Ma if the requisite capital can be found.

DMZ & Vicinity
Khu Phi Quân Sự và Vùng phụ cận

From 1954 to 1975, the Ben Hai River served as the demarcation line between the Republic of Vietnam (South Vietnam) and the Democratic Republic of Vietnam (North Vietnam). The Demilitarised Zone (DMZ) consisted of an area five km to either side of the demarcation line.

The idea of partitioning Vietnam had its origins in a series of agreements concluded between the USA, UK and the USSR at the Potsdam Conference, which was held in Berlin in July 1945. For logistical reasons, the Allies decided that Japanese occupation forces to the south of the 16th parallel would surrender to the British while those to the north would surrender to the Kuomintang (Nationalist) Chinese Army led by Chiang Kaishek.

In April 1954 in Geneva, Ho Chi Minh's government and the French agreed to an armistice among whose provisions was the creation of a demilitarised zone at the Ben Hai River. The agreement stated explicitly that the division of Vietnam into two zones was merely a temporary expediency and that the demarcation line did not constitute a political boundary. But when nationwide general elections planned for July 1956 were not held, Vietnam found itself divided into two states with the Ben Hai River, which is almost exactly at the 17th parallel, as their de facto border.

During the Vietnam War, the area just south of the DMZ was the scene of some of the bloodiest battles of the conflict. Dong Ha, Quang Tri, Con Thien, Cam Lo, Camp Carroll, the Rockpile, Khe Sanh, Lang Vay, the Ashau Valley, Hamburger Hill – these became almost household names in the USA as, year after year, TV pictures and casualty figures provided Americans with their daily evening dose of the war.

Since 1975, 5000 people have been injured or killed in and around the DMZ by mines and ordnance left over from the war. Despite the risk, impoverished peasants still dig for chunks of left-over metal to sell as scrap. The locals are paid the equivalent of US$0.03 (!) per kg of steel, US$0.38 per kg of aluminium and US$0.77 per kg of brass. Much of the metal is sold to Japan.

Orientation
The old DMZ extends from the coast westward to the Lao border; National Highway 9 (Quoc Lo 9) runs more or less parallel to the DMZ. The Ho Chi Minh Trail (Duong Truong Son), actually a series of roads, trails and paths, ran from North Vietnam southward (perpendicular to National Highway 9) through the Truong Son Mountains and western Laos. To prevent infiltrations and to interdict the flow of troops and materiel via the Ho Chi Minh Trail, the Americans established a line of bases along National Highway 9, including (from east to west) Cua Viet, Gio Linh, Dong Ha, Con Thien, Cam Lo, Camp Carroll, Ca Lu, the Rockpile, Khe Sanh Combat Base and Lang Vay.

The old bases along National Highway 9 can be visited in a day trip from Dong Ha. The road leading south-east from the Dakrong Bridge goes to the Ashau Valley (site of the infamous Hamburger Hill) and Aluoi. With a 4WD it is possible to drive the 60 rough km from Aluoi to Hué.

Travel Permit
Unfortunately, the local government in Quang Tri Province is now requiring that foreigners secure a separate travel permit to visit any places in the DMZ off National Highway 1. The charge for the permit is US$10 plus you must rent a car from the local government. Cars cost US$30, or you can rent a minibus for US$40. This rule applies even if you already have your own

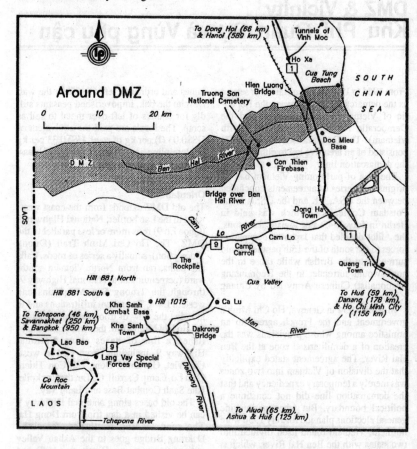

Around DMZ

0   10   20 km

To Dong Hoi (66 km)
& Hanoi (589 km)

Tunnels of
Vinh Moc

Ho Xa

Cua Tung
Beach

SOUTH
CHINA
SEA

Hien Luong
Bridge

Truong Son
National Cemetery

Doc Mieu
Base

D M Z

Ben   Hai   River

Con Thien
Firebase

Bridge over Ben
Hai River

Dong Ha
Town

LAOS

Cam   Lo   River

Cam Lo

Camp
Carroll

Quang Tri
Town

The
Rockpile

Cua Valley

To Huế (59 km),
Danang (178 km),
& Ho Chi Minh City
(1156 km)

Hill 881 North

Hill 881 South

Hill 1015

Ca Lu

Khe Sanh
Combat Base

Hien
River

To Tchepone (46 km),
Savannakhet (250 km)
& Bangkok (950 km)

Khe Sanh
Town

Dakrong
Bridge

Lao Bao

Lang Vay Special
Forces Camp

Dakrong
River

Co Roc
Mountain

LAOS

To Aluoi (65 km),
Ashua & Huế (125 km)

Tchepone River

rental car from elsewhere. You can secure these permits in the town of Dong Ha.

Warning!

The war may be over but death is still fairly easy to come by in the old DMZ. At many of the places listed in this section you will find live mortar rounds, artillery projectiles and mines strewn about. As tempted as you might be to collect souvenirs, *never* touch any left-over ordnance. Watch where you step. If the locals have not carted it off for scrap it means that even they are afraid to disturb it. White phosphorus shells – whose contents burn

fiercely when exposed to air – are remarkably impervious to the effects of prolonged exposure and are likely to remain extremely dangerous for many more years. If one of these shells happens to explode while you're playing with it, your whole trip will be ruined – and don't expect a refund from Saigon Tourist.

In short, be careful. Don't become a candidate for plastic surgery – or a statistic!

DONG HA
ĐÔNG HÀ
Dong Ha, the capital of newly reconstituted

Quang Tri Province, is at the intersection of National Highway 1 and National Highway 9. Dong Ha served as a US Marines command and logistics centre in 1968-69. In the spring of 1968, a division of North Vietnamese troops crossed the DMZ and attacked Dong Ha. The city was later the site of a South Vietnamese Army base.

Orientation

National Highway 1 is called Le Duan St as it passes through Dong Ha. National Highway 9 (the new American-built branch), signposted as going to Lao Bao, intersects National Highway 1 next to the bus station. Tran Phu St (old National Highway 9) intersects Le Duan St 600 metres west of (towards the river from) the bus station. Tran Phu St runs south for 400 metres until the blockhouse, where it turns westward.

There is a market area along National Highway 1 between Tran Phu St and the river.

Information

Tourist Office Quang Tri Tourism (Cong Ty Du Lich Quang Tri; ☎ 261) is the government-owned tourist authority for Quang Tri Province. The office is in the Dong Truong Son Hotel, three km from the city out on Tran Phu St. Cars and guides are available here, but you'd do better to arrange a guided visit to the area through Thua Thien-Hué Tourism in Hué.

French Blockhouse

Surrounded by captured American tanks and artillery pieces, the old French-built blockhouse (Lo Khot) was used by the French and later the American and South Vietnamese armies. The blockhouse is on Tran Phu St 400 metres from National Highway 1.

Places to Stay

The *Nha Khach Ngoai Thuong* is the cheapest place in town and very close to the centre. It's just to the west of the old French blockhouse. Rooms cost US$5 to US$6 and have attached bath, but there's cold water only.

The *Nha Khach Buu Dien Tinh Buu*

Quang Tri is a nice, quiet place with a pleasant courtyard and friendly manager. All rooms have attached bath with hot water and can accommodate four persons. There is a security guard on duty at night. The price for foreigners is US$15. This hotel is on the south side of town about one km from the centre.

The *Nha Khach Dong Ha* (☎ 361; 24 rooms) is a pleasant official guesthouse 300 metres west of the French blockhouse on Tran Phu St. Rooms with shared bath cost US$5 to US$10; private attached bath raises the tariff to US$15. Hot water is available.

The *Dong Truong Son Hotel* (☎ 415; 44 rooms) is three km out on Tran Phu St from the old French blockhouse. While it's not a bad place, the remote location means it's almost always empty – how it has managed to stay open for years without going bankrupt is a mystery. Room prices are from US$10 to US$25. All rooms have private bath and air-conditioning. It might be worth stopping in here to talk to the desk clerk who speaks excellent English and can help you find a guide for the DMZ.

Places to Eat

There are a number of eateries along National Highway 1 (Le Duan St) between the bus station and Tran Phu St. These places look rather run-down but the food is pretty good because of the fierce competition for the lucrative patronage of truckers. There are more places to eat on Tran Phu St between the blockhouse and Nha Khach Dong Ha.

If you are staying at the Nha Khach Buu Dien Tinh Buu Quang Tri (hotel) there is a pleasant restaurant just next door. The *Huong Vinh Restaurant* is run by a married couple (wife's surname is Huong, husband is Vinh) and their six daughters. The speciality of the house is barbecued beef cooked right at your table, served with lots of fresh vegetables. The cost for a huge meal for three people is under US$10.

The *Dong Truong Son Hotel* has its own restaurant which – like the hotel – is usually deserted.

Getting There & Away

Bus Buses from Hué to Dong Ha depart from An Hoa Bus Station. Citroën Tractions to Dong Ha leave from Dong Ba Bus Station.

In Dong Ha, Dong Ha Bus Station (Ben Xe Khach Dong Ha; ☎ 211) is at the intersection of National Highway 1 and National Highway 9. Vehicles to Hué depart between 5 am and 5 pm. There are buses to Khe Sanh at 8 and 11 am; to get to Lao Bao, change buses in Khe Sanh. There is service every Monday and Thursday to Hanoi; the bus departs at 5 am, arriving in Vinh at 6 or 7 pm and in Hanoi at 5 am the next day. Buses also link Dong Ha with Danang, Con Thien, Cua, Dien Sanh, Hai Tri and Ho Xa, which is along National Highway 1 about 13 km west of Vinh Moc.

Train Dong Ha Railway Station (Ga Dong Ha) is a stop for the Reunification Express trains. For ticket prices, see the Train section in the Getting Around chapter.

To get to the train station from the bus station, head south-east on National Highway 1 for one km. The railway station is 150 metres across a field to the right (south-west) of the highway.

Car Road distances from Dong Ha are:

Ben Hai River	22 km
Danang	190 km
Dong Hoi	94 km
Hanoi	617 km
Ho Chi Minh City	1169 km
Hué	72 km
Khe Sanh	65 km
Lao Bao (Lao border)	80 km
Savannakhet, Laos (Thai border)	327 km
Truong Son National Cemetery	30 km
Vinh	294 km
Vinh Moc	41 km

QUANG TRI
QUẢNG TRỊ

The town of Quang Tri, 59 km north of Hué and 12.5 km south of Dong Ha Bus Station, was once an important citadel-city. In the spring of 1972, four divisions of North Vietnamese regulars backed by tanks, artillery and rockets poured across the DMZ into Quang Tri Province in what became known as the Eastertide Offensive. They lay siege to Quang Tri City, shelling it heavily before capturing it along with the rest of the province. During the next four months, the city was almost completely obliterated by South Vietnamese artillery and massive carpet-bombing by US fighter-bombers and B-52s. The South Vietnamese Army suffered 5000 casualties in the rubble-to-rubble fighting to retake Quang Tri City.

Today, there is little to see in the town of Quang Tri except a memorial and a few remains of the moat, ramparts and gates of the citadel, once a South Vietnamese army headquarters. The Citadel is 1.6 km from National Highway 1 on Le Duan St (not to be confused with Le Duan St in Dong Ha), which runs perpendicular to National Highway 1. The ruined two-storey building between National Highway 1 and the bus station used to be a Buddhist high school.

Along National Highway 1 near the turn-off to Quang Tri is the skeleton of a church – it's definitely worth taking a look inside. It gives you the chills to see the bullet holes and know what took place here – a deadly fight between US forces and the VC.

Cua Viet Beach, once the site of an important American landing dock, is 16 km north-east of Quang Tri. Gia Dang Beach is 13 km east of town.

Getting There & Away

Bus The bus station is on Le Duan St (Quang Tri's north-south oriented main street) 600 metres from National Highway 1. Renault buses to An Hoa Bus Station in Hué leave at 5.30 am, 6.30 am, 8 am and noon. A Citroën Traction to Dong Ba Bus Station in Hué departs daily at 6.30 am. The daily bus to Khe Sanh leaves at 8 am. There is also service to Ho Xa.

DOC MIEU BASE
DỐC MIẾU

Doc Mieu Base, which is next to Nationa

Highway 1 on a low rise eight km south of the Ben Hai River, was once part of an elaborate electronic system (McNamara's Wall) intended to prevent infiltration across the DMZ. Today, it is a lunar landscape of bunkers, craters, shrapnel and live mortar rounds. Bits of cloth and decaying military boots are strewn about on the red earth. This devastation was created not by the war but by scrap-metal hunters, who have found excavations at this site particularly rewarding.

BEN HAI RIVER
SÔNG BẾN HẢI
Twenty-two km north of Dong Ha, National Highway 1 crosses the Ben Hai River, once the demarcation line between North and South Vietnam, over the decrepit Hien Luong Bridge. Until 1967 (when it was bombed by the Americans), the northern half of the bridge that stood on this site was painted red while the southern half was yellow. Following the signing of the Paris Cease-Fire Agreements in 1973, the present bridge and the two flag towers were built. A typhoon knocked over the flag pole on the northern bank of the river in 1985.

CUA TUNG BEACH
BÃI BIỂN CỬA TÙNG
Cua Tung Beach, a long, secluded stretch of sand where Vietnam's last emperor, Bao Dai, used to vacation, is just north of the mouth of the Ben Hai River. There are beaches on the southern side of the Ben Hai River as well. Every bit of land in the area not levelled for planting is pockmarked with bomb craters of all sizes. Offshore is Con Co Island which can be reached by motorised boat; the trip takes about 2½ hours.

Getting There & Away
There are no buses to Cua Tung Beach, which can be reached by turning right (eastward) off National Highway 1 at a point 1.2 km north of the Ben Hai River. Cua Tung Beach is about seven km south of Vinh Moc via the dirt road that runs along the coast.

VINH MOC TUNNELS
ĐỊA ĐẠO VĨNH MỐC
The remarkable tunnels of Vinh Moc are yet another monument to the tenaciousness of North Vietnamese determination to persevere and triumph – at all costs and despite incredible difficulties – in the war against South Vietnam and the USA. The 2.8 km of tunnels here, all of which can be visited, are the real thing, unadulterated (unlike the tunnels at Cu Chi) for viewing by tourists. A museum is being constructed on the site. A visit to the tunnels can be combined with bathing at the beautiful beaches which extend for many km north and south of Vinh Moc.

Local authorities who prefer not to lose any foreigners in the maze of forks, branches and identical weaving passageways are adamant that visitors enter the tunnels only if accompanied by a local guide. The tunnels have been chemically treated to keep snakes away. The entrance fee is US$0.75. Bring a torch (flashlight).

In 1966, the villagers of Vinh Moc found themselves living in what the US military called a 'free-fire zone'. Facing incessant US aerial and artillery attacks which rendered small family shelters ineffective, they began tunnelling by hand into the red clay earth. After 18 months of work (during which the excavated earth was camouflaged to prevent its detection from the air), the entire village of 1200 persons was relocated underground. The adults would go outside to fish and work in the fields; the old people and children stayed inside all the time. Supplies were delivered to the village on bicycles and by boat.

Later, the young and old were evacuated and the local young people, who continued to fish and plant, were joined by Viet Cong guerrillas whose mission was to keep communications and supply lines to nearby Con Co Island open. People began moving above-ground in 1969 but returned to the tunnels in 1972-73. A total of 11,500 tons of supplies reached Con Co Island and a further 300 tons were shipped to the South thanks to the Vinh Moc tunnels.

Other villages in the vicinity also built tunnel systems but none were as elaborate as the one at Vinh Moc. The poorly constructed tunnels of Vinh Quang village (at the mouth of the Ben Hai River) were crushed by bombs, killing everyone inside.

The tunnel network at Vinh Moc remains essentially as it looked in 1966, though some of the 12 entrances, seven of which exit onto the palm-lined beach, have been retimbered and others have become overgrown with foliage. The tunnels, which average 1.2 metres wide and are from 1.2 to 1.7 metres in height, were built on three levels ranging from 15 to 26 metres below the crest of the bluff. The deepest level was used by the Viet Cong fighters.

On both sides of the passageways are tiny chambers with arched ceilings, each of which housed a family. Water was drawn from wells (the water table is only five metres below the deepest tunnel). The centrepiece of the network is a long, narrow room on the middle level. It was used as a warehouse and conference hall and was big enough to seat 150 people, who would gather to sing or, from 1972 onwards, watch movies. Electric lighting was also added in 1972. The network included a medical clinic with obstetric facilities; over the years, 17 children were born in the tunnels.

The tunnels were repeatedly hit by American bombs, but the only ordnance that posed a real threat was the feared 'drilling bomb'. Only once did such a bomb score a direct hit, but it failed to explode and no one was injured; the inhabitants adapted the hole for use as an air shaft. The mouths of the complex that faced the sea were sometimes hit by naval gunfire.

Offshore is vegetation-covered Con Co Island, which during the war was an important supply depot. Today the island, which is ringed by rocky beaches, houses a small military base. The trip from Vinh Moc to Con Co takes 2½ to three hours by motorised fishing boat.

Places to Stay

There is no hotel at Vinh Moc but if you have a letter of introduction from Quang Tri Tourism you may be able to stay in a private house (don't bet on it, though). Accommodation is available at Cua Tung Beach, seven km to the south.

Getting There & Away

The turn-off to Vinh Moc from National Highway 1 is 6.5 km north of the Ben Hai River in the village of Ho Xa. Vinh Moc is 13 km from National Highway 1.

TRUONG SON NATIONAL CEMETERY
NGHĨA TRANG LIỆT SĨ TRƯỜNG SƠN

Truong Son National Cemetery is a memorial to tens of thousands of North Vietnamese soldiers from transport, construction and anti-aircraft units who were killed in the Truông Son Mountains (the Annamite Cordillera) along the Ho Chi Minh Trail (Duong Truong Son). Row after row of white tombstones stretch across the hillsides in a scene eerily reminiscent of the endless lines of crosses and Stars of David in US military cemeteries. The cemetery is maintained by disabled war veterans.

The soldiers are buried in five zones according to the part of Vietnam they came from; within each zone, the tombs are arranged by province of origin. The gravestones of five colonels (Trung Ta and Dia Ta) and seven decorated heroes, of whom one is a woman, are in a separate area. Each headstone bears the inscription 'Liet Si', which means 'martyr'. The soldiers whose remains are interred here were originally buried near where they were killed and were brought here after reunification, but many of the graves are empty, bearing the names of a small portion of Vietnam's 300,000 MIAs (soldiers 'missing in action').

On the hilltop above the sculpture garden is a three-sided stele. On one face are engraved the tributes of high-ranking Vietnamese leaders to the people who worked on the Ho Chi Minh Trail. At the bottom is a poem by the poet To Huu. Another side tells the history of the May 1959 Army Corps (Doang 5.59) which is said to have been founded on Ho Chi Minh's birthday in 1959 with the mission of constructing and maintaining a supply line to the South. The third side lists the constituent units of the May 1959 Army Corps, which eventually included five divisions. The site where the cemetery now stands was used as a base of the May 1959 Army Corps from 1972 to 1975.

Getting There & Away

The road to Truong Son National Cemetery intersects National Route 1, 13 km north of Dong Ha and nine km south of the Ben Hai River; the distance from the highway to the cemetery is 17 km. A rocky cart-path, passable (but just barely) by motorcar, links Cam Lo (on National Route 9) with Truong Son National Cemetery. The 18-km drive from Cam Lo to the cemetery passes by newly planted rubber plantations and the homes of Bru (Van Kieu) tribal people who raise, among other crops, black pepper.

CON THIEN FIREBASE
CĂN CỨ CỒN THIÊN

In September 1967, North Vietnamese forces backed by long-range artillery and rockets crossed the DMZ and besieged the US Marine base of Con Thien, which had been established to stop infiltrations across the DMZ and as part of McNamara's Wall (named after the US Secretary of Defense 1961-68), an abortive electronic barrier to detect infiltrators.

The Americans responded with 4000 bombing sorties (including 800 by B-52s) during which more than 40,000 tons of bombs were dropped on the North Vietnamese forces around Con Thien, transforming the gently sloping brush-covered hills that surrounded the base into a smoking moonscape of craters and ashes. As a result of the bombing the siege was lifted, but the battle had accomplished its real purpose: to divert US attention from South Vietnam's cities in preparation for the Tet Offensive. The area around the base is still considered too dangerous even for scrap-metal hunters to approach.

Getting There & Away

Con Thien Firebase is 10 km west of National Highway 1 and seven km east of Truong Son National Cemetery along the road linking National Highway 1 with the cemetery. Concrete bunkers mark the spot a few hundred metres to the south of the road where the base once stood.

Con Thien is 12 km from National Highway 9 and six km from Truong Son National Cemetery on the road that links Cam Lo with the cemetery. As you head towards the cemetery, the base is visible off to the right (east).

Six km towards National Highway 1 from Con Thien (and four km from the highway) is another US base, C-3, the rectangular ramparts of which are still visible just north of the road. It is inaccessible due to mines.

CAMP CARROLL
TRẠI CARROLL

Established in 1966, Camp Carroll was named for a US Marine captain who was killed trying to seize a nearby ridge. The gargantuan 175-mm cannons at Camp Carroll were used to shell targets as far away as Khe Sanh. In 1972, the South Vietnamese commander of Camp Carroll, Lieutenant Colonel Ton That Dinh, surrendered and joined the North Vietnamese army; he is now a high-ranking official in Hué.

These days there is not that much to see at Camp Carroll except a few overgrown trenches and the remains of their timber roofs. Bits of military hardware and lots of rusty shell casings litter the ground. The concrete bunkers were destroyed by local people seeking to extract the steel reinforcing rods to sell as scrap; concrete chunks from the bunkers were hauled off for use in construction. Locals out prospecting for scrap metal can point out what little of the base is left.

The area around Camp Carroll now belongs to the State Pepper Enterprises (Xi Nghiep Ho Tieu Tan Lam). The pepper plants are trained so that they climb up the trunks of jackfruit trees. There are also rubber plantations nearby. The road to Camp

Carroll leads on to the fertile Cua Valley, once home to a number of French settlers.

The turn-off to Camp Carroll is 11 km west of Cam Lo, 24 km east of the Dakrong Bridge and 37 km east of the Khe Sanh Bus Station. The base is three km from National Highway 9.

THE ROCKPILE

The Rockpile was named for what can only be described as a 230-metre-high pile of rocks. There was a US Marines lookout on top of the Rockpile and a base for American long-range artillery nearby. The local tribal people, who live in houses built on stilts, engage in slash-and-burn agriculture.

The Rockpile is 26 km towards Khe Sanh from Dong Ha.

DAKRONG BRIDGE
CẦU ĐẮC RÔNG

The Dakrong Bridge, 13 km east of the Khe Sanh Bus Station, was built in 1975-76 with assistance from the Cubans. The bridge crosses the Dakrong River (also known as the Ta Rin River). Hill-tribe people in the area live by slash-and-burn agriculture. Some of the tribespeople openly carry assault rifles left over from the war; this is against the law but the government seems unwilling or unable to do anything about it.

The road that heads south-east from the bridge to Aluoi was once a branch of the Ho Chi Minh Trail. Constructed with Cuban help, it passes by the stilted homes of the Brus.

ALUOI
A LƯỚI

Aluoi is approximately 65 km south-east of the Dakrong Bridge and 60 km west of Hué. There are a number of waterfalls and cascades in the area. Tribes living in the mountainous Aluoi area include the Ba Co, Ba Hy, Ca Tu and Taoi. US Army Special Forces bases in Aluoi and Ashau were overrun and abandoned in 1966; the area then became an important transshipment centre for supplies coming down the Ho Chi Minh Trail.

Among the better known military sites in the vicinity of Aluoi are landing zones Cunningham, Erskine and Razor, Hill 1175 (west of the valley) and Hill 521 (in Laos). Farther south in the Ashau Valley is 'Hamburger Hill' (Apbia Mountain). In May 1969, American forces on a search-and-destroy operation near the Lao border fought one of the fiercest engagements of the war here, suffering terrible casualties (hence the name); in less than a week of fighting, 241 American soldiers died at Hamburger Hill, a fact well publicised in the American media. A month later, after US forces withdrew from the area to continue operations elsewhere, the hill was reoccupied by the North Vietnamese.

KHE SANH COMBAT BASE
CĂN CỨ KHE SANH

Khe Sanh Combat Base, site of the most famous siege (and one of the most controversial battles) of the Vietnam War, sits silently on a barren plateau surrounded by vegetation-covered hills often obscured by mist and fog. It is hard to imagine as you stand in this peaceful, verdant land, with the neat homes and vegetable plots of local tribespeople and Vietnamese settlers all around, that in this very place in early 1968 took place the bloodiest battle of the Vietnam War. Approximately 500 Americans (the official figure of 205 American dead was arrived at by statistical sleight-of-hand), some 10,000 North Vietnamese troops and uncounted civilian bystanders died amidst the din of machine-guns and the fiery explosions of 1000-kg bombs, white phosphorus shells, napalm, mortars and artillery rounds of all sorts.

But little things help you to picture what the history books say happened here. The outline of the airfield remains distinct (to this day nothing will grow on it). In places, the ground is literally carpeted with bullets and rusting shell casings. And all around are little groups of local people digging holes in their relentless search for scrap metal (once, local scavengers say proudly, they unearthed an entire bulldozer!). And the US MIA Team, which is charged with finding the remains of Americans listed as 'missing-in-action', still visits the area to search for the bodies of the Americans who disappeared during the fierce battles in the surrounding hills. Most of the remains they find are Vietnamese.

History

Despite opposition from Marine Corps brass to General Westmoreland's attrition strategy (they thought it futile), the small US Army Special Forces (Green Beret) base at Khe Sanh, built to recruit and train local tribespeople, was turned into a Marine stronghold in late 1966. In April 1967, there began a series of 'Hill Fights' between the US forces and the well-dug-in North Vietnamese Army infantry who held the surrounding hills. In the period of a few weeks, 155 Marines and perhaps thousands of North Vietnamese were killed. The fighting centred on hills 881 South and 881 North, both of which are about eight km north-west of Khe Sanh Combat Base.

In late 1967, American intelligence detected the movement of tens of thousands of North Vietnamese regulars armed with mortars, rockets and artillery into the hills around Khe Sanh. The commander of the US forces in Vietnam, General Westmoreland, became convinced that the North Vietnamese were planning another Dien Bien Phu, a preposterous analogy given American firepower and the proximity of Khe Sanh to supply lines and other American bases. Pres-

---

Missing in Action (MIA)

An issue which continues to poison relations between the USA and Vietnam is that of US military personnel officially listed as 'missing in action'. Nearly two decades after US forces were withdrawn from Vietnam, there are still 2265 American soldiers whose bodies have not been found and who are therefore officially 'unaccounted for'.

The families of the missing are usually adamant – many believe that their loved ones are still alive and being held in secret prison camps somewhere in the jungles of Vietnam. POW-MIA groups in the USA continue to lobby Congress to 'do something'. It's a highly emotion-charged issue, one which is often cleverly exploited by some US politicians. 'No compromise', they insist, 'until Vietnam accounts for every one of the MIAs'.

But there are others who think that the POW-MIA groups are beating a dead horse. The figure of 2265 MIAs is almost certainly too high. About 400 flight personnel were killed when their planes crashed into the sea off the coast of Vietnam – the bodies were never recovered but they are still listed as MIAs. Many others were killed when their aircraft went down in flames over the jungle and no remains could be recovered. Still others were killed in ground combat, but the tropical jungle quickly reclaims a human corpse. Not much is said about the 300,000 Vietnamese who are also MIAs – all are almost certainly dead.

US Senator John Kerry is the chairman of a Senate committee exploring the MIA issue. After visiting Vietnam in November 1992, he called for a reappraisal of the US body count. During a press conference, he said 'you have certain instances in which this person was KIA (killed in action) and the body cannot be recovered...this standard has to be reviewed'.

Kerry added that in 1973, when Vietnam returned the last 590 American POWs, there were 37 soldiers believed to have been captured who were not among those released.

Could there still be some American troops being held prisoner in Vietnam? The Vietnamese government adamantly denies it, but their atrocious human rights record erodes their credibility. But as one observer noted, 'No one can be sure; perhaps the Vietnamese did keep some American prisoners after the war ended. But if I were them, I would have executed those prisoners long ago – keeping them around and risking discovery would be too much of an embarassment'.

In the meantime, MIA teams continue to comb the Vietnamese countryside with little success, at a cost to American taxpayers which has now added up to millions of US dollars. When private POW-MIA groups started circulating photographs showing US soldiers being held prisoner in a Vietnamese camp, there was a flurry of official investigations: The photos proved to be fakes. ■

ident Johnson himself became obsessed by the spectre of Dien Bien Phu: to follow the course of the battle, he had a sand-table model of the Khe Sanh plateau constructed in the White House Situation Room, and he took the unprecedented step of requiring a written guarantee from the Joint Chiefs of Staff that Khe Sanh could be held.

Westmoreland, determined to avoid 'another Dien Bien Phu' at all costs, assembled an armada of 5000 aeroplanes and helicopters and increased the number of troops at Khe Sanh to 6000. He even ordered his staff to study the feasibility of using tactical nuclear weapons.

The 75-day Siege of Khe Sanh began on 21 January 1968 with a small-scale assault on the base perimeter. As the Marines and the South Vietnamese Rangers with them braced for a full-scale ground attack, Khe Sanh became the focus of global media attention. It was the cover story for both *Newsweek* and *Life* magazines and appeared on the front pages of countless newspapers around the world. During the next two months, the base was subject to continuous ground attacks and artillery fire. US aircraft dropped 100,000 tons of explosives on the immediate vicinity of Khe Sanh Combat Base. The expected attempt to overrun the base never came, and on 7 April 1968 after heavy fighting, US Army troops reopened National Route 9 and linked up with the Marines, ending the siege.

It now seems clear that the Siege of Khe Sanh, in which an estimated 10,000 North Vietnamese died, was merely an enormous diversion intended to draw US forces and the attention of their commanders away from South Vietnam's population centres in preparation for the Tet Offensive, which began a week after the siege did. At the time, however, Westmoreland considered the entire Tet Offensive to be a 'diversionary effort' to distract attention from Khe Sanh!

A few days after Westmoreland's tour of duty in Vietnam ended in July 1968, American forces in the area were redeployed. Policy, it seemed, had been reassessed and holding Khe Sanh, for which so many men had died, was deemed unnecessary. After

everything at Khe Sanh was buried, trucked out or blown up – nothing recognisable that could be used in a North Vietnamese propaganda film was to remain – US forces up and left Khe Sanh Combat Base under a curtain of secrecy. The American command had finally realised what a Marine officer had long before expressed this way: 'When you're at Khe Sanh, you're not really anywhere. You could lose it and you really haven't lost a damn thing'.

Getting There & Away

To get to Khe Sanh Combat Base, turn northwestward at the triangular intersection 600 metres towards Dong Ha from Khe Sanh Bus Station. The base is on the right-hand side of the road, 2.5 km from the intersection.

KHE SANH TOWN
THỊ TRẤN KHE SANH

Set amidst beautiful hills, valleys and fields at an elevation of about 600 metres, the town of Khe Sanh (Huong Hoa) is a pleasant district capital once known for its French-run coffee plantations. Many of the inhabitants are Bru tribespeople who have moved here from the surrounding hills. A popular pastime among the hill-tribe women is smoking long-stemmed pipes.

Places to Stay

The guesthouse of the District People's Committee (Nha Khach Huyen Huong Hoa; ☎ 27 from the Dong Ha telephone exchange) has five rooms and about 20 beds. It is 300 metres south (towards Laos) from Khe Sanh Bus Station.

Getting There & Away

Khe Sanh Bus Station (Ben Xe Huong Hoa) is on National Highway 9, 600 metres southwest (towards the Lao frontier) from the triangular intersection where the road to Khe Sanh Combat Base branches off. Buses to Dong Ha depart at 7 am and around noon; the daily bus to Hué leaves at 7 am. There are two buses a day to Lao Bao; the first leaves at 6 am, the second whenever it is full.

The ticket window is open from 6 to 7 am; tickets for later buses are sold on board.

If and when the border with Laos is opened for trade and travel, the public transport situation in the area is likely to improve significantly.

LANG VAY SPECIAL FORCES CAMP
TRẠI LỰC LƯỢNG ĐẶC BIỆT LÀNG VÂY

In February 1968, Lang Vay (Lang Vei) Special Forces Camp, established in 1962, was attacked and overrun by North Vietnamese infantry backed by nine tanks. Of the base's 500 South Vietnamese, Bru and Montagnard defenders, 316 were killed. Ten of the 24 Americans at the base were killed; 11 of the survivors were wounded.

All that remains of dog-bone shaped Lang Vay Base are the overgrown remains of numerous concrete bunkers. Locals can show you around.

Getting There & Away

The base is on a ridge just south-west of National Highway 9 at a point 9.2 km towards Laos from the Khe Sanh Bus Station and 7.3 km towards Khe Sanh from Lao Bao Market.

LAO BAO
LAO BẢO

Lao Bao is right on the Tchepone River (Song Xe Pon), which marks the Vietnam-Laos border. Towering above Lao Bao on the Lao side of the border is Co Roc Mountain, once a North Vietnamese artillery stronghold.

Two km from the border post is Lao Bao Market, where Thai goods smuggled through the bush from Laos to Vietnam are readily available. Merchants accept either Vietnamese dong or Lao kip.

Getting There & Away

Lao Bao is 18 km west of Khe Sanh, 80 km from Dong Ha, 152 km from Hué, 46 km east of Tchepone (Laos), 250 km east of Savannakhet, Laos (on the Thai frontier), and 950 km from Bangkok (via Ubon Ratchathani). Lao Bao may eventually become an important border crossing for trade and tourism between Thailand and central Vietnam.

North-Central Vietnam
Bắc Trung Phần Việt Nam

The area north of the DMZ is the former North Vietnam. While the differences between north and south have faded since reunification in 1975, there is still evidence that there were once two different countries with two different political systems.

While the south enjoyed America's largesse which brought wartime prosperity, the north has never been anything but desperately poor – and still is. While the south was the scene of many (mostly small) land battles, it was the north that suffered from bombing – bomb craters and damaged buildings are still a feature in this part of Vietnam.

And there is also a perceptible change in attitudes – southerners disdain the northerners whom they see as provincial and backwards. For their part, the northerners think the southerners are aggressive money-grubbers. Both sides complain that they have trouble understanding what the other says – the two parts of Vietnam speak a sharply different, though mutually intelligible, dialect.

DONG HOI
ĐỒNG HỚI
The fishing port of Dong Hoi is the capital of Quang Binh Province. Important archaeological finds from the Neolithic period have been made in the vicinity. During the Vietnam War, the city suffered extensive damage from US bombing. When travelling on National Highway 1 north of the DMZ, note the old French bunkers and US bomb craters lining the route; both are especially numerous near road and rail bridges. The Vietnam-Cuba Hospital is one km north of town.

Information
Tourist Office The Dong Hoi Tourist Office is near the Hoa Binh Hotel in the centre of town.

Beaches
Most of Quang Binh Province is lined with sand dunes and beaches. There are dozens of km of beaches and dunes north of town and on a long spit of sand south of town. Nhat Le Beach is at the mouth of the Nhat Le River; another bathing site in the region is Ly Hoa Beach.

Places to Stay
The *Hoa Binh Hotel* is a large four-storey building, making it a veritable skyscraper by Dong Hoi standards. It's also the only place in town where foreigners are permitted to stay. All rooms have air-conditioning and hot water, and cost a whopping US$27.

Getting There & Away
Bus & Car Dong Hoi is 166 km from Hué, 94 km from Dong Ha, 197 km from Vinh and 489 km from Hanoi. Dong Hoi is on National Highway 1 and sees regular bus traffic. Road traffic between Dong Ha and Dong Hoi is light, especially after the early morning. North of the DMZ, much of National Highway 1 is under repair, which means lots of gravel, dust, mud and potholes.

There is a ferry crossing at Cua Gianh (also called Song Painh), which is 33 km north of Dong Hoi. The ferry is really just a small barge which is pushed and pulled by tugboats and there is often a long queue of vehicles – it can take an hour or more to get across.

Train Dong Hoi is a stop for the Reunification Express. For ticket prices, see the Train section in the Getting Around chapter.

PHONG NHA CAVE
ĐỘNG PHONG NHÃ
Phong Nha Cave, which is about 45 km north-west of Dong Hoi, is remarkable for its thousands of metres of passageways lined

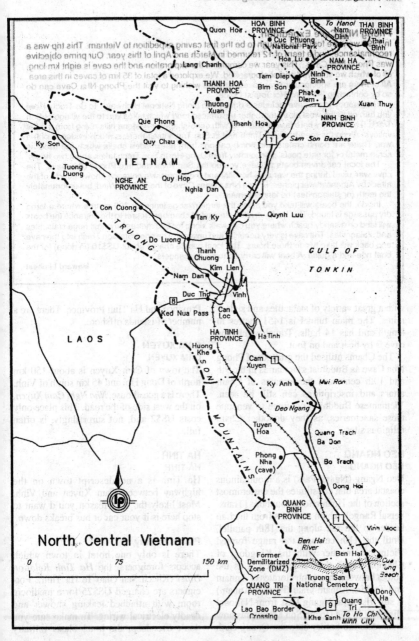

North Central Vietnam

0   75   150 km

Phong Nha Cave Expedition

In 1990 we were fortunate enough to be the first caving expedition to Vietnam. This trip was a reconnaisance, and a team of 12 returned in March and April of this year. Our prime objective was Phong Nha Cave...This year we completed the exploration and the cave is eight km long, all of which we surveyed and photographed. We explored a total of 35 km of caves in this area. All of them are spectacular river caves. Anyone wishing to visit the Phong Nha Cave can do so by contacting the Dong Hoi Tourist Office.

The journey to the cave includes a drive north along National Highway 1 to Bo Trach. Here you turn off to the west along a rougher unsurfaced road which takes you to the village of Son Trach. The scenery here is very beautiful with cone-shaped limestone hills rising from the flat valleys. Along the road from Bo Trach and in Son Trach itself there is much evidence of the war. There are bomb craters and bomb casings from unexploded shells which are used as scrap metal or for gate posts. The journey from Dong Hoi to Son Trach takes about two hours.

The local oar-driven boats will take you up the Son River and into Phong Nha Cave. The cave was used during the war as a hospital and the impressive entrance shows effects of the attack by American war planes. Phong Nha means Cave of the Teeth & Wind, but unfortunately the teeth (or stalagmites) no longer remain.

Inside, the boats will take you along the large river galleries for 700 metres where a large dry passage is found. This leads up into a decorated chamber. Nearer to the entrance the boats will land on a sandy beach where you can walk along for 500 metres amongst huge stalactites and stalagmites. The cave is very beautiful and unspoilt. The ride from Son Trach into the cave and back will take two to three hours. The local people charge about US$10 (in dong) for the boat ride and a guide. A boat will carry up to six passengers.

Howard Limbest

with a great variety of stalactites and stalagmites. The main tunnel is 1451 metres in length and has 14 halls. Travel within the cave is by boat and on foot.

The Chams utilised the grottoes of Phong Nha Cave as Buddhist sanctuaries in the 9th and 10th centuries; the remains of Cham altars and inscriptions can still be seen. Vietnamese Buddhists continue to venerate these sanctuaries, as they do other Cham religious sites.

DEO NGANG
ĐÈO NGANG

Deo Ngang (Ngang Pass) is a mountainous coastal area that constitutes the easternmost section of the Hoanh Son Mountains (Transversal Range), which stretches from the Lao border to the sea along the 18th parallel. Until the 11th century, the range formed Vietnam's frontier with the Kingdom of Champa. Later, the French used it as the border between their protectorates of Annam and Tonkin; Annam Gate (Porte d'Annam) is still visible at Ngang Pass from National Highway 1. The Hoanh Son Mountains now demarcate the border between Quang Binh Province and Ha Tinh Province. There are a number of islands offshore.

CAM XUYEN
CẨM XUYÊN

The town of Cam Xuyen is about 150 km north of Dong Hoi and 45 km south of Vinh. There is a guesthouse, *Nha Nghi Cam Xuyen*, on the west side of the road. This place only costs US$2 and, not surprisingly, is often full.

HA TINH
HÀ TĨNH

Ha Tinh is a nondescript town on the highway between Cam Xuyen and Vinh. Most likely the only reason you'd want to stop here is if your car or bus breaks down.

Places to Stay

There is only one hotel in town which accepts foreigners, the *Ha Tinh Relation Hotel* (Khach San Giao Te Ha Tinh). Foreigners are charged US$25 for a mediocre room with attached leaking shower and deadly electrical wiring. To make sure you don't oversleep, the hotel blasts military

Woman and pig, Cam Xuyen

music at 5 am. The hotel is one km east of National Highway 1 and is operated by the provincial tourism authority, Ha Tinh Tourism (Cong Ty Du Lich Ha Tinh; ☎ 6647).

VINH

VINH

The port-city of Vinh is the capital of one of Vietnam's most populous provinces, Nghe An. While there is almost nothing of interest in the city, it is a convenient place to stop for the night if you are going overland between Hué and Hanoi.

Nghe An and neighbouring Ha Tinh provinces are endowed with poor soil and some of the worst weather in Vietnam. The area frequently suffers from floods and devastating typhoons. The locals say, 'The typhoon was born here and comes back often to visit'. The summers are very hot and dry while during the winter the cold and rain are made all the more unpleasant by biting winds from the north.

The upland and highland regions of Nghe An, much of which is thickly forested, cover 80% of the province's territory and are home to Muong, Tai (Thai or Thay), Khmer, Meo and Tho hill-tribe people. Mountain fauna includes tigers, leopards, elephants, rhinoceros, deer, monkeys, gibbons and flying squirrels. Nghe An's agricultural products include wet-grown rice, sugar cane, tea, mulberry leaves, areca and pomelo.

A good source of information on Nghe An and Ha Tinh provinces is *Nghe Tinh: Native Province of Ho Chi Minh*, which is volume 59 of the *Vietnamese Studies* series published in English and French in Hanoi by Xunhasaba (State Enterprise for the Export-Import of Books, Periodicals & Cultural Commodities).

Vinh's relatively harsh climate has made much of Nghe An and Ha Tinh provinces one of the most destitute regions in Vietnam. The peasants who can be seen begging along National Highway 1 at Ngang Pass to the south of Vinh are known to be so utterly destitute that even domestic travellers give them money.

History

Nghe An and neighbouring Ha Tinh provinces (they were once combined into a single province called Nghe Tinh) are famous for their revolutionary spirit. Both Phan Boi Chau (1867-1940) and Ho Chi Minh (1890-1969) were natives of Nghe An Province. The Nghe Tinh Uprising (1893-95) against the French was led by the scholar Phan Dinh Phung (1847-95). The Nghe Tinh Soviets Movement (1930-31) began with a series of workers' strikes and demonstrations encouraged by the newly formed Indochinese Communist Party; by the summer of 1930, peasant associations (or soviets) had seized power in some areas. The French moved swiftly to suppress the unrest, employing aircraft to attack crowds of demonstrators. The Ho Chi Minh Trail began in Nghe An Province, and much of the war matériel transported on the Ho Chi Minh Trail was shipped via the port of Vinh.

Vinh's recent history has not been the happiest. It was a pleasant citadel-city during colonial days but was destroyed in the early 1950s as a result of French aerial bombing and the Viet Minh's scorched-earth policy. Vinh was later devastated by a huge fire. To

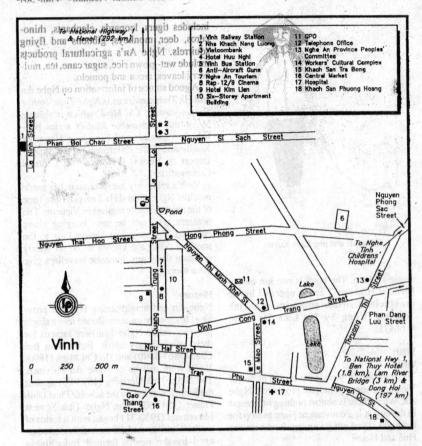

KEY

1 Vinh Railway Station
2 Nha Khach Nang Luong
3 Vietcombank
4 Hotel Huu Nghi
5 Vinh Bus Station
6 Anti-Aircraft Guns
7 Nghe An Tourism
8 Rap 12/9 Cinema
9 Hotel Kim Lien
10 Six-Storey Apartment Building
11 GPO
12 Telephone Office
13 Nghe An Province Peoples' Committee
14 Workers' Cultural Complex
15 Khach San Tra Bong
16 Central Market
17 Hospital
18 Khach San Phuong Hoang

Le Ninh Street

Phan Boi Chau Street

Nguyen Si Sach Street

Nguyen Phong Sac Street

Nguyen Thai Hoc Street

Le Hong Phong Street

To Nghe Tinh Childrens' Hospital

Pond

Lake

Trang Street

Phan Dang Luu Street

Dinh Cong

Trang

Lake

Ngu Hai Street

Vinh

0   250   500 m

Tran Phu Street

Gao Thang Street

Le Mao Street

Thuong Thi Street

To National Hwy 1, Ben Thuy Hotel (1.8 km), Lam River Bridge (3 km) & Dong Hoi (197 km)

Nguyen Du St

add icing on the cake, the US military obliterated the city in hundreds of air attacks and naval artillery bombardments from 1964 to 1972 which left only two buildings intact (the Americans paid a high price for the bombings – more US aircraft and pilots were shot down over Nghe An and Ha Tinh provinces than over any other part of North Vietnam).

After the war, Vinh was rebuilt with East German financial and technical assistance, which perhaps explains why the city's grim and rapidly dilapidating buildings suffer from a uniform lack of imagination.

Vinh's one salvation is its location on National Highway 1 almost exactly midway between Hué and Hanoi. Both foreign and Vietnamese travellers use Vinh as a convenient overnight stop, which benefits the hotel and restaurant business and gives small shopowners a chance to draw in customers.

Orientation

As National Highway 1 enters Vinh from the south, it crosses the mouth of the Lam River (Ca River), also known as Cua Hoi Estuary. Quang Trung St (which runs north-south) and Tran Phu St intersect one block north of

Vinh Central Market. Street address numbers are not used in Vinh.

Information

Tourist Offices The government-owned Nghe An Tourism (Cong Ty Du Lich Nghe An; ☎ 4692) is on Quang Trung St just to the north of Rap 12/9 cinema.

Phong Huong Dan Du Lich (☎ 4751) is a travel agent in the Hotel Kim Lien. This agent can even do international air-ticket reservations.

Money Vietcombank (Ngan Hang Ngoai Thuong Viet Nam; ☎ 2304) is at the corner of Le Loi and Nguyen Si Sach Sts.

Post & Telecommunications The post office is on Nguyen Thi Minh Khai St 300 metres north-west of Dinh Cong Trang St; it is open from 6.30 am to 9 pm.

International and domestic telephone calls can be made from the calling office (Cong Ty Dien Bao Dien Thoai), which is in a little building on Dinh Cong Trang St near the corner of Nguyen Thi Minh Khai St. The office, which is across the street from the Workers' Cultural Complex, is supposed to be open from 7 am to 9 pm. If no one is there, enquire at the cigarette stall next door or go into the telephone exchange building, which is across the field behind the calling office.

Emergency The general hospital is on the corner of Tran Phu St and Le Mao St.

Vinh Central Market

Vinh's main marketplace, Cho Vinh, is noteworthy for the limited selection of goods offered for sale. There are food stalls around the back. Vinh Central Market is at the end of Cao Thang St, which is the southern continuation of Quang Trung St.

Veterans' Vietnam Restoration Project Clinic

A building for surgery and physical therapy was built on the grounds of Nghe Tinh Children's Hospital in the fall of 1989 by a team from the Veterans' Vietnam Restoration

Project (based in Garberville, California) working alongside Vietnamese war veterans. The same group also constructed a medical clinic in Vung Tau. Nghe Tinh Children's Hospital (Benh Vien Nhi Nghe Tinh) is out Nguyen Phong Sac St (the continuation of Truong Thi St) and down a side street on the right (towards the south-east).

Workers' Cultural Complex

The Workers' Cultural Complex (Cau Lac Bo Cong Nhan), a huge structure at the corner of Le Mao St and Dinh Cong Trang St, is the centre of Vinh's cultural life. It includes a cinema, a theatre and a dancing hall in which concerts, plays, film screenings, dances and other events are held.

Anti-Aircraft Guns

Don't try to visit the field of anti-aircraft guns on Le Hong Phong St. It is not a museum dedicated to the glorious exploits of the people of Vinh in resisting the American imperialists. The guns, with their double barrels pointed skyward, are loaded and still ready to defend the city against aerial attack.

Birthplace of Ho Chi Minh

Kim Lien Village, where Ho Chi Minh was born in 1890, is 14 km nort-west of Vinh. The house in which he was born is maintained as a sacred shrine and can be visited. Nearby is a museum.

Beaches

Vinh is 15 km from the sea. Cua Lo Beach is 20 km from the city.

Places to Stay

There are plenty of hotels in Vinh, but only six are authorised to accept foreigners. Fortunately, the whole price range from budget to luxurious is covered.

The *Ben Thuy Hotel* (Khach San Ben Thuy; ☎ 4892) is on the south side of Vinh on Nguyen Du St (National Highway 1); 1.3 km towards the centre of Vinh from the bridge over the Lam River and 1.8 km towards the bridge from the intersection of Nguyen Du St and Truong Thi St. It's too far to walk from the railway station, but this is a very popular place with budget travellers who are travelling by. All rooms cost US$7. The hotel has a small restaurant.

Also on the south side of town is the *Khach San Phuong Hoang* on Nguyen Du St (National Highway 1). It's not the Hilton, but it's the cheapest in town at US$3 for a room with attached bath. Only cold water is available. The management seems to be very friendly.

Another budget hotel is the *Khach San Tra Bong* at the corner of Tran Phu and Le Mao Sts. All rooms have attached bath (but cold water) and cost US$5.

The *Nha Khach Nang Luong* is an old but friendly place near the intersection of Le Loi St and Phan Boi Chau St. This is the closest hotel to the railway station. Rooms with private bath (cold water) are US$8; with hot water it's US$10 and US$12.

The *Hotel Huu Nghi* is the second-largest in town. It's a big, glittering place with air-conditioning, hot water and in-house restaurant. Rooms cost US$20 to US$25. The hotel is on Le Loi St.

The *Hotel Kim Lien* is the largest hotel in Vinh and has everything; air-conditioning, hot water, moneychanger, travel agent, restaurant, massage services, the whole lot. All this luxury will cost you US$20 to US$30 for a double. The hotel is on Quang Trung St in the centre of town.

Places to Eat

There are a number of small restaurants on Le Ninh St just outside the gate to the railway station. The food stalls in Vinh Central Market are behind the main building.

Getting There & Away

Bus Vinh Bus Station (Ben Xe Vinh; ☎ 4127, 4924) is on Le Loi St about one km north of the Central Market; the ticket office is open from 4.30 am to 5 pm daily. Express buses to Buon Ma Thuot, Danang, Hanoi and Ho Chi Minh City depart every day at 5 am; express buses to Hanoi leave at other times

of the day as well. Non-express buses link Vinh with:

Bahai, Huong Son (Pho Chau), Cam Xuyen, Ky Anh, Cau Giat, Lat, Con Cuong, Muong Xen, Cua, Nghia Dan, Do Luong, Phuc Son, Dung, Pleiku (Playcu), Gia Lam, Que Phong, Hanoi, Quy Chau, Ha Tinh, Quy Hop, Hoa Binh, Trung Tam, Hué, Yen Thanh.

Train Vinh Railway Station (Ga Vinh; ☎ 4924) is one km west of the intersection of Le Loi and Phan Boi Chau Sts, which is 1.5 km north of the Central Market. The Reunification Express trains stop here. For ticket prices, see the Train section in the Getting Around chapter.

Car Road distances from Vinh are as follows:

Danang	468 km
Dong Hoi	197 km
Hanoi	292 km
Hué	363 km
Lao border	97 km
Thanh Hoa	139 km

National Highway 8, which begins in Vinh, crosses into Laos at 734-metre-high Keo Nua Pass.

Getting Around

There are relatively few passenger cyclos in Vinh because the people can't afford to ride them. To get around, you might try hiring an oversize cargo cyclo.

THANH HOA

THANH HÓA

Thanh Hoa is the capital of Thanh Hoa Province; in this region, National Highway 1 is lined with bomb craters, particularly near bridges and railway stations. There is a large and attractive church on the northern outskirts of town.

Thanh Hoa Province was the site of the Lam Son Uprising (1418-28), in which Vietnamese forces led by Le Loi (later Emperor Ly Thai To) expelled the Chinese and re-established the country's independence.

Muong and Red Tai (Thai) hill tribes live in the western part of the province.

Information

Thanh Hoa Tourism & Relations (Cong Ty Du Lich Va Giao Te Thanh Hoa; ☎ 52298, 52517) is the official government tourist authority for Thanh Hoa Province. The office is at 298 Quang Trung St.

Places to Stay

The *Khach San Thanh Hoa* is on the west side of National Highway 1 in the centre of town. Rooms cost US$5 and US$7. Don't mistake this place for the similarly named *Nha Khach Thanh Hoa* on the east side of the highway which does *not* accept foreigners.

Places to Eat

Soup shops, tea shops and a few restaurants can be found along National Highway 1, especially near the southern entrance to town.

Getting There & Away

Bus & Car Thanh Hoa city is 502 km from Hué, 139 km from Vinh and 153 km from Hanoi.

Train Thanh Hoa is a stop for the Reunification Express trains. For ticket prices, see the Train section in the Getting Around chapter.

SAM SON BEACHES
BIỂN SẦM SƠN

The two beaches at Sam Son, among the nicest in the north, are 16 km south-east of Thanh Hoa; they are a favourite vacation spot of Hanoi residents who can afford such luxuries. Near the bridge, which the US forces repeatedly bombed, are extensive fortifications and trenchworks. Accommodation ranges from basic bungalows to multi-storey hotels.

NINH BINH
NINH BÌNH

Ninh Binh is known to travellers mainly as a possible overnight stop on the way to Hanoi and a transit point to Hoa Lu. For information on Hoa Lu, see the chapter in this book called The North.

Places to Stay

There are two hotels, both on the west side of National Highway 1. The *Nha Hang Hoa Do* is both a restaurant and a hotel, and charges US$15 for a room. The *Khach San Hoa Lu* is nearby and also charges US$15.

Getting There & Away

Train Ninh Binh is a scheduled stop for the Reunification Express trains travelling between Hanoi and Ho Chi Minh City. For ticket prices, see the Train section in the Getting Around chapter.

Car Ninh Binh is 200 km north of Vinh, 61 km north of Thanh Hoa and 114 km south of Hanoi.

Hanoi
Hà Nội

A city of lakes, shaded boulevards and verdant public parks; where beggars fight over a plate of discarded noodles; where prosperous shopowners exemplify Vietnam's new economic reforms; the seat of power; where absolute power corrupts absolutely.

Hanoi (population 925,000), capital of the Socialist Republic of Vietnam, is different things to different people. Most foreigners on a short visit find Hanoi to be slow-paced, pleasant and even charming. Physically, it's a more attractive city than Ho Chi Minh City – there is less traffic, less noise, less pollution, more trees and more open space. Hanoi's centre is an architectural museum piece, its blocks of ochre buildings retaining the air of a provincial French town of the 1930s. The people of Hanoi are known for being more reserved – and at the same time more traditionally hospitable – than their southern compatriots.

No music! That's the big difference between Hanoi and the south. Where's the loud rock 'n roll, the schmaltzy top 10 hits?

Hanoi used to be notorious amongst travellers as a place to avoid. Many Western visitors (both backpackers and business people) have reported being harassed by the police, especially at the airport, where officials would arbitrarily detain and fine foreigners as they were trying to leave. This policy at last seems to have stopped, especially after severe diplomatic protests by Western embassies which have recently opened in Hanoi. It's also finally dawned on government officials that throwing foreigners into prison to extort money out of their families is not good for the tourist business, not to mention the country's image.

Getting business done in Hanoi is still more difficult than in the south, which is a major reason why the city, along with the rest of the north, is seeing less foreign investment. Resistance to reform is strongest amongst ageing officials. But attitudes are changing – geriatric revolutionaries in the prime of senility are being forceably retired. The younger generation – with no romantic attachment to the past – is only interested in the side of the bread which is buttered.

The first beneficiaries of the city's recent economic liberalisation have been the shop and restaurant owners. No longer is a shopping trip in Hanoi a journey to a large state department store specialising in empty shelves. The colour and liveliness has returned to the streets, buildings are being repaired and foreign companies are now looking to invest in joint-venture hotels. Hanoi, and the rest of the north, has great potential to develop export-oriented manufacturing industries – a potential as yet unrealised.

Whatever else Ho Chi Minh may have done, he created in north Vietnam a very effective police state. For four decades, the people of Hanoi and the north have suffered under a regime characterised by the ruthless exercise of police power; anonymous denunciations by a huge network of secret informers; the detention without trial of monks, priests, landowners and anyone else seen as a potential threat to the government; and the blacklisting of dissidents and their children and their children's children. This legacy of human rights violations has left its mark on the people of Hanoi, who seem complacent and even cowed compared to the dissatisfied and outspoken Saigonese. Perhaps they seem less discontented because the north has never experienced the war-time affluence US aid brought to the south; then again, the north has produced a steady haemorrhage of refugees.

Perhaps as a sign that the north is deter-

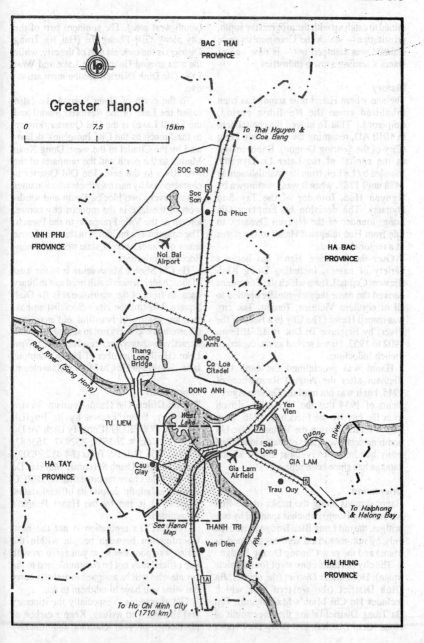

mined to catch up with the progressive south, prostitution – which the Communists once claimed was stamped out – is now one of Hanoi's leading growth industries.

History

The site where Hanoi now stands has been inhabited since the Neolithic period. Emperor Ly Thai To moved his capital here in 1010 AD, renaming the site Thang Long (City of the Soaring Dragon). Hanoi served as the capital of the Later Le Dynasty, founded by Le Loi, from its establishment in 1428 until 1788, when it was overthrown by Nguyen Hué, founder of the Tay Son Dynasty. The decision by Emperor Gia Long, founder of the Nguyen Dynasty, to rule from Hué relegated Hanoi to the status of a regional capital.

Over the centuries, Hanoi has borne a variety of names, including Dong Kinh (Eastern Capital), from which the Europeans derived the name they eventually applied to all of northern Vietnam, Tonkin. The city was named Hanoi (The City in a Bend of the River) by Emperor Tu Duc in 1831. From 1902 to 1953, Hanoi served as the capital of French Indochina.

Hanoi was proclaimed the capital of Vietnam after the August Revolution of 1945, but it was not until the Geneva Agreements of 1954 that the Viet Minh, driven from the city by the French in 1946, were able to return. During the Vietnam War, US bombing destroyed parts of Hanoi and killed many hundreds of civilians; almost all the damage has since been repaired.

Orientation

Hanoi sprawls along the banks of the Red River (Song Hong), which is spanned by two bridges, the old Long Bien Bridge (now used only by non-motorised vehicles and pedestrians) and the new Chuong Duong Bridge.

The city of Hanoi consists of four districts (quan): Hoan Kiem District (the centre); Ba Dinh District (the western area which includes Ho Chi Minh's Mausoleum); Hai Ba Trung District (along the river south of Hoan Kiem District); and Dong Da District

(south-west area). The southern part of the city along Giai Phong Rd (Hai Ba Trung District) is the tackiest part of the city, while the area around Hoan Kiem Lake and West Lake (Ba Dinh District) are the most attractive.

To the north of Hoan Kiem Lake (also called the Lake of the Restored Sword and the Small Lake) is the Old Quarter (known to the French as the Cité Indigène), delineated by the Citadel to the west, Dong Xuan Market to the north and the ramparts of the Red River to the east. The Old Quarter is characterised by narrow streets whose names change every two blocks. South and southwest of the lake is the modern city centre, known as the Ville Française to the French. The colonial-era buildings in this area house many of Hanoi's hotels, state stores and non-Socialist embassies.

Ho Chi Minh's Mausoleum is to the west of the Citadel, which is still used as a military base. In front of the mausoleum is Ba Dinh Square. Most of the city's Socialist embassies are nearby in beautiful old mansions (Western late-comers had to settle for far less attractive embassy quarters elsewhere). West Lake (Ho Tay), another of Hanoi's famous lakes, is north of Ho Chi Minh's Mausoleum.

Information

Tourist Office The Hanoi Tourism Service Company, better known by its English acronym TOSERCO (Cong Ty Dich Vu Du Lich Ha Noi; ☎ 263541, 252937, 263687; telex 411535 TLHT-VT; fax (84-4) 259209), is at 8 To Hien Thanh St (corner Mai Hac De St). Travellers have reported that TOSERCO is often unhelpful despite its official status; TOSERCO is run by the Hanoi People's Committee.

TOSERCO's reputation is not the best. Coordination between people within the office is so poor that what you agree on with one official may not be communicated to the people who will be assigned to actually carry out what you have hired them to do.

Get *everything* – especially the itinerary and all costs – in writing. Keep a carbon or photocopy of your contract and itinerary with you at all times; if they ask to see it, make sure to keep a copy for yourself.

You should also insist upon paying no more than one-third of your bill as a down payment and the balance at the end of the trip. Unfortunately, travellers' experiences indicate that during the tour, you may need the added bit of leverage which you'll lack if you're all paid up.

Travel Agencies There are plenty of travel agencies in Hanoi, both government and private, which can provide cars, book air tickets and extend your visa. Some of these places charge the same as TOSERCO and Vietnam Tourism, while others are only half the price. We've also heard disturbing reports of incompetent bunglers – especially some cafes – *losing* travellers' passports! Some agencies which have been recommended by travellers for low prices and good service include Anne Tourist Office, Ecco Vietnam, Especen Tourist Company, Oscan Enterprises and Pacific Tours. However, remember that good places can go bad, bad places can go bankrupt and new ones open – ask other travellers about their experiences. And finally, always compare prices before you put down the cash. The line-up of travel agencies includes:

Anne Tourist Office
 Dong Do Hotel, 27 Tong Duy Tan St (☎ 233275)
Ecco Vietnam
 50A Ba Trieu (☎ 254615)
Especen Tourist Company
 79 Hang Trong (☎ 266856)
Hanoi Tourism
 (Cong Ty Du Lich Ha Noi) 18 Ly Thuong Kiet St (☎ 254209, 257886; telex 411275 CTSC-VT; fax (84-4) 256418, 252800)
Oscan Enterprises
 60 Nguyen Du St (☎ 252690, 265859; fax (84-4) 257634)
Pacific Tours
 58B Tran Nhan Tong St (☎ 267942; fax (84-4) 254437)
Vietnam Tourism
 (Tong Cong Ty Du Lich Viet Nam), 54 Nguyen Du St (☎ 257080, 252986, 255963)
 branch office: 30A Ly Thuong Kiet St (☎ 255552, 264148; telex 411272 TCDL-VT; fax (84-4) 257583)

Vietnam Trade Union Tourism
 (Du Lich Tong Lien Doan Lao Dong Viet Nam) 65 Quan Su St (☎ 254112, 259508; telex 412270 TOCODO-VT)
Vung Tau Con Dao International Tourist
 136 Hang Trong St
Youth Tourism Centre
 (Trung Tam Du Lich Thanh Nien) 70B Hoang Hoa Tham (☎ 257112, 256987, 256989)

Money The Foreign Trade Bank (Ngan Hang Ngoai Thuong Viet Nam) is off Ly Thai To St, just north-east of the Government Guest House. Here it is possible to exchange US dollar-denominated travellers' cheques for US dollars cash. The commission charged for cashing travellers' cheques is 1½%. You can also change major hard currencies. Cash advances for Visa, Mastercard and JCB cards are possible to arrange.

Vietcombank has opened a new branch on the corner of Tran Binh Trong and Nguyen Du Sts, near Thien Quang Lake.

Jewellery shops near the shoe market (at the north-east corner of Hoan Kiem Lake) are the best place to seek the black market. Now that the bank rate is more or less in line with what you can get on the black market, it may not be worth the risk to squeeze that extra few percent from your dollars.

Post & Telecommunications The GPO (Buu Dien Trung Vong; ☎ 257036, fax 253525), which occupies a full city block facing Hoan Kiem Lake, is at 75 Dinh Tien Hoang St (between Dinh Le St and Le Thach St). The entrance in the middle of the block leads to the postal services windows where you can send letters, pick up domestic packages and purchase philatelic items; the postal services section is open from 6.30 am to 8 pm.

The same entrance leads to the telex, telegram and domestic telephone office (☎ 255918), which is to the left as you enter the building. Telex and domestic telephone services are available from 6.30 am to 8 pm; telegrams can be sent 24 hours a day.

International telephone calls can be made

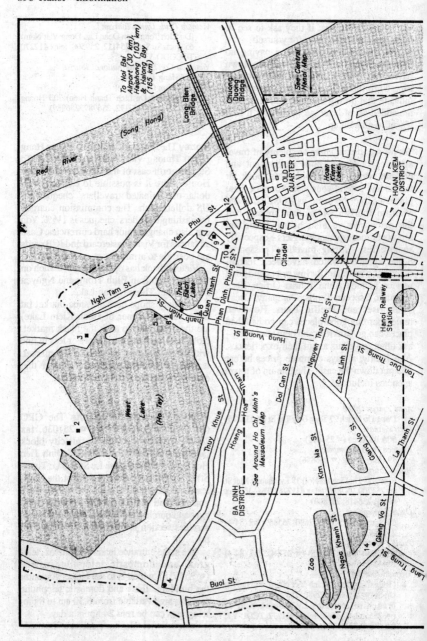

Wreckage of US B52, Hanoi (LG)

Top Left: One Pillar Pagoda, Hanoi (RS) Top Right: Tran Quoc Pagoda, Hanoi (RS)
Middle: Junk, Halong Bay (PS)
Bottom Left: Rickshaw, Hanoi (RM) Bottom Right: Flower Market, Haiphong (RS)

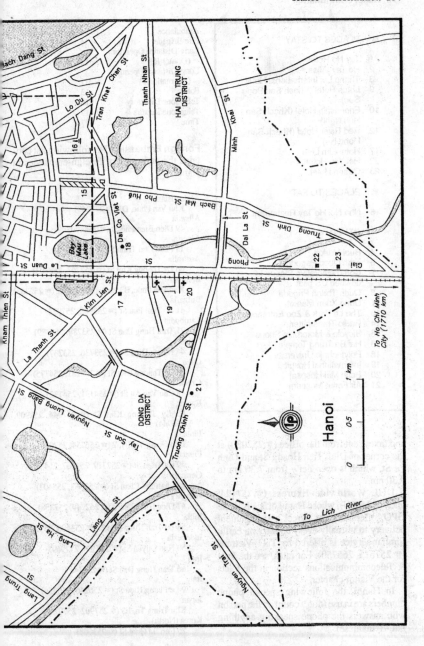

■ PLACES TO STAY

1 Tay Ho Hotel
2 Ho Tay Villas
3 Thang Loi International Hotel
9 Lotus Hotel (Khach San Bong Sen)
10 Friendship Hotel (Khach San Huu Nghi)
12 Red River Hotel (Khach San Hong Ha)
17 Hotel Kim Lien
22 Hai Yen Hotel
23 Queen Hotel

▼ PLACES TO EAT

5 Nha Noi Ho Tay Restaurant

OTHER

4 Buoi Market
6 Tran Quoc Pagoda
7 Commemorative Plaque to downed US pilot
8 Quan Thanh Pagoda
11 Dong Xuan Market
13 Thu Le Park & Zoo Entrance
14 Radio Transmitter
15 Bicycle & Motorbike Shops
16 Hai Ba Trung Temple
18 Polytechnic University
19 International Hospital
20 Bach Mai Hospital
21 Air Force Museum

Ambulance	15
Fire Brigade	14
Long-Distance Operator (Domestic)	10
Long-Distance Operator (International)	11
Police	13
Telephone Directory	16
Telephone Repairs	19
Time	17

Foreign Embassies The following list contains the addresses of foreign embassies in Hanoi:

Afghanistan
    Khu Van Phuc, D1 (☎ 253249)
Albania
    49 Dien Bien Phu St (☎ 254490)
Algeria
    13 Phan Chu Trinh St (☎ 253865)
Australia
    66 Ly Thuong Kiet St (☎ 252763, 252703)
Belgium
    Khu Van Phuc, B3, suites 201 & 202 (☎ 252263)
Bulgaria
    41-43 Tran Phu St (☎ 252908, 257923)
Cambodia
    71 Tran Hung Dao St (☎ 253788, 253789)
China
    46 Hoang Dieu St (☎ 253736, 253737)
Cuba
    65 Ly Thuong Kiet St (☎ 252281, 254775)
Czech
    13 Chu Van An St (☎ 254131, 254132)
Egypt
    85 Ly Thuong Kiet St (☎ 252944, 252909, 256944)
Finland
    B3b Giang Vo, F1, 2 (☎ 256754, 257096)
France
    49 Ba Trieu St (☎ 252719, 254367, 254368)
Germany
    25 Phan Boi Chau St (☎ 253663, 255402)
Hungary
    47 Dien Bien Phu St (☎ 252748, 252858)
India
    58-60 Tran Hung Dao St (☎ 253406, 255975)
Indonesia
    50 Ngo Quyen St (☎ 253353, 257969)
Iraq
    66 Tran Hung Dao St (☎ 254141)
Italy
    9 Le Phung Hieu St (☎ 256246, 256256)
Japan
    Khu Trung Tu, E3 (☎ 257902, 257924)
Korea (North)
    25 Cao Ba Quat St (☎ 253008)

and faxes sent from the office (☎ 252030) at the corner of Dinh Tien Hoang St and Dinh Le St, which is open daily from 7.30 am to 9.30 pm.

DHL Worldwide Express (☎ 257124; telex 4324 HN), whose Hanoi office is in the GPO, offers express parcel and document delivery to virtually every country on earth. Similar service is offered by TNT Vietrans (☎ 257615, 265750). For rates, see the Post & Telecommunications section in the Facts for the Visitor chapter.

In Hanoi, the following special phone numbers are in use (don't count on the person who answers the phone speaking anything but Vietnamese):

Laos
22 Tran Binh Trong St (☎ 254576). The consular section is on the 2nd floor of an unmarked yellow building opposite the FAO office at 40 Quang Trung St (☎ 252588)

Libya
Khu Van Phuc, A3 (☎ 253371)

Malaysia
Khu Van Phuc, A3 (☎ 253379)

Mongolia
39 Tran Phu St (☎ 252151, 253009)

Myanmar (Burma)
Khu Van Phuc, A3 (☎ 253369)

Netherlands
53 Ly Thai To St

Nicaragua
Khu Trung Tu, E1 (☎ 262214, 262216)

Palestine
Khu Trung Tu, E4 (☎ 252947)

Philippines
Khu Trung Tu, E1 (☎ 257948, 257873)

Poland
3 Chua Mot Cot St (☎ 252027, 253728, 252207)

Romania
5 Le Hong Phong St (☎ 252014)

Russia
58 Tran Phu St (☎ 254631, 254632)

Sweden
So 2, Duong 358, Khu Van Phuc, Quan Ba Dinh (☎ 254824, 254825)

Thailand
Khu Trung Tu, E1 (☎ 256043, 256053, 262644)

UK
16 Ly Thuong Kiet St (☎ 252349, 252710)

Yugoslavia (Serbia)
29B Tran Hung Dao St (☎ 252343, 253677)

Bookshops The Thong Nhat Book Store is near the Hotel Pullman Metropole on the corner of Ngo Quyen and Trang Tien Sts. It has a limited selection of books in Western languages published in Vietnam as well as postage stamps, posters, greeting cards and Soviet-produced art books and propaganda treatises. The Thong Nhat Book Store is open daily from 8 am to noon and 1 to 8.30 pm except on Mondays and Thursdays, when the store closes at 4.30 pm.

The Foreign Language Bookshop (☎ 257043) at 61 Trang Tien St is open daily from 8 to 11.30 am and 2 to 4.30 pm; it has Soviet art books and a lot of material in Russian. Similar published items are available at the State Bookshop (☎ 254282), at 40 Trang Tien St. It is open Monday to Saturday from 8 to 11.30 am and 2 to 8 pm except on Mondays and Thursdays, when it closes at 5 pm.

The State Enterprise for the Import & Export of Books & Periodicals (☎ 254067), better known by its acronym Xunhasaba, has a shop at 32 Hai Ba Trung St. Xunhasaba publishes the English and French-language *Vietnamese Studies* series. This is one of the best places to look for unusual books.

The office of the Foreign Languages Publishing House (☎ 253841) is at 46 Tran Hung Dao St. The offices of the State Company for the Distribution of Foreign Language Books (☎ 255376) are at 66 Trang Tien St.

Libraries The National Library (☎ 252643) is at 31 Trang Thi St; the Technical & Social Sciences Library (☎ 252345) is at 26 Ly Thuong Kiet St; the Army Library (☎ 258101) is on Ly Nam St.

Maps The Tourist Map *(Ban Do Du Lich)* of Hanoi, a masterpiece of four-colour printing, is widely available from bookshops (even in Ho Chi Minh City).

Emergency Both the French and Swedish embassies have physicians attached to their staffs.

The International Hospital (Benh Vien Quoc Te; ☎ 243728), where foreigners are usually referred, is on the western side of Giai Phong St a bit south of the Polytechnic University (Dai Hoc Bach Khoa). To get there, take bus Nos 4, 7 or 15 from the city centre. In winter, the hospital's outpatient clinic is open from 8 am to 12.30 pm and 1 to 4.30 pm; in summer, it is open from 7.30 am to noon and 1 to 4.30 pm. The staff speak English and French and are very helpful. There is an on-site pharmacy. Westerners must pay in US dollars.

Other hospitals in Hanoi include the Bach Mai Hospital (Benh Vien Bach Mai; ☎ 254385) on Giai Phong St near the International Hospital; the K Hospital (☎ 252143) at 43 Quan Su St; the E Hospital (☎ 254139) in Co Nhue (the Institute of Ophthalmology) at 38 Tran Nhan Tong St;

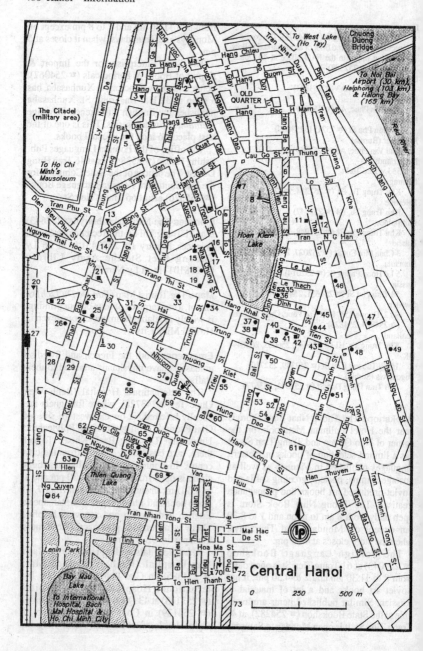

Central Hanoi

■ PLACES TO STAY

5	Phung Hung Hotel
10	Nam Phuong Hotel
11	Energy Service Centre
12	Binh Minh Hotel & China Southern Airlines
14	Dong Do Hotel
16	Phu Gia Hotel
21	Hoan Kiem Guest House
22	Dong Loi Hotel
24	Rose & Saigon Hotels
28	Khach San 30-4
29	Capital Hotel
38	Sophia Hotel & Restaurant
40	Bodega Café & Guesthouse
42	Hotel Bac Nam
43	Dan Chu Hotel
45	Hotel Pullman Metropole (Thong Nhat Hotel)
52	Hoa Binh Hotel
61	Hoan Kiem Hotel
67	Boss Hotel

▼ PLACES TO EAT

1	Piano Restaurant
2	Cha Ca Restaurant
3	Chau Thanh Restaurant
4	Restaurant 22
7	Thuy Ta Restaurant
9	Bittek Restaurant (Le Français)
13	Food Stalls
17	Cafe
20	Huong Sen Restaurant
40	Bodega Café
50	Small Restaurants
53	Small Restaurants
71	Restaurant 202
72	Hoa Binh Restaurant

OTHER

6	Shoe Market

8	Ngoc Son Temple & The Huc Bridge
15	St Joseph Cathedral
18	Palace Restaurant & Dancing
19	Aeroflot Office
23	German Embassy
25	Australian Embassy
26	Egyptian Embassy
27	Railway Station
30	Ambassadors' Pagoda
31	'Hanoi Hilton' Prison
32	19th December Market
33	National Library
34	Vietnam Airlines International Office & Air France
35	GPO & DHL
36	International Telephone Office
37	Traditional Medicines Pharmacy
39	State General Department Store
41	Foreign Language Bookshop
44	Thong Nhat Book Store
46	Foreign Trade Bank
47	Revolutionary Museum
48	Municipal Theatre
49	History Museum
51	Algerian Embassy
54	Indonesian Embassy
55	Vietcochamber
56	Indian Embassy
57	Iraqi Embassy
58	Immigration Police
59	Cambodian Embassy
60	French Embassy
62	Vietcombank
63	Lao Embassy
64	Kim Lien Bus Station
65	Lao Embassy Consular Section
66	FAO Office
68	Vietnam Air Lines Domestic Booking Office
69	Japanese Embassy
70	TOSERCO
73	Bicycle & Motorbike Shops

the Traditional Medicine Hospital (Y Hoc Dan Toc; ☎ 255662) at 29 Nguyen Binh Khiem St; the Vietnam-Germany Friendship Hospital (Huu Nghi Viet Duc; ☎ 253531) on Trang Thi St; and the Vietnam-Soviet Friendship Hospital (Huu Nghi Viet Xo; ☎ 252231) on Tran Khanh Du.

If you need a dentist, ask at the Thang Loi Hotel or Thang Long Hotel.

Visas At some point, the Interior Ministry decided to try out more liberal policies on individual travel but their policies keep changing. This makes it difficult to predict the kind of a reception your requests for visa extensions will receive in Hanoi, but at the time of this writing things were looking good.

The Immigration Police Office is at 87

Tran Hung Dao St; it is open Monday to Saturday from 8 to 11 am and 1 to 5 pm. Travellers have recently reported that this office is being cooperative (who says miracles don't happen?) and is being generous with visa extensions and exit visas (to cross by train into China). A few years ago this same office was responsible for expelling one of our Lonely Planet writers from the country.

Business people may be able to extend their visas through the Chamber of Commerce, Vietcochamber.

TOSERCO issues visa extensions to individual travellers with tourist visas. It charges US$20 for each visa extension. Visa extensions are normally granted for two weeks, and there seems to be no limit on how many times you can extend if you keep paying. Paperwork done through TOSERCO takes two days to clear. TOSERCO can also arrange for cars, guides and hotels.

Useful Organisations The head office of Vietcochamber (☎ 252961, 253023; telex 411257 VIETCO; fax (84-4) 256446), the Chamber of Commerce & Industry of Vietnam, is at 33 Ba Trieu St. The Trade Service Company, which is attached to Vietcochamber, also has its offices here. It can arrange business trips, assist business people with bureaucratic formalities (visa extensions, etc), book hotel accommodation anywhere in the country, arrange land transport of all sorts and provide translation services.

Business travellers might want to talk to the Vietnam Trade Information Centre (☎ 263227, 264038), 46 Ngo Quyen St.

The Ministry of Foreign Affairs is at 1 Ton That Dam St, near Ho Chi Minh's Mausoleum. English-speaking personnel can always be found at the North America Department (☎ 257279, 258201, extension 314 or 312). The Foreign Press Centre of the Ministry of Foreign Affairs (☎ 254697) is at 10 Le Phung Hieu St.

The International Relations Department of the Ministry of Information (☎ 253152; telex 4532 VNRT VT) is at 58 Quan Su St.

Aid Organisations There are a number of foreign aid organisations with offices in Hanoi. These include:

FAO (TC Luong Thuc Va Nong Nghiep)
  3 Nguyen Gia Thieu St (☎ 257208, 257239)
ICRC (UB Chu Thap Do Quoc Te)
  Hotel Pullman Metropole, 15 Ngo Quyen St (☎ 254454)
OMS
  Khu Van Phuc – A1 (☎ 257901, 252148)
PAM
  27-29 Phan Boi Chau St (☎ 257495, 257318, 254254)
UNDP (Chuong Trinh Cua LHQ Ve Phat Trien)
  27-29 Phan Boi Chau St, which is at the corner of Ly Thuong Kiet St (☎ 257495, 254254, 257318)
UNFPA (UN Fund for Population Control; Quy LHQ Ve Hoat Dong Dan So)
  Khu Giang Vo – Khoi 3 (☎ 254763)
UNHCR (Cao Uy LHQ Ve Nguoi Ti Nan)
  60 Nguyen Thai Hoc St (☎ 257871, 256785)
UNICEF (Quy Nhi Dong LHQ)
  72 Ly Thuong Kiet St, which is next to the Australian embassy (☎ 253440, 254222, 252109)
UNIDO (UN Industrial Development Organisation)
  27-29 Phan Boi Chau St, in the UNDP compound (☎ 257495, 257318, 254254)
WFP (World Food Programme; Chuong Trinh Luong Thuc The Gioi)
  27-29 Phan Boi Chau St, in the UNDP compound (☎ 257495, 257318, 254254)

Lakes, Temples & Pagodas
One Pillar Pagoda Hanoi's famous One Pillar Pagoda (Chua Mot Cot) was built by the Emperor Ly Thai Tong, who ruled from 1028 to 1054. According to the annals, the heirless emperor dreamed that he had met the Quan The Am Bo Tat (Goddess of Mercy) who, while seated on a lotus flower, handed him a male child. Ly Thai Tong then married a young peasant girl he met by chance and had a son and heir by her. To express his gratitude for this event, he constructed the One Pillar Pagoda in 1049.

The One Pillar Pagoda, built of wood on a stone pillar 1.25 metres in diameter, is designed to resemble a lotus blossom, symbol of purity, rising out of a sea of sorrow. One of the last acts of the French before quitting Hanoi in 1954 was to destroy the One Pillar Pagoda; the structure was rebuilt by the new government. The One Pillar Pagoda is on Ong Ich Kiem St near Ho Chi Minh's Mausoleum.

Dien Huu Pagoda The entrance to Dien Huu Pagoda is a few metres from the staircase of the One Pillar Pagoda. This small pagoda, which surrounds a garden courtyard, is one of the most delightful in Hanoi. The old wood and ceramic statues on the altar are very different to those common in the south. An elderly monk can often be seen performing acupuncture on the front porch of the pagoda.

Tours of Ho Chi Minh's Mausoleum end up at the One Pillar Pagoda.

Temple of Literature The Temple of Literature (Van Mieu) was founded in 1070 – four years after the Norman invasion of England – by Emperor Ly Thanh Tong, who dedicated it to Confucius (in Vietnamese, Khong Tu) in order to honour scholars and men of literary accomplishment. The temple constitutes a rare example of well-preserved traditional Vietnamese architecture.

Vietnam's first university was established here in 1076 to educate the sons of mandarins. In 1484, Emperor Le Thanh Tong ordered that steles be erected in the temple premises recording the names, places of birth and achievements of men who received doctorates *(Thai Hoc Sinh)* in each triennial examination, beginning in 1442. Though 116 examinations were held between 1442 and 1778, when the practice was discontinued, only 82 stelae are extant. In 1802, Emperor Gia Long transferred the National University to his new capital, Hué. Major repairs were last carried out here in 1920 and 1956.

The Temple of Literature consists of five courtyards divided by walls. The central pathways and gates between courtyards were reserved for the king. The walkways on one side were for the use of administrative mandarins; those on the other side were for military mandarins.

The main entrance is preceded by a gate on which an inscription requests that visitors dismount their horses before entering. Khue Van Pavilion, which is at the far side of the second courtyard, was constructed in 1802 and is considered a fine example of Vietnamese architecture. The 82 stelae, considered the most precious artefacts in the temple, are arrayed to either side of the third enclosure; each stele sits on a stone tortoise.

The Temple of Literature is two km west of Hoan Kiem Lake. The complex, which is 350 by 70 metres, is bounded by Nguyen Thai Hoc St, Tong Due Thang St, Quoc Tu Giam St and Van Mieu St. It is open from 8.30 to 11.30 am and 1.30 to 4.30 pm Tuesday to Sunday; the entrance fee is US$0.10. There is a small gift shop inside the temple.

Hoan Kiem Lake Hoan Kiem Lake is an enchanting body of water right in the heart of Hanoi. Legend has it that in the mid-15th century, Heaven gave Emperor Ly Thai To (Le Loi) a magical sword which he used to drive the Chinese out of Vietnam. One day after the war, while out boating, he came upon a giant golden tortoise swimming on the surface of the water; the creature grabbed the sword and disappeared into the depths of the lake. Since that time, the lake has been known as Ho Hoan Kiem (Lake of the Restored Sword) because the tortoise restored the sword to its divine owners.

The tiny Tortoise Pagoda, topped with a red star, is on an islet in the middle of the lake; it is often used as an emblem of Hanoi. Every morning around 6 am, local residents can be seen around Hoan Kiem Lake doing their traditional morning exercises, jogging and playing badminton.

Ngoc Son Temple Ngoc Son (Jade Mountain) Temple, founded in the 18th century, is on an island in the northern part of Hoan Kiem Lake. Surrounded by water and shaded by trees, it is a delightfully quiet place to rest. The temple is dedicated to the scholar Van Xuong, General Tran Hung Dao (who defeated the Mongols in the 13th century) and La To, patron saint of physicians.

Ngoc Son Temple is reached via wooden The Huc (Rising Sun) Bridge, painted red, which was constructed in 1885. To the left of the gate stands an obelisk whose top is shaped like a paintbrush. The temple is open daily from 8 am to 5 pm; the entrance fee is US$0.10.

West Lake Two legends explain the origins of West Lake (Ho Tay), which covers an area of five sq km. According to one, West Lake was created when the Dragon King drowned an evil nine-tailed fox in his lair, which was in a forest on this site. Another legend relates that in the 11th century, a Vietnamese Buddhist monk, Khong Lo, rendered a great service to the emperor of China, who rewarded him with a vast quantity of bronze from which he cast a huge bell. The sound of the bell could be heard all the way to China, where the Golden Buffalo Calf, mistaking the ringing for its mother's call, ran southward, trampling on the site of Ho Tay and turning it into a lake.

West Lake, also known as the Lake of Mist and the Big Lake, was once ringed with magnificent palaces and pavilions. These were destroyed in the course of various feudal wars. The circumference of West Lake is about 13 km.

Tran Quoc Pagoda is on the shore of West Lake just off Thanh Nien St, which divides West Lake from Truc Bach Lake. A stele here dating from 1639 tells the history of this site. The pagoda was rebuilt in the 15th century and in 1842. There are a number of monks' funerary monuments in the garden.

There are already a number of luxurious villas around West Lake, and you can expect more soon. Foreign investors see this as a likely spot for hotel development and are falling over each other to sign joint-venture agreements so the facilities can be completed before the expected floodtide of tourists arrives.

Truc Bach Lake Truc Bach (White Silk) Lake is separated from West Lake by Thanh

Nien St, which is lined with flame trees. In the 18th century, the Trinh Lords built a palace on this site; it was later turned into a reformatory for deviant royal concubines, who were condemned to weave a very fine white silk.

Quan Thanh Pagoda (also called Tran Vo Temple) is on the shore of Truc Bach Lake near the intersection of Thanh Nein St and Quan Thanh St. The pagoda, shaded by huge trees, was established during the Ly Dynasty (ruled 1010 to 1225) and was dedicated to Tran Vo (God of the North), whose symbols of power are the tortoise and the snake. A bronze statue and bell here date from 1677.

Ambassadors' Pagoda The Ambassadors' Pagoda (Quan Su; ☎ 252427) is the official centre of Buddhism in Hanoi, attracting quite a crowd – mostly old women – on holidays. During the 17th century, there was a guesthouse here for the ambassadors of Buddhist countries. Today, there are about a dozen monks and nuns at the Ambassadors' Pagoda. Next to the pagoda is a store selling Buddhist ritual objects.

The Ambassadors' Pagoda is at 73 Quan Su St (between Ly Thuong Kiet and Tran Hung Dao Sts); it is open to the public every day from 7.30 to 11.30 am and 1.30 to 5.30 pm.

Hai Ba Trung Temple The Hai Ba Trung Temple, founded in 1142, is two km south of Hoan Kiem Lake on Tho Lao St. A statue here shows the two Trung sisters (1st century AD) kneeling with their arms raised, as if to address a crowd. Some people say the statue shows the sisters, who had been proclaimed queens of the Vietnamese, about to dive into a river in order to drown themselves, which they are said to have done rather than surrender following their defeat at the hands of the Chinese.

Museums
In addition to the usual two-hour lunch break, it's worth knowing that almost all of Hanoi's museums are closed on Mondays.

History Museum The History Museum (Bao Tang Lich Su), once the museum of the École Française d'Extrême Orient, is one block east of the Municipal Theatre at 1 Pham Ngu Lao St. The building, constructed of reinforced concrete, was completed in 1930.

Exhibits include artefacts from Vietnam's prehistory (Palaeolithic and Neolithic periods); proto-Vietnamese civilisations (1st and 2nd millennia BC); the Dong Son Civilisation (7th century BC to 3rd century AD); the Oc-Eo (Funan) culture of the Mekong Delta (1st to 6th century AD); the Indianised kingdom of Champa (1st to 15th century); the Khmer kingdoms; various Vietnamese dynasties and their resistance to Chinese attempts at domination; the struggle against the French; and the history of the Communist Party.

Army Museum The Army Museum (Bao Tang Quan Doi) is on Dien Bien Phu St; it is open from 7.30 to 11.30 am only daily except Mondays. Outside, Soviet and Chinese weaponry supplied to the North are on display alongside French and US-made weapons captured in the Franco-Viet Minh War and the Vietnam War. The centrepiece is a Soviet-built MiG-21 jet fighter triumphant amidst the wreckage of French aircraft downed at Dien Bien Phu and a US F-111. The displays include scale models of various epic battles from Vietnam's long military history, including Dien Bien Phu and the capture of Saigon.

Next to the Army Museum is the hexagonal Flag Tower, which has become one of the symbols of the city. It is part of a Vauban-style citadel constructed by Emperor Gia Long (ruled 1802-19).

Air Force Museum This is one of the larger museums in Vietnam and, though seldom visited by foreigners, it's very worthwhile.

Many of the museum's exhibits are outdoors. This includes a number of Soviet MIG fighters, reconnaissance planes, helicopters and anti-aircraft equipment. Inside the museum hall are other weapons including

mortars, machine guns and some US-made bombs (hopefully defused). There is a partially truncated MIG with a ladder – you are permitted to climb up into the cockpit and have your photo taken. The museum has other war memorabilia including paintings of obvious Soviet design and portraits of Ho Chi Minh.

The Air Force Museum is on Truong Chinh St in the Dong Da District (south-west part of the city). From the railway station it's almost five km, a rather long cyclo ride.

Ho Chi Minh Museum The museum is divided into two sections, 'Past' and 'Future'. You start in the past and move to the future by walking in a clockwise direction downwards through the museum, starting at the right-hand side once at the top of the stairs. The displays are very modern and all have a message (eg peace, happiness, freedom, etc).

It's probably worth taking an English-speaking guide since some of the symbolism is hard to figure out (did Ho Chi Minh have a cubist period?). The 1958 Ford Edsel bursting through the wall (an American commercial failure to symbolise America's military failure) is a knockout.

The museum is the huge cement structure next to Ho Chi Minh's Mausoleum. Photography is forbidden. Upon entering, all bags and cameras must be left at reception.

Fine Arts Museum The building housing the Fine Arts Museum (Bao Tang My Thuat; ☎ 252830) served as the Ministry of Information under the French. It continues its propaganda function today: the museum's exhibits consist almost exclusively of politically correct folk art, sculpture, engravings and lacquerware by contemporary artists.

Most of the works on display are revolutionary in style and content, depicting heroic figures waving red flags, children with rifles, a wounded soldier joining the Communist Party, innumerable tanks and weaponry, and grotesque Americans. One lacquerware work depicts artillery pieces being hauled up a mountainside. Upstairs are a few examples of traditional crafts along with an incredibly intricate embroidery of Ho Chi Minh reading.

The Fine Arts Museum is at 66 Nguyen Thai Hoc St (corner Cao Ba Quai St), which is across the street from the back wall of the Temple of Literature; it is open from 8 am to noon and 1.30 to 4 pm Tuesday to Sunday.

Revolutionary Museum The Revolutionary Museum (Bao Tang Cach Mang) at 25 Tong Dan St presents the history of the Vietnamese Revolution.

Independence Museum The house at 48 Hang Ngang St (north of Hoan Kiem Lake in the Old Quarter), in which Ho Chi Minh drafted Vietnam's Declaration of Independence in 1945, has been turned into a museum.

Ho Chi Minh's Mausoleum

In the tradition of Lenin and Stalin before him and Mao after him, the final resting place of Ho Chi Minh is a glass sarcophagus set deep in the bowels of a monumental edifice that has become a site of pilgrimage. Ho Chi Minh's Mausoleum – built despite the fact that in his will, Ho requested to be cremated – was constructed between 1973 and 1975 of native materials gathered from all over Vietnam; the roof and peristyle are said to evoke either a traditional communal house or a lotus flower – to many tourists it looks like a cold concrete cubicle with columns. While reviewing parades and ceremonies taking place on the grassy expanses of Ba Dinh Square, high-ranking party and government leaders stand in front of the mausoleum.

Ho Chi Minh's Mausoleum is open to the public on Tuesday, Wednesday, Thursday and Saturday mornings from 8 to 11 am; on Sundays and holidays, it is open from 7.30 to 11.30 am. The mausoleum is closed for two months a year (usually from September to early November) while Ho Chi Minh's embalmed corpse is in Russia for maintenance.

Photography is permitted outside the building but not inside. All visitors must register and check their bags and cameras at a reception hall on Chua Mot Cot St; if possible, bring your passport for identification. Soundtracks for a 20-minute video about Ho Chi Minh are available in Vietnamese, English, French, Khmer, Lao, Russian and Spanish.

Honour guards will accompany you as you march single-file from near reception to the mausoleum entrance. Inside the building, more guards wearing snowy white bleached military uniforms are stationed at intervals of five paces, giving an eerily authoritarian aspect to the macabre spectacle of the embalmed, helpless body with its wispy white hair. The whole place has a spooky 'sanitised for your protection' atmosphere.

The following rules are strictly applied to all visitors to the mausoleum:

- People wearing shorts, tank-tops, etc will not be admitted.
- Nothing (including day packs and cameras) may be taken into the mausoleum.
- A respectful demeanour must be maintained at all times.
- For obvious reasons of decorum, photography is absolutely prohibited inside the mausoleum.
- It is forbidden to put your hands in your pockets.
- Hats must be taken off inside the mausoleum building. Although the rules do not explicitly say so, it is suggested that you don't ask the guards 'Is he dead'?

After exiting from the mausoleum, the tour will pass by the Presidential Palace, constructed in 1906 as the Palace of the Governor General of Indochina; it is now used for official receptions. Ho Chi Minh's house, built of the finest wooden materials in 1958, is next to a carp-filled pond. Just how much time Ho actually spent here is questionable – the house would have made a good target for US bombers had it been suspected that Ho could be found here.

Nearby is what was once Hanoi's botanical garden, now a park. The tour ends up at the One Pillar Pagoda (see the Lakes, Temples & Pagodas section earlier). If you're lucky, you'll catch the 'Changing of the Guard' outside Ho's Mausoleum – the

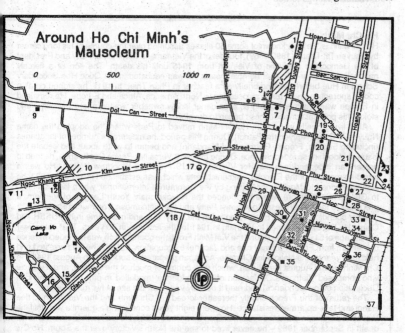

Around Ho Chi Minh's Mausoleum

0   500   1000 m

■ PLACES TO STAY

9   La Thanh Hotel
13 Giang Vo Hotel
14 Thang Long Hotel
30 Hai Yen Mini-Hotel
33 Mai Anh Hotel
34 Dong Loi Mini Hotel
35 Sao Mai Hotel

▼ PLACES TO EAT

11 Restaurant 79
15 Dong Do Restaurant
18 Phuong Nam Restaurant

    OTHER

1   Presidential Palace
2   Ho Chi Minh's Mausoleum
3   Ba Dinh Square
4   National Assembly Building
5   One Pillar Pagoda & Dien Huu
    Pagoda

6   Ho Chi Minh Museum
7   Reception for Ho Chi Minh's Mau-
    soleum
8   Ministry of Foreign Affairs
10 Belgian, Malaysian, Myanmar &
    Swedish Embassies
12 Finnish Embasssy
16 Exhibition Hall
17 Kim Ma Bus Station
19 Albanian & Hungarian Embassies
20 Romanian Embassy
21 Chinese Embassy
22 Lenin Statue
23 Flag Tower
24 Army Museum
25 Fine Arts Museum
26 Bulgarian Embassy
27 Mongolian Embassy
28 North Korean Embassy
29 Hanoi Stadium
31 Temple of Literature
32 Entrance to Temple of Literature
36 Market
37 Railway Station

Ho Chi Minh

Ho Chi Minh is the best known of some 50 aliases assumed over the course of his long career by Nguyen Tat Thanh (1890-1969), founder of the Vietnamese Communist Party and President of the Democratic Republic of Vietnam from 1946 until his death. The son of a fiercely nationalistic scholar-official of humble means, he was educated in the Quoc Hoc Secondary School in Hué before working briefly as a teacher in Phan Thiet. In 1911, he signed on as a cook's apprentice on a French ship, sailing to North America, Africa and Europe. He remained in Europe where, while working as a gardener, snow sweeper, waiter, photo retoucher and stoker, his political consciousness began to develop.

After living briefly in London, Ho Chi Minh moved to Paris where he adopted the name Nguyen Ai Quoc (Nguyen the Patriot). During this period, he mastered a number of languages (including English, French, German and Mandarin) and began to write about and debate the issue of Indochinese independence. During the 1919 Versailles Peace Conference, he tried to present an independence plan for Vietnam to US President Woodrow Wilson. Ho was a founding member of the French Communist Party which was established in 1920. In 1923, he was summoned to Moscow for training by the Communist International, which later sent him to Guangzhou (Canton) where he founded the Revolutionary Youth League of Vietnam, a precursor to the Indochinese Communist Party and the Vietnamese Communist Party.

After spending time in a Hong Kong jail in the early '30s and more time in the USSR and China, Ho Chi Minh returned to Vietnam in 1941 for the first time in 30 years. That same year – at the age of 51 – he helped found the Viet Minh Front, the goal of which was the independence of Vietnam from French colonial rule and Japanese occupation. In 1942, he was arrested and held for a year by the Nationalist Chinese. As Japan prepared to surrender in August 1945, Ho Chi Minh led the August Revolution, which took control of much of the country; and it was he who composed Vietnam's Declaration of Independence (modelled in part on the American Declaration of Independence) and read it publicly very near the site of his mausoleum.

The return of the French shortly thereafter forced Ho Chi Minh and the Viet Minh to flee Hanoi and take up armed resistance. Ho spent eight years conducting a guerrilla war until the Viet Minh's victory against the French at Dien Bien Phu in 1954. He led North Vietnam until his death in September 1969 – he never lived to see the North's victory over the South. Ho Chi Minh is affectionately referred to as 'Uncle Ho' (Bac Ho) by his admirers.

Uncle Ho may have been the father of his country, but he wasn't the father of any children, at least none that are known. Like his erstwhile nemesis, South Vietnamese President Ngo Dinh Diem, Ho Chi Minh never married. ■

amount of pomp and ceremony rivals the British equivalent at Buckingham Palace.

Old Quarter

The Old Quarter is demarcated, roughly speaking, by Hoan Kiem Lake, the Citadel, Dong Xuan Market and the ramparts of the Red River. As they have since the 15th century, the narrow streets of the Old Quarter bear names that reflect the business once conducted there: Silk St, Rice St, Paper St, Broiled Fish St, Vermicelli St, Jewellers' St, Paper Votive Objects St and so forth. This interesting area now houses a variety of small shops.

Dong Xuan Market

Dong Xuan Market is 1.3 km north of the northern end of Hoan Kiem Lake. State stores near the entrance offer a limited selection of outmoded goods; out the back are shops selling potted plants and live animals, including monkeys, mynah birds and parrots. Nearby are food stalls and vendors selling fresh vegetables. Near the main entrance there is a pharmacy specialising in traditional medicines, including alcohol-based snake syrups.

St Joseph Cathedral

Stepping inside neo-Gothic St Joseph Cathedral (inaugurated in 1886) is like being instantly transported to medieval Europe. The cathedral is noteworthy for its square towers, elaborate altar and stained-glass windows. The first Catholic mission in Hanoi was founded in 1679.

The main gate to St Joseph Cathedral is

open daily from 5 to 7 am and 5 to 7 pm, the hours when masses are held. At other times of the day guests are welcome but must enter the cathedral via the compound of the Diocese of Hanoi, the entrance to which is a block away at 40 Nha Chung St. After walking through the gate, go straight and then turn right. When you reach the side door to the cathedral, ring the small bell high up to the right of the door to call the priest to let you in. Across Nha Chung St from the diocese compound is a nunnery where about 30 older nuns live.

Hanoi Hilton

The 'Hanoi Hilton' is the nickname given to a prison in which US POWs – mostly aircraft crew – were held during the Vietnam War. Soon after they were captured, American pilots appeared on TV broadcasts shown around the world, confessing to their crimes and asking the US government to halt the bombing of North Vietnam. This strategy backfired – one of pilots blinked nervously at the camera while he spoke, spelling out the word 'torture' in Morse Code.

The high walls of the forbidding triangular building, officially known as Hoa Lo Prison, are pierced by precious few barred windows. The structure, which was constructed by the French in the early 20th century, is bounded by Hai Ba Trung, Tho Nhuom and Hoa Lo Sts. Photography is forbidden.

Long Bien Bridge

The Long Bien Bridge, which crosses the Red River 600 metres north of the new Chuong Duong Bridge, is a fantastic hodge-podge of repairs dating from the Vietnam War. American aircraft repeatedly bombed the strategic Long Bien Bridge (which at one time was defended by 300 anti-aircraft guns and 84 SAM missiles), yet after each attack the Vietnamese somehow managed to improvise replacement spans and return it to road and rail service. It is said that when US POWs were put to work repairing the bridge,

the US military, fearing for their safety, ended the attacks.

The 1682-metre Long Bien Bridge was opened in 1902. It was once known as the Paul Doumer Bridge after the turn-of-the-century French Governor General of Indochina, Paul Doumer (1857-1932), who was assassinated a year after becoming President of France.

Government Guesthouse

Formerly the Palace of the Governor of Tonkin, the ornate Government Guesthouse (☎ 255853) was stormed during the August Revolution of 1945; the wrought-iron fence surrounding the ornate building still shows marks from bullets fired during the battle. The guesthouse, which is now used to house highly favoured official guests and capitalist tourists (see Places to Stay below), is at 2 Le Thach St, across Ngo Quyen St from the Thong Nhat Hotel.

Thu Le Park & Zoo

Thu Le Park & Zoo (Bach Thu Thu Le), with its expanses of shaded grass and ponds, is six km west of Hoan Kiem Lake. The entrance is on Buoi St a few hundred metres north of Ngoc Khanh St. The zoo is open daily from 6 am to 6 pm; the entrance fee is US$0.10.

Co Loa Citadel

Co Loa Citadel (Co Loa Thanh), the first fortified citadel recorded in Vietnamese history, dates from the 3rd century BC. Only vestiges of the massive ancient ramparts, which enclosed an area of about five sq km, are extant. Co Loa again became the national capital under Ngo Quyen (reigned 939-944). In the centre of the citadel are temples dedicated to King An Duong Vuong (ruled 257-208 BC), who founded the legendary Thuc Dynasty, and his daughter My Nuong (Mi Chau). When My Nuong showed her father's magic crossbow trigger – which made the Vietnamese king invincible in battle – to her husband (who was the son of a Chinese general) he stole it and gave it to his father. With its help, the Chinese were able to defeat An Duong Vuong and his forces, depriving Vietnam of its independence.

Co Loa Citadel is 16 km north of Hanoi in Dong Anh district.

Golf

King's Valley is a golf course being built 45 km west of Hanoi. Membership is US$5000, but the club should be open to visitors.

Festivals

Tet, the Vietnamese New Year, falls in late January or early February. In Hanoi, Tet is celebrated in a variety of ways. A flower market is held during the week before the beginning of Tet on Hang Luoc St, near Dong Xuan Market. A two-week flower exhibition and competition takes place in Lenin Park beginning on the first day of the new year. On the fourth day of the new year, there is a firecracker festival in Dong Ky, a

---

Radio Hanoi & Jane Fonda

Hanoi's radio transmitter is nothing to see, but it's worth a historical footnote for the role it played in the war against the USA (the current transmitter is not the original one used during the war).

Those who are old enough to remember the Vietnam War will doubtless recall the radio broadcasts from Hanoi made by American movie actress Jane Fonda. Ms Fonda made only one live broadcast over Radio Hanoi, her famous speech to US pilots. Subsequent broadcasts played over the radio were tape-recorded speeches and conversations made during her stay in North Vietnam.

Jane Fonda went to North Vietnam on 15 July 1972 and returned to the USA on 29 July, travelling via Paris and Beijing. She was not the only US civilian to visit Hanoi during the war, but she was certainly the most famous. In spite of the fact that a war was raging, it was never illegal for US citizens to visit North Vietnam.

That almost changed. As a direct result of Jane Fonda's visit, Representative Ichord, Chairman of the House Internal Security Committee, proposed to amend the 1950 Internal Security Act to make it illegal for any US citizen to visit a country at war with the USA. The Ichord Amendment – later known as the 'Jane Fonda Amendment' – never passed.

Her visit continues to stir emotions to this very day. During WW II, an American woman known as 'Tokyo Rose' made propaganda broadcasts for the Japanese, and she was prosecuted for treason by the Americans when the war ended. Many veterans who served in Vietnam (and some members of Congress) felt that Jane Fonda's actions were no different, but she was never prosecuted. Not that it wasn't considered – even as late as 1984 the Justice Department under the Reagan administration looked into the matter but decided that Jane Fonda's trip to North Vietnam and her public speeches did not constitute a crime.

Just as Ms Fonda has her critics, she also has her defenders. There are those who say she was simply exercising her right to freedom of speech in speaking out against a war which was morally wrong. It's also only fair to mention that she made a sincere effort to visit the captured American pilots at the nearby 'Hanoi Hilton' prison, but her request for the visit was rejected by North Vietnamese authorities (New York Times, 29 July 1972, page 9).

An act of treason? Or a heartfelt wish to speak out against an unjust war? You can decide for yourself: the following public domain information is a transcript from the US Congress House Committee on Internal Security ('Travel to Hostile Areas', HR 16742, 19-25 September 1972, page 7671 – special thanks to CompuServe Military Veterans Forum):

[Radio Hanoi attributes talk on DRV visit to Jane Fonda; from Hanoi in English to American servicemen involved in the Indochina War, 1 pm GMT, 22 August 1972. Text: Here's Jane Fonda telling her impressions at the end of her visit to the Democratic Republic of Vietnam: (follows recorded female voice with American accent):]

This is Jane Fonda. During my two-week visit in the Democratic Republic of Vietnam, I've had the opportunity to visit a great many places and speak to a large number of people from all walks of life – workers, peasants, students, artists and dancers, historians, journalists, film actresses, soldiers, militia girls, members of the women's union, writers.

I visited the (Dam Xuac) agricultural coop, where the silk worms are also raised and thread

village three km north of Hanoi. A competition for the loudest firecracker is held, attracting gargantuan firecrackers up to 16 metres in length! On the 13th day of the first lunar month in the village of Lim in Ha Bac Province, boys and girl engage in *hat doi*, a traditional game in which groups conduct a sung dialogue with each other; other activities include chess, cock-fighting and firecrackers. Wrestling matches are held on the 15th day of the first lunar month at Dong Da Mound, site of the uprising against Chinese invaders led by Emperor Quang Trung (Nguyen Hue) in 1788.

Vietnam's National Day, 2 September, is celebrated at Ba Dinh Square (the expanse of grass in front of Ho Chi Minh's Mausoleum) with a rally and fireworks; boat races are held on Hoan Kiem Lake.

Places to Stay

The free market has only come to Hanoi very

---

is made. I visited a textile factory, a kindergarten in Hanoi. The beautiful Temple of Literature was where I saw traditional dances and heard songs of resistance. I also saw an unforgettable ballet about the guerrillas training bees in the south to attack enemy soldiers. The bees were danced by women, and they did their job well.

In the shadow of the Temple of Literature I saw Vietnamese actors and actresses perform the second act of Arthur Miller's play *All My Sons*, and this was very moving to me – the fact that artists here are translating and performing American plays while US imperialists are bombing their country.

I cherish the memory of the blushing militia girls on the roof of their factory, encouraging one of their sisters as she sang a song praising the blue sky of Vietnam – these women, who are so gentle and poetic, whose voices are so beautiful, but who, when American planes are bombing their city, become such good fighters.

I cherish the way a farmer evacuated from Hanoi, without hesitation, offered me, an American, their best individual bomb shelter while US bombs fell near by. The daughter and I, in fact, shared the shelter wrapped in each others arms, cheek against cheek. It was on the road back from Nam Dinh, where I had witnessed the systematic destruction of civilian targets – schools, hospitals, pagodas, the factories, houses, and the dike system.

As I left the United States two weeks ago, Nixon was again telling the American people that he was winding down the war, but in the rubble-strewn streets of Nam Dinh, his words echoed with sinister (words indistinct) of a true killer. And like the young Vietnamese woman I held in my arms clinging to me tightly – and I pressed my cheek against hers – I thought, this is a war against Vietnam perhaps, but the tragedy is America's.

One thing that I have learned beyond the shadow of a doubt since I've been in this country is that Nixon will never be able to break the spirit of these people; he'll never be able to turn Vietnam, north and south, into a neo-colony of the United States by bombing, by invading, by attacking in any way. One has only to go into the countryside and listen to the peasants describe the lives they led before the revolution to understand why every bomb that is dropped only strengthens their determination to resist.

I've spoken to many peasants who talked about the days when their parents had to sell themselves out to landlords as virtually slaves, when there were very few schools and much illiteracy, inadequate medical care, when they were not masters of their own lives.

But now, despite the bombs, despite the crimes being created – being committed against them by Richard Nixon, these people own their own land, build their own schools – the children learning, literacy – illiteracy is being wiped out, there is no more prostitution as there was during the time when this was a French colony. In other words, the people have taken power into their own hands, and they are controlling their own lives.

And after 4000 years of struggling against nature and foreign invaders – and the last 25 years, prior to the revolution, of struggling against French colonialism – I don't think that the people of Vietnam are about to compromise in any way, shape or form about the freedom and independence of their country, and I think Richard Nixon would do well to read Vietnamese history, particularity their poetry, and particularly the poetry written by Ho Chi Minh. [recording ends] ■

recently, with the result that most hotels are government owned and expensive. Even domestic travellers complain about a lack of low-priced accommodation, and for Western backpackers the situation is critical because the budget (read 'grotty') hotels are mostly off-limits to foreigners. While it is at least theoretically possible to pay less than US$10 per night for a double room, in practice expect to pay US$20 and consider yourself lucky if you get off cheaper.

As more private hotels open, competition should increase and prices should drop. Even now, bargaining is sometimes possible. Foreign joint ventures are being formed to build new accommodation, but this will mostly be in the up-market range. The situation should improve in the future, but for now it's difficult to get a decent hotel room in Hanoi at a decent price. Unlike Ho Chi Minh City, no neighbourhood in Hanoi has yet emerged as the centre for budget travellers.

Places to Stay – bottom end

The *Bodega Café & Guesthouse* at 57 Trang Tien St has a few rooms for rent on the 3rd floor at US$15 to US$20. Immaculately clean with a friendly staff, the hotel is so popular that they're opening an annexe (*Bodega II*) several blocks away at 41 Hang Bai St. If the Bodega is full, the staff will try to direct you to another guesthouse.

The *Trang Tien Hotel* at 35 Trang Tien St (just south-east of Hoan Kiem Lake near Bodega Café) costs US$7 for a double with shared bath, or US$10 to US$15 for a room with private bath. Don't be put off by the entrance which is along a dark alley – there is a security guard at the end of the alley at the hotel entrance and the alley is quite busy. This has become one of the most popular budget places in Hanoi, and the downstairs cafe is a favourite meeting place.

The *Sophia Hotel* (☎ 255069) is at 6 Hang Bai St, up the stairs from the restaurant. It is adequate but overpriced at US$20 for a double, with bathroom and hot water. The staff are friendly but fairly incompetent and seem somewhat averse to cleaning the

rooms. If the hotel is full, they will direct you to their other place, *Sophia II*, about three km away; prices there are about the same.

The *Dong Do Hotel* (☎ 233275; fax (84-4) 256569), 27 Tong Duy Tan St, is a popular place with budget travellers. Rooms cost from US$10 to US$40. This hotel is also the location of Ann Tourist Office which can arrange car rentals, air tickets, extend visas and perform other useful services.

The *Hoan Kiem Guest House* (☎ 268944; four rooms), 76 Hai Ba Trung St, should not be confused with the much pricier Hoan Kiem Hotel. This guesthouse is a fine privately run place to stay. Suite-like rooms with attached bath, hot water, colour TV and air-con cost US$20 for a double. The rooms are squeaky clean and the manager is very friendly.

The *Hoa Binh Hotel* (☎ 253315; 112 rooms), 27 Ly Thuong Kiet St, is centrally located. This old place has a certain crumbling elegance to it, though there are plans to do renovation work soon. Singles/doubles cost from US$18/22 to US$57/65. As for the in-house restaurant, the hotel's glossy brochure promises 'excellent cook-chiefs who won gold medal' and you can reach the upstairs restaurant 'by stairs of by modern Japanese lifts'.

The *Hai Yen Hotel* (☎ 291024; seven rooms) is at 126 Giai Phong St in the far south of Hanoi. Singles/doubles/triples cost US$12/15/17. It's good value though a bit far from the centre. This hotel is a Taiwanese joint venture and, not surprisingly, has a Chinese-speaking manager and a Chinese restaurant.

The *Giang Vo Hotel* (☎ 253407; about 300 rooms) consists of several five-storey apartment blocks in a large compound. One entrance to the hotel, which is 3.5 km west of the city centre, faces Giang Vo Lake; there is another entrance on Ngoc Khanh St. This is *the* most popular place with Vietnamese budget travellers, but foreigners are welcome if there is space. The dumpier rooms go for US$5 to US$6; rooms with air-con, fridge and hot water cost US$20. The Giang Vo Hotel is run by TOSERCO.

The *Phung Hung Hotel* (☎ 265555, 265556) is a bit over one km north of the railway station at 2 Duong Thanh St. Though not dirt-cheap, it has become fairly popular with backpackers. The hotel has a restaurant and bicycles for rent. Rooms cost US$15 and US$25. The Phung Hung belongs to TOSERCO.

The *La Thanh Hotel* (☎ 254123, 257057; about 100 rooms) is a French-era renovated structure two km west of Ho Chi Minh's Mausoleum at 218 Doi Can St. The lobby is interesting, filled with slot machines and billiards tables. This place is very popular with Chinese tourists and traders; the staff speak some English but they speak Chinese better. Budget rooms cost US$8 and US$12; rooms with colour TV cost US$14 to US$25.

The *Red River Hotel* (☎ 254911), also called *Khach San Hong Ha*, is at 78 Yen Phu St. This is a good place in the budget category. Doubles cost US$5, US$20, US$25 and US$35. The hotel is close to the Long Bien Bridge which crosses the Red River.

The *Phu Gia Hotel* at 136 Hang Trong St has a pleasant location next to Hoan Kiem Lake. Not much English is spoken, but it seems to be a popular place and is often full. Double rooms cost US$12 to US$45.

The *Sao Mai Hotel* (☎ 255827), 16-18 Thong Phong Alley, Ton Duc Thang St, is a pleasant mid-sized place less than one km south of the Ho Chi Minh Mausoleum. Double rooms cost US$20/25.

The *Dong Loi Mini-Hotel* (☎ 259173), 70 Nguyen Khuyen St, is very conveniently located for access to the railway station. This privately run guesthouse costs US$20 for a double.

The *Khach San 30-4* (☎ 252611; six rooms), 115 Tran Hung Dao St, is conveniently located opposite the railway station. It used to be a budget hotel, but at the time of this writing it was closed for renovation. When it reopens, it is possible the name will change and prices will escalate. Next door on Trang Hung Dao St is the *Capital Hotel*. Like Khach San 30-4, it was under renovation at the time of our visit.

After the time of our visit, a few travellers informed us of the opening of another yet-unnamed budget guesthouse at 76 Hang Trong St (just west of Hoan Kiem Lake) which costs US$5 to US$6 for a room with shared bath 'and hardly any water in the showers'.

Places to Stay – middle

The *Hotel Bac Nam* (☎ 257067; fax (84-4) 268998), 20 Ngo Quyen St, is a large guesthouse with an excellent restaurant. Double rooms cost US$20 to US$55. The location near Hoan Kiem Lake is very central.

The *Nam Phuong Hotel* is a small, pleasant place at 16 Bao Khanh St, a narrow street which leads from Hoan Kiem Lake to Hang Trong St. It costs US$35 a double, but has a TV and fridge in each room and is very clean. The staff are friendly.

The *Mai Anh Hotel* (☎ 232702), 109A Nguyen Thai Hoc St, is a very pleasant privately owned guesthouse. Rooms are quite plush and cost US$25.

The *Hai Yen Mini-Hotel* (☎ 265803; fax (84-4) 233813), 48 Hang Chao St, is another pleasant privately run guesthouse which charges US$30.

The *Binh Minh Hotel* (☎ 266441; fax (84-4) 257725), 27 Ly Thai To St, is a new place in the same building as the China Southern Airlines office. Doubles cost US$26 to US$40.

The *Energy Service Centre* (☎ 253169), 30 Ly Thai To St, is not a nuclear power station, but rather a decent hotel. As you might have guessed, it belongs to the Ministry of Energy. Rooms get progressively cheaper as you go upstairs. Top-floor rooms cost US$30; other rooms are US$40 to US$50. The hotel is opposite the office of China Southern Airlines.

The *Friendship Hotel* (☎ 253182) is also known as *Khach San Huu Nghi*. There is a bar, gift shop and other amenities. Singles cost US$38 to US$42 while doubles are US$46 to US$54. The hotel is a five-storey building at 23 Quan Thanh St.

The *Rose Hotel* (☎ 254438; fax (84-4) 254437), 20 Phan Boi Chau St, is also known as *Khach San Hoa Hong*. This attractive hotel is centrally located near the railway station and has singles/doubles from US$25/30 to US$48/52.

Adjacent to the Rose Hotel is the *Saigon Hotel* on the corner of Phan Boi Chau and Ly Thuong Kiet Sts. It was not yet ready to open at the time of this writing, but should be by the time you read this. Prices are expected to be similar to the Rose Hotel.

The *Hoan Kiem Hotel* (☎ 254204; fax (84-4) 268690), 25 Tran Hung Dao St (corner Phan Chu Trinh St), boasts a bar, souvenir shop, sauna and restaurant. Singles/doubles cost US$30/35 to US$44/48; triples are US$44 to US$57.

The *Hotel Kim Lien* (☎ 253064) is a former compound for Soviet workers, and still looks like it. No one here *yet* speaks a word of English and signs on the buildings are still in Russian. No doubt this place will see some renovation in the future. Rooms presently cost US$40, but for that price you might get a whole apartment with cooking facilities. The hotel is on the south side of Hanoi on Kim Lien St just west of the railroad tracks near Bay Mau Lake.

The *Queen Hotel* (☎ 291237, 291238), 189 Giai Phong St, is in the tacky south side of town near the railroad tracks. All rooms are doubles and cost US$30 to US$40. The hotel was undergoing a major expansion at the time of our visit, perhaps a sign of price rises to come.

The *Lotus Hotel* (☎ 4254017; telex 411222 KSBS-VT; 26 rooms) is also called the *Khach San Bong Sen*. Singles/doubles are US$38/44 plus 10% service charge, but breakfast is thrown in free. The five-storey building was built in 1990. The hotel is at 34 Hangbun St, north of the downtown area and near Truc Bach Lake. The location is conveniently near some of Hanoi's historical sites, as the hotel's glossy brochure says: 'You have five minutes only to visit to the remains of history celebrated view start from hotel.'

The *Ho Tay Villas* (☎ 258241, 254165; 68 rooms) has recently turned itself into a tourist hotel (it was once the Communist Party Guest House). The well-designed, spacious villas, set amidst a beautifully landscaped area on West Lake, were once the exclusive preserve of top party officials; but now, visitors bearing US dollars are welcome to avail themselves of the great facilities, excellent food and friendly staff. Even if you don't stay, it's instructive to visit to see how the 'people's representatives' lived in one of Asia's poorest countries. The 5.5-km trip from downtown Hanoi to the hotel takes about half an hour by bicycle. Singles/doubles cost from US$37/44 to US$44/50.

The *Tay Ho Hotel* (☎ 232380; fax (84-4) 232390) is in the West Lake area and offers the full range of facilities such as a swimming pool, rental cars, etc. Singles/doubles are US$40/45 and US$50/55.

The old but fully remodelled *Dong Loi Hotel* (☎ 255721; fax (84-4) 267999), also called Khach San Dong Loi, is at 94 Ly Thuong Kiet St. The door attendants wear crisp-white uniforms and greet you with 'Hello sir' or 'Hello madam.' Singles/doubles cost US$44/66.

The *Thang Long Hotel* (☎ 257796), a 10-storey building which overlooks Giang Vo (a small lake 3.5 km west of the city centre) was closed at the time of this writing for renovation. It should be open by the time you read this; expect prices in the mid to upper range.

The *Government Guesthouse* is one of the best of the mid-range places; the rooms are luxurious and enormous and have their own bathroom (with enormous bath), large double beds, mahogany writing desks and other paraphenalia, all for US$45 a double. Given the cost of some other places in Hanoi this is good value.

Places to Stay – top end

The *Boss Hotel* (☎ 252690; fax (84-4) 257634) is a new and luxurious place at 60 Nguyen Du St. The hotel faces Thien Quang Lake and is adjacent to the Vietnam Airlines international booking office. Rooms cost US$60 and US$66. Amenities include the Blue-Diamond Restaurant and VIP Lounge.

The *Thang Loi International Hotel* (☎ 268215; telex 411276 KSTL-VT; fax (84-4) 252800; 140 rooms) is also known as 'the Cuban Hotel' because it was built in the mid-1970s with Cuban assistance. The floor plan of each level is said to have been copied from a one-storey Cuban building, which explains the doors that lead nowhere. Around the main building are bungalows. The hotel is built on pylons over West Lake and is surrounded by attractive landscaping. All this luxury will cost you either US$47/60 or US$60/70 for singles/doubles. Among the amenities available are postal and telex services, a barber, a hairdresser, massage, tennis courts, gift shops and a swimming pool. The Thang Loi International Hotel is on Yen Phu St, 3.5 km from the city centre.

The *Dan Chu Hotel* (☎ 253323; fax (84-4) 266786) is at 29 Trang Tien St. Once called the Hanoi Hotel, it was built in the late 19th century. Singles/doubles cost US$40/46 to US$60/70. Breakfast is included in the tariff.

The *Hotel Pullman Metropole* (☎ 266919; fax (84-4) 266920), 15 Ngo Quyen St, is also known as the *Thong Nhat Hotel*. This is by far the most expensive hotel in Hanoi, considerably more costly than the luxurious villas out by West Lake. Doubles cost from US$129 to US$249, plus there is a 10% tax and service charge. The postal services counter is open from 10 am to 6 pm. The restaurant is ventilated by some three dozen ceiling fans; if they cranked them all up at once the food would get sucked into the chimney.

Places to Eat

Hanoi is disappointing after Ho Chi Minh City. Restaurants in the capital tend to be more expensive than elsewhere, the food lousier and the service lethargic. This is not to say that you're going to starve, but you won't find great cheap meals on almost every street corner as you do in Ho Chi Minh City. Many backpackers finally decide that the best way to enjoy a cheap meal is to pick up a loaf of delicious French bread, some salami, French cheese and a Coke or beer, then take it back to the hotel room to enjoy it.

The restaurants in the *Dan Chu Hotel* and the *Thong Nhat Hotel* are quite decent and the prices are surprisingly moderate (meals

Lunch in Hanoi

start at US$2). The *Hoan Kiem Hotel* has a limited menu, but the food is good and cheap. There is also an in-house restaurant in the *Hoa Binh Hotel*.

The *Sophia Restaurant* (☎ 255069) is at 6 Hang Bai St (between Hai Ba Trung St and Hoan Kiem Lake). Downstairs is a cafe; the restaurant proper is on the 2nd floor. The food is edible and priced in the mid range. The menu is simple but a big selling point is the French cheese. Deafening music drifts through the walls from the adjacent stereo shop.

The *Bodega Café* is down the street at 57 Trang Tien St; this place serves pastries and drinks and is particularly popular in the evenings.

There are a number of small eateries on Hang Bai St, at the corner of Ly Thuong Kiet St, and also nearby on Hai Ba Trung St, just around the corner from Hang Bai St.

Restaurant Bistrot (☎ 266136) at 35 Tran Hung Dao St is an excellent French restaurant with almost obscenely low prices. This place has a great ambience and is really in vogue with budget travellers.

Restaurant 202 (Nha Hang 202) is 1.5 km south of Hoan Kiem Lake at 202 Pho Hué. One of the best restaurants in the city, it is a favourite of the diplomatic community and has a vaguely French atmosphere. The menu is all European; serving sizes are small.

Across the street at 163 Pho Hué is the *Hoa Binh Restaurant*.

Near the railway station, the *Huong Sen Restaurant* (☎ 252805), run by Hanoi Tourism, is at 92 Le Duan St. There are a number of other places to eat in the immediate vicinity of the railway station, including a restaurant next to the lobby of the Dong Loi Hotel. There are quite a few small restaurants around Kim Lien Bus Station.

Restaurant 22 (also known as Quang An Restaurant) is at 22 Hang Can St. The entrance is through a narrow passageway and up the stairs. It has menus in Vietnamese, English, French, Italian and Swedish. As one traveller wrote:

...the best restaurant I found in Vietnam. Clean, tidy, with silver cutlery, tablecloths, friendly staff who speak English plus good meals and cheap prices.

Another favourite of the expat community is *Cha Ca Restaurant* at 14 Cha Ca St; it specialises in fish (in fact, cha ca means 'fried fish'). Cha Ca St, which is a two-block-long continuation of Luong Van Can St, begins about 500 metres north of Hoan Kiem Lake. The *Nha Thinh Restaurant* is at 28 Luong Van Can St.

Not far away at 50 Hang Vai St is the *Piano Restaurant*. One of its specialities is boiled crab. As the name suggests, it's a fun place with live music every evening starting at 7 pm.

The *Chau Thanh Restaurant*, a favourite of visiting journalists, is at 48 Hang Ga St. The food is excellent but the menu is all French – good luck! This is one of the few places in Hanoi open late at night (ie after 9 pm).

A current favourite for backpackers is the *Darling Café*, 33 Hang Quat St, not far from the corner of Hang Trong St. As well as Vietnamese dishes it has Western food like pancakes and fruit shakes. The Darling Café also organises day trips to various places like Halong Bay.

There are a number of food stalls in the alleyway between numbers 202 and 204 Hang Bong St. Nearby at 192 Hang Bong St

is a small restaurant. *Bittek Restaurant*, also known as *Le Français*, is off Hang Gai St at 17 Ly Quoc Su St; bittek means 'beefsteak'.

The *Thuy Ta Restaurant* at 1 Le Thai To St is a two-storey place overlooking Hoan Kiem Lake. It is about 200 metres south of the intersection of Le Thai To and Hang Gai Sts. The fare is limited to Vietnamese food, including what can best be described as Vietnamese chop suey.

Restaurant 79 is at 79 Ngoc Khanh St, which is a few hundred metres west of the Swedish Embassy.

The excellent *Phuong Nam Restaurant* is on Giang Vo St in Block I1, which is less than 200 metres west of the Hanoi Stadium and not far from the Ho Chi Minh Mausoleum.

The *Dong Do Restaurant* is on Giang Vo St next to the Exhibition Hall (Trien Lam Giang Vo); the food is mediocre. There are several small places to eat across Giang Vo St from the Exhibition Hall.

The *Nha Noi Ho Tay Restaurant* (☎ 257884) floats on West Lake (Ho Tay) just off Duong Thanh Nien St; it's very near Tran Quoc Pagoda. The atmosphere is very pleasant but the food is so-so and the prices high for what you get.

For some of the best French pastries and coffee in Vietnam, visit the *Pastry & Yogurt Shop* at 252 Hang Bong St near the centre.

There are lots of ice cream *(kem)* cafes along Le Thai To St by Hoan Kiem Lake.

Fresh vegetables can be purchased at the 19th of December Market (Cho 19-12), whose two entrances are opposite 61 Ly Thuong Kiet St and next to 41 Hai Ba Trung St. Dog meat is available from curb-side vendors a few hundred metres north of the History Museum on Le Phung Hieu St near Tran Quang Kha St.

In Dong Xuan Market there are food stalls as well as fresh produce vendors.

Entertainment

Municipal Theatre The 900-seat Municipal Theatre (☎ 254312), which faces eastward up Trang Tien St, was built in 1911 as an opera house. It was from a balcony of this building that a Viet Minh-run committee of citizens announced that it had taken over the city on 16 August 1945. These days, performances are held here in the evenings.

Workers' Cultural Palace The huge Workers' Cultural Palace complex (Nha Van Hoa Cong Nhan), built with Soviet aid and completed in 1985, houses libraries, classrooms, sports facilities, and a 1200-seat theatre. There are great views from the roof. It is on Tran Hung Dao St three blocks east of the railway station.

Dancing Dancing – both ballroom and disco – is all the rage with young Hanoi residents who can afford it. The Palace Restaurant is a popular locale on Nha Chung St (near Hoan Kiem Lake and the Aeroflot office). 'Soirées Dansantes' are held at the Thong Nhat Hotel every Saturday and Sunday night from 8 to 11.30 pm. The Dan Chu Hotel also has dancing.

Water Puppets This is a fantastic art form unique to Vietnam and Hanoi is one of the best places to see it. The Water Puppet Theatre (Nha Hat Mua Roi; ☎ 244545) is far from the centre at 32 Dong Truong Ching. Performances are held at 7.30 pm on Sundays and Thursdays.

Circus The endearingly amateurish State Circus often performs in the evenings in a huge tent near the entrance to Lenin Park (Cong Vien Le Nin). Many of the performers (gymnasts, jugglers, animal trainers, etc) were trained in Eastern Europe.

Karaoke Japanese culture comes to Hanoi. You can have your own karaoke booth and sing songs to yourself at the VIP Club (☎ 252690) which is in the Boss Hotel at 60-62 Nguyen Du St, Hai Ba Trung District. Meals can be delivered to your karaoke cubicle. There is supposed to be a 20% discount from 5 to 8 pm. The VIP Club also has slot machines.

Things to Buy

Bao Hung and Hai Van, at 1 and 1a Ly Quoc Su St, are great T-shirt shops; lots of Western customers seem to like the Ho Chi Minh T-shirts. Around Hang Bong/Hang Gai Sts are other T-shirt shops and places selling Viet Cong headgear. T-shirts cost US$2 to US$3.50 and either printed or embroidered ones are available. However, it might be worth keeping in mind that neither Ho Chi Minh T-shirts nor VC headgear are popular apparel with Vietnamese refugees and certain war veterans living in the West. Wearing such souvenirs while walking down a street in Los Angeles or Melbourne might offend someone, possibly endangering your relationship with the Overseas Vietnamese community, as well as your dental work.

Greeting cards with traditional Vietnamese designs hand-painted on silk covers are available around town for US$0.10 or so.

Attractive gold-on-scarlet banners, usually given as awards for service to the Party or State, can be ordered to your specifications (with your name or date of visit, for instance) at shops at 13 and 40 Hang Bong St. Souvenir patches, sewn by hand can also be commissioned at 13 Hang Bong St.

Hang Gai St and its continuation, Hang Bong St, are a good place to look for embroidered tablecloths and hangings; one shop you might try is Tan My at 109 Hang Gai St. Hanoi is a good place to have informal clothes custom-tailored. There are also a number of antique shops in the vicinity.

A good shop for silk clothing is Khaisilk, 96 Hang Gai St. The proprietor is fluent in French and English, and the clothes are modern and Western in design, unlike many of the clothes in other shops in the vicinity.

There is an outstanding shoe market along Hang Dau St at the north-east corner of Hoan Kiem Lake. However, it's difficult to find large sizes for big Western feet.

The government-run Vietnamese Art Association at 511 Tran Hung Dao St is where aspiring young artists display their paintings in hopes of attracting a buyer. Prices are in the US$30 to US$50 range after bargaining.

There are quite a number of stores in Hanoi offering new and antique Vietnamese handicrafts (lacquerware, mother-of-pearl inlay, ceramics, sandalwood statuettes, etc) as well as watercolours, oil paintings, prints and assorted antiques. Hanart (☎ 253045) at 43 Trang Tien St offers old ceramics, wood and stone figurines, lacquerware, mother-of-pearl inlay, ivory objects, carpets, etc. The Galerie d'Art at 61 Thi Trang Tien St is open from 8 am to noon and 2 to 7 pm daily; its specialities include watercolours, oils, puppets and prints. My Thuat Art Gallery is at 61 Trang Tien St.

Another store offering typical products of traditional Vietnamese artisanship faces Hoan Kiem Lake at 25 Hang Khai St. Studio 31, which is two stores away at 31 Hang Khai St, has a selection of paintings. There are small crafts shops at 53 and 55 Ba Trieu St. There is a souvenir shop for foreigners on the corner of Ly Thuong Kiet and Hang Bai Sts; it is open Tuesday to Sunday from 8.30 am to noon and 1.30 to 5.30 pm.

Tapes of Vietnamese music are available at Sun Ashaba, at 32 Hai Ba Trung St. There is a pharmacy (Hieu Thuoc Quan Hoan Kiem; ☎ 254212) specialising in traditional medicines – including something called Gecko Elixir – at 2 Hang Bai St (corner Hang Khai St). A little further west on Hang Khai St are several photographic shops; print film is plentiful and cheap.

For philatelic items, try the philatelic counter at the GPO (in the main postal services hall); it is run by the government philatelic corporation, Cotevina (Cong Ty Tem Viet Nam).

Hanoi's largest store is the State General Department Store (Bach Hoa Tong Hop), which is on Hang Bai St between Hai Ba Trung St and Hoan Kiem Lake. It's a good place to buy things, such as lacquerware items, mother-of-pearl inlay work and silverware. It has a better selection than most shops and has some of the cheapest prices in town. The prices are listed alongside the items, which are encased in glass cabinets (hence there's no need to haggle), and the attendants are reasonably prompt and efficient. Upstairs (amongst other things) is a counter selling chocolates. These chocolates are rather hilariously described on the wrapping as being 'as good as the Indonesian ones' and taste like mud.

Watercolour paints and brushes are available at a store at 216 Hang Bong St (corner Phung Hung St). Musical instruments can be purchased from shops at 24 and 36 Hang Gai St, and 76 and 85 Hang Bong St.

Russian watches and various old (or old-looking) timepieces can be bought in several places in central Hanoi, especially along Luong Van Can and Hang Gai Sts. Formerly very cheap, watch prices are escalating rapidly.

Getting There & Away

Air Vietnam Airlines has nonstop international flights between Hanoi and Bangkok (US$160 one way), Guangzhou (Canton), Nanning (China), Hong Kong and Vientiane (US$80). There are other international flights (via Ho Chi Minh City) including the following destinations: Kuala Lumpur, Manila, Paris, Phnom Penh (US$175) and Singapore.

Visitors arriving in Hanoi from Vientiane have reported having things disappear from checked baggage.

Even worse, immigration police at Hanoi's airport have recently been operating a scam in which they claim your visa is not valid, as your 'sponsor' (that is, your travel agent) has not submitted the necessary paperwork. In this case, the hapless foreigner needs a new sponsor to sign the arrival card. It just so happens that there is an authorised sponsor (travel agent) right there in the airport ready to sign your card for a US$50 fee (subject to bargaining). Not everyone gets hit with this scam – whether or not you fall into this rotten trap probably depends on who is on duty at the time, your nationality, and so on.

In short, customs and police officials at the airport have a reputation for arbitrariness and unpleasantness. Getting visibly angry will probably push them over the edge – be sweet and smiley even if you hate them. Remember, they've got God-like powers and they know it. With luck, you may be able to talk your way through an unpleasant encounter without having to shell out a wad of cash, but don't count on it.

The old x-ray machines, which were guaranteed to ruin your film, have been replaced recently by modern 'filmsafe' ones. They're the same brand used at Bangkok airport, so your film should be able to pass through them undamaged.

It is essential to reconfirm all reservations for flights out of the country. Even once you've gotten yourself to the airport, checked in and boarded your flight, don't uncork the champagne until the plane actually gets off the ground. Last minute 'technical problems' have been known to cause substantial delays.

Vietnam Airlines acts as sales agent for Lao Aviation (Hang Khong Lao) and Cambodia Airlines (Hang Khong Cam Bot). Domestic and international airline offices found in Hanoi are as follows:

Aeroflot
    2 Quang Trung St (☎ 256184)
Air France
    3 Quang Trung St (☎ 253484)
China Southern Airlines
    Binh Minh Hotel, 27 Ly Thai To St, Hoan Kiem District (☎ 269233, 269234; fax (84-4) 269232)
Pacific Airlines
    81 Tran Hung Dao St, Hoan Kiem District (☎ 265350)

Thai International Airways
    1 Quang Trung St (next to Vietnam Airlines)
Vietnam Airlines
    International (Phong ve Quoc Te Hang Khong Vietnam), 1 Quang Trung St (☎ 255284, 253842, 255229)
    Domestic (Phong ve Quoc Noi Hang Khong Vietnam), 60 Quang Trung St (☎ 255194, 253577)

The domestic flight schedule and one-way ticket prices are as shown in the table.

Destination	Schedule	Price
Danang	daily	US$80
Ho Chi Minh City	daily	US$150
Hué	Tue, Fri	US$80
Nha Trang	Thu, Sun	US$105
Pleiku	Tue, Fri	US$110

Bus Hanoi has several main bus terminals. Kim Lien Bus Station serves points south of Hanoi. Kim Ma Bus Station serves destinations that are north-west of the capital. Buses to points north-east of Hanoi leave from Long Bien Bus Station which is on the east bank of the Red River. Soviet-built buses seating 24 people can be chartered from the Kim Ma Bus Station; for more information, have a Vietnamese-speaker call 44227 or 43808. Buses can also be hired from Vietcochamber.

Kim Lien Bus Station (Ben Xe Kim Lien; ☎ 255230) is 800 metres south of the railway station at 100 Le Duan St (corner Nguyen Quyen St). The express bus (toc hanh) ticket office, which is open every day from 4.30 am to 5 pm, is across the street from 6B Nguyen Quyen St. There are express buses to:

Binh Dinh, Buon Ma Thuot (42 hours), Danang (24 hours), Gia Lai, Ho Chi Minh City (49 hours), Kontum, Nha Trang (39 hours), Quang Ngai (27 hours) and Qui Nhon (35 hours).

All the express buses leave daily at 5 or 5.30 am. According to an incentive plan, the driver must refund 10% of the ticket price if an express bus is two hours late and 20% if the bus is three or more hours late.

There are non-express buses from Kim Lien Bus Station to:

Bac Son, Bim Son (3½ hours), Chi Ne, Danang (about 24 hours), Do Luong, Dong Ha (20 hours), Dong Van, Guot, Ha Tinh, Ho Chi Minh City (60 hours), Hoa Binh (3½ hours), Hoa Mac (1½ hours), Hué (24 hours), Kim Bang, Ky Anh (12 hours), Nghia Dan, Phu Ly (12 hours), Sam Son Beaches (five hours), Thai Nguyen (2½ hours), Thanh Hoa (four hours), Thuong Tin (trains V81, T83 & ND1 depart from here), Tuyen Quang (6½ hours), Vinh (eight to 10 hours).

Most non-express buses depart between 4.30 and 5.30 am, though some, especially on shorter routes, leave later in the day.

Kim Ma Bus Station (Ben Xe Kim Ma; ☎ 252846) is opposite 166 Nguyen Thai Hoc St (corner Giang Vo St). Tickets should be purchased the day before departure for buses to:

Chi Ne, Son La, Co Tuyet, Tho Tang, Ha Giang, Thuan Chau, Hat Lot, Tuan Giao, Hoa Binh, Tuyen Quang, Moc Chau, Viet Tri, Phu Tho, Vinh Yen, Yen Bai.

Tickets for the following shorter runs are sold 15 minutes before departure:

Bac Ninh, Bat Bat, Da Chong, Dap Cau, Ni, Phuc Tho, Phuc Yen, Quang Oai, Son Tay, Tan Hong, Trung Ha, Xuan Hoa.

Train The Hanoi Railway Station (Ga Ha Noi; ☎ 252628) is opposite 115 Le Duan St at the western end of Tran Hung Dao St; the ticket office is open from 7.30 to 11.30 am and 1.30 to 3.30 pm only. Windows 2, 4 and 6 handle trains heading southward; tickets for trains to the east and north are available at windows 1 and 3. Tickets should be purchased at least one day before departure.

Besides the usual express and local trains linking Hanoi with Ho Chi Minh City, there are trains heading east to Haiphong (three to five hours), north-east to the Chinese border at Lang Son (six hours) and north-west to Pho Lu (10 hours) stopping short of the Chinese border at Lao Cai.

For more information on the Vietnamese train network and express train fares, see the Getting Around chapter. For information

about getting to Haiphong by train, see the next chapter (The North).

Car Land distances from Hanoi are as follows:

Ba Be Lakes	240 km
Bac Giang	51 km
Bac Ninh	29 km
Bach Thong (Bac Can)	162 km
Cam Pha	190 km
Cao Bang	272 km
Da Bac (Cho Bo)	104 km
Danang	763 km
Dien Bien Phu	420 km
Ha Dong	11 km
Ha Giang	343 km
Hai Duong	58 km
Haiphong	103 km
Halong Bay (Hong Gai)	165 km
Ho Chi Minh City	1710 km
Hoa Binh City	74 km
Hué	658 km
Lai Chau	490 km
Lang Son	151 km
Nam Dinh	90 km
Ninh Binh	42 km
Phat Diem	121 km
Phnom Penh, Cambodia	1964 km
Son La	308 km
Tam Dao Hill Station	85 km
Thai Binh	109 km
Thai Nguyen	80 km
Thakhek, Laos	576 km
Thanh Hoa	153 km
Tuyen Quang	165 km
Viet Tri	291 km
Yen Bai	182 km

Getting Around

To/From the Airport Hanoi's Noi Bai Airport is about 35 km north of the city. Road traffic from Noi Bai Airport to Hanoi crosses the Red River on the Chuong Duong Bridge, which runs parallel to the old road-and-rail Long Bien Bridge.

Buses from Hanoi to Noi Bai Airport depart from the Vietnam Airlines International Booking Office on Quang Trung St, around the corner from Trang Thi/Hang Khai Sts. The schedule depends on the departure and arrival times of domestic and international flights, but in any case the buses do not go very frequently. The schedule has a not very definite departure at 4.30 am and sometimes at 6, 7, 8 and 9 am and noon as well. The trip to Noi Bai takes 50 minutes. Bus tickets are sold inside the International Booking Office and cost US$2 for buses and US$3 for minibuses. It's advisable to book at least a day in advance. As a rule, these buses are *extremely* crowded.

Vietnam Tourism charges US$20 for a taxi ride to Noi Bai Airport; the same service costs US$33 from Hanoi Tourism. With bargaining you can usually get a better price (US$12 to US$15) by hiring a private taxi; they congregate in front of the Vietnam Airlines International Booking Office (☎ 255284), which is at the corner of Trang Thi and Quang Trung Sts.

Bus The tourist map of Hanoi includes bus lines in red. Service on many of the bus routes is rather infrequent.

Tram Like Saigon, Hanoi once had an electric tram system. Hanoi's trams were kept in service longer than Saigon's, but the system finally ground to a halt around 1990. You can still see the electric cables suspended above some of the streets. Nostalgia buffs might want to photograph these, because they will almost certainly be removed soon.

Taxi There are no taxis to be hailed in Hanoi, nor are there taxi stands as yet.

Car To hire a car with a driver, contact a major hotel, Vietnam Tourism, Hanoi Tourism, TOSERCO or Vietcochamber. A cheap Russian-built rental car can be had for about US$4 per hour, or US$25 per day (under eight hours and under 100 km), or US$0.25 per km. Small Japanese cars can be

rented for US$5 per hour, or US$35 per day, or US$0.35 per km. A mini-van can carry up to 12 people and be rented for US$6 per hour, US$40 per day, or US$0.40 per km.

Cyclo Cyclos are slightly cheaper in Hanoi than in Ho Chi Minh City (though not if you take one you find sitting in front of a major tourist hotel). The cyclos in Hanoi are also wider than the Ho Chi Minh City variety, making it possible for two people to fit in one vehicle and share the fare.

The cyclo drivers in Hanoi are even less likely to speak English than in Ho Chi Minh City, so take a map of the city with you. And finally, some travellers have reported problems:

Cyclo drivers in Hanoi are far more rapacious than their Saigon counterparts. I had a fingers bargaining session with one, only to discover at the end of the ride that he was bargaining dollars and I was bargaining dong! He got 5000d not US$5 – much to his disappointment – but I had to be very forceful to get away with it.

Bicycle The best way to get around Hanoi is by bicycle. More and more hotels are now offering these for rent; try the Phung Hung Hotel if your hotel doesn't have any. Bike rentals cost about US$1 per day.

If you'll be in town for more than a few days, you might consider buying a cheap Vietnamese-made bicycle which costs only about US$25. When you leave, you can give it to someone if it hasn't been stolen by then. There are dozens upon dozens of bicycle and motorbike shops along Pho Hué (Hué St) south of Restaurant 202. Bicycle parts are also available at shops near the intersection of Dien Bien Phu and Nguyen Thai Hoc Sts.

The North
Miền Bắc

Stretching from the Hoang Lien Mountains (Tonkinese Alps) eastward across the Red River Delta to the islands of Halong Bay, the northern part of Vietnam (Bac Bo), known to the French as Tonkin, includes some of the country's most spectacular scenery. The mountainous areas are home to many distinct hill-tribe groups, some of which remain relatively untouched by Vietnamising and Westernising influences.

All of the north is open to tourists now, even Americans – with requisite travel permits. The areas near the Chinese border – where heavy fighting took place during the Chinese invasion of 1979 – are considered militarily sensitive, but you shouldn't have too much difficulty getting a permit if you pay for a car, driver and guide. As for individual travel, it's becoming common in areas that get many visitors – Haiphong, Halong Bay and the railway to the Chinese border crossing at Dong Bang. In out of the way places that see few foreigners, getting a permit for individual travel might prove difficult. Try the private travel agents in Ho Chi Minh City and Hanoi.

Around Hanoi

PAGODAS
Thay Pagoda
Thay Pagoda (the Master's Pagoda), also known as Thien Phuc (Heavenly Blessing), is dedicated to Thich Ca Buddha (Sakyamuni, the historical Buddha) and 18 *arhats* (monks who have attained Nirvana); the latter appear on the central altar. On the left is a statue of the 12th century monk Tu Dao Hanh, the 'Master' after whom the pagoda is named; on the right is a statue of King Ly Nhan Tong, who is believed to be a reincar-

nation of Tu Dao Hanh. In front of the pagoda is a small stage built on stilts in the middle of a pond; water-puppet shows are staged here during festivals.

The pagoda's annual festival is held from the fifth to the seventh days of the third lunar month. Pilgrims and other visitors enjoy watching water-puppet shows, hiking and exploring caves in the area.

Thay Pagoda is about 40 km south-west of Hanoi in Ha Tay Province.

Tay Phuong Pagoda
Tay Phuong Pagoda (Pagoda of the West), also known as Sung Phuc Pagoda, consists of three parallel single-level structures built on a hillock said to resemble a buffalo. The 76 figures carved from jackfruit wood, many from the 18th century, are the pagoda's most celebrated feature. The earliest construction here dates from the 8th century.

Tay Phuong Pagoda is approximately 40 km south-west of Hanoi in Tay Phuong hamlet, Ha Tay Province. A visit here can easily be combined with a stop at Thay Pagoda.

Perfume Pagoda
The Perfume Pagoda (Chua Huong) is a complex of pagodas and Buddhist shrines built into the limestone cliffs of Huong Tich Mountain (the Mountain of the Fragrant Traces). Among the better known sites here are Thien Chu (Pagoda Leading to Heaven); Giai Oan Chu (Purgatorial Pagoda), where the faithful believe deities purify souls, cure sufferings and grant offspring to childless families; and Huong Tich Chu (Pagoda of the Perfumed Vestige).

Great numbers of pilgrims come here during a festival that begins in the middle of the second lunar month and lasts until the last week of the third lunar month; these dates usually end up corresponding to March and April. Pilgrims and other visitors spend their time here boating, hiking and exploring the caves.

The Perfume Pagoda is about 60 km south-west of Hanoi in Hoa Binh Province. It is accessible by road or river.

Van Phuc Pagoda

Van Phuc Pagoda, surrounded by hills considered noteworthy for their beauty, was founded in 1037. It is 27 km north-east of Hanoi in Ha Bac Province.

Buc Thap Pagoda

Buc Thap Pagoda, also known as Ninh Phuc Pagoda, is known for its four-storey stone stupa dedicated to the monk Chuyet Cong. The pagoda's date of founding is uncertain, but records indicate that it was rebuilt in the 17th and 18th centuries; the layout of the structure is traditional.

Buc Thap Pagoda is in Ha Bac Province not far from Van Phuc Pagoda.

Kiep Bac Pagoda

Kiep Bac Pagoda, also known as Ho Quoc Pagoda and Tran Hung Dao Dai Vuong Tu, is dedicated to Tran Quoc Tuan, an outstanding general of renowned bravery who helped Tran Hung Dao defeat 300,000 Mongol invaders in the mid-1280s. The pagoda was founded around the year 1300.

Kiep Bac Pagoda, recently restored, is in Hai Hung Province 61 km from Hanoi and 32 km from Bac Ninh.

Keo Pagoda

Keo Pagoda (Chua Keo) was founded in the 12th century to honour the Buddha and the monk Khong Minh Khong, who miraculously cured Emperor Ly Than Ton (ruled 1128-38) of leprosy. The finely carved wooden bell tower is considered a masterpiece of traditional Vietnamese architecture. The nearby dike is a good place to get a general view of the pagoda complex.

Keo Pagoda is in Thai Binh Province 9.5 km from the town of Thai Binh near Thai Bac.

TAM DAO HILL STATION
TRẠM TAM ĐẢO

Tam Dao Hill Station (elevation 930 metres), known to the French as the Cascade d'Argent (Silver Cascade), was founded by the French in 1907 as a place of escape from the heat of the Red River Delta. Today, the grand colonial villas are a bit run-down, but Tam Dao retains its refreshing weather, beautiful hiking areas and superb views. The Vietnamese regard it as the 'Dalat of the north', though in some ways it's even better because commercialisation hasn't had such an impact as in the south.

The three summits of Tam Dao Mountain, all about 1400 metres in height, are visible from the hill station to the north-east. Many hill-tribe people live in the Tam Dao region. The best times of the year to visit Tam Dao are generally from late May to mid-September and from mid-December to February.

The Tam Dao area is particularly rich in flora and fauna. Among the old-growth trees, giant ferns (some as tall as nine metres), camellias and orchids live an incredible variety of birds and butterflies as well as deer, gibbons, wild pigs, tortoises and rare snakes.

Remember that it is cool up in Tam Dao, and that this part of Vietnam has a winter. Come prepared.

Information

Tourist Office Tam Dao Tourism (Cong Ty Du Lich Tam Dao; ☎ 306) is in the Tam Dao Hotel.

Places to Stay

The *Tam Dao Hotel* (Khach San Tam Dao; ☎ 306) is the main place for foreigners to stay.

Getting There & Away

Tam Dao Hill Station is 85 km north-west of Hanoi in Vinh Phu Province. A bus or car from Hanoi takes about two hours.

HOA BINH
HÒA BÌNH

Hoa Binh City, which is the capital of Hoa

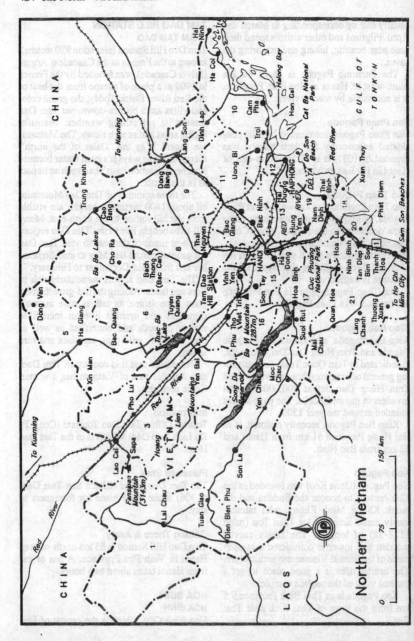

Northern Vietnam

```
┌─────────────────────────────────────┐
│    Provinces of Northern Vietnam     │
│                                      │
│    1   Lai Chau                      │
│    2   Son La                        │
│    3   Lao Cai                       │
│    4   Yen Bai                       │
│    5   Ha Giang                      │
│    6   Tuyen Quang                   │
│    7   Cao Bang                      │
│    8   Bac Thai                      │
│    9   Lang Son                      │
│    10  Quang Ninh                    │
│    11  Ha Bac                        │
│    12  Haiphong                      │
│    13  Hai Hung                      │
│    14  Hanoi                         │
│    15  Ha Tay                        │
│    16  Vinh Phu                      │
│    17  Hoa Binh                      │
│    18  Nam Ha                        │
│    19  Thai Binh                     │
│    20  Ninh Binh                     │
│    21  Thanh Hoa                     │
└─────────────────────────────────────┘
```

Binh Province, is 74 km south-west of Hanoi. This area is home to many hill-tribe people, including Muong and Thai. Hoa Binh can be visited on an all-day excursion from Hanoi, or as a stop on the long drive to Dien Bien Phu.

Hoa Binh is the site of a large dam on the Song Da River, creating Song Da Reservoir, the largest in Vietnam. This is part of a major hydroelectric scheme which generates power for the north, blessing Hanoi with excess electric capacity and freedom from the dry-season power failures which plague Ho Chi Minh City.

Unfortunately, Hoa Binh's paranoid security apparatus fears spies and saboteurs and doesn't take kindly to foreigners poking around the dam and reservoir site.

Information

Hoa Binh Tourism (☎ 37) has an office at 24 Tran Hung Dao St in Ha Dong, which is only 11 km from central Hanoi.

CUC PHUONG NATIONAL PARK
CÔNG VIÊN QUỐC GIA CÚC PHƯƠNG

Cuc Phuong National Park, established in 1962, is one of Vietnam's most important nature preserves. Though wildlife has suffered a precipitous decline in Vietnam in recent decades, the park's 222 sq km of primary tropical forest remain home to an amazing variety of wildlife, including 1967 species of flora from 217 families and 749 genera; 1800 species of insects from 30 orders and 200 families; 137 species of birds; 64 species of animals; and 33 species of reptiles. Among the extraordinary variety of life forms in the park are several species discovered here, including a tree known as *Bressiaopsis Cucphuongensis* and the endemic red-bellied squirrel *Callosciurus erythrinaceus Cucphuongensis*. Larger animals you may encounter range from the yellow macaque *(Macaca mullata)* to the spotted deer *(Cevus nippon)*.

In Con Moong Cave, one of the park's many grottoes, the stone tools of prehistoric humans have been discovered.

Cuc Phuong National Park, which is 70 km from the sea, covers an area about 25 km long and 11 km wide in the provinces of Ninh Binh, Hoa Binh and Thanh Hoa. The elevation of the highest peak in the park is 648 metres. At the park's lower elevations, the climate is subtropical.

Places to Stay

The rest house at park headquarters charges US$12 per night.

Getting There & Away

Cuc Phuong National Park is 140 km from Hanoi (via Ninh Binh); sections of the road are in poor condition. With a car, it is possible to visit the forest as a day trip from Hanoi.

HOA LU
HOA LƯ

Hoa Lu was the capital of Vietnam under the Dinh Dynasty (ruled 968-980) and the Early Le Dynasty (ruled 980-1009). The site was an attractive place for a capital city because of both its distance from China and the natural protection afforded by the region's landscape, parts of which are said to resemble Halong Bay without the water.

The ancient citadel of Hoa Lu, most of which has been destroyed, covered an area of about three sq km. The outer ramparts encompassed temples, shrines and the place where the king held court. The royal family lived in the inner citadel.

Today, there are two sanctuaries at Hoa Lu. Dinh Tien Hoang, restored in the 17th century, is dedicated to the Dinh Dynasty. Out the front is the stone pedestal of a royal throne; inside are bronze bells and a statue of Emperor Dinh Tien Hoang with his three sons. The second temple, Dai Hanh (or Dung Van Nga), commemorates the rulers of the Early Le Dynasty. Inside the main hall are all sorts of drums, gongs, incense burners, candle holders and weapons; to the left of the entrance is a sanctuary dedicated to Confucius.

Bic Dong Cave is in the village of Van Lam, a short boat trip away. The three sanctuaries here date from the 17th century.

Reaching Ninh Binh, turn west for 20 km. On the right there's a hut with a bar. Pay a toll, go ahead and then you can take a tiny rowing boat with an oarswoman. It's a beautiful landscape; high rocks, green with vegetation, rice paddies. The boat sails along a narrow canal amongst the fields. The silence is pure. Three times we passed grottoes. The trip may take two or more hours. Someone in our group compared this place to Halong Bay.

Mauro Grusovin

Getting There & Away
Train No train stops in Hoa Lu, but the Reunification Express stops in nearby Ninh Binh. From there, you'll need to find a car or motorbike, or have a very long walk.

Car Hoa Lu is at the southern edge of the Red River Delta in Truong Yen Village, which is in Ninh Binh Province. By car, the trip from Hanoi to Hoa Lu is 120 km due south and takes about two hours.

PHAT DIEM
PHÁT DIỆM
Phat Diem (Kim Son) is the site of a cathedral remarkable for its vast dimensions and unique Sino-Vietnamese architecture. The vaulted ceiling is supported by massive limwood columns almost one metre in diameter and 10 metres tall. In the lateral naves, there are a number of curious wood and stone sculptures. The main altar is made of a single block of granite.

Before 1954, the cathedral, founded by a Vietnamese priest named Six, was an important centre of Catholicism in the north, and there was a seminary here. Six's tomb is in the square in front of the cathedral. Nearby is a covered bridge dating from the late 19th century.

Phat Diem is 121 km south of Hanoi and 29 km south-east of Ninh Binh.

BA VI MOUNTAIN
NÚI BA VÌ
Ba Vi Mountain (elevation 1287 metres) is about 65 km west of Hanoi. There is a spectacular view of the Red River valley from the summit.

Haiphong
Hải Phòng

Haiphong, Vietnam's third most populous city, is the north's main industrial centre and one of the country's most important seaports. Greater Haiphong has an area of 1515 sq km and a population of 1,300,000; Haiphong proper covers 21 sq km and is home to 370,000 souls.

The French took possession of Haiphong, then a small market town, in 1874. The city soon became a major port; industrial concerns were established here in part because of the proximity of coal supplies.

One of the immediate causes of the Franco-Viet Minh War was the infamous French bombardment of the 'native quarters' of Haiphong in 1946 in which hundreds of civilians were killed and injured (a contem-

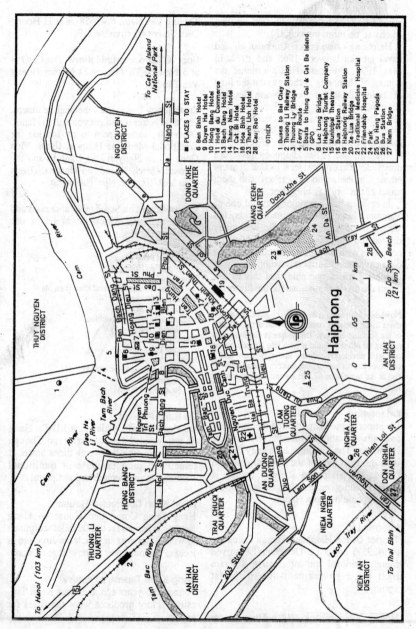

Haiphong

PLACES TO STAY

6   Ben Binh Hotel
9   Duyen Hai Hotel
10 Hong Bang Hotel
11 Hotel du Commerce
13 Bach Dang Hotel
17 Dang Nam Hotel
18 Cat Bi Hotel
16 Hoa Binh Hotel
23 Thanh Lich Hotel
28 Cau Rao Hotel

OTHER

1   Buses to Bai Chay Railway Station
2   Thuong Li Railway Station
3   Thuong Ly Bridge
4   Ferry route
5   Boats to Hong Gai & Cat Ba Island
7   GPO
8   Lac Long Bridge
12 Haiphong Tourist Company
15 Municipal Theatre
19 Haiphong Railway Station
20 Bus Station
21 Traditional Medicine Hospital
22 Friendship Hospital
24 Park
25 Du Hang Pagoda
26 Bus Station
27 Niem Bridge

To Cat Ba Island National Park

To Hanoi (103 km)

To Do Son Beach (21 km)

To Thai Binh

porary French account estimated civilian deaths at 'no more than 6000').

Haiphong came under American air and naval attacks between 1965 and 1972. In May 1972, President Nixon ordered the mining of Haiphong harbour to cut the flow of Soviet military supplies to North Vietnam. As part of the Paris Cease-Fire accords of 1973, the USA agreed to help clear the mines from Haiphong harbour; 10 US Navy mine-sweepers were involved in the effort.

Since the late 1970s, Haiphong has seen a massive outflux of refugees, including many ethnic Chinese, who have taken with them much of the city's fishing fleet.

In spite of being a major port and one of Vietnam's largest cities, Haiphong today is a sleepy place with little traffic and many dilapidated buildings. However, if Vietnam continues with economic reforms, Haiphong does have the potential to develop rapidly. A Haiphong travel pamphlet has this to say about the city's aspirations for the future:

Nowadays Haiphong is one of the creative and active cities in the socialist construction and in the defence of the socialist country. The people in Haiphong are sparing no effort to build it both into a modern port city with developed industry and agriculture and a centre of import and export, tourism and attendance and at the same time an iron fortress against foreign invasion.

Orientation

It's important to keep in mind that there are two railway stations within the city limits of Haiphong. The Thuong Li Railway Station is in the west part of the city, far from the centre. The Haiphong Railway Station is right in the city centre; this is the last stop for the train coming from Hanoi.

Information

Tourist Office Haiphong Tourist Company (☎ 42957) at 15 Le Dai Hanh St proved friendly, helpful and informative – a rare treat for a government-owned tourist agency!

Money Vietcombank (Ngan Hang Ngoai

Thuong Viet Nam; ☎ 47658) is at 11 Hoang Dieu St, not far from the GPO.

Post & Telecommunications The GPO is at 3 Nguyen Tri Phuong St (corner Hoang Van Thu St).

Emergency If you need medical treatment, you'd do better if you get yourself to Hanoi. Otherwise, some places to try include the Traditional Medicine Hospital (Benh Vien Dong Y) on Nguyen Duc Canh St and the Vietnam-Czech Friendship Hospital (Benh Vien Viet-Tiep) on Nha Thuong St.

Useful Adresses Some other addresses and phone numbers which might be of use include:

Communist Party offices
　Dinh Tien Hoang St
Municipal Library
　corner of Minh Khai and Dien Bien Sts
Municipal Museum
　Dien Bien St
Municipal People's Committee
　Hoang Dieu St
Municipal Theatre
　Tran Hung Dao St
Russian Consulate
　14 Minh Khai St (☎ 47611)
TNT Vietrans
　(☎ 47180, 47165)

Du Hang Pagoda

Du Hang Pagoda, which is at 121 Du Hang St, was founded three centuries ago. Though it has been rebuilt several times since, it remains a good example of traditional Vietnamese architecture and sculpture.

Hang Kenh Communal House

Hang Kenh Communal House on Hang Kenh St is known for its 500 relief sculptures in wood. The area in which the structure is located was once part of the village of Kenh.

Hang Kenh Tapestry Factory

Founded 65 years ago, the Hang Kenh Tapestry Factory produces wool tapestries for export.

Dang Hai Flower Village

Flowers grown at Dang Hai, which is five km from Haiphong, are sold on the international market.

Places to Stay

The most popular place with backpackers is the *Hoa Binh Hotel* (Peace Hotel) (☎ 46907, 46909), which is across from the railway station at 104 Luong Khanh Thien St. Double rooms with fan cost US$8; with air-con they're US$10. The hotel has an attached restaurant.

The *Cat Bi Hotel* at 29 Tran Phu St is also close to the railway station. Rooms cost US$15 and US$20.

The French-era *Hotel du Commerce* (☎ 42706, 42790), 62 Dien Bien Phu St, has singles/doubles from US$8/10 to US$30/35.

Directly across the street from the foregoing is the *Thangnam Hotel* (☎ 42820) at 55 Dien Bien Phu St. Singles/doubles start at US$12/16 and go to US$20. The hotel has a beauty shop and a restaurant.

The *Duyen Hai Hotel* (☎ 42157) at 5 Nguyen Tri Phuong St is moderately priced at US$12 for a single and US$15 to US$27 for a double.

The *Bach Dang Hotel* (☎ 42444), 42 Dien Bien Phu St, has rooms covering a wide price range from US$5 to US$38.

The *Hong Bang Hotel* (☎ 42229; telex 311252; 28 rooms), 64 Dien Bien Phu St, costs US$35 for a double room equipped with bath, refrigerator and colour TV. The hotel has a restaurant, steam bath and massage services.

The *Ben Binh Hotel* is just opposite the main ferry pier on the Cam River. All rooms for foreigners cost US$30.

If you don't mind being away from the centre, a quiet place to stay is the *Thanh Lich Hotel* (☎ 473161). It's at 47 Lach Tray St in a park-like compound. Rooms cost US$10.

To the south of the centre next to the highway heading towards Do Son Beach is the *Cau Rao Hotel*. It's a quiet but pleasant place, but not much English is spoken. Doubles cost US$10 to US$25.

Places to Eat

Haiphong is noted for its excellent fresh seafood, which is available from every hotel restaurant.

Getting There & Away

Air Vietnam Airlines flights depart Ho Chi Minh City for Haiphong daily except Thursday; the same aircraft returns to Ho Chi Minh City in the afternoon. A one-way ticket costs US$150.

Pacific Airlines flies between Ho Chi Minh City and Haiphong every Wednesday and charges the same fare as Vietnam Airlines.

Bus Occasional buses from Hanoi to Haiphong depart from the Long Bien Bus Station, which is on the east side of the Red River. Most travellers who go by public transport take the train, which is far more reliable.

Buses depart Haiphong for Bai Chay and Hong Gai (Halong Bay) from a bus station in the Thuy Nguyen District (north bank of the Cam River). To reach the Thuy Nguyen District, you must take a ferry (see Haiphong map).

Train One train to Haiphong departs from Hanoi at 5.50 am. Going the other way, there are two trains, departing Haiphong for Hanoi at 5.55 and 9 am. Haiphong is not on the main line between Hanoi and Ho Chi Minh City.

Car Haiphong is 103 km from Hanoi on National Highway 5. There are a number of bridge crossings where motor vehicles, bicycles, pedestrians and pushcarts share the bridge with trains. The bridges are only single-lane which means the two-way traffic has to alternate, and everyone has to get off the bridge when a train comes. The result is long delays. Allow at least 2½ to three hours for the one-way Hanoi-Haiphong trip. The round-trip fare by car will be at least US$60 unless you're very good at bargaining.

Boat Being a major sea and river port, Haiphong is well connected to the rest of

Vietnam by ferry. The boats tend to be slow and none too comfortable, but they certainly are cheap. You can even get to Hanoi by boat. The ferries most used by travellers are the one to Hong Gai (see Halong Bay section for details) and Cat Ba Island.

The boat schedule changes frequently so it's no use presenting it here. For some destinations, boats go only once or twice weekly. A trip to Ho Chi Minh City by boat would take at least a week, possibly require a few changes of boats and could be done for as little as US$10. Some possible destinations in northern Vietnam and boat fares include:

Destination	Price
Cat Ba	US$1.40
Dan Tien	US$3
Do Luong	US$2.40
Ha Tinh	US$3.20
Hanoi	US$1
Hong Gai	US$0.80
Nam Dinh	US$1
Ninh Binh	US$1.30
Phu Ly	US$1.30
Thai Binh	US$0.80
Thanh Hoa	US$1.60
Vinh	US$2.60

Around Haiphong

DO SON BEACH
BÃI BIỂN ĐỒ SƠN
The palm-shaded beach at Do Son, 21 km south-east of Haiphong, is the most popular seaside resort in the north and a favourite of Hanoi's expatriate community. The hilly four-km-long promontory ends with a string of islets. The peninsula's nine hills are known as the Cuu Long Son (Nine Dragons). The town is famous for its ritual buffalo fights, which are held annually on the 10th day of the eighth lunar month, the date on which the leader of an 18th century peasant rebellion here was killed.

Places to Stay & Eat
The Van Hoa Hotel at the very tip of the peninsula offers good views but a long walk to the beach. The hotel is built in Disneyland-style decor with two turrets – you almost expect to see someone walking around in a Mickey Mouse suit. Rooms are cheap at US$6.

Most hotels which can accept foreigners are similarly priced. Some places to try include the Do Son Hotel, Hoa Phuong Hotel, Hai Au Hotel and Khach San Cong Doan.

Cheap and good restaurants line the beach front.

CAT BA NATIONAL PARK
CÔNG VIÊN QUỐC GIA CÁT BÀ
About half of Cat Ba Island (whose total area is 354 sq km) and 90 sq km of adjacent inshore waters were declared a national park in 1986 in order to protect the island's diverse ecosystems. These include tropical evergreen forests on the hills, freshwater swamp forests at the base of the hills, coastal mangrove forests, small freshwater lakes, sandy beaches and offshore coral reefs. The main beaches are Cai Vieng, Hong Xoai Be and Hong Xoai Lon.

Cat Ba is a charming island and Vietnam's most beautiful national park. There are numerous lakes, waterfalls and grottoes in the spectacular limestone hills, the highest of which rises 331 metres above sea level. The growth of the vegetation is stunted near the summits because of high winds. The largest permanent body of water on the island is Ech Lake, which covers an area of three hectares. Almost all of the surface streams are seasonal; most of the Cat Ba's rainwater flows into caves, following underground streams to the sea and resulting in a severe shortage of fresh water during the dry season. Though parts of the interior of the island are below sea level, most of the island is between 50 and 200 metres in elevation.

Cat Ba Island is home to 15 types of mammals, such as the Francois monkey (Presbytis francoisi poliocephalus), wild boar (Sus scrofa), deer, squirrels and hedgehogs; and 21 species of birds, including hawks, hornbills and cuckoos, have been sighted. Cat Ba lies on a major migration route for waterfowl (ducks, geese, shorebirds) who feed and roost in the mangrove forests and on the beaches. The 620 species of plants recorded on Cat Ba include 118 timber species and 160 plants with medicinal value.

The waters off Cat Ba Island are home to 200 species of fishes, 500 species of molluscs and 400 species of arthropods. Larger marine animals in the area include seals and three species of dolphin.

Stone tools and bones left by human beings who lived between 6000 and 7000 years ago have been found at 17 sites on the island. The most thoroughly studied site is Cai Beo Cave, discovered by a French archaeologist in 1938, which is 1.5 km from Cat Ba Town.

Today, the island's human population of 12,000 is concentrated in the southern part of the island, including the town of Cat Ba (Cat Hai). They live from fishing, forest exploitation and agriculture, including the growing of rice, cassava, oranges, apples and lychees.

During February, March and April, Cat Ba's weather is often cold and drizzly, though the temperature rarely falls below 10°C. During the summer months, tropical storms and typhoons are frequent.

The charm of Cat Ba is spoilt a little by a woman who seemed to monopolise the place. We had to negotiate with her about the hotels, the food in the restaurant, the price of the bus to the ferry and the boat to explore Halong Bay. For the boat we paid US$70 for the whole day with seven people. Be sure to agree on an itinerary before you leave. The monopolist position of the woman is not in itself to be condemned. Had she had some degree of compassion, it would have been bearable. The fact is that this person was a walking contradiction to the word 'compassion'.

Twan van de Kerkhof

Places to Stay

There are three hotels on the island, all of which seem to be named the *Cat Ba Hotel*. Passing through the village, you enter a gate and a hotel is immediately to your left. There

is another hotel in the opposite corner of the bay. The first hotel (near the gate) is the better appointed of the two. The third place to stay is a basic beach hut. All three places charge US$2 to US$4. Electricity is only available from 6 until 9 pm.

Getting There & Away

Cat Ba National Park is 133 km from Hanoi and 30 km east of Haiphong. A boat to Cat Ba departs from Haiphong every day at 1.30 pm and returns the next day at 6 am; the trip takes about 3½ hours and costs US$1.40. The park headquarters is at Trung Trang.

Getting Around

On arrival at the pier, there should be a bus waiting to take you to Cat Ba Village for US$0.20. If the bus is not there, it takes approximately 30 minutes to walk the only road on the island.

HALONG BAY
VỊNH HẠ LONG

Magnificent Halong Bay, with its 3,000 islands rising from the clear, emerald waters of the Gulf of Tonkin, is one of the natural marvels of Vietnam. Visitors have compared the area's magical landscape of carboniferous chalk islets to Guilin, China, and Krabi in southern Thailand. These tiny islands are dotted with innumerable beaches and grottoes created by the wind and the waves.

The name Ha Long means Where the Dragon Descends into the Sea. Legend has it that the islands of Halong Bay were created by a great dragon who lived in the mountains. As it ran towards the coast, its flailing tail gouged out valleys and crevasses; as it plunged into the sea, the areas dug up by the tail became filled with water, leaving only bits of high land visible.

The dragon may be legend, but sailors in the Halong Bay region have often reported sightings of a mysterious marine creature of gargantuan proportions known as the Tarasque. More paranoid elements of the military suspect it's an imperialist spy submarine, while eccentric foreigners believe

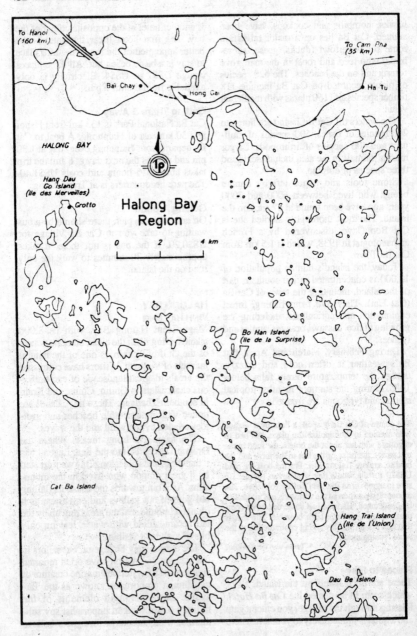

To Hanoi
(160 km)

To Cam Pha
(35 km)

Bai Chay

Hong Gai

Ha Tu

HALONG BAY

Hang Dau
Go Island
(Ile des Merveilles)

Grotto

Halong Bay
Region

0   2   4 km

Bo Han Island
(Ile de la Surprise)

Cat Ba Island

Hang Trai Island
(Ile de l'Union)

Dau Be Island

they have discovered Vietnam's own version of the Loch Ness monster. Meanwhile, the monster or whatever it is continues to haunt Halong Bay, unfettered by the Immigration Police, TOSERCO and the need for travel permits. Enterprising Vietnamese boat owners have made a cottage industry out of the creature, offering cash-laden tourists the chance to rent a junk and pursue the Tarasque before he gets fed up and swims away.

Halong Bay is in Quang Ninh Province, Vietnam's foremost coal-producing region.

Orientation

Halong Bay and its numerous islands sprawl out over an area of 1500 sq km, right up to the Chinese border.

Travellers focus on two accessible places which have accommodation, food and all other life-support systems. Bay Chai is the main transport hub and accommodation centre and also boasts a dirt-and-pebble beach and a few climbable hills in the vicinity.

A short ferry ride to the east is the fishing village of Hong Gai, which is more interesting and also has accommodation and food.

Much farther afield (near the Chinese border) is a beach resort at Tra Co, but it's seldom visited by foreigners.

Information

Tourist Office There is an office of Quang Ninh Tourism (Cong Ty Du Lich Quang Ninh; ☎ 46318, 46321) on Bai Chay St in the town of Bai Chay. This agency owns two hotels and can inform you about boat tours and the like.

Quang Ninh Tourism & Ship Chandler (Cong Ty Du Lich Va Cong Ty Tau Bien Quang Ninh; ☎ 46405, 46427; fax (84-33) 46226) owns four hotels and can provide similar services to the foregoing. It is on Bai Chay St in Bai Chay.

Grottoes

Because of the type of rock the islands of Halong Bay consist of, the area is dotted with thousands of caves of all sizes and shapes.

Hang Dau Go (Grotto of Wooden Stakes),

known to the French as the Grotte des Merveilles (Cave of Marvels), is a huge cave consisting of three chambers which you reach via 90 steps. Among the stalactites of the first hall, scores of gnomes appear to be holding a meeting. The walls of the second chamber sparkle if bright light is shined on them. The cave derives its Vietnamese name from the third of the chambers, which is said to have been used during the 13th century to store the sharp bamboo stakes which Tran Hung Dao planted in the bed of the Bach Dang River to impale Kublai Khan's invasion fleet.

Drum Grotto is so named because, as the wind blows through its many stalactites and stalagmites, visitors think they hear the sound of distant drumbeats. Other well-known caves in Halong Bay include the Grotto of Bo Nau and two-km-long Hang Hanh Cave.

Some tourist boats stop at Deu (Reu) Island, which supports an unusual species of monkey distinguished by their red buttocks. A few travellers also visit Ngoc Vung Island which has a red brick lighthouse.

Organised Tours

Vietnam Tourism in Hanoi offers rather expensive three-day tours to Halong Bay: it costs US$100 to hire a car (which can seat up to three people in addition to the driver and guide) for the round trip from Hanoi; room and board cost US$50 per person for two nights and three days; and Vietnam Tourism charges US$28 per hour (!) for a boat out to the island grottoes.

One foreigner booked a car with guide and driver from Vietnam Tourism and had this to say:

Your tour guide has been instructed to take you to the Vietnam Tourism designated hotel which is very expensive. If you go into town you can easily get a room for US$10. Do not let your driver or guide book a boat for you. He will charge about US$20 each for three hours (per person!). If you negotiate yourself with the boat driver you can get a tour from approximately US$3 for three people for three hours.

Alternately, take the ferry from Haiphong to Halong Bay and this takes you through the islands and saves you doing the tour, although not in as much detail.

Catherine Ryan

Places to Stay

Almost everyone making an excursion to Halong Bay spends at least one night in the town of Bai Chay.

The *Nha Nghi Cong Doan* (Workers' Guest House) is the cheapest place in Bai Chay and most popular with budget travellers. Rooms cost US$3 to US$5 per night.

Other places include the *Vuon Dao Hotel* and *Hai Quan Hotel* (Navy Hotel). The *Van Hai Hotel* is very central, but at US$8 to US$10 it's not great for the standard of accommodation (fan, shared bath but free cockroaches).

The *Bach Dang Hotel* is near the ferry pier and is one of the more up-market places in town. There are also many privately owned 'mini-hotels' costing US$15, US$20 and more. The *Halong Hotel* costs US$35 per night.

Alternatively, you can take a ferry over to Hong Gai which also has accommodation.

Getting There & Away

For well-heeled travellers, the usual way to get to Halong Bay is to take a car from Hanoi to Bai Chay, spend one night, take a boat tour the next day, spend another night in Bai Chay and then head back to Hanoi in the same car. Total time: three days.

For budget-minded backpackers, the usual method is to take a morning train from Hanoi to Haiphong, take the afternoon boat to Hong Gai (or spend the night in Haiphong), then a ferry to Bai Chay, spend one night (at least) in Bai Chay, take a boat tour around the bay, then a bus back to Haiphong, spend a night in Haiphong again and catch the morning train back to Hanoi. Minimum time: three days but usually more.

If you can find a group to share a car from Hanoi, this might be almost as economical as using public transport since you might save one night's accommodation in Haiphong.

Bus Buses from Haiphong to Bai Chay depart Haiphong from a bus station in the Thuy Nguyen District (north bank of the Cam River). The trip takes approximately two hours. The bus station in Bai Chay is about one km from the Halong Hotel.

Car Bai Chay is 160 km from Hanoi, 55 km from Haiphong and 45 km from Cam Pha. The one-way trip from Hanoi to Bai Chay by car takes at least three hours. The cost for a Hanoi-Bai Chay car (round-trip) is about US$100, and this price should include the driver's 'waiting time' (normally three days). Usually, you are responsible for your driver's food and accommodation expenses.

Boat Ferries depart from Haiphong harbour to Hong Gai three times daily at 6 and 11 am, and at 4 pm (schedule is subject to change!). The trip takes three hours one way and costs US$0.80. From Hong Gai there are frequent ferries to nearby Bai Chay.

Getting Around

Boat You won't see much unless you also take a boat to tour the islands and their grottoes. You needn't rent a whole boat for yourself – there are plenty of other foreigners who wouldn't mind getting together a small sightseeing group and it's even possible to go with a group of Vietnamese. A mid-sized boat can hold six to 12 persons and costs around US$6 per hour. Larger boats can hold 50 to 100 persons and cost US$10 to US$20 per hour. The large boats are government owned while the small ones are private. To find a boat, ask around the quays of Bai Chay or Hong Ga.

Note that there has been at least one reported robbery from a small boat – the foreign passengers lost all their money, passports, etc.

Sometimes a boat approaches and offers fish and crabs, but beware – these people may be robbers! They grabbed the bag of an English guy (with passport, money and cheques) and disappeared. Our tourist boat was slow and couldn't catch that fast boat. Two travellers we met reported that the crew of their boat stole some small things while they were swimming.

Helicopter If you've got the cash to burn, helicopters can be chartered for whirlwind tours of the bay. Of course, it's hard to imagine how you're going to get a good look at the grottoes from a helicopter unless the pilots are *really* skilled. The staff at Quang Ninh Tourism in Bai Chay say they can arrange this; other possible sources of helicopters include Vietnam Tourism, TOSERCO and Vietnam Airlines.

The Far North
Miền Cực Bắc

The northernmost parts of Vietnam have only recently been opened to foreigners, mainly because of security problems along the Chinese border.

It wasn't always so. China was a good friend of North Vietnam from 1954 (when the French departed) until the late 1970s. China's relations with Vietnam began to sour shortly after reunification as the Vietnamese government became more and more friendly to the USSR, China's rival. There is good reason to believe that Vietnam was simply playing China and the USSR off against each other, getting aid from both.

In March 1978, when the Vietnamese government launched a campaign in the south against 'commercial opportunists', seizing private property in order to complete the country's 'socialist transformation', the campaign hit the ethnic-Chinese particularly hard. It was widely assumed that behind the Marxist-Leninist rhetoric was the ancient Vietnamese antipathy towards the Chinese. One former Chinese restaurant owner from Saigon described what it was like when the government seized his business in 1978.

Government officials from Hanoi came and catalogued every table, chair, chopstick, glass, plate and dish in my restaurant. Thereafter, if I broke a glass, I had to pay for it, even though everything had originally been purchased with my own money.

The anticapitalist and anti-Chinese campaign caused as many as 500,000 of Vietnam's 1.8 million ethnic-Chinese to flee the country. Those in the north fled overland to China while those in the south left by sea. At least in the south, creating Chinese refugees proved to be a lucrative business for the government – refugees typically had to pay up to US$5000 each in 'exit fees' to be allowed to leave. In Saigon, Chinese entrepreneurs in 1979 had that kind of money – refugees in the north were mostly dirt-poor.

In response, China cut off all aid to Vietnam, cancelled dozens of development projects and withdrew 800 technicians. Vietnam's invasion of Cambodia in late 1978 was the icing on the cake – Beijing was alarmed because the Khmer Rouge were close allies of China. China's leaders – already worried by the huge build-up of Soviet military forces on the Chinese-Soviet border – became convinced that Vietnam had fallen into the Russian camp which was trying to encircle China with hostile forces.

Carrying wood near Phy Ly

In February 1979, China invaded northern Vietnam 'to teach the Vietnamese a lesson'. Just what lesson the Vietnamese learned is not clear, but the Chinese learned that Vietnam's combat-hardened troops were no easy pushover. Although China's forces were withdrawn after 17 days and the operation was officially declared a 'great success', most observers soon realised that China's People's Liberation Army (PLA) had been badly mauled by the Vietnamese. The PLA is believed to have suffered 20,000 casualties in the 2½ weeks of fighting. Ironically, China's aid to Vietnam was partially responsible for China's humiliation by the Vietnamese forces.

Officially, such past 'misunderstandings' are ancient history – trade across the Chinese-Vietnamese border is booming and both countries publicly profess to be 'good neighbours'. In practice, China and Vietnam remain highly suspicious of each other's intentions. Continued conflicts over who owns oil-drilling rights in the South China Sea is an especially sore point. China has neither forgiven nor forgotten its humiliation at the hands of the Vietnamese army, and has relentlessly been building up its military ever since. Thus, the Chinese-Vietnamese border remains militarily sensitive, though the most likely future battleground will be at sea.

LANG SON
LANG SƠN
Lang Son (elevation: 270 metres) – capital of mountainous Lang Son Province – is in an area populated largely by ethnic minorities (Tho, Nung, Man and Dao), many of whom continue their traditional way of life. There are also caves 3.5 km from Lang Son, near the village of Ky Lua.

However, the real attraction of Lang Son is neither ethnic minorities nor scenery. The town has long served as an important trading post and crossing point into China. Since 1992, the Vietnamese government has been permitting foreigners to exit Vietnam overland by this route. Unfortunately, entering Vietnam by this route is more difficult but it is possible. See the Getting There & Away chapter (Land section) for details on entering Vietnam this way.

Lang Son was partially destroyed in February 1979 by invading Chinese forces; the ruins of the town and the devastated frontier village of Dong Dang, 20 km to the north, were often shown to foreign journalists as evidence of Chinese aggression. Today, though the border region is still mined, fortified and heavily guarded, Sino-Vietnamese trade seems to be in full swing again. This has greatly benefited Lang Son, which has become a booming market town.

Information
Money There's a thriving black market in Lang Son. Not only is the unofficial banking system able to exchange US dollars and dong, but Chinese renminbi is also on the menu. While it is possible to bargain a little, the exchange rates offered are usually not bad at all (perhaps this will change when they've seen more foreigners).

In case you've still got leftover dong, it is possible to change money on the Chinese side too.

Travel Permits & Visas As an exit point from Vietnam, Lang Son is now of great interest to Western travellers. However, unless you hold a Vietnamese or Chinese passport, it is still not permitted to enter Vietnam this way. It seems likely though this policy will eventually change. No doubt this would become an extremely popular route with travellers if the border was more open.

If you wish to exit Vietnam via Lang Son, this must be authorised on your visa. If your visa shows a different exit point, you can usually get a change made in Hanoi or Ho Chi Minh City at the Foreign Ministry office. However, you also need a travel permit if you want to exit Vietnam via Lang Son, and getting the permit is not something you can do yourself. For this reason, it's best to pay a Vietnamese travel agency to do all the paperwork (both visa change and travel permit), which should cost around US$20.

Getting There & Away

Bus Buses to Lang Son depart Hanoi's Long Bien Bus Station around 6 am. The cost is US$5 and the journey takes roughly six hours over a bone-jarring road.

There are two checkpoints along the way and locals can get searched very thoroughly though they usually go easy with foreigners. The situation seems even worse when going the other way (towards Hanoi) – the police are known to rip luggage open with knives and confiscate 'contraband' from China. Even if you are personally spared, the searches can cause long delays and it's really a depressing sight – Vietnamese people in tears pleading with the police. On the other hand, it's an educational experience – just think of how much worse it was in the old days before 'reform' and 'openness'.

From Lang Son to the border at Dong Dang is another 20 km with yet another police checkpoint along the way. Other than walking, the cheapest way to cover this distance is to hire a motorbike for US$1. There are also army jeeps willing to take you. Make sure they take you to Huu Nghi Quan – there are a few other checkpoints but this is the only one where foreigners can cross.

Train There is one train daily departing Hanoi at 9.30 pm and arriving in Lang Son at 3.30 am. These inconvenient hours make the bus a preferred mode of transport. As with the bus, arriving by train in Lang Son leaves you 20 km from the border and you'll need to hire a motorbike.

There is much talk of running an international train directly from Hanoi to Nanning, China. It would certainly make sense to do so, but 'sense' is not a strong point of bureaucrats.

Car The 150 km highway between Hanoi and Lang Son is in lousy condition and most passenger cars do not have sufficiently high-ground clearance to negotiate this road safely. For this reason, jeeps, trucks and minibuses are the vehicles of choice. Chartering a jeep costs around US$80 to US$90. A minibus costs around US$120 but could

well prove cheaper if you can get together five or six passengers to share the cost. While trucks are capable of making the journey, this seems like an uncomfortable alternative.

Despite the expense, renting a private vehicle is not a bad idea since you can be driven right to the border crossing at Dong Dang.

To/From China No matter what means of transport you use to reach the Vietnamese border, there is a walk of 600 metres from the Vietnamese border post to 'Friendship Gate' on the Chinese side. Expect to be searched thoroughly at the border – there's quite a problem with drug smuggling. After you've crossed into China and cleared all customs hassles, it's a 20-minute drive to Pinxiang by bus or share taxi (US$3) from where you can get a train to Nanning, capital of China's Guangxi Province. Trains to Nanning depart Pinxiang at 8 am and 1.30 pm. More frequent are the buses (once every 30 minutes) which take four hours to make the journey and cost US$3.

CAO BANG
CAO BẰNG

Cao Bang City is the capital of Cao Bang Province, many of whose inhabitants are members of the Tho, Nung, Dao and Meo national minorities. Principal products of the region include beef, pork, goats, zinc and lumber. The area is known for its waterfalls and grottoes.

Cao Bang is 272 km north of Hanoi.

BA BE LAKES
HỒ BA BỂ

The Ba Be Lakes are an area of waterfalls, rivers, deep valleys, lakes and caves set amidst towering peaks. The lakes, which are about 145 metres above sea level, are surrounded by steep mountains up to 1754 metres high. The 1939 Madrolle Guide to Indochina suggests getting around the area 'in a car, on horseback, or, for ladies, in a chair', meaning, of course, a sedan chair.

Ba Be (three bays) is the name of the

southern part of a narrow body of water seven km long; the northern section of the lake, separated from Ba Be by a 100-metre-wide strip of water sandwiched between high walls of chalk rock, is called Be Kam. The Nam Nang River is navigable for 23 km between a point four km above Cho Ra and the Falls of Dau Dang, which consist of a series of cascades between sheer walls of rock. Pong Tunnel is almost 300 metres in length and 30 to 40 metres high.

Getting There & Away

The Ba Be Lakes are in Cao Bang Province not far from the borders of Bac Thai Province and Tuyen Quang Province. Ba Be is 240 km from Hanoi, 61 km from Bach Thong (Bac Can) and 17 km from Cho Ra.

The North-West
Miền Tây Bắc

SON LA
SƠN LA

Son La, capital of a province of the same name, is 308 km west of Hanoi. The area is populated mainly by hill tribes, including the Black Tai (Thai or Tay), Meo, Muong and White Tai. Vietnamese influence in the area was minimal until this century; from 1959 to 1980, the region was part of the Tay Bac Autonomous Region (Khu Tay Bac Tu Tri).

Son La was once the site of a French penal colony where anti-colonialist revolutionaries were held.

There is a basic hotel in the town of Son La. Almost all travellers journeying between Hanoi and Dien Bien Phu spend the night here both coming and going. The food in Son La is poor – bring some from Hanoi.

DIEN BIEN PHU
ĐIỆN BIÊN PHỦ

Dien Bien Phu was the site of that rarest of military events, a battle that can be called truly decisive. On 6 May 1954, the day before the Geneva Conference on Indochina

was set to begin half a world away, Viet Minh forces overran the beleaguered French garrison at Dien Bien Phu after a 57-day siege, shattering French morale and forcing the French government to abandon its attempts to re-establish colonial control of Indochina.

Dien Bien Phu (population 10,000), capital of Dien Bien District of Lai Chau Province, is in one of the remotest parts of Vietnam. The town is 16 km from the Lao border in flat, heart-shaped Muong Thanh Valley, which is about 20 km long and five km wide and is surrounded by steep, heavily forested hills. The area is inhabited by hill-tribe people, most notably the Tai and Hmong. Ethnic Vietnamese, whom the government has been encouraging to settle in the region, currently comprise about one-third of the Muong Thanh Valley's population of 60,000.

For centuries, Dien Bien was a transit stop on the caravan route from Burma and China to northern Vietnam. Dien Bien Phu was established in 1841 by the Nguyen Dynasty to prevent raids on the Red River Delta by bandits.

In early 1954 General Henri Navarre, commander of the French forces in Indochina, sent a force of 12 battalions to occupy the Muong Thanh Valley in order to prevent the Viet Minh from crossing into Laos and threatening the Lao capital of Luang Phabang. The French units, one-third of whose members were ethnic-Vietnamese, were soon surrounded by a Viet Minh force under General Vo Nguyen Giap consisting of 33 infantry battalions, six artillery regiments and a regiment of engineers. The Viet Minh force, which outnumbered the French by five to one, was equipped with 105-mm artillery pieces and anti-aircraft guns carried by porters through jungles and across rivers in an unbelievable feat of logistics. The guns were emplaced in carefully camouflaged positions dug deep into the hills that overlooked the French positions.

A failed Viet Minh human-wave assault against the French was followed by weeks of intense artillery bombardments. Six battalions of French paratroops were parachuted into Dien Bien Phu as the situation worsened, but bad weather and the Viet Minh artillery, impervious to French air and artillery attacks, prevented sufficient reinforcements and supplies from arriving by air. An elaborate system of trenches and tunnels allowed Viet Minh soldiers to reach French positions without coming under fire. After the idea of employing American conventional bombers was rejected – as was a Pentagon proposal to use tactical atomic bombs – the French trenches and bunkers were overrun. All 13,000 men of the French garrison were either killed or taken prisoner; Viet Minh casualties are estimated at 25,000.

Today, the site of the battle is marked by a small museum. The headquarters of the French commander, Colonel Christian de Castries, has been recreated and nearby there are old French tanks and artillery pieces. One of the two landing strips used by the French is extant. There is a monument to Viet Minh casualties on the site of the former French position known as Eliane, where bitter fighting took place. A memorial to the 3000 French troops buried under the rice paddies was erected in 1984 on the 30th anniversary of the battle.

At present, the Vietnamese government is considering a request by French veterans of Dien Bien Phu that they be allowed to restage their paratroop drop of almost four decades ago.

The scenery is incredible. You pass through Hmong and Black Tai villages where they stare at you as much as you stare at them. There is not much to see at the battlefield itself but the museum presents the incredible story of Vietnamese determination. You might want to bring some food – local food consists of rice, fried pig fat and huge piles of fresh mint washed in water that made us sick. Back in Hanoi I splurged after all the bumps of the road by having a tonic water with ice at the Metropole and then sneaking into their completely empty swimming pool.

Ingrid Muan

Getting There & Away

Air Dien Bien Phu has an airport and at one time had regular flights, but these are no longer running. A tour group might be able to arrange a charter flight. Given the increas-

ing number of foreign tourists visiting Vietnam, it's hard to imagine that Vietnam Airlines will continue to ignore this potentially lucrative route, but for the moment it's moribund.

Bus The bus may be cheap but not really much fun – they are so packed that it's doubtful you'll get to admire the splendid scenery. Furthermore, the buses we've seen looked awfully dangerous (you need good brakes in these mountains).

Jeep Getting there is half the fun: as it nears Dien Bien Phu, the road winds through beautiful mountains and high plains inhabited by hill tribes (notably the Black Tai and Hmong) who still live as they have for generations. Between Hoa Binh and Son La, the road passes by tea plantations and orchards.

The 420-km drive from Hanoi to Dien Bien Phu takes two full days. In other words, a minimum of five days is required for an overland expedition from Hanoi to Dien Bien Phu: two days to get there, a day to visit the area, and two days to come back.

The reason why it takes so long is because the road is in abysmal condition. A normal passenger car would have a very difficult time making it, and no sane driver would attempt it. If it's been raining recently, mud will create additional problems.

A two-wheel drive truck or bus *might* make it, but could easily get stuck in the mud or break down. The only passenger vehicle which can comfortably negotiate this highway is a jeep. A Russian-built jeep (of which there are many in Hanoi) can seat four passengers plus the driver. It's also possible to find a Russian-built military van, equipped with 4WD, which can hold more passengers than a standard jeep.

The going rate for renting a jeep to Dien Bien Phu and back is at least US$500. Enquire at travel agencies or your hotel about jeep rentals.

Other vehicles mechanically capable of doing this journey would include 4WD trucks and 'off-road' motorcycles (with powerful engine, knobby tires and raised exhaust pipes). Finding either of these options in Hanoi would probably prove difficult.

LAO CAI
LÀO CAI

Lao Cai is also the major town at the end of the rail line and right on the Chinese border. At the time of this writing, foreigners were unable to get an exit visa to leave Vietnam by this route, nor were visas being issued permitting entrance to Vietnam at Lao Cai.

Practically no foreigners come to Lao Cai, and most who do are usually hopefuls who think they can bluff their way across the border. This doesn't seem to work, and the foreigners are invariably turned back. Although the police here have generally been amiable towards Westerners, we do not suggest sneaking across the border – both Vietnam and China look considerably less charming from the inside of a prison.

The only reason why we are reporting on how to get to Lao Cai is because we want to be optimists – in the future this border crossing might open to foreigners. If so, Lao Cai will no doubt become a major destination for travellers journeying between Hanoi and Kunming, the scenic capital of China's Yunnan Province.

The scenery around Lao Cai is beautiful and the people very friendly. However, they

have not yet seen many foreigners and therefore are *intensely* curious. If you drop in, expect to be treated like a visitor from another planet.

Places to Stay

There are no hotels in Lao Cai or nearby villages. The few odd foreigners who have shown up are usually offered a place to stay in a local person's house. Of course, some sort of payment is expected, but it will certainly be cheap.

There is a hotel in Pho Lu adjacent to the small square in front of the railway station. While it looks reasonably clean from the outside, the beds lack mattresses, there is no shower and just one toilet for the whole place.

Getting There & Away

Probably for security reasons, passenger trains currently do not go all the way to Lao Cai but terminate at Pho Lu, 40 km away. While there are trains going all the way to Lao Cai from Hanoi, these are only for hauling freight.

There are three trains daily from Hanoi to Pho Lu, but two arrive in the middle of the night. The most useful train departs Hanoi at 7 am and arrives in Pho Lu at 5.30 pm. In Pho Lu, you can transfer to another train that is waiting at the station. This is a very basic train with only small wooden benches on the long sides of the carriages. This train takes about an hour to get to a tiny village about 10 km from Lao Cai. The best way to get from the village to Lao Cai is to hire a motorbike for about US$1.20.

A train departs Pho Lu at 6.20 pm and arrives in Hanoi at 4 am.

SAPA
SA PA

Sapa is an old hill station built in 1922 in a beautiful valley (altitude: 1600 metres). Don't forget your winter woollies – Sapa is known for its cold, foggy winters (down to 0°C). Thanks to the chilly climate, the area is known for its temperate-zone fruit trees (peaches, plums, etc) and gardens for raising medicinal herbs which are sold in the markets of Hanoi and Ho Chi Minh City.

Surrounding Sapa are the Hoang Lien Mountains, nicknamed the Tonkinese Alps by the French. These mountains include Fansipan (also spelled Phan Si Pan), which at 3143 metres is Vietnam's highest peak. The summit sees few visitors – foreigners are an extreme rarity and Vietnamese people hardly have the financial resources for mountaineering holidays. Fansipan is nine km from Sapa and reachable on foot.

Some of the more well known sights around Sapa include Thac Bac (Silver Falls) and Cau May (Cloud Bridge) which spans the Muong Hoa River.

Due to its proximity to the border, Sapa was the scene of some fighting during the Chinese invasion of 1979. Some of the buildings were damaged and have not yet been repaired. At the moment, Sapa only gets a handful of visitors but this is expected to change.

Getting There & Away

The gateway to Sapa is Lao Cai, 29 km from Sapa. Buses do make the trip occasionally but are infrequent. The roads are in poor condition and the ideal vehicle would be a jeep.

It is entirely possible to combine a trip to Sapa with a trip to Dien Bien Phu, though it would be rough going on some of these mountain roads. Again, a jeep would be the ideal vehicle.

Glossary

Agent Orange – a toxic and carcinogenic chemical herbicide used heavily during the Vietnam War

am & duong – Vietnamese equivalent of Yin & Yang

Annam – old Chinese name for Vietnam meaning 'Pacified South'

ao dai – national dress of Vietnamese women (and men)

arhat – monk who has attained nirvana

ARVN – Army of the Republic of Vietnam (the former South Vietnamese army)

bang – congregation (in the Chinese community)

bonze – Vietnamese Buddhist monk

Buu Dien – Post Office

Cai Luong – modern theatre

Caodaism – indigenous Vietnamese religious sect

can – 10-year cycle

can danh – brown (literally, 'cockroach wing')

cay son – tree from whose resin lacquer is made

Champa – Hindu kingdom dating from the late 2nd century AD

Chams – the people of Champa

Cochinchina – the southern part of Vietnam during the French colonial era

chu nho – standard Chinese characters (script)

chu nom – also *nom*, Vietnamese script

crachin – fine drizzle

cu ly – fern stems used to stop bleeding

cyclo – pedicab or bicycle rickshaw (from French)

dau – oil

dikpalata – gods of the directions of the compass

dinh – communal meeting hall

DMZ – the misnamed 'Demilitarised Zone', a strip of land which once separated North and South Vietnam

doi moi – economic restructuring or reform

DRV – Democratic Republic of Vietnam (the old North Vietnam)

fu – talisman

Funan – see Oc-Eo

ghe – long, narrow rowboat

giap phep di lai – internal travel permit

gom – ceramics

hai dang – lighthouse

Han Viet – Sino-Vietnamese literature

Hat Boi – classical theatre in the south

Hat Cheo – popular theatre

Hat Tuong – classical theatre in the north

ho ca – aquarium

Ho Chi Minh Trail – route used by the NVA and VC to move supplies to guerrillas in the south

hoi – 60-year period

ho khao – sort of residence permit needed to attend school, seek employement, own farmland, home, business, etc

Honda om – motorbike taxi

huyen – rural district

Indochina – Vietnam, Cambodia and Laos. The name derives from the influence of Indian and Chinese cultures on the region

kala-makara – sea monster god

kalan – sanctuary

khach san – hotel

Khmer – ethnic Cambodians

Kich Noi – spoken drama

Kinh – Vietnamese language

Kuomintang – or KMT, meaning 'Nationalist Party'. The KMT controlled China from around 1925 to 1949 until defeated by the communists. The KMT still controls Taiwan.

ky – 12-year cycle

lang tam – tombs
Lien Xo – literally 'Soviet Union'; used to call attention to a foreigner
linga – stylised phallus which represents the Hindu god Shiva
Liberation – the 1975 takeover of the South by the North; what most foreigners call 'reunification'

mandapa – meditation hall
moi – derogatory word meaning 'savages', mostly used regarding hill-tribes people
mukha linga – linga with a painted human face on it (from Sanscrit)

naga – a giant snake, often depicted forming a kind of shelter over the Buddha
Nam Phai – For Men
napalm – jellied petrol (gasoline) dropped and lit from aircraft, with devastating effect
nha hang – restaurant
nha khach – hotel or guesthouse
nha nghi – guesthouse
nha thuoc – pharmacy
nha tro – dormitory
NLF – National Liberation Front; official name for the Viet Cong
nom – see chu nom
Nu Phai – For Women
nuoc mam – fish sauce, added to almost every dish in Vietnam
nuoc suoi – mineral water
nuoc dua – coconut milk
NVA – North Vietnamese Army

Oc-Eo – Indianised kingdom (also called Funan) in southern Vietnam between 1st and 6th centuries

pagoda – traditionally, an eight-sided Buddhist tower, but in Vietnam the word is commonly used to denote a temple
Phoenix Programme – or Operation Phoenix; a controversial programme run by the CIA, aimed at eliminating VC cadres by assassination, capture or defection
PRG – Provisional Revolutionary Government, the temporary communist government set up by the Viet Cong in the South. It existed from 1969 to 1976

quan – urban district
Quoc Am – modern Vietnamese literature
quoc ngu – Latin-based phonetic alphabet in which Vietnamese is written

rap – cinema
Revolutionary Youth League – the first Marxist group in Vietnam and predecessor of the Communist Party; founded in 1925 by Ho Chi Minh in Canton, China
Roi Can – conventional puppetry
Roi Nuoc – water puppetry
ruou – wine
RVN – Republic of Vietnam (the old South Vietnam)

son then – black
SRV – Socialist Republic of Vietnam (Vietnam's current official name)
Strategic Hamlets Programme – an unsuccessful programme of the US army and South Vietnamese government in which peasants were forcibly moved into fortified villages to deny the VC bases of support

Tet – the Vietnamese lunar new year
thanh long – dragon fruit
tinh – province
thuac bac – Chinese medicines
thung chai – gigantic round wicket baskets sealed with pitch; used as rowboats.
toc hanh – express bus
Tonkin – the northern part of Vietnam during the French colonial era; also name of a body of water in the north (Tonkin Gulf)
Truyen Khan – traditional oral literature

VC – Viet Cong or Vietnamese Communists. Considered a derogatory term until recently
Viet Minh – League for the Independence of Vietnam, a nationalistic movement which fought the Japanese and French but later became fully communist-dominated

xang – petrol
xe dap loi – wagon pulled by bicycle
xe Honda loi – wagon pulled by a motorbike
Xe Lam – three-wheeled motorised vehicle

Index

MAPS

TEXT

Map references are in **bold** type.

Keep in touch!

We love hearing from you and think you'd like to hear from us.

The Lonely Planet Newsletter covers the when, where, how and what of travel. (AND it's free!)

When...is the right time to see reindeer in Finland?
Where...can you hear the best palm-wine music in Ghana?
How...do you get from Asunción to Areguá by steam train?
What...should you leave behind to avoid hassles with customs in Iran?

To join our mailing list just contact us at any of our offices. (details below)

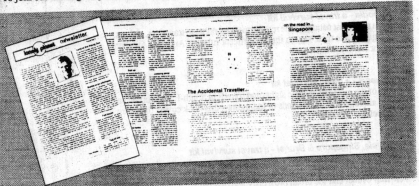

Every issue includes:

- a letter from Lonely Planet founders Tony and Maureen Wheeler
- travel diary from a Lonely Planet author - find out what it's really like out on the road
- feature article on an important and topical travel issue
- a selection of recent letters from our readers
- the latest travel news from all over the world
- details on Lonely Planet's new and forthcoming releases

Also available Lonely Planet T-shirts. 100% heavy weight cotton (S, M, L, XL)

LONELY PLANET PUBLICATIONS
Australia: PO Box 617, Hawthorn, 3122, Victoria (tel: 03-819 1877)
USA: Embarcadero West, 155 Filbert Street, Suite 251, Oakland, CA 94607 (tel: 510-893 8555)
UK: Devonshire House, 12 Barley Mow Passage, Chiswick, London W4 4PH (tel: 081-742 3161)

Guides to South-East Asia

South-East Asia on a shoestring
The well-known 'yellow bible' for travellers in South-East Asia covers Brunei, Burma (Myanmar), Cambodia, Hong Kong, Indonesia, Laos, Macau, Malaysia, the Philippines, Singapore, Thailand and Vietnam.

Bali & Lombok - a travel survival kit
This guide will help travellers to experience the real magic of Bali's tropical paradise. Neighbouring Lombok is largely untouched by outside influences and has a special atmosphere of its own.

Cambodia - a travel survival kit
As one of the last nations in the region opens its doors to travellers, visitors will again make their way to the magnificent ruins of Angkor. Another first for Lonely Planet!

Indonesia - a travel survival kit
Some of the most remarkable sights and sounds in South-East Asia can be found amongst the 7000 islands of Indonesia – this book covers the entire archipelago in detail.

Malaysia, Singapore & Brunei - a travel survival kit
Three independent nations of amazing geographic and cultural variety – from the national parks, beaches, jungles and rivers of Malaysia, tiny oil-rich Brunei and the urban prosperity and diversity of Singapore.

Myanmar (Burma) - a travel survival kit
Myanmar is one of Asia's most interesting countries. This book shows how to make the most of a trip around the main triangle route of Yangon–Mandalay–Bagan, and explores many lesser-known places such as Bago and Inle Lake.

Philippines - a travel survival kit
The friendly Filipinos, colourful festivals, and superb natural scenery make the Philippines one of the most interesting countries in South-East Asia for adventurous travellers and sun-seekers alike.

Thailand - a travel survival kit
This authoritative guide includes Thai script for all place names and the latest travel details for all regions, including tips in trekking in the remote hills of the Golden Triangle.

Singapore - city guide
Singapore offers a taste of the great Asian cultures in a small, accessible package. This compact guide will help travellers discover the very best that this city of contrasts can offer.

Bangkok - city guide

Bangkok has something for everyone: temples, museums and historic sites; an endless variety of good restaurants, clubs, international culture and social events; a modern art institute; and great shopping oppurtunities. This pocket guide offers you the assurance that you will never be lost...or lost for things to do in this fascinating city!

Also available:

Thai phrasebook, *Thai Hill Tribes* phrasebook, *Burmese* phrasebook, *Pilipino* phrasebook, *Indonesian* phrasebook, *Papua New Guinea Pidgin* phrasebook, *Mandarin Chinese* phrasebook and *Vietnamese* phrasebook.

Mail Order

Lonely Planet guidebooks are distributed worldwide. They are also available by mail order from Lonely Planet, so if you have difficulty finding a title please write to us. US and Canadian residents should write to Embarcadero West, 155 Filbert St, Suite 251, Oakland CA 94607, USA; European residents should write to Devonshire House, 12 Barley Mow Passage, Chiswick, London W4 4PH; and residents of other countries to PO Box 617, Hawthorn, Victoria 3122, Australia.

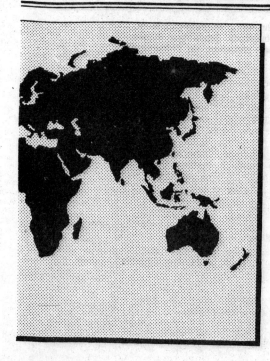

Indian Subcontinent
Bangladesh
India
Hindi/Urdu phrasebook
Trekking in the Indian Himalaya
Karakoram Highway
Kashmir, Ladakh & Zanskar
Nepal
Trekking in the Nepal Himalaya
Nepal phrasebook
Pakistan
Sri Lanka
Sri Lanka phrasebook

Africa
Africa on a shoestring
Central Africa
East Africa
Trekking in East Africa
Kenya
Swahili phrasebook
Morocco, Algeria & Tunisia
Moroccan Arabic phrasebook
South Africa, Lesotho & Swaziland
Zimbabwe, Botswana & Namibia
West Africa

Central America
Baja California
Central America on a shoestring
Costa Rica
La Ruta Maya
Mexico

North America
Alaska
Canada
Hawaii

South America
Argentina, Uruguay & Paraguay
Bolivia
Brazil
Brazilian phrasebook
Chile & Easter Island
Colombia
Ecuador & the Galápagos Islands
Latin American Spanish phrasebook
Peru
Quechua phrasebook
South America on a shoestring
Trekking in the Patagonian Andes

Europe
Dublin city guide
Eastern Europe on a shoestring
Eastern Europe phrasebook
Finland
Iceland, Greenland & the Faroe Islands
Mediterranean Europe on a shoestring
Mediterranean Europe phrasebook
Poland
Scandinavian & Baltic Europe on a shoestring
Scandinavian Europe phrasebook
Trekking in Spain
Trekking in Greece
USSR
Russian phrasebook
Western Europe on a shoestring
Western Europe phrasebook

Lonely Planet Guidebooks

Lonely Planet guidebooks cover every accessible part of Asia as well as Australia, the Pacific, South America, Africa, the Middle East, Europe and parts of North America. There are five series: *travel survival kits*, covering a country for a range of budgets; *shoestring guides* with compact information for low-budget travel in a major region; *walking guides*; *city guides* and *phrasebooks*.

Australia & the Pacific
Australia
Bushwalking in Australia
Islands of Australia's Great Barrier Reef
Fiji
Melbourne city guide
Micronesia
New Caledonia
New Zealand
Tramping in New Zealand
Papua New Guinea
Bushwalking in Papua New Guinea
Papua New Guinea phrasebook
Rarotonga & the Cook Islands
Samoa
Solomon Islands
Sydney city guide
Tahiti & French Polynesia
Tonga
Vanuatu
Victoria

South-East Asia
Bali & Lombok
Bangkok city guide
Myanmar (Burma)
Burmese phrasebook
Cambodia
Indonesia
Indonesia phrasebook
Malaysia, Singapore & Brunei
Philippines
Pilipino phrasebook
Singapore city guide
South-East Asia on a shoestring
Thailand
Thai phrasebook
Vietnam
Vietnamese phrasebook

North-East Asia
China
Mandarin Chinese phrasebook
Hong Kong, Macau & Canton
Japan
Japanese phrasebook
Korea
Korean phrasebook
Mongolia
North-East Asia on a shoestring
Seoul city guide
Taiwan
Tibet
Tibet phrasebook
Tokyo city guide

West Asia
Trekking in Turkey
Turkey
Turkish phrasebook
West Asia on a shoestring

Middle East
Arab Gulf States
Egypt & the Sudan
Egyptian Arabic phrasebook
Iran
Israel
Jordan & Syria
Yemen

Indian Ocean
Madagascar & Comoros
Maldives & Islands of the East Indian Ocean
Mauritius, Réunion & Seychelles

The Lonely Planet Story

Lonely Planet published its first book in 1973 in response to the numerous 'How did you do it?' questions Maureen and Tony Wheeler were asked after driving, bussing, hitching, sailing and railing their way from England to Australia.

Written at a kitchen table and hand collated, trimmed and stapled, *Across Asia on the Cheap* became an instant local bestseller, inspiring thoughts of another book.

Eighteen months in South-East Asia resulted in their second guide, *South-East Asia on a shoestring*, which they put together in a backstreet Chinese hotel in Singapore in 1975. The 'yellow bible' as it quickly became known to backpackers around the world, soon became *the* guide to the region. It has sold well over half a million copies and is now in its 7th edition, still retaining its familiar yellow cover.

Today there are over 120 Lonely Planet titles in print – books that have that same adventurous approach to travel as those early guides; books that 'assume you know how to get your luggage off the carousel' as one reviewer put it.

Although Lonely Planet initially specialised in guides to Asia, they now cover most regions of the world, including the Pacific, South America, Africa, the Middle East and Europe. The list of *walking guides* and *phrasebooks* (for 'unusual' languages such as Quechua, Swahili, Nepalese and Egyptian Arabic) is also growing rapidly.

The emphasis continues to be on travel for independent travellers. Tony and Maureen still travel for several months of each year and play an active part in the writing, updating and quality control of Lonely Planet's guides.

They have been joined by over 50 authors, 54 staff – mainly editors, cartographers, & designers – at our office in Melbourne, Australia, 10 at our US office in Oakland, California and another three at our office in London to handle sales for Britain, Europe and Africa. In 1992 Lonely Planet opened an editorial office in Paris. Travellers themselves also make a valuable contribution to the guides through the feedback we receive in thousands of letters each year.

The people at Lonely Planet strongly believe that travellers can make a positive contribution to the countries they visit, both through their appreciation of the countries' culture, wildlife and natural features, and through the money they spend. In addition, the company makes a direct contribution to the countries and regions it covers. Since 1986 a percentage of the income from each book has been donated to ventures such as famine relief in Africa; aid projects in India; agricultural projects in Central America; Greenpeace's efforts to halt French nuclear testing in the Pacific and Amnesty International. In 1993 $100,000 was donated to such causes.

Lonely Planet's basic travel philosophy is summed up in Tony Wheeler's comment, 'Don't worry about whether your trip will work out. Just go!'